VIETNAM

VIETNAM

A New History

CHRISTOPHER GOSCHA

BASIC
BOOKS

New York

CONTENTS

ACKNOWLEDGMENTS

Over the last fifty years, a wide range of scholars has produced an exciting body of scholarship on Vietnam. Without access to it, I would have never been able to write this book. In many ways, I'm standing on their shoulders and I hope that I have done them justice in the pages that follow. It is impossible to cite each of them here; the list would go on for pages. While they may not always agree with everything I advance, I wish to thank them and those who kindly took the time out of their busy schedules to read and comment on draft chapters, provide references, or make suggestions for improving the book. In no particular order, they are: Agathe Larcher, Nola Cooke, Liam Kelley, Li Tana, Philip Taylor, Kathlene Baldanza, George Dutton, Jon Heit, Mark Lawrence, Keith Taylor, Christopher and Susan Bayly, Shawn McHale, Geoff Wade, Phi Van Nguyen, François Guillemot, Sophie Quinn-Judge, Nguyen Quoc Thanh, Tuong Vu, Nasir-Carime Abdoul, Philippe Papin, David Marr, Charles Keith, Peter Zinoman, Olga Dror, Emmanuel Poisson, and William Turley.

A NOTE ON TERMS

Words matter. Most problematic of all in this book is the word 'Vietnam' itself. While tribes referring to themselves as 'Viet' emerged in around the third century BCE from present-day southern China to the Red River valley, at no time before 1802 did these people ever call their kingdoms, dynasties, or states 'Vietnam'. Upon creating a unitary state running from the Red River basin to the Mekong delta in 1802, Emperor Gia Long had first wanted to call his new country 'Nam-Viet' or the 'Viet of the South'. Worried that the use of this term implied expansionist designs on China's southern territories, the Chinese emperor reversed the word order to form the term 'Viet-Nam' (which I render in English simply as 'Vietnam'). In 1804, Gia Long accepted this Chinese-devised coupling as recognizing the independent state he had just created running from north to south. The Chinese continued to refer to it by their old appellation dating from Tang times, 'An-Nam', meaning the 'Settled Land of the South'. The term Vietnam did not last long under the Nguyen, however. In 1813, the court briefly revived the term Dai Viet (Greater Viet) and, in 1838, Gia Long's son, Minh Mang, who ruled after him, changed the kingdom's name to Dai Nam (the Greater South). Subsequent Nguyen rulers used this term until mid-1945. 'An artificial appellation then', Alexander Woodside writes of the term 'Vietnam', 'it was used extensively neither by the Chinese nor by the Vietnamese'. The word only took off when nationalists like Tran Trong Kim and Ho Chi Minh used 'Vietnam' as the name for the nation-states they declared independent in 1945.[1]

Further complicating the matter is the multitude of Vietnams under study in this narrative. Not only is the use of the term Vietnam for the period prior to 1945 anachronistic (except between 1802 and 1813), but the question also arises as to which Vietnam we mean. From the seventeenth century onward, two 'Vietnams' existed: one in the Red River delta based around Hanoi, the other expanding into the Mekong delta with its capital in Hue. The same problem arises after 1945, when Ho Chi Minh's Democratic Republic of Vietnam competed with Bao Dai's Associated State of Vietnam and Ngo Dinh Diem's Republic of Vietnam. For the sake of clarity, I use the term Red River Vietnam or Dai Viet to refer to the Vietnamese polity that first emerged in the north and lasted in one form or another until the late eighteenth century. For the period between the seventeenth and eighteenth centuries, when civil conflicts gave rise to the region fracturing into several polities, I distinguish among them by speaking of 'Trinh Vietnam', 'Nguyen Vietnam', and 'Tay Son Vietnam'. These were the three main military houses at odds with each other. This shorthand allows me to maintain clarity without burdening the reader with confusing qualifying statements. For the French colonial period, there was no Vietnam and I have mainly refrained from using the term, except from the point in time when nationalists began to revive it from the start of the twentieth century. For the post-1945 period, I use the term 'Vietnam' to refer to the nation-states run by leaders such as Ho Chi Minh, Bao Dai, and Ngo Dinh Diem. However, when referring to these states, I will use the proper terms for each—the Democratic Republic of Vietnam, the Associated State of Vietnam, and the Republic of Vietnam, respectively. I will not use the terms 'Viet Minh', 'les Viets', or 'Viet Cong' to refer to the 'Vietnamese communists'. Nor should we resort to the politically charged term 'Saigon regime' for the Republic of Vietnam. This is not an ideological bias on my part. Rather, these words obscure a complicated but in the end fascinating story of contested sovereignties.

Finally, 'Vietnam'—whatever its name, shape, or form—has never been an ethnically homogeneous polity. A wide range of ethnic groups—and they did not become 'ethnic minorities' ('*dan toc thieu so*') until the emergence of nation-states in the mid-twentieth century—dominated large parts of present-day Vietnam. These peoples occupy an important place in the history of modern Vietnam and cannot be simply subsumed under the homogenizing, nationalist term 'Vietnamese'. For centuries, they were not 'Vietnamese', and many still do not want to be. Chapter 14 of this book is specifically the story of these non-Viet peoples. When I need to make an ethnic distinction between the two groups, I will use the word 'Viet' instead of 'Vietnamese', much as one distinguishes the 'Han', the ethnic Chinese majority in China, from other ethnic groups there, such as the Tibetans or Uyghers. Again, this is not mere political correctness on my part. Words count, and by using them precisely and carefully, they can help us to shed new light on the complexity of Vietnam in a plural rather than singular or homogenizing sense. That said, I have done my best not to let these semantic concerns muddle the narrative or side-track readers. There will admittedly be times when the words 'Vietnam' or 'Vietnamese' as well as 'China' and 'Chinese' appear in my narrative in a general way, because not to have done so would have simply risked losing the reader.

LIST OF ABBREVIATIONS

ARVN: Army of the Republic of Vietnam

ASEAN: Association of South East Asian Nations

ASV: Associated State of Vietnam

BIC: Banque de l'Indochine or Bank of Indochina

CCP: Chinese Communist Party

CIA: Central Intelligence Agency

COSVN: Central Office of Southern Viet Nam (the communist party's apparatus in southern Vietnam)

DRV: Democratic Republic of Vietnam

FCP: French Communist Party

FULRO: Front unifié de lutte des races opprimées or United Front for the Struggle of Oppressed Races

GDP: Gross Domestic Product

GMD: Guomindang, or Chinese Nationalist Party

ICP: Indochinese Communist Party

MAAG: Military Assistance Advisory Group

MACV: Military Assistance Command, Vietnam

MEP: Missions étrangères de Paris or Paris Overseas Missions

MRP: Mouvement républicain populaire or the Popular Republican Movement

NLF: National Liberation Front of South Vietnam (under communist control)

PAVN: People's Army of Vietnam (under communist control)

PLAF: People's Liberation Armed Force (army under communist control operating below the seventeenth parallel)

PRG: Provisional Revolutionary Government of the Republic of South Vietnam (under communist control)

RV: Republic of Vietnam

SEATO: South East Asia Treaty Organization

SRV: Socialist Republic of Vietnam

SV: State of Vietnam

TLVD: Tu Luc Van Doan or the Self-strengthening Literary Movement

UNHCR: United Nations High Commissioner for Refugees

Viet Minh: *short for* Viet Nam Doc Lap Dong Minh, or Vietnamese Independence League

VNQDD: Viet Nam Quoc Dan Dang or Vietnamese Nationalist Party

VWP: Vietnamese Workers Party (replaced the ICP in 1951)

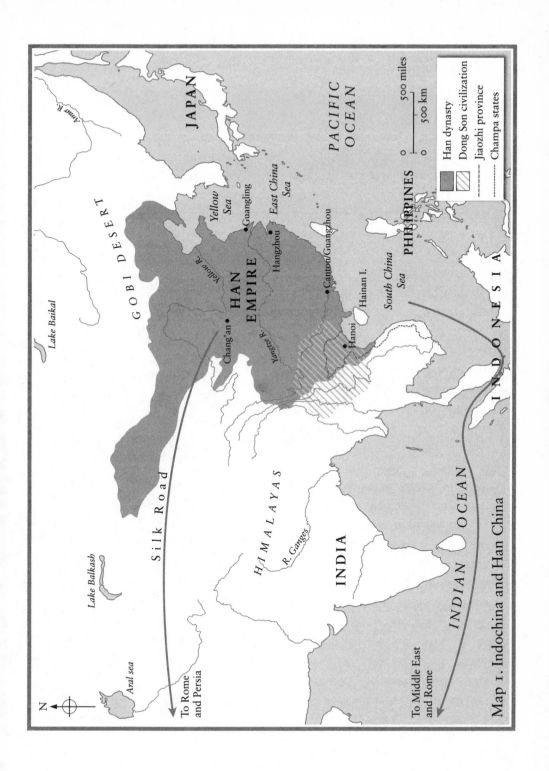

Map 1. Indochina and Han China

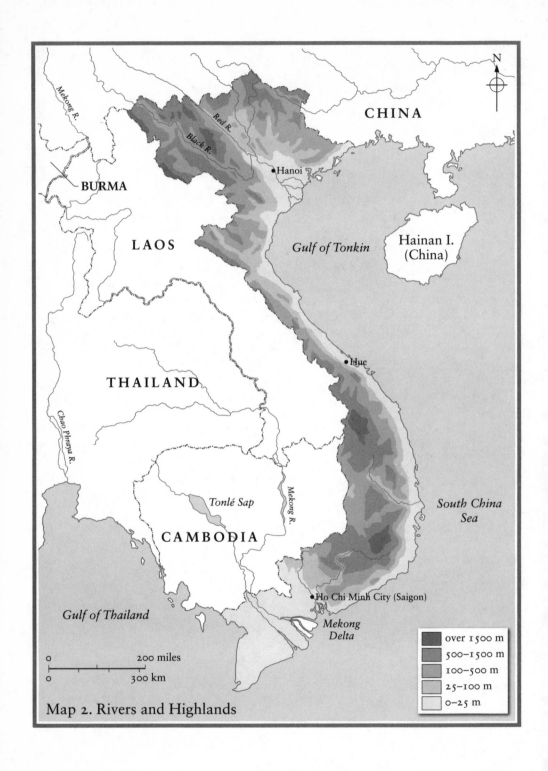

Map 2. Rivers and Highlands

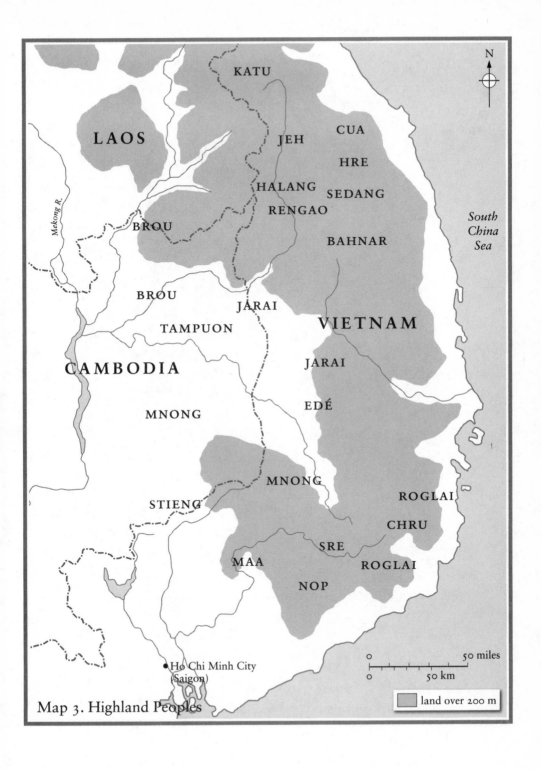

N

KATU

LAOS

CUA

JEH

HRE

HALANG   SEDANG

RENGAO

BROU

BAHNAR

South
China
Sea

BROU

JARAI

VIETNAM

TAMPUON

JARAI

CAMBODIA

EDÉ

MNONG

MNONG

ROGLAI

STIENG

CHRU

SRE

ROGLAI

MAA

NOP

Mekong R.

• Ho Chi Minh City
(Saigon)

0   50 miles

0   50 km

Map 3. Highland Peoples

land over 200 m

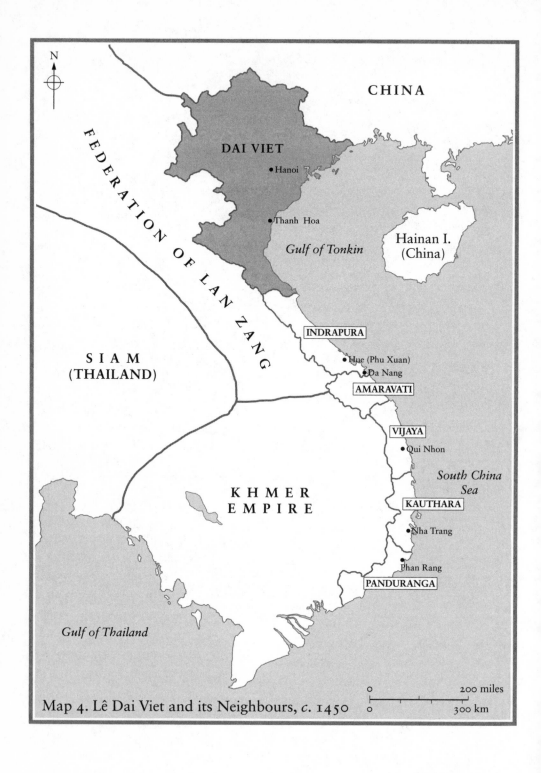

N

CHINA

FEDERATION OF LAN ZANG

DAI VIET

• Hanoi

• Thanh Hoa

Gulf of Tonkin

Hainan I.
(China)

SIAM
(THAILAND)

INDRAPURA

• Hue (Phu Xuan)
• Da Nang

AMARAVATI

VIJAYA

• Qui Nhon

South China
Sea

KHMER
EMPIRE

KAUTHARA

• Nha Trang

• Phan Rang

PANDURANGA

Gulf of Thailand

Map 4. Lê Dai Viet and its Neighbours, c. 1450

0
0
200 miles
300 km

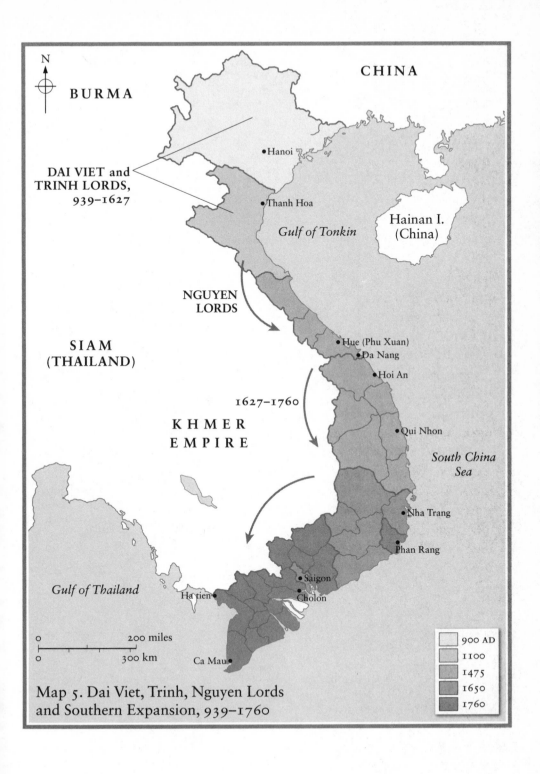

N

BURMA

CHINA

DAI VIET and
TRINH LORDS,
939–1627

• Hanoi

• Thanh Hoa

Gulf of Tonkin

Hainan I.
(China)

NGUYEN
LORDS

SIAM
(THAILAND)

• Hue (Phu Xuan)
• Da Nang

• Hoi An

1627–1760

KHMER
EMPIRE

• Qui Nhon

*South China
Sea*

• Nha Trang

• Phan Rang

Gulf of Thailand

Ha tien •

• Saigon
• Cholon

0   200 miles

0   300 km

Ca Mau •

	900 AD
	1100
	1475
	1650
	1760

Map 5. Dai Viet, Trinh, Nguyen Lords
and Southern Expansion, 939–1760

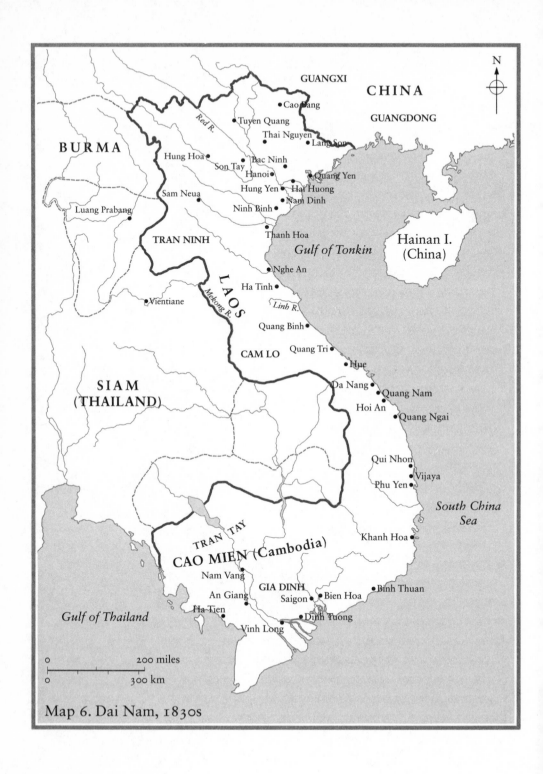

N

GUANGXI

CHINA

GUANGDONG

• Cao Bang

• Tuyen Quang

Thai Nguyen •

• Lang Son

BURMA

Red R.

Hung Hoa •

Son Tay •

Bac Ninh •

• Quang Yen

Hanoi •

Hung Yen •

Hai Huong •

Sam Neua •

• Nam Dinh

Ninh Binh •

Luang Prabang •

Thanh Hoa •

Gulf of Tonkin

Hainan I.
(China)

TRAN NINH

• Nghe An

LAOS

Ha Tinh •

• Vientiane

Mekong R.

Linh R.

Quang Binh •

CAM LO

Quang Tri •

SIAM
(THAILAND)

• Hue

Da Nang •

• Quang Nam

Hoi An •

• Quang Ngai

Qui Nhon •

• Vijaya

Phu Yen •

South China
Sea

TRAN TAY

Khanh Hoa •

CAO MIEN (Cambodia)

Nam Vang •

An Giang •

GIA DINH

Saigon • • Bien Hoa

• Binh Thuan

Gulf of Thailand

Ha Tien •

• Dinh Tuong

Vinh Long •

0   200 miles

0   300 km

Map 6. Dai Nam, 1830s

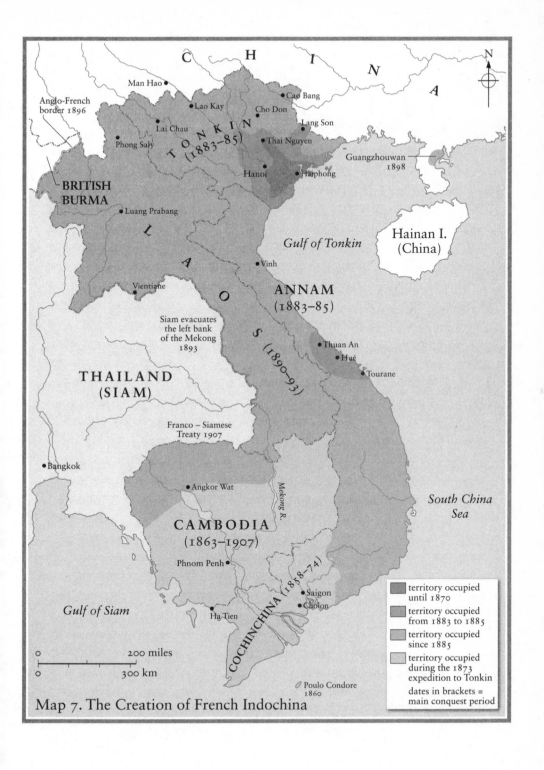

C H I N A

N

Man Hao •

Anglo-French
border 1896

• Lao Kay

Lai Chau •

T O N K I N
(1883–85)

• Cao Bang
Cho Don •
• Lang Son
Thai Nguyen •

Phong Saly •

Hanoi •

• Haiphong

Guangzhouwan
1898

BRITISH
BURMA

• Luang Prabang

L

Gulf of Tonkin

Hainan I.
(China)

A

O

• Vinh

Vientiane •

Siam evacuates
the left bank
of the Mekong
1893

S

ANNAM
(1883–85)

(1890–93)

• Thuan An
• Hué

• Tourane

THAILAND
(SIAM)

Franco – Siamese
Treaty 1907

South China
Sea

• Bangkok

• Angkor Wat

CAMBODIA
(1863–1907)

Mekong R.

Phnom Penh •

Gulf of Siam

• Ha Tien

COCHINCHINA (1858–74)

• Saigon
• Cholon

0   200 miles

0   300 km

Map 7. The Creation of French Indochina

Poulo Condore
1860

territory occupied
until 1870

territory occupied
from 1883 to 1885

territory occupied
since 1885

territory occupied
during the 1873
expedition to Tonkin

dates in brackets =
main conquest period

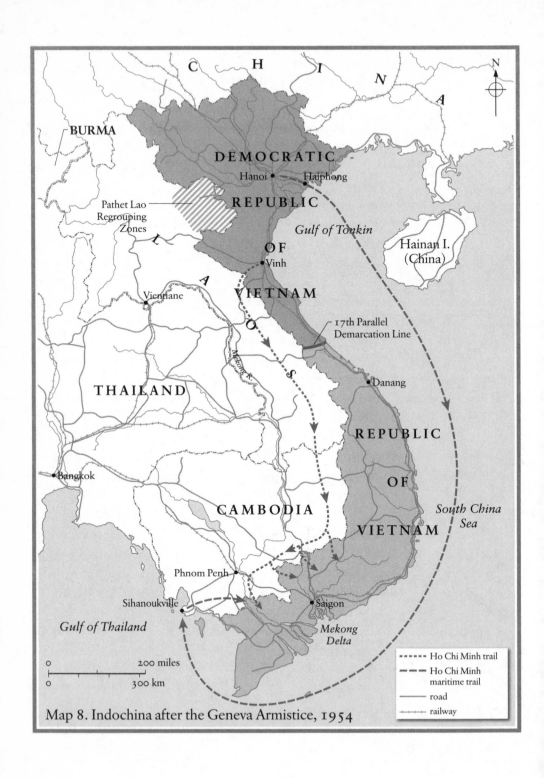

Map 8. Indochina after the Geneva Armistice, 1954

BURMA

C H I N A

N

DEMOCRATIC

Hanoi · · Haiphong

Pathet Lao
Regrouping
Zones

REPUBLIC

Gulf of Tonkin

Hainan I.
(China)

OF

Vinh

L A O S

Vientiane

VIETNAM

17th Parallel
Demarcation Line

THAILAND

Danang

Mekong R.

REPUBLIC

OF

· Bangkok

CAMBODIA

South China
Sea

VIETNAM

Phnom Penh

Sihanoukville

Saigon

Gulf of Thailand

Mekong
Delta

0   200 miles
0   300 km

········ Ho Chi Minh trail
− − − Ho Chi Minh
        maritime trail
——— road
+−+−+ railway

THE MANY DIFFERENT VIETNAMS

MOST AMERICAN READERS will remember 'Vietnam' as the decade-long war that bogged down the US Army in a struggle to prevent the Soviet and Chinese communists from marching into Southeast Asia. The Vietnam War ended in a humiliating defeat for the United States in 1975, and to this day, images of helicopters scrambling to evacuate people from the US Embassy in Saigon to aircraft carriers waiting off the Vietnamese coast remind Americans of that loss.

However, the United States was hardly the first 'great power' to send their warships into the waters off Vietnam's coastline. Indeed, if Vietnam is recognizable to so many today, it is largely because this small country is located in one of those coveted parts of the world where the 'great powers' repeatedly collide. Attracted by trade with the Indian Ocean and determined to project its power by sea, the Chinese empire ruled northern Vietnam for almost a thousand years beginning around the first century BCE. The Chinese saw in Vietnam a gateway for trading with Southeast Asia and tapping into Indian Ocean markets extending to the Middle East. The Vietnamese regained their independence in the tenth century but briefly lost it again to the Chinese in the early fifteenth century as the Ming dynasty sent its armadas across the Indian Ocean as far as Africa and the Red Sea.

Meanwhile, a new set of imperial powers soon expanded into the region via the Pacific and Indian Oceans. This initially European imperialism assumed a particularly aggressive form in the nineteenth century when the French colonized Vietnam and the British confiscated Singapore, Burma, and Malaya. Meanwhile, the Americans crossed the Pacific Ocean to take the Philippines from the Spanish while the Japanese focused their colonial attention on Korea and Taiwan. Together, these colonial powers also divided up the long Chinese coastline into enclaves, treaty ports, and concessions.

The French were perfectly aware of the strategic importance of their Vietnamese colony in this wider imperial competition, perched as it was at the spot where the Indian and Pacific Oceans and the Eurasian continent converge. At the turn of the twentieth century, they finished building the deep-water port of Cam Ranh Bay, located off the southeastern coast of Vietnam. Russian warships dispatched from the Baltic to stop Japanese colonial expansion into China and Korea gathered there before being defeated by the Japanese at the Battle of Tsushima in 1905. Following the Japanese invasion of China in 1937, President Franklin Roosevelt closely followed Japanese movements down the Chinese coastline and imposed an embargo on Tokyo as Japanese imperial troops started occupying Vietnam in 1940. His fears of a wider Japanese thrust southward were well founded. In early 1942, having attacked Pearl Harbor and occupied all of Vietnam, the Japanese then concentrated their ships in Cam Ranh Bay before attacking Southeast Asia and striking as far as the Andaman and Nicobar Islands in the Indian Ocean. Created in 1942, the American 7th Fleet helped roll back the Japanese empire and remained to protect America's postwar control of the Pacific and Indian Oceans. The 7th Fleet first called on Vietnam in 1950 to reassure the French following the Chinese communist victory of 1949. The Americans went on to station the bulk of their naval forces in Cam Ranh Bay during the Vietnam War. And when they withdrew from the country in April 1975, the Russians took over.[1]

Today, geopolitical tensions are again on the rise in the waters off Vietnam's coast. For the first time since the Ming recalled their armada from the Indian Ocean in 1433, the Chinese are actively seeking to expand their naval presence into the Pacific. The United States is in conversation with its former enemies in Vietnam about how best to respond. The Russians have taken a renewed interest in Vietnam and Cam Ranh Bay since the end of the Cold War, and, worried by growing Chinese naval power, the Japanese are also improving their ties with the Vietnamese. Vietnam remains to this day at the center of intense global rivalries, and it is tempting to view the country and its history in terms of the conflicts of the 'great powers'.

The problem, however, is that such accounts of Vietnam are driven by the views of those who coveted, occupied, and fought over this country. By casting Vietnam as a former colony or a strategic zone, or reducing it to a single war or a series of wars, the history of Vietnam becomes the story of its relationship with—outside powers. There is nothing necessarily wrong with an external take on Vietnam's past. However, such accounts tend to present the history of this country in rather one-dimensional ways: Vietnam was acted upon by the big powers; it was not quite an actor itself. In the great power account, Vietnam is the victim of colonization and domination, never a colonizer or a conqueror itself. Its own internal divisions, ethnic diversity, and conflicts are obscured.

Things are changing, however. Thanks to a flood of new research on Vietnam in recent years, the opening of the country to the outside since the 1980s, and the distance now separating us from the heated political debates generated by Western intervention in the 1950s, 1960s, and 1970s, it is now possible to write a new history of Vietnam. This book tries to do just that. It still takes into account this country's position in a coveted part of the world where empires collide, but it also emphasizes Vietnam's own role in shaping its history and highlights the country's extraordinary diversity and complexity.

Most importantly, it emphasizes that there has never been one Vietnam but several remarkably varied ones. During the seventeenth and eighteenth centuries, at least two polities existed, one anchored in the Red River delta around Hanoi, another pushing southward past Hue into the plains of the Mekong. Vietnam only appeared in something of its present S-like form when, in 1802, the emperor of the Nguyen dynasty, Gia Long, following decades of civil strife, united the country. Even then, Vietnam hardly remained inert. Until the 1840s, Nguyen leaders fairly successfully tried to expand their imperial state to include Cambodia and swathes of today's eastern Laos, declaring the empire of Dai Nam (the Greater South) as they did so.

French colonizers had no qualms about invoking earlier Dai Nam imperial pretensions to justify their own colonial expansion up the Mekong River in search of a Chinese Eldorado. However, if the Indochinese Union they announced in 1887 placed Vietnam, Laos, and Cambodia within the same colonial structure, the French divided Vietnam territorially into three separate sub-units—Cochinchina (the south), Annam (the center), and Tonkin (the north). Between 1862 and 1945, the independent Nguyen state that had unified Vietnamese lands in 1802 was no more. That changed as the Second World War drew to a close in 1945, toppled French Indochina, and nationalists declared the independence of Vietnam and reaffirmed its territorial unity along the lines largely established by Gia Long. Such unity was, however, short-lived. Decolonization, the Cold War, and civil conflicts intersected violently to divide Vietnam into several competing states between 1945 and 1975. In its entire history, Vietnam has only existed in its present national form for about eighty-three years and some months (as of 2016)—never before 1802, for forty-three years in the nineteenth century, six months in 1945, and for forty years since 1976. The 'great power' take on the Vietnamese past tends to overlook this multiplicity.[2]

The expansion of Red River Vietnam southward into populous areas also transformed this country into a mosaic of peoples, languages, and cultures. Ethnic Viet, or the *kinh*, may constitute the majority of the Vietnamese population today (85.7 percent in 1999), but they share the national territory with over fifty other ethnic groups. Centuries before the *kinh*—'the people of the capital'—moved out of the Red River basin, the Tai, Jarai, Cham, Khmers, and others were the dominant populations in the highlands which hug the Red River lowlands, along the central coast, and throughout the Mekong delta. Until the late fifteenth century, the history of Vietnam below the Red River—even within it—was a very non-Viet one. There was no 'S' shape to Vietnam. And well into the twentieth century, the non-Viet peoples now living within Vietnam's borders outnumbered the *kinh* in the highlands, an area comprising over half of the country. It is precisely its multiple territorial forms, ethno-cultural heterogeneity, and diverse colonial experiences—Chinese, French, and Vietnamese—that make the history of Vietnam so fascinating.[3]

Specialists inside and outside Vietnam know this, and scholars are increasingly fascinated by the country's diversity. This new general history moves in similar directions. Rather than positing one Vietnam, one homogeneous people, one history, one modernity, or even one colonialism, this book investigates Vietnam's past through its multiple forms and impressive diversity.[4] Let us take a closer look at what this might mean.

MULTIPLE VIETNAMS

Until recently, Vietnam has commonly been understood to mean today's Socialist Republic of Vietnam (SRV), first declared independent by Ho Chi Minh in September 1945 as the Democratic Republic of Vietnam (DRV). The conventional narrative moves rapidly from the French attack on Nguyen Vietnam in 1858 to the emergence of the Democratic Republic of Vietnam in 1945 by way of a discussion of French conquest, colonial development, and modernity, and the rise of Vietnamese anticolonialism, nationalism, and communism. Ho Chi Minh stands out as the main character in this narrative of modern Vietnam, allowing historians to follow him (and his Vietnam) from Saigon in 1911 to Paris in 1919, and then on to Moscow and Hong Kong as he embraces communism as the best 'road' to attaining Vietnam's national independence in 1945. This popular account then culminates in the French and American military defeats in Indochina as the DRV marches to final victory over the Republic of Vietnam in 1975. It's the story of one Vietnam.

American journalist Frances FitzGerald's highly influential and Pulitzer prize-winning book, *Fire in the Lake*, went furthest in establishing what has become the standard account of modern Vietnam in the English language. Even before the communist victory in 1975, she had proclaimed Ho Chi Minh's Vietnam as the real one. Not only were the Americans supporting the wrong Vietnamese leaders, first Bao Dai, the French-backed leader of the Associated State of Vietnam, then Ngo Dinh Diem, who replaced it with the Republic of Vietnam in 1955, but in so doing they were also placing themselves on the wrong side of history—Vietnamese history, as defined by FitzGerald, as being a timeless, deep-seated culture of resistance to foreign invasion and colonial domination which Ho and his Vietnam incarnated. Like other righteous rulers before him, in FitzGerald's hands, Ho became the rightful new sovereign, who had emerged in a time of great disorder to seize the 'Mandate of Heaven', with the support of the people. Published at the height of the anti-war movement, *Fire in the Lake* sought above all to show how the Americans and their empire, just like the French and theirs, were doomed to failure.[5]

Whether one is for or against American intervention in Vietnam, there are serious problems in terms of how American-focused accounts of the wars like this represent the Vietnamese past. By assuming that Ho Chi Minh's Vietnam of 1945 incarnated a timeless, traditional Vietnam with its roots deep in an antiquity which was destined to win in the present, FitzGerald gives us a very essentialized, unchanging Vietnam. This teleological framing of the Vietnamese past prevents us from seeing the multiplicity and complexity of Vietnamese historical experience and the different possibilities for the future that were present at the time. Communist nationalists led by Ho Chi Minh were certainly important, as this book will demonstrate; but communist Vietnam was but one of several possibilities. No history of this country is complete without taking into account competitor states and their leaders, such as French Vietnam (1858–1955) under men like Albert

Sarraut, Pierre Pasquier, and Léon Pignon; the Associated State of Vietnam led by Bao Dai (1949–1954), the Republic of Vietnam forged by Ngo Dinh Diem, Nguyen Van Thieu, and others (1955–75), and highland Vietnams marshalled by Léopold Sabatier, Deo Van Long, and Y Thih Eban.

These alternative polities undeniably failed, often miserably so, but their stories spanning more than a century deserve our attention if we are to understand today's Vietnam. After all, Ho Chi Minh's Vietnam had to engage with each in order to prevail, starting with Sarraut's in the 1910s. As one astute observer put it in relation to the American Civil War, 'to exclude all thoughts of the alternative is to lose contact with how it felt to peer into the inscrutable future'. In short, it is no longer necessary to write the history of 'Vietnam' as the unique story of the winners. We need to recognize that the history of Vietnam, like any other place in the world, is a series of interlocking forces and people, occurring and acting at specific points in time and space, each generating its own range of possibilities and eliminating others at the same time. So let us try in the pages that follow to peer into the Vietnamese past with at least a few 'thoughts of the alternatives'.[6]

Modern Vietnams

We might also try to think of 'modernity' in similar terms. Much ink has been spilled over the rather slippery notions of the 'modern' and 'modernity', to say nothing of 'postmodernity'. For many, 'modern' simply means something 'recent', not 'old'. For partisans of *this* periodization, the nineteenth and twentieth centuries usually fit the bill best for delineating modern Vietnam as something recent. For others, 'modern' refers to a specifically Western historical transformation which culminated in Europe and North America in the nineteenth century with the advent of industrialization, urbanization, secularization, scientific and bureaucratic rationalization, capitalism, and the rise of the nation-state. One can quibble over a precise definition—and there may never be one—but most would agree that these are the main ingredients making the 'modern'.

According to this school of thought, Western colonial expansion in the nineteenth and twentieth centuries exported these components to the non-Western world in one form or another. It could be done independently as in the case of Japan, Thailand, and Turkey, or it could arrive through direct Western colonial connections as in Vietnam, Burma, or Algeria. Until recently, most histories of modern China began in 1842, with the Chinese defeat at the hands of the British during the First Opium War. Only then, the story goes, did China embark on the road to 'modernization' and 'progress'. As one specialist of China has pointed out, we tend to use the term 'un-modern' to refer to 'what existed in Europe before 1800 and what existed in the rest of the world until Europeans arrived and changed the way people did things or alternatively, until European ideas and opportunities were made available to people in other parts of the world to adopt and adapt to fit their local situations'. The history of 'modern Egypt' starts the same way, with Napoleon Bonaparte's invasion in 1798 and the opening of the country to the West.[7]

A number of scholars writing on Vietnam and colonial Indochina subscribe to this Western-centric conception of modernity and its accompanying periodization. Pierre Brocheux goes so far as to make the French 'colonial moment' the cornerstone of his recent history of modern Vietnam. In their landmark general history of French Indochina, he and co-author Daniel Hémery insist on the modernizing nature of the French colonial project. While they certainly recognize colonialism's exploitative character and the importance of pre-colonial Vietnam's achievements, the authors conclude nonetheless that French colonialism introduced modernity in the form of infrastructure, urbanization, science and medicine, capitalist development, bureaucratic rationalization, and the nation-state. Like the 1842 date for those writing on China or 1798 for Egypt, Brocheux and Hémery's account begins with the point of Vietnam's colonial contact with the French in 1858. More than anything else, they argue, French colonialism created modern Vietnam from that point in time. They are by no means alone. I myself once attached similar importance to French colonial modernity in the making of Vietnamese nationalism at the expense of exploring pre-existing connections and modernities.[8]

That Western colonialism was a major modernizing force in Vietnamese history, few would disagree. I do not. However, the periodization, defining, and framing of all that is modern in Vietnam in such terms comes with real problems. For one, they create a 'great divide' in Vietnamese history between a 'pre-colonial' or a 'pre-French' past and a much more detailed 'nineteenth- to twentieth-century Vietnam' during which the country becomes 'modern'. Secondly, by assuming that modern Vietnam began with the French attack of 1858, we lose sight of the complex set of pre-existing historical phenomena and a plurality of 'lost' or 'multiple modernities' that went into the making of a series of 'new Vietnams'. The meritocratic Confucian examination system and the rational though contested bureaucracies it nurtured were essential components of modernity present in China, Korea, and Vietnam. Voltaire waxed lyrically over China's laws, institutions, and secularism in the eighteenth century, contrasting them favorably to the things he so wanted changed in France. Thirdly, far from replacing the pre-existing bureaucracy and its civil servants, French administrators often grafted their colonial state on to it as an effective mechanism of social control, an efficient method of political administration, and a source of information without which 'the colonial moment' would not have lasted for long. French efforts to develop Vietnam's roads, canals, dikes, and the lucrative Asian rice trade also built on pre-existing projects. Minh Mang's reign in the early nineteenth century deserves perhaps more than a footnote in the history of 'modern Vietnam'. His administrative policies were aimed at territorial integration, state centralization, bureaucratic rationalization, economic development, and ideological homogenization. This is not to say that he achieved all of this (he did not!), but rather to suggest that modernity is not an all-or-nothing phenomenon. It exists in multiple forms, at different points in time and space, and often blends with and builds upon pre-existing ones. It can disappear as fast as it arrives. It can even co-exist with the 'un-modern'. French *and* Vietnamese women did not obtain the right to vote until 1945.[9]

While there is no need to construct an Asian-centered approach to modernity in the place of the Western-centered one, it is useful to keep these wider spatial and temporal considerations in mind in the pages that follow, for they allow us to see the Vietnamese past in new ways. This is why I have intentionally left open the precise timing of modernity's birth in Vietnam, rather than insisting that 'modern' Vietnam only emerged from 1858 onward. This makes room for multiple modernities, colonial grafts, and wider connections that the Franco-centric approach misses. It is admittedly a more complicated story, pushing 'the modern' further into the past than most are accustomed, but such an open-ended periodization makes it a much more interesting one. One of the reasons why the brief Chinese colonization of Vietnam in the early fifteenth century was so important was because it provided the Vietnamese with access to some of the most modern gunpowder weapons of the time, a sophisticated bureaucratic model, and a colonial ideology needed for their own rethinking and building of a new Vietnam long before the French arrived on the scene.[10]

IMPERIAL VIETNAMS

This latter point is important; for by starting in 1858 one would not know that today's Vietnam is the product of its own colonial history, not just the French one. One need only look a little before 1858 to see that the French were not the first colonizers in the Mekong delta or the Red River basin. The latter zone, the cradle of Vietnamese civilization, was part of a Chinese empire for a millennium. Once independent of China, the Vietnamese began building and pushing their own empire southward, establishing protectorates over far-flung regions, promoting settlement colonies, alternating between 'direct' and 'indirect' methods of rule over distant, multi-ethnic peoples, testing cultural assimilation, and developing their own *mission civilisatrice*. They were far from finished when the French arrived. And rather than stopping Vietnamese expansion in its tracks, the French often reinforced the Vietnamese imperial project in many places by making them their privileged partners in building another colonial state. The French colonial project in Indochina thus carried within it a second, pre-existing Asian one, that of the Vietnamese themselves. These intersecting imperial projects are central to understanding modern Vietnam.

Some will object to this focus on 'pre-French', Asian empires in the making of modern Vietnam. However, such critics forget that colonial connections and empire-states were not unique to the West or to the nineteenth century. They are part of a wider global history made up of empires running from one end of Eurasia to the other since antiquity. Qing colonial expansion into central Asia—Tibet, for example—in the eighteenth century is vital to understanding China today. Indeed, by ignoring the role of pre-existing Asian colonialisms, we fail to pick up on the complexity of countries such as China and Vietnam and the novelty of their territorial forms. This wider view of imperial projects helps to guard against projecting homogenizing notions of ethnicity and national identity back into and on to a much more diverse and, in the end, fascinating past. It also provides a glimpse into state formation as a work in continual progress and sheds light on how power operated in Vietnam across time and space before, after, and often right through '1858'. And lastly, like their Chinese, Russian, American, and French counterparts, Vietnamese colonialism generated a complex historical experience marked by violent confrontations with indigenous peoples whom they conquered as well as peaceful exchanges with them, each of which has had important ramifications to this day. Today's nations are often the historical products of pre-existing, multi-ethnic empires. Vietnam, like the United States and the Russian Federation, is the product of several imperial pasts, including its own.[11]

DIVIDED VIETNAMS

The need to go beyond 1858 is important for a final reason of periodization. For if one ventures one last time beyond this conventional date, it becomes rapidly clear that Gia Long's creation of a unitary Vietnam in 1802 was in fact more the exception than the rule. After breaking with each other violently in 1627, the Trinh and Nguyen military lords came to rule Vietnam as two separate states (but under the nominal unitary rule of the Le dynasty) until the Tay Son brothers charged out of the central highlands to add a third polity in the late eighteenth century. That is over a century and a half of a divided Vietnam. There was thus nothing necessarily aberrant about the existence of 'two Vietnams' during the second half of the twentieth century. Nor was the twentieth century the only time during which Vietnamese fought each other. Internecine conflicts racked Vietnam in the seventeenth and eighteenth centuries (and long before), some of which expanded into regional conflagrations with the Thais and the Chinese, as they would in the late twentieth century. Nor was inter-ethnic violence unheard of as non-Viet peoples, like the Cham, Tai, and the Khmer, resisted Vietnamese conquest, or attacked the Viet to expand their own empires. The implications of all of this are important to understanding Vietnam to this day.[12]

While this book admittedly zooms in on the nineteenth and twentieth centuries, the three pre-1858 chapters provide more than just rapid 'historical background' on the 'pre-French period'. They are an important part of this book's goal of providing a new account of the plurality of Vietnams from the past to the present, one that avoids creating a great divide at the 'French colonial moment' of 1858, between 'East' and 'West', 'modern' and 'un-modern', 'before' and 'after', 'unified' and 'divided', 'Viet' and 'non-Viet'. Some will object that by exploring Vietnam's colonial, diverse, and divided past, I'm engaging in a postmodernist fetish for 'deconstructing' or, worse, that I will end up legitimating 'conservative' justifications for foreign intervention in Vietnam. I politely disagree. If I take issue with anything in the politics of writing the Vietnamese past, it is a persistent tendency inside and outside Vietnam to exceptionalize it. This is particularly the case in

American diplomatic history where the Vietnam War remains central to critiquing—or defending—'American empire' and 'American exceptionalism'. While I have no problems taking American empire and nationalism to task, I do not believe that we have to exceptionalize the Vietnamese and their past to do so. Those who do so run the risk of practicing a form of Western-centered Orientalism that Edward Said warned us against.[13]

Balancing all this has been extraordinarily difficult. I have inevitably left out things some would have wanted to see. I certainly could have solved this problem by increasing the size of the book and the level of detail. However, I remain convinced that bigger is not always better. The reader will be the judge of how well I have done. Will specialists of Vietnam find anything of interest for them in this book? I do hope so, for I owe each of them my deepest gratitude. For those specifically wishing to teach and study from this book, I have created a website which includes an online bibliography and material on the historiographical debates about Vietnam, as well as short essays on differences in interpretation among scholars. It is on my home page at www.cgoscha.uqam.ca.

CHAPTER 1

NORTHERN
CONFIGURATIONS

In the spring of 1694, Shilian Dashan, a Buddhist abbot in charge of the Changshou Monastery in the southern Chinese port city of Guangzhou (Canton), received two letters from Vietnam—one from a former disciple now serving as the Dai Viet court's advisor on Buddhist matters, the other penned by the ruling lord himself, Nguyen Phuc Chu. Since assuming power a few years earlier, the Vietnamese ruler had been trying to bring this highly regarded missionary to Hue to help spread the Buddhist church. Part of it was personal; Chu wanted to believe. Part of it was also designed to legitimate royal power and reinforce Nguyen state-building in a very contested land. To convince the Chinese master of his sincerity, Nguyen Phuc Chu insisted in his missive: 'I now devote myself to burning incense and meditation' and 'humbly beg the master of the Way to change his mind and agree to travel. Only then will our kingdom prosper.'[1]

It apparently worked, for a year later Dashan and his team of over a hundred people landed in today's central Vietnam. The Chinese monk immediately set to work, performing the rites making Nguyen Phuc Chu his first Vietnamese disciple, before initiating the royal family, court officials, and various elites into Buddhism. Dashan presided over the establishment of new temples and the renovation of others. He advised court officials and the Nguyen lord on Buddhist doctrine and statecraft, essential to helping the Nguyen make a new Vietnam, independent of the one further north from which it had initially sprung.

Dashan could not have sailed back to China in 1696 without realizing that there was not one 'Dai Viet', but in fact two hiding behind that name— one which had been anchored in the Red River delta for centuries and still was, the other moving its way southward past Hue. Based in Guangzhou and having proselytized extensively in Asia, Dashan would have also known how overland and seaborne routes had long connected both of these Vietnams to China, the South Seas, and the Indian Ocean. Chinese traders and monks had been crisscrossing these areas for centuries, spreading Buddhism from India to Korea, Japan, and the Red River lands. Confucianism and Daoism had arrived in these countries through similar channels. And as our Chinese Buddhist missionary returned to his monastery, he would have also known that another group of religious men, Christians, were also hard at work in this part of the world where so many people, routes, and ideas intersected. This is where the story of Vietnam's past in this chapter begins, in this open zone running between today's central Vietnam and southern China.

IMPERIAL CONFIGURATIONS

A Mosaic of a Hundred Viet
The area of the Red River delta and the hills that line it from three sides is considered today to be the cradle of Vietnamese civilization, the sacred land from which today's Vietnam traces its national heritage back for thousands of years. Viewed from above, it's a beautiful sight to behold: emerging from the cragged reliefs of southern China, the Red River slowly winds its way through a rice-terraced delta, then past the capital of Hanoi before emptying into the Gulf of Tonkin. For thousands of years, the low-lying Red River basin has been home to diverse peoples arriving via the eastern coast and overland from the surrounding hills. Austro-asiatic peoples moving into mainland Southeast Asia by way of southern China are thought to have been among the first to arrive in this area during the Neolithic period (10,000–2,000 BCE). Similar migrations occurred to the west, where three other waterways parallel the Red River's descent into Southeast Asia—the Irrawaddy crossing Burma into the Andaman Sea, the Chao Phraya flowing through Thailand to the Gulf of Thailand, and the Mekong that winds its way slowly from Tibet to Saigon.

Some of the earliest settled agricultural communities appeared in the Red River plains from around 3,000 BCE as climatic changes began drying parts of what had until then been a very swampy place. As it did, rice cultivation spread in from northern areas in the Yangzi valley. Over time, thanks to the development of dikes and canals, inhabitants began to control flooding and used irrigation for double-cropping. Such intensive, wet-rice agriculture supported larger populations, as did early maritime exchanges with Asia. Dominant families emerged, clans united into tribes, and more complex socio-political institutions evolved. The spread of metal- and bronze-casting technology allowed craftsmen to make agricultural tools, weapons, and a variety of art objects as cloth production flourished.

Peoples inhabiting this area participated in a wider civilization covering large swathes of present-day southern China and mainland Southeast Asia. Archeologists refer to it loosely as the Dong Son culture. Thanks to archeological excavations, radiocarbon dating, and historical linguistics, we know that this civilization thrived roughly between the sixth century BCE and the second century CE, extending from the Red River plains to today's northeastern Thailand and northward into southern China's Yunnan province. Its bronze drums, which one can see on display in the National Museum in Hanoi today, were used for religious and political purposes. These drums, some of which boast pictures of elegant cranes, have come to symbolize Dong Son's brilliance and, for many, the origins of Vietnamese national identity. While the Vietnamese village of Dong Son, where many of these artifacts have been unearthed, was an important production site in this prehistoric civilization, the fact that peoples living far beyond present-day northern Vietnam produced similar ones during the same era complicates such nationalist claims.[2]

The Dong Son civilization was home to a vibrant collection of peoples and cultures, but it was not always a pacific region or a unified one. As one group eyed the riches of another, conflicts inevitably arose. Local metal and bronze production meant that weapons were available. Ambitious rulers organized warrior classes to expand their territories and control populations. Local polities rose and fell as small dynasties, tribes, and their strongmen clashed. Indeed, Dong Son drums were often made with war in mind. As far as we know no one ruler ever gained the military upper hand or projected the charismatic force needed to create a single 'Dong Son federation' extending from southern China to northern Vietnam. Some scholars have suggested that power was perhaps organized locally around a collection of charismatic military leaders or kings. A local balance of power tended to prevail. Central control would have thus remained diffuse and moved through a multi-centered array of small territories, 'a patchwork of often overlapping *mandalas*, or "circles of kings"', who, in turn, often relied upon a spirit world to legitimate their rule. New research, however, suggests that a powerful, centralized political authority emerged in the third century BCE in Co Loa near Hanoi. A complex of walls, moats, and ramparts supported a surprisingly important urban population for the time. The large amounts of labor needed to build and defend such a center also suggest that Co Loa achieved a high level of political, social, and economic organization that may have allowed it to dominate other Dong Son locations concentrated in the Red River valley.[3]

The nature of this ancient state formation continued to evolve when the 'Chinese' Qin (221–206 BCE) and especially the Han dynasts (206 BCE–220 CE) dominated and then began unifying warring tribes concentrated between the Yellow and Yangzi rivers into a single imperial core state. At the center—between heaven and earth—stood one divine leader, the emperor, equipped with a mandate from heaven. In theory, he ruled the empire through a bureaucratic state and military capable of holding and administering large swathes of multi-ethnic territories. Upon assuming power, Qin and Han emperors soon dispatched their forces southward to conquer new lands. Access to people and resources was essential to perpetuating the imperial state as it expanded from its core area outward. This, in turn, required authorities to devise an array of direct and indirect methods for ruling distant and multi-ethnic lands and peoples.[4]

Casting themselves as the leaders of a universal empire, Chinese rulers, imperial officers, colonial administrators, and their explorers viewed the peoples they encountered south of the Yangzi (as well as in the Central Asian steppes) with a combination of curiosity, arrogance, disgust, and fear. Like the Romans also hard at work building an empire on the other side of Eurasia, the Han coined a range of terms to describe the inhabitants living beyond their empire's confines, people they considered to be bereft of superior Han civilization and thus worthy of conquest. The Romans borrowed the Greek term for 'barbarian' to distinguish themselves from those living outside the civilizing domain of the empire. Han authorities used the terms *yi*, *man*, and others to make sense of those living outside the civilizing confines of the 'central country', *zhong guo*. They also used the characters for 'beyond' and 'across' to describe those living below the Yangzi. One such term was 'Yue' ('Viet'), meaning 'those from beyond'. Chinese officials often coupled it with the word for the 'south', '*nan*', to indicate its geographical relationship to the Middle or Central Kingdom, giving us *Yue Nan* (Viet Nam) or *Nan Yue* (Nam Viet). The Chinese annals confirm, too, that there was never a single 'Yue/Viet' state, but rather a collection of dynastic and tribal polities operating across much of southern China into the Red River basin. Many had fled into this area in 333 BCE when the Qin destroyed an ancient Yue state located along China's middle-eastern coast.

At one point, the Han used the characters Bai Viet or Bach Viet to refer to the 'Hundred Viet' tribes located in what they now increasingly viewed as a 'borderland' below the Yangzi River.[5]

ENTER THE CHINESE EMPIRE[6]

It was during this shifting geopolitical context, as Chinese rulers began incorporating southern lands into their own protean imperial formation, that 'Vietnam' enters the Chinese empire and with it the written historical record. Vietnamese writing in the fifteenth century asserted that in 257 BCE, a local king named An Duong Vuong united the Lac Viet and Au Viet tribes into a single polity in the Red River area called Au Lac. It consisted of peoples coming from the delta and its surrounding highlands. While it is likely that An Duong Vuong took control of the Co Loa center located near today's Hanoi, this early state did not last long. Around 170 BCE, it fell to a rogue Han general based in Guangzhou named Zhao Tuo. Without the consent of the court, he carved out a separate borderland polity and named it the land of the 'Southern Viet' (Nam Viet/Nan yue). It included the Co Loa area of the Red River delta as well as parts of Guangdong and Guangxi provinces.[7]

Zhao Tuo's regime lasted little longer than its Au Lac predecessor, as Han imperial troops moved in. In 111 BCE, the Han dynasty formally incorporated these southern 'yi' lands, consisting of Viet and non-Viet peoples, into their imperial state as a military commandery. Despite a few brief periods of independence, the people of the Red River remained there until the tenth century as China's frontier province of Jiaozhi (Giao chi in Vietnamese). Initially, Jiaozhi included the Red River delta and much of today's Guangdong province, the highlands as well as the deltas. In the late fifth century CE, the Chinese reduced the province's borders to today's upper Vietnam.[8]

Control of this southern province was of major concern for the Han. Partly this stemmed from the attraction of its fertile plains and agricultural production; but trade also pulled imperial strategists southward. The Qin and Han had both extended canal building toward the southern coast in order to profit from international commerce coming from the South Seas and the Indian Ocean, what they often combined into one term as the 'Southern Seas' or Nanhai. The coast of today's northern Vietnam provided an excellent opening for trading with Southeast Asia, the Indian subcontinent, the Middle East, and as far as the Mediterranean. This attraction of the Southern Seas is worth keeping in mind here and for later periods, for just as the overland Silk Road connecting China to the Roman and Parthian empires drew the Chinese empire deeper into the Central Asian steppes to the north, so too did the Indian Ocean's markets, peoples, and products pull it southward into the Red River toward Southeast Asia. In 231 CE, a Han administrator in Jiaozhi was categorical about Vietnam's commercial value, writing to his superiors that agricultural taxes yielded little revenue compared to international trade: 'This place is famous for precious rarities from afar: pearls, incense, drums, elephant tusks, rhinoceros horns, tortoise shells, coral, lapis lazuli, parrots, kingfishers, peacocks, rare and abundant treasure enough to satisfy all desires. So it is not necessary to depend on what is received from regular taxes in order to profit the Central Kingdom.' The Chinese would in turn export highly sought-after products to international customers, including ceramics, tea, and silk.[9]

Like their Roman and Parthian counterparts, Han imperial armies could be massive and conquest was often brutal, despite the lofty civilizing missions proffered by their emperors. Those 'barbarians' who refused to submit to imperial power often paid with their lives. Survivors found themselves jailed, banished, demoted, or homeless. Pragmatic-minded Han authorities realized, however, that such hard-handed methods would get them nowhere in the long run. Blind military conquest and assimilation without a political endgame were costly affairs and only created a sea of hate from which the 'barbarians' would recruit their own armies. Perceptive colonial officials also realized that while the empire circulated Han administrators, officers, and settlers to work in the south, their numbers would never be large enough to operate the state effectively at the lower, yet vital levels of the administration in which few spoke Chinese. One Chinese administrator posted to the south bemoaned the gap between colonial theory and practice in a report: 'Customs are not uniform and languages are mutually unintelligible, so that several interpreters are needed to communicate. . . . If district level officials are appointed, it is the same as if they were not'.[10]

Located far from the metropolis, many Han authorities had no choice but to accommodate local leaders by offering them a role in the provincial administration. Rather than defeating aristocratic families, warlords, or shamans, compromises were reached and concessions were made. Outside the provincial capital, colonial authorities used pre-colonial administrative structures, kinship networks, and cults to rule indirectly, regardless of the orders they received from on high calling for uniformity and assimilation. Over time, the court eventually opened the doors of the imperial army, administration, and academies to Red River Viet as a way of instilling loyalty, building legitimacy, and ruling effectively.

While resistance to Chinese imperial expansion was real, so was the desire of many Viet to build a better life from within the empire. This was often the case for groups that had been marginalized under pre-existing orders and saw a chance to reassert themselves and their projects in the new balance of power and within the new imperial formation. Well into the twentieth century elite Viets would serve at the highest levels of the Chinese state and army. Equally important, Han cultural, technological, military, and political modernity proved attractive, especially when it could be used to promote local interests, trade, and identities. As a result, over the centuries, a new Sino-Viet or Sinitic elite emerged in the provincial capital near today's Hanoi, while much less 'Sinicized' chieftains and aristocratic families continued to exercise power at the local levels. But without the collaboration of these local Sinitic elites and rural lords who knew the land, the people, and its languages, the Chinese imperial moment would never have lasted a millennium.[11]

Vietnam achieved a new level of development as a part of China. The foreign trade defended by our Han administrator above continued to drive change. But contrary to what he asserted, so did agriculture. In fact, by the second century CE, agricultural production had developed sufficiently enough to support a population of around one million people. New farming techniques and tools spread along with improved methods of diking and irrigation. Local manufacturing produced glassware from potash for local consumption and export. Bronze drum decorations reveal organized spinning and weaving production, based in part on slave labor. Drum-casting became a lucrative business with Red River manufacturers supplying them to nearby non-Han leaders who often used them as symbols of their local authority. The Chinese court taxed trade, agriculture, and manufacturing, with some of the revenue going to Jiaozhi lords.[12]

Empires have always served as motors for change. They connect and circulate peoples and move ideas, material cultures, and languages, and not just theirs. They can also serve as a process for accelerating integrative, technological, cultural, and economic change. A thousand years of Chinese rule spread many aspects of Han culture into Jiaozhi. Chinese administrators introduced new notions of law, time, and space (legal codes, calendars, measures, weights, maps, etc.) as well as bureaucratic statecraft, weapons, paper, and a character-based writing system to accompany it. Elite Red River culture changed with the introduction of Chinese-inspired royal architecture, music, art, and culinary practices, including the use of chopsticks. Thousands of Chinese settlers also moved into the delta during the colonial period, bringing with them a collection of new ideas, technologies, and words. Intermarriage was common, as were mixed offspring and bilingualism. Like the Middle English born of the Norman conquest of England in the twelfth century, a similar 'Middle-Annamese' arose in colonial Vietnamese towns, allowing many Chinese words to enter the Viet language during that time. The imperial connection also introduced ideas coming from further abroad. From its Indian birthplace in the fifth century BCE, for example, Mahayana Buddhism travelled the Silk Road with traders and missionaries and, through southern China and the coast, entered Vietnamese history through Jiaozhi province. Indian missionaries also visited and more than one Vietnamese monk went abroad for religious study in the native land of the Buddha.[13]

The Confucian repertoire of enlightened monarchy, good governance, and social harmony also circulated southward. In its simplest form, Confucianism turned on three basic relationships: subjects owed loyalty to the king; sons behaved with piety toward their fathers; and wives expressed submissive fidelity toward their husbands and sons. In theory, this male-dominated family hierarchy served as the bedrock for building an ideal government and harmonious social order. Just as sons submitted to their fathers, so too should subjects loyally serve their ruler. Ancestor veneration—whereby the living performed pious rituals ensuring the proper afterlife of deceased family members and royalty—reinforced this. The Chinese relied on Confucianism to erect centralized bureaucratic states and spread Confucian culture, after centuries of political instability and social disorder. This included the development of a modern civil service and examination system based on merit instead of court, family, aristocratic, or military connections. The importance and utilization of Confucianism ebbed and flowed over time and space. As a repertoire, it was a collection of techniques and guiding principles for regulating state and society.[14]

What deserves emphasis here, viewed from a comparative world history perspective, is four things. Firstly, despite nationalist claims to the contrary, there is nothing particularly surprising about Vietnam's entry into and extended participation in the Chinese imperial state. Like the Au Lac Viet peoples facing the Han from the third century BCE onward, Celtic Gaul came under Roman attack in 121 BCE, with Julius Caesar subduing the area in 51 BCE. For half a millennium, the Romans ruled what became 'France' as a number of provinces. Like its Chinese counterpart, the Roman empire served as a vehicle through which institutions, laws, architecture, religions, and the Latin-based writing system spread into Gaul and other conquered lands. Not unlike the use of Latin in Europe, Chinese characters became the written language of bureaucratic politics and religious expression in East Asia, including Vietnam. Chinese characters (*hanzi*) served as the models for the development of writing scripts in Korea (*hangul*), Japan (*kanji*), and Vietnam (*han tu* or *chu han*). Each word in *han tu* or Sino-Vietnamese is a Chinese character, but read with a Viet pronunciation. Viet elites also used Chinese characters later to construct an indigenous demotic script, *chu nom*, adjusted to represent spoken Vietnamese. A millennium of Chinese imperial rule features in the Vietnamese past, just as the Roman empire helped shape French history.[15]

Secondly, whether in western Eurasia or on its eastern side, such transfers of power never worked out so easily on the ground. Chinese imperial power in Vietnam tended to be channeled through a few, small urban sites and handled by literate Sino-Vietnamese elites living in these administrative hubs. Few imperial channels fed directly into the countryside, where the majority (and largely illiterate) rural population resided. While elites had adopted many Chinese loan words in the 'Middle-Annamese' they spoke, the Mon-Khmer Vietnamese language (and others) resonated throughout the rest of the Red River delta. If imperial authorities wanted to reach this part of Vietnam, they had to connect to the pre-existing grid, staffed by local lords familiar with Sinicized ways, but operating in their languages and according to their customs. Located on the outermost rim of the empire, the majority rural population of Red River Vietnam, dominated by a dozen or so aristocratic families, lived in a spiritual realm where they venerated a host of deities and spirits reaching back into the depths of time. It was also a realm into which Buddhism had inserted itself, sometimes seeming as if it had always been there.[16]

The process of Confucianization certainly began in Vietnam under Chinese rule, but it remained a largely urban, administrative, and elite male experience. Moreover, because urbanization in Jiaozhi remained minimal under Chinese rule, the line between elite and popular religions and cultures was never drawn sharply. They overlapped. Viet elites in Hanoi may have been well versed in the Confucian canon and taken pride in writing Chinese characters, but they were just as often at ease in the composite religious world of Buddhist monks, spirits, genies, and cults. To return to the Eurasian comparison, it was not because the Roman Emperor Constantine backed Christianity in the fourth century or a Frankish tribal leader named Clovis was baptized a century later that all Europeans or Frenchmen suddenly became 'Christians'. They did not. It took a lot of time. The same is true for 'Confucian' East Asia and Vietnam. If anything connected the Vietnamese to China, indeed the rest of Eurasia during this early period, it was this world of spirits, local cults, deities, soothsayers, and millenarian beliefs permeating the lives of elites and commoners alike.[17]

Thirdly, next to these cultural transfers, stood force. Not all emperors were benevolent father figures. Many used their armies to get what they wanted, regardless of the effects locally. Onerous labor requirements, heavy taxation, and corruption were sources of social discontent and revolt. Colonial culture and statecraft often collided with pre-existing political formations, privileges, cultures, identities, and languages. Resistance broke out often when the Chinese court pursued assimilationist policies or tried to impose direct rule instead of remembering the advantages of accommodation, flexibility, and indirect rule. The Trung sisters have gone down in history for their heroic rebellion between 39–43 CE. Fueling their defiance was the imperial execution of one sister's husband against the backdrop of unpopular assimilation policies aimed at the local aristocratic class. The arrival of more Han settlers may have also triggered the revolt by removing local elites from positions of power, threatening their social status and landed interests. The Chinese emperor dispatched General Ma Yuan, who smashed the revolt before quelling another just to the north.[18]

Lastly, imperial rule transformed the colonial elites, both Chinese and Vietnamese. Over the centuries, Chinese settlers, army officers, and administrators who spent long periods of time in the empire's south married into local families, picked up local languages, traded, and sometimes just wandered about. In so doing, they distanced themselves physically, culturally, even mentally from the imperial center. Han army officers invading the south were shocked to find a former Qin official 'with his hair in a bun and squatting on the ground'. One Chinese poet in the eighth century opened a poem on life in Vietnam as follows: 'I have heard it said of Jiaozhi, that

southern habits penetrate one's heart. Winter's portion is brief; three sea-
sons are partial to a brightly wheeling sun.' He then mused about how the
warlord Zhao Tuo had created an independent southern land a thousand
years earlier. Indeed, Chinese settlers, officials, and their offspring could
join forces with Viet elites to promote their shared interests, including independence from imperial rule. This tended to occur when the Chinese
capital encountered difficulties, allowing rogue officers to take the initiative
in the borderlands. Some of these rebels were 'Chinese'; others were 'Vietnamese'. Oftentimes they were both. It didn't really matter. What counted
most was their ability to garner local support, often from this spiritual world
swirling beneath their feet, in order to transform military force into lasting
political change. In 544 CE, with the Chinese court locked in civil violence
to the north, a certain Ly Nam De led a rebellion against corrupt imperial
rule before creating another Nam Viet kingdom. This Jiaozhi man had long
been a magistrate in the Chinese administration, was trained in the Confucian classics, and descended from Chinese settlers. Similar strongmen
asserted themselves across the southern confines of the Chinese empire.
Nam Viet independence was, in the end, short-lived. In 602 CE, the Chinese
re-established control over their coveted maritime province and its agricultural heartland. However, Viet and Sino-Vietnamese elites continued to
hold high positions in Chinese Jiaozhi for another three hundred years.[19]

Independent Dai Viet
Jiaozhi province ultimately left the Chinese empire in the tenth century to
become an independent state. A series of intertwined factors explain this
key event in Vietnamese history. Firstly, the shattering of the Tang dynasty
in 907 (if not earlier) weakened the imperial court's hold over its distant
provinces, allowing local elites or warlords to take things into their own
hands. Colonial governors, without clear instructions from above or sufficient military force on the ground, looked on helplessly or ran for cover.
Secondly, the attack on the imperial order in the Red River did not come
from nomads descending from the Central Asian steppes on the scale of
the Mongols and the Manchus who would later seize China. Dissent came
from within the colonial order itself, from local military and administrative elites (the two often overlapped) convinced that they could do better
without the Tang. In 939, Ngo Quyen, a high-standing prefect and general
in Jiaozhi province, took advantage of the disintegration of Tang power to
rally his men, beat back an enemy naval attack, and secure the province's

independence. That enemy attack, in fact, came from a very similar state based in Guangzhou whose leaders had declared their independence from the vanishing Tang to create the 'Great Viet' in 917 before changing it to the 'Southern Han' a year later. Ngo Quyen did not secure national independence from 'China', but rather from a sibling rival state in this overland and maritime zone shared by Vietnam and China. Within a century, Ngo Quyen's men spoke of their own Dai Viet, or 'Greater Viet'.[20]

Ngo Quyen also owed his victory to a rapidly changing regional balance of power on his other flanks. As a former general on China's southern border, he and others like him would have been acutely aware of the rise of a host of neighboring states, several of which had become very powerful over the centuries. To the south, the Khmer and Cham had built expansionist states, whose leaders were not particularly keen on seeing this unprecedented Dai Viet state cut off their lucrative trade with the Chinese, crowd them out of the Indian Ocean market, or even deny them the Red River basin in the event that the Chinese actually packed their bags and left. To the west and northwest, federating Tai (not to be confused with Thai) polities drawing on increasingly large populations and caravan trading routes asserted themselves politically and militarily. In the eighth century, a particularly powerful Tai state emerged in Yunnan province named Nanzhao. When Tang officials threatened its profitable overland trade in horses in exchange for Vietnamese salt (two very important products), Nanzhao troops marched on the Jiaozhi capital in 846, 860, 862, and stayed for two years in 863. The Tang were already in trouble in the south before Ngo Quyen secured independence at the Battle of the Bach Dang River in 938. To the north, the weakening of the imperial hold over non-Han areas in Guanxi had already ushered in a number of chieftains moving toward self-reliance and *de facto* self-rule. Ngo Quyen clearly had models to emulate. Finally, the importance of Jiaozhi as the main trading port with the Indian Ocean declined under the Tang in favor of areas located further north. All of this would have encouraged local military men, lords, and officials to turn on the empire from the inside, while Tang strategists might have been willing to let it happen.[21]

In any case, taking power was one thing, holding on to it quite another. Regional powers like the Cham and Khmer continued to pose real threats to the fledgling Viet state and a Chinese counter-attack was always a real possibility. Just as important were a dozen or so Red River lords who had always been there and were not going to sit by idly as Ngo Quyen consolidated his power at their expense. The rapid Tang withdrawal of its military and colonial personnel created a power vacuum which these lords sought to exploit as much as Ngo Quyen. And as is so often the case in times of decolonization, civil war quickly broke out. For half a century, different groups scattered across the plains into the highlands of Jiaozhi. They competed with each other until a certain Ly Thai To emerged victorious and, in 1009, formed a dynasty carrying his family's name.[22]

All of these families seeking to transform colonial Jiaozhi province into an independent Dai Viet state faced similar challenges—to what extent does one rely on the pre-existing colonial order and Chinese statecraft to rule independently? Should one create something entirely new or fall back on something that had never disappeared? How does one legitimate and structure a new postcolonial polity ideologically, religiously, and historically? Could one family or one charismatic leader rule a state for more than a generation against local lords who had never really been defeated? Or was it time to use a major world religion like Buddhism to structure, build, and impose a more centralized form of exercising power?[23]

While early military leaders like Ngo Quyen and Ly Thai To embraced monarchy as their core model, they all had to confront these deeper questions in one form or another. One of the first problems to solve was the question of political legitimation. After all, who could convincingly demonstrate, in 939 or 1009, a direct line of kinship to a royalist past and a founding monarch after a thousand years of Chinese rule and without ancient Viet records available to confirm much? No one. So Dai Viet kings did what so many others in their same positions had been doing from one end of Eurasia to the other. They carved out a mythic past, their past, and connected it to their present and its political needs. The court sent its annalists back in time to find the first rulers. They found them in the person of Co Loa's An Duong, and then pushed deeper into the depths of time to resurrect the Van Lang, Phung Hung, and Hong Bang monarchs—who may or may not have actually existed. It didn't matter. Making the myth did.[24]

Secondly, although the Dai Viet annalists did their best to prune their history of its colonial content, they were nonetheless at ease in Chinese characters, needed Chinese sources to find their past, and used Chinese history to authenticate their own. Indeed, by creating a Vietnamese antiquity on par with the origins of China itself, complete with an array of references to ancient Chinese history, dynasties, and philosophers, Dai Viet monarchs could further reinforce royalist legitimacy, much like medieval kings in Europe who consciously reconnected themselves and their states to the 'first' glorious Roman empire. Just as Charlemagne and his successors would cast themselves as the new Romans, Caesars (czars, kaisers, etc.), Vietnamese kings represented themselves as 'Han', the leaders of their own 'middle kingdoms', and the 'sons of heaven' in every way on a par with Chinese culture, statecraft, and, above all, antiquity. The challenge for the Vietnamese (as well as the Japanese and Koreans) was that the Chinese empire, unlike its Roman counterpart, endured; indeed, it is still with us. Once independent, the Gauls and Germans never had to worry about the Romans coming back to challenge their empire-building or heap ridicule on their legitimation stories. In any case, some Viet monarchs would succeed better than others at inventing the past; but there was nothing 'fake' about the process. And the fact that Dai Viet annalists invented their traditions in Chinese and based on Chinese sources made it no less authentic than that of their European counterparts using Latin and Roman archives.[25]

Thirdly, kings needed to tap into the rural cults, deities, heroes, genies, and their ritual circuitry in order to connect and then project their symbolic image to everyone, from elite members to villagers, and back into this eternal past (to which they were, in fact, largely foreigners). Rulers needed the spirits to 'declare' their support for the new ruler, or the new monarch needed to impose his story of spiritual support in order to exert control over his new subjects. It was a common political strategy throughout the Chinese empire; Chinese administrators in Jiaozhi had practiced it for centuries and the Vietnamese maintained it. Through dreams, miracles, and prophecies, rulers carefully searched out spirits that could be mobilized and often humanized to support the political cause. Buddhist monks often lent a helping hand, given that they moved through this spiritual realm so effortlessly. Completed in the early fourteenth century, the *Departed Spirits of the Viet Realm* recounts in one instance how the mythical King Phung Hung had provided the supernatural aid propelling Ngo Quyen and the Viet people to independence in the tenth century. Facing a Chinese attack from the north, Phung Hung revealed in a dream to Ngo Quyen that he should not fear, for 'I have sent ten thousand regiments of spirit soldiers to strategic places, where they are ready to lie in ambush.' And so it was. Having defeated the enemy, Ngo Quyen built a great temple and a royal cult in honor of this Phung ancestor. The fourteenth-century account concludes that this 'had gradually become an old ceremony', confirming, in fact, its recent invention.[26]

Creating a monarchy, equipping it with a royalist identity, myths, and ceremonies, and defending it with military power, backed up by spiritual soldiers, did not, however, mean that an operational state necessarily followed. Early Dai Viet did not emerge from a thousand years of Chinese rule fully equipped with a centralized bureaucracy running on a state-of-the-art Confucian motor. The Tang had pulled out the majority of their civil servants and the Chinese had never pushed an ideal Confucian order down to the grassroots level in Jiaozhi in any case. Neither the Ly (1009–1225) nor their successors, the Tran (1225–1400), could get rid of powerful aristocratic or military families that emerged with and drew strength from so much war. Nor could they bend the spiritual world to their political will overnight, despite what they wrote in their books or built as shrines. While both dynasties incorporated Confucian practices inherited from the colonial period, especially in diplomatic relations with China, their states turned on a fragile royalist alliance with the local nobility and the owners of large estates who continued to rule largely as before. Peasants might have become royal subjects instead of colonial ones; but they continued to interact with these local lords and especially the spirits and monks moving around them all. They did not march necessarily in lockstep with the new Ly and Tran rulers whose thrones only really controlled core areas around Hanoi.

Unsurprisingly, some of Dai Viet's most effective leaders tended to have one foot in the court and the other in the countryside, where Buddhism and the spiritual world had long been mixing. The first Ly king was a Buddhist. Educated in a pagoda school, he knew his religious texts and understood how the clergy operated through a collection of monasteries spread across the land and in collaboration with the surrounding cults and spirits. Upon coming to power, Ly Thai To began elevating Buddhism to an official religion, with the king in charge of the monastic order and working in alliance with its monks to bring in prosperity, the faith, and, hopefully, more effective political and economic control. Vietnamese monks helped him in this endeavor 'to guard the royal territory'. One such ruler required his subjects to refer to him as an incarnation of the Buddha. Others used Buddhism to create royal cults with 'gold cast images of King Phan [Brahma] and De Thich [Indra]' whom the Ly monarch 'attended in ritual'. These rulers had much in common with their royalist counterparts at work in Cambodia (Angkor), Thailand (Sukhothai), and Burma (Pagan); but such practices were also to be found in China, Japan, and Korea.[27]

Unsurprisingly, Ly rulers also sought to attract and unify local, pre-existing spirits moving across the land and channel them, their rituals, and deities and soothsayers toward the center of political power. In the eleventh century, following a revelation, the Ly king discovered the protective power of the Lady God of the Earth. He ordered the erection of a shrine to her in the capital in order to connect the spiritual realm to his own political base. Lastly, the Ly used inter-state and inter-clan marriages to ensure good diplomatic relations with powerful neighbors and consolidate political control internally. The Ly and Tran invested in agricultural development through the construction of more and better dikes and canals. As a result, the Red River population increased rapidly, thanks to better harvests and a steady and sufficient rice supply.[28]

While a religiously minded state based on inland agricultural and rapid demographic growth developed around Hanoi, a different tendency emerged in coastal Dai Viet where the commercial take-off of China's Song Dynasty (960–1279) transformed the Gulf of Tonkin once again into a vibrant commercial hub. The shifting of the Song capital southward to Hangzhou in 1126 in the face of nomadic threats coming from the Eurasian steppes reinforced this. The Song's robust cultural, intellectual, and commercial activities moved down the coast. And as Chinese trade with the Indian Ocean grew, a multi-ethnic collection of coastal traders moved into Dai Viet and began serving as intermediaries for the export of Chinese ceramics and silks to Cham, Khmer, island Southeast Asian, and Middle Eastern markets. Elegant Vietnamese-made ceramics also flourished and found homes deep in the lands of the Indian Ocean. Commercial movements became so intense that the Dai Viet port of Van Don emerged at the center of an array of exchanges going up and down the coast from southern China and Hainan Island to northern Champa's port near Vijaya in today's Qui Nhon. Local merchants referred to this area bordering Dai Viet as the Jiaozhi Ocean. Local demand reinforced this commercial activity, which, in turn, attracted more people from China, Champa, and beyond.[29]

While the Ly monarchy loosely ruled all of the country from around Hanoi, coastal merchants, travelers, and immigrants introduced a host of new ideas, products, and technologies. Cham art found homes in the Ly, Tran, and early Le dynasties. Cham music could move the Ly court deeply: 'Its sound was so mournful and sorrowful that it brought tears to listeners' eyes', wrote one witness. Little wonder. Many were prisoners of war. But

Cham Hinduist ideas also found their way into Red River villages, whose populations used them to create their own local cults. Southern Chinese traders and Song political refugees fleeing the thirteenth-century Mongol conquest of China often carried with them their arts, culture, and political ideas, including some very Confucian ones. They also arrived with paper, printing presses, and literati who helped develop such ideas along the coast and found many a local convert at ease in Chinese and literate in classical characters. Zen Buddhism had also extended its roots along the coast. Shilian Dashan, our Chinese monk from Guangzhou, was anything but an exception in the seventeenth century. He was the product of a very maritime Buddhism with roots deep in the past.[30]

Early Dai Viet thus embodied a dual track in its early independent development: The inland capital of Hanoi ruled over the agricultural plains and mountains, while remaining connected via the Red River to the vibrant seaborne trade of the Indian Ocean. The leaders of a new dynasty, the Tran, arose from this coastal world to rule Dai Viet from Hanoi between 1225 and 1400. They were Buddhists, but they were also well versed in this coastal Song Confucianism. They were themselves the descendants of prosperous Fujian traders and fishermen, who had moved into maritime Dai Viet and intermarried with the Ly family. This alliance was symbolically significant. Not only did it facilitate the Tran acquisition of the Buddhist throne in Hanoi, but it also fused the inland, agriculturally focused Dai Viet with its coastal, outward-looking commercial half. This gave rise to a dynamic state, capable of making the most of its agricultural heartland and its international trade.[31]

It also made it a coveted land. The Tran had to fight off powerful Cham attacks from the south on several occasions. They then had to join their coastal competitor to repel even stronger Mongol offensives coming by land and sea in the thirteenth century. Lest we forget, the Mongols wanted to extend their massive Eurasian empire running from Persia to China down the Vietnamese coast in order to reach Southeast Asia's Spice Islands. The Cham and the Vietnamese contained them at the Red River, while the Japanese and the Javanese did so by the sea.[32]

Like their Burmese and Thai counterparts moving from inland river capitals in Pagan and Sukhothai to ones in the deltas of the Irrawaddy (Rangoon) and Chaophraya (Ayuthia and Bangkok), something similar started to occur under the Tran, who shuttled between Hanoi and their coastal palace. The capital remained in Hanoi, but the Tran nonetheless reoriented it toward the coast. The Song had already moved their capital to the coastal town of Hangzhou. Politically, the Tran also opened a breathing space for more Confucian-minded literati and statesmen who saw in Song Confucianism a more effective way of creating a modern state and civilization than the Buddhist kind some had started to scorn privately. The Tran remained Buddhist believers, but that commitment did not prevent them and many of those working for them from promoting Confucianism as an alternative way of organizing state power and legitimating royalty. Under the Tran, Confucian and Buddhist approaches toward statecraft intermingled and sometimes entered into competition. The question as to which would ultimately prevail was never resolved before the Ming Chinese (1368–1644), having finally overthrown their imperial masters, the Mongols, invaded Vietnam in yet another attempt to grow the Chinese empire.[33]

Ming and Dai Viet Imperial Projects[34]

The Ming may have thrown the Mongols out of China in 1368, but they were as determined as their 'world conquerors' to push China's imperial control into Southeast Asia. Not only did they march their armies into Hanoi in 1406 to re-impose Chinese rule, but, like the Mongols, they also sent their soldiers deep into the non-Han highlands crossing Yunnan, into the Tai polities like Lanna, and as far as today's northern Burma. In these southern highlands spreading across Yunnan, the Ming dusted off the *tusi* or 'native chieftan system' to rule indirectly. And that system of indirect rule for the Tai would extend well into the twentieth century.[35]

Parallel to their overland thrusts into upper Southeast Asia, the Ming also sent their armadas deep into the Southern Seas, determined to establish a maritime order to their liking. Admiral Zheng He, himself a Muslim from Yunnan, led a series of naval expeditions through the Straits of Malacca, into the Indian Ocean as far as the east African coast and Mecca. To assert control over the spice trade in Southeast Asia, Chinese ships opened fire on Malacca a century before the Portuguese did. The Ming used tribute and trade to further the creation of an informal empire. Backing all of this up were very modern advances in shipbuilding and gunpowder technology. Chinese vessels thus carried commercial goods as well as tens of thousands of troops. Indeed, in the fifteenth century, the Ming armed forces were the most lethal in Asia, equipped with sophisticated cannons, guns, pistols, and grenades. The Europeans were not the only ones seeking to create 'gunpowder empires' or the first to bring new forms of modernity, statecraft, and violence to the region. The Chinese were.[36]

The Vietnamese knew it arguably better than anyone else. Between 1407 and 1428, precisely the time during which the Ming pushed their imperial expansion southward hardest, Dai Viet returned to the Chinese empire as its thirteenth province, essential to further Chinese expansion by land and sea. For better or for worse, this was a watershed in modern Vietnamese history. On the one hand, Ming re-conquest of Dai Viet was militarily harsh and the imposition of direct political rule and cultural assimilation all too real. Upon arriving, the Ming burned Dai Viet books in an attempt to reset the Vietnamese clock to Chinese imperial time. Scores of Chinese bureaucrats debarked to run the province, pushing local leaders out of the way and scorning 'barbarian' customs as they did so. Few of these officials could speak Vietnamese and saw no reason to do so. Jiaozhi, in their view, was and should be part of the northern empire.[37]

The result was predictable: resistance and collaboration. Opposed to such heavy-handed rule and sidelined from power, in 1418 a group led by Le Loi retreated to their southern bases in today's Thanh Hoa and Nghe An provinces to take up arms against the Chinese occupation. The Ming reaction was swift and brutal: sending in tens of thousands of well-armed troops to crush the resistance. However, as resistance forces captured modern Chinese arms and copied their military science and gunpowder-production techniques (they could read Chinese), Le Loi's officers began transforming their ragtag forces into an increasingly strong military force. Le Loi's partisans also began to use Chinese bureaucratic techniques to organize and deploy tens of thousands of their own troops. Under Le Loi's command, after a decade of war, the Vietnamese drove the Ming out of the country in 1427, in battles that went beyond simple 'guerilla warfare'. As short as their rule was, the Ming ironically helped the Vietnamese achieve a modern military revolution of their own; one which they turned on the colonizer and would use to build a new state.[38]

Chinese gunpowder and weapons were not the only things attracting Vietnamese attention. So did the Ming bureaucratic model and the civil service on which it turned. During those twenty years, the Chinese established a host of Confucian-minded schools and training academies. By 1408, the Chinese had already created forty-one sub-prefectures and 208 counties operating along Chinese administrative practices. The Ming burned Vietnamese books, but they also re-introduced the Confucian canon, print technology, and paper, as well as their legal code, and with it notions of statecraft. Collaboration thus appealed to a certain segment of the Dai Viet elite, who could use the Ming texts and methods to promote a very Vietnamese agenda, including a Confucian revolution some had been pushing for from coastal areas for decades.[39]

This was even true for the anticolonialists. Upon taking back Dai Viet and declaring himself emperor, Le Loi and his successors revamped the Dai Viet state according to the Confucian model. Le Loi and others saw the chance to do what had always escaped their predecessors—establish centralized control over an often unwieldy country. He and his descendants promoted Confucian statecraft through the construction of more academies and schools, the acceleration of the civil service examination program, and the promulgation of a Le law code with Confucian characteristics. New laws reduced the power of aristocrats by reducing private land ownership and assigning control of individual villages to the state. A new fiscal system allowed revenues to go directly to the central government. Provincial administrators took over increasingly from the lords in the countryside, while the Le kept on many of those who had collaborated with the Ming. They needed them and this would help ensure their loyalty.[40]

Leading the charge would be one of Le Loi's best-known descendants, Le Thanh Tong (1460–97). This dynamic monarch thoroughly reformed the Confucian examination system and introduced Chinese-derived legal and criminal codes. He established the National College to train a loyal bureaucratic elite who were to be dispatched across the land to spread Confucian norms at grassroots levels by ensuring popular loyalty to this political ideology both in society and within the local bureaucracy. In 1463, he initiated the standard triennial Confucian examination as Buddhism faded from elite politics. To further sideline the Buddhists, the court issued a new pantheon of official heroes for everyone to worship. The idea was to diffuse a state ideology to all levels of society; but controlling the spiritual world would always remain a challenge.[41]

The Chinese also offered an imperial model. While the Le successfully repulsed Chinese colonization, they borrowed many things from their former overlords in order to build an empire of their own. This included the title of emperor (*hoang de*), modern military science, gunpowder technology, and a bureaucratic model for organizing territory and people. And by actively participating in the East Asian Confucian world, a 'Domain of Manifest Civility', the Vietnamese also acquired a powerful colonial ideology

and hierarchical ethnography elevating them to a higher civilizational order. This East Asian civilization separated them from the surrounding,
non-Han, uncivilized 'barbarians', and in so doing provided them with the
justification they needed to conquer others, forgetting conveniently that
they themselves had sprung from this barbarian world. This is why, when
the Viet conquered, they often claimed to do so in the name of a civilized
and superior *Han* civilization, of which they wanted to be a part. It does
not mean that the Viet wanted to 'be Chinese'. Claiming to spread Han
civilization served as a process of colonial legitimation, similar to the Frankish postcolonial 'barbarians' in Europe who presented themselves as new
Romans, justifying their conquests by claiming to be a part of this superior
Roman culture and history. The difference, again, was that Rome had disappeared in Europe, but China remained in Asia. This is why independent
Vietnamese rulers could claim to be 'Han' and 'emperors' as they expanded
their imperial state, while the Chinese, annoyed by this Vietnamese refusal
to join the 'real' Middle Kingdom (their empire), had to 'de-civilize' them
and reduce them to kings and, sometimes, imperial subjects.[42]

While building demographic pressures in the Red River delta pushed
the nascent Vietnamese empire southward, Dai Viet leaders, like the Mongols and the Chinese, were well aware of the importance of the Indian
Ocean trade. Indeed, one of its main hubs was located just south of the
newly independent Vietnamese state, in the Cham ports of Qui Nhon and
Hoi An. The Cham and Vietnamese had fought each other repeatedly in
the past, but this time the Le would not be content to withdraw once victory
was achieved. In 1470, in a remarkable edict on Champa, Le Thanh Tong
laid out in great, often vitriolic detail why the Vietnamese had to destroy
Champa, not just for security reasons, but also as part of a wider civilizing
mission in order to '[r]espectfully bring the Mandate of Heaven, and do
the work of striking and killing those cruel people'! True to his word, one
year later, Le imperial armies crushed the Cham in Vijaya, took their port at
Qui Nhon, and colonized their lands in today's central Vietnam. This date
symbolized the beginning of an aggressive Vietnamese colonial expansion
using state-of-the-art weapons. And the conquest of Vijaya apparently paid
off: the export of Vietnamese and Cham ceramics rose dramatically after
this date.[43]

No one knew at the time where it all would end up, but it was quite clear
that there was an impetus to move southward down the coast and westward
and northwestward into the surrounding massifs from whence the Viet had

initially come. In 1479, Le imperial armies struck deep into Tai territories in today's Laos and northwestern Vietnam, marching through Tran Ninh and Dien Bien Phu, getting as far as Burma before pulling back like the Ming before them. Many imperial soldiers received orders to stay behind to create military farms and garrisons. Soldiers farmed the land and kept it secure at the same time. Tax records show a steady rise in the Viet population in these conquered areas. And like the Ming colonialists they so despised for using brute force so indiscriminately, Dai Viet commanders could do the same. As a Vietnamese report on the conquest of one unfortunate 'barbarian' polity reads:

> 1479: Attacked Bon Man again. The Duke of Ky, Le Niem, served as the general leading an army of 300,000 [. . .] The army went over the pass, the [chief] Cam Cong fled and died. [Our army . . .] burnt their capital, took their garrisons, and burnt their granaries. Before this [attack], Bon Man had 90,000 households; in this operation almost all of them starved or were killed and only 2,000 people remain. They thus surrendered [to us] and Cam Dong, one of their race, was appointed as the Pacification Commissioner, and [Viet] officers were appointed to rule the area. But Cam Dong later rebelled again.

The Vietnamese were colonizers, too.[44]

Catholic Vietnam
Many were also Catholic. Indeed, our Buddhist master, Shilian Dashan, was not the only missionary working in Vietnam in the late seventeenth century. Traveling on Iberian trading ships, European missionaries had begun debarking in Asia shortly after the Portuguese took Malacca in 1511. The first landed in Vietnam in the early seventeenth century. Most were Jesuits who had fled persecution in Japan, where the new Tokugawa rulers viewed them as threats to their control over a still very contested country. In 1620, the French Jesuit Alexandre de Rhodes joined a small mission in Red River Dai Viet, where he proselytized until his expulsion a decade later. He then moved southward to spread the word.[45]

To facilitate the spread of Christianity, European missionaries and their Viet partners developed a writing system for transcribing Vietnamese into the Roman alphabet. In 1651, de Rhodes published the first Portuguese-Latin-Vietnamese dictionary. This early Romanization system—known as *quoc ngu* or the 'national language'—became the writing system in twentieth-century Vietnam. But until then, the Vietnamese elite and the missionaries trying to reach them continued to use Chinese characters (*han tu*) or the indigenized character-based writing system known as *chu nom*. Like their Buddhist counterparts, Catholic missionaries excelled in learning the majority language of the rural lowlands, Vietnamese. Their success depended on it.[46]

Catholicism made limited though significant inroads in Vietnamese society. Vietnamese rulers were never able to expel the Christians as effectively as the Tokugawa Japanese had in the seventeenth century. European missionaries moved in and around Vietnam during this time, building country churches and congregations. By the mid-eighteenth century, around 300,000 Vietnamese Catholics lived in the Red River valley, despite the court's hostility. Numbers were much smaller in the south, never exceeding 15,000 prior to the eighteenth century (and not exceeding 100,000 by the early nineteenth century). Vietnamese Catholics remained a minority of the estimated 7.5 million people living in Vietnam by the late eighteenth century.[47]

Wars, difficult socio-economic conditions, famine and disease facilitated conversions among the poor. Many peasants turned to Christianity, attracted by its perceived healing powers, the promise of salvation and an afterlife, and its embrace of all souls regardless of social status. Immigrants leaving family and friends behind to carve out new lives on the often-hostile southern frontier found a reassuring sense of solidarity in Catholic communities and churches. Many Christian notions of spirituality and miracles dovetailed with pre-existing beliefs in the supernatural and occult. The cult of the Virgin Mary, for example, found a place among coastal fishermen and sailors in Tonkin, who had long venerated the protecting 'Mother of the Sea' (*Thien phi*). The ethnographically well-informed Jesuit Father Adriano di St Thecla wrote a riveting, if heretical account of the synergy and commonality between European Christianity and indigenous spirit practices and cults in China and Vietnam.[48]

However, Vietnamese Catholics, like their Buddhist counterparts, were more than a collection of the rural down-and-out. Many a Catholic soldier served in the army. Viet elites, including high-ranking Confucian mandarins, also converted, attracted by Christianity's moral code and notions of rectitude. One of the court's sharpest reformist mandarins in the nineteenth century, Nguyen Truong To, was Catholic. And if China's Shilian Dashan could help Lord Nguyen Phuc Chu grow Buddhism at the turn of the eigh-teenth century, a remarkable Vietnamese Jesuit, Philiphê Binh, travelled to Lisbon and stayed there for three decades defending Catholicism and the Jesuit order operating in Tonkin. Lastly, the French bishop Pigneau de Béhaine spent much of his adult life evangelizing in Vietnam and help-ing Chu's illustrious descendant, Gia Long, regain his country during the eighteenth-century Tay Son wars discussed below. While little came of this in the end, he played an instrumental role in the signing of a treaty between Gia Long and Louis XVI in 1787.[49]

In short, religions, like empires, are globalizing forces. Confucianism, Buddhism, and Catholicism all emerged within Vietnam via Asian and in-ternational connections and in response to local conditions and spiritual needs. And Catholicism also had to interact with that deeper substrate of cults, spirits, diviners, sects, fortune-tellers, and millenarians. But it was not necessarily any more a 'foreign' creation than Confucianism. Nor was it 'French' or a French colonial importation.[50]

MILITARY RULE AND SHATTERED SOVEREIGNTIES

The postcolonial confidence, the rapid internal state building, and the imperial expansion that flowed from the Le victory over the Ming in the fifteenth century did not last. The Confucian revolution that was theoret-ically supposed to create a modern centralized state from the top down had limits in practice. Centuries-old aristocratic families did not sur-render easily. Confucianism ebbed and flowed depending on the socio-economic circumstances, the leaders, and the political conjunctures. Rapid territorial expansion created its own problems as it distanced the court from the periphery and provided new opportunities for the emer-gence of competing power bases in the borderlands as well as non-Viet anticolonial revolts. Renewed civil wars coupled with never-ending co-lonial conquests meant that military leaders and their families continued to hold considerable privileges and power, including access to troops, weapons, and alternative loyalties. The Le, the Trinh, and the Nguyen military houses all heralded from the newly colonized lands of the then southern province of Thanh Hoa. The Le in particular had connections to the highlands in Laos and never really made peace with the coastal Dai Viet or trusted the Chinese.

A House Divided Against Itself

Things began to fall apart for the Le in the sixteenth century, when the dynasty's failure to reinvigorate the monarchy and balance the interests of these powerful military families on which its rule turned led to crisis. In 1527, contested succession to the throne and deepening factionalism saw a military clan from the coastal north, the Mac, make a grab for power. Mac Dang Dung overthrew the Le emperor, declared himself ruler, and created a new dynasty in his name. Opposition from the Le's two main military backers in the south—the Nguyen and the Trinh clans—was immediate. General Nguyen Kim joined forces with his son-in-law Trinh Kiem to restore the Le by bringing the court to Thanh Hoa. From there, they launched attacks against the Mac, progressively pushing them out of Hanoi and into northern areas around Cao Bang province where the Ming continued to support this deposed royal family.

Sovereignty shattered further when personal ambition got the better of Trinh Kiem, who turned on the forces of his Nguyen ally, Nguyen Kim, when the latter died at the hands of the Mac. The Trinh wanted power. Rather than risk a three-way civil war or put his family at risk, Nguyen Kim's son, Nguyen Hoang, requested a military transfer to newly conquered areas in Quang Tri. Trinh Kiem gladly obliged, happy to get him out of the capital they had recovered from the Mac. In 1558, Nguyen Hoang and much of his entourage left for the then faraway south—today's central Vietnam. Three military houses now ruled a divided Vietnam—the Mac along the Sino-Vietnamese border, the Trinh in the Red River delta, and the Nguyen in the southern colonial borderlands. While the Trinh and the Nguyen supported the Le emperor, the Trinh family now pulled the strings. By proclaiming himself 'king' (*vuong*) in 1599, Trinh Kiem's successor made it clear that this military house had no intention of sharing power. The Trinh used the Le emperor and the associated ritual of emperorship (*hoang de*) to legitimate their rule, much as the Tokugawa military house had maintained the Japanese emperor upon taking power in 1603. In both countries, the emperor was, for all intents and purposes, a prisoner.

Although the Trinh never developed the political equivalent of Tokugawa Japan's military government, the *bakufu*, this Viet family ruled through what was in reality a military regime and political culture. Military officials loyal to the Trinh king rather than any kind of Confucian bureaucracy ensured public order and loyalty. The Trinh presided over elaborate military rituals and temples, banners, and oaths of loyalty to maintain order. In 1600, having returned to the north to defeat the Mac for good, Nguyen Hoang acquiesced to the Trinh ascendency, pledged loyalty to the Le emperor, and then returned to the south. While he did not know it at the time, he and his family would go on to build a second Vietnam along the imperial frontier.[51]

By all accounts, Nguyen Hoang appreciated the beauty of the land he encountered in the south, was seduced by its exoticism, and attracted by the riches it promised to the hard-working soul. The bustling port of Hoi An, its vibrant trade with the Indian Ocean, and the mosaic of local, regional, and international travelers, merchants, and missionaries impressed him. Chinese, Arabs, Persians, Japanese, and Europeans had long visited this ancient trading town the Vietnamese had taken from the Cham. As one eminent scholar has nicely put it, 'Talent and ability began to count for more than birth and position. This was, in effect, an escape from ancestors, an escape from the past. For Nguyen Hoang, the result was a greater reliance on his own abilities, a shifting of the burden of moral choice from the past to the present'. This man and those putting their faith in him made something of a leap of faith, even if they maintained their ties to the north. They began to imagine a new 'way of being Vietnamese', a state of mind from which another southern polity could spring.[52]

These areas to the south of the Red River delta were not, however, blank spaces. Millions of people lived in the lowland areas embracing the South Seas to the east, the highland massifs just to the west of Hue, and areas extending across the Mekong delta to the Gulf of Thailand. Between 1000 BCE and 200 CE, an impressive Sa Huynh culture had thrived in present-day central and southern Vietnam, paralleling, even interacting with its prehistoric counterpart to the north, the Dong Son civilization. Sa Huynh's craftsmen produced a wide variety of iron tools, weapons, and ornaments. The kingdoms of Funan and Chenla were the first to create loosely organized mandala-like polities in the Mekong delta (1–9 CE). Whereas the Viet in the north had borrowed Confucianism, Buddhism, and characters from China, the people of Funan in the south tailored Hinduism, Buddhism, and Sanskrit print culture coming from India to local needs. Thanks to the port of Oc Eo in the Mekong province of today's An Giang province, Funan was at the center of trade routes linking it to the Chinese and Indian Ocean empires.

Other states subsequently emerged in this region. At its apogee in the fourteenth century, the Cambodian empire of Angkor based near the Tonle Sap ruled large swathes of lower mainland Southeast Asia. Cambodian mastery of a sophisticated hydraulic system allowed for increased population growth, urbanization, and sophisticated political formations and extraordinary artistic and architectural achievements. For some, Angkorian civilization marked 'the largest complex of low-density urban development in the preindustrial world' with a population of one million people. This vigorous empire certainly mobilized people, promoted Buddhism, and spread Pali- and Sanskrit-based writing systems across areas located between the Chaophraya and Mekong deltas.[53]

In areas north of the Mekong centered around the port of Hoi An the dynamic kingdoms of Champa emerged in the seventh century, mentioned in passing above and discussed in detail in chapter 14. The Cham ruled territories running roughly from modern Ha Tinh province south to Da Nang, including lowland and upland territories. Cham resources, markets, trade, and populations turned this coastal federation into a prosperous and culturally diverse land. Asian and Middle Eastern traders regularly visited this entrepot. Arab and Persian merchant ships had been trading along the Vietnamese coasts for centuries. These traders plying the Indian Ocean introduced Hinduism, Buddhism, and Islam to the Cham.[54]

Along the coast, Ming maritime movements triggered an early wave of Chinese immigrants to the region. And when the Ming ended their maritime expeditions in 1433 and focused their attention on Central Asia, the Japanese increasingly stepped in (while local southern Chinese merchants kept coming). Soon European traders, adventurers, and missionaries were circulating throughout the region, introducing new ideas, products, weapons, and religions. Malay and Arab peoples called this region, bordered by China at one end and India at the other, the 'lands below the winds'; the Chinese named it the 'Southern Seas'; the Indians 'the Golden Peninsula'; and the Europeans imagined the 'Land beyond the Ganges' before European geographers called it 'Indo-China'. Since the Second World War, we now refer to it as 'Southeast Asia'.[55]

The Imperial State in a Southern Form

It was in these culturally diverse and populated lands that Nguyen Hoang began building a new imperial state, a continuation of the earlier Le one, but increasingly under autonomous Nguyen control. By the end of the seventeenth century, through the use of superior technology, force, persuasion, and an array of alliances, the Nguyen took over what remained of Champa, transforming it into the new province-protectorate of Thuan Thanh. Much the same happened in the Mekong delta as Nguyen lords extended their rule. Indeed, with the demise of Angkor in the fourteenth century, a new generation of Burmese, Thai, and Viet state-builders all began moving southward into the fertile alluvial basins of the Irrawaddy, Chaophraya, and Mekong rivers, attracted by the agricultural riches and the international trade. Armed with modern military technology, the Thais and the Nguyen rolled back the Khmer empire in the eighteenth century and entered into close contact with each other for the first time in doing so.[56]

A range of factors pushed and pulled Viet settlers southward. Firstly, the Nguyen lords were military men and the *de facto* government they crafted and administered was always a very martial one. Like the Le, the Nguyen encouraged their soldiers sent in to conquer new territories to remain there at the head of military colonies. Their families could join them and the Nguyen provided them with land to till upon demobilization. Tens of thousands of prisoners of war also ended up in the south. They provided indentured labor but, with good conduct, regained their liberty, land, and a new future in the south. To promote immigration, Nguyen lords also offered plots of land to poor peasants from the increasingly crowded Red River delta.

To help them, the Nguyen recruited Ming loyalists who had fled the Manchu conquest of China in 1644. Thousands of them sought refuge in Taiwan and the Mekong delta. Around 3,000 Ming loyalists helped the Nguyen lords extend their political and economic control into the area of present-day Saigon, transforming it into the administrative region of Saigon-Gia Dinh in 1698. Further south, another Ming supporter, Mac Cuu, turned the area of Ha Tien in the Gulf of Thailand into a prosperous and semi-autonomous realm. He ended up joining the Nguyen and helped them to incorporate this vibrant commercial and strategic area into their kingdom. These new colonies attracted more Chinese refugees, traders, and immigrants. Intermarriage was common and their children (called *Minh huong* or 'those who are loyal to the Ming') worked in the Nguyen civil service.[57]

That said, Nguyen colonization of the south did not occur overnight, in one military swoop, or in a single wave of settlers. Viet settlers trickled southward in slow, almost imperceptible movements over long periods of time. This meant that 'middle grounds' emerged in conquered Cham and Cambodian lands. Hardly a majority at the outset, Viet immigrants had no choice but to live in Cham towns and villages with the local peoples. Writing in 1644, one Nguyen chronicler reported that areas around Hoi An are 'all settled by Chams [while] the immigrants [Vietnamese] are still sparse'. As in Jiaozhi, intermarriage, collaboration, and borrowings between the settlers and the indigenous peoples were common. They frequented the same markets. The northern Dai Viet court had long borrowed from the Cham. Lowland Viet settlers and Chinese merchants traded with highlanders such as the Jarai and Hre. If the Vietnamese spread their language, religious practices, and culture, many Viet settlers also adopted Cham agricultural technology, spiritual beliefs, food, and music.[58]

Nguyen expansion into these areas also necessitated flexibility and compromise. Although violent conquest may have opened new lands and futures for Viet settlers, the Nguyen simply did not have enough soldiers to ensure security all the time and everywhere, or adequate numbers of bureaucrats to rule over such vast and far-flung regions. And they always had to keep a watchful eye on the Trinh to the north. The Nguyen did what so many colonizers do; they adopted indirect forms of colonial rule in the form of protectorates and military territories. They carefully maintained the pre-existing administrations and a collage of non-Viet elites through whom they administered these territories. They struck alliances through intermarriage, showered gifts on those who cooperated, and consciously appropriated Cham shrines, rituals, and deities if it helped them legitimate their rule and attract local support.[59]

Imperial expansion in Vietnam did not solve internal political competition among Vietnam's military houses, however. On the contrary, by the eighteenth century, a *de facto* independent Nguyen imperial polity had emerged in the south, quite different from the one in northern Vietnam from which it had sprung. Vietnamese now called this southern domain 'Dang Trong', the 'inner region': in contrast to 'Dang Ngoai' or the 'outer region', meaning the Trinh-run state of Dai Viet in the north. In theory, both regions constituted a greater Dai Viet unitary state with the Trinh military house in charge and the Le emperor serving as a symbol of continued dynastic unity. But the fiction of all of this could last for only so long, as the Nguyen kept building what was in practice a quite separate Dang Trong empire-state running southward from the Gianh River to the Mekong delta with its capital in Hue. In 1613, in his deathbed statement to his son, Nguyen Hoang warned him that if an accord could not be struck with the Trinh, 'Then you must strive to guard and protect our territories and await a suitable opportunity. Do not forget these, my commands.'[60]

His descendants did not. In 1620, tensions came to a head between the long-divided military houses when the Nguyen refused to pay taxes to their Trinh masters in Hanoi. This act of fiscal defiance was in fact a declaration of political secession. Civil war followed in 1627, when the Trinh attacked the Nguyen headquarters in Hue. The northern Vietnamese organized seven campaigns against the Nguyen. All of them were failures, with the last ending in 1672. Military stalemate ensued, leading to a century of relative calm as the Nguyen continued building another Vietnam. Indeed, as Nguyen Phuc Chu's invitation to Shilian Dashan the Buddhist abbot revealed, by the late seventeenth century the Nguyen wanted their own state. Undeterred by Qing China's refusal to accord diplomatic recognition, Chu cast the first royal seal establishing a Nguyen monarchy in 1709. In 1744, his descendent mounted the newly created royal throne in Hue. This self-assurance confirmed what everyone knew since the start of the civil wars in 1627: two Dai Viets existed. What no one in Hanoi or Hue saw coming was a third force led by three rebel brothers who bolted out of the central Vietnamese highlands, rallied large armies to their cause, and in so doing upended a chronically fragile Vietnamese order. The Nguyen survived, barely, to return to power in 1802. The Trinh and the Le did not.

CIVIL WAR AND THREE VIETNAMS: THE TAY SON REBELLION[61]

Starting in 1771, three angry brothers rode a wave of socio-economic discontent to power across Vietnam. In so doing, they renewed the simmering civil war between the Trinh and the Nguyen, sparked regional conflicts with the Thais and Chinese, forged unprecedented alliances with Khmers, Chams, and upland peoples, and drew Europeans into the fray for the first time. There had been signs for some time suggesting that all was not well. Unable to establish accurate censuses in regions they administered badly or had only recently colonized, the Nguyen struggled to generate revenues. Foreign trade had declined notably in the 1750s, denying the dynasty one of its main sources of revenues. To compensate, leaders increased taxes, to the point where they became onerous. These fiscal demands extended into the central highlands, spreading socio-economic discontent among non-Viet peoples. As in China, bi-metallism exacerbated rural unrest in Nguyen Vietnam. When Hue could no longer import copper from Chinese and Japanese mines to cast its coins, the Nguyen turned to a cheaper zinc substitute. Not only did they impose this cheaper money on the population for making transactions for rice, but they also demanded that it be accepted and exchanged at parity with copper cash. Unsurprisingly, peasants hoarded rice rather than selling it for depreciating zinc coins. The result was predictable: the overall rice supply available plummeted, prices rose, and hunger began to stalk the kingdom. At the same time, the court increased its demands on commercial farmers in the Mekong delta to produce and send more rice northward. One of the regions hit hardest by these policies was in Quy Nhon, where the Tay Son revolt started.[62]

Without well-staffed, -trained, and sufficiently paid civil servants, the court was often blind to the anger spreading across the lowlands and into the hills. Faced with high taxes, Cham anticolonialism resurfaced in the Quy Nhon area, near their ancient capital. Underpaid local administrators in the highlands were often tempted by competing alliances, loyalties, and corruption. The teacher of the Tay Son brothers was a former Nguyen administrator with a grudge: he had been reprimanded and demoted by the court, unjustly so, in his eyes. He was arguably the one who sparked the whole fire by urging his former pupils to revolt.

What we do know is that in 1771, in a small village called Tay Son, located in the highlands looking down on the port of Qui Nhon, three Nguyen clan brothers, Nhac, Lu, and Hue, launched a revolt against high taxes and corruption. It spread like wildfire as the Nguyen court scrambled to stop them by calling in the army. The Trinh were delighted to see their arch-rivals under siege and immediately dispatched their own troops to the Gianh Son Pass to put down the rebellion in the name of a unified Dai Viet. In their rush, however, the Trinh forgot their own problems in the Red River, not least of all recurrent bouts of severe famine and equally destabilizing revolts.

Pragmatic, the Tay Son signed a truce with the Trinh to keep them at arms' length in Hue while the brothers focused their attention on wiping out the Nguyen heading southward into the Mekong delta. The Trinh accepted. They preferred to let the Tay Son destroy the Nguyen so that they could tend to their own problems in the north, confident that they could deal with the Tay Son brothers later. The brothers thus pressed on, forcing Nguyen troops to flee to the Gia Dinh-Saigon region and as far as Bangkok. Fighting went on back and forth in the Mekong delta and the Gulf of Thailand. In a near fatal blow, in 1777 the Tay Son killed the Nguyen monarch and much of his family holed up in the Saigon area. Five years later, the

Tay Son massacred some 10,000 Chinese there for supporting the newly crowned prince, Nguyen Phuc Anh, the future Emperor Gia Long, who barely escaped into the Gulf of Thailand and on to Bangkok.

Reassured by their military victories, the Tay Son brothers grew ever bolder. So much so that, in 1778, Nhac proclaimed himself ruler of the Nguyen kingdom. Significantly, he chose as his new capital the Cham city of Vijaya, near Qui Nhon. From this point on in time, there existed three political centers for 'Vietnam'—that of the Tay Son based in Vijaya, the surviving Nguyen holed up in the Mekong delta, and the Trinh in Hanoi. They all paid lip service to the powerless Le emperor, whose only real function was to reassure the Chinese that the Le were still there and to serve as a symbol of a mythic Dai Viet unity which everyone knew to be a sham.

Having repelled a Thai attack in 1785, the Tay Son brothers finally set their sights on Hanoi. After routing the Trinh army, Nguyen Hue marched victoriously into the Red River in 1786. Here too famine, recession, corruption, and divided loyalties created conditions that helped this Tay Son brother vanquish the second military house of Dai Viet. In 1788, Nguyen Hue declared himself Emperor of Dai Viet, adopting the reign name of Quang Trung and doing away with the Le dynasty. This was too much for the Chinese, who maintained a tributary relationship holding them to protect the Le imperial house. When a Qing army entered the Red River delta to restore the Le, war immediately followed. In a historic victory celebrated to this day, Quang Trung expelled the Chinese and ruled Dai Viet from Hanoi until his death in 1792.

As historic as it was, Tay Son rule did not survive its new emperor. The loss of the dynamic and the militarily gifted Quang Trung as well as infighting within the Tay Son entourage sapped morale and undermined effective governance. Personal rivalries and territorial fragmentation were such that it is impossible to speak of a truly unified Tay Son Vietnam between 1788 and 1792. The brothers fell back on pre-existing, engrained patterns of military rule under the guise of monarchy and tended to divvy up the country into regional fiefdoms.[63]

They also had a formidable foe in the person of Gia Long, who brought the Nguyen state back from the brink of extinction. Tenacious, this young man had carefully bided his time, building up an impressive array of local and international alliances. Charismatic, he forged close relationships with southern strongmen, religious leaders, the Chinese community, and non-Viet groups. He promised them considerable autonomy and privileges in the postwar era in exchange for their collaboration. He outdid all of his rivals in securing diplomatic and military aid from an array of Asian and European governments, merchants, arms dealers, missionaries, and the like. By the time the Tay Son revolt was running out of steam in the north, Gia Long had assembled an army and navy in the south that rolled its way northward to crush the house of Tay Son for good.

In many ways, the Tay Son revolts remind us of the Taiping rebellion that would roar out of southern China in the mid-nineteenth century. Like the leaders of the 'Kingdom of Great Peace' in China, though on a much smaller scale, the Tay Son brothers rode a massive wave of popular discontent, forged pragmatic alliances with non-Viet populations, tapped into religious networks, and worked the social margins of bandits and criminals with great success. Their millenarian promises of a better future attracted massive support. While they disappeared in 1801 as rapidly as they had appeared three decades earlier, the social fury they unleashed and the shattering of political sovereignties they left behind were as transformative as that which the Taiping achieved in China. By marching from one end of Vietnam to the other, the Tay Son opened the way to a wider southern-dominated unitary state, which Gia Long assumed upon his final victory over the Tay Son in 1802. As a high-ranking Nguyen official put it accurately in 1806: 'It is true that in our country of Viet, from ancient times to the present, this territory had never before been as broad and vast as this.' This is how modern Vietnam acquired its current S-like form.[64]

But that unity came at a high price, as it would in the twentieth century. In a dirge for the fallen civil war soldiers, Nguyen Du, one of Vietnam's greatest poets, captured the suffering caused by thirty years of death and destruction. He spoke of the young who had gallantly ridden off to fight but who died without children to tend to their souls:

There were proud men who followed glory's path—they warred and hoped to conquer all the world. Why talk about the heyday of their might? Remember their decline, their fall, and grieve ... Killed young, they've left no heirs—they drift unmourned as headless ghosts that moan on nights of rain. Defeat or triumph lies in Heaven's scheme—will ever those lost souls escape their fate?[65]

CHAPTER 2

A DIVIDED HOUSE AND A
FRENCH IMPERIAL MERIDIAN?

GIA LONG'S SUCCESSORS, emperors Ming Manh and Thieu Tri, followed international events closely as they each tried to bring a long-
divided Vietnam under control during their respective reigns (Ming Mang,
r. 1820–41; Thieu Tri, r. 1841–7). Between 1823 and 1846, the Nguyen court
dispatched at least twenty official delegations to island Southeast Asia, what
the Vietnamese called the 'southern lands', to gather information. Others
went to China. Emperor Ming Mang put some of the best and brightest in
charge of these fact-finding missions and could even make exceptions for
those who had been on the wrong side of his family's victory in 1802. The
pro-Tay Son ties of Phan Huy Chu's family did not prevent him from leading an important mission to China in 1831 and another one to Indonesia
in 1832. A decade later another northern emissary with a less-than-perfect
résumé, Cao Ba Quat, left for the southern lands on a similar fact-finding
mission. With the Opium War underway, the latter provided a detailed
and alarmist account of the Western threat. The British 'Red Hairs', he
warned, were now expanding their colonial control and naval power from
Singapore to Hong Kong. The Nguyen rulers read these reports closely,
questioned their advisors carefully, and pondered what the expansion of
Western power in Asia could mean for their country.[1]

Internally, Minh Mang ruled with an iron fist, convinced that it was
the only way to bring order to this Vietnam that had never existed before. He respected his father, but the inefficiencies of the empire he had
inherited exasperated him and he dedicated his reign to fixing them. As
his ambassadors travelled abroad, the emperor embarked upon one of the
most audacious and far-reaching state-building projects since the Le dynasty in the fifteenth century. This meant transforming what remained a
very militarized polity into a Confucian-structured civilian government. It
meant bringing into line many Le, Trinh, and Tay Son partisans who had
never really accepted the Nguyen victory of 1802. It meant assimilating and

civilizing non-Viet peoples. And it meant taming this unruly spiritual world that had moved south with centuries of colonial expansion and transformed into something quite unique as it connected with Cham, Khmer, maritime, river, and highland spirits.[2]

Revolutions always come with a price, however, especially when they occur at unpredictable international conjunctures. Minh Mang's was no exception. Upon his death in 1841, he left behind a deeply fractured country that his successors did not have the time to heal. In 1854, just a few years before the French attacked, Cao Ba Quat died leading a rebellion against the court he had served. Then Le Duy Phung, an angry Catholic with the restoration of the Le on his mind and hungry peasants in his ranks, asked the French for help. While the French turned him down and the Vietnamese emperor had him executed, Vietnam remained a very divided house, as Europeans began to move menacingly into the Southern Sea.

HOLDING IT TOGETHER

Vietnam under Gia Long

When Nguyen Phuc Anh adopted the name of Gia Long and declared himself emperor of an unprecedented Vietnamese unitary state in 1802, he was deeply aware of the fragility of this new political entity and the explosive tensions that could still tear it apart. Unlike his counterparts in Thailand and Burma, who had also emerged victorious after decades of civil war in the eighteenth century, Gia Long stepped more lightly when it came to imposing central control. During his reign between 1802 and 1820, he maintained many of the flexible, moderate, and pragmatic wartime policies that had enabled him to take all of Vietnam. He allowed the Cham to keep their protectorate status and king. The large Khmer populations continued to practice Theravada Buddhism, speak their language, and run local affairs without molestation. The Chinese in Saigon-Gia Dinh, who had suffered greatly during the civil war, prospered under the victorious Nguyen emperor they had supported, as did the Catholic missions.

That said, Gia Long knew he had to establish some sort of order and consolidate a lasting hold on this new Vietnam, the northern part of which his family had never ruled. In the early years, he did what any victor does—he left his occupying army and officers in charge of maintaining order until he could bring in his own people, determine who in the *ancien régime* could be trusted, and figure out more generally what would be the best model for building a new state. He maintained the Nguyen monarchy declared by his ancestors in 1744 and authorized the creation of a restoration myth to connect it to a timeless royalist tradition. Unlike the Ly, Tran, and his own predecessors, however, Gia Long refused to elevate Buddhism to a national religion. Despite his time in Thailand and friendship with the Chakri Buddhist king there, the Vietnamese monarch never attempted to form a royalist alliance with the Buddhist church, its clergy, monasteries, and schools in order to centralize rule and push its power down to the grassroots. And he rejected out of hand suggestions that he should give Catholicism a try.

More secular-minded, Gia Long turned to Confucianism and Chinese models of statecraft as the best way for bringing all of Vietnam under his family's rule. To this end, he issued a new law and penal code based closely on the Chinese model, defining correct social relations and laying out the nature of the state along Confucian lines. He restored a regional examination system that had fallen by the wayside during the war. New Confucian academies and schools reappeared across the land to train elites for government service. He dispatched envoys and diplomats to China, including the future author of *The Tale of Kieu*, Nguyen Du, to study what the Chinese were doing and bring back texts and ideas that could be used in a Vietnamese context. In a bid to show his northern critics that the Nguyen were just as 'Confucian' as their predecessors he created an imperial capital in Hue worthy of its name by closely modeling it on the Chinese one in Beijing.[3]

But once again, theory and practice are two very different things. It was not because Gia Long chose Confucianism as his preferred political model that it became operational overnight. It did not. Gia Long was a military man and proud of it. He had never had the time himself to undergo any formal Confucian training in his youth and probably never gave it any serious thought. He had built his reputation, his army, and his extraordinary victory in 1802 on pragmatism, personal initiative, deal-making, and the power of his word. Secondly, Gia Long knew just how fragile this new Vietnam born of thirty years of war was. The Trinh and Tay Son armies might have disbanded, but loyalties remained deeply divided. The wounds of war might have healed, but the scars remained. Hate and vengeance often lurked beneath a veneer of tranquility. The victorious emperor did not help when he tracked down all of the remaining Tay Son leaders he held responsible for killing his family and then killed what remained of theirs. Thirdly, Gia

Long knew the political, military, and economic power of regional lords. His family was one of them and he had helped a new group emerge from a wartime power base in the Mekong delta. Indeed, Gia Long's longtime ally and dear friend in Gia Dinh-Saigon, General Le Van Duyet, effectively ruled the south after 1802. The emperor rewarded other wartime allies with high-ranking positions in the center and the north. This is why, despite issuing a new Confucian law code, resurrecting the civil service exams, and creating a capital with its own Chinese 'forbidden city', the emperor kept a very military regime in place on the ground. For central Vietnam, the court ruled through four military camps and eleven military provinces. For northern and southern Vietnam, the emperor administered five such provinces respectively. During Gia Long's reign, military lords were as much a part of Vietnamese political culture as was the Confucian monarchy. This duality reached back to the rise of the Mac, the Trinh, and the Nguyen houses in the fifteenth century, if not earlier.[4]

Nguyen political appointees thus tended to dominate the top positions in the postwar state, regardless of the outcomes of civil service exams. Many Le, Trinh, and Tay Son civil servants and advisors withdrew, refusing to serve the new dynasty. But many stayed on out of necessity or conviction to create this unprecedented Vietnam. Such men included Nguyen Du, Phan Huy Chu, and Cao Ba Quat. And of course, Gia Long never had or trained enough officials to run the lower levels of the northern bureaucracy. He maintained pre-existing civil servants in place as long as they continued to do their jobs faithfully.

But as Cao Ba Quat's revolt would show, Gia Long had to exercise great caution in this northern land where so many elites had served the Trinh, the Le, and even the Tay Son. Indeed, former Tay Son supporters had scattered all over central and northern Vietnam, running into the highlands. None of these groups necessarily saw 1802 as a definitive victory. Nor did they subscribe to the new dynasty's restoration myth which placed the Nguyen of Hue at the center of a seamless Vietnamese tradition they all knew to be patently false. Many considered the Le, the Red River, and Hanoi to be the real repositories of Vietnamese identity, history, and culture. Loyalty thus remained a constant problem. Nguyen Du's *Tale of Kieu* tells the story of the tragic destiny of a heroine who sold herself into prostitution in order to save her family, but some also read it as a subversive reflection on the fate of those who had to serve a dynasty that was never really theirs, never truly legitimate. Rather than attacking all of these forces head on and risking renewed civil war, Gia Long reformed rather than remade what remained a royalist military regime with Confucian characteristics.[5]

The new emperor did promote greater centralization and state control in other ways. He clamped down on all sorts of social and religious unrest. He presided over the creation of new roads, dikes, and canals in order to promote economic development and unity. The construction of the 'mandarin route', the precursor to today's Highway 1, reflected the Nguyen desire to connect the new Vietnam. By circulating administrators from north to south—and vice versa—he sought to stitch the different Vietnams into one administrative body. A new postal service moved information, decrees, and reports across the land, as did the circulation of a standard currency. Gia Long continued military and civilian colonization programs as the best way of increasing agricultural production and relieving population pressures, but his state also cleared land and built dikes. Defense spending remained a priority. Between 1778 and 1819, the Nguyen state produced over 1,482 ships for war and trade while several French-style Vauban fortresses went up along the Vietnamese coast.[6]

Minh Mang's Revolution?[7]

Gia Long's son, Minh Mang, was a very different type of leader. Born in 1791, he was too young to have remembered much of the civil war, nor of the near-extinction of the dynasty at the hands of the Tay Son. While he certainly respected what his father and his allies had done, the new emperor was a firm believer in creating a strong civilian-run state instead of the military one he had inherited. He deplored this hybrid system in which 'failures were seen as achievements and nothing was seen as something'. Minh Mang shared his father's view that a royal alliance with Buddhism was inoperable, and certainly not with Catholicism, which the young emperor seems to have despised from an early age. Trained in the classics, he saw Confucianism as the best political ideology for making Vietnam work, but only on the condition that he achieve what his father had been unable to do—dismantle the military state, eradicate local privileges and warlordism, terminate special rule for non-Viet peoples, subordinate religions, rituals, and their spirits to state control, and then Confucianize the state and society from the top down. Rational to the point of obsession, intelligent like few before him, Minh Mang devoted his twenty-year reign to creating a modern, centralized state. Ruthless, he would let nothing get in the way of that goal.[8]

Essential to getting this project off the ground was the reintroduction of the Confucian ministerial service, the civil service examination system, and the selection of regional and provincial leaders based on merit, transparency, rotating assignments, and bureaucratic loyalty. In 1821, only a year after assuming the throne, the young emperor established provincial exams on a regular, triennial basis and then opened the metropolitan exam in Hue to the best and brightest, regardless of their regional location or their family's past. In so doing, he sought in part to assuage northerners who resented his father's reliance on southerners and military men to run the Red River. He was also betting that the more Confucian-minded northern elite, both the Le and Trinh, would welcome the rebirth of the examination system, providing them with a stake in this new Vietnam and a reason to shift their loyalties to the Nguyen for good. Like the Le, Minh Mang saw in Confucianism, its exams, and the bureaucracy undergirding it, a powerful instrument for political integration and an administrative vehicle for diffusing the court-centered ideology to the lower levels, to local officials and villagers alike.

Mirroring the Thai and Burmese rulers building modern states to the west, Minh Mang agreed that centralized authority turning on rational bureaucratic control could allow for more efficient economic development. Taxes on people and trade would provide the money needed to invest in major infrastructure projects, purchase foreign imports, and pay the salaries of the expanding civil service. Better bureaucratic control extending down to lower levels would allow for the mobilization of the large amounts of labor needed to build new dikes, roads, and bridges. The emperor also supported efforts to promote international trade. He knew that decades of war had allowed an illicit commerce to develop independently of state control. (His father had benefitted from this in wartime.) The emperor accordingly cracked down on the smuggling of rice and opium and in its place promoted state-run commerce with Singapore, China, and the West through approved Chinese, Vietnamese, and European merchants. The Nguyen organized the large Chinese trading community into congregations so as to better control and tax them. The sale of opium now went through a state-controlled Chinese monopoly.[9]

The expansion of European colonialism into the region reinforced this internal consolidation. Minh Mang knew that the Westerners arriving in the wake of Napoleon's defeat in Europe in 1815 were very different from the ones who had helped his father. In 1819, the British acquired Singapore as a colony and overseas base, while the Dutch expanded their direct hold over Indonesia's interior. In the mid-1820s, when the British extended their rule from India into Burma by force of arms, Minh Mang urged his Chakri counterpart to support the Burmese—rejecting the request of a Burmese delegation in Saigon seeking an alliance against the Thais. He dispatched dozens of missions into Asia, one reporting back from British Calcutta in 1830. The emperor always had an eye on the rapidly changing international situation.[10]

But what concerned him most was consolidating his hold over Vietnam. Ironically, the source of the greatest armed resistance to his revolutionary project was not in the foreign north, but in his own southern backyard from whence his father had conquered all of Vietnam and where he had been born. Upon taking the throne in Hue in 1802, Gia Long had left powerful military men in charge of the south. Foremost among them was Le Van Duyet, Gia Long's charismatic general, close friend, and godfather to Minh Mang. General Duyet and his officers ruled the south for the Nguyen. Though fiercely loyal to their emperor, they also enjoyed considerable privileges in the southern delta, ruling over local fiefdoms and maintaining their own troops. Indeed, behind this southern general stood an array of other people and interests. They included Catholic missionaries, Chinese merchants, non-Viet peoples, local strongmen, and probably Buddhist millenarians too. Most of them had served Gia Long during the Tay Son wars and appreciated the local autonomy they had received in return. Few of them were 'Confucians'. In fact, the Confucian examination system could only get you so far in this part of the country, where deal-making and heterogeneity were a fact of life. But where General Duyet and his southern entourage saw this as politics as usual and never dreamed of revolting, Minh Mang began to see these people and their looser politics as an obstacle to the modernization, centralization, rationalization, and homogenization of the Vietnam he was determined to build. This is how southern loyalty began to transform into southern sedition and separation.

Upon coming to the throne, the young emperor bided his time; but he let it be known that change was on its way, everywhere. In 1824, General Le Van Duyet intimated to a friend during a trip to Hue to defend Catholic allies in trouble with the court and explain why the Vietnamese should forge an alliance with the Burmese that:

The court recruits civil officials and wants to make a proper ruling system with them. Both of us have risen in the world from a military background.

We only know straight expression and quick action, thus violating manners or official rules, sometimes. We are originally different from them. We had better give up our positions [. . .] to avoid possible mistakes.[11]

The two southern generals tendered their resignations, but Minh Mang wisely refused them. He waited until Duyet died in mid-1832 before making his move in the south, although he had already begun dismantling the military government from Quang Binh upward. As he did so, he replaced it with a civilian-run system based on provinces and governors with the court in charge and the civil service exams in operation. To those tempted by revolt, he sent a clear message that same year, ordering that the surviving male descendants of the Tay Son brothers were to be arrested and executed *pour l'exemple*. In 1833, with General Duyet finally gone, the emperor decreed the abolition of the semi-autonomous southern military regime based in Saigon-Gia Dinh and ordered its replacement with a civilian government ruling over six provinces with civil governors at the helm. The emperor now divided the kingdom of some eight million people into thirty-one provinces and 283 districts, all falling under three regional administrative groupings: *Nam Ky* (South), *Trung Ky* (Center), and *Bac Ky* (North). To mark the start of this revolutionary project, he changed the name of the country to 'Dai Nam', the land of the Greater South.

This administrative transformation included the ideological unification of the civil service and society through the twin policies of 'cultivation' (*giao hoa*) and 'Sino-Vietnamese acculturation' (*han phong hoa*). In 1834, the court promulgated the Ten Articles edict, requiring mandarins to honor Confucian commandments such as filial piety, respect for elders, and moral obligations to the emperor. Civil servants received instructions to explain and apply these edicts at the village level as an instrument of social control. Minh Mang cracked down on heterodox religious beliefs and practices, especially but not exclusively in the Mekong delta, where an astonishing mosaic of religions, millenarian movements, cultures, ethnic groups, and loyalties reigned. He countered these by promoting state-sponsored ancestor worship. To this end, the emperor presided over the creation of a vast network of temples, altars, shrines, indeed an entire pantheon of officially approved heroes, all of which sought to associate the local populations with the court. Minh Mang had no problems grafting this state religion on to local Cham and Buddhist spirits and deities if it reinforced the court's legitimacy and thus reached the people. But religion had to be under his state's control.[12]

Minh Mang reversed his father's indirect rule over non-Viet peoples. Viet civil servants increasingly assumed the administration of Khmer villages, ending centuries of protectorates and indirect rule. Land was surveyed and taxes applied to non-Viet peoples who had been exempted or lightly imposed upon in the past. Accompanying the establishment of direct rule over the Cham were the efforts made to assimilate all non-Viet peoples to a Sino-Vietnamese Han culture, the Vietnamese language, Chinese characters; in short, an inclusive 'Dai Nam' identity defined from the capital, from the top down, as part of an East Asian Han civilization. The court required Khmer children in Hue to learn Vietnamese, use chopsticks, and wear Viet-style clothes. Pre-existing Khmer Theravada temples started to disappear as Sino-Vietnamese Mahayana pagodas appeared in their place. By advocating Han 'cultivation' and 'acculturation', the Vietnamese emperor sought to legitimate local state-building and colonial assimilation. And when the Khmer rose up, Minh Mang smashed them just as he crushed the Cham, Catholics, or anyone else who defied (or even appeared to defy) his control over state power and ideology.[13]

Like the Le in the fifteenth century, Minh Mang's internal state-consolidation manifested itself externally in the form of aggressive colonial expansion. In 1835, the emperor terminated the vestigial political power of the Cham by formally incorporating Panduranga into the Nguyen administration (see chapter 14). In 1813, in response to the Cambodian king's request for help to dislodge the Thais, Gia Long had already dispatched General Le Van Duyet to Phnom Penh and placed Cambodia under a protectorate. But in the 1830s, Cambodia proper became a province of the Dai Nam empire. Minh Mang's court dispatched Confucian-trained Viet governors and civil servants to administer provinces and districts throughout Cambodia. Hue authorities controlled military and economic affairs and applied there many of the same assimilationist policies used against the Khmer minority described above. The court levied taxes, issued orders to build roads, encouraged Viet and Chinese immigration westward, and even hoped to substitute Mahayana Buddhism for its Theravada version inside Cambodia. The Nguyen expanded control over areas in eastern Laos, too, including Samneau, Savannakhet, and Tran Ninh. By 1840, the empire of Dai Nam already looked a lot like French Indochina. Imperial expansion and state consolidation often went hand in hand in modern Vietnam.[14]

Like his predecessors, Minh Mang justified the conquest of Cambodia on Han cultural grounds borrowed from the Chinese. Only superior

Confucian culture and institutions could civilize the 'barbarian' (*cao mien* or *man*) Cambodians, he argued. As members of an East Asian Confucian world, the Vietnamese had a duty to introduce modern Sino-Vietnamese administrative institutions and civilization to Cambodia. The Nguyen would bring superior technology to better exploit the riches of this country. And long before the French had done so, the Vietnamese court had already portrayed the Khmers as 'lazy' and 'disorganized'. As Minh Mang explained the Vietnamese *mission civilisatrice* to his commanding general in Cambodia in the 1830s:

> The barbarians [in Cambodia] have become my children now, and you should help them, and teach them our customs. . . . I have heard, for example, that the land is plentiful and fertile, and that there are plenty of oxen (for plowing) . . . but the people have no knowledge of [advanced] agriculture, using picks and hoes, rather than oxen. They grow enough rice for two meals a day, but they don't store any surplus. Daily necessities like cloth, silk, ducks and pork are very expensive [. . .] Now all these shortcomings stem from the laziness of the Cambodians [. . .] and my instructions to you are these: teach them to use oxen, teach them to grow more rice, teach them to raise mulberry trees, pigs and ducks. [. . .] as for language, they should be taught to speak Vietnamese. (Our habits of dress and table manners must also be followed. If there is any outdated or barbarous custom that can be simplified, or repressed, then do so).[15]

But behind the civilizing mission stood colonial force. Dai Nam mistreatment of Khmer laborers recruited to build the great Vinh Te Canal in the Mekong delta in the early 1820s had already led to a brief but violent revolt. Nguyen troops crushed it, but Minh Mang's renewed efforts in the 1830s to transform Cambodians into loyal Dai Nam subjects sparked revolts among both discontented elites and hungry peasants. When the authorities in Hue moved to do away with Theravada monasteries and suppress the Khmer monarchy altogether, anticolonial resistance surged, increasingly backed by the Thais. This eventually allowed the Cambodians to regain a fragile Thai- and Dai Nam-backed independence in 1848. (The death of Minh Mang in 1841 helped.) While the territorial limits of the Nguyen state returned roughly to those of 1802, had the Thais not intervened the borders of present-day Vietnam and Cambodia would have been very different.[16]

Minh Mang's territorial consolidation was not limited to the south, however. A policy no less aggressive occurred in non-Viet areas in the northern highlands of Tuyen Quang, Thai Nguyen, Cao Bang, and Lang Son. Until Minh Mang, Vietnamese emperors had followed the Chinese lead in ruling indirectly over these multi-ethnic borderlands. This system, called *tusi* in Chinese and *tho ty* in Vietnamese, allowed hereditary Tai leaders to continue administering their people and lands in exchange for their loyalty to the Vietnamese empire, payment of taxes, and support in wartime. In 1829, Minh Mang did away with this hereditary system in favor of one judged more modern and centralized with his state-trained Viet mandarins at the helm. However, local resistance to this revolutionary change in exercising power was immediate. A local chief, Nong Van Van, led a two-year revolt in 1833–5. Minh Mang's troops would squash it, but the emperor would end up allowing the Nong family to maintain its local leadership. The emperor had no choice. He needed this family's collaboration in order to rule such distant areas of the empire. Direct administration was impossible in these faraway lands and there were never enough Viet civil servants to be found in Hue who were willing to serve in such an alien environment (see chapter 14).[17]

The question, however, was whether Minh Mang's successors could keep such audacious internal state-building and aggressive colonial expansion on track at the same time as imperially minded Europeans were moving deeper into the region, including a resurging France. While Minh Mang's revolution of the 1830s established the administrative foundations of this unprecedented Vietnam, his policies generated anger, divisions, and resistance among elites and their constituencies from the Red River and Mekong deltas deep into Laos and Cambodia. Minh Mang's successors, Thieu Tri and Tu Duc in particular, never had the time to heal these wounds, which covered so much of the country. And the French would take advantage of this divided Vietnamese house in order to promote their own colonial cause.

Vietnamese Catholicism and Minh Mang's State-Building Project

The pretext the French would use to justify their attack on the Nguyen in 1858 was the court's persecution of Catholics. However, in 1802 no one could have predicted such a scenario. Gia Long might not have trusted the Catholics and certainly had no intention of becoming one, but his relationship with them was better than any other monarch in Vietnamese history up to that point. Many European missionaries and Viet Christians had helped him to regain his kingdom and unify the country. In exchange, Gia Long accorded them considerable postwar privileges, not least of all the right to practice their religion freely and rebuild their devastated Church. The emperor allowed his Catholic advisor during the Tay Son wars, Bishop Pigneau de Béhaine, to be buried in Saigon. He delivered a funeral oration praising his friend for all that he had done for the country. Little wonder that European and Vietnamese Catholics continued to recognize the legitimacy of Nguyen rule. And in any case, Catholics never exceeded 5 percent of the total Vietnamese population.[18]

What transformed Catholicism into a major problem was the collision of two separate projects occurring against the backdrop of European colonial expansion into Asia. The first was the reinvigorated Catholic mission in Dai Nam following the restoration of the Catholic monarchy in France in 1815 and in the context of the religiously liberal Vietnam emerging under Gia Long. The second was Minh Mang's Confucian-inspired revolution designed to eliminate heterodox threats to rule from Hue and to place Dai Nam and all of its religions under the emperor's tight control. This is why trouble between Catholics and the Vietnamese court only became a divisive problem during Minh Mang's administrative revolution in the 1830s—not before. Let us focus first on how Catholicism became such a problem for Minh Mang's state-building project and then turn to the international conjuncture in order to understand how and why the French found it a useful pretext to justify colonial conquest.

While Minh Mang never hid his personal disdain for Catholicism and would go after Catholics with a vengeance, he was not necessarily singling them out for persecution, at least not at the outset. He pursued others who challenged or appeared to challenge his revolution with the same ruthlessness. This included southern warlords, Cham and Khmer anticolonialists, and defiant peasants, as well as Vietnamese Buddhists and Muslims. In the early 1830s, he sent his troops to attack Cham Muslims who declared a *jihad* on the Nguyen for Minh Mang's attack on Islam and who made a last stand to save their land from Vietnamese colonization. Minh Mang crushed Buddhist-minded revolts in the Mekong delta and did the same in Nguyen Cambodia, all the while seeking to promote and impose a Confucian orthodoxy in the place of all of this 'heterodoxy'. In January 1833 the emperor issued the first kingdom-wide prohibition of Catholicism. A series of subsequent edicts ordered the destruction of churches and the dispersion of congregations and required Vietnamese believers to recant or submit to royal power. Many Catholics, Europeans and Vietnamese, fled the country or headed into the highlands. Others fell into government hands. This attack on religion was an essential part of the wider administrative revolution discussed above, reaching from the Chinese border in the north to the Mekong delta in the south.[19]

What sent Vietnamese Catholicism down a particularly dangerous path and politicized it profoundly was missionary participation in the Le Van Khoi revolt in the south between 1833 and 1835. Le Van Khoi was the adopted son of General Le Van Duyet. Opposed to Minh Mang's efforts to take control of the south following his father's death, Khoi solicited the support of various groups who also resented their increasing loss of autonomy and religious freedom. Khoi quickly found allies among the Chinese settler community, exiles from northern Vietnam, and even among disgruntled Nguyen civil servants. Catholics, both Vietnamese believers and European missionaries, joined him in the hope that he would restore the religious freedom they had enjoyed under Gia Long. They had nothing to lose, given the emperor's recent decrees and the hard-handed methods he used to enforce them.[20]

In May 1833, the southern insurrection began when Le Van Khoi called on people to oppose Minh Mang and remember what his father, the 'great general' Le Van Duyet, had done. It was, this time and not before, a southern, separatist call to arms. It also confirmed Minh Mang's worst fears. In any case, the revolt spread rapidly until all six provinces of the south—called Nam Ky under Minh Mang's 1833 administrative reform—were in rebel hands. Catholics, Muslims, Buddhists, Cham, Khmer, and Chinese joined its ranks. It took Minh Mang's imperial army over two years to smash the revolt and retake the citadel from the rebels holed up in Saigon. Khoi died before falling into imperial hands. However, the emperor showed no mercy toward the survivors. Of the prisoners taken in Saigon, 1,200 men and women were buried alive. Minh Mang ordered Le Van Duyet's tomb in Saigon to be razed to the ground. The emperor held this family responsible for having planted the seeds of southern secession. That said, it could be argued that the emperor's inflexible methods had created a separatist problem where there had never truly been one. The emperor was, after all, born a southerner himself . . .

Although Christians were but one group among several opposed to the emperor's policies, their participation in this revolt convinced Minh Mang that Catholics were inimical to his ability to rule and had to be uprooted once and for all. The public execution of dozens of Vietnamese and European missionaries implicated in the southern revolt, including the gruesome one of Father Marchand, served as a warning to all that he would brook no opposition to his rule. While Minh Mang's son would temporarily moderate these policies, state-sponsored persecution of Catholics continued until the signing of a treaty with the French in 1862.[21]

This was where Minh Mang's methods intersected with both the international situation and a French domestic situation that transformed the issue of Catholics in Vietnam. Firstly, this intensive attack on Vietnamese Catholicism coincided with a renaissance of French imperial expansion, to which we will return below. Secondly, imperial persecution of Christians occurred just as French Catholicism and missionary activity in particular was undergoing something of a nineteenth-century renaissance. The restoration of the Bourbons to the French throne in 1815 meant the resurgence of the Catholic Church and of its missionary work, both of which had suffered during the revolutionary and Napoleonic wars. Nowhere was this better seen than in the creation in France in 1822 of the Association de la propagation de la foi (Association for the Propagation of the Faith) and its prolific press, the *Annales*. Run initially by the Missions étrangères de Paris (MEP) in Paris and backed by the Vatican, this association and its magazine reported widely on the missions, their work, and needs. From the 1830s onward, the MEP and new Catholic media outlets provided readers with detailed accounts of missionary suffering at the hands of the 'cruel' Nguyen. By the time of his death in 1841, Ming Manh was well known to French Catholics as a 'bloodthirsty' and 'barbarian' despot. The lurid details of the ruler's persecution of missionaries attracted a larger readership, solicited sympathy, and generated sizeable financial contributions for the MEP mission operating clandestinely in Vietnam. This and the revival of French Catholicism further strengthened the MEP in Vietnam with the dispatch of a new generation of mainly French missionaries. Highly energized, these young men resumed their proselytizing with zeal. This, in turn, only confirmed Minh Mang's fears that the Catholics were a fifth column, when that had not, initially, been the case.[22]

Lastly, Nguyen persecution of Catholics coincided with the coming to power in 1852 of Napoleon III and the beginning of the Second Empire in France. Not only was Napoleon III a Catholic monarch, but he was also set on making France a global imperial power. This boded ill for the security of Dai Nam, whose leaders failed to grasp how their continued persecution of Catholics in this rapidly changing international context could transform Vietnamese Catholicism into the pretext Napoleon III needed to attack Vietnam. The Nguyen also persecuted Muslims, but they could do this with impunity—the Ottoman empire was in no position to intervene on their behalf in the 1850s in faraway Asia. It was Vietnam's disaster that—on the far side of the world—political and technological changes were happening that suddenly gave Catholics a powerful and determined sponsor.[23]

Internal Instability and International Threats

Minh Mang's successors, Thieu Tri (1841–7) and Tu Duc (1847–83), did their best to hold Vietnam together following the death of their illustrious predecessor. In the face of dual internal and external threats, they increased their control over foreign affairs, with the Europeans being of particular concern. The court monitored the Opium War, which allowed the British to colonize Hong Kong in 1842 and then join in an international colonial coalition in charge of treaty ports and concessions running down China's entire coast. The French obtained a concession in Shanghai in 1847. The Americans did too. In that same year, the French navy intervened in Da Nang to free Catholic missionaries, inflicting a humiliating defeat on the Nguyen. The court reacted by limiting travel abroad for its subjects and sought to control foreign trade by confining it to specific ports and licensing Chinese merchants to serve as intermediaries.

Was this the 'closing off' of Vietnam under the Nguyen? It was not so much that the Nguyen were turning inward or isolating themselves from the outside world, as that they were trying to keep the coastal colonization of China from extending straight into Vietnam. They also wanted to control access to international contacts, ones which internal foes could use against them to reverse their father's revolution, or worse. The Nguyen must have been aware of the Chinese Qing dynasty's inability to keep precisely such international contacts and trade out of the hands of political competitors residing along the southern coast, most notably Ming loyalists, pirates, religious millenarians, and a stream of unemployed, hungry peasants. Nguyen efforts to control external contacts also had much in common with the *sakoku* or 'locked' foreign policy that the Tokugawa house had adopted in seventeenth-century Japan to stop the Portuguese from arming the Shogun's internal rivals. It may not have been suited to the international context of the nineteenth century, but there was a logic to what the Nguyen were doing and, as in Japan, 'locked' did not necessarily mean 'closed'.

More than anything else, the Nguyen wanted to monopolize contacts with the outside. This is why the state-sponsored rice trade with Singapore and southern China continued to flourish, as did commerce with Hainan, Thailand, and Cambodia. Nguyen rulers continued to purchase and adapt Western military technology and weapons to their local needs. Until the 1830s, Vietnam was home to a surprisingly modern shipbuilding industry. In 1838, the emperor purchased a Western steamship and ordered his engineers to learn how to make one. In fact, the emperor informed his subordinates of the importance of mastering modern naval warfare: 'I indeed have a cursory knowledge of one or two of the tactics of the Western countries, but I want you all to examine them and become familiar with them . . . and make your findings and calculations into books. We will order soldiers to study them day and night.' Meanwhile, the Nguyen continued to dispatch diplomatic missions abroad to report on international events, including a delegation led by the Catholic advisor Nguyen Truong To (a firm believer in implementing far-reaching reforms of a Western kind). Unlike the Japanese, however, Thieu Tri and Tu Duc never really had enough time before the French attacked to realign reform away from its Confucian trajectory toward a capitalist-minded one. Instead, they found themselves scrambling from one crisis to another. And like the Qing, the Nguyen not only had to deal with the outside world, but they continued to encounter challenging problems inside, not least of all deep factionalism in the court.[24]

Environmental problems also undermined the ability of the Nguyen to hold Vietnam together as the French huddled off the coast. Natural disasters, drought, hunger, and disease undermined popular support for the court at this crucial conjuncture. A massive cholera epidemic spread across the kingdom in the late 1840s, combining with famine to kill an estimated 8 to 10 percent of the rural population, roughly 800,000 deaths out of a total estimated population of eight million people. Vietnam was not China, but, proportionally, this environmental tragedy ranked among the deadliest ones marching across the Asian continent at that time. The court struggled to supply rice and relief to the poor all the while taxing them in order to generate badly needed revenue. The peasants were selling their lands to rich landholders in order to survive, and land concentration in the north increased while the potential tax base decreased. Revenues then declined as peasant unemployment took off. Unable to pay civil servants adequately, corruption spread while loyalties realigned, further weakening Hue's authority. A vicious cycle ensued.[25]

The Nguyen monarchy did its best to provide emergency relief through aid, as well as through land and welfare policies. Maintaining, improving, and expanding dikes were important concerns for rulers, as was the maintenance of a network of granaries to get people through tough times. State-sponsored shelters for the poor and the elderly existed and there was no attempt to stigmatize poverty. Non-governmental charity groups, mutual aid societies, and relief programs did their best to help the poor, filling in where the state could not. Buddhist clergy across the country did their best to alleviate the suffering. One Buddhist offshoot was particularly active in the south during the cholera epidemic of 1849, the Buu Son Ky Huong sect (or the Mysterious Fragrance of the Precious Mountain). However, as suffering spread, conversions to Buddhism in the Mekong delta took off, something that only reinforced Hue's opposition to religious meddling in state affairs. Meanwhile, in an ever-stronger financial position thanks to revived Catholicism in Europe and generous donations, MEP missionaries continued their own religious and charitable activities outside state control. And this, as well as increased Catholic conversions among the poor, further fed the 'religious problem'. Minh Mang's successors responded with repression.[26]

However, the very fact that these religious groups continued to function in spite of repeated prohibitions left no doubt that the Nguyen were not in full control at the local level or able to alleviate, much less defuse, major socio-economic problems, hunger above all. In all, some 415 revolts arose to challenge the Nguyen emperors during the first six decades of the nineteenth century. To shore up support, Tu Duc issued decrees exhorting the population to respect state-sponsored tutelary spirits and remain loyal. Between 1848 and 1883, Hue printed some 13,000 certificates, of which over 8,500 applied to villages from Quang Tri northward, but only 3,000 for southern villages. Northern loyalty to the court had clearly become a major concern.[27]

Rural unrest worsened, loyalties eroded, and new forms of accommodation had thus begun to form as the international situation changed rapidly in the 1850s and the possibility of external intervention and foreign support of local actors increased. In 1854, Cao Ba Quat led his revolt against the court in the name of a Le restoration. Other loyalists teamed up with Catholics, who had already been realigning their relationships with the West as bloody Nguyen persecutions continued. Le Van Duy's overtures to the French in the early 1860s were driven by the suffering Catholics had endured since the 1830s; but driven too by a wave of peasant hunger sweeping through the countryside. Many Khmer, Cham, and Tai anticolonialists saw the possibility of recovering their earlier independence via foreign intervention against the Nguyen. When the French attacked Vietnam as part of a renewed European assault on China during the Second Opium War (1857–60), the Nguyen state not only remained a politically divided house, but it was also a socially exhausted one.

A FRENCH COLONIAL MERIDIAN AND THE IMPLOSION OF DAI NAM[28]

French Colonial Expansion into Asia

The French intervened in southern Vietnam in 1858 for a number of reasons. Spreading Catholicism was among the least important of them. Most importantly, colonial possessions provided national and international prestige. Napoleon III firmly believed this. Between 1852 and 1871, through an activist and interventionist foreign policy, he did everything possible to re-establish his country's *grandeur* at the global level. His successful participation with the British in the Crimean War (1854–6) against Russia confirmed the return of a European-minded France, as did his meddling in Italian affairs and Papal politics. Outside of Europe, Napoleon sought to build an empire capable of rivaling that of the British, but in fact he could also pursue the same goal in collaboration with the British, as in the Crimean, and especially as the Second Opium War showed in Asia. He promoted the French colonial presence in Algeria, personally traveling to the colony in 1860 and again in 1865. With the United States mired in civil war during that same period, he intervened in Mexico to establish a French sphere of influence in the Americans' backyard. The campaign ended in a fiasco; but it signaled his determination to make France a global player.

Secondly, the French might have lost their North American empire to the British in the Treaty of Paris in 1763 and their continental one upon Napoleon's defeat in 1815, but wider forces flowed out of the eighteenth and early nineteenth centuries, such as the industrious and industrial revolutions and the related emergence of new forms of banking, financing, and insurance. These pushed France in expansionist directions long before the Third Republic took over. Driving this new 'imperial meridian', as scholars of British imperialism have put it, were proactive merchants, bankers, financiers, insurers, shipbuilders, and free-trade minded theorists. These 'gentlemen capitalists' in Britain and France pushed their governments to open global markets to European industries and finance and to pursue increasingly aggressive colonial policies in Asia in particular. Major French banks and companies established offices in the concessions and ports their government gained during the Opium Wars. Many of the French traders, bankers, and financiers pushing Napoleon III to intervene in Vietnam were already deeply involved in China and others parts of East Asia, indeed the world. These businessmen probably held Napoleon III's attention for longer than any French missionary telling horror stories about cruel Vietnamese rulers. No account of the French conquest of Vietnam can be fully understood without taking into account the resurgence of Atlantic imperialism in the nineteenth century, its connection to the coastal colonization of China, and the rise of a French 'meridian' in the Afro-Asian world. The French were part of this 'Great Divergence' that saw Western states, including Japan, push a new economic order on the rest of the world through the creation of formal and informal empires of a capitalist nature.[29]

Napoleon III did not need much convincing. The emperor fully supported the industrialization and modernization of France. Industrial expansion and financial institutions thrived under the Second Empire, whose leader sought to promote French commercial interests through foreign trade and conquest, formally and informally. He was convinced that colonies would provide much-needed markets for finished industrial products as well as supplying primary materials at bargain prices. He was sympathetic to the emergence and needs of new French banks, insurance companies, and their global expansion. The collapse of older industries, notably Lyon's silk manufacturing in the mid-nineteenth century, reinforced commercial pressure to penetrate the Asian market. Lyonnais capitalists were involved in what one scholar has called 'municipal imperialism'.[30]

Unsurprisingly, naval expansion became a priority both for Napoleon III and those promoting the colonial project. Prestige, commercial, and colonial expansion depended on it. In order to trade with the Far East, however, the French needed strategic bases from which they could fuel and repair their ships, protect their commercial exchanges, and eventually attack. The French possessed Algiers in the Mediterranean and a concession in Shanghai, but they depended on British goodwill for access to China via Singapore and Hong Kong. Admiral Prosper de Chasseloup-Laubat, the Minister of the Navy and Colonies during the vital period between 1860 and 1867, was a vocal supporter of the colonization of southern Dai Nam. Saigon or Danang, he continually repeated to anyone who would listen, could serve as France's Hong Kong. Moreover, he insisted to the emperor, the Mekong River starting in Saigon could provide an independent water route to the Chinese Eldorado they all wanted to reach. The French ruler listened.

Lastly, the general scramble for Asian colonies in the mid-nineteenth century pushed Napoleon to act. The Second Empire's attack on Dai Nam in 1858 coincided with the India Act a year earlier, which formally transferred most of the Indian subcontinent from the private imperial hands of the East India Company to the British Crown. Between 1852 and 1885, the British completed their colonization of Burma, transforming it into a province of British India. To the east, the Americans sent Admiral Perry and his 'black ships' to Japan in 1854 with an ultimatum to open the country to trade or suffer the consequences. (The former enemies of the Tokugawa overthrew the Shogun and created a new regime, that of the Meiji, whose leaders were determined to industrialize and colonize on a par with the West.) In April 1857, Napoleon III formed a special committee on Cochinchina—the European term for Nguyen Vietnam—and consulted extensively with missionaries, business leaders, and concerned ministers about possible colonial expansion into the Mekong valley. It was in this regional and global context that French missionaries implored their 'Catholic emperor' to intervene on their behalf. Napoleon was sensitive to what they were saying, not only because of his own Catholicism but because their persecution would provide him with the perfect pretext for intervening in Cochinchina in 1858, as it would in Lebanon in 1860 and Korea in 1866.[31]

All of this is why, whatever his reasons, Emperor Tu Duc could not have selected a year worse than 1857 to execute two Spanish missionaries. At the end of the year, having attacked Guangzhou with the British during the Second Opium War, Admiral Charles Rigault de Genouilly received authorization to launch a punitive raid against Dai Nam, together with the Spanish based in their colony in the Philippines. The French attack on Vietnam was part of the wider Atlantic assault along the East Asian coastal arc running from Shanghai to Saigon. A year later, in September 1858, de Genouilly led a joint Franco-Spanish attack on Danang and occupied the small port town. In early 1859, backed by the French government, the navy expanded its offensive to include Saigon. French forces occupied the town after heavy fighting, before pushing into the surrounding provinces. France was now engaged in its most important colonial war of conquest since the one undertaken in Algeria (1830–47).

The French Conquest of Vietnam

The imperial capital city, Hue, was on its own against the French. Qing China was no more in a position to assist its southern tributary ally than the Ottomans had been able to help their North African subjects in Algeria or hold the line against the Europeans in the Crimea. The Qing themselves were facing a combined Franco-British coastal assault during the Second Opium War (1856–60). Moreover, the massive Taiping peasant rebellion originating from Guangzhou was threatening to bring down the entire Qing dynasty from the inside (1850–64). To the west, the Thais refused to help the Vietnamese in Cochinchina, keen not to give the Europeans a pretext to invade. The Vietnamese thus fought alone against the French in Nam Ky until 1862, when the Hue court finally signed the Treaty of Saigon, ceding to the French the three eastern provinces of southern Dai Nam (Gia Dinh, My Tho, and Bien Hoa). Emperor Tu Duc ordered his forces to cease fighting and reversed the policy of persecuting Catholics in all territories remaining under Hue's control. Determined to reach China, the French further expanded their hold on the Mekong delta region, when, in 1863, they established a protectorate over Cambodia and eyed up Lao territories on both sides of the Mekong. In 1867, the French then also occupied the three remaining western provinces of Nam Ky as the French colony of Cochinchina started to take shape.

Tu Duc believed that he could regain his lost southern provinces through negotiations by according favorable trading rights and treaty ports to the French. The Chinese had done this; he could do the same. He sent a mission to Paris to negotiate the return of the three provinces in exchange for coastal concessions. (He never recognized the French occupation of the three other provinces.) The problem, a classic one, was that the emperor's advisors were divided into 'peaceful' and 'warlike' factions. His decision to sue for peace rather than continued war in 1862 caused widespread dissatisfaction and sapped his authority at a crucial moment in Vietnam's history. During the regional examinations held in Hue in late 1864, candidates openly opposed the court's conciliatory policy toward the French and linked that subject to the need to destroy Catholics, who they felt were on the enemy's side. This defiance was such that the emperor had to call in imperial troops to disperse his own officials. Further investigation revealed that this event was part of an attempt to start a war, wipe out the Catholics once and for all, and replace the ruler, if need be. While all felt they had the best interests of the country in mind at the moment of its greatest need, divided loyalties now penetrated the highest levels of the government itself. To make matters worse, as a childless emperor, Tu Duc's untimely death in July 1883 brought longstanding and extremely divisive succession problems into the open.

Tumultuous events in Europe ended the Second Empire's expansion up the Mekong. Napoleon's disastrous defeat at the hands of the Prussians in 1870 marginalized the French in Europe, reignited civil unrest in France, and gave rise to a nascent yet fractious Third Republic. In Cochinchina in the 1870s, however, French navy men remained at the helm and they often operated independently of the divided metropolitan ruling class. Joining them were merchants and bankers. All of these men shared a desire to find a river route to reach the Chinese market. When French exploration teams headed by Francis Garnier and Doudart de Lagrée finally concluded that the higher reaches of the Mekong were un-navigable, they shifted their attention to the Red River region.

These increasingly brash merchants and admirals took the lead in expanding their colonial interests beyond Cochinchina, nudged by the financial and commercial lobbies discussed above. They had all found their place in the new French Republic as if little had changed in 1870. In 1873, Admiral Marie Jules Dupré, Governor of Cochinchina, dispatched Francis Garnier to Hanoi to obtain the release from the Dai Nam authorities of a French merchant, Jean Dupuis. Keen to trade with southern China, Dupuis had tried to sail up the Red River without authorization. Garnier was sympathetic to this enterprise and Dupré tacitly backed both of them. However, negotiations broke down as Garnier moved to seize control of Hanoi, declare the Red River open to navigation, and threaten unilaterally to impose a French protectorate over Tonkin.

While Tu Duc sought to negotiate a way out of full-scale war, local Vietnamese commanders enlisted the support of Chinese irregulars of diverse ethnic origins called the Black Flags to attack Garnier's men. Hostilities therefore began without either the nascent Third Republic's leaders or even the Vietnamese emperor in Hue authorizing the attacks. The Black Flags overwhelmed Garnier's small force and killed the explorer. The Third Republic was unwilling to go any further—not least because of the real risk of war with China. The government in Paris reined in its officials on the ground. The violence in Hanoi had, however, forced Hue to recognize formally the loss of all of Cochinchina (now including the three western provinces of Nam Ky) in a second treaty signed in Saigon in 1874. For the time being, French troops withdrew from the north, trade on the Red River resumed, and Dai Nam remained independent, albeit in its reduced form.

French nationalist and colonialist policies became more aggressive after 1877, when the republicans consolidated their power over the Legitimists (monarchists). At the helm of the metropolitan government was Jules Ferry, one of republican France's most celebrated leaders. He was determined to break with France's monarchical and Catholic past in favor of replacing it with an equally ardent Republic. The French were no longer subjects of a monarchy or the Church, but rather citizens of a modern nation-state, based on democratic institutions and the separation of Church and state. As prime minister (1880–81, 1883–5), he pushed through legislation establishing secular public education, supported major infrastructure programs integrating the country, and helped make Paris and the French language the center of national life.

Ferry was also the republic's most vocal colonial advocate. Pushing him, like Napoleon III earlier, was the colonial lobby of banking, financial, and insurance interests. Economic stagnation in France also led politicians and business leaders to agitate for renewed colonial expansion. The French economy experienced a long period of recession between 1873 and 1897, reaching a low point in 1884–5. Trade deficits were chronic. Protectionism was on the rise in Europe and the Americas. Colonies, many leaders concluded, or at least hoped, could provide the export markets and sources of growth that they so desperately wanted. Revealingly, in 1881, the government detached the question of the 'colonies' from the navy and attached it briefly to the Ministry of Commerce. In 1875, influential French financiers focused their attention on Asia by creating the Bank of Indochina ('Banque de l'Indochine', also known as the BIC). This increasingly powerful institution helped underwrite the colonial development of what became French Indochina and issued its unique currency—*la piastre indochinoise*—until 1955. It also financed private and public investment throughout Asia, into China, and much further still during the twentieth century. The French bank Crédit agricole is, in part, a descendant of the Bank of Indochina.[32]

The Third Republic and Jules Ferry's justifications for colonial expansion differed little from those of the Second Empire and the British: geopolitics, national prestige, and liberal economics. Ferry may have added the notion of a special republican *mission civilisatrice* to underscore the noble, liberal-minded goals of republican colonial ideology, but in practice this differed little from the British notion of the 'white man's burden'. Social Darwinism and a hodgepodge of nineteenth-century racialist theories helped French republicans justify why the 'strong' and the 'white' should rule over the 'weak' and the 'colored'. And French republican colonial expansion relied on the use of brute force, just like the British, the Americans, and countless others before them in world history.

Ideologically, however, French republicans used empire in ways the British did not. After the humiliating defeat of 1870 and now faced with the reality of German preeminence in continental Europe, republicans saw in colonial expansion a way of affirming a new sense of national identity and 'grandeur' which they badly wanted. For nationalist leaders on the left *and* the right, the idea of La plus grande France (or Greater France) took on an ideological life of its own, with remarkable staying power in elite circles until the late twentieth century. Although French public opinion remained overwhelmingly uninterested in colonial expansion and its wars to maintain the empire, government ministries and colonial lobbies joined forces to promote a favorable colonial ideology in France through the organization of exhibitions, art shows, travel and tourism, books, newspapers, and educational information. Meanwhile, a wide range of scientific, geographical, and medical associations became interested in the non-Western world which colonialism introduced and the laboratories, specimens, and art objects it could provide. The impact of 'empire' on the ordinary Frenchman or woman was minimal, but its effect on officials, administrators, officers, and scholars was not.[33]

Few republican leaders expressed philosophical or moral opposition to suspending their belief in the rights of man when it came to conquering the rest of Vietnam. Ferry had already led the charge against Tunisia in 1881 and Madagascar two years later. Unlike his predecessors, however, Ferry was ready to risk war with China in Asia to get his way over Dai Nam. He got his chance when another naval officer, Henri Rivière, implicitly backed by colonial authorities in Saigon, led a small contingent to Hanoi in late 1881, ostensibly to free merchants held by Dai Nam authorities. In a replay of Garnier's hubris, Rivière was convinced that he could easily take control of Tonkin, and thereby force Paris to follow suit. In April 1882, he occupied the Hanoi citadel. The Dai Nam court sent troops, Black Flag soldiers backed them, and, most importantly, this time China agreed to honor its tributary obligations. In mid-1882, the Qing dispatched troops to their southern border, where they occupied vital Dai Nam border towns such as Lang Son and Son Tay. Undaunted by this Chinese display of force, Rivière confidently marched on. But once again, things did not go according to plan. As Chinese troops looked on, Vietnamese and Black Flag troops routed the Frenchman's contingent.

While Rivière had created yet another fiasco in Tonkin, he was right about one thing: the Third Republic was committed to colonial expansion in Asia. Upon taking over the premiership for the second time in February 1883, Ferry transformed Rivière's defeat into a heroic moment of truth which required the French government to commit itself to achieving victory and building an Asian empire. War resumed in July–August 1883, when Admiral Amédée Courbet arrived at the head of naval forces. To force the Nguyen hand in the north, he attacked the capital of Hue and achieved a bloody victory over the imperial army on the beaches of Thuan An. The French writer and active naval officer Pierre Loti accompanied French troops into the heat of battle at Thuan An. He watched '*la grande tuerie*' (the 'slaughter' is how he put it) from the ship's deck. He noted the shells raining down on the adversary, walked among the Vietnamese corpses strewn across the dunes after the French victory, and interviewed French soldiers about 'what they had just done'. Based on all of this, he wrote a very disturbing series of articles on the violence of colonial conquest, the nature of men at war on both sides, speaking of both the humanity and inhumanity on display that day: 'We killed a lot; it was almost robbery'. Outraged by Loti's less than heroic account of republican soldiers committing war atrocities, Ferry ordered Loti to be discharged from the army.[34]

Thanks to this military success, French diplomat and leading colonial architect Jules Harmand obtained from the Nguyen court their signatures on the Treaty of Hue in August 1883 which ceded Tonkin to the French as a newly created protectorate. As Harmand warned the Nguyen court in the aftermath of the battle of Thuan An, failure to conclude a treaty meant annihilation:

> Now, here is a fact which is quite certain; you are at our mercy. We have the power to seize and destroy your capital and to cause you all to die of starvation. You have to choose between war and peace. We do not wish to conquer you, but you must accept our protectorate. For your people it is a guarantee of peace and prosperity; it is also the only chance of survival for

your government and your Court. We give you forty-eight hours to accept or reject, in their entirety and without discussion, the terms which in our magnanimity we offer you. We are convinced that there is nothing in them dishonorable to you, and, if carried out with sincerity on both sides, they will bring happiness [sic] to the people of Vietnam. If you reject them, you must expect the greatest evils. Imagine the most frightful things conceivable, and you will still fall short of the truth. The Dynasty, its Princes and its Court will have pronounced sentence on themselves. The name of Vietnam will no longer exist in history.[35]

Tough talk and one battle victory was not enough however to ensure Dai Nam's submission, however. The Black Flags stayed put in the north, allied with local Vietnamese forces refusing to lay down their arms. Most importantly, just across the border, Chinese forces remained in their positions. The Qing court still rejected the French right to remove Dai Nam from the Middle Kingdom's orbit. Like their mid–twentieth-century successors, the Qing were not keen on having hostile and expansionist-minded foreigners on their southern doorstep. Hostilities resumed when Courbet attacked the border town of Son Tay, hoping to defeat local Black Flags and Chinese troops before Qing China could send in reinforcements. Sporadic fighting continued into 1884 as the French increased the size of their contingent. After Son Tay, the French-occupied Bac Ninh. Unwilling to go any further, the Qing ultimately agreed to negotiate and signed the Tianjin Accord in May 1884. In so doing, they renounced their tributary relationship with Dai Nam and recognized the French protectorates in Dai Nam, in Annam and Tonkin. The Chinese withdrew their troops, leaving Lang Son in Vietnamese hands. A 'second' Treaty of Hue (called Patenôtre) entered into effect in June 1884, allowing the French to take over the whole of Dai Nam. The signature of this treaty also obliged the Hue court to melt down the seal presented by the Qing to Gia Long which symbolized the tributary relations which had bound the two countries for half a century. Although connections between China and Vietnam would remain, the French had extricated Dai Nam from its tributary position in the East Asian order in order to link it through treaties to a new imperial nation-state directed from Paris.[36]

However, French colonial conquest was still incomplete. The reoccupation of frontier towns did not go as planned when local Chinese commanders at Bac Le refused to budge. Rather than ironing out differences through diplomatic channels, French commanders preferred issuing ultimatums and using force. Ferry's government demanded the immediate Chinese evacuation of Tonkin and the payment of a 250 million franc indemnity to help cover the costs of conquest. Outraged by Chinese recalcitrance, the French blockaded and then attacked a number of southern Chinese ports. The navy even moved on Taiwan. What had been until now a rather local-ized colonial war of conquest suddenly set off a wider regional conflict and confirmed yet again the wider context of the French conquest of Vietnam and its connections to China.

This expansion led to increased political opposition in the National Assembly to Ferry's 'obsession' over Tonkin. (His adversaries ridiculed him as *Ferry le Tonkinois*.) Events came to a crescendo on 28 March 1885, when Ferry received a pessimistic telegram informing the French govern-ment that the army had abandoned Lang Son and that a Chinese attack on the delta was imminent. In reality, no such Chinese attack was in the works. Nor was the temporary evacuation of Lang Son an impediment to French progress in occupying the border towns. However, news of the 'fall of Langson' raised fears of a 'colonial Sedan' (which was where the Prus-sians had surrounded Napoleon III and his army in 1870). What interested Ferry's opponents most was the chance to bring down the prime minister over Tonkin. Ferry ardently defended his colonial policy, setting out all the reasons why the Republic had to grow its empire; but in the end it did not prevent a vote of no confidence and the fall of his government in April 1885 over a war that was already over.

This is why the disappearance of Ferry's government did little to change the outcome of Franco-Chinese relations or the destiny of Dai Nam. De-spite what they had argued against Ferry, his conservative adversaries were hardly anticolonialists. More than anything else, the Langson affair had served internal political needs in France. The new government quickly achieved a favorable settlement with the Chinese. Ferry's nemesis, Georges Clémenceau, would go on to champion the Republic's colonial cause. Wor-ried by simultaneous Japanese aggression in Korea, the Qing reaffirmed the validity of the Tianjin Accord with the French. In June 1885, a formal peace treaty ratified by the French Senate ended the Sino-French war. Dai Nam no longer existed as an independent state.[37]

To the west, the French also dismantled Thailand's tributary relation-ships with Lao states located throughout the Mekong River valley. Al-though ships could not navigate the Mekong all the way into China, the

British conquest of northern Burma nonetheless determined the French to secure their control over this waterway to the Chinese border. Relying on diplomacy, force, and exploratory missions, such as the one led by Auguste Pavie, the French contested and rejected Thai claims to these tributaries. In the end, however, force was necessary to remove them from Bangkok's own colonial hold. In 1893, the French dispatched gunboats up the Chao Phraya River to Bangkok, trained their cannons on the Chakri Royal Palace, and blockaded the Thai coast when the court refused to comply with an ultimatum to cede left-bank Lao territories.

The Bangkok court was no more ready to go to war in 1893 than Hue had been a decade earlier. Thai King Rama V had no independent Asian allies to whom he could turn: Burma was British, Qing China was imploding, the Japanese and the Americans were determined to join the colonial club in Asia, while the British had their own designs on his kingdom. The Thai king signed a treaty in October recognizing the French colonization of what would become Laos—a collection of military territories and kingdoms (Luang Prabang, Champassak, and Vientiane) organized loosely in the form of a protectorate. In 1907, the Thais further ceded the Cambodian provinces of Sisophon, Battambang, and Siemreap, the home of the magnificent Angkor Wat temple complex, to the French. Rather than go to war over Thailand, the French and the British left it independent as a buffer state.[38]

By the end of the nineteenth century, colonial conquest in Asia had destroyed centuries-old states, reshaped internal political and social relations, destabilized populations, and reconfigured the geopolitical map of Asia. A concert of Asian nations largely centered on imperial China vanished with the Qing dynasty in 1911, and a new one would not truly appear until after the Second World War as Chinese nationalists of all kinds struggled to create a nation-state on top of a centuries-old imperial empire which seemed to be falling apart like that of the Romans before it. As the Thais and Japanese rapidly moved to create independent nation-states based on the Western model, the French, Dutch, and British began building imperial ones on the vestiges of the states they had confiscated. For the French, this colonial state would be known as 'Indochina'.

CHAPTER 3

ALTERED STATES

Having signed the Treaty of Saigon in 1862, Emperor Tu Duc was convinced that he could negotiate the return of the three southern provinces in Dai Nam which he had just ceded to the French, and thereby avoid a more destructive war. His viceroy for the south, Phan Thanh Gian, agreed and travelled to Saigon to open talks with the French along these lines. What neither saw coming was the refusal of the commander of the southern forces, Truong Dinh, to stand down. Born in 1820, Dinh was the son of an imperial army officer from central Vietnam stationed in the south. He joined the army like his father and established a military colony in the delta like so many settlers before him. He loved the land, and following the French attack in 1858, he faithfully mobilized a six thousand-strong guerilla force to defend it. Impressed, Tu Duc put him in charge of the southern 'righteous army'.

Truong Dinh fought well, but when the emperor's emissary asked him to stop so that the court could negotiate the return of the lost provinces, the young officer replied that it was his duty to carry on in the name of king and country. He warned the sovereign's viceroy that negotiations would get them nowhere. As it turned out, he was right. In 1867, empty-handed, the viceroy Phan Thanh Gian committed suicide after having failed to stop the French from taking all of Cochinchina. Dinh had already taken his own life as enemy troops had closed in on him. Two of the emperor's servants had failed in two different ways to stop the creation of a new colonial state in the Mekong delta.[1]

Making French Cochinchina

There was no 'French Cochinchina' before Emperor Tu Duc had signed over three of his six southern provinces to Napoleon III in 1862. Until then, these six provinces constituted the 'southern region' of Dai Nam, known as Nam Ky since Minh Mang's administrative changes of 1833. The

Portuguese had first started to popularize the term 'Cochinchina' in the early sixteenth century to refer to all of Le Vietnam (which was then limited to the Tonkin delta). Starting in the seventeenth century, European Catholic missionaries circulating throughout the region adopted this term to describe the southern Nguyen state that had broken away from the north. In the eighteenth century, European missionaries, merchants, and travelers used the term Cochinchina widely to describe this ever larger southern state. Christian missionaries may have been the first to connect this term to the six southern provinces created in 1833 in order to administer their own religious activities accordingly. What we do know is that the French government first began to appropriate the term politically in 1858 during the 'Cochinchinese campaign'. The appearance of the first official bulletin in 1862, the Bulletin officiel de l'expédition de Cochinchine, confirmed that Nam Ky was becoming French Cochinchina along the lines laid out by Minh Mang's administrative reforms thirty years earlier.[2]

At the start, no one in the French ruling class knew where their colonial foothold in the eastern Mekong delta would lead them. Political leaders in Paris had issued no master plan to authorities on the ground which would trace the road from the 1862 Treaty of Saigon to the Indochinese Union of 1887. In fact, metropolitan signals were often mixed, communications between Saigon and Paris poor, and oceanic and wireless telegraphy still largely non-existent. Although the Suez Canal opened in 1869, it took weeks before ships arrived in Saigon with news of the fall of the Second Empire. Even then instructions remained vague as the Third Republic only slowly emerged. Uncertainty and contingency counted for as much as any grandiose colonial theories and geopolitical calculations in the making of French Cochinchina and what later grew into French Indochina.

As we know, French conquest began in the south and moved northward. The Treaty of Saigon (1862) ceded to the French the three eastern provinces of Bien Hoa, Gia Dinh (Saigon), and My Tho (Dinh Tuong). The French also obtained the island of Poulo Condor on which they built their notorious penitentiary. In 1863, Cambodia became a protectorate ruled from Saigon, essential to protecting Cochinchina, promoting French influence up the Mekong, and containing Thai expansionism eastward. By 1867, military occupation had expanded French Cochinchina to include the three remaining provinces of southern Dai Nam—Chau Doc (An Giang), Ha Tien, and Vinh Long. In January 1863, the French government placed the administration of their Cochinchinese territories in the hands of a powerful governor based in Saigon, assisted by a Consultative Council in charge of running what was, from 1865, officially called 'la Cochinchine française'. The navy played a leading role in building and administering this still-embryonic colonial entity. Until the 1870s, Navy officers monopolized the governship and reported directly to the Ministry of Navy and Colonies. Admirals dominated the Consultative Council and ran the interior ministry which was in charge of the administration of both European and indigenous offices. After thirty years of Nguyen civilian rule, military men were once again in charge of an imperial project in the Mekong delta.[3]

Conquest was one thing. Building a colonial state from the ashes of war was quite another. The disruptive effects of French conquest were profound. Civilians had fled their villages and towns as troops clashed and fires burned. Rice production and its transport declined precipitously as hunger spread. By early 1860, one missionary reported from the delta that thousands had already perished: 'There are entire provinces where poor people as well as the rich are reduced to consuming the grass of the fields and tree roots.' Many officials loyal to the Nguyen abandoned their posts, paralyzing the administration and its ability to alleviate such suffering. In April 1862, Admiral Louis Bonard reported soberly to his superiors: 'To this point, nothing has been done in Cochinchina to prepare for the future. We have destroyed a great deal, we have practically disorganized everything. Makeshift actions are all that have been taken thus far. Ruin is all that one sees among the towns that were once inhabited and commercially vibrant, like Saigon and its surrounding areas, which are now burned, ravaged, and depopulated.' Although the Nguyen army was on the run, Bonard concluded that '[i]n reality, we don't control the conquered country'.[4]

The disappearance of so many high-ranking and well-trained Nguyen civil servants was a real problem. It denied the new conquerors access to sources of information and badly needed administrative intermediaries. After all the Nguyen mandarins knew the country, its languages, and people infinitely better than the French. In 1878, the estimated total population of Cochinchina's six provinces (60,000 square kilometers) numbered 1.6 million people, comprising 1.5 million ethnic Viet, 100,000 Khmers, 10,000 Stieng, 9,500 Cham, and 36,000 Chinese. Totaling only around 2,000 people (excluding the armed forces) by 1900, the Europeans might have been at the top of the new colonial ladder, but they lived in an ocean of strangers. Protracted guerilla warfare, including attacks on Vietnamese officials cooperating with the French, only further undermined efforts to exert control.[5]

Early admiral-governors like Bonard and La Grandière applied direct and indirect methods of rule to govern. The withdrawal of so many Vietnamese civil servants meant that French inspectors had to step in at the provincial level. But rather than dismantling the lower levels of the Nguyen civil service (districts, cantons, and villages), Bonard tried to keep local elites in place. There were hardly enough trained Frenchmen to keep everything in hand. Moreover, because metropolitan leaders insisted that the colonies pay for themselves, relying on the pre-existing administration would keep costs down. As one of the governor's associates later recalled, 'Admiral Bonard arrived in Saigon in November 1861 and immediately proclaimed the principle of government by the indigenous for the indigenous'. Under the supervision of French inspectors, backed by the military and hastily organized indigenous militias, district and village-level mandarins continued to collect taxes, police, and arbitrate local disputes. The admirals certainly believed firmly in the need to transform their Asian subjects through France's superior civilizing power; but the transition from military occupation to a functioning colonial administration required them to be pragmatic and to adjust to local customs and procedures as much as to remaking the colonized in the French image. The French could not immediately impose direct assimilationist rule over Cochinchina. They simply did not have the means on the ground to do so.[6]

Moreover, indirect rule had support in very high places in the Second Empire. In French Algeria, Chasseloup-Laubat and Napoleon III had both backed the organization of indigenous government as an official policy. Napoleon had personally supported the creation of the *Bureaux arabes* ('Arab offices') as part of his grand strategy of ruling indirectly through local elites in Algeria. Between 1844 and 1870, French officers ran these offices, using Arab authorities, their families, and patron–client networks to gather intelligence, collect taxes, police the populace, and adjudicate locally. Chasseloup-Laubat now fully approved the desire of naval officers to rule Cochinchina through indigenous structures and loyal elites—'like the heads of our Arab offices in Algeria'.[7]

To this end, Admiral Bonard created the Consultative Committee on Indigenous Affairs. Through it, a handful of French inspectors (mostly former naval officers) spread across the delta, filling the provincial posts abandoned by the Nguyen. Bonard personally approved the translation into

French of the Gia Long law code, so that inspectors might know Nguyen customs and use the dynasty's legislation effectively in winning over and administering mandarins who had stayed on at the lower echelons of the indigenous bureaucracy.

The French also deployed direct forms of rule in their new Cochinchinese colony, since the still independent northern provinces in Dai Nam (Annam and Tonkin) continued to control the traditional supply of mandarins from Hue. The last thing the admirals wanted to do in any case would be to import bureaucrats from 'enemy' Annam or Tonkin. They thus had no choice but to step in and, as time progressed and pre-existing civil servants retired or left, fill vacancies in the indigenous Cochinchinese bureaucracy with greater numbers of non-Confucian-trained civil servants, with French-educated ones, and with French inspectors. However, by recruiting and often promoting non-qualified Vietnamese to positions of power in the rural bureaucracy, the French disrupted local politics and social relations. Interpreters with no Confucian civil-service training found ways of rendering themselves particularly indispensable. Ton Thu Tuong was one example among many at the time. Although he had failed the civil service examinations under the Nguyen, he accepted work with the admirals, and, in exchange, became a high-ranking prefect in Cochinchina. He urged others to do likewise.[8]

Local strongmen in the Mekong delta also offered their services to help the French keep the colonial peace on the cheap. The problem was that many of these men did not necessarily have the interests of the people (or even the colonial state) in mind. Some developed their own fiefdoms, practiced extortion, and often did so with the implicit support of the French. Several were illiterate. Such collaboration in colonial state-making certainly provided attractive upward social mobility for men like Tuong; but it also created local animosities which, as in earlier periods of Vietnamese history, would not be forgotten easily. As one French administrator soon lamented:

> Our new officials, both through instruction and education, are, in general, infinitely inferior to the old [mandarins]. They are not in the least scholars, nor imbued with Confucian doctrine. In the first years of conquest one takes men of goodwill that one finds in one's hands. Fidelity counts more than capacity ... many would not have been given employment as simple clerks formerly.[9]

Like the Nguyen before them, the French also relied upon Chinese merchants and their regional networks to help them consolidate their hold over the delta. Upon landing troops in Danang in 1858, French officers began recruiting Chinese traders in Cholon, the 'big market', to supply their armies with beef from Cambodia. They also needed them to import rice from the delta to feed the local populations coming under French control. Before becoming famous for his military exploits in Tonkin, Francis Garnier had administered Cholon and developed close relationships with the Chinese trading community based there. He had done much to support what would become modern Vietnam's largest and best-known 'Chinatown'. And, like their predecessors, the French also welcomed Chinese immigration. The Chinese population in Vietnam increased from 25,000 in the early 1860s to 120,000 in 1904 and 201,000 in 1911. The overwhelming majority lived in Cochinchina, where colonial development would always attract far more Chinese settlers than French ones.[10]

The well-connected Fujian trader, Ban Hap, is a case in point. During the Cochinchinese campaign, he built up a prosperous business supplying French forces with food. Thanks to French political support and Chinese capital from Singapore, Ban Hap remained in Cochinchina after the war and invested heavily in Saigon's emerging real estate market, commerce, and the opium trade. In fact, he purchased the state license allowing him to run the colony's opium monopoly. Thanks to his networks and contacts, he imported opium from across Asia for sale to a mainly Chinese clientele. In so doing, he provided the nascent colonial state with arguably its single most important source of revenue at the time. Ban Hap's importance was such that when he faced bankruptcy at one point, the government bailed him out. The governor had been worried that this Asian businessman's downfall would have 'compromised the colony's finances' and 'ruined part of the local commerce'. Ban Hap's cooperation was such that the French ensured the education of his children in the metropole and supported his wish to become a French citizen.[11]

If there was much continuity between the French and Vietnamese colonial experiences, there was also great change. The transformation of the small town of Saigon into a major commercial center and the Cochinchinese capital is instructive. Founded by the Cambodians, propelled by the Chinese, and colonized by the Nguyen, Saigon was in fact home to only a few thousand Chinese and Vietnamese on the eve of French conquest. Violent clashes during the French assault emptied the town of its population and destroyed all but one of the forty small villages comprising it. Between 1859 and 1862, Saigon was a ghost town. It 'had ceased to be Annamese but had not yet become French' is how one officer described it. But that changed rapidly. With the guarantee of the 1862 treaty and attracted by Chinese commercial activity next door in Cholon, the French immediately began transforming Saigon into Cochinchina's capital and main port. While no one knew it at the time, in so doing they also ensured that this small administrative town would become the major urban center of modern Vietnam. Admiral Bonard and his successors presided over the digging of a series of canals to drain the insalubrious marshes which inundated the area. The government approved concessions and authorized the sale of land. Ban Hap built one of the rare multi-story houses at the time, a sure sign of his social ascent. By 1867, 15 kilometers of roads lined a rapidly expanding colonial center as governors went on something of a spending spree. French Saigon was soon home to the Botanical Gardens, a modern naval shipyard, the Arsénal, and the Avalanche warehouse which handled goods leaving and entering the port. Links to the metropole and the rest of the world evolved rapidly. In 1862, one of the first French steamships, *L'Impératrice,* arrived in Saigon. The Merchant Shipping Company (Compagnies des Messageries maritimes) soon began providing shipping services to Yokohama, Hong Kong, Bangkok, Aden, and Marseille.[12]

Most of the original Viet denizens of Saigon never returned to their homes, having found themselves on the wrong side of colonial conquest. In fact, the first to settle down in postwar French Saigon were 3,000 Catholics, most of whom had been evacuated from Danang with the French army in 1860. Others moved into the city to escape the violence against them in the countryside. They needed French protection and the French needed their cooperation. In 1863, the first new Catholic church building in decades appeared in Saigon. By 1869, the total population of Saigon equaled 8,000 people, including an increasing number of European civil servants, merchants, and missionaries. Almost all of them were men. As the population increased, hotels, restaurants, and stores appeared. The same was true in bustling Cholon, which catered to the growing Chinese clientele. The admirals erected the first in a series of buildings for administration during this time, including the Palais Norodom, the Governor of Cochinchina's headquarters.[13]

Such large-scale projects cost money, however. And given that the French government expected the Cochinchinese authorities to finance local development, the majority indigenous population ended up assuming the fiscal burden. Governors immediately turned to 'direct contributions' from the people, mainly in the form of personal and land taxes levied on them, as well as 'indirect' ones, such as their licensing of monopolies. Thanks to the pre-existing Nguyen land registry records (*dia ba*), the French collected their first property taxes via the local administration. The French required peasants to pay this tax in the new colonial currency, *la piastre*, and not in kind, thereby further expanding the monetary economy throughout the countryside. Topographical teams spread across the delta to plot and register new lands and verify existing ones. The introduction of the état-civil, a certified legal document containing a person's vital information, aimed to increase central state control and to improve upon the pre-existing one. Authorities also collected a 'personal tax', which was in reality a tax on registered members of villages. Revenue from land and personal taxes increased from 1.5 million francs in 1865 to 2.1 million in 1867.[14]

Other sources of income were the state-run monopolies on alcohol, gambling, and opium. The opium license generated large amounts of revenue, tripling from 500,000 francs in 1862 to 1.5 million in 1865. Between 1874 and 1877, it generated 3.2 million francs. If the income from the gambling and prostitution monopolies is added to this, Cochinchina reaped 4.2 million francs in monopoly income in 1878, and 6.7 million in 1881. Opium largely financed the creation of French Cochinchina.[15]

Rice was also important. Under the Nguyen, the Mekong delta had produced rice for export to southern China as well as for internal consumption. The French, however, firmly redirected production toward the export market. In the early 1870s, the total cultivable land area in Cochinchina equaled 300,000 hectares, of which 250,000 were in rice production. Given that the French did little draining of marshy land outside Saigon before 1900, the increase in exports could only have come from lowering the supply available for internal consumption or from halting the pre-existing black market in rice. Regardless, the peasant population—not the French taxpayer— paid the highest price for financing French Cochinchina's development in terms of taxes and rice production, while the Chinese community's opium addicts bore the brunt of that particular monopoly. Moreover, by depriving Dai Nam of its crucial Mekong rice basket, food became scarce in the still independent kingdom to the north, further undermining its internal stability.[16]

The making of French Cochinchina also deeply affected the Vietnamese language, a major transformation in the history of modern Vietnam. For one, the durability of any colonial project depends on access to reliable information in order to know the conquered population. The French naval officers taking over in the Mekong delta knew next to nothing about the 1.5 million people suddenly under their control. Through the Catholic missions a few Frenchmen spoke Vietnamese. Although a handful of high-ranking Vietnamese officials like Ton Thu Tuong spoke French well, hardly any lower- and middle-ranking mandarins did. To complicate matters, French officials soon realized that while civil servants used their native Vietnamese when speaking amongst themselves at home or in the market, they consigned their written bureaucratic correspondence to classical Chinese characters. This may have pleased Orientalist naval officers, such as Paul Philastre and Louis-Gabriel Aubaret (who translated and annotated the Gia Long law code), but it baffled their superiors, who could not imagine setting up a colonial civil service based on this 'hieroglyphic' language. Prejudices against Chinese culture were legion among officers who were at that very time also involved in carving up the Middle Kingdom. To Bonard, the use of Chinese was 'incompatible with all progress'.[17]

Admirals initially turned to missionaries for help. The hope was that Catholics could provide a reliable supply of interpreters at ease with French. The problem, at least at the outset, was that relatively few Viet Catholics actually knew French. European missionaries preached in Vietnamese and taught the indigenous clergy the language of the Church—Latin. In the early days, it was not uncommon for naval officers to dust off their grammar-school Latin to communicate with the Viet clergy using paper and pen. A precious exception to this rule was the remarkable Catholic polyglot, Petrus Truong Vinh Ky, who had first trained in Penang, the Vatican's seminary for Southeast Asia. Fluent in French, he helped governors from Bonard to Paul Bert in interpreting, translating, in short, understanding the country. As one contemporary nicely put it, he was Cochinchina's first 'Annamese civil servant'. Indeed, interpreters soon constituted a new and invaluable class of bureaucrats in French Cochinchina, with their names appearing early on in the official gazettes alongside those of their French counterparts.[18]

That said, one man could not do it all. And missionaries caused as many problems as solutions. Perhaps the single most important (and unintentional) missionary contribution to the colonial cause was the Romanized writing system developed in the seventeenth century for transcribing Vietnamese via the Latin alphabet. *Quoc ngu* or, word for word, the 'national script', was attractive to colonial authorities for several reasons. Firstly, admirals realized that a Latin alphabet would allow French administrators to learn Vietnamese more easily and rapidly than Chinese characters. Secondly, no one in the field at the time truly believed that local elites would suddenly begin to speak or write in French. So much so that Bonard saw in the spread of *quoc ngu* the possibility of creating 'a language that all the Franco-Annamese people will understand'. Thirdly, deprived of the Nguyen civil service exams, the admiralty pushed the Latin script in order to train badly needed Vietnamese interpreters and bureaucrats as rapidly as possible. Lastly, by breaking away from Chinese characters, this Romanized script would help remove Viet elites from their Chinese civilizational orbit and orientate them toward their French future. The last two reasons turned out to be the most important.[19]

The colonial promotion of *quoc ngu* was certainly assimilationist in design. However, its main goal was to create a more efficient form of administrative control, rather than necessarily turn the Cochinchinese into Frenchmen. Admirals immediately opened language schools teaching the Latin script to interpreters, civil servants, and, later, tens of thousands of children. They gave the governance of several early schools to Petrus Ky and other French-speaking Catholics. In April 1865, Petrus Ky received authorization to publish the first *quoc ngu* newspaper in modern Vietnam, the *Gia Dinh Bao* (*Gia Dinh News*). Unsurprisingly, it published colonial decrees, instructions, and statistics; but it also produced articles on sociocultural subjects before it closed in 1909. From 1882, *quoc ngu* officially replaced Chinese characters for reproducing in translation official French correspondence relating to the colony. To be sure, the use of Chinese characters continued into the twentieth century (as did the demotic script, *chu nom*), but the mechanics of colonial institutionalization and the practical requirements of local administration and an education system designed to feed it had introduced a Romanized script that would ultimately emerge victorious over the character writing systems. The irony is that Vietnamese nationalists—like their Indonesian counterparts adopting a Dutch-sponsored Latin script—would soon turn *quoc ngu* against the colonizers and use it for their own cultural and state-building projects.[20]

Making Annam-Tonkin French[21]

From their base in Saigon, the admirals pushed for the conquest of the remainder of Dai Nam. And although the Cochinchine des Amiraux (the 'Cochinchina created by the admirals') disappeared in 1879 when the Third

Republic appointed a civilian governor for Cochinchina, French republicans were as colonially minded as their predecessors. This time, however, the French conquerors were taking over the entire Nguyen state, including the monarchy at the top in Hue. French troops sacked the capital in 1885, sending the young emperor Ham Nghi fleeing into the countryside with his regents. In his place, General Philippe de Courcy named a new emperor under colonial tutelage. As the French general bluntly reported on the new balance of power—'We will now have them execute decisions made outside of their control'.[22]

Vanquished Dai Nam—consisting of 'Annam' (the center) and 'Tonkin' (the north)—became a French protected state. The Patenôtre Treaty of 1884 served as the legal text upon which French rule over Annam-Tonkin rested until 1945. As a colonial protectorate, Dai Nam lost its internationally recognized sovereignty. The court could no longer direct its diplomatic relations or field an independent army. However, in theory, the Hue-based emperor maintained the power to run Dai Nam's internal affairs of state, including the civil-service examination system and the bureaucracy it supplied. With French approval, the colonially consecrated Emperor Dong Khanh dispatched a viceroy to Hanoi to continue administering mandarins in the north. In 1886, in Hue, Paul Bert replaced General de Courcy as the civilian resident general (résident général). The Ministry of Foreign Affairs attended to the protectorate of Annam-Tonkin, while the Ministry of the Navy and Colonies remained in charge of Cochinchina-Cambodia. Administratively, two separate French colonial structures existed and the colonized had to have their papers in order to travel from one to the other.

Continued Viet resistance to French conquest and republican ideological proclivities for centralized control effectively transformed the protectorate into a very complicated and messy form of *de facto* direct and indirect rule. In a bid to weaken stubborn royalist opposition to their rule, the French further split the protectorate of Annam-Tonkin into two separate territorial units, each ruled by a resident general from Hue and Hanoi, respectively. In 1897, the French closed the office of the viceroy in Hanoi, thereby severing Hue's institutional link to its northern territories. French commissioners (résidents supérieurs) now directly assumed the selection of local mandarins for Tonkin and Annam. As of 1897, the French had effectively sectioned the unitary Vietnam of 1802 into three territorial and administrative units—Cochinchina, Annam, and Tonkin. This would become a major point of contention for nationalists in the twentieth century.[23]

However, the appearance of powerful commissioners in Tonkin and Annam does not mean that the French brushed aside the pre-existing mandarinate at local level. The combined population of Annam-Tonkin exceeded
ten million people, seven times greater than that of Cochinchina in the
1860s. Like the admiralty in the south, republican colonizers needed the
native mandarinate to rule indirectly at the district and village level. And indirect rule was always cheaper. Lofty republican promises to assimilate and
civilize their colonized subjects never worked out so easily on the ground.
In fact, French officials in charge of running Annam and Tonkin did their
best to rehabilitate and reform the pre-existing civil service and examination
system in order to rule more effectively. In 1907, the future governor general
of Indochina, Pierre Pasquier, waxed lyrically over 'this admirable provincial administration that constitutes a marvelous instrument of governing'.
In 1896, 55 percent of the provincial mandarins in Tonkin had begun their
careers before the arrival of the French and over 70 percent were graduates
of the Nguyen examination system. French colonial rule was as much a graft
on to the past as it was a break with it. Little wonder the Confucian-based
exams continued to operate in colonial Annam and Tonkin until 1919. In
French Indochina, as in the Vietnamese colonial state preceding it, the policies of 'association/indirect rule' and 'assimilation/direct rule' were never
mutually exclusive. They overlapped and changed over time and across
particular spaces and also at different levels of the administration as circumstances required and conjunctures changed. The interplay of these two colonial policies was an essential part of the making of modern Vietnam. And
so was the question of colonial collaboration, to which we must now turn.[24]

COLONIAL COLLABORATION AND CHOICE

Colonial collaboration is a complex phenomenon and a very sensitive
one—and not just in Vietnam. We have encountered it in earlier periods of
Vietnamese history, under a millennium of Chinese imperial rule and as a
part of Vietnam's own colonial expansion. We will come across it again in
wartime. Collaboration is almost always 'occupier-driven', to borrow Jan
Gross' definition for Europe during the Second World War, and established
and administered through the conqueror's threat or use of superior military
force, which impacts profoundly upon local choices, loyalties, and a range
of social and political relationships. It could mean cooperating with the

occupier in order to survive difficult, indeed, life-threatening situations: the need to feed and care for one's family and loved ones is always an essential consideration in such troubled times, often trumping ideological beliefs. Secondly, as we have already seen in this book, by forcing regime change, occupiers provide a chance for marginalized groups to advance their political and social agendas. Intentionally or not, new occupiers often revive long-dormant debates and exacerbate pre-existing socio-political tensions in new ways. Lastly, collaboration is never static; it changes as the occupier's strength weakens, the likelihood of outside intervention increases, or the international balance of forces shifts. And as it does so, strategies of cooperation and resistance to the occupiers change accordingly. This does not excuse purely self-interested collaborators. These people existed in Vietnam as they did in France, and throughout world history.[25]

But not all peasants, mandarins, or even kings who stayed on to work under the French were simple traitors at the outset. They were, above all, vanquished. The French monopolized the use of modern violence and did not hesitate to employ it. The bloodletting at Thuan An in 1883 described by Pierre Loti in chapter 2 was not an isolated event. Given the asymmetrical nature of the battlefield, the rapid collapse of the Dai Nam army left civilians with little choice but to collaborate with the occupier, retreat into the hills, or risk serious bodily harm. People resisted, both elite and common folk (as the case of Truong Dinh above shows). But the French army and their Vietnamese allies often responded to such resistance with extreme violence, burning villages and pagodas to the ground with no consideration of the impact on individual lives, possessions, and subsistence. And for the men, women, and children caught in the crossfire, choices rarely appeared in black and white. Drawing upon oral sources collected from the rural poor who had survived the French assault in the late nineteenth century, Father Léopold Cadière captured the dilemma poignantly:

> For the poor inhabitants of the country, farmers, fishermen, loggers, those souls who relied on forest products for their subsistence, how painful, how worthy of pity was their fate! Caught between the rebels and our troops, they didn't know what to do. We were told of the mayor of Kim Lu, who 'would for a long time not see his village'. Was he shot or simply imprisoned for many months, for failing to provide the information wanted of him? His case was a typical one. He represented the large number of those poor Annamese who, putting aside their nationalist feelings, were victims of events.

There were certainly among them people considered by our sentinels to be traitors, rebels, and enemies. But there were also many people who acted or refused to act out of fear, or who said nothing because they knew nothing.[26]

In *The Sacred Willow*, Duong Van Mai Elliot's history of her northern family, the author provides an empathetic account of her great-grandfather's dilemma as a rising young mandarin faced with a profound change in power relations triggered by the French conquest. While the ability of the author really to penetrate the innermost feelings of her great-grandfather is questionable, Duong Van Mai puts her finger on the difficult decisions scores of mandarins had to make when she writes:

> In 1884, when the French consolidated their hold over the north, my great-grandfather had just begun his mandarin career, having become District Magistrate in Ha Dong province in 1883. The goal he had struggled for was finally within his grasp. Yet, as fate would have it, the moment of triumph would become clouded only months later by the loss of independence. He stayed in this position for three years, but his heart was not in it. He resigned in 1886, using his mother's illness as an excuse, the first of many resignations during his career. Although he was forced to resume government service time and again, either in response to official summonses that he could not turn down, to meet his family's heavy financial burdens, or to do whatever good he could as a mandarin for a country in its hour of need, my great-grandfather did so with reluctance. For the rest of his life, until his retirement, he would feel the conflicting pull of what scholars at the time called 'engagement' and 'withdrawal'. Should he, as a scholar trained to serve the court and the country, join the government and risk getting stigmatized by collaborating with the French? Or should he abstain from dealing with affairs of state, even if he could make some difference, and keep his reputation intact? He would also struggle with the issue of loyalty, a value that scholars considered central to their lives. Could he, in 'engaging', separate loyalty to the court from loyalty to France, which controlled it? And could he, as a mandarin, be loyal to the people and their welfare, without also furthering the interests of France?[27]

There were other reasons explaining accommodation. For centuries Viet political loyalties had been split. Upon unifying a deeply divided country in 1802, Gia Long sidelined northern officials who had served the Trinh and the Le. By helping or not opposing the French war on the Nguyen, several marginalized elites now saw a chance to reassert their influence and promote their social mobility under the French. One northern mandarin, Hoang Cao Khai, lent his knowledge, contacts, and militia to French 'pacification' in the late nineteenth century. In exchange, the French catapulted him to the position of imperial delegate for Tonkin. Without the French occupation, Hoang Cao Khai's family would have never become the political force it did during the next century. Moreover, many non-Viet people in the central highlands saw in collaboration with the French the chance to protect themselves from centuries of ethnic Viet colonization and carve out a new independent future. The man who was to betray Emperor Ham Nghi in 1888 was a member of the Muong tribe who resented the heavy-handed Nguyen colonial rule which had been in place since the 1830s.[28]

Creating French Indochina

French reliance on the indigenous administration and elite did not prevent the Third Republic from creating a single colonial state under one authority. In 1887, the French government formally approved the creation of the Indochinese Union (Union indochinoise). Until 1945, this colonial state incorporated Cochinchina, Cambodia, Annam, Tonkin, and, from 1893, Laos (or what would become Laos). In all, it ultimately covered 740,000 square kilometers and counted over sixteen million people by 1913. In 1888, the cities of Hanoi, Haiphong, and Danang joined Saigon as directly administered colonies subject to metropolitan law. Appointed by Paris and based in Hanoi, a governor general ruled what became commonly known by the turn of the century as French Indochina, l'Indochine française. Assisting him was the Upper Council of Indochina, which consisted of five directors in charge of the colonial state's main services. From 1891, the governor general received his orders directly from one source, the Ministry of Colonies.[29]

The governor general's powers were considerable. He established the union's budget and presided over the entire administration—both the Indochinese central services (communications, justice, customs, and police) and the local administration of each of the protectorates, colonies, and military territories. Though the French never created an 'Indochinese Army' like the British-sponsored one in India, in 1886 the Native Guard (Garde indigène) was born to ensure internal security, buffeted by an amalgam of security services and militias. The decision to make Hanoi the administrative capital of Indochina shifted the political center of gravity away from the poles of Saigon (French Cochinchina) and Hue (Dai Nam) back to the

Red River delta, as it had been in a much earlier period. The governor of Cochinchina in Saigon became a 'lieutenant governor', subservient to the governor general now appointing him. Unsurprisingly, many European politicians, merchants, and civil servants in Cochinchina decried this re-appropriation of their powers and revenue streams. But there was little they could do. Unlike Le Van Duyet's opposition to Minh Mang's consolida-tion of the south, there would be no rebellion on the part of the 'French Cochinchinese'. A resolution in the 1890s calling for Cochinchinese seces-sion from the Indochinese Union failed. Settlers were few in number and were no match for the colonial army.

As in Algeria, French settlers in Cochinchina welcomed the advent of the Third Republic. Shared republican ideals united some; but rising metropolitan immigration and settler opposition to the admiralty's (per-ceived) protection of the 'indigenous' was the most important factor. Set-tlers warmly welcomed the first civilian governor of Cochinchina, Charles Le Myre de Vilers, applauding his decision to emasculate the Indigenous Affairs office. Much to their relief, de Vilers also replaced the Gia Long law code with the French one, began implementing French civil law, and pre-sided over the introduction of the Code de l'indigénat, allowing for efficient repression and ensuring the legal primacy of French 'citizens' over native 'subjects'. Moreover, the Third Republic—not the Second Empire—for-mally annexed all of Cochinchina as a colony in 1874, much to the delight of the French community concentrated there.[30]

While Cochinchina never became a French department like Algeria, the Third Republic created the Colonial Council of Cochinchina (Conseil co-lonial de Cochinchine)—the only one of its kind in Indochina. It consisted of sixteen (later eighteen) members and its powers were heavily stacked in favor of French citizens and based on universal suffrage (for French *male* citizens). Only six male Vietnamese could be elected to the council from a college of electors consisting of delegates chosen by village notables. Even then, those nominees needed French approval to run for office and few could speak French in the early years of the colony's existence, which was a serious handicap. The council had the power to establish the local bud-get and to seat a Cochinchinese deputy in the French parliament. With the admirals out of the way and direct rule on the rise, European settlers now enjoyed greater power over the indigenous. Hardly surprisingly, land alienation of the indigenous population in Cochinchina increased dramati-cally from 1880 onward, as it had in Algeria under republicans. In the end,

Hanoi may have become home to the Indochinese government, but Saigon-Cholon remained the center of European settler power and the colony's commercial hub.[31]

A decade later, having put to rest royalist resistance (see below), the Third Republic redoubled its efforts to consolidate Indochina. Leading the charge was the highly motivated Paul Doumer. Thanks in part to his service as a minister of finance in France, he arrived in Indochina in 1897 with a government loan of 200 million francs and a mandate to give real life to the colony. He set to work immediately, equipping the general government with core departments in charge of finances, customs and monopolies, public works, agriculture and trade, the postal and telegraph service, and so on. A devoted republican, Doumer further centralized control over the civil service, the budget, and the tax code. In 1897, he abolished the viceroy's position in Hanoi and reduced the monarchy's powers in the north to almost nil. The lieutenant governor in Cochinchina lost his control over the southern budget. Doumer maintained and extended the direct and indirect taxes which applied to Cochinchina to all of Indochina. He created three powerful state monopolies in opium, salt, and alcohol. Between 1899 and 1922, opium accounted for 20 percent of Indochina's budget, confirming again the continued importance of this drug in underwriting colonial development.

The 200 million franc loan from the Third Republic allowed for substantial investment in major infrastructure and public works projects. The Bank of Indochina provided financing for much of the remainder of the costs and made huge profits in doing so. As an indication of French government and this bank's joint strategic interests, the governor general ensured that train tracks were laid from Hanoi to Kunming in southern China (at the same time that the Russians were building a railroad across Manchuria to the north). Indeed, the implosion of the Qing and the scramble to carve up China still weighed heavily on French colonial priorities into the early twentieth century. Work also began on a line from Hanoi to Haiphong, transforming the latter into modern Vietnam's most important northern port. Major investment also went into the building of dikes in the Red River and the draining of tens of thousands of hectares of marshland in the Mekong delta. By the turn of the century, French Indochina had become a reality.

Again, the Indochinese peasants bore the brunt of this colonial development. Doumer developed a global system of taxation that increased the fiscal burden on the rural population which was heavily enforced, and exacerbated by the fact that the French cadastral methods were not always that modern. His expansion of the salt and alcohol monopolies accentuated rural poverty, as did the arbitrary requisitioning of peasant labor, *la corvée*, essential to realizing these grandiose public works projects. In other words, the French taxpayer did not finance the making of colonial Vietnam. Nor did the small French settler population. The Indochinese did—the Vietnamese, Cambodians, and Laotians.[32]

Resistance, Monarchy, and Choice

The stability and legitimacy of French rule remained fragile as long as any Vietnamese, from north to south, continued to resist. And many did so, and, they did so heroically. The 'pacification' of Cochinchina lasted a decade, during which resistance to the French was often fierce. Although the court in Hue sued for peace in the treaty in 1862, it could not call off local commanders and officials determined to fight on. Following the loss of its southernmost territory, several high-ranking advisors to the court argued more vocally in favor of war. The most outspoken of them, the mercurial Ton That Thuyet, counseled against further concessions and urged the emperor to prepare for war. As Tu Duc's health deteriorated in 1883, Thuyet increasingly asserted his influence and backed the young Prince Ham Nghi as the heir to the throne. In late 1883, Thuyet got his wish and had Ham Nghi named as emperor. However, the young emperor only ruled for 1884 and part of 1885 until the French took over by force. On the night of 4 July 1885, as the French stormed the capital, Thuyet and his allies secretly smuggled Ham Nghi out of Hue to a safe base in the nearby highlands. From there, the boy emperor issued the edict calling on officials and scholars to take up arms against the foreign invaders, to support the emperor, and restore the country's independence.

It was a call to arms. Copies of the '*Can Vuong*' ('Save the King') edict circulated northward to Tonkin and southward into the Mekong delta. The emperor and his regents urged mandarins to mobilize their areas for war. For the first time, the throne openly sanctioned popular resistance. Given the low levels of urbanization in Dai Nam and the existence of a civil service structure which returned many trained, mid-level mandarins to their native villages and districts, the Can Vuong movement could draw upon considerable patron–client, student–teacher, and kinship ties to generate support in the countryside. Many local mandarins and scholars rallied entire villages through such relationships. Others obtained local acquiescence in providing food, shelter, and recruits. This helps explain why anticolonialists managed to keep the royalist resistance going for years, despite the capture of the emperor in exile, Ham Nghi, in 1888.[33]

Despite the propaganda they distributed, French officials knew they were not dealing with a bunch of 'bandits' and 'pirates'. They also realized that as long as they failed to harness control of the man who represented the legitimate monarchy to the Vietnamese (and not just the royal puppet figure who remained in Hue, Emperor Dong Khanh), the success of the entire colonial project remained vulnerable. To one French officer, Emperor Ham Nghi (r. 1884-5) 'represented in the eyes of the people the patriotic struggle against the foreigner'. Even Jules Harmand, the colonial strategist ready to annihilate the Nguyen if need be, believed that deep patriotic forces linked subjects and mandarins to their emperor and drove the resistance. It also explains why he was so determined, despite the tough talk, to win over this heroic elite by providing them immediately with a privileged partnership in the building of Indochina. This perception among high-ranking colonial administrators of a tightly knit and patriotic Vietnamese identity helps explain why, on the one hand, the French emasculated their own colonial emperors for fear that they might turn on them, and, on the other hand, did their best to use the monarchy, convinced that, if handled and mobilized adroitly, the sovereign could serve as the living symbol through which the French could associate this patriotic people with their rule. To put it another way, French republicans may have done away with their own kings at home, but they latched on to colonial monarchy in Vietnam early on and would not let go for decades.[34]

One of the most remarkable royalist officials staying behind to lead the fight against the French for over a decade was Phan Dinh Phung. Born in 1847 in Ha Tinh province, Phung heralded from an illustrious mandarin family reaching back twelve generations to the Le dynasty. In 1876-7, he passed the regional and metropolitan exams with great distinction, arguing in a dissertation set by Tu Duc that the court should emulate Japan's military modernization. Despite getting into trouble with Ton That Thuyet over tricky succession matters, Phung emerged as the leader of the Can Vuong movement, while Thuyet travelled to China in search of aid from the Qing and ended up staying there.

The French did everything in their power to arrest Phan Dinh Phung and defeat his supporters. The legitimacy of their colonial state depended on it. Governor General Jean-Marie de Lanessan counted on Hoang Cao Khai and his royalist connections to do this. Khai had known Phung from their childhood days. In 1885, Khai drew upon his village contacts to send a message to Phung (whose men operated in the surrounding mountains). In his letter, couched in the powerful Confucian language of the mandarin class, Khai urged his old friend to give up. It was futile to resist and, if he did, it would only bring further suffering upon the people. Khai also threatened to dig up all of Phung's family tombs and dismember his recently captured brother *pour l'exemple*. Phung received the letter, but he apparently scoffed at it, assuring his inner circle that he would never cross over. No longer was it possible to think only of one's family, he told them. One now had to think of saving 'all the other brothers of our country'. Phung's contempt for Khai's collaboration and the French message he had delivered was intense. Defiant, Phung instructed his fellow countryman 'if anyone carves up my brother, remember to send me some of the soup'. 'There is only one way for me to die now,' he concluded.[35]

For the next decade, Phung joined forces with royalists in western An-nam and the remote hills of Tonkin in organizing a network of resistance bases, purchasing arms from abroad, or making them locally when that was possible. He entered into contact with another anticolonialist, Hoang Hoa Tham, who would lead the resistance in the name of the true emperor in the northern province of Bac Giang. Phung relied on regional ties in Ha Tinh and Nghe An to launch hit-and-run attacks on the French. As a result, between 1885 and 1895, the French had to commit large numbers of troops to patrolling the rough terrain of Annam and Tonkin.

Life in the maquis, however, took its toll. Disease, cold, and isolation sapped morale and weakened the body. Comrades tired and returned home to a life of seclusion. Some were captured. Others defected. In 1893, hoping to lift spirits across the land, Can Vuong forces launched a full-scale attack on the provincial seat of Nghe An governed by Hoang Cao Khai. It ended in defeat as the partisan frontal assault came under a barrage of enemy cannon fire, with devastating consequences. Phung's inner circle began to dwindle, while the French and their Vietnamese associates jailed Phung's family, dug up his ancestors' tombs as promised, and terrorized those villagers who supported the royalists or were simply suspected of assisting the 'rebels'. As more resistance leaders fell or lost heart, Phung realized that the move-ment could not last. Sensing that his enemy might be ready to surrender, Hoang Cao Khai quickly drafted another French-approved missive which recognized the righteousness of Phung's decision to remain loyal to the monarchy, but stressing again that it was now imperative to think of the welfare of the people: 'Who has ever heard of men who were loyal to their emperor but forgot the people's aspirations'? Khai queried. Should Phung continue to resist, then 'not only will the population of our village be destroyed but our entire country will be transformed into a sea of blood and a mountain of bones'. In his reply, Phung reminded his childhood friend that the French—not the royalists—were responsible for the change in the balance of power and the suffering it had caused in all of the country: 'Our rivers and our mountains have been annexed by them at a stroke and turned into a foreign territory. These events affected the whole country, the entire population. It is not any particular region or any particular family alone that has suffered this trial.'[36]

In 1896, Phan Dinh Phung died of dysentery. (Disease, not battle, exacted the heaviest toll on both Vietnamese resistance and French colonial troops.) With this loss, the Can Vuong movement disintegrated. In 1897, Doumer initiated his policies to turn French Indochina into a fully operational colonial state. He simultaneously severed the court's control over Tonkin, named Hoang Cao Khai as a (powerless) viceroy, and emasculated what remained of the colonially controlled monarchy in Hue. The French allowed Hoang Cao Khai and his followers to dig up Phan Dinh Phung's grave, burn his corpse, and shoot it out of a cannon as a symbolic gesture designed to discredit the royalist resistance and intimidate those who would oppose the new rulers.

Nationalists in the twentieth century would, of course, venerate Phan Dinh Phung as a national hero and excoriate the collaborator Hoang Cao Khai for selling out the nation in its hour of greatest need. Indeed, the Can Vuong movement provided later generations with the martyrs they needed to build a national pantheon based on heroic resistance to foreign invasion. It was heroic, and it did exist, but the Can Vuong movement was not a nationalist movement. It remained a royalist, restoration-minded one. Nor did it promote a modernizing social agenda. Phan Dinh Phung might have admired the Japanese, but he is on record as having argued against adopting Western reforms while serving in Tu Duc's court. The disappearance of the Can Vuong movement in 1896 and the French takeover of the monarchy in Hue that same year meant that a new generation of Vietnamese would have to rethink the link between 'monarch' and 'subject', the nature of postcolonial governance, as well as the territorial shape of an independent Vietnamese state that no longer existed.[37]

CHAPTER 4

RETHINKING VIETNAM

P RINCE CUONG DE was the direct descendant of the senior branch of the Nguyen dynasty and proud of it. He worshiped his venerable ancestor, Gia Long. Born in 1882, Cuong De saw himself as the next in line to rule and as the emperor who would modernize Vietnam. The French of course did not necessarily see it this way and passed him over in favor of a host of seemingly more docile candidates, culminating in the crowning of Bao Dai in 1926. Anticolonialists, however, turned to Cuong De precisely because of the royalist legitimacy they felt he could confer on their efforts to drive out the French and remake Vietnam. In 1906, the patriot Phan Boi Chau brought the young prince to Japan to serve as the figurehead for a series of associations-in-exile and governments-in-waiting.

Cuong De, however, always marched to his own drum. He closely followed colonial and international developments from his position of exile, moving from Tokyo to Guangzhou by way of Bangkok, waiting for a favorable conjuncture to present itself. He recruited supporters from inside Vietnam and searched out new allies wherever he could. In 1913, thanks to German support and attracted by the liberal policies of the new Governor General of Indochina, Albert Sarraut, Cuong De travelled to Berlin to let the government know that he was ready to negotiate. The French never took him or his reformist ideas seriously and the prince never trusted the French again. He turned permanently instead to the Japanese, convinced that they would free Vietnam from its colonial hold and restore him and his rightful branch of the royal family to the throne.

In the end, Cuong De lost his bet when the Japanese failed to support him during their occupation of Indochina during the Second World War. He died in exile in Tokyo in 1951, a broken and bitterly disappointed man. But at the turn of the twentieth century, he and hundreds of others looking to free their country had no way of knowing what the future would bring. Cuong De's itinerary took him to Asia. Others travelled to the West. Some went to Moscow, while many more stayed in Vietnam. Some gambled that the French would help them to remake Vietnam. Others were convinced it would be a futile effort.[1]

REFORMISM AND CHANGE:
ASIAN CONNECTIONS, IMPERIAL ALLIANCES

East Asian Reformism

The consolidation of Paul Doumer's Indochina at the turn of the century did not sever Vietnamese elites from their Asian world. Indeed, until the end of the First World War, a wide-range of reform-minded mandarins turned to the surrounding region as much as to France for models of successful economic, political, and scientific modernization and information about regional and world events. At the outset, Japan was a particularly attractive model. Since the seventeenth century, Tokugawa rulers had relied on mainly Dutch traders to provide them with books and information on European science and thought. This school of 'Western studies' (*rangaku*) contributed to the country's take off when Meiji leaders assumed power in 1868. Three decades later, fellow Asians marveled at the revolutionary transformation of Japan into a modern nation-state, with military power and economic force increasingly on par with the West. Thousands flocked to Tokyo to see for themselves, including several hundred Vietnamese.

There was more to this Asian connection for these Vietnamese than the attraction of the Meiji miracle, however. Linguistically, neither the French language, nor the colonially backed Romanized script, *quoc ngu*, could replace the elite's centuries-old use of Chinese characters overnight. Until the First World War, most Vietnamese discovered the ideas of Montesquieu and Rousseau in Chinese translation rather than in the French original. This was particularly true in Annam and Tonkin, where the Confucian-based civil-service examination was longest established and relayed in Chinese characters for the greatest period of time. (It was eliminated in 1919.) This meant that most of the young male elite continued to study in Chinese ideograms (in the hope of passing the exam and landing good jobs). Although *quoc ngu* and French developed earlier in Cochinchina, it was not until the 1920s that colonial schools truly began producing a new generation of Vietnamese at ease in both. Lastly, until the French created the redoubtable political police in 1917, the Sûreté générale, determined anticolonialists could readily use false papers and ingenious disguises to board visiting ships bound for Hong Kong, Guangzhou, Shanghai, Tokyo, and Yokohama.[2]

Asia also continued to flow into colonial Vietnam. The French may have terminated Hue's tributary missions to Beijing, thereby ending the court's ability to import books and information directly from China, but they provided a substitute by accelerating Chinese immigration to the colony. Many of the Chinese living in Indochina and elsewhere were avid readers of 'new books' (*hsin-shu*) and sympathetic to well-known mainland reformers such as Liang Qichao and Kang Youwei. Some of these overseas communities ('*huaqiao*') traced their origins back to seventeenth-century Ming loyalists who had fled Qing conquest in 1644. Chinese nationalists, opposed to the same dynasty for two and a half centuries, later often found natural allies among these overseas Chinese communities. The father of modern China, Sun Yat-sen, travelled widely between Singapore and San Francisco, making stopovers in Saigon and Hanoi in the early 1900s. He solicited donations, enrolled young recruits, and established nationalist associations among the Chinese diaspora. Vietnamese anticolonialist memoirs repeatedly mention Chinese traders and skippers shuttling them all over Asia well into the 1950s.[3]

This also meant that there was no shortage of Chinese language books, papers, reformist pamphlets, religious texts, and translations available in Chinese bookshops and associations in French Indochina. While few Vietnamese mandarins could actually speak Chinese, they could communicate via 'brush conversations' and increasingly frequented Chinese bookshops in search of these new publications they could easily read. As one French official reported at the time: 'The majority of Chinese residents in Indochina are in sympathy with the [Chinese] revolutionary party, and it is in part by means of the journals they receive, as well as their remarks and their conversations, that they contribute to the spread of new ideas among the Annamite population'. In 1910, the French were shocked to learn that mandarins in the provinces were still reading the works of Liang Qichao and Kang Youwei, thanks to Chinese skippers carrying papers and books from one port to another (as they had done for centuries). Meeting them on the docks were trusted couriers, who quickly shuttled these materials to waiting mandarins. As another worried colonial official described the last step, nicely, 'Thanks to their knowledge of characters, the literati re-copy the articles which interest them. These are then put under their robes and smuggled to the most distant villages'.[4]

That Chinese reformist ideas attracted Vietnamese attention is hardly surprising. Reformers in China and Vietnam confronted many of the same problems, not least the struggle against imperial aggression and the quest to unlock the keys of Western modernization. However, as noted above, a major shift occurred in this China-centered East Asian world. Thanks to its rapid modernization (free of foreign domination), Meiji Japan (1868–1912) sought to replace the seemingly sick Chinese imperial giant. By the turn of the century, the Meiji navy had not only inflicted a military defeat on the Qing over Korea and had colonized Taiwan, but Japan had also become the home to an array of organizations promoting a Japanese-centered Asia based on common cultural and racial ties. The possibility that the Chinese empire would implode seemed likely for many.

Liang Qichao, Kang Youwei, and Sun Yat-sen travelled to Japan in the hope that Meiji would help them against the Qing and provide students with the modern knowledge and military science needed to build a new China. The Japanese defeat of the Russians in 1905—the victory of a 'yellow race' over a 'white' one—further shifted the center of gravity eastward, convincing many that the Europeans were not invincible and that there was an Asian way out of the Social Darwinian dead end (which held that 'white' stood for both 'right' and 'might'), and that it had started in Japan. In 1905, Sun Yat-sen created the Chinese Revolutionary Alliance headquarters in Tokyo, the precursor of the Chinese Nationalist Party (Guomindang, or GMD). Liang established schools the Qing would have never authorized back home. The Japanese operated the East Asian Higher Preparatory School: one of its pupils was a certain Zhou Enlai. Meanwhile, Chiang Kai-shek studied in the Imperial Japanese Army Academy Preparatory School. Both men would become leaders of twentieth-century China and each would play a part in shaping Vietnam's twentieth-century destiny.[5]

Vietnamese elites were part of these wider movements. This was certainly the case for the great literati, Phan Boi Chau (1867–1940) and Phan Chu Trinh (1872–1926). Both men had been born in the heart of the Nguyen dynasty and had come of age during the violent French conquest of their country. Like their fathers, both men had diligently studied classical Chinese until their twenties and prepared tirelessly for the civil service exams. In the end, however, neither made a career in government. Each in his own way was determined to rethink a Vietnam that was no more. Disappointed by Tu Duc's failure to implement reforms, both became avid readers of new books and closely followed events in Asia and the world. Trinh would distance himself from Chau's support of armed liberation and confidence in the Japanese. He turned instead to the French to implement Western change. Like Cuong De, both men gambled on their foreign allies and each would be bitterly disappointed. But neither could know it at the time.

Phan Boi Chau and the Asian Sources of Vietnamese Reformism
Freed from family obligations in 1900 by the death of his father, Phan Boi Chau went to work immediately. Travelling tirelessly from north to south, he discussed what was to be done with like-minded friends, veterans of the Can Vuong movement, reformist mandarins, and patriotic youths who had flocked around him. In 1904, he united supporters into a study group called the Vietnam Modernization Society (Viet Nam Duy Tan Hoi). Unsurprisingly, Chinese reformist texts were high on everyone's reading list. Royalists were welcome, too. Chau's prestige was such that he easily recruited the Nguyen prince, Cuong De, to the society and made him honorary president in order to attract the widest possible support. While the Vietnam Modernization Society never went very far ideologically, it was more forward-looking than the restoration-minded Can Vuong movement led by Phan Dinh Phung. Exchanges focused on the need to implement wide-ranging socio-economic reforms. It differed too in that the new group's leaders were determined to send students abroad.

Chau initially placed great hope in Japanese promises of uniting East Asian peoples of the 'same culture and common race' into a liberating and modernizing force. In late 1904, the Modernization Society dispatched him to Japan on a fact-finding mission. Chau landed in Yokohama in early 1905 as the Russo-Japanese war reached its climax. He quickly befriended Liang Qichao and, thanks to an indefatigable writing brush, explained the sad plight of the Vietnamese people and his group's desire to obtain Japanese assistance to expel the French and modernize the country. Well aware of Japan's imperial ambitions, Liang warned his counterpart of the dangers of relying too heavily on the Japanese and their Pan-Asianism. He advised Chau to focus first on reform, on educating the young, and awakening the patriotism of the people. 'Your country should not be concerned about not having a day of independence,' he counseled, 'but should be concerned about not having an independence-minded people.' Liang knew what he was talking about. China was in much the same situation. He was himself bringing students to study in Japanese schools and military academies.[6]

Liang's warning about Meiji's expansionist ambitions did not deter Chau from soliciting military aid. Chau contacted a wide range of Japanese politicians, diplomats, officers, and intellectuals. This included the future Japanese prime minister Inukai Tsuyoshi, Okuma Shigenobu, who was to be prime minister twice, and General Fukushima Yasumasa, Director of the Shimbu Military Academy. All of these meetings in 1905 occurred against the backdrop of Japan's victory over the Russians and Tokyo's entry into the Western-centered concert of nations. In his meeting with Shigenobu, Chau lauded Japan's emergence as a world power, but reminded him of Tokyo's Asian responsibilities:

Vietnam is not on the European continent, but the Asian [one]. Vietnam is common to Japan in race, culture, and continental positioning, yet the French gangsters are left to spread their bestial venom without fear. Hence the French are unaware that Asia already has a major power, already has Japan. The strength of Japan has been felt in the Northwest, all the way to the Qing and to the Russians. Why then has Japan allowed the French to trample over Vietnam without trying to help us?[7]

The Japanese had no intention of moving militarily against the French over Indochina, not in 1905 in any case. They were focused instead on rolling back the Chinese imperial hold in East Asia and consolidating their own colonial gains in Taiwan, Korea, and Manchuria. Improving diplomatic relations with the West helped them do that. Phan Boi Chau could send students to study with them, but no more.

It was in this wider Asian context that the 'Go East' ('*Dong Du*') study-abroad program began sending Vietnamese students to Japan. Chau wrote letters and tracts urging families to send their sons. Back in Vietnam, he knocked on doors and found considerable support among reform-minded mandarins in Annam and Tonkin. So much so that, in 1907, Governor General Paul Beau conceded privately that those travelling to Japan were mainly the sons of mandarins keen on learning. Yet the Go East movement was not just an Annam and Tonkin affair. Wealthy landowners and pro-Nguyen royalists in Cochinchina also provided financial support and recruits. Gilbert Tran Chanh Chieu was a well-known Mekong landowner, entrepreneur, and naturalized French citizen. He encouraged southern youth, including his son, to study in Japan. Chieu personally travelled to Hong Kong in 1907 to discuss ways of modernizing the country and funding study abroad.

Meanwhile, to attract students, Prince Cuong De drew upon latent royalist sympathies among southern families that had supported his grandfather's victory of 1802. In all, between 1906 and 1909, around 300 Vietnamese studied in Japanese schools and military academies. For the first time since the late 1850s, Viet elites from all three areas of former Dai Nam met to study and rethink their country, not in Paris, but in Tokyo. Indeed, more Vietnamese were studying abroad in Japan than in France at this time.[8]

Time in exile also allowed older men like Phan Boi Chau to rethink Vietnam without fear of arrest or censorship. Besides taking care of students and getting Prince Cuong De to Japan, one of the most important things Chau did was to write texts to 'awaken the people'. Taking Liang's advice to heart, he put pen to paper to provide some of the foundational texts of modern Vietnamese nationalism. This meant closely reading Japanese, Chinese, and Western materials in search of models, styles, and comparisons. Tokyo libraries and bookshops and his numerous encounters in East Asia provided him with a gold mine of information. One of the most important things he realized was that in order to explain the sad state of his country in the present and imagine a new future, he had to return to, indeed rethink, the past. The result was the publication in 1905 of *The History of the Loss of Vietnam*. In it, Chau lambasted the Nguyen for losing the country and failing to implement reforms in time. He celebrated the Can Vuong heroes who had resisted valiantly and condemned those who had collaborated. He focused on the evils of French colonialism, detailing the terrible effects of Doumer's tax and labor demands on the common people. To communicate his 'awakening' message more effectively, Chau dropped much of the flowery style and arcane allusions of the Confucian tradition to write in direct, hard-hitting prose. Although he was still writing in characters, he and others realized that in order to communicate their message to a wider audience, they had to recalibrate their prose and their own ways of thinking. In the last section, Chau turned to his 'Future Vietnam', insisting that all of the people had to join hands to save the country, regardless of class, religion, or race. Liang Qichao published the book and distributed copies among the overseas Chinese. In fact, Chau's history of Vietnam ended up stirring Chinese patriots as much as Vietnamese ones. Sun Yat-sen was so alarmed by what he read that he warned his compatriots in southern China to beware of the dangers that could befall them as Doumer laid train tracks for Kunming. Chau took fifty copies of his book home, where they were recopied, increasingly translated into *quoc ngu*, always circulated clandestinely, and sometimes read out loud to interested villagers.[9]

In short, Phan Boi Chau's exile in Japan allowed him to rethink Vietnamese history in increasingly national forms. In his 'Letter from Abroad Written in Blood', he focused again on the evils of French colonialism and urged his readers to wake up before it was too late. He criticized the monarchy and the mandarinate for failing to save the country and to help the people in their hour of greatest need. He argued that a new type of community was in order: a national one by which the pre-existing bond between 'emperor' and 'subject' would be replaced by one associating the 'people' with the 'nation'. It was at this point that Chau and others began to use new Atlantic revolutionary terms to communicate ideas based on Meiji models and Japanese loan-words, such as 'revolution' (*cach mang*), 'nation' (*quoc gia*), and 'citizen' (*dan quoc*). 'Why was our country lost?' he asked rhetorically. 'First, the monarch knew nothing of popular affairs; second, the mandarins cared nothing for the people; and third, the people knew only of themselves.' And yet the people had built the 'the foundations of our country'. The conclusion was obvious: 'The people are in fact the country, the country is the people's.' He repeated the same mantra in another national history of Vietnam and undoubtedly in hundreds of conversations. He also reminded readers that the Viet had themselves once been great colonizers, the conquerors of Champa. Now, he lamented, the tables had been turned. They were the colonized, who could disappear as the Cham had under Vietnamese rule.[10]

In the end, the Go East and Vietnam Modernization Society movements were short-lived. In 1907, the French and the Japanese concluded a treaty by which Tokyo recognized French sovereignty over Indochina in exchange for France's recognition of Japan's imperial interests further north. The outbreak of tax revolts less than a year later led the French to increase pressure on Tokyo to expel the Vietnamese, and the Japanese complied. In March 1909, Phan Boi Chau left Japan to regroup among a group of overseas Vietnamese based in Thailand. A year later, the Japanese transformed Korea into a colony. Bitterly disappointed, Chau understood that Japan was as colonial-minded as the Western powers and would be of no further help. However, by providing Vietnamese émigrés with a safe haven to reside, to access new information, and to study, write, and interact with a range of Asian reformers, the Japanese had contributed to the Modernization Society's ability to rethink the past, make better sense of the tumultuous present, and start to imagine a new future. This vision of a 'Future Vietnam' only existed in the imagination at that point, and it meant different things to different people. It was nonetheless an important turning point in the making of modern Vietnam.

A Colonial 'J'accuse'? Phan Chu Trinh and a Republican Contract

Phan Chu Trinh was as fascinated by Japan as was Phan Boi Chau. In 1906, the two toured Tokyo together, meeting with Japanese officials and urging young Vietnamese to study hard. Each agreed that the introduction of Western-style education à la Meiji was indispensable to the country's renaissance. Both enthusiastically cited Fukuzawa Yukichi's educational reforms as a model to emulate. Beyond the quest for modernity, however, the two Phans differed greatly in their approaches. Trinh did not share his counterpart's desire to seek Japanese military assistance. He recoiled at Chau's increasing talk of achieving national liberation through violent means, and he saw little need to work with royalty like Cuong De. Trinh chose instead to cooperate with the French to remake Vietnam.[11]

Besides his differences with Chau, Trinh had other reasons for making this choice. He saw in a colonial alliance the best way to achieve the reforms the Nguyen had botched in the nineteenth century. By conquering Dai Nam, Trinh reasoned, the French had changed power relations, to the detriment of the monarchy, not necessarily a bad thing since he considered the throne to be the single greatest obstacle to change. Moreover, France seemed to offer a model for reform as promising as the Japanese one. Like their Meiji counterparts, French republicans were equally determined to create a new France, a modern nation-state, complete with a mass education system, national military service, and an infrastructure capable of turning 'peasants into Frenchmen'. And where Chau found inspiration in Japanese-centered Pan-Asianism, Trinh was enthralled by French-championed republicanism, the universal rights of man, the idea of representative government, and welcomed the *mission civilisatrice* which promised to extend such progress to the Republic's empire. Lastly, unlike Meiji's resurrection of its long-dormant monarchy, the French had done away with their monarchy in favor of a constitutional democracy.[12]

Phan Chu Trinh's republicanism owed a great deal to two young French friends and dedicated republicans in Hanoi, the journalist Ernest Babut and the captain Jules Roux. Both were members of the Hanoi branch of the League of Human Rights (Ligue des droits de l'homme) established in 1903. Roux spoke Vietnamese well and advocated the development of *quoc ngu* and modern education in Indochina. In 1905, Babut launched the first *quoc ngu* newspaper in Hanoi, the *Dai Viet Tan Bao* (*Modern Dai Viet Times*), in which Trinh's earliest writings appeared. Babut was also a member of the French socialist party and a Freemason (Phan Chu Trinh later became one). While the League of Human Rights, Freemasons, and socialists hardly embraced decolonization, they advocated colonial reform and representative politics, and firmly believed in France's *mission civilistrice*.[13]

Phan Chu Trinh also sought to use this conjuncture and the colonizers to reform on his terms. This included his well-known goals of introducing Western studies, a mass educational system, instruction in French and *quoc ngu*, industry and commerce, and representative forms of government. However, Trinh wanted more than just a 'colonial Meiji'. Though he could never say it publicly, he wanted to use the French to help him accomplish a colonial revolution—the overturning of the monarchy. It is unclear where Trinh's visceral hate of the monarchy originated, but it was real. In his memoirs, Phan Boi Chau wrote that during their travels together in East Asia in 1906, they argued repeatedly over which came first: relying on the French to reform Vietnam or driving them out of it. For Trinh, the emperor had to go, and if the French could help on that score, then the choice was clear. As Chau recalled later:

> He and I kept company in Kwangtung [Guangdong] for more than ten days. Every day when we talked about the affairs of our country, he singled out for bitter reproach the wicked conduct of the monarchs, the enemies of the people. He ground his teeth when talking about the ruler of the day, who was bringing calamity to the country and disaster to the people; as much as to say that if the system of monarchical autocracy were not abolished, simply restoring the country's independence would bring no happiness.[14]

In place of the monarchy, Chau wrote, Trinh argued in favor of republicanism: 'Once popular rights have been achieved, then we can think about other things.' Trinh's collaboration with the French thus turned on his desire to use the French to push a very Vietnamese revolution, the overthrow of the monarchy and the creation of a colonial republic.

Rather than trying to wake up Chau's trustworthy mandarins or locate the nation in the past, Trinh realized that the only way his plan would ever work was by stirring the republican conscience of his colonial rulers. This meant painting the autocratic mandarinate in the worst possible light, deploring everyday French brutalities against the Vietnamese, and then holding the highest authorities to the implementation of an indigenous policy based on their republican ideals. This is exactly what Trinh did in early 1907, when the scholarly journal, the *Bulletin de l'Ecole française d'Extrême-Orient*, ran his open letter to the Governor General of Indochina, Paul Beau (1902–8). In this historic document, Trinh explained to Beau that he had travelled the country from north to south and what he saw was heart-wrenching—the regression of the Vietnamese into a state of barbarity and their near racial extinction. He had no choice, he explained, but to inform authorities of the terrible suffering of the people and the need for immediate and real reform on their part.[15]

For Trinh the corrupt and despotic mandarin class ruling the countryside with impunity was at the core of this suffering. By disemboweling the monarchy but leaving it in place, the French had effectively removed any sort of institutional control over these 'parasites'. They were now free to enrich themselves and exploit the population. Theoretically, he agreed, the protectorate had dispatched French delegates to keep them in line. In practice, however, these immoral beings did whatever they pleased. Ignorant of the Vietnamese language, customs, and village politics, French commissioners were either unaware or unwilling to intervene as long as the taxes and *corvée* arrived on time. They needed these bad mandarins.

Secondly, Trinh continued, French insensitivity and brutality toward the overworked peasants, including the beating of many to death, hardly reflected well on lofty republican ideals and colonial humanism. Verbal insults and daily acts of violence against the indigenous were legion, he said (and they were). Peasants ran for cover when they saw a Frenchman coming, he pointed out. And it wasn't just the European settlers who were to blame. Haughty colonial officials often humiliated good mandarins and, in so doing, dissuaded them from reporting abuses or suggesting solutions. Meanwhile, the corrupt ones continued to ingratiate themselves, always bearing good news to the colonizers. The situation in the countryside was, Trinh concluded, dire. And by entrusting these corrupt bureaucrats with collecting onerous taxes and *corvée*, the French were responsible for the hate and suffering 'piling up' across the land.

This was strong language. No Vietnamese elite had ever dared to address the colonizer in such terms. And yet Trinh wrote to Beau because he

had no other means to make himself or his people heard. There was no colonial parliament. The press remained in its infancy and heavily censored.
He also made his move at this time because he knew that the governor general was involved in developing colonial reforms based on the principle of
'association'. This was not the word Trinh wanted to hear, for indirect rule
would leave his hated mandarins in power: 'And you still want to increase
the power of these men by confiding to them the realization of the reforms
for which our salvation depends! Don't you understand they will never apply them, except to make money.'

A former literati himself, Trinh knew perfectly well that not all mandarins were 'bad', nor were they as anti-modern as he had portrayed them in
his missive to Beau. But his goal in crafting this letter was not to present an
objective study of the mandarinate or rural conditions. He wanted above
all to jolt the French into action by convincing the republican governor
general that his emerging 'native policy' ('*politique indigène*') had to extend
basic human rights to the colonized and deal with the problem of a corrupt
monarchy. Much like Ferhat Abbas in Algeria, who denied the reality of Algerian nationalism in favor of egalitarian republican assimilation, Trinh believed that a similar colonial contract could work in Vietnam, but only if the
French made good on their own republicanism. Then, he concluded, 'the
only thing the Annamese would fear would be seeing the French leave Annam to its own devices'. It was an extraordinary gamble designed in large
part to bring down the pre-existing Vietnamese monarchy. Like Chau's Pan
Asianism, Trinh's colonial alliance with the French was riddled with contradictions and not a little naiveté; but, then again, collaboration was as important as anticolonialism in the making of modern Vietnam. And colonial
collaboration often carried within it revolutionary indigenous projects.

Mandarin Reformism and Colonial Fear
The two Phans were not alone in their quest for change; and all mandarins
were not corrupt, conservative, or anti-modern. Nor were the French or the
Japanese the first to introduce notions of modernity or reform to Vietnamese elites. A large number of officials working for the Nguyen dynasty on
the inside had long been interested in good government, reform, and modernization. The fifteenth–sixteenth century Le dynasty is a case in point.
And as harsh as they often were, Minh Mang's reforms had sought to ra-
tionalize and modernize Vietnam. In the late 1860s, the Catholic adviser to
Emperor Tu Duc, Nguyen Truong To, pleaded for far-reaching economic,

social, and even political reforms along Western lines. These included sending students abroad for Western studies, expanding the education system, revamping financial, judicial, and administrative institutions, developing modern science, agriculture, and commerce, and even creating a national writing system based on *chu nom*: 'Have we not talented persons able to devise a script which will transcribe our national language?' he asked.[16]

Nguyen Truong To failed to convince the last emperor of the need to reform, but that does not mean that reformist debates within the mandarinate necessarily disappeared under French rule. Another of Tu Duc's reform-minded advisors, Dang Xuan Bang, kept making the case for change. By the early 1900s, he and others had begun establishing private schools and organizing informal seminars in their spare time to teach modern ideas and practices to young and old. Classes offered instruction in French, Chinese, and *quoc ngu*, as well as in mathematics, physics, and geography. These officials had access to Western and Asian reformist writings in Chinese translation (some of which appeared in the civil service exams in Hue). Other mandarins received authorization from colonial authorities to study abroad in France. The French created the Colonial Academy in Paris in the late nineteenth century to train Indochinese elites in modern ways. That the future Ho Chi Minh applied (unsuccessfully) to study there is hardly surprising. And although colonial exhibitions in France (in 1907, 1922, 1930–31) certainly pushed a political and Orientalist agenda, they also allowed a range of elite Vietnamese to 'go West' to study European ways, procure information, and make new contacts. Vietnamese reformism at the turn of the century thus encompassed a wide range of sources, choices, ideas, models, and people. There were never two, one-way roads leading straight to 'modern Vietnam'—one 'Asian/Phan Boi Chau' ('*Dong Du*'), the other 'Western/Phan Chu Trinh' ('*Di Tay*'). Rather, different trajectories intersected, recalibrated, and shifted over time and space. Some had already developed inside Vietnam before the French had arrived; others connected to the outside world whether the French liked it or not.[17]

Nowhere is this more evident than in the creation in early 1907 of the Tonkin Public School (the Dong Kinh Nghia Thuc). In fact, twentieth-century Vietnam's first modern school was neither a colonial nor an anti-colonialist creation. The two Phans did not make it. Nor did the French. This Western studies school was a northern-based, mandarin initiative modeled on Fukuzawa Yukichi's educational policies mentioned above. The term '*Nghia Thuc*' is the Vietnamese translation of the Japanese term,

'*Keio Gijuku*', which refers to a non-fee-paying private school established and paid for from public donations. Knowledge of it came from Go East travellers to Japan and reformist writings circulating in Chinese. But it drew, too, upon a centuries-old Sino-Vietnamese tradition of creating private schools for teaching classical studies. Within months, this school attracted some four hundred students, young and old alike. The dapper French-trained civil servant and interpreter, Nguyen Van Vinh, was there in full Western attire, as were local mandarins sporting their Confucian garb, but nonetheless keenly aware of what was at stake.[18]

Uniting them all was a burning desire to learn and discuss new ideas and necessary reforms. Dong Kinh classrooms offered conferences on and instruction in mathematics, geography, and science (a particularly hot subject). Students studied French and *quoc ngu*. Most (not all) agreed that Chinese characters no longer sufficed. Reformists building this school wanted a written language designed less to associate the elite with an East Asian civilizational sphere operating in characters than to educate and associate the masses inside the country with new forms of social organization via the spoken language they all shared. The Romanized script increasingly appeared as a powerful tool of modernization and socialization. As one Dong Kinh slogan read: '*Quoc ngu* is the saving spirit in our country, we must take it out among our people'. More literati also began to study French. History lectures attracted large gatherings as speakers sought to distance the Vietnamese past from its civilizational association with China in favor of crafting a distinct history, a unique set of heroes, indeed a separate cultural identity. Phan Boi Chau's writings from abroad circulated in Nghia Thuc circles, while Phan Chu Trinh was a popular guest speaker. And there is no reason not to think that Chau drew many of his nationalist ideas from texts being produced *inside* Vietnam.[19]

As elsewhere in Asia, much effort went into promoting social and cultural change along Western lines. This is evident in the titles of many of the texts the Nghia Thuc produced, such as *Civilization and New Learning* or *The Indictment of Corrupt Customs*. The former called upon young Vietnamese to break with the Confucian past and embrace the modern world. Several teachers argued that the East had become stagnant while the West was now the most dynamic part of the world. And it wasn't long before many began to see Confucianism as an obstacle to the modernization and Westernization of the country. In another major shift, women entered the classrooms for the first time as traditional social relations loosened. Change even manifested itself corporally as part of the 'Haircutting Chant' shows, recited by Nghia Thuc adepts:

> Comb in the left hand,
> Scissors in the right,
> Snip, snip, clip, clip!
> Watch out, be careful,
> Drop stupid practices.
> Dump childish things,
> Speak openly and frankly,
> Study Western customs,
> Don't cheat or bluff,
> Don't lie.
> Today we clip.
> Tomorrow we shave![20]

However, this early attempt at modern education and socio-cultural change on Vietnamese terms did not last long. When a revolt broke out in February 1908 against excessive *corvée* demands—just as Phan Chu Trinh had warned—the French did the only thing they knew how to do: they cracked down violently as it spread. The discovery of a plot to poison French troops a few months later only led to more repression as scared European settlers demanded swift and decisive action. Rather than reflecting on the socio-economic causes of this discontent and devising appropriate policy measures, fear got the better of the French, and not just among the small settler community. A special criminal commission set up on Paul Beau's watch sentenced thirteen Vietnamese plotters to death and many more to long prison terms. Phan Chu Trinh—the Third Republic's most sincere indigenous collaborator—was soon breaking rocks on the prison island of Poulo Condor. Vietnam's dedicated republican remained in the 'colonial Bastille' until 1911, when the French shipped him off to France. Colonial authorities quickly closed the Nghia Thuc school for good.[21]

The Imperial Trajectories of Vietnamese Reformism, Exile, and Labor

Phan Chu Trinh was not the only person the French wanted to get out of Indochina. Early on, the French dispatched tens of thousands of Vietnamese laborers to work on commercial plantations, mines, and in colonial offices in New Caledonia, New Hebrides, Polynesia, and Reunion Island.

Others followed imperial itineraries taking them to French North Africa and South America. Moving in parallel to these workers were several thousand Vietnamese political prisoners, whom the French banished to colonial prisons and penal colonies as far away as Guyana and Guadeloupe. The French exiled their rebellious emperors, most notably Ham Nghi, Thanh Thai, and Duy Tan, to Algeria and Reunion Island, while promising elite members, mandarins, and wealthy students pursued advanced studies in the metropolis.

These imperial-wide movements gave rise to some interesting encounters. First stationed in Algeria at the turn of the twentieth century as an agricultural specialist trained in France, the future Constitutionalist, Bui Quang Chieu, met the deposed emperor, Ham Nghi, in Algiers and maintained a long correspondence with him on how best to modernize Vietnam. Ky Dong, a brilliant Vietnamese young man who was undertaking his secondary studies in Algiers, also befriended Ham Nghi when he was there. Ky Dong's return to Vietnam in 1896 did not last long, however. When the French connected him to anticolonialist rebels, they exiled him to Polynesia, where he took up art and became a good friend to the artist Paul Gauguin. Many of these exiles were transformed by their experience and returned home to play a role in the making of a new Vietnam in 1945. This was the case for Dong Sy Hua, a colonial plantation worker in the French Pacific, who joined the resistance. Another exiled emperor, Duy Tan, died in a plane crash in 1945 in central Africa, trying to make it home to reclaim his throne. Ex-political prisoners from Guyana returned in 1963, as did 50,000 Vietnamese from northeast Thailand.[22]

A small, maritime, and increasingly politicized Vietnamese working class also emerged, as French and international shipping companies employed more and more sailors, deckhands, cooks, and laundry boys to handle the goods and passengers crossing the Indian Ocean. The Merchant Shipping Company (Compagnies des Messageries maritimes) and the United Shipping Company (Compagnies des Chargeurs réunis) probably employed annually one thousand Vietnamese sailors, who sailed the world from Saigon to Shanghai, Osaka to Singapore, and then on to the Atlantic through Djibouti, Aden, and the Suez Canal. Cochinchinese, Annamese, and especially Tonkinese worked on the ships' decks together. They also joined hands with Chinese workers. Not all of them became revolutionaries; most worked to feed themselves and their families. But a handful encountered new ideas, people, and associations, including notions of organized labor, as they moved from one port city to another. It was a motley crew, to be sure, but it was where revolutionaries like Phan Boi Chau and Ho Chi Minh would go to gather information, avoid police detection, and think about Vietnam in different ways. A future communist leader, Ton Duc Thang, came from this maritime working class. A Trotskyist debarking in Marseille in the 1920s left a lively description of the men who helped him make all the right connections. He was most impressed by a certain Hon, a colonial sailor turned drug trafficker who was running opium from one side of the Mediterranean to the other: 'Hon is cunning at getting things in under the noses of customs officials'.[23]

The First World War globalized imperial movements and demands for political reforms in unprecedented ways. Although the French were at first reluctant to bring any Vietnamese soldiers to the metropolis in the light of repeated revolts and defiant emperors, the intensification and entrenchment of the conflict left them no choice. They badly needed men to help supply and fight on the Western Front as well as to work in munitions factories to provide the massive amounts of weapons this industrial conflagration required—artillery shells, guns, bullets, and uniforms. In all, the French recruited and dispatched 90,000 Vietnamese to France, where 50,000 worked in local factories and the other 40,000 proceeded to the front. Many served in combat positions. The Vietnamese were part of a larger mobilization bringing almost a million colonial subjects to France, including British subjects from India. Joining them, too, were tens of thousands of workers from Spain, Italy, and especially China.[24]

This gave rise to a fascinating wartime situation in which non-French male workers joined a very feminized French workforce on the factory floors. Although French authorities carefully organized and disciplined the workplace in order to meet wartime needs, fraternization and even mixed unions emerged from this multi-ethnic labor mobilization. Racist attitudes of hostility toward foreigners, and above all fears of colonial men mixing with French women while Frenchmen fought at the front, were real. So were class fears in French unions like the CGT that this colonial labor force would take working-class jobs. But there was no denying the transformative impact of this wartime mobilization as almost a hundred thousand Vietnamese veterans returned to Indochina hoping to start a new life. Some wanted French citizenship; most expected good jobs and upward social mobility. Several hoped to modernize Vietnam along Western lines, despite the barbarity they had just witnessed in Europe.[25]

Most Vietnamese reformists supported the war effort in the hope that the colonizers would now have to make good on their promises of political and social reform. They had a debt to pay. Cultural luminaries like Nguyen Van Vinh, Duong Van Giao, and Phan Van Truong dusted off their initial training as interpreters and served as intermediaries for administering the Vietnamese troops and laborers in France. Phan Chu Trinh lent his personal support to colonial efforts to recruit Vietnamese men for the war effort, and this despite the fact that the French had thrown him in jail in September 1914 for six months on trumped-up charges of colluding with Prince Cuong De and the Germans. Vietnamese administrators, some of them sharing Trinh's reformist dreams, but most acting on French orders, mobilized the local administration in the protectorates of Annam and Tonkin to provide the majority of recruits the French needed in record time.

Vietnamese elite members like Phan Chu Trinh were also aware of a parallel reformist trend that had developed at the highest levels of the French army in the person of General Théophile Pennequin. Having served throughout the empire and with such well-known colonial conquerors as Lyautey, Galliéni, and Pavie, Pennequin rose to the top of the army and head of colonial troops in Indochina in 1911. A devout republican, he was also a man born in the 1840s who could have served in one of Napoleon III's Arab Offices in Algeria, such was his belief in association and the respect of local cultures. He was also a fine observer of colonial policies in other empires, notably that of the Americans in the Philippines. He worried that trouble in China could spill into Indochina. And if the French did not give more of a voice to Vietnamese elite members in actually running the colony, including the army, then they should not count on them to help keep Indochina French in times of trouble. Close to Jules Roux, himself a friend of Phan Chu Trinh, Pennequin had followed Vietnamese reformism and witnessed the violent revolts that had ended in so many executions in 1908 and Trinh's exile. He cringed at the French settler disdain for the Vietnamese.

Whereas his counterpart, General Charles Mangin, advocated a Force noire ('black army'), using mainly Senegalese troops to help France fight in the event of war, Pennequin asked for the creation of a mainly Vietnamese Armée jaune ('yellow army'). Not only would it defend Indochina and France in times of need, but it would also promote some Vietnamese to positions of command and provide the French with loyal partners with whom they could build a new and, eventually, independent Indochinese state. The general's ideas enthralled Vietnamese reformers. Trinh threw his full support behind the general at the same time as the French settler community vehemently denounced him for arming the 'barbarians' from the inside. The French government would study Pennequin's plans. But when the First World War broke out, the leadership in Paris and Hanoi insisted that the Vietnamese had not 'evolved' sufficiently to adopt Pennequin's project. Rather than sending the Armée jaune to fight on the Western Front, the French preferred sending the bulk of Vietnamese as factory workers and logistical supply hands.

It is hard to underestimate the significance of the Great War for Vietnamese reformists. In exchange for their defense of France, Vietnamese of all political colors expected the French to make good on their promises of change. It is no accident that Duong Van Giao's remarkable history of the Indochinese during the First World War called on the French to adopt a new 'native policy'. This is precisely what the authors of the *Revendications du peuple annamite*—Phan Chu Trinh, Phan Van Truong, and Ho Chi Minh—requested in 1919; not independence, but republican reformism. But instead of sending Pennequin to Hanoi to build a new Indochinese state in collaboration with reformist members of the elite and thousands of returning veterans, the French sent Albert Sarraut. His answer to the *Revendications* was a policy of enlightened Franco-Vietnamese collaboration and colonial monarchy.[26]

SARRAUT AND THE MAKING OF AN INDOCHINESE STATE

The Policy of Franco-Vietnamese Collaboration

As Pennequin's Armée jaune project shows, the French were no more monolithic in their reformist thinking and state-building plans than the Vietnamese. Nor did colonial policy in Indochina operate independently of the center, other parts of the empire, or without connection to neighboring colonial states. Caught off guard by the revolts of 1908 and troubled by the heavy-handed repression used to stop them, a remarkable debate ensued among metropolitan leaders. For the first time, important parliamentarians and colonial policy-makers realized that it was not enough to conquer, exploit, and punish. Paul Bert and Paul Doumer may have created a more centralized administration and extricated the revenue and labor needed to do so, but it had come at a great cost for the colonized. Four decades after the admirals had first landed in Cochinchina, the events of 1908 made it clear to many in Paris that the French colonial presence in Indochina still lacked legitimacy among peasants and elite alike.

Why did metropolitan leaders take particular notice of events in Indochina at this time? Ideology was one reason. The Dreyfus affair (1894–1906) and the rise of French socialism under Jean Jaurès were energizing republicanism, as was the advent of a modern, activist press in the Third Republic. Disgusted by the repressive measures used in 1908, the socialist Francis de Pressensé and vice-president of the newly created League of Human Rights in France (1898) asked how the republic could use extra-judicial means in Indochina to execute Vietnamese and still remain true to its principles at home. Though the Vietnamese were colonial subjects, they were humans too, he and others insisted. Like-minded deputies deplored a long list of colonial abuses. Maurice Viollette, a Freemason and colonial reformer, stated that the French could not claim to be 'a superior race' by committing rape, murder, and battery in Indochina. Deputies also criticized onerous taxation, oppressive monopolies, and excessive labor coercion as unworthy of the republic. In a series of debates between 1908 and 1911, many in Paris came to agree with Phan Chu Trinh's message: 'French policy will fail unless it is a pro-indigenous one.' And the only way republicans could remain true to their core values was by implementing a workable policy of association with the Vietnamese, including legal guarantees of their individual rights.[27]

The result was the decision to dispatch Albert Sarraut to serve as Governor General of Indochina with a mandate to implement far-reaching reforms. Born in 1872, Sarraut heralded from a powerful republican newspaper family. His father was a Freemason and militant republican. A member of the Radical Socialist Party (which was the name of the republican party in France at that time) himself, Sarraut's ascension in French politics had been meteoric. He voted for the law of 1905 separating Church and State and was a committed Dreyfusard (he carried a wound from a duel to prove it!). That he had no colonial experience was irrelevant (nor had Doumer). Also shocked by the events of 1908, the Minister of Colonies, Adolphe Messimy, wanted change. So much so that Messimy and Sarraut apparently met with Phan Chu Trinh in Paris to discuss the latter's colonial 'J'accuse' of 1907 discussed above.

Like many of his socialist counterparts at the time (and this well into the twentieth century), Sarraut believed deeply in republican exceptionalism and its colonial mission, convinced that a unique humanism distinguished French colonialism from other (inferior) types in the past and present. But, like his backers in Paris, Sarraut was also a pragmatist. He knew that reform was essential to preventing revolution and preserving the empire. And he was an astute observer of geopolitics. His arrival in Indochina coincided with the rise of Japan and the fall of the Qing in China in late 1911. He closely followed the creation of the Republic of China under Sun Yat-sen. Intelligence reports apprised him of the Asian context in which Vietnamese anticolonialism and reformism had been circulating. He knew that Phan Boi Chau had recently moved to southern China, where he actively sought Chinese republican support for his Go East study-abroad program for young Vietnamese to travel to Japan. Sarraut was astonished to learn that mandarins inside and outside the colony were still conceptualizing reform in East Asian, not French, terms.

Lastly, the international context also explains this surge in liberal reformism in the Third Republic. In particular, the rise of a colonial-minded Japan, Germany, Britain, and United States convinced Sarraut that the Vietnamese had choices. It was no accident that Prince Cuong De pointed out in his 1913 letter to Sarraut the specific cases of Canada and Australia as models of colonial reform. The French were but one possible partner among several suitors, and republicans never ceased to justify their continued presence in Indochina by insisting that things would be even worse if others took over. Sarraut's worst nightmare was that a war in Europe would end with the Indochinese house in German hands.

Phan Boi Chau certainly hoped that another Franco-German conflagration in Europe would favorably change power relations in Indochina. Chau met often with German agents in Asia, while Cuong De travelled to Berlin, from where he wrote his letter to Sarraut. Indeed, the outbreak of war in Europe in 1914 offered Phan Boi Chau and Cuong De hope. The royal family in Hue also took note. Indeed, in 1916, France's latest colonial emperor, Duy Tan, tried to escape his glasshouse to join Chau's ranks on the outside. Although the French caught him and exiled him promptly to Reunion Island, Duy Tan's colonial treason made it clear that elite collaboration at the highest level of the protected state was hardly guaranteed. A year later, a prison uprising occurred in Thai Nguyen province and spread to the countryside. It took the French six months to re-establish order. Fear, both in official circles and among the settlers, continued to run high. Maurius Moutet, a feisty lawyer and the future Minister of Colonies, had to fight tooth and nail to get his friend, Phan Chu Trinh, out of French prison in 1914.[28]

It was in this context that Albert Sarraut began implementing a wide range of reforms during his two mandates, which dominated the second decade of the 1900s (1911–14, 1917–19). Although his overall goal was to preserve French rule, he was sincere in his desire to improve the relationship between the French and the Vietnamese. Upon his arrival, he studied a little Vietnamese under Roux, promoted the first Vietnamese into the European civil service ranks, tried (unsuccessfully) to require French administrators to learn Vietnamese, and made a point of listening to native elite members and treating them as humans. Many such Vietnamese saw reason for hope in Sarraut's nomination and gestures. Most of the European settler community, however, worried that this new breed of republicans—especially these socialist, humanist, and reform-minded governors—would 'go native' on them as the admirals had (allegedly) done before them and Pennequin was doing now. A wall of white silence greeted Sarraut when he stepped off the boat in Saigon in 1911.

Three goals drove government-backed reforms for Indochina—the elaboration of an official policy of Franco-Annamese collaboration, the introduction of a series of indigenous reforms, and the further rationalization of the colonial state. There was nothing particularly new about any of this. Worried by the Meiji miracle and the rise of Japan, Governor General Paul Beau had promoted just such an indigenous policy during his mandate (1902–8). He had established a modern Franco-Indigenous school system, reformed the mandarinate, and liberalized the penal code. He introduced a system of consultative chambers in Tonkin for selecting provincial mandarins and created an Indochinese university to produce a French-trained elite class. However, the revolts of 1908 had reversed much of this, as colonial fears had rolled back liberal reform.

With strong government backing, Sarraut was determined to go forward with the creation of a functioning Indochinese state. He asserted tighter control over the budget, revamped administrative borders, and streamlined the civil service. He presided over the creation in 1917 of the powerful political police, the Sûreté générale, which was essential to policy formulation, social control, and repression. This went together with the establishment of a rejuvenated indigenous affairs bureau for formulating and applying his liberal native policy. A remarkable group of men, including the head of the political police, Louis Marty, served him faithfully as the governor tried to

increase the power of the native elite class by expanding deliberative local councils in Annam-Tonkin and opening the Cochinchinese Colonial
Council to more southern Vietnamese. Sarraut also promoted some judicial reforms favoring individual and indigenous rights, pushed through fiscal and cadastral changes to lighten the tax burden on the rural poor, and
ended rampant concession grants to the European population. He restored
the Indochinese university and promoted modern Franco-Indigenous education to re-situate elites within the French orbit. Nowhere was the break
with the past more evident than in 1919 when Sarraut presided over the
closing of the centuries-old, Confucian exam system.[29]

Charismatic and articulate, Sarraut was also a master of propaganda.
His team promulgated new press laws and authorized the publication of
more newspapers, books, and translations in order to promote colonial
reform and a Franco-Vietnamese future devoid of its old East Asian ties.
Worried by German attempts to turn Asian opinion against the French,
Sarraut initiated what was for all intents and purposes the start of a concerted *francophonie* strategy. Modern photography, cinema, theater, and
radio would help win over hearts and minds. However, Sarraut also wanted
to make good on Phan Chu Trinh's call for more freedom of expression by
opening the press to trustworthy members of the indigenous elite. This
would provide them with a modern instrument and public forum through
which they could express their needs. The press would also allow the colonized to speak out against a settler community that had long dominated
the press. Censorship certainly continued under Sarraut, but he was often
aghast at European behavior and language toward the colonized. Inadver-
tently, by expanding the colonial press, Sarraut also allowed a wide range
of colonized subjects—Chinese, Indians, Cambodians, Lao, and Vietnamese—to engage each other in exchanges and shape colonial opinion in new
and unforeseen ways.[30]

This was the context in which Sarraut's team recruited a remarkable
group of reform-minded Vietnamese allies and placed them at the head
of major government-backed newspapers in southern, central, and northern Vietnam. They included such men as Pham Quynh, in charge of the
Nam Phong (*Southern Wind*, in Tonkin); Nguyen Van Vinh at the *Dong
Duong Tap Chi* (*Indochina Review*), *Trung Bac Tan Van* (*Northern Central
News*), and *L'Annam nouveau* (*New Annam*, also in Tonkin); Bui Quang
Chieu and Nguyen Phu Khai at the *La Tribune indigène* (*Native Tribune*,
in Cochinchina); and later Huynh Thuc Khang at the *Tieng Dan* (*Voice of*

the People, in Annam). Like Phan Chu Trinh, these reformers bet on colonial republicanism, reformism, humanism, and collaboration. Even Phan Boï Chau saw hope in Sarraut, leading him to write a pamphlet in 1917 he would later regret and one which nationalist historians would like to forget: 'On Franco-Vietnamese Collaboration'.[31]

The title of Chau's essay is significant because one of the pillars of Sarraut's mandate was his ardent desire to enshrine reform in an official policy of collaboration. The governor understood the Vietnamese desire to play a greater role in the administration of their affairs and the country the French had violently taken from them. He also knew that the Vietnamese had supported the French during the First World War and expected a liberal colonial policy in return. In 1919, he delivered a speech in Hanoi to 3,000 Vietnamese elite members before returning to France to become their Minister of Colonies and the Republic's most important colonial thinker since Jules Ferry. In it, he reiterated the French commitment to reform and its unique colonial mission. But he went further, insisting that Indochina had to be more than just an administration. It had to become an operational state, acting for its own interests within the French empire. Decision-making had to be located in Indochina, not the metropole. Economic development had to benefit the colonized as much as the colonizer. Sarraut promised political change. He held out the promise of increased colonial democracy, an Indochinese charter, a federation to hold its different parts together, and eventual self-government. He was fond of repeating that the 'colonies are states in the making', adding quickly that only a genuine policy of Franco-Vietnamese cooperation could ensure this.[32]

Many Vietnamese took Sarraut seriously that day, translating and commenting at length on his speech. His plans for building an Indochinese federation with its own decision-making powers, shared with the Vietnamese, convinced many that there was finally a future in working with the French. The French certainly hoped so, as the exhausted Third Republic looked to its empire to help it recover economically from the Great War and remain a great power. It is no accident that Sarraut published his colonial treatise, 'On the Development of the Colonies' ('*La mise en valeur des colonies*'), in 1923. To put it another way, colonial reformism, development, and federalism did not emerge from the Second World War, but rather in the wake of the 1908 revolts and the First World War. Sarraut's vision of a Franco-Vietnamese Indochina was riddled with contradictions, a great deal of naïveté, and would fail miserably by the 1940s. But no one at the time knew this, and Indochina was an idea as much as a state with which all Vietnamese would have to contend.

Becoming Indochinese?

In fact, many Vietnamese took Sarraut so seriously that they came remarkably close to rethinking their political future in Indochinese terms. While few in modern Vietnam can imagine such a thing today, it was hardly a far-fetched idea at the time. After all, pre-French Vietnam was the product of centuries of colonial expansion itself. Le Thanh Tong and Minh Mang were not only remarkable modernizers and state-builders; they and their descendants had also been ambitious colonizers. Moreover, what the Third Republic offered in terms of a special relationship in Indochina was a largely Franco-Vietnamese partnership. The French never offered an alliance to Cambodia or Laos before the Second World War. Convinced that they had to offer something to the Vietnamese in order to obtain their collaboration and thwart Thai expansionism, the French intentionally pushed the Vietnamese elite to remember their own imperial past and to think in Indochinese terms in the present. In 1885, Jules Harmand, a leading proponent of association, laid out the premise for promoting a policy of dual colonialism in Indochina at the very moment when he demanded that the court in Hue surrender completely:

> The day that this race understands that its historical ambitions can, thanks to us, come to fruition in ways that it never before imagined; when [the Annamese] sees our aid allows him to take vengeance for the humiliations and defeats that he has never forgiven his neighbors; when he feels definitely superior to them and sees his domination expand with ours, only then will we be able to consider that the future of French Indochina is truly assured.[33]

Lastly, there were practical reasons explaining the French decision to cast Indochina in Franco-Vietnamese terms. Simply put, the colonizers needed local partners to help them operate the Indochinese state on the ground. The Europeans never numbered more than 35,000 during the entire colonial period (unlike the one million living in Algeria by 1954) and the Europeans resided overwhelmingly in eastern Indochinese towns. The French had increased Chinese immigration, but most were from the rural poor of southern China, and the last thing the French wanted to do was to import a Chinese elite to help run their colonial state. The French thus trained tens of thousands of overwhelmingly ethnic Viet civil servants, housed them, paid them regularly and covered their travel costs between Hanoi and Vientiane and Saigon and Phnom Penh, where they worked in the Indochinese colonial administration. In Cambodia, new roads linking Cochinchina to Cambodia saw the Viet population grow there, from 79,050 in 1911 to 140,220 in 1921. Of the sixteen Indochinese bureaucrats working in the town hall of Phnom Penh in 1913, fourteen were Viet and two Khmer. For similar reasons, the ratio of Viet bureaucrats in Laos increased too. By the early 1930s, the Viet occupied 54 percent of the posts offered by the administration. This was in spite of the fact that by the late 1930s the non-Viet populations in Laos constituted 98 percent of the population. By 1937, this immigration was such that there were 10,200 Viet living in Vientiane, but only 9,000 Lao.[34]

Similar demographics characterized the emerging working class in colonial Indochina. Faced with over-population problems in Tonkin and northern Annam, the French began shipping Tonkinese and Annamese laborers to southern Indochina to clear the jungle and to labor on rubber plantations. In the mid-1920s, three new roads linking Laos to northern Annam allowed for the easier transportation of Annamese laborers to Thakhek and Savannakhet. The overwhelming majority of the workers on rubber plantations in Cambodia and mines in Laos were ethnic Viet. Far from stopping Vietnamese expansion westward, French colonialism often promoted it.[35]

The French colonial project thus carried within it a second, pre-existing Asian one. While the French may have disrupted the Nguyen civil service of the nineteenth century, they opened up new possibilities for young Vietnamese graduates in the western Indochinese bureaucracy in the twentieth. These young graduates did not take over the protected royal administration of the Cambodians, but helped run the Indochinese state at federal level as secretaries, customs and security agents, mailmen, clerks, and telegraph operators. Colonial Indochina thus became a functional territorial space, state, and identity for the Viet operating it on the ground. There was one important exception to this Viet occupation and administration and that was in the highlands where the French increasingly tried to avoid using them (see chapter 14).

The formation of the Indochinese Constitutionalist Party under the direction of Bui Quang Chieu was one of the first signs that things were running along colonial lines. As editor of the party's official mouthpiece,

La Tribune Indigène, and one of France's best allies since Phan Chu Trinh, Chieu took Sarraut seriously when the latter talked of building an Indochinese federation. The Constitutionalists applauded the idea of giving greater 'autonomy, decentralization and freedom of action' to an Indochinese state and welcomed the privileged place they would occupy in the colonial alliance. They applauded Sarraut's promise of creating 'a constitutional charter' with 'all the structures needed for a modern state'. This transformation was necessary if the colony were to become an 'autonomous country' and if 'its Annamese personnel [were to] become Indochinese citizens'. Others took the French Indochinese model and connected it to a colonial Vietnamese past in order to justify continued, indeed accelerated Vietnamese expansion—with the French—in the present. In 1921, the Indochinese Constitutionalist Party defended the concordance between Vietnam and Indochina in clear terms:

> We do not deny these [non-Viet] races' intrinsic qualities or the right to present their problems within the Indochinese Union. But given the overwhelming majority of the Annamese in this country and the importance of their population, the forces behind their expansion continue. Given the more advanced state of their civilization and, finally, their historic rights, they occupy clearly the most important place in the concerns of the protecting country [France] in her colonizing mission in Indochina. The Annamese [. . .] are thus first in line for historic, ethnographic and geographic reasons which would be childish to deny and against which it would be futile to argue. In Indochina [. . .], it's the law of the majority that rules [. . .], within the French Indochinese Union our supremacy is the logical consequence, the very nature of things.[36]

By the 1930s, Vietnamese entrepreneurs and politicians pushed for increased immigration westward in order to take the population pressure off Annam and Tonkin. In an essay entitled 'From the Annamese Nation to the Indochinese Federation', budding capitalist Pham Le Bong wrote that 'in studying the history of the Annamese nation, one also has the impression that [Annam] is the unachieved history of Indochina'. Even leading intellectuals and politicians of the time, not least of all Pham Quynh and Nguyen Van Vinh, could think of themselves in remarkably Indochinese terms. Part of this shift was designed to force the French to do away with indirect methods of rule, including the monarchy, in order to implement truly republican institutions of an assimilationist kind, even if it meant doing so in Indochinese terms. This is how nations begin to take form, in ways we may not expect today, but that did not seem so strange at the time. This is also why it is dangerous to assume that modern Vietnam has always existed in its current form. It could have been and indeed once had been something very different.[37]

Republican Monarchy? The Birth of the Bao Dai Solution

The French simultaneously pushed in other directions depending on the political stakes. For one, French republicans may have done away with kingship in France, but they had no intention of letting go of their colonial emperors in Hue. Indeed, French republicans considered Vietnamese kingship to be an important part of their policy of indirect rule and association. The French were so shaken by Duy Tan's near escape from Hue in 1916 (not to mention his father's earlier attempt in 1907) that they decided to mold their own colonial emperor in the form of a little boy named Bao Dai. That Albert Sarraut was the architect of this first 'Bao Dai solution' after the First World War should come as no surprise. The governor was only too aware of the dangers of anticolonialist attempts to turn the Vietnamese monarchy against the French. He was convinced, like his good friend, Commissioner to Annam, and specialist of ancient Vietnam, Pierre Pasquier, that the Nguyen royal family and mandarinate on which it rested continued to exercise great influence over the majority peasant population, thereby making it a powerful cultural instrument of colonial control and mass participation. Sarraut was no royalist, but like scores of republicans following in his footsteps, he made major ideological compromises within the republic's empire in order to keep Vietnam French. And this is why Phan Chu Trinh's dream of overturning the Nguyen monarchy with the help of the Third Republic discussed earlier would be an utter failure. In a letter to Sarraut in 1922, Pasquier privately ridiculed Trinh's idea of creating an 'Annamese republic' in association with the French.[38]

Anti-communism also explains Sarraut and the French Republic's willingness to think in monarchical terms. Since the October Revolution in Russia in 1917 and the creation of the Comintern two years later, Sarraut, now Minister of Colonies, carefully watched the Soviet Union's revolutionary moves across the globe and into colonial Asia. Long before American Cold War warriors began speaking of the need to 'contain' Sino-Soviet communism, Sarraut had already called for the creation of a 'holy colonial alliance' to block the spread of communism into the Western imperial world.[39]

In the wake of the First World War, Sarraut and Pasquier went to work to shape a loyal colonial monarch. Knowing that Emperor Khai Dinh was terminally ill, they convinced him to allow his son to come to them for a modern upbringing. In 1922, Pasquier wrote detailed instructions concerning the raising and education of the young prince. This process had to begin in France, he said, but culminate in Annam. Bao Dai had to be modern (French) and traditional (Annamese) at the same time. To this end, Sarraut and Pasquier took Bao Dai from his family, entrusted him to a French one, and sent him to France, where he was raised and educated in the finest aristocratic fashion. Before sending him off to France, however, Pierre Pasquier reminded the future emperor of his colonial conception and guardianship: 'Young prince, always remember the day on which you received the mark of your future destiny, on that day two grand figures looked down on you, to smile at you, to protect you: ancient Annam and the sweet and beautiful France, in all of her glory and radiance'.[40]

Bao Dai spent nearly a decade in France, where Sarraut watched over him. Before returning him to Vietnam to help deal with a new set of revolts, the French had refashioned Bao Dai for colonial purposes which extended far beyond his native Annam. In an extraordinary *mise en scène* opening the International Colonial Exhibition of 1931, the emperor is dressed in traditional royal dress and plays his traditional, exotic part in this well-studied ritual celebrating the empire. Bao Dai sits at the center of the inaugural ceremony of the colonial exhibition in the Permanent Colonial Museum (Musée permanent des colonies), built for the occasion and which one can still visit today in Vincennes. The young emperor shares the VIP section with the likes of Marshal Lyautey, while the president of the republic delivers the opening speech (see photos 9 and 10). No other colonial emperor or king experienced such an invitation or such a display. Not only did the Nguyen emperor embody the special colonial relationship between France and Vietnam, but at that time he symbolically represented the empire (through the visible intermediary of his person) for the Third Republic. Colonial monarchy is part of modern Vietnamese history, but it is also part of the history of modern France. Bao Dai was the French Third Republic's colonial monarch. This was exactly what the reformists led by Phan Chu Trinh did not want.

CHAPTER 5

THE FAILURE OF COLONIAL
REPUBLICANISM

O N 1 JANUARY 1929, the leader of the Constitutionalist Party and leading French ally since the First World War, Bui Quang Chieu, stepped up to the podium in Calcutta to address the closing session of the Indian Congress Party. Jawaharlal Nehru, the future prime minister of independent India and then General Secretary of the Indian National Congress, had invited Chieu and his fellow Constitutionalist, Duong Van Giao, to attend this event (Nehru knew Giao through family connections and earlier meetings in Europe). As Chieu adjusted the microphone, the Indian audience welcomed the head of the Constitutionalist Party with hails of 'Indochinese! Indochinese!' Chieu assured his 'frenetic' audience that 'the Annamese are with you entirely in your struggle against imperialism'. 'Your liberty is not only an Indian affair,' he continued, 'it is the concern of all of humanity because you represent a third of the human race [. . .] We bring to you, messieurs, the most ardent wishes of the Annamese people for the victory of your noble efforts. Long Live India! Long Live Liberty!' Chieu even enjoyed a brief meeting with Mahatma Gandhi, who expressed his support of the Annamese people.

Upon returning to Saigon, Bui Quang Chieu wrote glowingly of his Calcutta trip in a series of travel notes. He praised the Indian National Congress, the success of colonial democracy in British India, and the model it could provide to republican-minded Vietnamese like him. But Chieu's sudden interest in India and Gandhi's non-cooperation with the British struck more than one reader as hypocritical. After all, this was one of France's most faithful followers, a longtime believer in Sarraut's policy of 'Franco-Annamese collaboration'. A naturalized French citizen, Chieu served as vice president of the Cochinchinese Colonial Council, but had done little to turn it into a more representative Indochinese congress.

Chieu disingenuously claimed that he had known nothing about India before leaving Indochina, though his paper, *La Tribune indochinoise*, had long covered British reformism and the question of 'dominion status' for

India and others. Other Vietnamese most certainly followed events in India attentively too. In 1926, Phan Boi Chau wrote admiringly of Gandhi's non-cooperation and held it up as a model for the Vietnamese to emulate. Vietnam's most prominent republican, Nguyen An Ninh, saw in Gandhi's non-cooperation proof that colonial rule, whether British or French, was untenable without the participation of the people. French readers meanwhile recoiled at Chieu's praise of British colonial democracy, attacking Chieu for even suggesting that the British could be better colonizers than they. But for Vietnamese republicans, the Indian example served as a counter-example to Sarraut's much touted, but, in the end, empty policy of Franco-Annamese collaboration. Without the institutional reforms on which the Indian Congress turned, it was nothing more than a bluff. Bui Quang Chieu knew it, but even after his India trip he remained on course, unwilling to challenge the French on their failed republicanism, scared, no doubt, to lose his privileges. But this decision would cost him his life in 1945, as Vietnamese nationalists, radicalized by decades of failed colonial reformism as much as international communism, went after and destroyed moderates whom they did not trust. The irony is that many powerful French administrators had themselves never trusted their most faithful 'collaborators', not Bui Quang Chieu, not even their own colonial emperor Bao Dai. There was no equivalent to Nehru in Vietnam in 1945. There was no Indochinese version of the Indian Congress. There was little real trust within the politics of Franco-Vietnamese collaboration.[1]

THE LIMITS OF COLONIAL DEMOCRACY: ACT 1. THE CONSTITUTIONALISTS[2]

Things could have been different. Albert Sarraut's 1919 promise of a republican-minded contract with the Vietnamese raised the hopes of many that reform was finally going to happen. This was of particular interest to the members of an emerging Vietnamese bourgeois class in Cochinchina. This included landowners, entrepreneurs, upward-moving civil servants, and highly educated professionals (doctors, lawyers, and pharmacists). As their economic power and social status grew, so too did their demands for a greater role in decision-making. Most resided in the bustling urban center of Saigon-Cholon. They spoke French, embraced Western culture, sent their children to French high schools, and some enjoyed metropolitan citizenship. Having grown up in Cochinchina, they had no direct experience of the Confucian examination system or the mandarinate still operating in Annam and Tonkin. In fact, they wanted to abolish what remained of it in the southern countryside in order to introduce a French-style direct administration which was judged to be more modern.

These assimilationist practices were not always crass efforts to mimic the colonizer. Holding metropolitan citizenship allowed these members of the elite to skirt around, via the law, a colonial system which made them second-class citizens in their own country (despite the fact that they were as 'civilized' and as 'intelligent' as the European settlers they crossed in the streets and competed with in placement tests). As in Algeria and Madagascar, French citizenship allowed the 'natives' to participate more effectively in colonial institutions dominated by the miniscule French population. Thanks to metropolitan citizenship, those Vietnamese in Cochinchina could own newspapers and avoid censorship more easily. Naturalization could also protect them from arbitrary arrest, unlawful prosecution, and special commissions, as Gilbert Chieu's recent trial had demonstrated. He had supported the anticolonialist, Phan Boi Chau, but avoided jail thanks to his French citizenship.

The rise of a bourgeois class is an important milestone in the history of modern Vietnam. This new social group was increasingly interested in capital accumulation and real estate acquisition, the expansion of trade and industry, upward social mobility, and the leisure accompanying it. Few, by the 1920s, had any interest in reviving the monarchy, despite the Nguyen dynasty's southern roots. Representative politics and expanded access to colonial decision-making attracted them most. Who were they? Some of the best-known names of those in this new and more confident class included Bui Quang Chieu, Nguyen Phu Khai, Nguyen Phan Long, and Duong Van Giao. A protégé of Pierre Loti, Nguyen Phu Khai had studied in France. A rich landowner, he created the first Vietnamese-owned rice mill in 1915, helped organize a boycott against Chinese traders in 1919, and, as part of this burgeoning economic nationalism, joined in the creation of the country's first 'Vietnamese bank'. Thanks to Sarraut's support, Khai established the *Tribune indigène* in 1917, thereby providing a voice to these southerners determined to work with the French to remake the country, economically and politically.

A French citizen, Bui Quang Chieu trained abroad as an agricultural engineer. Upon his return, he rose rapidly in the Indochinese civil service, joined the staff of the *Tribune indigène*, and wrote prolifically in favor of republican reformism and the need to accord the Cochinchinese elite a greater role in colonial governance. Nguyen Phan Long did much the same in his paper, the *Echo annamite* (*Annamese News*), while Duong Van Giao had studied law in France and pushed for increased native representation in colonial institutions. This was not an exclusively southern affair, however. One of modern Vietnam's first capitalists heralded from the north. The indefatigable Bach Thai Buoi rose from rags to riches at the turn of the century, thanks to his shipping and mining businesses. He, too, challenged pre-existing Chinese commercial interests, as an emerging Vietnamese business class affirmed itself.

These bourgeois elites built on Phan Chu Trinh's reformist project. This included attaining greater freedoms of association, press, and travel; the establishment of the rule of law through judicial reform; and the ending of the colonizers' monopolies upon alcohol and opium. In addition to promoting Western education and commercial modernization, they also sought to expand white-collar careers in the civil service beyond interpreting jobs, to liberalize the requirements for acquiring metropolitan citizenship, and to transform the Nguyen villages' own administrative bodies into elected municipalities along French lines. Thanks to more liberal laws afforded by Cochinchina's status as a colony and backed by Sarraut's team, these men created the Indochinese Constitutionalist Party in 1923, the first of its kind in Vietnam. Given their considerable financial support of France during the First World War (through fund-raising for it or loans made to it), these southerners trusted Sarraut to go forward as Minister of the Colonies in the elaboration of an Indochinese constitution or congress which would guarantee expanded colonial democracy. No one had forgotten the governor-general's historic promise of 1919: 'We must increase native representation in the existing local assemblies, create native representation in assemblies where it does not yet exist, and enlarge the native electoral body that will designate its representatives in such a way that the native representatives are increasingly the direct emanation of the population and no longer the administration's delegates.' This was the foundation of a colonial democracy that many, not just the Constitutionalists, could accept.[3]

In the southern colony, this meant obtaining increased representation in local municipalities and on the Cochinchinese Colonial Council in particular. The road leading to such an expansion of political participation, however, was lined with obstacles, not least of all the European settler community. As in Algeria, the French in Indochina were largely opposed to according metropolitan citizenship to members of the native elite or to broadening the native electorate. In the settlers' eyes, the extension of even limited voting rights to the most 'civilized' Vietnamese raised the specter of the 'native masses' running the Europeans out of the colony—legally. The Europeans interpreted any concession to the colonized as a loss. Republican governors certainly pushed through reforms over the heads of such opposition, and a variety of native commissions and representative chambers emerged in Cochinchina, Annam, and Tonkin. However, colonial authorities refused the native elite any real decision-making power. The French nominated the so-called 'native delegates', who only were allowed to hold consultative or advisory roles. They could not vote on budgets or establish quotas for the payment of the *corvée*, even though the non-European population provided the overwhelming bulk of the tax revenue and labor. In Annam, the monarchy often objected to introducing representative politics, reluctant to lose what little power it still possessed. And when peasants revolted against onerous taxes and *corvée* requirements, as they had done in 1908, the French backtracked on expanding native representation.

The French were not all to blame, however. The Constitutionalists never endorsed universal suffrage. In fact, they wanted to limit the native right to vote and French naturalizations to a small social group of elite members like themselves. When the question arose of granting French citizenship to thousands of largely illiterate Vietnamese who had served in France as workers and soldiers during the war, Bui Quang Chieu objected. In fact, the Sarraut-inspired decree of 1922 expanding the Cochinchinese electorate from 1,500 to 20,000 individuals went beyond what the Constitutionalists had initially requested. They certainly welcomed this reform as well as its expansion in the number of native seats on the Cochinchinese Colonial Council from six to ten. They threw themselves into local politics, mobilized their papers, and increased the number of Constitutionalists on the council. However, they never sought to enfranchise the entire population. They denied the right to vote to women, even those of their own class.

On the whole, the Cochinchinese Constitutionalists remained bourgeois reformers, operating from the urban centers and focused primarily on promoting the interests of their class in a delicate balancing act with the settler population and the colonial authorities. Depending on the issues coming before the council and local municipalities on which they sat, the Constitutionalists could oppose or support local French politicians. In

1919, for example, many supported Ernest Outrey, a trade-oriented settler politician, in his bid to remain Cochinchina's deputy to the French national assembly. Several European traders, editors, and politicians also took sides with the Constitutionalists during the boycott of the Chinese. And, depending on the issues, French and Constitutionalists might clash when it came to debating important economic matters such as the Saigon port authority, colonial monopolies, and infrastructure development. However, by defining their interests narrowly in urban and class terms and by betting on French goodwill to implement their desired reforms, the Constitutionalists found themselves in the difficult position of having to prove their faithfulness to the French, and even siding with them in times of trouble, for fear of being treated as *anti-français* or nationalists. They feared that both labels would undermine their socio-economic status and reformist project.

They did. French settler politicians and journalists did their best to keep these Vietnamese in their place and to prevent Sarraut's promises from ever coming to fruition. While Sarraut and his successors in Indochina were hardly pro-settler, their failure to implement real reforms undermined the Constitutionalists and others betting on colonial republicanism. Fearful of losing control, a string of leftist governors in the 1920s imposed strict regulations on the opening of new secondary schools, closed the faculty of law at the University of Hanoi, cracked down on private schools of a modern kind in Annam and Tonkin, and maintained strict censorship, and limits on freedom of travel, assembly, and thought. When one of their strongest allies, Pham Quynh, tried to form a political party in Tonkin in 1926, the French refused him the permission to do so.

Even the advent of a left-dominated government, the Cartel des Gauches (or 'Cartel of the Left', 1924–6), in France and the dispatch of the socialist Alexandre Varenne to run Indochina did little to expand representative politics. Varenne created the Chamber of People's Representatives (Chambres des représentants de l'Annam et du Tonkin) for Annam and Tonkin, as well as the Grand Council of Economic Interests (Grand Conseil des Intérêts économiques). While each allowed its members to voice their opinions and to debate local, mainly economic, issues, both remained strictly advisory bodies and their members could not set their own agendas. Bui Quang Chieu travelled to France at this time, confident that change was finally in the making. But he returned home disappointed, especially when he saw what the British were doing in India. This disillusionment was widespread. In 1928, Huynh Thuc Khang, a pro-French reformer who had gone to jail with Phan Chu Trinh during the 1908 peasant revolts, became the president of the Chamber of People's Representatives for Annam. At the outset, he was hopeful that the introduction of colonial democracy to the countryside would bring badly needed change by providing the rural poor with a voice in decision-making and allowing local leaders to bypass the moribund monarchy. In a bitter speech in 1928, he criticized the French for failing to address seriously any of the major pleas coming from the 'people's chamber':

> Entrusted with the confidence of my constituents, I have assumed, thanks to the civilizing policy of the government, the responsibility of a people's representative for the past two years [...] Yet, during the last two years the government has not once given heed to any of our requests, failing thereby to reassure the people that this new institution is different from the absolute rule they had experienced in the past. The people, consequently, have lost their confidence in us. Neither do they believe any longer in the government. We ourselves have often heard uttered by our constituants comments such as the following: 'The name does make use of the words, "representatives of the people", but the reality simply yields a new mandarinate'.[4]

Irritated, the Commissioner of Annam shot back that all was fine, insisting that 'the people are busily working in total peace'. Khang resigned, humiliated and distrustful. In 1946, he would become the president of postcolonial Vietnam's first National Assembly.

Significantly, the French never considered expanding their single most important democratic institution in the colony—the Cochinchinese Colonial Council—northward to establish a pan-Vietnamese or an Indochinese-wide colonial parliament or congress. Until 1949, French Vietnam thus remained a hodgepodge of colonies, protectorates, and military territories. Pham Quynh asked in 1930 whether the French wanted to turn 'Vietnam' into a fully assimilated colony, like Algeria, or maintain it as a protectorate by allowing an autonomous Vietnamese state to exist within the French empire, as they did in Morocco. The French never provided a clear answer, but they systematically refused any attempt to unify Cochinchina, Annam, and Tonkin into one administrative 'Vietnamese' body. Sarraut and his successors certainly spoke of creating an Indochinese federation whenever trouble was in the air, but it never occurred before the Second World War in reality.[5]

As Bui Quang Chieu pointed out in his travel notes of 1929, this was in stark contrast to the Indian National Congress created by the British in 1885. During the interwar years in particular, the British had increasingly allowed Indian elites to organize electoral campaigns, participate in provincial elections, and increasingly partake in colonial decision-making. Some in Indochina may have mocked Gandhi's pacifism, but many Vietnamese understood that this ascetic man and his trusted ally, Nehru, were transforming the Congress from an elitist, bourgeois urban party into a mass-based rural organization with provincial committees. Of course, reformism, whether British or French in design, sought to avoid decolonization. However, by failing to develop or allow institutions and mass parties capable of reaching into the countryside, the French left the field open to others while hemming in their most faithful partners all the time. When large-scale revolts broke out again in 1930–31, organized religious, nationalist, and communist parties mobilized along mass lines, while French republicans repressed the indigenous people, reversed reforms, and desperately tried to revive the very monarchy in which so few Vietnamese believed. And by their own refusal to widen politics to the working and peasant classes, the Constitutionalists, including Bui Quang Chieu, missed a golden opportunity to create a mass party like the Indian nationalists. To young nationalist eyes, the Constitutionalists now started to pass for colonial collaborators of the worst kind. Modern bourgeois Vietnamese republicanism was stillborn.[6]

THE POLITICIZATION OF A NEW ELITE: THE YOUNG

The French, the Constitutionalists, and the monarchists alienated another segment of the population, an increasingly politicized and nationalist-minded one by the 1920s—that of the educated young. This new generation heralded overwhelmingly from urban centers, not just Saigon, but also Hanoi, Vinh, Haiphong, and a host of growing provincial and district towns. A few could claim working-class and peasant backgrounds, but most were the privileged sons and daughters of mandarins, civil servants, professionals, and entrepreneurs. Pham Van Dong and Nguyen Thi Minh Khai, future communist leaders, as well as the novelist and nationalist Nhat Linh, all heralded from mandarin families. This younger generation was also the first to experience the Franco-Indigenous school system. Many graduated from the much-admired French high schools in Saigon

(Chasseloup-Laubat) and Hanoi (Albert Sarraut). By 1925, this French-trained, urban intelligentsia counted around 5,000 individuals, doubling to 10,000 a decade later. They worked in the civil service and liberal professions. Many were teachers and journalists. Nguyen Thai Hoc, the founder of the Vietnamese Nationalist Party in 1927, was a schoolteacher, as was Vo Nguyen Giap (who led the Vietnamese to victory in battle over the French at Dien Bien Phu in 1954).[7]

A two-pronged linguistic revolution also marked the emergence of this generation as a political force. For the first time in centuries, an entire group of young elite members no longer formally studied Chinese characters, but was now speaking, reading, and writing quite fluently in a new foreign language—French. Unlike the two 'Phans', young Vietnamese graduates now read Rousseau in the original and discovered and easily understood an array of global ideas in French translation. However, the colonial classrooms also reinforced this generation's mastery of a *second* written language—their own. From the start, the French pushed the Romanized writing system for Vietnamese in the civil service, schools, and colonial barracks. On the eve of the Second World War, 10 percent of the Vietnamese population of almost twenty million people could read newspapers in *quoc ngu*.

Further facilitating the politicization of this new intelligentsia was the introduction of state-of-the-art printing presses, a renaissance in print culture, and improved means of transportation and communications. The number of French and *quoc ngu* newspapers, pamphlets, and books in circulation during the interwar period exploded. Despite their efforts to censor *quoc ngu* papers and control ideas, the French realized that there was little they could do to put the genie back in the bottle. Sarraut may have promoted French and *quoc ngu* in the 1910s in order to sever Vietnam membership from China's civilizational orbit, but little did he realize that, within a decade, this script would become a powerful tool for shaping a wide range of local opinions and identities—national, religious, and cultural (see chapter 12).[8]

A fiery young man who had returned from Paris led the charge. His name was Nguyen An Ninh. Born in Cochinchina in 1900, Ninh was a product of the colonial education system. A graduate of Chasseloup-Laubat, he spoke French beautifully and wrote it elegantly. He translated Rousseau's *Social Contract* into *quoc ngu*. He obtained his undergraduate degree in law in Paris in 1921. He travelled widely in France and Europe and developed a keen interest in politics, nationalism, journalism, philosophy, and religion.

Although he fraternized with Phan Chu Trinh in Paris, Ninh shared little of Phan's faith in colonial collaboration.[9]

Nguyen An Ninh began to express his doubts publicly upon returning to Saigon in 1922. Armed with a French-language newspaper like none other before it—*La Cloche fêlée* (*The Cracked Bell*), he wrote a string of hard-hitting articles and incisive essays designed to wake up his generation and to lay bare the glaring contradictions of republican colonial rule and its twisted discourse for all to see. In 1923, he penned 'The Ideal of the Annamese Youth', in which he argued that the redemption of the country now depended on the young, both individually and collectively. Most importantly, he insisted, the youth had to act. 'Life is action', he wrote. 'To say action is to say effort. To say effort is to say obstacles. And they are many, the obstacles to our ambitions, the greatest of them being ourselves.' If the youth could create a new set of ideals, 'their ideals', then they could create a new culture, a new Vietnam, free of colonial domination and the weight of the past. Sarraut's Franco-Vietnamese collaboration and reformist talk was a bluff, he insisted. And the *mission civilisatrice* upon which it rested? A colonial myth designed to legitimate and perpetuate indefinitely foreign rule, for the French would always cast the Vietnamese as children, necessarily incapable of ruling themselves.[10]

For Ninh and others like him, the liberation of Vietnam from foreign domination went hand in hand with the unshackling of the individual from what was judged to be a suffocating Confucian tradition. By 1930, young Vietnamese intellectuals were attacking 'Confucianism' and 'tradition' for stifling individual freedoms and thought. As one of Ninh's contemporaries wrote: 'It is Confucianism which in the past elevated Vietnam to the rank of civilized nations. It is also Confucianism which has brought Vietnam to the brink of perdition'. In other texts, Ninh focused on collective action and the need to develop a national culture in opposition to the colonial one. He zeroed in on the brutality of French conquest, objecting to the dismemberment of the country into three parts. He reminded his young readers that the Vietnamese had never lacked heroes. Individual men and women had stood up in the past to resist a thousand years of Chinese occupation; they could do it again. He resurrected the Trung sisters and their resistance against the Chinese in the first century CE and recast them as heroines to emulate in the present. In place of colonial myths, Ninh (and others) wanted national ones. In a 1925 text called 'The French in Indochina', Ninh produced a long list of revolts, from that of the Trung sisters to the most recent one—the attempt by Pham Hong Thai to assassinate the governor general during the latter's visit to Guangzhou. Although Pham Hong Thai failed, drowning while trying to escape, Ninh held him up as proof of a young Vietnamese who had acted on an ideal, driven by a deep-seated resistance culture, and, though Ninh did not say it, capable of serving as a martyr to emulate, individually, collectively, and, above all, now. In short, nationalism and anticolonialism were spreading rapidly among this young urban class that Ninh embodied so well; another turning point in the making of modern Vietnam.[11]

The increasing radicalization of the young interacted with the sinking of colonial reformism. Ninh's initial hope that the French would help the youth dissipated completely as the leftwing government in the Cartel des Gauches and Alexander Varenne in particular failed to make good on Sarraut's political promises and transform 'association' into something more than a never ending word game to mask unchanging colonial rule, and the use of fear as its weapon. At some time in 1925, Ninh concluded that the French were hostile to any form of substantial reform. His generation had no choice but to act to free itself and the country. On 30 November 1925, he issued a call to arms:

> Liberty is to be taken; it is not to be granted. To wrest it away from an organized power, we need to oppose to that power an organized force [. . .] When we ask for reforms, we acknowledge the authority of the established regime. But if they are refused to us, let us know how to organize ourselves. Let us not put any faith in the policy of association that is much talked about these days. To associate, at least there must be two sides, and only equals. Let us say to the government to wait until we have the same liberty and the same rights as those with which it wants us to associate.[12]

The Governor of Cochinchina, Dr Cognacq, had already summoned the young man to his office and warned him: 'There must not be intellectuals in this country. The country is too simple. If you want intellectuals, go to Moscow. Be assured that the seeds you are trying to sow will never bear fruit'. It is doubtful that the governor believed everything he said, for his own intelligence services were reporting that those sympathetic to Ninh's cause included not just 'intellectuals', but also peasants, traders, rural teachers, paramedics, colonial civil servants, and students. What French authority figures like Cognacq failed to grasp was that the elite young were fast losing faith in colonial republicanism and reformism. Hardly an accident, in late

1925 Nguyen An Ninh and his new co-editor, Phan Van Truong, changed the motto appearing at top of each issue of *La Cloche fêlée* from its designation as the 'Medium of Propaganda for French Ideas' to a subversive quote from Mencius: 'The people are everything; the state has but a secondary importance; the prince is nothing'. This came as Sarraut and Pasquier did their best to fashion a new colonial emperor in the person of Bao Dai. The disconnect spoke volumes about the poverty of French colonial policy and their inaction at this critical juncture.[13]

In the end, Ninh remained an ideas man more than an organizer of the masses. He often dreamed of being a Vietnamese Gandhi, but was always content to play the part of the gadfly in the end. His fearless critique of French injustices landed him repeatedly in jail. He did, however, get to relish his role in catalyzing the young into a political force for the first time in the history of Vietnam. This began in 1926 when a series of events converged to spur thousands of young people to defy the French. The arrest and trial of Phan Boi Chau in late 1925 became a *cause célèbre* for this generation, as had Phan Chu Trinh's return from France. Despite briefly falling for Sarraut's policy of collaboration, Chau remained a hero for the young, one of the rare individuals to have stood up, resisted, and sacrificed so much individually for the collective cause. When Varenne realized that he was making a martyr out of the man by putting him on trial in 1926, the governor quickly commuted Chau's harsh sentence and shuttled the aging revolutionary off to Hue to live out the rest of his days in solitude. Meanwhile, the police arrested Nguyen An Ninh, closed his newspaper, and, in so doing, further enraged his disciples.

Little wonder that the death (from natural causes) of Phan Chu Trinh in March 1926 brought students into the streets. In Saigon alone, around 100,000 people took part in Trinh's funeral cortège, arguably the largest public manifestation to have ever occurred in Vietnam to that date. Wearing black armbands, the youth used this occasion of public mourning to vent their anger and air their political grievances. Workers' strikes also occurred in Saigon and elsewhere over the next year. When the French sanctioned many who had demonstrated, schools rapidly became politicized sites as scores of students boycotted their classes. In Cochinchina alone, the colonial authorities expelled over a thousand students as Constitutionalists like Bui Quang Chieu and monarchists like Pham Quynh looked on apprehensively, refusing to make the nationalist leap of faith. Many of these burgeoning radicals would not forget this.

From this point onward, the lines were quickly being drawn in the sand. Not all students went on strike or risked expulsion; but those who did suddenly found themselves on the wrong side of the law and often at odds with their parents, many of whom thought that they had lost their Confucian minds. Colonial authorities certainly agreed, not least the new governor general in 1928, Pierre Pasquier. A longtime administrator and dedicated monarchist, this conservative man disdained these young *déracinés* as much as Cognacq. He prided himself on his deep knowledge of Vietnam and of the Vietnamese. Pasquier immediately implemented educational policies designed to re-root the young in their true 'Confucian culture' and 'moral order'. His erudite history *L'Annam d'autrefois* (*Ancient Annam*) reappeared in print at the very moment that this young generation began to rethink Vietnam in new ways.[14]

One of the most important lessons these young elites learned was that opposition to colonial power required the creation of political parties that could operate clandestinely and take the national message to the countryside—to the 'people', as Ninh's slogan put it. In 1927, a group of nationalist-minded teachers, students, journalists, civil servants, and merchants in the north tried to do just that when they established the Vietnamese Nationalist Party, known by its acronym, VNQDD (Viet Nam Quoc Dan Dang). While it shared the same name as the Chinese Nationalist Party (the GMD), the VNQDD was a very Vietnamese affair. Nguyen Thai Hoc and Pham Tuan Tai, both schoolteachers, and Nguyen Khac Nhu, an older, reformist-minded mandarin scholar, formed the core of the party. Initially, VNQDD leaders called on the French to make good on Sarraut's reformism and to recognize the Vietnamese people's basic human rights. While the party certainly relied on Leninist organizational principles (as did the GMD), the Vietnamese Nationalist Party was a non-communist nationalist movement. Its main goals were national independence and territorial unification (Tonkin, Annam, Cochinchina), economic development of a socialist kind, and the creation of republican government based on popular sovereignty and the rule of law.[15]

The VNQDD's members also had a penchant for brash and violent action. Many were convinced that the socio-economic suffering in the countryside was such that the masses would easily be made to follow them. A spark was all that was needed. The assassination of a notorious French labor recruiter in early 1929 was intended to do that. But instead of triggering an uprising, the killing of this man set off a spiral of colonial repression that pushed the leadership into further, ultimately fatal action. On the night of 9 February 1930, as the police moved in, Vietnamese Nationalist Party leaders organized a daring attack on the French garrison in Yen Bay in Tonkin. It was a miserable failure; there was no peasant uprising. Instead, the French arrested scores of members of the VNQDD, including Nguyen Thai Hoc. Those who escaped fled to southern China, where they would largely remain under the tutelage of the Chinese Nationalist Party until returning to Vietnam in 1945.[16]

The Vietnamese Nationalist Party's daring action shook the colonial state. Fear once again guided colonial policy as Pasquier unleashed his security services. Unlike the violent conquest of the nineteenth century or the crackdown of the 1908 revolts, French repression in 1930 triggered anti-colonial demonstrations in the metropolis for the first time. This occurred at the same time that the republic was trying to sell the empire to the French people by bringing it to them at the colonial exhibition outside Paris in 1931. Metropolitan journalists also began covering colonial affairs more closely and critically. Louis Roubaud's 'Viet-Nam: la tragédie indo-chinoise' provided a riveting, even subversive, account of the VNQDD. Roubaud met with colonial authorities, interviewed Vietnamese Nationalist Party prisoners, and, in the company of Indochina's top policeman, Paul Arnoux, witnessed the execution of Nguyen Thai Hoc. Roubaud was so moved by what he saw that day that he included the word 'Viet-Nam' on the cover of his book, one of the first times it had ever appeared in French: 'Viet-Nam! Viet-Nam! Viet-Nam! Thirteen times, I heard that scream before the guillotine at Yen Bay'. Nguyen Thai Hoc's fiancée, Nguyen Thi Giang, committed suicide a few weeks later, leaving a double suicide note, one for her lover, the other for her country.[17]

Roubaud understood that these men and women were not 'pirates' or, despite the colonial spin, 'communists'. He pointed out in fact that these nationalists were a lot like the French. When he asked a high-ranking Vietnamese Nationalist Party leader if he were a communist, the young man scornfully shot back: 'I'm a republican just like you. What I wish for my country is that which you have obtained for yours: a democratic government, universal suffrage, liberty of the press, the recognition of human rights and those of the citizen, and, for starters, independence'. Backed by a special commission, the republic guillotined him a few days later. Days before his own execution, Nguyen Thai Hoc had addressed a letter to the French National Assembly, in which he explained that Varenne's failure to move on any reforms had led him to act. There was no reason not to take him at his word. With these executions, the French had effectively crushed yet another manifestation of Vietnamese republicanism, the non-communist one. Seventy years after taking Saigon, colonial legitimacy remained as fragile as ever and Sarraut's policy of Franco-Annamese collaboration of 1919 was little more than an empty shell. But by failing to work with moderate nationalists, even anticommunist ones, the French pushed them in radical directions.[18]

Ho Chi Minh and Global Communism[19]

Ho Chi Minh was no exception to this rule. His birth name was Nguyen Tat Thanh, 'he who is sure to succeed'. Ho was certainly not 'born Red'. He was born into a Confucian-minded family in Annam in 1890. He had one foot in the world of the two Phans and the other in that of Nguyen An Ninh and Nguyen Thai Hoc. The son of a high-ranking mandarin, he was set to follow in his father's footsteps. Like so many others in the protectorates, he diligently studied Chinese characters and the Confucian classics in preparation for the civil service exams. His father's transfer to Hue also meant that Ho came of age in the royal capital. He entered the prestigious National College (Quoc Hoc) there, created to train modern civil servants for the imperial government. He learned the basics of *quoc ngu*, picked up some French, and may have experienced the newly introduced Franco-Indigenous curriculum. His studies ended abruptly in 1909, however, when, in a drunken rage, his father's beating of a subject ended in the poor man's death. Ho's father lost his job and with it Ho's own chances of becoming a mandarin.

On his own, the young man left for Saigon. While we do not know what was driving him southward, Ho was hardly apolitical. As an important mandarin, Ho's father had crossed paths with a variety of Vietnamese luminaries. And from his location in Hue, Ho must have witnessed the peasant revolts of 1908. A spy later told the French that Ho 'claims that with his own eyes he saw the Vietnamese coming empty-handed to the Commissioner for Annam's office to protest against the heavy labor contribution [. . .] and that the crowd was fired on to disperse it'. That the authorities at the National College reprimanded him for criticizing such repression suggests that Ho, like so many others, wanted to do something. Whatever it was, he had clearly concluded that the answers lay abroad. In Saigon, he landed a job as a cook on a French liner, the *Admiral Latouche-Tréville*, as it steamed westward across the Indian Ocean, through the Suez Canal, and into the Mediterranean. Upon arriving in Marseille in 1911, he applied to the Ecole Coloniale, but his father's sins blocked again his access to the civil service. Undeterred, Ho kept his job on the *Latouche*, traveling back and forth across the Atlantic, even working as a housekeeper in New York to make ends meet.[20]

Ho's international movements were hardly unique at the time. By the turn of the century, people and information were moving across the planet in unprecedented ways and with greater alacrity as globalization intensified. The opening of the Suez Canal in 1869, the expansion of more shipping lines between the East and the West, the laying of transoceanic communication cables, and the spread of wireless telegraphy had all increasingly connected the world. The demand for labor had also increased as colonial states across the globe expanded and industrialization spread further. This, in turn, facilitated the movements of massive numbers of people and of Asians in particular. Between the mid-nineteenth century and 1940, two and a half million Chinese moved to British Singapore and Malaya. Most were laborers working on colonial plantations. Tens of thousands migrated to the Pacific islands, the Caribbean, and the Americas. European wars also accelerated Asian movements westward. As we saw in chapter 4, almost 100,000 Vietnamese served in wartime France. Several thousands stayed on after the war while more Chinese and Vietnamese workers would arrive in the 1920s, marking the takeoff of the Chinese and Vietnamese diasporas in France. Meanwhile, French shipping lines, such as the Compagnies des messageries maritimes and the Compagnies des chargeurs réunis, moved thousands of Vietnamese sailors around the world. Associations popped up in port towns on both sides of the Atlantic, serving as meeting places and relays for exchanging information, mail, people, and ideas. Like so many other revolutionaries, Ho relied on sailors for information, contacts, and transportation.[21]

Having closed Phan Boi Chau's Go East program to study abroad in Japan in 1909, the French also sought to channel the movement of the young elite toward the Indochinese University in Hanoi and establishments in France. When Ho landed in Marseille, he found that there were a dozen young Vietnamese studying in the metropole. Phan Chu Trinh was there, keeping company with Phan Van Truong and Nguyen The Truyen. Phan Van Truong was the first Vietnamese to obtain a law degree at the Sorbonne.

When he wasn't teaching Vietnamese to colonial administrators in Paris, he penned articles for various papers. He was a fierce republican and advocate of colonial reform whose activities landed him in prison on several occasions. He created with Phan Chu Trinh the Fraternity of Compatriots (Fraternité des compatriots) in 1912, then the Annamese Patriots Group (Groupe des Patriotes annamite) in 1919. A member of the French Socialist Party, Nguyen The Truyen joined the others in calling on the French to make good on their reformist promises. And although he did not settle down in Paris until mid-1919 (he had preferred to reside in New York and London), Ho Chi Minh stopped over regularly in France. He followed the course of the First World War closely and worked with Phan Van Truong, Nguyen The Truyen, and Phan Chu Trinh. These men helped Ho to make the right connections, widened his perspectives, challenged his ideas, and helped him prepare his first articles in French.

Ho's travels also brought him into contact with a wider range of reformists and anticolonialists moving westward like him, not least of all Korean nationalists he met in the United States and Chinese ones in France, including Zhou Enlai. Thanks to his improving English, French, and 'brush conversations' in Chinese characters, Ho learned that the Koreans were lobbying President Woodrow Wilson to support their independence cause at the Versailles peace conference. The Chinese also hoped that Wilson's talk of self-determination would apply to Asia. Korean nationalists submitted their petition to the conference on 12 May 1919. The Algerian nationalist Emir Khaled submitted one to Wilson on 23 May 1919. Inspired, Ho arrived in Paris in June and joined immediately with Phan Van Truong and Nguyen The Truyen to submit a Vietnamese petition. Ho Chi Minh did not write the famous '*Revendications du peuple annamite*' ('The Demands of the Annamese People') in 1919 alone. They all did.[22]

Unlike the Koreans, these Vietnamese did not ask the French or the Americans for independence. Rather they asked the French to honor their reformist promises. In mid-1919, Ho still believed in republican reformism. He became a Freemason, a socialist, and a member of the Human Rights League. During a brief audience with Sarraut, he urged the governor to keep the promises he had made in Hanoi in April 1919. But like Truyen and Truong, Ho was increasingly exasperated by the contradictions in republican colonial policy and discourse. In a tense conversation with Phan Chu Trinh, Ho warned that if real reform did not come soon, then the Vietnamese would have to take their rights back by force: 'We are men and we

should be treated that way. All those who refuse to treat us as their equals
are our enemies'. Trinh countered that the implications of his words were
immense: 'What do you want our unarmed countrymen to do against the
Europeans and their weapons? Why should people die uselessly without
any result?' This was not the last time that this question would confront
Vietnamese nationalists.[23]

Over the next year, Ho Chi Minh abandoned Phan Chu Trinh's blind
faith in colonial reformism. More than anything else, Ho's discovery of the
Russian Revolution, Marxism, and especially Lenin's theses on colonialism
provided him with a cogent explanation of his country's plight and offered
a way out. For Lenin, international capitalism not only exploited the working class in Europe, but it also attained its highest level of development in
the form of global imperialism in the non-Western, unindustrialized world.
Capitalist countries needed colonies as sources of cheap primary materials
and as captured markets for their finished products. Capitalism's oppression of the European working class and the Afro-Asian colonized were thus
two sides of the same theoretical coin. To break their chains, Lenin said,
workers and colonial peoples had to unite their forces against their common, two-headed enemy—international capitalism and imperialism. At a
time when it was clear that Wilson was not going to push decolonization
beyond Europe, the Soviets appeared to many (but not to all) as the only
great power interested in the non-Western colonized. In 1919, Lenin created the Comintern (the Communist International organization) to direct
and support the development of communist parties across the globe. In
July 1920, the Comintern approved Lenin's colonial theses; Ho learned of
them from the pages of *L'Humanité*.

Others were making this leftward journey in France. Zhou Enlai, Li
Lisan, and Deng Xiaoping from China, for example. Ho also collaborated
with fellow colonial subjects from Madagascar, Dahomey, and Algeria.
Together many of them published articles in the *Le Paria* (*The Pariah*)
newspaper, condemning colonial abuses across the empire and calling for
revolutionary change. What distinguished Ho from other Vietnamese radicals at the time was that he seized this moment of conjuncture and the
favorable conditions in France to take the revolutionary high ground. His
communist conversion, political activism, and personal determination
were so successful that he attended the groundbreaking Tours Congress
in December 1920 (when French socialists and communists went their
separate ways). He fully approved of the communists' decision to break

with the 'bourgeois' Social-democrats (the SFIO, the Section française de l'Internationale ouvrière, widely referred to as the socialists) and to create the French Communist Party (FCP) under the auspices of the Comintern based in Moscow. Not only did Ho become a founding member of the French communist movement (like Nguyen The Truyen), but in so doing he was also betting heavily that the metropolitan FCP—backed by the Comintern—would now serve as a powerful motor in France for pushing revolutionary change throughout the empire. This was a key strategic linkage for Ho: In his address to the Tours congress, he implored the FCP leadership to support the anticolonial struggle in the French empire, not just among French workers.[24]

Ho also realized that communism offered an international network of support and training within which he and his plans for Vietnam could grow. In mid-1923, he travelled to Moscow, the newest *locus* of revolutionary interchange after Tokyo, Guangzhou, and Paris. In October, he spoke at the International Peasants Conference there and joined the Peasant International's *presidium*, or permanent council. He enthusiastically embraced Nikolai Bukharin's idea of relying on the peasantry as a massive revolutionary force in colonial and semi-colonial countries like Vietnam and China. He also agreed with the Comintern that the best way to proceed at this stage was to build national fronts with the revolutionary bourgeois class, just as Chinese communists were doing.

Vietnam differed from China, however, in that the Comintern considered Indochina to be part of the French imperial state and thus that it should be administered by the French Communist Party through the two organizations of the Intercolonial Union and the Committee for Colonial Studies in Paris. Ho knew this and had already joined both. The problem, as Ho had feared from the start, was that French communist support for colonial communism was lukewarm at best (Ho must have been aware of French leftist fears during the Great War of letting in too many 'foreign workers'). Indeed, one of the main reasons he left for Moscow in 1923 was to lobby the Comintern to pressure the FCP to honor its anticolonialist pledge. Reassured by the Comintern's growing interest in the peasantry and commitment to revolution in China (now that the chance of a workers' revolution in Weimar Germany seemed increasingly remote), Ho focused his energies on getting to southern China. His wish was finally granted in 1924 when the Comintern allowed him to travel to Guangzhou and work in the offices of the Russian Telegraphic Agency (later TASS). However, Ho was not a *bona fida* Comintern agent and the Soviets were much more interested in China than Indochina. The Comintern had already presided over the creation of the Chinese Communist Party (CCP) in Shanghai in 1921. But this was certainly not a bad thing, given Indochina's location on China's southern flank, connected by a series of maritime and overland routes. What counted most for Ho was reaching Guangzhou and staying on good terms with the Comintern, the CCP, and the Chinese Nationalist Party in order to get a Vietnamese communist party off the ground, with or without the French Communist Party.[25]

Southern China offered Ho a favorable revolutionary laboratory and recruiting ground. Since 1911, Guangzhou had become the capital of Phan Boi Chau's 'Vietnam abroad'. Southern China was also the area where French colonial influence extended furthest, as the French-operated Hanoi-Kunming railway attested. This colonial presence was such that 7,000 Vietnamese civil servants and workers moved to the Yunnan and Guangxi provinces, increasing the Vietnamese diaspora in southern China to around 10,000 individuals. Thanks to his father's connections, Ho immediately entered into contact with Phan Boi Chau and recruited a number of his best disciples. One of them, Ho Hoc Lam, worked on Chiang Kai-shek's general staff and helped Ho secretly build up his networks until he took power in 1945. Chiang Kai-shek had taken over the leadership of the Chinese Nationalist Party following Sun Yat-sen's death in 1923 (and was to become the leader of the Republic of China between 1928 and 1949). Ho also renewed contact with Zhou Enlai, now teaching in the Whampoa Military Academy outside Guangzhou. Zhou helped Ho enroll dozens of young Vietnamese into Chinese Nationalist Party/Chinese Communist Party schools and military academies. Sun Yat-sen had presided over the creation of the first united front between the Chinese nationalists and communists in 1923. Few other Vietnamese organizations, except the Catholics, could match the communists in their global movements and connections at this point in time.

Ho lost no time in creating a new revolutionary party for Vietnam in Guangzhou. Following the Comintern's model for China, he presided over the creation of the Vietnamese Youth League in 1925 and a newspaper of the same name. Picking up on his earlier work in Paris, he fine-tuned his *quoc ngu* style, penning easy-to-follow articles, essays, and pamphlets on a wide range of social, economic, political, and revolutionary topics. The politicization of the urban youth which Nguyen An Ninh had spearheaded since 1923 was a godsend. Between 1925 and 1927, dozens of young, well-educated Vietnamese found their way to Guangzhou, where Ho inducted them into the Youth League, enrolled some in the Whampoa academy, and dispatched others to Moscow for advanced studies. Pham Van Dong joined the Youth League; Le Hong Phong travelled to the Soviet Union. The future General Nguyen Son studied at Whampoa before making the Long March with the Chinese Communist Party. Of course, not all of them came under Ho's wing. Another group made its way to Moscow via France, bypassing Ho's control. And, just as importantly: separate proto-communist groups popped up inside Vietnam and gained traction with the rise of this nationalist-minded youth and the fall of the Vietnamese Nationalist Party. The brilliant lexicographer and Marxist intellectual, Dao Duy Anh, is one notable example. The Trotskyists also became a real political force in Cochinchina during the 1930s.

All the while Ho kept lobbying the Comintern to let him create a communist party in Vietnam. The French Communist Party wanted to do this in Paris and had begun creating nationalist front parties there like the Etoile Nord Africaine under the Algerian Messali Hadj and the Annamese Independence Party under Nguyen The Truyen. Ho disagreed and probably still doubted the FCP's commitment to revolutionary change within the empire. For him, communism could not remain a purely diasporic and metropolitan affair (which was a major difference between Vietnamese and Algerian communism). The outbreak of civil war between the Chinese Nationalist Party and the Chinese Communist Party in southern China in 1927 delayed efforts to create a unified party as Ho and his disciples ran for cover. Ho returned to Moscow and then sailed for Thailand to live, work, and recruit followers again, this time among the 50,000 Vietnamese living along the Mekong there. He carried no clear directions from Moscow, however. As the Vietnamese Nationalist Party prepared to launch their attack on the French garrison at Yen Bay and the economic Great Depression bore down on Indochina, Ho seized the moment to create a unified communist party from among the different groups that had sprung up inside Indochina and among the Vietnamese of the diasporas running from Udon Thani in northeast Thailand to Guangzhou in southern China.

Complicating his task was the arrival of a parallel group of younger Vietnamese who had made their way to Moscow and joined the Comintern independently of Ho's control. Most important among them was Tran Phu. He arrived in Moscow as Stalin consolidated his power and imposed a strict proletarian line on the international communist movement in 1928.

Tran Phu received instructions to create a party for Indochina along those lines. The problem was that Ho was still operating as if the nationalist line of approach still applied. In February 1930, convinced he was doing the right thing, Ho organized a unification conference in Hong Kong from which the Vietnamese Communist Party emerged. Upon arriving in the British colony a few months later, Tran Phu criticized Ho's action, accusing him of ignoring the Comintern's proletarian line in favor of a narrow, nationalist one. Ho accepted, even recognized his error, but he was relieved above all that the Comintern finally stood behind the creation of the Indochinese Communist Party (ICP) in October 1930. Less than a year later, the ICP became an official member of the Comintern, independent of the FCP. Ho then travelled to Thailand and Singapore to help build the Thai and Malayan parties, relying on his CCP and Comintern contacts to do so, as well as the growing Chinese and Vietnamese immigrant and working-class populations in the region. The mandarin's son from Annam had become a truly global revolutionary, helping to spread communism not only to Indochina, but also to other parts of Asia.[26]

Like the Vietnamese Nationalist Party had done, the Indochinese Communist Party encountered stiff colonial surveillance inside and outside Indochina. And like their nationalist competitors, the communists also had a penchant for brash, violent action. Encouraged by the Chinese communist creation of revolutionary Soviets to the north and convinced that rural suffering was peaking under the Great Depression, the ICP helped organize peasant revolts in Nghe An and Ha Tinh provinces, briefly establishing a dozen Soviets of their own. Revolts also broke out among workers on the Phu Rieng rubber plantation in Cochinchina and strikes occurred in urban centers in central and southern Vietnam. In all, the French counted 125 peasant demonstrations in thirteen of colonial Vietnam's twenty-one provinces. The French cracked down brutally. In a sign of things to come, Pasquier authorized the air force to bomb protesters at the cost of hundreds, perhaps thousands, of civilian lives. In Nghe Tinh province alone, 3,000 peasants may have perished. And disgruntled First World War veterans were involved, too.[27]

In all, French repression in 1930–31 was such that it destroyed the Vietnamese Nationalist Party and effectively pushed the center of gravity of the nascent Vietnamese communist movement toward Cochinchina and its surrounding Asian bases. Massive colonial arrests also concentrated Vietnamese communists and nationalists in prisons, most notably on the island of Poulo Condor. Paradoxically, rather than disrupting communist ties, the French reinforced them by placing militants from all over the country in a national microcosm behind bars. Like Catholic missionaries imprisoned by the Nguyen, communist prisoners organized meticulous ideological training sessions, deepened their universal faith, and forged some of the most important bonds upon which the future communist party state would turn. It was also in colonial prisons that tensions between Vietnamese communists and nationalists turned violent for the first time. For the communists, internationalism and nationalism went together. For many in the Vietnamese Nationalist Party, however, communism was a foreign ideology that had to be combatted as fiercely as colonialism. When communists stepped up their efforts to convert VNQDD leaders to this new faith, fistfights occurred in cellblocks, adumbrating civil wars to come and mirroring the one that was already ripping apart southern China. Vietnamese communism, anticommunism, and nationalism were to mix violently long before French colonialism collapsed. And again, by attempting to destroy anticommunist nationalism because of its anticolonialism, the French only strengthened the communist hand.

Unlike in 1908, the French republican reaction to the revolts of 1930–31 did not lead to any immediate liberalization of colonial policy. In fact, much the opposite occurred. In tandem with his repressive policies, Pasquier joined forces with Sarraut in Paris to return their colonial emperor, Bao Dai, to Hue as quickly as possible. (The French government had sent him to France in the 1920s for his formal education.) Rather than create an Indochinese congress to coopt anticolonialists as the British were doing in India, Pasquier and Sarraut sought to resurrect the monarchy. In a private letter to Pasquier in 1932, Sarraut insisted that the governor general had to mobilize the young emperor (and the mandate of heaven he incarnated) in order to rally the people against those who would turn the peasants against the French. 'I tell you all this, my dear Pasquier, with considerable emotion, for I cannot reconcile myself to the thought that we might bungle the experience we are creating with him [Bao Dai . . .]. We must protect his person, we must protect his authority.' No sooner had Bao Dai returned to Annam in September 1932 than Pasquier sent him on a series of carefully orchestrated imperial tours to areas recently shaken by strikes and revolts. Like Sarraut, Pasquier was convinced that the peasants in revolt remained innately conservative and deeply attached to their young emperor. By bringing him out of the palace and sending him toward the 'people', Pasquier and Sarraut were convinced that they, not their Vietnamese opponents, could maintain the support of the 'masses'.[28]

The Minister of the Colonies, Paul Reynaud, backed the Bao Dai 'experiment'. He agreed, too, that a carefully controlled rejuvenation of the monarchy would allow the French to win over the support of some of their most faithful collaborators calling for political change. In 1931, during Reynaud's visit to Indochina, Pham Quynh implored the minister to grant the Vietnamese at least one reform: the right to create a 'Vietnamese kingdom with a modern constitution within an Indochinese state endowed with an appropriate federal charter, under the guidance of France—that, [Your] Excellency, is a reform [. . .] which fully answers our intimate national demands'.[29]

No such federation emerged, but the French did agree to allow the reform-minded Bao Dai to head up a royalist government for Annam in 1933 in tandem with their trusted ally, Pham Quynh, and a young Catholic reformist governor from Phan Thiet named Ngo Dinh Diem. However, when Bao Dai and Diem pushed for some of the real reforms discussed above, including the elaboration of a constitution and the honoring of the protectorate treaty, meaning indirect rule, Pasquier refused. Diem resigned, understanding that the French would not even support an anticommunist Catholic reformist or the constitution-minded emperor if they appeared to call into question colonial rule in the minutest way. When Pasquier died in a plane crash in 1934, Diem focused on his religious activities while the emperor retreated into the forest on hunting trips rather than playing the walk-on part of a collaborator. The first Bao Dai solution was stillborn. The French trusted no one.[30]

THE LIMITS OF COLONIAL DEMOCRACY:
ACT II. THE POPULAR FRONT

Colonial conservatism seemed to recede with Pasquier's death in 1934 and the rise of another leftwing coalition government in France (1936-8), known as the Popular Front. Vietnamese nationalists ranging from the Constitutionalists to the communists felt that a ruling government of socialists, communists, and leftist republicans in France would finally push through the reforms so many had wanted since the turn of the century. The Popular Front's leader, Léon Blum, reinforced such expectations when he presided over major reforms in France, including the right to collective bargaining, annual leave for workers, and the forty-hour working week. Blum's nomination of Maurice Moutet to run the Ministry of Colonies provided hope that change just might happen. This was the man who had dared to defend Phan Chu Trinh.[31]

The far left in Cochinchina was particularly well placed to take advantage of the French Popular Front. The relaxation of colonial repression in Indochina under the Popular Front certainly helped radicals rebuild in all of Vietnam. But the French destruction of nationalist and communist networks in Annam and Tonkin in the early 1930s under Pasquier had shifted radicalism's center of gravity firmly to the south. There, starting in 1934, a remarkably active group of French-trained Trotskyists and communists, allied with none other than Nguyen An Ninh, did the two things Cochinchinese law allowed them to do more easily than in the northern protectorates: establish political newspapers in French and run candidates for office in the Colonial Council of Cochinchina against the Constitutionalists. They did both things extremely well for the next five years. Ninh led the charge again by creating the landmark militant paper *La Lutte* (*The Struggle*). In it, he and his radical allies focused squarely on the plight of the urban poor, the workers, and peasant laborers. By this time, the Vietnamese working class numbered around one million underpaid laborers, concentrated in the south. Secondly, the *La Lutte* group successfully ran its candidates against the Constitutionalists and gained them places on the Colonial Council and in the Saigon municipal elections, determined to expand their influence through these institutions (and with the support of the urban working class). Lastly, the shift in the Comintern's line to united-front tactics following Hitler's rise to power in 1933 condoned the Indochinese Communist Party's participation in the French Popular Front, so much so that Stalinists and Trotskyists could not only operate legally in Indochina, but they were able, briefly, to join forces (unthinkable anywhere else in the communist world to my knowledge!) before later turning on each other violently.

The advent of the Popular Front in 1936 reinforced *La Lutte*'s reform program and encouraged the Vietnamese left to embrace colonial democracy, despite its limitations. The model rapidly spread northward as the Blum government loosened restrictions on publishing in the protectorates of Annam and Tonkin and released a large number of political prisoners, both communists and non-communists. Communists in particular (there were hardly any Trotskyists outside Cochinchina) created the newspaper *Le Travail* (*Labor*) in Hanoi, which soon attracted the participation of Vo

Nguyen Giap and Truong Chinh, the Indochinese Communist Party's future military commander and secretary general. Inspired by the *Lutteurs*, northerners organized for their own candidates to run in the municipal elections in Hanoi.

Non-communist republicans associated with Nhat Linh, Hoang Dao, and Khai Hung's 'Literary Self-strengthening Movement' (Tu Luc Van Doan or TLVD [for more detail, see chapter 12]) also supported candidates for the Hanoi city council and the people's chamber of Tonkin. Admirers of the legendary socialist Jean Jaurès, Nhat Linh and Khai Hung supported SFIO candidates, while the local branch run by Louis Caput opened its doors to Vietnamese members, like Hoang Minh Giam, for the first time. Vietnamese across the left (and not just communists) believed that the Popular Front coalition government in power in France would finally implement major social legislation and expand democratic institutions, including the freedom of the press and the extension of the Cochinchinese Colonial Council to all of Indochina (instead of the consultative people's chambers in Annam and Tonkin). Vietnamese non-communists were probably also hoping that the transition to a democratic socialist-minded state would prevent the increasingly powerful communists from creating a potential dictatorship, as in the Soviet Union.

The Blum government seemed to be open to major reform when it announced the dispatch of a special Inspection Commission for the Colonies (Commission d'enquête dans les colonies). In response, the *Lutteurs*, Constitutionalists, those belonging to the Literary Self-strengthening Movement, the Indochinese Communist Party, and others formed an Indochinese Congress to investigate, organize, and eventually submit a wide range of reforms to the government. Initiated by the *Lutteurs*, the congress operated thanks to a collection of 'action committees' whose leaders dispersed across the colony to identify problems and propose *cahiers de voeux*, first draft reform proposals. While it was not a political party, the congress associated disparate social and political actors from all over Indochina for the first time. It also moved the thinking of the urban elite into the countryside.

During its short lifespan, the Popular Front introduced some major social reforms, including the approval of a labor code and an increase in workers' salaries. But in the end, the Popular Front failed to implement any significant political reforms. It did not expand representative institutions or create the Indochinese federation promised by Sarraut and his acolytes. The question of further enfranchising the native population remained a dead letter, despite the fact that the Indian Congress had achieved one of its greatest victories in 1937 by running candidates successfully in provincial elections. That the French leftist ruling class was incapable of even moderate political reform was clear when Marius Moutet, Minister of Colonies, ordered the closing of the Indochinese Congress in September 1936 and, when that failed to slow things down, authorized the incarceration a year later of many of the very Vietnamese who had once welcomed his governor general, Jules Brévié, into power with fists clenched in the air as a sign of Leftist solidarity. The Third Republic had squandered its last chance to make good on colonial reformism along the lines used by the British or the Americans who had just promised Filipinos a 'commonwealth' as a better way of indirectly maintaining an empire. Already, in 1931, a well-informed French police inspector warned his superiors that they 'no longer have anyone with us'.

> The mandarins, to whom we have only ever given an insufficient moral and material position, serve us only out of prudence, and anyway cannot do very much. The bourgeoisie probably does not want communism, but it still considers that it could be—as in China—put to excellent use externally, even if it is worthless internally. The educated youth is entirely against us, as is the immense and miserable population of workers and peasants. Truly, something more than simple repression is needed here. It is undoubtedly necessary to reform the material order. But it is no less necessary and urgent to restore calm to people's souls. For that, it is necessary to govern and not be content with shortsighted administration. The reforms needed must be carried out immediately.[32]

French decision-makers, whether conservatives like Cognacq and Pasquier, or liberal humanists like Sarraut and Moutet, clearly had excellent intelligence services and analysis at their disposal. The problem was not there. The problem was the inability of republican officials across the political spectrum to grasp the importance of implementing the moderate political reforms requested by Phan Chu Trinh in 1907, suggested by Théophile Pennequin in 1911, and promised by Albert Sarraut in 1919, if only to hold off decolonization or to allow it to proceed on terms favorable to the French. This closing of the French official mind—despite the fact that French public opinion showed little real interest in empire—would have disastrous consequences for the Vietnamese people during the rest of the twentieth century.[33]

CHAPTER 6

COLONIAL SOCIETY
AND ECONOMY

IN FEBRUARY 1936 there was a semi-final match of the Bédier football tournament in Vientiane, Laos. The mainly Vietnamese Amusporta club was playing the Lao Police Sport. The winners would go on to compete for the championship title. Supporters from the large Vietnamese community were there; but mainly Lao fans filled the stands, including some of the country's best-known elite and royal family members. Things got ugly when a Vietnamese player carded by the Lao referee protested vehemently, outraging Lao fans. A few punches apparently flew before the Vietnamese forfeited the game and quickly disappeared.

The issue was not over though; it continued in the press for several more weeks. One anonymous Vietnamese spectator wrote in to criticize the Lao referee for bad officiating. He accused certain Lao authorities in the stands of inciting their fans to attack the Vietnamese players, to 'beat them senseless' and 'kill them'. The referee, Thao Bong, shot back that he had done his best to control a very physical match and did not want to 'deepen the rift already dug by certain of your compatriots between the Annamese and Laotians'. Lao fans, he added, had not appreciated the wild gesticulating one Vietnamese player had demonstrated before them earlier in the match.[1]

There was nothing exceptional about this match between the Vietnamese and the Lao. In Cochinchina, football games had become so physical after the First World War that the sporting commission temporarily banned matches between the French and the Vietnamese. But that did not stop teams and their supporters from organizing their own meetings, often with the Vietnamese playing on French teams for lack of players. We know that the Lao Police Sport team was only 'four-fifths aboriginal' (i.e. four-fifths Laotian). The rest were certainly Tonkinese, Annamese, or Cochinchinese. In the 1920s, French players even lifted their glasses in Saigon to honor a deceased Vietnamese comrade. Football matches generate racist, nationalist, and violent exchanges; but they can also produce moments of intense personal joy and fraternization. Vietnam, colonial or not, was no exception.

But perhaps more than anything else, this small incident revealed the extent to which an Indochinese-wide colonial state had begun to circulate and connect diverse peoples in ways never dreamed by Minh Mang or his imperial-minded Vietnamese predecessors. Playing against each other in countless unreported matches in Vientiane were ethnic Viet and Lao civil servants, police officers, tax collectors, and of course their children. Vietnamese played with and against Chinese, Indian, and Khmer players throughout the Mekong delta. The French had built the roads connecting Laos and Cambodia to Vietnam, which would move the Vietnamese to Vientiane and Phnom Penh to push pencils. But with increased colonial connections came frictions. When the Lao fans rushed on to the pitch in 1936, the French were preparing a law to slow down Viet immigration to Laos. And just as Lao and Khmer elites demanded control of Viet immigration in their countries, the Vietnamese were trying to end the privileged positions of the Chinese and the Indians in eastern Indochina.

COLONIAL ECONOMY

As new as these Asian movements were, the French did not start with a *tabula rasa* when they conquered Indochina in the late nineteenth century. In Vietnam, they grafted many of their policies on to pre-existing ones—land registry systems, taxation schemes, opium, alcohol and salt monopolies, *corvée* practices, and canal, dike, and irrigation networks. Organizing Chinese immigration was certainly no French creation. And while the French amplified Vietnam's trading relations with Asia, they did not connect Vietnam to the outside world for the first time. The Cham, Highlanders, Viet, Chinese, Japanese, Arabs, Persians, Indians, Thai, and Portuguese had already done this. The French did, however, accelerate and expand this process. They invested deeply in their Indochinese colony between 1862 and 1954, and it mattered. Between 1888 and 1918 alone, the metropolis poured 249 million gold francs into industry and mining in Indochina, 128 million into transportation, 75 million into commerce, and 40 million into agricultural development. In so doing, the French initiated important economic and social changes, essential to understanding modern Vietnam.[2]

Infrastructure and Transports

Infrastructure development is a case in point. The French built on, expanded, and transformed pre-existing infrastructure and roads. They built new ones. The Nguyen had first built the mandarin route in the early nineteenth century to consolidate their administrative hold on a still contested and deeply divided Vietnam. This road circulated civil servants from one end of the country to the other and helped improve commercial exchanges. The French paved it over with the Route Coloniale (RC) no. 1 for much the same reasons. But they went further, by creating a network of asphalted roads and secondary gravel ones linking rural areas to urban centers. They also connected Vietnam to Laos and Cambodia as never before. In 1943, French Indochina boasted 32,000 kilometers of practicable roads, of which 5,700 kilometers were asphalted. Eighteen thousand vehicles, cars, buses, and trucks buzzed down these roads, by the end of the 1930s transporting an estimated forty to fifty million people annually. The image one Frenchman evoked of a bus moving people down the road is a memorable one: 'It's like a piece of the local market, a particularly concentrated one, that starts moving down the road: men, women, baskets, pigs, birds, shouts, smells, betel spit. It's all there, people pouring out of the [bus's] windows, pressed to its hood and making up its human roof . . .'[3]

Bourgeois Vietnamese purchased their own cars. Then, as now, automobiles were the visible markers of social success and racial equality with the colonizers. Nguyen Phan Long, a well-known journalist, politician, and landowner, loved to show off his collection of automobiles and travelled widely throughout Indochina in the 1920s. The future novelist Marguerite Duras loved pretty cars too, but she found herself shunned by French students in her high school when they saw her beau behind the wheel—'Unfortunately Léo was Annamese, despite his wonderful car'. With better transport, modern tourism emerged. And as it did, French, European, Asian, and Vietnamese travelers discovered Indochina's marvels, including Angkor Wat, thanks in no small part to the Madrolle travel guides they often carried with them. Perceptions of time and space changed as people moved in new ways and at faster speeds. One young Vietnamese civil servant travelling through the highlands in the early 1930s put his finger on something important when he admitted: 'It's Annam, but it's not Annam. I don't know quite how to explain it. One doesn't quite feel Annamese in the Highlands'. Perhaps it was because this world had never been so 'Vietnamese'. The cooler weather of the highlands attracted French settlers and civil servants, who, together with Vietnamese laborers, turned Dalat into a hill station and vacation spot for those seeking shelter from the heat and forests to rest or hunt wild game. Gardens around Dalat also began producing and exporting to all of Vietnam a wide variety of fruits and vegetables previously unknown to the country, such as strawberries.[4]

The emergence of a modern rail system also circulated products and people and connected territories in new ways, but not necessarily in Vietnamese or Indochinese ways. Indeed, French capital investment, colonial strategists, and the Bank of Indochina first laid tracks from Hanoi to Kunming (1901–11) as part of the grand design to create a French sphere of influence in southern China. The French also constructed rail segments in Cambodia, Cochinchina, and Annam. Passenger cars moved millions of people and created a new group of railway workers from whom another communist party secretary would come, Le Duan. While the Thais pushed their railways toward the Mekong in the 1920s in order to pull Lao and Cambodians toward Bangkok, the French relied on their network of roads to bind eastern and western Indochina together. Colonial routes 6 and 13 cut from Hanoi to Saigon via the Mekong valley. To this day, no railroad traverses the Mekong valley.[5]

Fluvial transportation expanded greatly in the Red River and Mekong deltas. In 1881, the River Transport Company for Cochinchina (the Messageries Fluviales de Cochinchine) began operations in the Mekong, offering transport from Saigon-Cholon to Vientiane by the turn of the century. By 1930, this company operated 200 steam-powered longboats (*chaloupes*). Similar boats and small barges chugged up the Red River to Lao Cai; others passed through secondary branches. In all, in 1928, 2,600 vessels measuring 16 tons or more, 191 longboats, and 21 motorized barges weighing between 50 and 350 tons plied Indochinese waterways and estuaries. By the 1930s, outboard motors propelled vessels at greater speeds, stuffed with all sorts of goods, grains, animals, and people. Meanwhile, along Vietnam's long coastline (3,260 km), the Chinese junk trade continued moving rice, animals, and people from one place to another, carrying on to Guangzhou and Bangkok. Already in 1864, 25,000 mainly Chinese skippers were operating junks transporting rice from the Mekong delta to hungry mouths in northern Vietnam and southern China. And until the Second World War, Chinese-operated junks along the littoral remained the cheapest and fastest way for moving rice from Cochinchina to Tonkin. The French only connected Hanoi to Saigon by rail in 1936.[6]

The French improved on and expanded the number of Vietnamese canals on which so much of the rice production depended for irrigation and
transportation. By 1930, the French had constructed 4,000 km of new canals in the Mekong, improving irrigation and lowering transportation costs.
This canal network allowed Chinese merchants in particular to move rice
from paddies deep within the delta to their steam-powered mills in Cholon.
In the northern and central parts of the country, the French improved upon
pre-existing dikes to protect double-cropping rice growing areas against
devastating floods and the famines that almost always followed in their
wake. New dikes helped protect 115 million hectares of crop-growing land
in 1945 (up from 20 million in 1885), while new canals brought water to
parched areas of Annam.[7]

The twin cities of Saigon and Cholon had already become the most important Vietnamese port under the Nguyen. While Saigon never became
a French Hong Kong, the French dredged and widened its harbor and
created a separate deep-water port in Cam Ranh Bay, making it France's
preeminent forward base in East Asia. Maritime routes linked Indochinese
ports to the French concession in Shanghai and their establishments in
Pondicherry and then on to Marseille via the Suez Canal (opened in 1869).
By the end of the 1930s, the rice and rubber trade made Saigon-Cholon
France's sixth most important port, handling a total traffic of 2.1 million
tons of merchandise in 1937. The French also transformed Haiphong into
a vibrant port, linking it overland to nearby mines and using this northern outlet to connect the Gulf of Tonkin to southern China, thanks to the
Yunnanese railway line running to Kunming. These colonial, private, and
strategic investments in infrastructure, transportation, and ports contributed greatly to the economic development of Vietnam and its geopolitical
importance. It's no accident that Russian war ships gathered in Cam Ranh
Bay before being defeated by the Japanese at the Battle of Tsushima in 1905.
The Japanese would concentrate their ships in the same deep-water port
before attacking Southeast Asia in 1942. The Americans stationed the bulk
of their naval forces in Cam Ranh Bay during the Vietnam War before the
Soviets took over during the Third Indochina War.[8]

Commercial Rice Expansion: Asian Modernity
at Work in French Indochina

The rice trade constitutes one of the most important components of
the Vietnamese economy to this day. While the colonial infrastructure

improvements mentioned above certainly helped make Vietnam the third most important rice exporter in the world after Thailand and Burma before 1940 (and second only to Thailand today), the Chinese and the Vietnamese operated this sector of the economy. The French found it much more convenient and profitable to let Chinese intermediaries continue collecting, milling, and exporting rice grown by mainly Vietnamese farmers in the Mekong delta. After all, the French settlers were a miniscule population of 35,000 individuals. Most of them lived and worked in urban centers and those who lived in the countryside were mainly involved in growing rubber, coffee, and tea. The overwhelming majority of those opening new rice plantations in the south were Vietnamese landowners (many of whom had first gained their land under the Nguyen) and tens of thousands of poor Vietnamese agricultural laborers and newly arrived immigrants hoping to eke out a better living. The opening of more southern land under the French from 1900 and increased demands for agricultural laborers attracted more Vietnamese from the overpopulated north and center, as did the promise of a better future. The French did anything but slow a centuries-old flow of ethnic Viet toward the south. They accelerated it, not least of all by increasing the Vietnamese birth rate via better health care and hygiene. The southern population increased from 2.2 million in 1895 (1.7 million in 1880) to 2.8 million in 1900 and 5.6 million in 1943.[9]

The French taxed the prosperous rice trade and provided financial and technological support to Chinese and Vietnamese merchants and growers. Loans were forthcoming and steam-operated mills rapidly replaced older methods. The amount of land under cultivation increased from 700,000 hectares in 1880 to 1.2 million hectares in 1900, and 2.2 million hectares in 1930. Rice exports increased accordingly from 130,000 tons in 1870 to 1,797,000 tons in 1928, before dropping off to 1 million in the depressed economy of 1933. In northern Vietnam, where there was little more virgin land to open up, the French expanded hydraulic works to water double-cropped fields and expanded the dikes to protect them against flooding. The basic subsistence of the population in Annam and Tonkin depended on these capital investments as well as imports of Cochinchinese rice, as the terrible famine of 1944–5 would demonstrate. The population of Tonkin grew from a total of 6.2 million people in 1886 to almost 10 million in 1943. In Annam, the number grew from 5.5 million in 1911 to 7.2 million in 1943. In all, the Vietnamese population grew from 14.7 million in 1921 to 22.6 million in 1943.[10]

Those benefitting from the lucrative rice trade were not those laboring in the fields, but rather the Chinese merchants, Vietnamese landowners, and the colonial state which taxed both. In 1938, big landowners held 45 percent of the Mekong rice land, 42.5 percent went to medium-sized plantations, and small landowners held only 12.5 percent of rice-growing land. Harder to establish is the size of a floating rural labor force; but it surely numbered in tens of thousands. The French did little to stop the concentration of land from being mainly in the hands of wealthy landowners (a pattern which dated from Nguyen times), while metropolitan interests blocked the industrialization of Indochina and the chance to create urban factory jobs to absorb the rural unemployed. The French never seriously considered implementing land reform. Nor did any of the Vietnamese in the Cochinchinese Colonial Council, many of them large landowners like Nguyen Phan Long and Nguyen Van Thinh, see any reason to insist on it. And in the absence of real political parties or a truly representative parliamentary body through which the majority peasant population could elect officials, there was little chance of passing even minor land reform laws.[11]

The Development of the Colonial Plantation Economy

If Asians dominated the commercial rice economy, the French ran the lucrative rubber plantations. By the turn of the twentieth century, processed rubber, known as latex, was used in the production of a wide variety of commercial products, many of them industrially produced, such as erasers, boots, gloves, conveyor belts, and, increasingly, tires. Brazil was the original home of rubber trees (*hevea brasiliensis*) until the British got hold of seeds in the 1870s and began growing their own trees in London laboratories and then in their colonies in Africa, India, and Southeast Asia. In the early 1890s, French scientists working at the Botanical Gardens in Saigon obtained specimens from the British in Malaya and the Dutch in Indonesia and rapidly confirmed that rubber trees could grow in Cochinchina and Cambodia. Meanwhile, industrial demand for rubber in France increased steadily. The Michelin brothers created their rubber factory there in 1888 and patented the original removable pneumatic tire three years later, first for bicycles and then cars.

Attracted by the growing demand for rubber, private individuals and companies began planting rubber trees near Saigon. Plantations soon emerged throughout the basalt-rich red soil or *terres rouges* of Cochinchina,

Cambodia, and southern Annam, including the surrounding highlands. As world demand for processed rubber increased even more after 1918, metropolitan capital was invested heavily in the development of large French plantations, which by 1930 controlled over 90 percent of the *terres rouges*. Firms like Michelin, Groupe Rivaud, and the Bank of Indochina held majority stakes in the commercial rubber economy, buying up land, clearing it and investing in the expensive machinery needed to transform raw rubber into latex. The amount of land devoted to rubber production increased from 200 hectares in 1908 to 126,000 hectares in 1940, making French Indochina (by the late 1920s) the third largest rubber exporter after British Malaya and the Dutch East Indies. During the boom years of the 1920s, French plantations and the firms invested in them made enormous profits. Michelin owned and operated its own plantation at Phu Do Rieng.[12]

Like the commercial rice economy, the rubber plantations ran on cheap, mainly ethnic Viet sweat. In collaboration with colonial authorities, plantation owners organized the recruiting and transportation of many northern Vietnamese to work on southern plantations. In 1942, some 133,000 mainly ethnic Viet laborers toiled on rubber plantations in Cambodia and Cochinchina. Twelve-hour days were common. Pay was pitifully low and housing conditions miserable. While it is true that infirmaries and health care were introduced to ensure healthy (thus operational) bodies, independent oversight was lacking. Plantation owners tended to be all-powerful. Abuses were legion and death from exhaustion and mistreatment was common. Many workers returned to Annam and Tonkin at the end of their contracts. Others stayed on in the south, while some fled from their bosses at great personal peril. Tran Tu Binh, a dirt-poor Catholic from the north, signed a contract that took him to work in this 'hell on earth', the Michelin plantation in the Phu Do Rieng. He later became a top-ranking communist and published a damning, if highly politicized, account of the life of Vietnamese laborers: 'Oh, it's easy to go to the rubber and hard to return. Men leave their corpses, women depart as ghosts'.[13]

Other types of plantation crops emerged, too. While the Chinese had long commercialized sugar cane and pepper production in southern Indochina, the French developed coffee production in Tonkin with the introduction of Arabica trees in 1888. From there, the French and a handful of Vietnamese growers spread coffee plants to other areas of the highlands, where they do well to this day. By 1930, Arabica plants dotted over 10,000 hectares of land were producing 1,500 tons of coffee for annual export. By 1940, that number had increased to 2,900 tons, of which 2,000 tons went abroad. The remaining 900 tons went on domestic consumption, as more and more mainly urban Vietnamese took to drinking coffee for the first time. Starting with vigor after the First World War, the French introduced tea plants to the red soils of southern Annam, especially in the Kontum, Pleiku, and Darlac provinces. On the eve of the Second World War, 3,000 hectares of land produced tea leaves. While French and increasingly Vietnamese producers never competed seriously with the Chinese or British at the international level, they nevertheless sold 812 tons of black tea to the metropole and their North African colonies.[14]

The French exploited large mineral reserves and coalfields located in northern Indochina. The industrialization of Japan as well as internationally financed coastal enclaves in southern China increased the demand for coal to fire steam-operated plants. The port of Haiphong was located near these fields and coal and minerals moved by train to Haiphong and from there to Asian markets by ship. The Bank of Indochina mobilized much of the investment funds needed to get these capital-intensive commercial enterprises up and running. In 1888, the French Society for Tonkin Coal (Société française des Charbonnages du Tonkin) received a license to exploit the coalfields in Hong Cai and Dong Trieu, joined by the Dong Trieu Coal Council (Charbonnages de Dong Trieu) in 1916. By the early 1900s, French Indochina exported 200,000 tons of coal. This increased to almost two million tons by 1940, making Indochina the biggest coal exporter in Asia after Japanese Manchuria. The French exploited other minerals commercially, including zinc and silver in Tonkin and Laos. Chinese, Viet, and non-Viet highlanders worked as laborers in the coalfields of Tonkin and Laos. The future General Nguyen Binh would recruit his first soldiers from the Tonkin coalfields in mid-1945. Tran Quoc Hoan, the future head of communist Vietnam's security forces, joined the party while working in Lao silver mines in the early 1930s. The Indochinese mining proletariat tended to be ethnically Viet.[15]

An Economic Federation and the Bank of Indochina

Upon conquering all of Vietnam in the 1880s, the French created a centralized state based in Hanoi and referred to it as the Indochinese Union. While this colonial state was a heterogeneous entity in so many ways, on the economic front it was a remarkably integrated customs, monetary, and budgetary union. Paul Doumer empowered the governor general to elaborate and submit one budget for all of Indochina, the General Budget for the Indochinese Union (Budget général de l'Union indochinoise). The colonial state also imposed one common tariff for all of Indochina's component parts. There were no internal prerogatives or exceptions, not even for Cochinchina. The Indochinese *piastre* served as the entire colony's currency from 1885. Separate currencies for 'Vietnam' or 'Cambodia' did not exist. Only the French could determine the *piastre*'s exchange rate. With a very brief exception after the First World War, the *piastre* remained on the silver standard until 1930. With the Great Depression, the government pegged the Indochinese *piastre* to the French franc at the rate of 1 *piastre* to 10 francs. But in an extraordinary arrangement, the Bank of Indochina, a private commercial bank, issued the *piastre* through its own note-issuing mechanism, the Institut d'émission (a mint).

Created in 1875, the BIC worked closely with the French government underwriting the economic and financial development of French Indochina. While the colonial government generated revenues through a variety of taxes, monopolies, and government loans, the Bank of Indochina also provided major capital investment from its investors and consortium banks for the development of the rice, rubber, and mineral sectors in Indochina. If much has been written about the role of 'gentlemanly capitalism' in the making of the British empire, in Indochina the financial class in France ran the BIC as a privileged consortium, working in alliance with the colonial government, but without having to take orders from it. Besides allowing the Bank of Indochina to issue the *piastre*, in 1888 the government entrusted its reserve funds to it. The bank charged a 2.5 percent interest fee and also had the right to dip into this fund for short-term speculation. And it did. When the Japanese finally overthrew the French in March 1945, the BIC held 200 million *piastres* of French Indochina's money. The Japanese were as careful as the French to respect this bank's autonomy in order to keep the colony up and running. Even the Vietnamese who took over during the August Revolution left the Bank of Indochina and its reserves in place, which was considered by some to have been a colossal mistake (though it's uncertain the Japanese would have let Vietnamese revolutionaries get anywhere near this bank, had they tried to take it over).

When the Great Depression struck the world economy and with it, Indochina, the BIC absorbed bankrupt companies, plantations, and real estate through its subsidiaries, the Indochinese Land Bank (Crédit foncier indochinois) and the Indochinese Real Estate Office (Société immobilière indochinoise). The Bank of Indochina had become a formidable financial and real estate powerhouse by the 1930s. The Vietnamese were not the only ones to deplore the BIC's seemingly unchecked power. Marguerite Duras railed in her semi-autobiographical novel, *The Sea Wall*, against the bank's confiscation of European settler lands and homes. Indeed, the Bank of Indochina made no distinctions based on race in confiscating the property of those who defaulted on loans they had taken out in the golden days of the 1920s. The BIC went on to expand its interests and those of its stockholders through investments in Asia, especially in China, and then across the globe. Supported by a conglomeration of other French banks, in turn supported by the government, the Bank of Indochina became one of France's biggest banks.

Vietnamese nationalists were well aware of the colonial hold over the economy and the *piastre indochinoise* in particular. This is why the independent government led by Ho Chi Minh from mid-1945 onward went to such great lengths to issue its own independent currency, the *dong*. The French, meanwhile, held out tooth and nail against Bao Dai's efforts to liberate his country's currency from the French *and* the BIC (see chapter 10), and attacked Ho Chi Minh's currency during the Indochina War. The French infuriated their nationalist partners in mid-1953 when the metropolitan government unilaterally decided to devaluate the *piastre* without consulting them. The French only truly let go of Indochina in December 1955, when they agreed to close the Bank of Indochina's Institut d'émission and stop printing the Indochinese *piastre* for good.

COLONIAL SOCIETY

Diversity, Tensions, and Interactions

The Indochinese Union of 1887 turned on a collection of protectorates, colonies, military territories, special urban regimes, and a mindboggling number of legal identities for different peoples, living at different times, in different places of the colonial state. Those residing within the protectorates of Annam and Tonkin, for example, were 'French-protected subjects' (*protégés français*), whereas those living in the Cochinchinese colony were 'French subjects' (*sujets français*). The city of Hanoi was a legal colony within the northern protectorate. Much of the northern highlands were

separate military zones, administered by French officers, whereas the central highlands excluded ethnic Viet administrators in favor of French and
highlander civil servants.

The French added to Indochina's ethnic diversity by allowing thousands of their citizens to settle, work, and acquire land there. Those Français
d'Indochine (French Indochinese), as they increasingly styled themselves,
numbered around 35,000 individuals on the eve of the Second World War.
In 1940, 17,000 (mainly) French people resided in Saigon, 6,000 in Hanoi,
and over 2,000 in Haiphong. The rest lived in smaller Indochinese towns.
While French women arrived in greater numbers around 1900, the French
colonial population was predominantly masculine. Most of the Français
d'Indochine were civil servants or officers in the colonial army. Perhaps a
thousand worked in the cities as traders, businessmen, and entrepreneurs.
Several thousand were planters, plantation owners, and missionaries scattered across the countryside. Although the French were the smallest ethnic
minority in Indochina, they stood at the top of the colonial ladder. Joining
them were perhaps a hundred Americans, mainly businessmen, diplomats,
and Protestant missionaries. In 1889, the United States appointed a commercial officer to Saigon to represent American interests in Indochina. The
British already had one.[16]

While the French often relied on nineteenth-century racialist theories
to develop their legal categories, they also drew on pre-existing classifi-
cation systems that had little to do with race and everything to do with
the everyday practicalities of ruling diverse peoples. For one, the French
maintained the Nguyen dynasty's congregation system (*bang*) for administering the large Chinese populations, numbering almost a half a million
by the 1920s. This regime required Chinese immigrants to belong to one of
the following 'congregations' or 'groups' which would correspond to their
dialect or initial place of residence in southern China—Guangzhou (Canton), Fujian, Hakka, Hainan, and Chaozhou. In 1871, the French adopted
and even expanded the congregation system in order to administer other
immigrant groups such as the Indians. Rather than collapsing the Chinese
identity and making them into 'Cochinchinese subjects' (the Chinese were
concentrated in the south), the French classified them as 'Asian foreigners'
(*Etrangers asiatiques*) in 1864, and again in 1871. Legal Chinese residents
could own property, open businesses, and work; but they also paid a much
higher tax rate. There was again continuity between the Nguyen and French
imperial regimes, with revenue generation being a top priority for both.[17]

Like the Chinese, the Japanese had long interacted with Vietnam. In the early seventeenth century, Japanese traders plied the South China Sea, stationing agents in the thriving port city of Hoi An (known then as Faifoo), until Tokugawa leaders restricted such overseas movements. This policy changed in the late nineteenth century when the new Meiji leaders opened up the country, embarked upon rapid industrialization, and allowed their subjects to trade and emigrate. In the late nineteenth century, a few hundred Japanese moved to Saigon, Hanoi, and Haiphong. Most were prostitutes whose clients were the European soldiers involved in colonial conquest. The First World War changed this, however. Allied with the French against Germany, Tokyo improved its terms of trade and, as it did so, Japanese entrepreneurs, bankers, and businessmen opened offices in Indochina. The first Japanese consulate began operations in Hanoi in 1920. Diplomats immediately ended the prostitution business and focused on promoting commercial interests, with considerable success. And despite persistent fears of the 'yellow peril', the French classified the Japanese living in Indochina as 'Europeans', based on their 'civilizational' parity with the West.[18]

Indians from the French enclave of Pondicherry (and Karikala) emigrated to French Indochina. Most were Christians; some were Hindus and Muslims. Having joined the French empire in the late seventeenth century, Pondicherrians were well versed in French administrative practices and located much closer to Indochina than the metropole. Indeed, Pondicherry had served as the main base from which the French attacked Cochinchina in the late 1850s and recruited many Indians to help them supply and feed the Expeditionary Corps. The French considered these Indian subjects to be more reliable than the recently conquered Cochinchinese (whose administrators had largely abandoned their posts) and recruited French-speaking Indians in the 1860s to help run this new French colony in Asia. More Indians arrived in the 1880s, when legal changes (within the French colonial establishments where they dwelled) allowed those from Pondicherry to become fully fledged French citizens much more easily than their Indochinese counterparts. This, in turn, facilitated inter-empire movements toward Indochina, in which French politicians in Cochinchina solicited Pondicherrian French votes (some said bought them) in the Cochinchinese Colonial Council. By the 1920s, as many as 10,000 Indians resided in Indochina.[19]

Fluent in French, the Pondicherrians worked as magistrates, customs officials, and tax collectors. A handful served as prison guards to watch over mainly ethnic Viet inmates. Others moved into the police as lower and mid-level agents. Indian merchants, shopkeepers, and moneylenders (often referred to pejoratively as 'Chettys' or 'Chettiars') also played an important commercial role in the countryside, lending money and serving as pawnbrokers. They thus interacted with the rural populations and did so in the Vietnamese language. Cochinchinese colonial authorities administered the Indians via congregations, but divided them according to their religion (Christian, Muslim, and Hindu), always noting whether they came from French or British India. The idea that the settler community in colonial Vietnam was *only* French is very misleading.[20]

Even the colonizing population was not quite as homogenous as one might expect. The French Corsican community administered its own papers, language classes, clubs, and sporting events, much like the Cantonese in Saigon or the Irish and Scottish in the British empire. Through such social activities, they maintained their ties to the Ile de Beauté and promoted a separate sense of a Corsican identity. In all, Indochina counted around 1,500 Corsicans during the interwar period. Like the Pondicherrians, they filled a range of positions in the colonial civil service, working as magistrates, policemen, and wardens. Some were shopkeepers. The Franchini family ran the legendary Hôtel Continental in Saigon until 1975. The French from Brittany and Bordeaux also administered separate associations, bulletins, and thus maintained a sense of their original local identities.[21]

This panoply of colonial identities gave rise to some revealing social encounters in daily life. As one testy Pondicherrian reminded the Corsican judge standing before him in a Saigon courtroom one day: '*Monsieur, nous étions français cents ans avant vous*'—'Sir, we were French one hundred years before you'. True, but such moments of inter-imperial pride always cut both ways. Vietnamese elite members, for example, resented the privileged position many Pondicherrians (and Chinese) settlers seemed to hold in the colonial world. How could the French accord citizenship to the Indians, but not to the equally enlightened Vietnamese? Racially minded Vietnamese could not believe that the French would allow such a dark-skinned people to rule them, let alone marry their daughters. As one former Indian resident in Saigon later recalled the Vietnamese putting their case to him: 'The French are the colonizer [*sic*]. But you are the colonized people like we are. How can you work with them to colonize us?'[22]

But the Vietnamese were not always on the losing end of these imperial configurations. In the 1930s, Laotian and Cambodian nationalists asked how the French could use Vietnamese bureaucrats to administer western

Indochina like Minh Mang had done in the 1830s? After all, the French had justified their colonization of Cambodia on the grounds that they were 'saving' the Khmers from Thai and Vietnamese colonization. Modern Laos' first nationalist, Prince Phetsarath, rebuked both the French and the Vietnamese in one quip in 1931: 'First of all, all confidence in French promises fades away and the [idea of the] Indochinese Federation appears to the weakest nations in the [f]ederation like an eye wash designed to allow the Annamese to rule over the others, under the protection of the French flag'. What everyone forgot in making such analogies was that Indochina was an imperial constellation. It turned on precisely such diverse alliances, ethnic heterogeneity, internal colonizations, and social constructions. And where the Vietnamese took the Indians to task for collaborating with the French, the Laotians and Cambodians criticized the Vietnamese for doing the same thing.[23]

None of these nationalist objections among France's colonial subjects, however, stopped interactions from occurring 'among the races'. People crossed borders one after the other, all the while slipping out of one identity into another, as we all do. Cambodian nationalists may have lamented the continued Vietnamese immigration southward and westward under the French, but King Sihanouk's father spoke Vietnamese fluently, while the well-known Cambodian nationalist Dap Chhuon had a Vietnamese wife. Mainly masculine immigration from the late nineteenth century among the Chinese, French, Indian, and Vietnamese settlers (in Laos and Cambodia) led to unions with local women. The Franco-Corsican founder of the Hôtel Continental, Mathieu Franchini, married Le Thi Trong from My Tho province. His son defends Corsica's national identity to this day. The constant flow of European colonial soldiers through the colony from 1858 to 1956 gave rise to a large number of live-in partnerships or *concubinage*. The Vietnamese word for 'girl', *con gai*, rapidly became in colonial parlance a synonym first for a 'concubine', then a 'prostitute'. And though prostitution proliferated in French Saigon and Hanoi, it was by no means the monopoly of European men or the French colonial army. Nor was the problem of venereal disease, as modern Vietnam's greatest writer, Vu Trong Phung, demonstrated in a series of riveting publications.[24]

These relationships produced several thousand Franco-Vietnamese children by the time of the Second World War, referred to in French as *Eurasiens* or *métis*, meaning children of mixed descent. Until the 1930s, European colonial society tended to shun those born out of wedlock, most of whom tended to live with their Vietnamese mothers, far from the 'civilizing' influence of the French community. Vietnamese social norms, especially in the countryside from whence most of these impoverished women came, were often just as intolerant. The fact that many *Eurasiens* were born to unknown fathers also meant that they could not obtain French citizenship easily, making their integration into the French settler society all the more difficult. Opposed to the idea of *métis* children living 'lost' among the 'natives', private and state-sponsored French welfare societies later tried to change this. They scoured the Indochinese countryside, removing dozens of *métis* children, sometimes by force, from their Vietnamese mothers and placed them in orphanages, special military academies, and usually bestowed them with French citizenship.[25]

Eurasiens born of legal unions were usually in a better situation. Not only did they enjoy French citizenship, but they also tended to come from wealthier families, enjoyed higher levels of education, and integrated into the French community much more easily. William Bazé and Henri Chavigny de Lachevrotière, for example, became powerful figures in the settler community, owned property, and ran influential newspapers. Lachevrotière's father had grown up in Quebec and Martinique; his mother was Tonkinese. He and Bazé were indefatigable defenders of the colonial order and of the Français d'Indochine. Of course some *métis* went in the opposite direction. Jean Moreau, the son of a colonial bureaucrat, joined the nationalist movement in 1945 and holds full Vietnamese citizenship to this day. Although no official number exists (colonial authorities refused to create a separate '*métis*' legal category), there were probably around 20,000 *Eurasiens* living in Indochina on the eve of the Second World War, some classified as 'French', others as 'natives', scattered throughout the cities and countryside.[26]

Albeit rarely at the time, French women sometimes married Vietnamese men. The future diplomat-at-large for Ho Chi Minh, Dr Pham Ngoc Thach, married a Parisian medical practitioner, while in 1946 Ho's Catholic minister of economic affairs, Nguyen Manh Ha, wedded the daughter of a man who was a high-level member of the French Communist Party and a deputy in the National Assembly. These couples met in the metropole. Things were different in Indochina, however, where the French settler community tended to disapprove of such unions, convinced that they threatened the racial hierarchy upon which the colonial order rested. When the French classmates of the future novelist Marguerite Duras learned that she was dating a very wealthy Vietnamese boy named Léo, they 'definitively distanced themselves from me. Those who frequented me until then dared no more to compromise themselves in my company'. Colonial society was doubly harsh on Duras, whose poor white (*petit blanc*) family from the countryside placed her at the bottom of the colonial ladder: 'At the time I knew Léo, we were able to get by and pay the Chettys [Indian money-lenders] by selling them each month our only remaining jewelry and furniture. We did this out of sight'.[27]

Though hardly studied, inter-Asian unions vastly outnumbered the Franco-Vietnamese ones, as did their *métis* offspring. And yet there was nothing new about such unions. Almost two thousand years before the French arrived on the scene, Chinese settlers, colonial administrators, and imperial soldiers in the Han Red River delta had married into local families. They and their children played important roles in the making of northern Vietnam and its language. The same was true in the south. The Nguyen lords welcomed those Chinese fleeing the Manchu conquest of the Ming dynasty in 1644. The Vietnamese referred to them as *Minh huong* ('Ming loyalists'). One such refugee, Mac Cuu, first established something of an independent kingdom in the Gulf of Thailand, not far from Ha Tien. His Vietnamese wife gave him a son, Mac Thien Tu, who entered the service of the Nguyen lords, integrated his father's orphaned 'Ming kingdom' into the Nguyen empire, and in so doing helped the Vietnamese expand their territorial control further into the Mekong delta at the expense of the Khmers. The Vietnamese colonizers were no more homogeneous in their colonial practices than the Chinese before them or the French after them.

Although Gia Long, upon uniting Vietnam in 1802, divided the Chinese into congregations in order to control and tax them more effectively, he allowed Chinese men to continue marrying Vietnamese women. However, the Nguyen adopted assimilationist policies toward their children, whom they now classified as *Minh huong*. Upon reaching adulthood, the state required these Sino-Vietnamese children to leave their father's congregation and live among the Vietnamese population, or, for the time being, in special *Minh huong* villages. They could not travel to China to study, nor could they dress in Chinese ways. The Nguyen ensured their collaboration by opening the civil service to them and exempting them from military service. Many occupied high-level positions in the southern administration, as Trinh Hoai Duc did. In so doing, he helped integrate the Mekong delta administratively into modern Vietnam.

Sino-Vietnamese marriages continued under the French, who accelerated Chinese immigration. By 1921, Cochinchina was home to 64,500 (declared) *Minh huong* offspring. A decade later the number reached 73,000, surely an underestimation. The French, however, reversed Nguyen efforts to assimilate *Minh huong* children into the Vietnamese population. They transformed them instead into Foreign Asians and taxed them accordingly, mainly for economic reasons, not racial ones. With the rise of a Vietnamese merchant class at the turn of the twentieth century, budding entrepreneurs like Bach Thai Buoi challenged Chinese commercial influence in shipbuilding. Bourgeois politicians in the Constitutionalist party joined ranks with some of them to organize a boycott of Chinese goods in 1919. Others clamored for the nationalization of these 'Foreign Asians' and '*Minh huong*' into 'Vietnamese citizens'. Neither request went far. Again, this was a colonial state, not a national one.[28]

Things were different in China, which had never lost its formal independence and began to assert its national control over the large overseas populations historically concentrated in Southeast Asia. Starting in 1909, the Qing government insisted that any child born of a Chinese father would become, *jus sanguinis*, a Chinese national, regardless of their place of birth. But it was only in the early 1930s, with the emergence of the Republic of China under Chiang Kai-shek in 1928, that the French finally agreed to sign accords allowing *Minh huong* children to choose their nationality upon reaching their majority. The French also agreed to re-categorize Chinese 'nationals' in Indochina as 'privileged foreigners' and to allow the Republic of China to establish consulates in Vietnam. This was a major legal victory for Chinese republicans, but not for the Vietnamese. Although Ho Chi Minh's government administered Chinese affairs in the territories it controlled during the First Indochina War, the French refused to let their Vietnamese partners do so before 1955.[29]

Most Sino-Vietnamese marriages occurred between Chinese men and Vietnamese women. Unlike their French counterparts, most (but not all) Chinese settlers learned to speak Vietnamese or grew up bilingual, thereby facilitating interactions with the majority lowland Vietnamese population. Relatively few Vietnamese men married Chinese women. However, Vietnamese men going to China to work on the French-supervised Yunnanese Railway or in French colonial offices in Shanghai and Kunming did. This was also true of several Vietnamese anticolonialists who moved to southern China. Ho Chi Minh married a Chinese woman from Guangzhou during his time in China. And Vietnamese immigration to western Indochina and northeast Thailand also produced mixed unions and *métis* children. The father of modern Laos, Kaysone Phoumvihane, was the son of a Vietnamese colonial civil servant and a Laotian mother. Prince Souphanouvong married a Vietnamese woman whom he met as a colonial engineer in Annam in the 1930s. Harkening back to the way that marriage practices were used by Dai Viet leaders to forge alliances with the Cham, Khmer, and Lao, Ho would rely on these Indochinese unions to help build associated states in Laos and Cambodia in the late 1940s (and discussed later on in this book).[30]

The French stamped their presence on cities like Saigon through architecture and urban planning and development. The imposing Palais du Gouverneur (built between 1868 and 75) located on Khoi Nghia Nam Ky Street today was the home of French colonial power until it transferred to Hanoi at the turn of the century. The Bank of Indochina stood in the heart of Saigon, an impressive structure for the time and a testament to its role in building French Indochina. Large avenues soon lined the city, with Rue Catinat (built in 1865) serving as French Saigon's first major artery. A series of French- and Asian-style buildings, shops, and export-import offices quickly appeared. Provençal villas characterized the residential sector of Saigon (and Hanoi) as the European population and the Vietnamese bourgeoisie expanded. The metropolitan architect, Ernest Hébard, gave colonial Saigon greater coherence, combining French and indigenous architectural forms. Though the lines were never strictly drawn, on the eve of the Second World War, French Saigon consisted of a business center, an administrative sector, the French quarter, a Vietnamese one, and a variety of cultural attractions. The French erected colonial monuments, named streets after famous conquerors, and advertised their goods and services in French newspapers and on Radio Saigon.

In daily life, the Vietnamese continued to converse in their native tongue as multilingual Chinese and Indian vendors shifted effortlessly from one language to another. Storefront windows in Cholon's Chinatown announced their goods and menus in characters as a cacophony of southern Chinese dialects resonated from one congregational area to another (the different 'Chinese' used Cantonese or Vietnamese to communicate among themselves). While several Vietnamese merchants continued to use Chinese characters to advertise their goods, especially those practicing traditional medicine, by the 1930s most were moving to the Romanized script, *quoc ngu*.

New social classes emerged in French Vietnam. Although the Chinese continued to dominate the commercial class in Vietnam, a handful of Vietnamese entrepreneurs emerged. Like Bach Thai Buoi, Le Phat Vinh and Truong Van Ben challenged Chinese commercial influence in textiles and rice husking, while Le Van Duc created perhaps the first Vietnamese insurance company. French-employed civil servants, lawyers, translators, and teachers acquired equal status with the members of the mandarin elite they had increasingly sidelined. They had a harder time, however, establishing equality with their French counterparts, whose salaries were almost always higher than the 'native' ones. No Vietnamese person ever became a commissioner at the provincial level, let alone at the regional one, before 1945. Landlordism increased under the French and, unlike in the past, the landlords moved to the cities. In all, an estimated 9,000 rich Vietnamese—mainly landowners and entrepreneurs—lived in urban Vietnam by 1930. Loosely defined, the urban middle class numbered 920,000 individuals.[31]

The rural poor working in French Saigon and Hanoi had it hardest. Dressed shabbily, they lived in rough quarters inside the city and on its outskirts. Their wages were pitifully low and the French outlawed any sort of organized labor. Most came from the countryside and relied on their rural connections to cope with accidents or loss of employment. Many rural migrants found work on construction sites. Others filled a myriad of backbreaking jobs serving as rickshaw drivers, maids, servants ('boys'), cooks ('*bep*'), waiters, waitresses, and street vendors and sweepers. And yet, the rural poor flooding into shantytowns on the outskirts of Saigon and into the Vietnamese quarters were vital to Saigon's takeoff in modernization, as well as its 'Vietnamization'. By the 1930s, a working class had emerged in Vietnam numbering in the hundreds of thousands, most working in urban construction, mining, and on plantations. These workers suffered much more from the economic crisis of 1929 than other classes. And while the Popular Front had introduced some reforms for workers, strikes and trade unions remained illegal.[32]

RELIGIOUS VIETNAM

The almost constant state of war over Vietnam during the second half of the twentieth century has understandably focused attention on the post-1945 period on political, diplomatic, and military matters discussed later on in this book. However, missing from this focus on the wars is the vital importance of religions and religious change during the colonial period. Some of them, like Buddhism, Catholicism, and even the 'political religion' of Confucianism, have roots deep in the past, as we have seen in earlier chapters. Others, like the Hoa Hao, Cao Dai, and Protestant faiths, were as new to Vietnam as communism.

The secularist-minded Third Republic and many of its highest-ranking colonial administrators in Indochina were as wary of organized religions as their Confucian predecessors and communist successors. Ironically, when it came to ruling the eastern half of Indochina, the French preferred to rely on the Confucian-calibrated civil service, even in Cochinchina, when it suited them. Highly influential and powerful colonial administrators like Pierre Pasquier and Léon Pignon were convinced that Confucianism, above all the monarch and his mandarins, was the key to 'understanding' and ruling Vietnam administratively. Confucianism was the 'real' Vietnam. Pasquier, who served in Vietnam for over thirty-five years and worked closely with the monarchy in Hue cast Vietnam as a miniature replica of China. He was convinced that the Confucian 'son of heaven' in Vietnam resonated from on high right down to village level, could be used to maintain order, and, through the intermediary of the person of the emperor, mobilize peasant support for French rule. He admired and promoted the mandarinal administrative system. It is no accident that the 'Bao Dai solution' was the brainchild of this very Confucian French mind. Colonial administrators in Vietnam never attempted to use Mahayana Buddhism, its schools, monastic order, and organizations to administer people and territories as they did Theravada Buddhism in Laos and Cambodia. Nor did they ever come to trust Vietnamese Catholics.[33]

Buddhist Vietnam[34]

Although the French were as distrustful of Buddhism as Minh Mang, they could do little more than he to stop this religion's growth. Local authorities and police informers kept tabs on religious leaders and attitudes and arrested troublesome monks when things seemed to get out of hand. Ironically, the French also contributed to something of a Buddhist revival during the interwar years through the colonial introduction of modern communications (presses, newspapers, and radios), the construction of better roads and means of transportation, and the expansion of *quoc ngu*. Combined, this led to an explosion in the number of Buddhist publications (sutras,

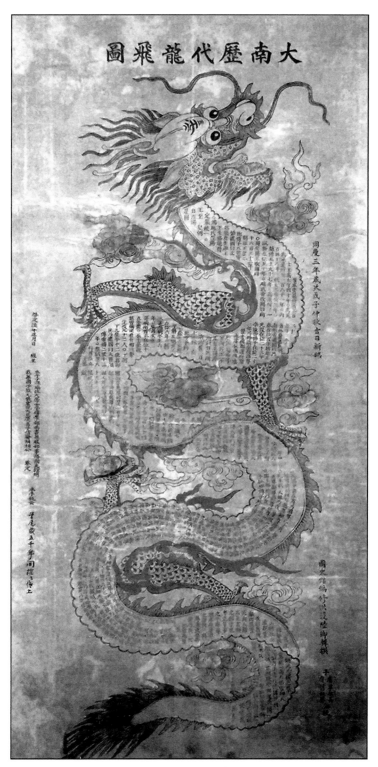

1. A stylized map of Vietnam, from the reign of Minh Mang.

2. Entrance gate to the Imperial City, Hue, Vietnam.

3. Entrance to the tomb of Minh Mang.

4. Two captured Black Flag militiamen, 1885.

5. Arrival in Saigon of Paul Beau, governor-general of Indochina 1902–7, engraving by Charles Georges Dufresne from *Le Petit Journal*, November 1902.

6. Man-Tien women at a market, Upper Tonkin, 1902.

7. Soldiers and trackers posing with the heads of men accused of poisoning French troops, Tonkin, 1908.

8. Inauguration on 6 September 1910 of the memorial to French and Annamese soldiers who died during the 1909 campaign.

9. Exiting the Colonial
Exhibition at Vincennes,
1931: Albert Sarraut (left),
Bao Dai (center), and
Pierre Pasquier (right).

10. Opening of the Colonial Exhibition, Vincennes, 1931. Bao Dai is seated in center.

11. Japanese troops en route to occupy Lang Son, September 1940.

12. Rokuro Suzuki, Japanese Consul.

13. A 1944 official French government brochure on Indochina.

14. A Japanese soldier posts the first proclamation issued by the Allied Control Commission, Saigon, 1945.

15. Vo Nguyen Giap, Jean Sainteny, and General Philippe Leclerc, Hanoi, 17 June 1946.

16. Vo Nguyen Giap and Ho Chi Minh, Battle of Dien Bien Phu, May 1954.

prayer books, and texts) and their transmission to a larger and increasingly literate audience, not just in the cities but also in the countryside, thanks to expanded primary education. This, in turn, reinforced Vietnamese religious efforts to consolidate, organize, and grow the Buddhist faith.

Connections with the Buddhist world outside Indochina also strengthened its renewal inside it. Monks and lay people participated in international congresses and closely followed (through books and papers) Asian efforts to strengthen Buddhism as a spiritual, social, national, and international force. Reform-minded Vietnamese monks were most interested in Chinese efforts to re-tailor Buddhism to the needs of a rapidly changing world. Vietnamese religious leaders devoured Buddhist reformist texts coming from Guangzhou and Shanghai. Highest on their reading list were the writings of the leader of the Buddhist revival movement in China, Taixu (1890–1947). This reformer called for a more human, socially engaged, and modernizing Buddhism. Starting in the 1920s, he urged monks to go toward the people, to tailor Buddhism to their needs, and to those of the nation. The clergy had to energize the church through compassion and social action, he insisted. This could be done through the creation of charitable and relief organizations to help the poor, the orphaned, and the hungry; through the building of religious schools to train novices in the way of the Buddha; and via the establishment of clinics to heal the sick. Reform, Taixu said, also depended on creating a streamlined monastic order, or *sangha*. Only a modern Church could train, control, and administer such a renewed religion at the national level. He discussed all of this in scores of lectures, books, and articles published in China and among the overseas Chinese in Southeast Asia.[35]

Indeed, thanks to Chinese bookstores in Indochina, Vietnamese monks, many of them still quite capable of reading Chinese characters, procured Taixu's writings and translated scores of Chinese Buddhist publications into *quoc ngu*. Taixu's program struck many Vietnamese Buddhists and young reform-minded monks as highly relevant to the situation in Indochina. Monks like Thich Nhat Hanh Do Nam Tu and Thien Chieu embraced Taixu's ideas and began promoting his reforms in a bid to respond to and make sense of the rapid transformation of Vietnamese society and the chronic suffering in the countryside. They found inspiration and models in Taixu's seminal text, *The Reorganization of the Sangha System* (1915). These efforts and others bore fruit during the interwar period, which was symbolized by the establishment of new Buddhist associations: the first for Cochinchina in 1931, the second in Annam a year later, and a third in Tonkin in 1934, each theoretically in charge of provincial chapters. Vietnamese Buddhists developed a host of relief and charity organizations, many of which helped during the great famine of 1944–5. Hundreds of religious schools appeared to train a new generation of monks and nuns in the correct Buddhist canon and practices. Although this restructuring was admittedly easier said than done, by the 1930s a unified and increasingly structured Buddhist Church emerged in Vietnam. Reformers established the Quan Su Temple near the train station in Hanoi, which rapidly became the hub for Buddhism reformism. It is today the home of the Vietnamese National Buddhist Congregation. The French tolerated many of these efforts as long as they remained apolitical, but never had the means in any case to stop their growth locally.[36]

Women played a particularly important role in the development of Buddhism in twentieth-century Vietnam, as they had earlier. They contributed money and donated land to open new monasteries and schools. Many ran the charity organizations. Buddhist schools trained more nuns than ever before in Vietnamese history. The northern nun, Hue Tam, was an ardent supporter of the Buddhist reform movement. In 1935, Nguyen Thi Hai travelled to India to participate in a major Buddhist congress. The renewal of Buddhism was also linked to wider debates over the role of women in the church and in society and the need to create a national and socially sensitive church. Indeed, the revitalization of Buddhism provided the rural poor with a powerful message of liberation and salvation, making it a socio-political force with which to reckon.[37]

The Hoa Hao and Cao Dai Faiths of the Mekong Delta[38]
This was particularly true in the Mekong delta, where Buddhist messianism was at its strongest and had long mixed with a tradition of peasant millennialism and mysticism to produce breakaway schools of faith. Besides being a mosaic of peoples, cultures, and religions, the southern delta had also long been a colonial society where the Nguyen had promoted large-scale private landlordism and plantations. The Nguyen accorded concessions to soldiers and loyal elites, who, in return, would help the imperial hub of power, Hue, control these newly conquered territories. However, this concentration of commercial rice land in the hands of the few also meant that peasant landlessness ran high as the population increased and, with it, the potential for social discontent. In the early 1840s, the acting financial

commissioner for the province of Vinh Long informed the emperor that 70 to 80 percent of the villagers in his province were landless. If families in the Red River delta could turn to communal lands in times of difficulty and owned more than one half of the available farmland there, such publicly shared lands were largely absent in Cochinchina, and farmers owned only one third of the land in the south.[39]

Peasant misery existed elsewhere in Vietnam, to be sure, but when hunger became unbearable in the south, spurring local leaders to action, it did so within a unique socio-cultural context. Self-proclaimed holy men often appeared at this time, as they did in Thailand, Burma, and Cambodia. Several evoked the name of the Buddha messiah Maitreya in order to rally the famished behind them. This savior would create a new kingdom and put an end to suffering on earth. These 'millenarian machines' also mobilized religious support for imminently socio-economic demands—the reduction of taxes, the free sale of agricultural produce, or the cancellation of rural debts. With tens of thousands of desperate peasants standing behind them, they could force the ruling class to listen. In the late 1840s, in the midst of a massive cholera epidemic that killed perhaps as many as a million people, a mystic in the delta, Doan Minh Huyen, initiated a millenarian movement known as the Dao Buu Son Ky Huong (the 'Way of the Strange Fragrance from the Precious Mountain'). Huyen cast himself as a living Buddha, a *maitreya*, sent into the world to end suffering and to bring salvation. Crowds flocked to hear him. Many attributed supernatural powers to him. Others said he could heal the sick. Like the Taiping rebellion threatening to bring down the Qing dynasty in the 1850s to make way for the heavenly kingdom, this Precious Mountain movement worried the court profoundly and pointed up the volatility of the Mekong delta in times of profound socio-economic crisis.[40]

The French did little to alleviate the landlessness problem in the south, where they expanded the plantation system on an unprecedented scale as discussed above in this chapter. Nor did the southern population remain unchanged. It increased from 1.7 million in 1880 to 4.4 million in 1930. Unsurprisingly, the French also had to confront religious mystics leading revolts and trying to build religious kingdoms on waves of peasant anger surging across the delta. Between 1911 and 1913, a southern mystic, Phan Xich Long, launched an intermittent, millenarian rebellion near Saigon-Cholon. He claimed to be the descendent of the rebel emperor, Ham Nghi, whom the French had shipped out of the country in the late 1880s (see chapter 3). He simultaneously cast himself as the 'living Buddha'. He and others like him found support among the rural poor, landless peasants, and disgruntled civil servants. The Phan Xich Long rebellion, though easily smashed, served as a warning to the authorities that these millenarian, mystic-minded leaders could mobilize tens of thousands of people. And these 'living Buddhas' were not as backward or as *fou* ('mad') as secular colonial, nationalist, and communist elites often painted them. They, too, knew how to tap into modern organizational techniques, print media, and use *quoc ngu* to spread their message.[41]

This was certainly true of the Cao Dai faith, founded by Le Van Trung in 1926. Trung inspired a group of Vietnamese civil servants, landowners, and peasants, who were attracted by his messianic message. The two words 'Cao Dai' evoke in Vietnamese the supreme or elevated being, which brings peace, harmony, and salvation to the world. It is called the Dai Dao Tam Ky Pho Do (which translates officially as the 'Way of the Highest Power'). This belief system is hierarchically structured and based organizationally on the model of the Roman Catholic Church. A *'Ho Phap'* ('pope') leads the Cao Dai Church, with its 'Holy See' based in Tay Ninh province located on the Cambodian border.

Like reformist Buddhism, Cao Dai leaders embraced a progressive program calling for greater equality between men and women, closer relations between the landowning and peasant classes, and the belief that colonization was punishment for failing to follow core Cao Dai teachings now located in a faraway past. Pham Cong Tac, a civil servant in Phnom Penh, resigned his post in 1928 and returned to Tay Ninh, the cradle of the religion, to help Trung run the rapidly expanding faith. Following Trung's death in 1935, Pham Cong Tac extended his influence and, in 1938, became the movement's supreme spiritual leader. The Cao Dai faith's embrace of the mystic and the ritualistic attracted a large following in the south. It also tapped into pre-existing religions inside Vietnam, borrowed from foreign ones, and combined them all into a unique faith symbolized by the left eye of God open within the Cao Dai triangle.

The French closely monitored the rapid development of the Cao Dai faith, worried by its social alliances, politicization, and its ability to garner massive support in the countryside. With extraordinary speed, the Cao Dai Church counted between 500,000 and one million believers, out of a total Cochinchinese population of 4.4 million people. During the Second World War, Pham Cong Tac welcomed the chance to expand the faith thanks to the Japanese occupation and the change in the balance of power this promised. Worried by just such a scenario, the French first incarcerated Pham Cong Tac in Vietnam and then shipped him off to Madagascar. This did not stop the expansion of the faith and, following the Japanese overthrow of the French in March 1945, Cao Dai leaders mobilized their armed militias and entered the fray of nationalist politics when the Japanese capitulated a few months later.

Another faith to emerge in the Mekong delta was that of the Hoa Hao. In July 1939, Huynh Phu So, a nineteen-year-old from the village of Hoa Hao in Chau Doc province, revealed during the course of a mystic experience that he was a Buddhist holy man. His mastery of Buddhist teachings impressed all. His charisma was by all accounts electrifying. Those present spoke of his supernatural powers, serenity, and compassion. Even the meaning of his native village 'Hoa Hao'—'conciliation' or 'concord'—seemed to confirm the legitimacy of this young man with the piercing eyes and the message he revealed. Two other factors also allowed him to expand what could have remained a localized cult into a major southern faith. Firstly, he could draw upon local Buddhist beliefs and the centuries-old popularity of the Maitreya Buddha to renew the millenarian promise of a coming golden age. Secondly, like Pham Cong Tac, Huynh Phu So could tap into real rural discontent among the landless and unemployed masses, many of whom were looking for a savior and the promise of a better world to help them make it through the difficult economic times of the 1930s.

Huynh Phu So was less interested in building a structured Church like that of the Catholics, Cao Dai, Mahayana Buddhists, or communists. He emphasized rather the pure, spiritual core of Hoa Hao Buddhism (Phat giao Hoa Hao). This also makes it harder to know just how many people joined him. By the time the Japanese started moving into northern Indochina in 1940, the French estimated that Huynh Phu So had several thousand followers concentrated in the provinces of Tan Chau, Chau Doc, and Long Xuyen. The French thought him crazy, and interned the 'bonze fou' (mad monk) in a psychiatric ward in Saigon (where he promptly converted his Vietnamese doctor to the faith). What really worried the French were the Japanese, who successfully intercepted So during his transfer to Laos and protected him from French arrest. By March 1945, when French Indochina collapsed under the Japanese, the Hoa Hao faith counted around 100,000 believers, several thousand of whom he had already begun organizing into militias. Unlike the communists, whose failed uprising in 1940 ended in almost complete destruction, the combined Hoa Hao and Cao Dai forces emerged from the Second World War as major politico-military actors, controlling together perhaps as much as 20 percent of the delta's total population.

Catholic Vietnam[42]

Vietnamese Catholicism also changed greatly during the colonial period. From the sixteenth century on, seaborne trading routes opened by the Iberians had debarked thousands of European missionaries in Asia. By the late seventeenth century, around 100,000 Vietnamese (mainly concentrated in the north) had converted to Catholicism. These numbers increased slowly over the years as Catholicism spread southward into the Mekong delta with the Nguyen. In 1945, out of a total population of around 30 million people, 1.6 million Vietnamese were Catholics. There were undoubtedly very real problems and mistrust between Catholics and their secular rulers from the time of the sixteenth century onward. As we saw, European missionaries and many Vietnamese Catholics did indeed look to the French for help against Minh Mang's attack on them.

However, this does not mean that colonial and Catholic interests were identical or that this early collaborative relationship between missionaries and colonizers remained static until 1945. The Vietnamese Church changed greatly between Napoleon III's conquest of Cochinchina in 1862 and Ho Chi Minh's declaration of the independence of Vietnam in 1945. The relationship between French missionaries and the French colonial rulers in Indochina also changed. Napoleon III might have been a fervent Catholic (and that's debatable), but his republican successors were anything of the sort. By the turn of the century, almost all of the French administrators in Indochina were secularist-minded, anticlerical products of the Third Republic. Paul Doumer and many other high-ranking colonial administrators like him were Freemasons. Albert Sarraut was a leading member of the Radical Socialist Party, a Dreyfusard, and an ardent supporter of the laws separating Church and State in France at the turn of the century.

While it would be wrong to conclude that all republican administrators necessarily became the enemies of Catholics in the empire, the alert ones realized upon their arrival overseas how hard it would be to adhere to Léon Gambetta's warning in 1876 that anticlericalism should *not* be exported to the empire. Many a zealous republican journalist, educator, lower-ranking officer, and civilian administrator remembered Gambetta best for his call to arms against the French Catholic clergy—'*Le cléricalisme, voilà l'ennemi!*' Rather than seeing the missionaries as allies in building colonial Indochina, many considered them unpatriotic and disloyal. Several were convinced that these Roman Catholic missionaries threatened the Third Republic's special civilizing mission in Indochina. Colonial officials, police services, and anticlerical journalists kept close tabs on missionary publications, proselytizing efforts, and connections with the Vatican and other Asian Churches, especially in China and the Philippines. French missionaries, most of whom still operated under the Missions étrangères de Paris, realized that they had to keep on good terms with colonial administrators if they were to keep their Church up and running.

The countryside, where the missions had always been most active, was the main site of conflict between the colonial state and the Catholic missions. On several occasions, local administrators concluded that they could not trust some missionaries to serve as the intermediaries for administering faraway territories and peoples. While colonial officials appreciated the impressive knowledge, contacts, and languages the European missionaries could marshal, they just as often doubted their political loyalty. Léopold Sabatier, a dedicated French civil servant working among the Rhadé people in the highlands, intensely distrusted French priests and their Vietnamese faithful. They were, in his view, unfit to administer territories in the highlands. In another instance, one French priest responded to his critics that he had always done his best to spread the republican message into the highlands and in so doing had brought tens of thousands of non-Viet people into the colonial fold. And many French priests did support the colonial project. But when attacked for failing to teach French to their Vietnamese followers, some missionaries lost patience. Standing before the Cochinchinese Colonial Council, one Father Mossard declared: 'Dare I add that the Vietnamese who know French are, with rare exception, those who love the French the least, who respect them the least, and who, fundamentally, are the most hostile to them?' Furious, one of the ethnic Viet republicans sitting on the council shot back that this was an attack on 'all Vietnamese who, like me, received the benefits of French civilization. Monseigneur Mossard clearly is accusing us of being traitors'. Not quite, but the French priest should have held his tongue, for the council revoked his subsidy. As for not teaching French, it had nothing to do with missionary anti-republicanism or insufficient French nationalism. What counted most for religious leaders in Vietnam was spreading the word of God in Vietnamese (and other languages besides French). Buddhists, Cao Daists, Hoa Hao, nationalists, communists, and even Pierre Pasquier understood this.[43]

However, the colonial republic's problems with Catholicism came less from the French missionaries than from Vietnamese Catholics and the Vatican in Rome. Like those pursuing other religions, a growing number of Vietnamese Catholics asserted their desire to take control of their Church and grow it on their terms and in their language. The rise of print culture, increased literacy in *quoc ngu*, and expanding roads and improved transportation facilitated this. Catholic papers, pamphlets, and booklets flourished during the interwar period, mainly printed in *quoc ngu*. Reinvigorated religious instruction produced a new generation of indigenous priests and nuns, while the expansion of Catholic schools helped spread the faith among the younger generations. Although Vietnamese priests were as a rule hostile to communism, progressive trends in global Catholicism, France, and Indochina led to a more socially conscious, center-left brand of Catholicism as clergy and lay people organized youth, workers, and peasants into associations. And as for other faiths, nationalism was very much a part of this religious transformation of Vietnamese Catholicism. To French dismay, a handful of Vietnamese priests like Father Mai Lao Bang in Nghe An province helped the Vietnamese patriot Phan Boi Chau in the early 1900s organize the dispatch of young men to Japan to study and drive out the French.[44]

The French were equally troubled by their inability to stop Vietnamese Catholics from moving within a wider Roman Catholic world in search of new ideas, models, and sources of international support. Indeed, the Vatican was a real problem for French republicans well into the 1950s. Particularly worrying was Rome's decision after the First World War to distance the Catholic Church from colonialism. Faced with an increasingly secular Europe, papal strategists concluded that the center of gravity of Catholicism was shifting rapidly toward the non-Western world and with it the future of the Church. Reports of colonial abuses in European empires and the association of European missionaries with Western colonialism convinced religious authorities that it was imperative to indigenize the non-Western Church. Just as worrisome was the rise of communism in a new state spanning all of Eurasia, the Soviet Union. The creation of the Comintern (the Communist International organization) in 1919 which preached a new type of universal secularism reinforced the Vatican's willingness to change its global tack. And of course the accelerating 'de-christianization' of Western Europe only reinforced the Church's interest in the non-Western world.[45]

The Vatican moved with surprising alacrity. Benedict XV's 1919 apostolic letter 'Maximum Illud' and Pius XI's 1926 encyclical 'Rerum Ecclesiae' authorized the indigenization of the Church in the non-Western world. Rome's emissaries immediately informed local European missionaries in China, Vietnam, and elsewhere that they should prepare to turn over the Church to the local clergy and support the efforts mentioned above to invigorate a Vietnamese Catholic Church. In Vietnam, this meant the training, designation, and ordination of local bishops. Despite colonial and even European missionary resistance, Rome successfully dispatched an apostolic delegate to Indochina in 1925 to preside over the 'Vietnamization' of the Church there. French republican leaders could do little to stop the Vatican. On the one hand, who among them could seriously accuse the Pope of being 'pro communist'? On the other hand, the Third Republic's all-out secular assault on the Church's powers and property in France removed any leverage French leaders might have used to make Rome toe the colonial line. As Rome's new delegate wrote in the late 1920s: 'Times having evolved, indigenous priests must be second to none to extend more effectively the kingdom of Christ'.[46]

This is not what French republican colonialists wanted to hear. In effect, the Vatican was implementing a genuine policy of association by letting the Vietnamese run their own Church in collaboration with Rome. This was precisely the type of colonial policy Vietnamese moderates wanted and the French had been promising since the regime of Governer General Paul Beau, but had never implemented. Sarraut had raised hopes enormously after 1918; but nothing tangible had come of French association. While the Catholic Church and its elite remained heavily Eurocentric, sometimes racist, and almost always paternalistic, the Vatican's indigenous policy trapped French republicans in their own discourse and inertia. French authorities were anything but elated in 1933, when Pope Pius XI ordained Nguyen Ba Tong as its first Vietnamese bishop in Saint Peter's Basilica in Rome. Tong returned to a hero's welcome in Vietnam. Newspapers splashed his picture on their front pages. Even non-Christian Vietnamese expressed pride in Rome's decision to trust one of them. As the French ambassador to the Vatican wrote perceptively in a 1933 dispatch, 'We would have difficulties making the Vatican understand our opposition to the elevation of one of our colonial subjects to ecclesiastic honors and Episcopal functions. We present ourselves voluntarily as the most liberal of colonizers; the expression "indigenous politics" and "politics of association" come from us. How could we justify finding this to be a poor method simply because it is the Vatican that is applying it'? Confronted with massive revolts and the rise of communism in China and Vietnam, colonial authorities watched helplessly as Rome proceeded to indigenize the Vietnamese Catholic Church before their eyes. Ironically, the Pope was better at implementing a form of 'association' in Vietnam than the French Third Republic was.[47]

Significantly, support for the indigenization of Catholicism and the application of indigenous rule to Vietnam's Catholic Church came from influential Catholics at the court in Hue, most notably from Nguyen Huu Bai and Ngo Dinh Kha. Both had accepted collaboration with the French on the understanding that the protectorate treaty would allow the monarchy to continue to administer and reform the country in association with the French, not on orders from them. They were aghast at the way the French had humiliated, dethroned, and exiled the 'rebel' emperors Thanh Thai and Duy Tan. While it is unclear to what extent the two things were linked in their minds, Kha and Bai welcomed Rome's indigenization of the Church and used it to increase pressure on the French to respect the protectorate treaty which allowed indigenous rule via the monarchy. Ngo Dinh Kha had raised his children in this patriotic tradition which had included Catholics as well as Buddhists. Upon the death of Ngo Dinh Kha in 1925, Nguyen Huu Bai took his friend's sons under his wing, Ngo Dinh Diem and Ngo Dinh Thuc. The Ngo brothers grew up in this patriotic milieu, one that was initially for the monarchy and pro association.

The revolts of the early 1930s changed French policy. Caught off guard by massive peasant uprisings and worried by the rise of Soviet-backed Vietnamese communism, Sarraut and Pasquier agreed to let these royalists administer a new government in Annam which would be more in accordance with the protectorate treaty. Pasquier also agreed to let their colonial monarch, Bao Dai, trained in France, return to run a protectorate government in Annam. With Nguyen Huu Bai's support, Ngo Dinh Diem joined Bao Dai's government in 1934. However, Pasquier rapidly changed his mind and ended the first Bao Dai solution, when he realized that Bao Dai, Ngo Dinh Diem, and Nguyen Huu Bai were serious about administering indigenous affairs in line with the protectorate treaty. Angered by French bad faith and especially their attack on Bai, Diem resigned while Bao Dai withdrew from public affairs. Although Bai died before he could savor the moment, in 1938 another one of his adopted sons, Ngo Dinh Thuc, became a bishop. Thuc never hid his patriotic views and used the Vatican's support and policies to prod the French (when he could) to respect indigenous rule properly. More than anything else, the rise of the Ngo brothers in the 1930s symbolized the shift from the royalist patriotism of their fathers to the emergence of a strongly nationalist Catholicism involved in politics, whether the French or other Vietnamese liked it or not.[48]

While this Catholic anticolonialism co-existed uneasily with the simultaneous emergence of Vietnamese communism during the 1930s, Vietnamese Catholics, Buddhists, Cao Dai supporters, Hoa Hao followers and others shared one thing in common with the communists—the desire to secure the country's full independence. We should thus not be surprised that they were all elated when Ho Chi Minh stepped before the crowd in Hanoi on 2 September 1945 to declare Vietnam's independence. On 1 November 1945, one of Vietnam's rising Catholic stars from Phat Diem, Le Huu Tu, was ordained as a bishop without the interference of colonial administrators or the presence of a single European missionary. Intensely anticolonialist, Le Huu Tu joined Bao Dai and Pham Cong Tac in accepting Ho Chi Minh's invitation to serve as a supreme advisor to the new national government. Like the communists, Buddhists, Hoa Hao followers, Cao Dai supporters and Catholics were also nationalists.[49]

CHAPTER 7

CONTESTING EMPIRES AND NATION-STATES

THE SECOND OF September 1945 was a hot, muggy day in Saigon. Starting in the morning, a well-known southern radical, Tran Van Giau, tried his best to preside over a massive demonstration of 200,000 people to celebrate Vietnam's independence declaration. The participants included men and women, young and old, rich and poor, workers and civil servants. Starting on the outskirts of town, they all converged on Norodom Square in downtown Saigon. The highlight of the day was scheduled for the afternoon when loudspeakers would broadcast live Ho Chi Minh's address to the nation which would announce the creation of the Democratic Republic of Vietnam (DRV) and its declaration of independence.

The organizers had also learned earlier that day that the first Allied teams were about to arrive to accept the Japanese surrender. Men and women immediately plastered the town square with banners and posters reading in English, Chinese, and Russian: 'Down with Fascism and Colonialism', 'Vietnam Has Suffered and Bled under the French Yoke', 'Long live the USSR and the USA', and 'Long Live Vietnamese Independence'. British, Chinese, American, Russian flags, and the DRV's red one with a yellow star in the middle hung from administrative buildings. The French tricolor was conspicuously absent. The French were not among the Allied powers authorized to accept the Japanese defeat.

Powerful emotions mixing nationalist invincibility and colonial insecurity were swirling all over Saigon that day. Dozens of French families watched with fear and curiosity from their balconies as the Vietnamese poured into the square below them to chant independence slogans. But the crowd's playful exuberance suddenly turned into anger when the organizers failed to broadcast Ho's independence speech from Hanoi. Some muttered that it was colonial sabotage, as others began to eye the French staring down from above. Then, as the crowd began to disperse, shots rang out. French and Vietnamese both ran for cover as pandemonium seized the square. Some hotheaded Vietnamese attacked French houses and fired on the nearby cathedral as the DRV security forces tried (with little success) to maintain order. A dozen French people perished in the violence, including a French priest known for his charitable work among the poor of Saigon.

During the entire time, the armed Japanese sentries and soldiers looking on from the sidelines did little to maintain order in a country they had ruled throughout the Second World War. They refused to free the French soldiers they had vanquished a few months earlier. And now defeated themselves, they refused to take orders from anyone but the Allies. Two shattered empires were on display on that hot Saigon day for all to see, one French, the other Japanese. And no one knew, as Ho Chi Minh declared Vietnam's independence in Hanoi, what would come next. Would the 'new French' freed from the German imperial grip in Europe be able to empathize with the aspirations for independence of their former colonial subjects or would Free France's Charles de Gaulle insist upon reasserting his country's own colonial domination to erase the humiliating defeat of 1940 and thus reinforce France's own national identity, international prestige, and economic recovery?[1]

GLOBAL WAR AND THE FALL OF TWO EMPIRE

The French and Japanese were not fated to clash over control of Indochina. Despite Japan's military victory over the Russians in 1905 and French fears of a *péril jaune*, both countries had normalized their diplomatic relations in 1909 following Japan's expulsion of Phan Boi Chau's Go East movement and the latter's recognition of French sovereignty over Indochina. In return, Paris had no trouble recognizing Japan's colonization of Korea in 1910 and membership in the 'Great Powers' club. Japan's entry into the First World War on the side of the Allies kept relations on an even keel, as did its postwar participation in the League of Nations and collective security arrangements in the Asia–Pacific region.[2]

All that changed in the late 1920s. With the advent of the Great Depression and the rise to power of an authoritarian military class, Japan's relative political and economic liberalism vanished rapidly. The country's new military leaders abandoned collective security and engagement in the international system, convinced that the country's survival depended on renewed colonial expansion and going it alone in Asia as Depression-driven tariff barriers went up around the world. In making this choice, however, militarists put their country on a collision course with the Western imperial powers in Asia, not just the French, but also the Europeans and Americans. China, however, bore the immediate brunt of renewed Japanese colonial aggression. As Chiang Kai-shek's army advanced northward from its southern stronghold to defeat warlords opposed to the creation of a unified China, strategists in Tokyo concluded that they had to attack before China could consolidate. In 1931, as the French crushed anticolonial revolts in Indochina, the Japanese army invaded mineral-rich Manchuria. When the League of Nations objected, Tokyo withdrew its membership in order to continue its colonial offensive. In 1937, the international community looked on as the Japanese imperial army invaded China, took control of the coastline running to the Indochinese border, and pushed Chiang Kai-shek's republican government into southwestern China. This occurred against the backdrop of the emergence in 1933 of another expansionist-minded authoritarian state on the other side of the Eurasian continent, Nazi Germany. And just as the Japanese sought to create a 'new order' in Asia, the Nazis wanted to do much the same in Europe. Two years after the Japanese invasion of China, the Germans set Europe ablaze by attacking Poland.[3]

The French were no more prepared to go to war with the Japanese over Indochina than they were capable of defending France against the Germans. In June 1940, the French capitulated to the Germans, while the majority of republican deputies, including figures such as Albert Sarraut, signed over full powers to Marshal Philippe Pétain. The Third Republic was dead. In its place, Pétain assumed the leadership of the French State, better known as 'Vichy France', named for the town from which it soon operated. The Vietnamese had confronted superior French power in the mid-nineteenth century, and now the French found themselves in a similar situation. Many resisted the Germans, notably Charles de Gaulle, who fled to London, then on to Algiers following the Allied liberation of North Africa in late 1942. Most kept their heads down, while others saw a chance to promote revolutionary projects which had been marginalized under decades of republican rule. In October 1940, for example, Pétain promoted a policy of collaboration with Hitler and initiated the 'National Revolution', which included the termination of democratic politics, the reinvigoration of the Catholic Church, and the promotion of authoritarian rule based on agrarian identity politics. 'Work, Family, and Country' became the famous slogan. Mass propaganda drives, youth mobilization campaigns, and a cult of personality centered on the grandfatherly Pétain sought to inculcate such values. Meanwhile, authorities adopted anti-Semitic laws and took a hard line toward the left.[4]

Like his predecessors, Pétain attached great importance to the empire, both strategically and ideologically. However, the exportation of the National Revolution to Indochina was complicated by the fact that the French were not the only ones in charge. The Japanese had been following European events closely, keen to take control of the Indochinese overland and maritime bridge to Southeast Asia. Control of the Red River delta, its routes and the railway running from Hanoi to Kunming would allow Tokyo to further cut off Chiang Kai-shek's government in Yunnan province from international suppliers. Worried by Japan's assault on China, the Americans (and the Soviets) had already increased their support of the besieged Chinese Republic and warned the Japanese not to strike into Tonkin, keenly aware of the geopolitical importance of Vietnam.[5]

In a complex series of events which began with the French capitulation to the Nazis in June 1940 (ushering in the new Vichy government), Germany's Axis ally, Tokyo put pressure on the French authorities in Hanoi to allow Japanese troops to enter Tonkin. In July, the new French authorities named Admiral Jean Decoux Governor General of Indochina, instructing him to maintain French sovereignty over the colony. In the fall, as Pétain moved France closer to Germany, Decoux received orders to allow the Japanese to station 6,000 troops in Tonkin. In exchange, the Japanese recognized French sovereignty over Indochina. French collaboration with Nazi Germany—Tokyo's main Axis partner from September 1940—opened the way to a troubled but unique imperial condominium in Indochina, in which two imperial powers, one Asian, the other European, now ruled. At the heart of this dual arrangement was the Japanese preference to administer Indochina indirectly through the French in order that they might focus on more important military matters.

Despite their shared anticommunism, disgust for democracy, and antipathy for the Anglo-Americans, rightwing French and Japanese rulers were reluctant and distrustful allies. Clashes between their troops were always a real possibility. Decoux saw little to emulate in the Japanese ideologically and did everything in his power to maintain French sovereignty and promote the National Revolution to the detriment of Japan's Greater Co-Prosperity Sphere and Pan-Asiatic propaganda. But, as in Europe, French territory in Indochina was in reality under foreign occupation. Decoux got his first taste of this when the Japanese supported the Thais in their phony war against the French over control of western Indochina, stepping in to ensure that Bangkok 'won', despite a French naval victory. In May 1941, left with no choice but armed resistance and the possibility of losing Indochina entirely, Decoux ceded large swathes of western Cambodia and Laos to Thai expansionists and in so doing undermined the territorial integrity of French Indochina. The Japanese also secured a new agreement with the French which placed the rest of the colony under Tokyo's military jurisdiction. The Japanese could now station 75,000 troops in southern Indochina. They also administered monetary policy and extracted rice and natural resources there, with the collaboration of French authorities and the Bank of Indochina.

Alarmed by Japan's expansion into Southeast Asia via Vietnam, President Franklin D. Roosevelt responded by freezing Japanese assets in the United States and led an embargo against Tokyo. The Japanese replied by preparing a surprise attack on the American naval forces in the Pacific in order to expand further southward in search of oil and rubber. Meanwhile, the Germans prepared to strike eastward deep into Eurasia's midsection. Following the German invasion of the Soviet Union in June 1941, the Japanese attacked the American Pacific Fleet at Pearl Harbor in December and moved into all of Southeast Asia. The Americans entered the war, focusing first on Europe as the Japanese used their Indochinese bases to overthrow the British in Malaya (December 1941), Singapore (February 1942), and Burma (January–May 1942). American rule in the Philippines came to an end during December 1941 to May 1942, as did Dutch control over Indonesia by March 1942. Vietnam was now part of a world at war, carrying with it the seeds of great historical change and terrible human suffering.

Vichy's collaboration was essential to Tokyo's ability to rule Indochina. As long as the French honored their mutual agreements and provided the required food, labor, and natural resources, Japanese authorities were content to rule indirectly through the pre-existing colonial administration. Decoux both signed authorizations for, and approved rice transfers to the Japanese, and reported to them. It is uncertain, however, if the French grasped how some 15,000 Indochinese elite members and millions of increasingly hungry peasants may have interpreted such joint colonial collaboration. Firstly, while Decoux prided himself on keeping Indochina French despite foreign occupation (just as Pétain claimed to do in the metropole), it was clear to any thinking Indochinese that he did so because the Japanese allowed him to do so. Secondly, that a 'yellow race' could so easily dominate a 'white one' debunked for good Social Darwinian arguments which had often been used to justify European colonial rule. Vietnamese rickshaw drivers serving customers in Saigon would have understood that the Japanese soldiers strolling down Rue Catinat had upended the colonial order and the racist assumptions on which it rested. Thirdly, by collaborating with the Japanese, the French failed to honor duly signed international legal agreements binding them to defend their Asian colony. For the Vietnamese, who were accustomed to repeated legal arguments justifying colonial rule, the failure to honor this contract ruined the legitimacy of colonial claims and later French attempts to reassert them.

The Japanese left equally negative impressions. Despite all the talk of liberating the 'Asian/yellow' people from 'Western/white' colonial exploitation since the days of Meiji, the undeniable truth was that the Japanese colonialists had intentionally left the 'white man' in power in Indochina. By choosing to rule Indochina through the French, the Japanese even abandoned their most loyal Vietnamese allies in their hour of greatest need. When diehard lieutenants of Phan Boi Chau's Go East program tried to seize power in the fall of 1940, the Japanese let the French crush them, rather than help the nationalists. Tokyo even refused to put their longtime ally, Prince Cuong De, on the throne in Hue, preferring not to disrupt the existing monarchy under Bao Dai and to risk undermining stability in Indochina. Cuong De died in Japan in 1951, a bitter and abandoned man. Worst of all, Japanese rule triggered a famine that would kill over a million Vietnamese peasants by 1945 (see below). In Indochina, the so-called 'Co-prosperity Sphere' (the term had been coined by the Japanese imperial government to describe a bloc of Asian nations which were to be led by them) was riddled with contradictions.[6]

The same was true for French efforts to promote their national revolution in Indochina. Admiral Jean Decoux faithfully applied anti-Semitic laws and clamped down on republicans and their associations in Indochina (Freemasons, the League of Human Rights, and the Popular Front). In their place, he promoted the fascist-minded French Legion of Soldiers and Volunteers for the National Revolution (Légion française des Combattants et Volontaires de la Révolution nationale). Thanks to volunteers from the European settler community, its ranks increased from 2,637 members in early 1942 to 6,576 by mid-1943, meaning about 25 percent of the total European population. Although some Vietnamese admired Hitler and dabbled with fascism, there is no evidence that Vichy authorities or activists sought to incorporate such rightwing Vietnamese nationalists into their fascist-minded Légion. Vichy did little of substance to break down the racially configured colonial divide between rulers and ruled.[7]

Vichy did roll back what little democracy the Third Republic had introduced to Indochina. Upon his arrival, Decoux rescinded those Popular Front reforms which had been designed to increase the democratic participation of local 'indigenous councilors' in the municipal assemblies of Saigon, Hanoi, and Haiphong. He now simply appointed people to those positions. In November 1940, Decoux presided over the dissolution of all Indochinese assemblies, including the Colonial Council of Cochinchina. Although Decoux dusted off Sarraut's idea of creating an Indochinese federation, he gutted it of any remaining liberalism. The Federal Indochinese Council, created in mid-1941, relied exclusively on staunchly pro-French 'notables', all twenty-five of whom the governor named. The Japanese never required any of these antidemocratic measures. In 1943, Decoux justified his policy in terms fully in line with metropolitan (Vichy France) authoritarianism:

> No doubt on the French side, some beneficiaries of the old regime will regret seeing their opportunities for democratic machinations disappear. But the wholesome element [. . .] will accept with satisfaction a reform marking the government's desire to apply to Indochina the principles used to restore our [Patrie . . .] None of those who recognize the dangers of elections [. . .] can interpret this reform as a regression. [On the Indochinese side . . .] the evolved Indochinese element, in other words the key to indigenous opinion, has embraced wholeheartedly the principles of the National Revolution, and never had any delusions about the powers of former assemblies in the first place.[8]

This was woefully inaccurate. By brushing aside a half-century of Vietnamese calls for meaningful representation in decision-making, Decoux further alienated a wide section of the Vietnamese elite, including the pro-French Constitutionalists like Bui Quang Chieu. Hounded by the police, younger republicans like Nguyen Tuong Tam fled to China to join the Vietnamese Nationalist Party. A few elected to work with the Japanese. The politically minded leaders of the Hoa Hao and Cao Dai religious faiths, Huynh Phu So and Pham Cong Tac, used Japanese power and protection to politicize, mobilize, and eventually arm their followers, something which the French had tried to block for years.

The only Vietnamese card Decoux would consider was the one his predecessors had been using for decades, the monarchy, and its indefatigable Vietnamese defender, Pham Quynh. In 1942, this man published a front-page article in the newspaper *La patrie annamite* (*The Annamese Nation*) which embraced the royalist ideas of French fascist Charles Maurras. Quynh insisted that Vietnam had to return to its traditional Confucian values in order to ensure stability. The source of disorder for Quynh was, as for Maurras, modern individualism and the ideas that Jean-Jacques Rousseau had unfortunately sown in young Vietnamese minds across the land. Quynh and Decoux were convinced that a return to Confucian values and the monarchy could attract popular support in the countryside and ensure stability in these troubled times. For Quynh, the monarchy was the 'most perfect form of government'. Quynh shared Maurras' critique of democracy and agreed that the monarchy was the manifestation of a *nationalisme intégral*, or a 'deep nationalism'.[9]

Like Pasquier and Sarraut, Decoux approved of the resurrection of a monarchical government based in Hue and made Pham Quynh Minister of the Interior. But once again this project went nowhere, not least because the Confucian 'son of heaven' was uninterested and not prepared to be a dupe. Bao Dai kept Decoux at bay, avoiding imperial tours designed to increase his 'prestige' among the people. More importantly, the monarchy had no chance of success as a counter-revolutionary device as long as the French refused either to unite the kingdom they had truncated or to endow its indigenous sovereign with some semblance of power. Decoux authorized the use of the word 'Vietnam' to manipulate patriotic sentiments and increased salaries for Indochinese civil servants to win over their continued support, but Vietnam remained divided and the Vietnamese elite had even less of a voice in the colony than under the Third Republic. Decoux's team may have marched tens of thousands of Vietnamese youngsters across Indochina shouting '*Maréchal, nous voilà!*' ('Marshal, here we are!'), but the Japanese, Cao Dai, and Hoa Hao did so, too. And it all rang hollow for now middle-aged Vietnamese nationalists, not least of all for the champion of the Vietnamese youth and the man Vichy let die in a Poulo Condor prison cell on 15 August 1943, Nguyen An Ninh.

Things were different in Laos and Cambodia, where the French promoted for the first time a policy of Franco-Lao and Franco-Cambodian

collaboration in order to contain the Thais. Undeterred by Bao Dai's pas-
sive resistance, Decoux turned to a dynamic young Cambodian prince
named Norodom Sihanouk. He made him King of Cambodia in 1941 and
then sent him out of the palace and across the countryside. Through a series of carefully orchestrated imperial tours, the young emperor cast his
gaze upon his people as they were invited to look upon him. If Bao Dai de-
tested these tours in Vietnam, Sihanouk never forgot this lesson in modern
kingship and its nationalist power. In fact, he would turn it against his colonial overlords in 1953. When a journalist asked him in the 1960s if the Vichy
years had influenced him in any way, Sihanouk responded: 'Yes, strangely
enough again, it was thanks to Admiral Decoux, I have to say. From the moment I ascended to the throne, he pushed me to visit my kingdom in order
to know it and to be closer to its people. I admit that at least on this matter,
he provided good counsel'.[10]

The governor general also travelled to Luang Prabang to meet King Sisavang Vong. In a move to counter further Thai claims to Lao territories,
Decoux entrusted to the king the administration of the amalgam of Lao
kingdoms and military territories which the French had colonized at the
turn of the century. In fact, Decoux allowed Sisavang Vong to rule over an
increasingly unified Lao territorial body, one we recognize today as 'Laos',
but one which had never existed as such in the past. Significantly, the same
governor general refused to the Nguyen emperor in Annam that which he
had just accorded to the Lao one in Luang Prabang—the right to rule over
a unified Vietnam, one which *had* in fact existed, if only for a few decades,
before the French arrived.[11]

THE END OF THE SECOND WORLD WAR AND
THE BIRTH OF A 'NEW VIETNAM'

The 9 March Coup and the Vietnamese Race for Power
Like Pétain's French state in Europe, Decoux's colonial one in Asia did not
survive the war. By mid-1943, both the Germans and the Japanese were in
trouble. The Soviet counter-offensive into Eastern Europe and the Allied
landing in Normandy in mid-1944 liberated France from German occupation and allowed Charles de Gaulle to declare and run the provisional
government of the French Republic. Like his predecessors, de Gaulle was
sensitive to the strategic importance of empire. In his radio address from

London in 1940, he had already insisted that 'France does not stand alone. She is not isolated. Behind her stands a vast empire'. Indeed, once liberated by the Allies in late 1942, Algeria had become the 'French' home to de Gaulle's government-in-exile. As the leader of liberated France itself from mid-1944, de Gaulle now had to show the Allies that his new government was determined to fight the Axis powers. It was crucial to validating de Gaulle's claim to Indochina. And that Roosevelt had been talking of placing Indochina under an international trusteeship made this all the more important.

Decoux, however, balked at the idea of fighting the Japanese, loathe to take orders from anyone, including de Gaulle, and convinced that only he could save Indochina. Again, like Pétain, he was wrong. The Japanese were taking no chances as they watched the Allies start to shift their undivided attention from Europe to Asia (technically, the Americans had already been dealing with Asia since Pearl Harbor, but now they could throw everything they had at the Japanese, including the atomic bomb). In fact, by early 1945, the Americans were well on their way to retaking the Philippines. On 12 January, a US naval task force attacked the Vietnamese coast, confirming Japanese fears of an imminent Allied landing. On 9 March 1945, doubtful of the continued collaboration of the French in Indochina, the Japanese launched a *coup de force*, overthrowing eighty years of French rule in a matter of days. Backed by the Japanese, Bao Dai announced Vietnam's independence in the form of the 'empire of Vietnam'. His prime minister, Tran Trong Kim, presided over the unification of the country for the first time in almost a century. The country was free of French rule, but not the Japanese. Although the government under Tran Trong Kim crumbled when the Japanese capitulated in mid-August 1945, during its three months' existence it started rolling back decades of colonial rule by nationalizing education, culture, and the civil service, at the same time as it did its best to cope with a deadly famine rolling through the countryside.[12]

Meanwhile, to the north, Vietnamese nationalists and communists were closely following events from southern China. Convinced the Japanese would lose, they now saw the opening they needed to transform their 'Vietnams abroad' into a nation-state inside the country. We know that Ho Chi Minh was to win this race, when he would announce Vietnam's full independence on 2 September 1945. But it is worth remembering that Ho was not necessarily well positioned at the start to win that contest. For one, the Kim government could have held, despite its association with the Japanese.

(Nationalist leaders like Sukarno would manage to do so in Indonesia). Secondly, Ho was not inside Vietnam. Unlike Mao Zedong, the leader of the Chinese Communist Party, Ho had spent all of his revolutionary career outside Indochina. He did not return to Vietnam or re-establish his pre-eminence within the Indochinese Communist Party until 1941 at the earliest. Some of the most active and articulate communists operated inside the country clandestinely, or were doing hard time in Poulo Condor. Although Ho had played a crucial role in getting the party off the ground in 1930, he was but one among several influential communists, none of whom was necessarily ready to elevate him to the top of the party's leadership. Moreover, few people outside of this communist core and a handful of extremely well informed intelligence officers could have even recognized Ho had he walked into Hanoi or Saigon. He had no popular support. He had to create it from scratch.

Ho Chi Minh's brilliance resided first and foremost in his uncanny ability to manoeuver himself into the right place at the right time. He was particularly good at assessing, connecting, and tailoring changes at the international and regional level to realities in Vietnam. He knew when it was crucial to act, as well as when it was best to wait patiently and lie low. He read newspapers and listened to the radio religiously. His knowledge of foreign languages (Chinese, French, Russian, English, and Thai) strengthened his effectiveness. His interpersonal skills were unparalleled, as was his impressive *carnet d'adresses*, allowing him to call in favors, recruit loyal disciples, and make vital connections in cities, towns, villages, and ports reaching from Paris and Marseille to Hong Kong and Guangzhou by way of Udon Thani and Singapore.

In 1934, having spent two years in a Hong Kong prison, Ho Chi Minh skillfully regained his freedom and returned to the Soviet Union, leaving younger revolutionaries aligned with Nguyen An Ninh's *Lutteurs* to lead the party inside Vietnam. During his long stay in Moscow, he assiduously studied the Marxist–Leninist canon, pledged allegiance to Stalin, and improved his Russian. He read everything he could about the situations in China and Vietnam and sent instructions to the party in Indochina. Using a pen-name, he published articles in leftist papers in Vietnam warning his colleagues of the dangers of Trotskyism and arguing in favor of Stalin's show trials. But what mattered most to Ho as the war began in the Pacific was getting back to southern China and building up a broad nationalist front—his real specialty—that could catapult Vietnamese communists to power. Then he and the party could dedicate themselves to radical social revolution, but not before.[13]

Ho's chances improved as the Japanese and Germans pushed the world—and with it, the communist bloc—toward global war and a new series of alliances and tactics. Most importantly, the Comintern's shift in line in 1935 from promoting 'class struggle' and 'international proletarianism' to building up national fronts and international alliances against the fascists strengthened Ho's hand immensely and helped his efforts to return to Asia. The Comintern's changing policy toward China helped even more. Faced with Japanese invasion, in December 1936 Chinese communists and nationalists created their second united front (the first had been created by Sun Yat-sen in 1923). Stalin backed this and Ho benefitted directly from it. With the Comintern's blessing, Ho arrived in northern China in 1938. After meeting with Chinese communists now operating in Yan'an, he joined the Chinese Communist Party's Eighth Route Army, working as a communications specialist. He arrived in Yunnan province in early 1940, where he immediately reactivated a wide range of contacts. He renewed his long-standing friendships with Zhou Enlai and Ho Hoc Lam, the latter being the Go East veteran still attached to Chiang Kai-shek's general staff. Ho also resumed his work soliciting the support of the Vietnamese diaspora, ingratiating himself to Chinese nationalist leaders in the south, extending his hand to both non-communist Vietnamese nationalists and to communist leaders inside Indochina.[14]

Several events occurring inside Indochina further strengthened Ho's hand indirectly. The French decision to outlaw communism in France and Indochina in September 1939 forced the Indochinese Communist Party to go underground. Many members ended up in prison or on the run. The French repression of the communist uprising in Cochinchina in late 1940 wrecked the party in the south and in so doing transferred the party's center of gravity northward to clandestine bases in Tonkin (led by Truong Chinh) and in southern China (led by Ho Chi Minh). The arrival of militants like Pham Van Dong and Vo Nguyen Giap in southern China in 1940 allowed Ho to establish direct links with these lieutenants and, through them, the interior of Vietnam. Nguyen An Ninh's death in 1943 further sealed the demise of southern radicalism and removed the man who might have easily competed with Ho Chi Minh for the nationalist and revolutionary mantle. Southern leftists lost their monopoly over Vietnamese politics, thus opening the way to northern domination of radical politics for decades to come.

This would turn out to be a major political shift in the history of modern Vietnam.

Ho Chi Minh skillfully used the second united front in southern China to position himself in the right place. He knew that Chinese nationalist leaders and generals in control of the frontier with Indochina needed Vietnamese communists and nationalists to create their own united front in order to help defeat their common enemy, the Japanese. Like Mao Zedong, Ho Chi Minh was in total agreement with this Comintern-approved tactical alliance. Anticommunist Vietnamese leaders in southern China were less convinced, but depended on their Chinese Nationalist Party big brothers to operate in China and, they hoped, take power in Vietnam upon Japanese defeat. With varying degrees of success, Chinese nationalist leaders in charge of the border like Zhang Fakui and Siao Wen prodded both the leader of the Vietnamese Nationalist Party in China, Vu Hong Khanh, and the leader of a new party called the Vietnamese Revolutionary Alliance (Viet Nam Cach Mang Dong Minh Hoi), Nguyen Hai Than (see below), into joining forces with Ho Chi Minh in the common struggle against the Japanese. Ho thus joined a Vietnamese nationalist front in 1936 (in the image of the Chinese Communist Party–Chinese Nationalist Party united front). With a blessing from Chinese nationalists worried by Japan's move into Indochina in late 1940, Ho moved his entourage to the Sino-Vietnamese border, promising to take part in the resistance to the Japanese. (He would also redouble his contacts with communists in Tonkin.) In remote Cao Bang province, Ho's lieutenants set up camp in the limestone caves in Pac Bo. And in February 1941, Ho walked into northern Vietnam for the first time since leaving Saigon by boat thirty years earlier.

Just as important, Ho re-asserted his leadership within the communist party through the same united front tactics he had used in the mid-1920s in southern China. In meetings with Tonkin-based leaders trying to keep the Indochinese Communist Party afloat, Ho explained the Comintern's united front policy and insisted on the importance of building up just such a front, but under communist control. He did not insist on leading the ICP or seeking revenge for those who had accused him of 'narrow nationalism' in the 1930s. Instead he endorsed Truong Chinh's position as the party's secretary general. Chinh had emerged as a leading theorist in Hanoi during the Popular Front period and published an important treatise called 'The Peasant Question' with Vo Nguyen Giap in 1938. Ho could have easily invoked his Comintern credentials to justify replacing Chinh, but he must have known that such a visible position at the head of the party would have undermined his ability to build up the nationalist front and win over non-communist support.[15]

In 1941, as the world moved toward a truly global war, Ho made his move. From bases along the Sino-Vietnamese border, he and his entourage presided over the ICP's historic eighth plenum on 10–19 May 1941. This meeting and the documents it produced officially shifted the party's line from proletarian internationalism to national liberation. This meant creating a broad national front which was focused on securing Vietnam's independence, regardless of divisions of class, race, sex, or political affiliation. Talk of radical agrarian revolution, including land reform, disappeared. The new front emerging from this historic meeting was the Vietnamese Independence League (Viet Nam Doc Lap Dong Minh, better known as the Viet Minh). In many ways, the Viet Minh replaced the pre-existing one set up in China in 1936, but it now put the communists at the helm inside Vietnam, not in southern China, where Chinese nationalist leaders and their Vietnamese allies could have easily interfered.

Little wonder Vu Hong Khanh and Nguyen Hai Than were convinced that the Viet Minh was a communist creation. It was. But the communists had no intention of letting their anticommunist nationalist competitors trap them in an anticommunist nationalist front backed by the Chinese Nationalist Party. Control and the expansion of a separate nationalist front were vital to winning the race for power. Where the non-communist Vietnamese parties in southern China erred massively was in their refusal to transfer their national front to Vietnam. By failing to do so, they allowed the Viet Minh to organize bases and mobilize people in upland areas of Vietnam and the delta for four years. Viet Minh agents were also in a better position to start opening granaries for famished peasants and penetrating the Tran Trong Kim government. Moreover, by betting entirely on the Chinese to put them in power in Vietnam, non-communist Vietnamese badly underestimated Ho's proven ability to turn the united front strategy against his anticommunist adversaries, knowing that their Chinese backers would let him do it, focused as they were on their more pressing problems in China itself.

On the inside, Ho Chi Minh and his team did everything in their power to transform the front and with it the communist party into the defenders of the nationalist cause within the country. They began printing clandestine papers and distributing propaganda wherever they could safely. On 6 June 1941, Ho issued his 'Letter from Abroad', echoing the title of the letter Phan

Boi Chau had written 'in blood' from Japan three decades earlier. In 600 easy-to-understand *quoc ngu* words, Ho called upon the Vietnamese to take up arms: 'In such painful tormenting conditions shall we simply fold our arms and wait to die? No absolutely not! More than twenty million descendants of the Lac and Hong are determined not to be perpetual slaves without a country!' Ho travelled throughout the northern hills, testing for the first time his ability to connect with people, many of them non-Viet, presenting himself as the defender of the nationalist cause, and preparing his cadres to move decisively and rapidly to take power when the right moment came.[16]

Whether he predicted it or not, the German invasion of the Soviet Union in June 1941 only strengthened his hand against any who might have doubted his insistence on a nationalist front. The dissolution of the Comintern in 1943 and the Soviet Union's life-and-death struggle against the Nazis ensured that there would be no direct interference from Moscow (or its Vietnamese allies) to Ho's rise to the top of the party. And given that the Soviets were now engaged in the Grand Alliance with the Americans against the Axis powers, there was nothing stopping Ho from soliciting American aid in southern China. The American Office of Strategic Services in China recruited many Vietnamese, including the personable and English-speaking Ho, to provide intelligence about the Japanese and to help rescue downed American pilots. The British were doing the same thing in dealing with the Malayan Communist Party, including its Vietnamese leader Lai Tek. And Ho offered the same thing to the Chinese Guomindang, in Chinese—intelligence on the Japanese enemy—further ingratiating him with many of the Chinese officers who would arrive in Hanoi in 1945.

Meanwhile, inside Vietnam, following the Japanese-instigated March 1945 coup, non-communist nationalists supportive of Bao Dai and his prime minister, Tran Trong Kim, mobilized the young, tore down colonial monuments, renamed streets after such figures as Nguyen Thai Hoc, and promoted a heroic, independent and unitary Vietnam with roots in the far-away past as essential to building a new national identity. However, in the eyes of Vietnamese nationalists perched on the northern border, the Tran Trong Kim government remained a creature of the Japanese. Like the Indochinese Communist Party, the Vietnamese Nationalist Party and the Vietnamese Revolutionary Alliance leaders had every intention of eliminating it once the war ended.[17]

What mattered most for Ho, however, was positioning the Viet Minh inside the country, so that the miniscule communist party of some 5,000 members (of whom at least half were sitting behind colonial bars) could take power at the propitious moment. Unlike the Vietnamese Nationalist Party and the Vietnamese Revolutionary Alliance, the Viet Minh quickly went to work recruiting members and building up organizations in remote northern areas free of Franco-Japanese patrols. For communist nationalists, this meant winning over local leaders and village headmen, and creating 'national salvation associations' to group different social groups—farmers, women, landowners—together under the Viet Minh umbrella. In most cases, it simply meant being in a position to take over the local colonial administration when the Japanese would inevitably surrender. Along the northern border, Vo Nguyen Giap began building a tiny liberation army. The American Office of Strategic Services provided some arms and military training as part of the broader fight against the Japanese. Meanwhile, Truong Chinh administered an underground network in Hanoi which cultivated contacts with intellectuals, civil servants, and youth groups, all the while trying to prepare his lieutenants to take control of the capital and provincial towns once the Japanese were defeated. Non-communist nationalists in China did little of this type of work. In the south, however, the situation was very different. The communists there had never truly recovered from the failed uprising of 1940 and had little, if any real contact, with northerners. Non-communist religious nationalists led by the Cao Dai and Hoa Hao led the way in organizing territory and mobilizing people.

Back in the north, the Indochinese Communist Party leadership carefully monitored the course of the war at the international, regional, and local levels. Party strategists certainly welcomed the Japanese overthrow of the French on 9 March 1945. The disappearance of the redoubtable colonial police allowed Ho's team to push deeper into Vietnam, setting up headquarters in the village of Tran Trao. However, like de Gaulle facing the Nazis in France, Ho understood that only Allied victory over the Japanese, generally viewed as sure to happen in 1946 or 1947, would provide the opportune moment for taking power. What neither de Gaulle or Ho or Vu Hong Khanh saw coming was the rapid Japanese capitulation on 15 August following the American nuclear bombings of Hiroshima and Nagasaki. But when news of it came via the radio, Ho lost no time. The ICP immediately issued the call for a general uprising as de Gaulle's intelligence officers and the non-communist nationalists in China looked on helplessly. On 19 August, the Viet Minh seized power in Hanoi and the northern provincial capitals before extending its control southward over Annam and Cochinchina by the end of the month. These events are collectively known in Vietnam today as the 'August Revolution of 1945'.

In an equally historic event, on 30 August, Bao Dai, the last emperor of the Nguyen dynasty, formally abdicated. He and his prime minister, Tran Trong Kim, could have asserted themselves at this time, like several others in similar positions in Southeast Asia in August 1945, but they did not. In a carefully choreographed ceremony, Bao Dai handed over the dynastic seal and sword to the newly constituted provisional government of Vietnam led by Ho Chi Minh. The emperor abandoned his title and name to become the simple citizen 'Vinh Thuy'. He even served as an advisor to Ho. His actions gave a powerful source of legitimacy to Ho Chi Minh and his fledgling government. Bao Dai's colonial king-makers were speechless. He must have been forced to do it, they repeated one after another. And yet the emperor had personally written a missive to Charles de Gaulle begging France's liberator to recognize the Vietnamese right to independence:

> I would ask you to understand that the only way to maintain French inter-
> ests and France's spiritual influence in Indochina is to recognize frankly
> Vietnamese independence and to renounce any idea of re-establishing sov-
> ereignty or a French administration in any form whatsoever. We could so
> easily get along and become friends if you could stop claiming [the right]
> to become again our masters.[18]

Given the importance the French had always paid to their colonial mon-archs, especially this one, it is impossible that de Gaulle was unaware of Bao Dai's letter. For the first time in his life, France's colonial emperor had openly challenged the French. And the French now found themselves in the sorry position of having no Vietnamese partner with whom to rebuild their lost colonial state. In August 1945, individually or on communist party orders, Viet Minh agents executed France's most faithful allies, Bui Quang Chieu and Pham Quynh.[19]

That said, despite Ho Chi Minh's shrewd positioning of the party and the timely abdication of Bao Dai, there was nothing necessarily inevitable about the communist-engineered 'August Revolution'. As Mao Zedong fa-mously quipped, 'Had the Japanese never invaded China, the communists would have never taken power'. The same could be said of their Vietnamese counterparts. Moreover, the ICP was not as in control of events at the time as its defenders—and anticommunist detractors—would like us to believe today. As in earlier periods of Vietnamese history, famine, more than anything else, ushered in change. This was particularly the case in central and northern Vietnam during the Japanese occupation. Increased population pressure, falling rice-paddy output, poor weather and cultivation methods, and a shift to industrial crops all combined to reduce the 1944 rice crop in Tonkin and in the northern central provinces of Thanh Hoa and Nghe An drastically. To make matters worse, the French and the Japanese refused to reduce taxes on farmers, thereby increasing the burden placed upon them, without offering the peasants incentives to produce more. Meanwhile, the French and the Japanese stockpiled rice for themselves. As the supply of rice fell, its price skyrocketed on the black market, greatly exceeding the officially set price. Farmers hoarded rice in order to meet their own needs rather than sell it at the official price. The only way to head off famine was to transport rice to the north from the comparatively rice-rich south. However, Allied bombers had severed the north–south railway and destroyed bridges, just at the same time as submarines were keeping coastal shipping to a minimum. Junks and parts of the railway could have been used, but Japanese officials were more concerned with the war in the Pacific as the Allies concentrated on destroying the rest of the Axis. French authorities failed to provide any solutions.[20]

The result was that from December 1944 until about May 1945, famine swooped down on Tonkin and upper Annam, killing about one million Vietnamese. An estimated 10 percent of the population in this crucial area perished in a five-month period preceding the 'August Revolution'. In many ways, Viet Minh leaders rode a famine-driven wave of angry peasant hunger to power in mid-1945, opening granaries as they raced across the provinces to take control of the colonial administration the French and Japanese had abandoned in their defeat. Bao Dai and the Tran Trong Kim government's rural administrators had little chance of surviving this massive social surge. In the eyes of the famished, the provincial and district notables were part of the problem, the ones who had stockpiled rice while their families slowly starved to death. These people became the visible objects of peasant wrath and many paid with their lives. Without war and the famine it produced, Vietnamese communists might well have never taken power in August 1945.[21]

THE END OF WORLD WAR AND THE
RISE OF A 'NEW FRANCE'

De Gaulle's government was badly out of touch with these events. Unlike
the British and the Americans, Free French intelligence services had refused as a matter of policy to cooperate with the 'natives', thereby denying
postwar French leaders an invaluable source of information on events inside Indochina and the opportunity to make partners for reconstructing
peace in the future. Like so many in the French ruling class, Gaullist policy
makers first in Algiers, then in Paris, were convinced that republican reformism and colonial humanism would be enough to rebuild the empire
and placate nationalist calls for independence. Nowhere was this more
evident than during the conference at Brazzaville (in the French Congo)
held in early 1944. Attending this meeting were governor generals, mainly
from Africa, and the representatives of the Provisional French Consultative Assembly. Japanese control of Indochina prevented any Indochinese
presence. No Asian or African colonial subjects participated. One of the
leading architects of Gaullist colonial policy, Henri Laurentie, argued that
France had to adopt a more liberal policy if the French were to maintain
their sovereignty against rapidly emerging nationalist elites contesting the
empire from within. The main change approved at Brazzaville was to move
the empire away from the principle of assimilation and toward federalism
(though it had never been exclusively 'assimilationist' in Indochina). Federalism would accord more autonomy to the restless elite through the creation of local parliaments with expanded electoral colleges, all the while
allowing the French to remain in charge of the imperial state, its foreign
affairs, and defense.[22]

For the Gaullists, Indochina would be the litmus test for colonial federalism. On 24 March 1945, hardly two weeks after the Japanese overthrew
the French, the provisional government of the French Republic issued its
first major public statement on policy toward Indochina. Based on the federal ideas developed at Brazzaville, the declaration heralded the creation of
a pentagonal Indochinese Federation which would regroup Tonkin, Annam, Cochinchina, Laos, and Cambodia into one colonial state. The federal structure would give each local state a greater level of autonomy, via the
creation of state governments under the direction of a French high commissioner (the new name for the governor general). This Indochinese Federation would in turn be linked to other French colonial states like Algeria, via

its membership in the 'French Union', the new word for the empire which was now to be a much more structured and interconnected one. Indeed, the French Union would eventually acquire an empire-wide consultative assembly based in Paris.

There is no evidence that the French revisited General Théophile Pennequin's reformist ideas of the 1910s for a policy of transition to an independent Indochinese state which was nonetheless still associated with the French, or the American creation in 1935 of a commonwealth which included the Philippines and was designed to do the same thing. The Gaullists had no intention of creating the equivalent of a British commonwealth of nations in which colonial states such as Canada, Australia, New Zealand, and latterly India acceded to full independence while remaining loosely in the imperial dominion. Nor did the French have any intention of uniting Tonkin, Annam, and Cochinchina into one territorially unified sub-state—'Vietnam'—within the Indochinese Federation. Laos, however, maintained the territorial unity which Decoux had accorded it. And, in 1946, Laos and Cambodia recovered the territories the Thais had taken from them in 1941.[23]

The problem was that the Indochina Declaration proved badly out of touch with events. Most obviously missing was any mention of the Japanese destruction of French Indochina two weeks earlier. Nor did it take into account the independence or the unification of Vietnam declared by Bao Dai. In fact, rather than pondering the meaning of Bao Dai's letter defending Vietnamese independence quoted above, de Gaulle ordered his new high commissioner, Admiral Georges Thierry d'Argenlieu, to retake all of Indochina, by force if need be, at the same time as the general searched out a new colonial emperor through whom he could legitimate this second war of colonial conquest. In an astonishing irony, de Gaulle selected the very emperor whom the French had deposed thirty years earlier for colonial treason—Duy Tan. The plan failed when Duy Tan perished in a plane crash in late 1945, but the French governmental obsession with colonial monarchy was clearly alive and well as the Fourth Republic came falteringly into being.[24]

The disconnect between French and Vietnamese nationalist thinking could not have been greater than when Ho Chi Minh stepped up to the microphone on 2 September 1945 and declared before tens of thousands of Vietnamese the independence of all of Vietnam. In an extraordinary transformation, Ho was no longer the angry young man arguing with Phan

Chu Trinh in Paris. Sporting a wispy beard and dressed simply, he now intentionally played the role of the wise humanist Confucian grandfather, or *'cu Ho'*, a man of the people. Papers carried his picture on the front page, for Ho was almost completely unknown inside Vietnam before mid-1945. His anticolonialism remained as ardent as in Paris, but he carefully hid his internationalist communist faith and connections in order to embody the national desire for independence and lead its bid toward it. When he asked his 'compatriots' that day if they could hear him as he prepared to read the country's declaration of independence, the crowd roared back with a resounding *'Co!'* (*'Yes!'*). Communist though he most certainly was, Ho had every intention of ensuring that the communists were seen as the true defenders of the nationalist faith, and creating a personality cult was an essential part of that project. Two new nation-states and two new nationalist leaders had thus emerged from the Second World War—the French Republic under de Gaulle and the Vietnamese one under Ho. Both men had real charisma and both held opposing yet strong feelings about the future of this Asian territory. This was a very dangerous mix.[25]

The Second French Colonial Conquest

General de Gaulle could not, however, do as he pleased in 1945. The European-dominated international system of the late nineteenth century was very different from the order emerging out of world war in 1945. It was clear to all that the Americans and the Soviets had emerged as the two most important powers in the international system, dominating both ends of Eurasia as never before in world history. If the Soviets occupied most of Eastern Europe at the war's end, the Americans were particularly well positioned in Atlantic Europe and in Pacific-Asia. In East Asia, they administered Japan, had re-established their hold over the Philippines, and occupied southern Korea. The Japanese overthrow of Western colonial states across Southeast Asia had deeply undermined European dominance, whose governments in any event did not have the financial means to compete with the Americans. Although the Soviets sent troops into Manchuria and upper Korea, Stalin's attention remained mostly focused on Europe, above all, Germany. Fearful that Mao's troops would take over China, the Americans helped Chiang Kai-shek reoccupy large swathes of the country following the Japanese defeat. And whatever his weaknesses, Chiang Kai-shek's wartime alliance with the Americans provided the Republic of China with a new voice in postwar Asian affairs.[26]

The opposite was true of the French. Having been knocked out of the war at the start, the French could hardly hope to retake their Indochinese colony as easily as the British restored their colonial presence in Southeast Asia (the increasingly popular term coined from the British South East Asia Command during the war). Moreover, Gaullist relations with Roosevelt were never good. French marginalization in the Allied decision-making was such that de Gaulle was not even privy to many of the Allied decisions concerning the fate of Indochina. A critical example was the decision taken during the Potsdam Conference in July 1945 by Roosevelt, Stalin, and Churchill which allowed the British to occupy and accept the Japanese surrender in Indochina below the sixteenth parallel while the Republic of China would do the same above that line. In early September 1945, British and Indian troops under the command of General Douglas Gracey began landing in Saigon, while Chinese troops led by General Lu Han established their headquarters in Hanoi. American OSS officers landed in Hanoi and Saigon in search of prisoners of war as the State Department began preparations to re-open its diplomatic offices there.[27]

Ho Chi Minh was keenly aware of the advantages and disadvantages of this war-generated internationalization of Indochina and marginalization of France. But if he had adroitly exploited changes in power relations in order to take power in August a few days after the Japanese capitulation, he knew that these same forces could undo his nascent nation-state and with it the Indochinese Communist Party's fragile hold on power. Ho knew, too, that de Gaulle would do everything in his power to turn the Chinese, Americans, and British against his nascent republic.

De Gaulle was not alone in that endeavor. Accompanying Chinese troops moving into Tonkin and northern Annam in September 1945 were the nationalist leaders of the Vietnamese Nationalist Party, Vu Hong Khanh, and of the Vietnamese Revolutionary Alliance, Nguyen Hai Than. They were counting on their Chinese partners either to overthrow Ho and his government or, if the Chinese insisted on maintaining a national united front, that the Chinese would force the Vietnamese communists to accept a coalition government. (During February 1946, Chiang Kai-shek seriously considered giving the order to his officers in Hanoi to overthrow Ho in favor of their non-communist Vietnamese allies, but in the end refrained from doing anything.) In the south, communist leaders like Tran Van Giau and Pham Ngoc Thach did their best to cooperate with the British. Cooperation among Vietnamese in the south was no easier than in the north, as southern communists struggled to survive in a nationalist coalition with religious groups and Trotskyists whose leaders deeply distrusted the ICP.[28]

It was in this complex context that de Gaulle dispatched his delegates to Indochina with clear orders to re-establish French sovereignty. These men entered into negotiations with the British, Chinese, and Vietnamese with the aim of resuming French control. The British, worried about the preservation of their own Asian empire, but also keen to maintain order on the ground, allowed local French forces to execute a *coup de force* in Saigon on 23 September 1945, pushing the Democratic Republic of Vietnam's southern forces into the countryside as the arriving Expeditionary Corps under General Philippe Leclerc began taking control of the major cities, routes, and bridges in southern Indochina. However, French forces did not do this alone. The British used Indian Gurkhas to help establish order while Japanese soldiers joined the French in combat operations against the Vietnamese below the sixteenth parallel.[29]

The Vietnamese resisted French colonial re-conquest from the outset, but did so in an extremely complicated situation. In December 1945, Nguyen Binh, a former prisoner of Poulo Condor and member of the Vietnamese Nationalist Party, took charge of southern forces for the Democratic Republic of Vietnam. While no one knew it at the time, a thirty-year war for Vietnam had begun, in the south, on 23 September 1945. North of the sixteenth parallel, however, the presence of the Chinese occupation forces continued to protect the DRV against an immediate colonial attack. As onerous as Chinese nationalist occupation most certainly was for the Vietnamese, Chinese republican troops—not Chinese communist ones—helped Ho keep his fledgling nation-state intact. Thanks to the Chinese decision not to overthrow Ho Chi Minh's government, until December 1946 DRV authorities were able to consolidate their state, mobilize the population, and create an army free of direct French intervention. For both the French and Vietnamese, foreign forces were vital to their abilities to promote their respective states in post-Second World War Indochina.[30]

The French understood this and did their best to secure the rapid withdrawal of Chinese forces. Increasing Chinese hostility toward the DRV in early 1946 led Ho to a similar conclusion. In late February, an agreement was reached whereby the Chinese agreed to withdraw their troops in exchange for special privileges for their nationals living in Indochina and the relinquishment of French colonial concessions and privileges in China. The French agreed. The Chinese insisted, however, that the replacement of their troops by French ones required both the French and the Vietnamese to reach an accord first. Local Chinese authorities wanted to avoid the outbreak of a destabilizing war on their watch, as had happened to the British on 23 September 1945. As a result, on 6 March 1946, the French and the Vietnamese signed a preliminary accord, by which Ho Chi Minh accepted that Vietnam would join the Indochinese Federation as a 'free state'. The French would be able to station 15,000 troops above the sixteenth parallel, but also had to agree to organize a referendum on the question of the unification of Cochinchina with the rest of Vietnam. The DRV, as a free state, would be able to run its own government, parliament, and finances, but not its foreign affairs, defense, or currency. Significantly, part of the accord also stipulated that the French forces would withdraw from the DRV within five years. This effectively allowed Ho to defend himself against anticommunist, nationalist charges that the communists were selling out the nation. It was also in this precise context that Ho muttered to a French counterpart that it was 'better to sniff French crap for five years than to have to eat Chinese dung forever!' That said, the agreement was a nightmare for non-communist nationalist leaders because it guaranteed the withdrawal of their main backer, the Chinese. Against the wishes of his own party, Vu Hong Khanh signed the accords with Ho and his French counterpart, Jean Sainteny, probably under heavy Chinese pressure or out of political naivety or both. The nationalist opposition was now vulnerable to attacks from both the French and the DRV.[31]

Although the accords allowed the French and the Democratic Republic of Vietnam to strengthen their respective military positions as the Chinese withdrew, they also offered a chance for peace. Ho understood this and threw himself into finding a negotiated settlement that would result in Vietnam's decolonization. A real problem turned, however, upon the question of the status of Cochinchina. The French now controlled much of it. Ho lost his bet when follow-up conferences designed to resolve the Cochinchina question failed, first in Dalat and then in France in mid-1946. The failure of the French and the Vietnamese to find a peaceful solution to the status of Cochinchina allowed colonial hardliners in Indochina like Thierry d'Argenlieu to take matters into their hands, making a compromise solution increasingly difficult to achieve. In a desperate move, Ho pleaded with Marius Moutet, a member of the Socialist Party and in charge of the Ministry of Overseas France (formerly known as the Ministry of Colonies), whom Ho knew from his Paris days, to sign a preliminary accord in

September 1946. It would prescribe, among other things, a ceasefire in the south. Moutet agreed, but the lack of political will in France, exacerbated by ever-changing governments in Paris, allowed local authorities in Indochina to apply de Gaulle's instructions to the letter, rolling back the DRV's national sovereignty in favor of the colonial federation. Such brinkmanship led to serious clashes in Lang Son and Haiphong in November 1946, before the Vietnamese lashed out in Hanoi on the evening of 19 December 1946. Long spoiling for a fight, local French authorities were all too ready to reply with force. Full-scale colonial war started that evening in Hanoi.

Civil War Begins

Wars of decolonization almost always spawn civil violence as different groups vie for control over the postcolonial state and its ideological soul. The first to challenge the communist claim to Vietnam were their former anticommunist nationalist enemies from the colonial prisons and southern China, above all the Vietnamese Nationalist Party. However, upon coming to power in mid-1945, the Democratic Republic of Vietnam could not immediately unleash its security services against the opposition. Any premature moves ran the risk of alienating potential allies across the political spectrum and from within the colonial state the communists were so desperately trying to take in hand. Most importantly, the occupation of northern Vietnam by Chinese republican troops had meant that the Indochinese Communist Party needed to be extremely careful. Chinese commanding officers in Tonkin, such as Lou Han, Zhang Fakui, and Siao Wen, had long supported non-communist Vietnamese anticolonialists in southern China. They knew perfectly well that Ho was a Comintern-trained communist with longstanding links to the Chinese Communist Party.

Who, exactly, constituted the opposition in the north in 1945? Three parties stand out: the Vietnamese Nationalist Party led by Vu Hong Khanh, the Dai Viet, or the Greater Vietnam coalition under Truong Tu Anh's leadership, and the Vietnamese Revolutionary Alliance marshaled by Nguyen Hai Than. None of them were pro French; all of them were nationalist; and each was anticommunist. We have already encountered the Vietnamese Nationalist Party and the Vietnamese Revolutionary Alliance. Greater Vietnam was a non-communist, nationalist coalition of urban, mainly northern elite members who had come together during the Popular Front period. This party consisted of republican nationalists such as Nguyen Tuong Tam and more authoritarian-minded ones like Truong Tu Anh. However, the outbreak of the Second World War led the French to crack down on these nationalists. Many of Greater Vietnam's leaders ended up in prison, fled to southern China, like Nguyen Tuong Tam, or went underground to work against the French, with or without Japanese backing.[32]

The communist core of the Democratic Republic of Vietnam had no love lost for any of these men and that feeling was fully shared by anticommunists. In the days following its seizure of power in August 1945, before the Chinese arrived to intervene, the communists jailed dozens of their opponents who had 'collaborated' with the Japanese and sinned against the Indochinese Communist Party. The chief of the DRV police has described how he toured a jail where he viewed with great satisfaction the incarceration of several dangerous 'traitors' who 'had blood debts' toward the people and the party. The security services arrested leading non-communist politicians such as Tran Trong Kim, Ngo Dinh Khoi, Ngo Dinh Diem, and Pham Quynh. The Viet Minh executed Ngo Dinh Khoi and Pham Quynh. Only Ho Chi Minh's personal intervention saved Khoi's brother, Ngo Dinh Diem from a similar fate. In all, several thousand enemies of the communists 'failed to survive abductions' in the wake of the August insurrection of 1945. As in China, such violence hardly built trust or facilitated cooperation between communist and non-communist nationalists following the Japanese defeat.[33]

The arrival of the Chinese occupying forces put a brake on the executions and delayed the start of what would have surely become a full-blown civil war in October 1945. Determined to deny the Chinese any pretext for overthrowing the fledgling government, the communists swallowed hard and allowed the opposition to organize propaganda drives, operate newspapers, publish political cartoons satirizing the communists and even ones which ridiculed Ho Chi Minh, the 'father' of the new nation. Never in the history of twentieth-century Vietnam, neither under the French colonialists nor the Vietnamese communists, did the press and opposition operate so freely. Thanks to the Chinese security umbrella, these parties widened their memberships, mobilized youth groups, and recruited for their militias. Opposition leaders decried what they considered to be the communist monopoly on power. They called for the creation of a truly nationalist coalition, with non-communists holding key ministries. Their wish was granted on several occasions, thanks to Chinese pressure. It was all part of their bid to roll back communist efforts to define the foundations of the state, national identity, and power at this crucial conjuncture.

Civil war erupted when the Chinese finished pulling the bulk of their troops out of upper Vietnam in mid-June 1946. Within a few weeks, the communists unleashed the security forces against the Vietnamese Nationalist Party, Vietnamese Revolutionary Alliance, and Greater Vietnam in Hanoi, while Vo Nguyen Giap used his emerging army against nationalist troops located in the countryside. In July, the DRV security forces descended upon the opposition's headquarters, offices, and presses in Hanoi. In the Red River area, the government sent its army northward to recover provincial towns held by the opposition parties as their Chinese protectors withdrew across the border. As one Democratic Republic of Vietnam officer later described the civil violence he witnessed in a small border town: 'On the right side of the building a man emerged with a gun in his hand, a bayonet attached to it. He's three meters from me when I put him in my sights, throw myself to the ground, and shoot. He stood there, his gun in the air, looking at me, and then he collapsed'. Vietnamese were now killing Vietnamese, as civil war returned to Vietnam for the first time since the eighteenth century. The French did not start this. It was a Vietnamese affair. It was also the first in a long line of civil conflicts that would mark modern Vietnamese history until 1975. As one anticommunist nationalist later recalled the violence that took his father from him: 'Patriotism at the highest degree gives to some an almost unimaginable will to survive, but it also encourages people of the same forefathers to kill their compatriots more eagerly and savagely. That is a reality of the armed conflict from 1945 to 1975 in Viet Nam'.[34]

In the south, two religious groups posed a major problem for the DRV— the Cao Dai and the Hoa Hao. As we saw earlier, the Cao Dai faith is a syncretic, monotheistic religion, combining elements of Taoism, Buddhism, Confucianism, Christianity, and humanism. The Cao Dai Church emerged in the wake of the First World War, and under its main leader, Pham Cong Tac, had adopted an increasingly political trajectory during the 1930s. The colonial police arrested Pham Cong Tac because of his links to the Japanese and his attempts to create an autonomous religious state and militia. The treatment of the leader of the Hoa Hao faith followed a similar track. It had emerged in the late 1930s in the Mekong delta. Its messianic leader, the young and dashing Huynh Phu So, drew heavily upon local Buddhist beliefs to build this millenarian religious movement with its roots deep in the past. The Japanese backed Huynh Phu So, and had put pressure on the French to release him from captivity. With the defeat of the Japanese, Hoa

Hao and Cao Dai leaders joined the DRV in opposition to the return of the French.

This cooperation did not last for long, however. Religious leaders of both groups were wary of the DRV's communist core and the idea of subordinating their forces to any control other than their own. The French quickly picked up on this tension as they returned to the Mekong delta and sought to rebuild their Indochinese house. Determined to turn anyone they could against the DRV, the French had no problems forgetting about the past. They immediately released Pham Cong Tac from the state of exile in Madagascar which they had imposed upon him, and returned him to the Mekong delta region in mid-1946 on the condition that he rally his church and people to the French cause. Pham Cong Tac agreed. On 8 January 1947, as the Expeditionary Corps retook Hanoi street by street, Pham Cong Tac signed an accord with the French and, within a few weeks, thousands of his followers began to cross over to the French side as the DRV scrambled to hold together their national coalition in the south.

The Democratic Republic of Vietnam's leadership authorized its representatives to contact the Cao Dai leadership secretly in a bid to stop the defections to the French. Talks occurred in January 1947, but to no avail. The Cao Dai asked the DRV to pull out of their home base in Tay Ninh province; the latter refused, invoking their sovereignty over all of the south. Things went immediately from bad to worse, as the Democratic Republic of Vietnam's security and military forces became involved in another civil war, this time with Cao Dai forces armed and supplied by the French secret services. By June 1947, most of the Cao Dai's forces had crossed over to the Franco-Vietnamese side, but not without leaving behind a trail of blood.[35]

Civil violence broke out almost simultaneously with the Hoa Hao. At the outset, Huynh Phu So was a special delegate in the Democratic Republic of Vietnam's southern administration. However, when he began to ally his followers, not alongside but with the Dang Dan Xa, a Hoa Hao political party independent of the DRV's control, relations between the two sides deteriorated rapidly. More importantly, like Pham Cong Tac, Huynh Phu So was also loathe to submit his military forces to the DRV's national control. And his religious antipathy toward communism was well known. When Huynh Phu So entered into secret negotiations with the French secret services in early 1947, southern DRV leaders reacted with violence. Tay Ninh province was rapidly slipping from the Democratic Republic of Vietnam's control, and, with it, hundreds of thousands of people. In April

1947, tensions between the Hoa Hao and the DRV were so bad that the latter decided to execute the church's spiritual leader, Huynh Phu So, in what had to be one of the biggest political blunders it ever committed. It created a sea of hate.[36]

A year later, the French successfully rallied yet another southern group to their cause, the brigands turned patriots known as the Binh Xuyen and named for the small village outside Saigon from whence they came. Ironically, this group led by Bay Vien had caused the French security services headaches during the interwar period. Arrested for theft, Bay Vien ended up in Poulo Condor, where he learned from political prisoners what the word 'Vietnam' really meant. He also saw with his own eyes the latent civil war already building behind colonial bars between communists and non-communists. The Binh Xuyen embraced the nationalist cause in 1945, but distrusted communists and the leader they had chosen to run the military show in the south, Nguyen Binh. Bay Vien finally broke with the DRV in mid-1948 as French intelligence officers adroitly steered his entourage toward the creation of an anticommunist state led by Bao Dai (see chapter 8).

That said, loyalties and strategies did not remain static. Unlike the civil war in the north, communism was not the only thing dividing the Vietnamese in the south. The creation of a modern, unitary nation-state, and the incorporation of what had been the separate colony of Cochinchina, was also a major source of friction. Local leaders, peoples, and identities often opposed the DRV government's attempt to assert central control and impose a new national identity over the south. The French would try to turn this friction to their advantage by according special privileges and autonomy to particular groups, hoping to divide in order to rule. But the Cao Dai, Hoa Hao, and Binh Xuyen were actors too, perfectly capable of 'playing' the colonizers to their advantage in order preserve their autonomous proto-states in the delta. It was only in 1955, during the Battle of Saigon, that Ngo Dinh Diem would finally achieve what Nguyen Binh had failed to do in 1947—to defeat the Hoa Hao, Cao Dai, and Binh Xuyen in order to create one sovereign nation-state, the Republic of Vietnam. It was no accident that Diem drove out the French at the same time.

CHAPTER 8

STATES OF WAR

N GUYEN BINH GREW up poor in the northern province of Hai Hung. He dropped out of school at an early age and drifted to Haiphong in search of work. In 1926, he tried his luck in Saigon, where he found jobs as a laundry boy and dockworker. He also discovered nationalist politics, joining a local branch of the Vietnamese Nationalist Party (VNQDD). Two years later, the colonial police caught up with him and sent him off to Poulo Condor. Binh's street smarts served him well in the rough-and-tumble world of the colonial prison. Overcrowding was rampant as massive arrests flooded cells with communists and nationalists after the revolts of the early 1930s. Both these groups wanted the French out of their country, but neither trusted the other. Ideological differences got so bad that Binh lost one of his eyes in a cell-block brawl before the new Popular Front government in France freed many political prisoners, including Binh.

Although Binh declined offers to leave the Vietnamese Nationalist Party, some of the most important Vietnamese communists knew who Binh was when he resurfaced in the north years later at the head of an armed group of miners trying to take over the coast near Haiphong from the defeated Japanese. When word of such exploits reached the new president of Vietnam in September 1945, Ho Chi Minh invited him to the capital and made Binh an offer he could not refuse—the command of the armed forces of the Democratic Republic of Vietnam in the Mekong delta. Nguyen Binh's prewar knowledge of the south, legendary charisma, meticulous organizational skills, and burning nationalism trumped his non-communism. Dressed in a Japanese military gabardine and boots, with a long Mikado sabre hanging from his side, Binh accepted Ho's offer and left for the south in late 1945.

The similarities to the political situation of the 1860s (discussed in chapter 3) are striking. Ho needed Binh to fight an angry war against the reinvading French, but the president also needed his southern general to stop fighting when ordered, so that the government could negotiate a way out of full-scale war. Unlike Truong Dinh (Tu Duc's commander in the south eighty years earlier), Nguyen Binh respected Ho's orders to cease fighting

in October 1946. But like Truong Dinh, Nguyen Binh had no faith in the invaders' desire to stop fighting. After the brutal French assault on Haiphong
in November 1946, he warned the commanding general in the north, Vo
Nguyen Giap, to forget negotiations and to begin a scorched earth-policy
from then onward: 'When we will have won, we will rebuild.' As it turned
out, Binh was right. The French wanted war; but this time they had badly
underestimated their adversaries, and it would cost everyone dearly.[1]

REMAKING COCHINCHINA AS A COLONIAL WEAPON[2]

The French had no idea when they dislodged the DRV authorities in Saigon in September 1945 that they were embarking on a war that would end
their colonial presence in Indochina a decade later. Although the Second
World War had generated great global change, leaders of all political colors
in France continued to see the maintenance of their empire as an essential,
achievable, and an entirely legitimate goal. Vichy and Gaullist France had
both relied heavily on the empire during the war. With the Allied liberation of France in 1944, continued control of Indochina and North Africa
would help the new French leadership rebuild their war-torn country economically and allow it to remain a player on the world scene. Even French
communists eyeing power in August 1944 concurred that the government
should not bow to any attacks that 'would undermine its sovereignty as a
great power, nor its strict right to administer overseas territories under its
control'.[3]

For the French in 1945, there was nothing necessarily inevitable about
decolonization. The new political class taking over in Paris was willing to
reform colonial structures; but leaders on the left and right had no intention of liquidating the empire in Indochina or of transforming it into an
independent member of a commonwealth as Winston Churchill's Labor
successor did for India. Charles de Gaulle ordered the re-conquest and the
re-establishment of colonial sovereignty to all of Indochina. The Brazzaville
Conference of 1944 and the Indochina Declaration of 1945 discussed in
the previous chapter would serve as the blueprints for rebuilding France's
Asian colony in the form of a pentagonal Indochinese federation within
a French Union. As de Gaulle, the liberator of France, thundered to one
of the rare Indochina specialists who dared to give a warning about the
dangers of ignoring Vietnamese nationalism: 'Dear Professor, we will win

because we are the strongest'. There was much continuity in French colonial thinking.[4]

As in the nineteenth century, the military had the job of re-conquering Indochina and rebuilding the colonial state. General Philippe Leclerc, the commander-in-chief of the newly constituted Expeditionary Corps for the Far East, presided over the re-occupation of Indochina as his troops began debarking in southern Vietnam in October 1945. When the former Governor General Albert Sarraut declined the offer to run postwar Indochina, de Gaulle named a naval officer as high commissioner, Admiral Georges Thierry d'Argenlieu. Another military man, Jean Cédile, arrived in Saigon in September as Commissioner of Cochinchina, and, with the support of the British, did his best to re-establish French sovereignty. In the north, Jean Sainteny, Sarraut's son-in-law, landed in Hanoi as the Commissioner of Annam and Tonkin.

The French armed forces did what every army does when involved in colonial conquest—they immediately became involved in state-making. Once troops had dislodged enemy forces, officers began restoring new provincial and district administrations and village councils. The government's instructions to commanding officers in the field were clear: 'to re-establish everywhere a Franco-Annamese administration like the one prior to 1939'. Most welcome were former Vietnamese civil servants, ones who had avoided the Democratic Republic of Vietnam (DRV), left it, or got off the fence once it was clear that the balance of power had favorably changed. Their bilingualism, contacts, and detailed knowledge of the local administration and villages made them priceless intermediaries for the French officers, who, with a few exceptions, knew little of Indochina.[5]

Unlike the situation in the nineteenth century, these newly arriving officers could also rely on a group of French colonial civil servants to help them. These men had served for years in Indochina. Whereas many in the British colonial service in Southeast Asia had perished under the Japanese or were sidelined by the arrival of a new generation of colonial administrators, the Japanese had kept on the colonial civil service in Vichy Indochina until March 1945 (in order to rule indirectly through the French). Despite icy first encounters with Gaullists suspicious of such collaboration, the practical matters of colonial conquest almost always trumped intra-French ideological differences. Cédile, Sainteny, and Thierry d'Argenlieu needed these experienced French administrators as badly as they did the Vietnamese notables in the countryside. Few in the end were purged. As a member of the special committee in charge of this question said of one zealous defender of Pétain's former national revolution: 'He's a monarchist, a Maurrassian. He has his views, but we can't hold them against him'. Instead they transferred him into the army as a political advisor. In 1948, he became the chief of cabinet to the high commissioner in Saigon. 1945 was not always a point of rupture in French colonial rule. Again, there was much continuity.[6]

Indeed, these French Indochinese hands not only returned to their positions, but they actually advanced their careers and exercised great influence over colonial policy and state-building. Who were they? Highest on the list was Léon Pignon, a graduate of the elite Colonial Academy. He had begun his administrative career in Indochina in the early 1930s under Pierre Pasquier. He returned to France in the late 1930s, joined the Free French, and became one of de Gaulle's top colonial advisors in Algiers. He participated in the Brazzaville Conference and helped craft the Indochina Declaration. He returned to Indochina in 1945 as the highest-ranking political advisor to Jean Sainteny and High Commissioner Georges Thierry d'Argenlieu, and then became high commissioner himself in 1948. Upon arriving in Hanoi, he immediately contacted his longtime colleagues and, thanks to his Resistance credentials, began recruiting them into the new colonial project. Pignon's close collaborator and specialist in colonial law, Albert Torel, began fleshing out the Indochinese Federation and its constitution. Marcel Bazin and Charles Bonfils rebuilt the police and security services, while Jean Cousseau helped resuscitate the pre-existing administration. Despite their different politics and wartime experiences, these administrators were all agreed, like the Gaullists they joined, that they had to restore the colonial order and that the Indochinese Federation was the best way to do it. Deeply influenced by the ideas of Sarraut and Pasquier, not to mention a heavy dose of Orientalism, these men were also diehard supporters of colonial monarchy, convinced that the peasant masses were deeply conservative and would follow their kings once order was restored. The only thing the peasants wanted, Torel told anyone who would listen, was 'the return of French peace'.[7]

Unable to retake northern Indochina at the outset, French authorities concentrated first on creating the federal state for Indochina and its local governments below the sixteenth parallel. The Indochinese Federation would consist of eleven administrative bodies each run by a French commissioner (these bodies would cover economy, security, political affairs, diplomacy, etc.). A new French high commissioner (the former governor general) would lead the federal government, assisted by five more commis-

sioners (formerly résidents supérieurs) in charge of each of the five territorial governments of the federation—Cochinchina, Annam, Tonkin, Laos,
and Cambodia. Although plans began for creating an Indochinese parliament to provide an increased voice for the colonized in local affairs, the
French controlled the colony's diplomacy, defense, and commerce. The
Indochinese *piastre* remained the official currency. Ho Chi Minh's new national currency, the *dong*, would have to go, as would the Democratic Republic of Vietnam's government bulletin which announced its decrees. On
3 January 1946, the Indochinese Federation's official bulletin (the Journal
officiel de la Fédération indochinoise) appeared in Saigon. Two states, one
national under Ho Chi Minh in the north (see chapter 7), the other colonial
under Thierry d'Argenlieu in the south, co-existed and were in competition
with each other in 1945-6, violently in the south, indirectly in the north.
Each entity claimed territories and people it did not fully control in the
other's domain. It was an explosive condominium of rival sovereignties that
simply could not last.[8]

Leclerc's men quickly overthrew the nationalist government Son Ngoc
Thanh had created in Cambodia under the Japanese in mid-1945. Having
been crowned by Vichy and then sidelined by the nationalists, King Norodom Sihanouk was only too happy to welcome the French back while the
Indochinese administrators were thrilled to have a monarch on their side. A
preliminary accord signed in January 1946 made Cambodia the first of the
five projected free states ('*Etats libres*') to join the emerging Indochinese
Federation. A few months later, with the withdrawal of the Chinese, the
French reoccupied Laos, drove out the Lao Issara ('Free Lao') government
that had taken power, and signed another preliminary accord adding Laos
(and a second monarch, Sisavang Vong), as the second of the five projected
free states.

From Saigon, Colonel Cédile began assembling a provisional government for what the French still considered to be their formal colony of
Cochinchina. Unlike in Laos and Cambodia, however, the French had no
emperor to whom they could turn. Bao Dai had joined the nationalists. So
had the southern leaders of the Cao Dai, Hoa Hao, and Binh Xuyen. The
assassination of Sarraut's 'faithful few', Bui Quang Chieu and Pham Quynh,
further reduced the field and left many moderates sitting on the fence. A
former Constitutionalist, Nguyen Phan Long, steered clear of the French in
1945, warning them of the dangers of their hostility to 'Vietnam'—the word
that everyone now knew to mean a unitary nation-state.

The French settler population did anything but stand still. Europeans had lived in Cochinchina since the late nineteenth century and by 1945 were concentrated in its urban centers. Like their counterparts in Algeria, they were hostile to the rise of colonial nationalism and tried to contain it at every turn. The advent of a nation-state would end their privileged positions at the top of the colonial ladder. Most also opposed the democratization of colonial institutions, fearful that the 'native' majority would vote them out of Indochina. Compared to the European population in Algeria, whose numbers in 1954 totaled one million out of a total 'native' population of eight and a half million (11.5 percent), in 1945 only 32,000 French lived among a population of twenty-four million in 'Vietnam', a miniscule 0.13 percent. Moreover, the Japanese occupation had humiliated the settlers and the Democratic Republic of Vietnam's one-month chaotic rule over the south had struck fear into their hearts. The outpouring of joy the French showed upon welcoming General Leclerc to Saigon in October 1945 was as real as the shame one young nationalist felt on witnessing French troops arrive in Hanoi to start replacing withdrawing Chinese ones six months later: 'On the sidewalks French civilian residents of Hanoi stood cheering. On the balcony each one of us was brushing away tears'. Emotions on all sides ran high.[9]

Leading figures in the French community like William Bazé, Maurice Weil, and Henry de Lachevrotière lost no time presenting themselves to arriving Gaullist officials as the experts on all things Indochinese. Bazé and Lachevrotière published the main newspapers for French settlers in Saigon; had important economic interests in the Mekong delta; and were both the offspring of Franco-Vietnamese marriages. All three had avoided the stain of collaboration during the war and forged good relationships with Gaullist officers. Although these local politicians welcomed de Gaulle's desire to re-establish colonial rule by force, a federation was not enough. Aware of their vulnerability, settlers promoted a strategy of Cochinchinese separatism designed to prevent the colony's absorption into any Vietnamese unitary state—colonial, national, or federal. For Weil, Bazé, and Lachevrotière, this meant insisting on Cochinchina's special legal status as a French colony and playing up the uniqueness of the 'south'. Pignon's civil servants backed them and together they brought Cédile and Thierry d'Argenlieu on board. Separatism seemed all the more necessary for all of them when the French government agreed in the March 1946 accords to hold a referendum on the unification of Cochinchina with the unitary 'Vietnam' of the DRV above the sixteenth parallel. Not only would this transform French Indochina into a triangular entity (DRV Vietnam, Laos, and Cambodia), but it would also force the settlers and French civil servants to share power with Ho Chi Minh's entourage in a unitary colonial Vietnamese state housed within an Indochinese federation. Such a modification was illegal, they insisted, since, as a colony, only the French parliament could change Cochinchina's status.

From mid-March, this triumvirate—the French settlers, the High Commissioner, and his Indochinese hands—accelerated its efforts to create a local Cochinchinese government as the next 'free state' of the Indochinese Federation, before any referendum could be organized or Ho could reach a separate deal in France to unify 'Vietnam'. The settlers formed Cochinchinese political parties, mobilized their papers for the separatist cause, recruited like-minded 'native' southerners (usually those with French citizenship), and fired off scores of petitions to politicians in Paris to make sure that Cochinchina remained French and retained its own identity. Separatist journalists fanned a virulent 'anti-Tonkinese' campaign in the press. For them it was important to stress that Cochinchina was unique, different from its northern counterpart, and to promote the idea that 'Cochinchinese' and 'Tonkinese' Vietnam were so different that the unification of these two territories (Cochinchina and DRV Vietnam) would be impossible. In so doing, they conveniently forgot that the 'native Cochinchinese' had substantially migrated to Cochinchina from the north over the centuries. Even Lachevrotière's mother had been born in Tonkin.

The triumvirate leaders understood that they could not establish an 'all white' Cochinchinese regime. Faced with a *de facto* national government in Hanoi, as well as many pro-unification Vietnamese moderates in Saigon, not to mention the infinitesimal French population, they felt compelled to bring on board like-minded southerners for a Cochinchinese solution to work. Settlers turned to ethnic Viet elite members with whom they had worked before 1945. Most were bourgeois, large landowners, held French citizenship, shared the settlers' anticommunism, had served in the French army, or had protected the French population against Japanese and nationalist molestation. Thanks to his Freemason contacts, Maurice Weil had the greatest success in recruiting a core group of 'native' partners, like Nguyen Van Thinh and Nguyen Van Xuan.[10]

These southerners had their own reasons for joining, however. Nguyen Van Thinh was a doctor, a Freemason, and head of the Democratic Party.

A committed republican, he was convinced that the new leadership in France would finally introduce long-promised democratic reforms that would protect bourgeois interests the best. He wanted, above all, to end the chaos the Japanese and the Democratic Republic of Vietnam had unleashed over the summer. He spurned national revolution and its attendant radicalism. He was a large landowner and a major rice-grower (who had tried to organize famine relief for northern peasants in 1944–5). His close collaborator, Nguyen Van Xuan, was also a Freemason and a colonel in the French army (Pétain had personally decorated him for bravery during the First World War). A member of the French Socialist Party, he too believed that this 'new France' would implement liberal change. Nguyen Van Tam was a hard-working rural administrator whose virulent anticommunism attracted everyone in the triumvirate community. In 1940, he had played a central role in helping the colonial police smash the communist uprising in Cochinchina. His hate for the communists was visceral. His loyalty to the French was unshakeable. The Japanese tortured him for it, and that was before forces loyal to the DRV killed two of his sons, something Tam never forgave. He had committed himself to helping the French return. All of these men had ties to the French and important economic interests to protect; but they were not a monolithic or static group.

Thierry d'Argenlieu accepted the settlers' separatist strategy and their Cochinchinese recruits as long as that fitted with de Gaulle's orders to rebuild a pentagonal Indochinese federation. Like so many French officers of the time, the admiral had also served in the empire and shared settler hostility toward the rise of native nationalism. In February 1946, Thierry d'Argenlieu supported the creation of the Cochinchinese Consultative Council under the leadership of the (French) Commissioner for Cochinchina. Like his Vichy predecessor, the high commissioner appointed all the council's members on the recommendation of the Cochinchinese commissioner, Jean Cédile. Nguyen Van Thinh became its president, seconded by Nguyen Van Xuan. But what troubled the triumvirate most was that Ho Chi Minh could try and go around them all, by reaching a deal in Paris to make Cochinchina a part of 'DRV Vietnam' and keep it in the federation for a few years, in order to try and nudge the French out later on. This was exactly what Ho hoped to do by holding the French to the accords which they had signed in March 1946. And this is also why, on 1 June, the day after the DRV president left for France, the high commissioner announced the creation of the Provisional Government of the Republic of Cochinchina *without* formal approval from Paris. This was the first of several *faits accomplis* the French authorities in Saigon engineered to prevent an accord on Cochinchina from being reached above their heads in Paris.

That said, the high commissioner had no intention of transferring power to a Cochinchinese government either. The French ruled through the federal level, being in charge of the colony's security, budget, diplomacy, and defense. The Cochinchinese solution was designed foremost to serve as a weapon to protect the colony from the nationalists and as a lever to force the French government's hand if need be. As DRV and French delegates met in Fontainebleau to follow up on the March accords, Thierry d'Argenlieu and his Indochinese supporters unilaterally organized a conference in Dalat in the summer of 1946 to move ahead on the Indochinese Federation, including the consolidation of Cochinchina as a 'free state' within that polity. Paris acquiesced again, ensuring the failure of the negotiations in Fontainebleau. Led by Lachevrotière and Bazé, the settlers organized a vocal lobby to push the separatist cause—the Union for the Defence of French Achievements in Indochina (Union pour la défense de l'oeuvre française en Indochine). Cochinchina, they repeated, was a French colony and thus had to remain autonomous in the federation. There could be no referendum, no unification, and there was no place for it in for the DRV.

This was a very hard line leading straight to war and Thinh, Xuan, and their like-minded allies began to plead for moderation during the Fontainebleau Conference. They objected to the ethnic divisions the triumvirate promoted, its implacable opposition to negotiations with Ho, and started talking about the need to bring union-minded, non-communist Cochinchinese moderates on board in order to expand the government's support beyond the French settlers. Widely read newspapers in Saigon favorable to the cause of union had already been making the case for negotiations. However, such talk drew the immediate wrath of the Cochinchinese French, who suspected these moderates of 'nationalism' and condemned their policy as dangerous 'appeasement'. Politicians like Thinh suddenly found themselves suspected of being 'anti French' by one group and 'anti-Vietnamese' by the other. Compared to Ho, who could openly embrace the nationalist cause, symbols, myths, and a state, Thinh could do little. Timid and uncharismatic, he had no popular support among the southern Vietnamese. His only political base and military guarantee was that of the triumvirate. Unlike Le Van Duyet's revolt against Minh Mang's unification project in the early 1830s, it was French settlers who led the southern separatist charge in the late 1940s. Meanwhile, Vietnamese moderates distanced themselves, unwilling to compromise themselves with such colonial hardliners or run the risk of assassination by DRV supporters. For many Francophile Viet, it was this ferocious colonial hostility to Vietnamese nationalism even in its tamest forms that led them to avoid the French or to join the DRV, not their support of communism.[11]

Nguyen Van Thinh was extremely naïve to think he could change the triumvirate's tack. He learned this in November 1946, when his opponents on the Cochinchinese Consultative Council demanded that he reshuffle his cabinet by the fifteenth of the month in order to get rid of the 'appeasers' and 'nationalists'. Colonial authorities closed pro-unification newspapers, imposed strict censorship, and harassed those favorable to negotiations with Ho. When Thierry d'Argenlieu refused to meet a desperate Nguyen Van Thinh on 9 November, the president now recognized his Cochinchinese republic for what it really was—a colonial political weapon designed to stop all Vietnamese nationalists, including himself. Upon arriving at work the next morning, Thinh asked his collaborators not to disturb him as he walked into his office. There he quietly threw one end of a rope around the lock of an elevated window, fastened the other around his neck, and hung himself. The note he left behind read: 'If the majority of our people did not understand me, I want you my friends, the intellectuals from the North, South and Center, you who carry the destiny of the country on your shoulders, to stop playing a criminal wait-and-see game. You must react. I die in order to show you the path of duty, liberty, and honor'. This would not be the last non-communist nationalist to die in such tragic circumstances, trapped by powerful partners, overcome by events, and misled by political naiveté.[12]

Thinh's suicide did nothing to halt Saigon's march to war against Ho Chi Minh's Vietnam. Two weeks later, Thierry d'Argenlieu, fully backed by his new general, Jean Valluy, focused their attention on the north when they challenged the Democratic Republic of Vietnam's right to collect customs duties in Haiphong. (It was a perfect example of how one state moved in on the other's sovereignty.) In so doing, these men intentionally transformed what could have easily remained a minor altercation into a pretext for conquering this strategic port city by force and setting off a war. When the Vietnamese delayed, Valluy authorized the shelling and aerial strafing of Haiphong and its surroundings on 23 November, resulting in 3,000 mainly civilian deaths. One month later, the DRV Vietnamese lashed out in Hanoi

to protect their shrinking territorial sovereignty. At 20:00 hours on the evening of 19 December, their backs to the wall, they attacked. Full-scale war
in Indochina was now underway. The high commissioner now had the excuse he needed—Vietnamese 'perfidy'—to force the French government's
hand (a liberal-minded socialist, Léon Blum, was taking over in Paris) and
destroy the nation-state which was blocking the restoration of French sovereignty to all of Indochina. From the sidelines, the now retired de Gaulle,
the man most responsible for starting the First Indochina War, cheered on
his admiral, as did the old Indochina hands led by Léon Pignon. The high
commissioner immediately prohibited the official use of the term 'Vietnam'
in favor of 'Cochinchina', 'Annam', and 'Tonkin'. To colonial minds, one
said 'Annamese', not 'Vietnamese', with the semantic significance being all
about territorial sovereignty. The French did not go to war on 19 December
1946 in order to stop communism. They went to war to stop Vietnamese
nationalism and to rebuild their Indochinese colonial state. And had war
not happened on the nineteenth, it would have occurred on another day.[13]

Meanwhile, French authorities sought feverishly to win over groups dis-
enchanted with the DRV. In early January 1947, as fighting continued in
Hanoi, the mastermind of French policy in Indochina, Léon Pignon, wrote
to the high commissioner: 'Our goal is clearly fixed: Transfer to the internal
Annamese level the quarrel we have with the Viet Minh party and involve
ourselves as little as possible in campaigns and reprisals which must be the
work of the native adversaries of this party [. . .].' Within weeks, French
civil and military officials opened secret negotiations with the Cao Dai, Hoa
Hao, and Binh Xuyen leaders in the south. That the first two groups had
collaborated with the Japanese and that the third had massacred French
civilians in Saigon in September 1945 mattered little in this classic divide-
and-rule strategy. By mid-1947, the French had rallied most of the Cao Dai
and Hoa Hao forces (the Binh Xuyen crossed over to support them a year
later), setting off a ferocious, albeit already simmering civil war with the
Democratic Republic of Vietnam supporters in the south. (See chapter 7).[14]

A SAVAGE WAR OF SOVEREIGNTIES[15]

What the French could not fathom as Valluy's troops went on the attack
in 1947 was that the Democratic Republic of Vietnam would survive the
assault, assert its territorial sovereignty, continue to build an army capable

of protecting it, and mobilize hundreds of thousands of people to maintain a state of war. Upon taking power in mid-1945, the DRV leadership did everything possible to train, outfit, and deploy an army. The protective cover provided by the Chinese occupation troops contributed greatly to this process. In mid-1946, the Vietnamese Defense Force (Ve Quoc Doan), the first independent Vietnamese army since the late nineteenth century, came to life. The Defense Force numbered around 100,000 troops, with 60,000 active in the north and 40,000 in the south. It operated under a general staff and was divided into organizational units (mainly battalions and platoons). Added to this were around 50,000 young militiamen and women operating mainly in the cities at the outset. Unsurprisingly, many came from Franco-Japanese youth and colonial scouting organizations.[16]

All of them were badly trained, poorly armed, and militarily inexperienced. With the outbreak of full-scale war, the army received strict instructions to avoid set-piece battles with the French, whose superior firepower and experience could destroy the fledgling army at the time when the state needed it most. Guerilla warfare was the *mot d'ordre*. Texts on partisan struggles in the Soviet Union, Maoist China, and the French Resistance during the Second World War circulated widely in *quoc ngu* translation. The head of the fledgling army, Vo Nguyen Giap, adapted Maoist ideas to the Vietnamese context while the party's general secretary, Truong Chinh, explained why their resistance would inevitably win by relying on its own strength and self-sufficiency. Japanese fighters who had crossed over to the DRV cause, European deserters, and colonially trained Vietnamese officers provided crash courses in military science and command. Meanwhile, dozens of French-trained technicians and engineers created cottage industries to produce rudimentary but operational guns, grenades, and even bazookas. What they couldn't produce they tried to recover from the enemy, or import clandestinely from the French-occupied zones. Until the Chinese communist victory in late 1949, the Democratic Republic of Vietnam had no committed foreign backers and few modern arms.[17]

None of this stopped the government from militarizing the villages it controlled, creating militias, flooding villagers with hate-filled nationalist propaganda, or even organizing war games for children. Besides harassing the Expeditionary Corps with hit-and-run operations, the DRV also launched attacks on those who they thought would collaborate with the French and their state-making project. The government had already assigned this task to their commander-in-chief in the south, Nguyen Binh.

This legendary, one-eyed non-communist from Tonkin we met above directed a war of terror against provincial and districts towns to ensure that the Vietnamese did not participate in French separatism or undermine the national government's control over people, resources, and territory. By 1947, the southern military and security services had killed hundreds of colonially trained Vietnamese bureaucrats who had been working with the French and kept even more on the sidelines. This is where Vietnamese partisans hurt the French most during the first half of the conflict—on the administrative front. As in the late nineteenth century, the French had little choice but to employ under-qualified people in their place, with all the risks this entailed for good governance and colonial legitimacy.[18]

Hanoi and Saigon became important strategic targets, too. Hanoi, the former capital of French Indochina and now of the DRV, was the site of a brutal two-month urban battle which initiated the thirty-year-long war for Vietnam. Between 19 December 1946 and 17 February 1947, two thousand young civilian militiamen running on high levels of patriotism, but with few arms and little experience, held out in a maze of streets, houses, and shops making up the capital's old quarter, as French tanks and paratroopers moved in under the cover of artillery barrages and aerial bombing. On the outskirts of the town, a handful of DRV battalions did their best to block French reinforcements rushing in by road. Intense firefights resulted. When the battle ended, the Democratic Republic of Vietnam had lost around a thousand civilian militiamen and soldiers. The French probably lost 500 soldiers. The old quarter of Hanoi lay in a heap of rubble and remained largely deserted until 1948. If sovereignty over the capital had returned to the French, the battle nonetheless allowed the DRV to transfer its national capital to the countryside, along with several thousand civil servants, engineers, radio operators, nurses, and doctors.[19]

Saigon was just as important. Between 1946 and 1950, Nguyen Binh conducted a terrorist assault on Saigon, targeting French installations and Vietnamese collaborators. Bombs went off in milk bars, while agents lobbed grenades where settlers were living. In April 1946, in a spectacular raid designed to stop separatists in the south, Binh's commandos blew up part of the French naval arsenal built in the 1860s. 'Destroying Saigon', he told his subordinates later, 'is a legitimate and humane action'. While this 'grenading' of the city never halted Saigon's bustling activities, it affected the way people went about their daily lives. Protective fencing and iron mesh went up around establishments. 'All of Saigon has shut itself up behind bars', the French war correspondent Lucien Bodard later recalled. 'It was then that Saigon became something of a prison. It wrapped itself in wire netting—boutiques, bistros, and dancing halls enrobed themselves in a veil of metal. Safe on the inside, the French could hear the detonations as they ate and drank'. One Chinese restaurant owner serving a settler clientele finally decided to 'enclose his establishment in a thick wall of iron'. One dined in peace, but one did so 'in a cage'.[20]

Vietnamese civilians in the countryside had no such cages to protect them in a war that was in so many ways all about them. And this is why the First Indochina War is not a simple tale of urban terrorism, rural counter-insurgency, or the well-known story of two armies locked in an epic showdown at Dien Bien Phu. It was above all a sustained and increasingly savage battle about controlling people, occupying territory, gathering information, and building states—in the cities to an extent, but especially in the countryside. Unlike the European wars pitting two pre-existing states and their conventional armies against each other in a battle to knock the other out, the Indochina War was the home to embattled embryonic states, colonial, national, and hybrid ones, each of which was determined to contest or indeed suppress the other's sovereignty. Armies thus fought not just to defeat the adversary's troops in the field, but also to extend their states' control in the most minute of ways on the ground, in collaboration with frontline administrators, security services, and propagandists. The French army would carry this baggage with them to Algeria; the Vietnamese would soon take it to Laos and Cambodia, and, like the Chinese, export their models of control still further into the non-Western world.[21]

In the countryside, where in 1945 at least 80 percent of the Vietnamese population resided, civilians did their utmost to keep themselves, their families, and their loved ones out of harm's way. The French Expeditionary Corps doubled in size from 53,000 troops in January 1946 to 110,245 in 1947 before reaching its peak of 204,000 men in 1954. Most of the troops came from outside France—above all from French Africa and from Vietnam itself. Seventy-three thousand battle-hardened troops from the Second World War's European front served in the French Foreign Legion during this conflict. Together, the southern militias of the Cao Dai, Hoa Hao, and Binh Xuyen counted 50,000 men and women (perhaps more) organized into militias, outfitted and armed by the French. The Expeditionary Corps rolled into villages in jeeps, armored trucks, and tanks. Troops touted machine guns, lobbed grenades, and carried flamethrowers as barking German shepherd dogs pulled at their chains during search-and-destroy missions. Officers radioed in mortar barrages, while the air force dropped paratroopers, bombs, and, from 1950 onward, American-supplied napalm.

Despite the advantages of such firepower, French forces were spread too thinly to control all of Indochina all of the time. When paratroopers launched the attack at Cao Bang in October 1947 to capture Ho Chi Minh's retreating forces, the nationalist government and army simply melted into the jungle. French troops soon found themselves dispersed over vast, rugged territories they could never hold for long, for lack of sufficient numbers. As a result, the remote hills of the north, the deepest jungles of the Mekong, and a vast stretch of central Vietnam were left still in the hands of the Democratic Republic of Vietnam. Commanders in Indochina would repeatedly request more troops, but the French government could hardly match the resources in men and materials that the Americans would later deploy. French commitments to other parts of their disintegrating empire made it harder for the regime to free up men and machines. In 1947, troops destined for Indochina had to divert to Madagascar to smash the nationalist resistance there. And yet Paris refused to impose military service on its population in France or to allow their Vietnamese allies to create their own army until 1951. The DRV also avoided imposing the draft until late 1949, for fear of alienating populations whose support it needed.

As a result, neither the French and their allies, nor the Democratic Republic of Vietnam and theirs, ever possessed sufficient force or weapons to control all of Vietnam all the time. Instead they all administered competing, archipelago-like states, whose sovereignties and control over people and territories could expand and shrink as armies moved in and out and the balance of power shifted accordingly. Borders among these competing states expanded and contracted like sponges being squeezed. In 1952, the DRV only administered 25 percent of the southern population as opposed to 75 percent in central Vietnam and 53 percent in the north. Of the total estimated population of 22.3 million people living in Vietnam in 1950, the Democratic Republic of Vietnam controlled perhaps half of them. Even in supposedly French-controlled villages, the DRV often sent in its security agents, spies, and administrators during the night to affirm their sovereignty and then ceded the same zones during the day to their adversaries. But it could work the other way, too. This also meant that hundreds of thousands of villagers passed from the control of one state to another during the First Indochina War—and often back again, several times. And this perpetual transfer of sovereignty and the attendant people was hardly a peaceful one. All of this affected religious fiefdoms and highland zones, too. Out of loyalty, fear, or a rational calculus to ensure security, villagers dealt with a variety of agents running these invisible but very real and always perilous middle grounds. As one nationalist later recalled, these were spaces where sovereignties intermeshed and gun-toting administrators competed for people's loyalty:

> Still, life in the buffer zone became more and more difficult and risky. In every village, there were some people who worked as spies for either side. In my village, a man of thirty years old volunteered to play a double agent to protect the village from both French and Viet Minh terrorism. With help from villagers, he regularly reported military intelligence information to the French by a 'secret letter box', an intermediary, in the adjacent village. At the same time, he provided the Viet Minh intelligence services with what he collected in the French-controlled areas. Sometimes the French paid him money for his information. Among the teen[ager]s, I was the only one he trusted. He told me about some of his tasks in exchange for my help in writing short messages for reports. I was sure that my village had some others who worked for both sides. Owing to these spies, my village was not terrorized in the second half of 1949.[22]

Like French mayors faced with heavily armed German soldiers patrolling their villages a few years earlier on, in the Second World War, more than one Vietnamese village headman repelled collaboration with the 'resistance' since it could draw reprisals of the worst kind from the occupiers. Indeed, as colonial 'pacification' rapidly turned into a drawn-out affair, angry French Union troops unable to let loose their firepower on their invisible adversaries adopted increasingly violent measures toward nearby civilian populations suspected of harboring, feeding, or protecting enemy combatants. The discovery of enemy propaganda or Democratic Republic of Vietnam-stamped papers in a village, but above all the loss of one soldier to a guerilla sniper or booby trap, could spark a frenzy of violence against nearby civilians. This included the bombing and burning of entire villages as well as the indiscriminate killing of men and women, young and old. The use of torture spread throughout the French army quickly—at what rate, no one knows, but both French and non-communist Vietnamese memoirs leave no doubt that it was all too real. The Democratic Republic of Vietnam authorities also tried to bring the use of torture under control, especially against other Vietnamese. Rape became a disturbing weapon used by the Expeditionary Corps, as did summary executions. Young Vietnamese women who could not escape approaching enemy patrols smeared themselves with any stinking thing they could find, including human excrement. Decapitated heads were raised on sticks, bodies were gruesomely disemboweled, and body parts were taken as 'souvenirs', and Vietnamese soldiers of all political colors also committed such acts. The non-communist nationalist singer, Pham Duy, wrote a bone-chilling ballad about the mothers of Gio Linh village in central Vietnam, each of whom had lost a son to a French army massacre in 1948. Troops decapitated their bodies and displayed their heads along a public road to strike fear into those tempted to accept the Democratic Republic of Vietnam's sovereignty. Massacres did not start with the Americans in My Lai, or the Vietnamese communists in Hue in 1968. And yet, the French Union's massacre of over two hundred Vietnamese women and children in My Trach in 1948 remains virtually unknown in France to this day.[23]

In such bloodstained asymmetrical encounters, choice and loyalty were rarely written in black-and-white or heroic terms. Vietnamese villagers did what millions of civilians had just done across Eurasia during the Second World War: they hid, dug tunnels, turned camouflage into an art form, lied through their teeth, wet their pants, or said whatever their interrogators told them to say to escape severe bodily harm. Most grabbed their children and ran. Many local administrators left their jobs, carefully crossing from 'free' to 'occupied' zones, and vice versa. Property owners abandoned their land. Peasants fled the countryside in ever larger numbers, leading to ever-greater levels of urbanization, a trend that would reach astonishing levels as violence intensified further under the Americans. The population of Saigon-Cholon tripled from 500,000 in 1939 to 1.7 million in 1954. War, not industrialization, explains this phenomenon. Those who could, mainly the urban rich and well-connected, started to leave Vietnam or sent their children abroad. One thing is certain: between 1945 and 1954, civilians in the countryside died in far greater numbers than any other social group, including regular troops. The DRV could never unleash such violence against civilians in France, who remained completely safe from and largely uninterested in France's colonial war in Indochina. No Vietnamese government has ever revealed how many deaths their populations suffered;

but the number of 500,000 offered by one of the Democratic Republic of Vietnam's officers at the end of the First Indochina War seems reasonable, indeed a minimum, since we have no estimates for civilian deaths in the other states opposed to the DRV. One highly respected French scholar put the number of war dead at one million.[24]

This militarization and brutalization of Vietnamese society created a sea of hate, surging on waves of raw human emotion. Ideology certainly counted in the decisions people made, as did family ties and intimate friendships; but young men, women, and even children often joined one side or the other because of traumatic experiences, such as the murder, rape, or torture of a loved one. European settlers who lost family members to unspeakable atrocities committed by the Vietnamese in Saigon in September 1945 and in Hanoi in December 1946 learned to hate in ways they never could have imagined a few years earlier. Madeleine O'Connell, the daughter of Irish immigrants who had come to Indochina to make their future, armed her plantation in the Mekong delta and herself so heavily that DRV agents referred to her as 'Madame Cannon'. Democratic Republic of Vietnam agents killed her in a firefight on Christmas Day in 1947 in order to send a message to settlers to get out. Enraged, her children dug in and hung on until 1975 (as did 15,000 other French settlers). Vietnamese children also witnessed extraordinary violence and were too often subject to it. Of the 175-strong children's guard ('*Ve ut*') participating in the Battle of Hanoi as guides and messengers, one third died. A veteran of the wars for Vietnam, Nguyen Cong Luan speaks in chilling detail of the horrific things he witnessed as a child and to which he grew all too easily accustomed. 'Even the animals', he recalled, knew how to get out the way of French-led patrols:

> Whenever the French [Union] soldiers came, all kinds of sounds subsided. Even domestic animals—beasts of burden, pigs, and dogs—seemed to try to make the least noise. All kept quiet and acted frantically as if they could apprehend [the] fear conveyed by the behavior of panic-stricken villagers. Most dogs ran about to find a nook of safety in dense bamboo groves. Some pigs sneaked into concealed holes when their owners yelled, 'French coming!' Two of the dozen buffaloes in my village would act accordingly to the shout 'Lie down!' when they were under fire while fleeing the village. When the French [Union] soldiers were gone and the villagers returned to their normal activities, all those animals became lively again and made their usual noises and sounds.[25]

War-generated hate manifested itself in language, too. The dehumaniza-
tion of the Vietnamese was such that the French army was soon using the
term '*les Viet*' to refer not only to the faceless enemy, but even to the majority population over which troops were instructed to re-establish colonial
control. War correspondents like Lucien Bodard and veterans like Marcel
Bigeard and Erwan Bergot popularized it in French. One can hear the term
used in France to this day (though not necessarily in the same negative or
racist way). The DRV combatant learned to infuse the ancient word '*giac*'
(bandit) with extremely powerful emotions to dehumanize the French enemy, while the term '*Viet gian*' (traitor) criminalized those Vietnamese 'collaborating' with the French in ways difficult to convey strongly enough in
English. Anticommunist nationalists, working with or against the French,
used the word '*Viet cong*' (Vietnamese communist) to describe pejoratively
Ho's Vietnam long before the American army and press corps globalized
it in English. Post-1945 Vietnamese history cannot be reduced simply to
'war'. However, the savage, sustained violence the Indochinese conflict unleashed directly influenced Vietnamese mentalities, society, and the states
emerging from it. The French and the very transnational army that did most
of the fighting for them did not emerge unscathed either. Veterans from
Senegal and Algeria carried 'things' with them long after this war ended.
They also left behind some 200,000 children, who struggled tragically to
find their place in Vietnamese societies that wanted to forget them much as
the French shunned children born of Franco-German unions during the
Second World War.[26]

THE DEMOCRATIC REPUBLIC OF VIETNAM (1945-50): A COLONIAL GRAFT?

So what was this state that opposed the French, other Vietnamese states,
and then the Americans, so fiercely? For all its nationalist rhetoric, the
Democratic Republic of Vietnam was in many ways a colonial creation at
the outset. Upon taking power, nationalists did everything in their power
to make the colonial state theirs before the colonizers could return. This
was hardly surprising. Nationalists across the Afro-Asian world did much
the same. In 1945-6, however, republican Chinese troops of occupation—
not communist ones—also contributed to the success of nationalist state-
building by preventing the French from returning immediately to areas

above the sixteenth parallel and by refusing to overthrow the Democratic Republic of Vietnam. Pragmatism once again trumped ideology in modern Vietnam, this time between Chinese non-communists and Vietnamese communists.[27]

Many colonially trained Vietnamese bureaucrats stayed on in their jobs in 1945–6, whether they were moved by nationalism, indecision, or simply driven by the need to put food on the table. A veteran later recalled how his father, a French-trained railway attendant, continued working under the Democratic Republic of Vietnam as if nothing that revolutionary had occurred: 'He worked for the revolution, still as a civil servant. He did not work for the sake of ideology but just out of the diligent, conscientious devotion of a civil servant. He just continued to follow his profession and to do his job.' Many, of course, supported the new national government on patriotic grounds. Literate young people at ease in *quoc ngu* found a new source of upward mobility and careers as the national government turned to them to fill new and vacant jobs. Many found employment in newly created mass organizations run by the Viet Minh. DRV state-building was always weaker in the south, however, where the French returned immediately, and they and their Vietnamese allies were always stronger there.[28]

Nowhere was the interface between the colonial and the national more evident than in the pages of the Journal officiel de l'Indochine as it imperceptibly became the Cong Bao Dan Quoc Viet Nam, the Democratic Republic of Vietnam's government bulletin. Past issues of the Cong Bao provide a day-by-day, decree-after-decree account of how the young Vietnamese republic assumed operation of the colonial state's people, services, offices, and materials, as it went about transforming them in national ways. Decrees instructed civil servants to remain in their jobs. Government authorities resumed trade, reopened forms of transport, and continued the telephone, telegraph, and postal services. Rice finally circulated to help alleviate the recent famine. Decrees authorized the requisition of the Pasteur Institutes, the Ecole Française d'Extrême Orient, hospitals, colonial primary and secondary schools, as well as the Indochinese University. High on the list, too, were colonial printing presses, newspapers, radios, paper, and typewriters, essential to the bureaucratic paper flow. Other edicts established the national flag (a yellow star plastered against a red background) and anthem while colonial street names changed to national ones. In a bid to shore up popular support, the government did away with several colonial taxes, including the much-resented head tax, but maintained others essential to the financial well-being of Vietnam. The Democratic Republic of Vietnam even relied on the colonial police infrastructure and lower-level staff to help in building, consolidating, and protecting its own security and intelligence services.[29]

But all was not a colonial graft. Territorially, nationalists did not announce a Republic of Indochina. They could have. The Javanese, after all, had become 'Indonesian'. In mid-1945, the national idea of Vietnam prevailed, not least of all because Lao and Khmer elites wanted nothing to do with Indochina—which was, for them, a Vietnamese as much as a French colonial structure. The majority of Vietnamese nationalists wanted 'Vietnam' and its unification. Gone were the colonial terms for 'Tonkin', 'Annam' and 'Cochinchina'. In their place appeared the officially sanctioned nationalist terms: 'Bac Bo', 'Trung Bo', and 'Nam Bo'. A good nationalist said 'Vietnamese' in 1945, not 'Annamese'. New history books celebrating Vietnam's heroic national past and timeless patriotic resistance poured off the presses, praising the heroic Trung sisters and ancient Vietnamese resistance to foreign domination. School children began singing patriotic songs while young scouts saluted Ho Chi Minh. That said, this seemingly national space was not necessarily the same one that had existed before the French arrived. In establishing colonial frontiers by force in the late nineteenth century, the colonizers accorded large swathes of land and people to 'Cochinchina', 'Annam', and 'Tonkin' at the expense of others. Although Vietnamese nationalists vehemently contested the division of Vietnam into three parts, they rarely disputed the colonially established outside edges of the country, including the maritime ones in the South Seas and the Gulf of Thailand.

A modern nation-state required a homogeneous citizenship for those who belonged to it. Whereas the French had created a hodgepodge of legal categories for their 'colonial subjects', the new republic established an inclusive definition of citizenship transforming almost all of those residing within its territory into Vietnamese nationals ('*dan cong Viet Nam*'). Significantly, this legislation also transformed national minorities ('*dan toc thieu so*') into citizens. In 1946, the ministry of the interior required all Vietnamese who were eighteen and over to carry citizenship cards. Similar cards existed for mass organizations such as the Viet Minh and the Indochinese Communist Party. In theory, identification papers provided decision-makers with a better knowledge of their populations. They allowed for the more efficient allocation of resources, the recruitment of manpower and soldiers, and the organization of the census needed to prepare a budget and set taxes. And of course the Democratic Republic of Vietnam used such cards to incorporate parts of the population into its political realm. However, this bureaucratic modernity was not a simple colonial carryover from the French. Twentieth- century Vietnamese politicians drew upon pre-existing Sino-Vietnamese models of administration in building the postcolonial state. Village councils continued to operate as they had under the French or even the Nguyen.

Like their Chinese counterparts, Vietnamese communists also relied on a united front to help them control and mobilize people. Ho Chi Minh was the driving force behind the creation of the Viet Minh in 1941. Through it, the communists took power in August 1945 and created the DRV state. They intentionally kept the Viet Minh alive as a political party and simultaneously transformed it into a mass nationalist organization. The communists used it to incorporate, control, and mobilize as many parts of Vietnamese society as possible, with the triple goal of running a state, a war, and eventually a communist revolution. Though small in numbers at the outset, dedicated party militants relied on young patriotic but mainly non-communist volunteers to organize an impressive network of national salvation associations, federations, and unions based on religious affiliation (Catholics, Buddhists, Cao Dai followers), gender and age (women's and youth federations), ethnicity (the overseas Chinese and Khmer), and professional status (workers, civil servants, artists, and peasants). Anticolonialism and national independence guided them. Friends, schoolmates, sweethearts, and family connections did more to build up these organizations in the late 1940s than the ability to cite the Marxist-Leninist canon, while French brutality increased membership better than any single propaganda drive or pamphlet the communists could concoct.

Unlike the Front de libération nationale (Front for National Liberation) that would fight the French over Algeria, the communists ran the Viet Minh nationalist front, and it mattered. The problem was that many Vietnamese intellectuals and bourgeois nationalists avoided the Viet Minh precisely because of its communist core. This, in turn, undermined the Indochinese Communist Party's ability to bring people into its fold. Like those repelled by the French colonial hold over Cochinchina in the south, hundreds of highly trained and badly needed non-communist patriots climbed on the fence in the north because of the Democratic Republic of Vietnam's communist hue. Of course French colonial and Vietnamese anticommunist propagandists were only too happy to keep them there, by transforming the 'Viet Minh' into a synonym for 'the communists'. The Chinese republic's occupation allowed the opposition to publish newspapers, organize political parties, and speak in public against the communists, the Viet Minh, and even Ho Chi Minh.[30]

The need to widen the national front became critical for the Indochinese Communist Party in mid-1946 with the departure of the Chinese army and the subsequent outbreak of civil war above the sixteenth parallel. In May 1946, as the communists mobilized the army and the police to destroy the anticommunist opposition parties, the government, pushed by the Indochinese Communist Party, created a new national front called the Association of United Vietnamese People (the Hoi Lien Hiep Quoc Dan Viet Nam) or the Lien Viet for short. Ho was honorary president of this 'super' national front, which regrouped all patriotic individuals who had not yet joined the Viet Minh within it. From this point, the Viet Minh existed in an even more confusing relationship with the Lien Viet until the latter formally absorbed it in 1951.

Despite their ideological differences, Vietnamese nationalists of all political colors agreed on one thing—the importance of running a modern, independent state complete with a presidency, cabinet, ministers, and a parliament. The Japanese-backed government led by Tran Trong Kim had already demonstrated this. Days after delivering the declaration of independence on 2 September, Ho Chi Minh signed universal suffrage into law and called for national elections to form a constituent assembly, an official government, and for the purpose of the elaboration of Vietnam's first constitution. Lively debates characterized the organization of the first national elections in January 1946. This experiment in postcolonial democracy gave birth to the country's first national assembly in March. The chairman of the parliament was none other than the man the French had so badly humiliated through their failure to allow for fuller colonial democracy after 1918, Huynh Thuc Khang. The DRV leadership also wanted a parliament in order to demonstrate to liberal-minded Vietnamese and to the colonialists that they were on the side of modern republicanism.

While there is no denying the authenticity of the debates surrounding the creation of Vietnam's first constitution and national assembly, this early experiment in multiparty politics was largely forced on the communists, due to their own weakness, the Chinese nationalist presence, and the need to show the French and the world that they were more nationalist and democratic than communist and dictatorial. Chinese protection allowed the opposition parties to publish newspapers, assemble publicly, and criticize the communists. Under Chinese pressure, Ho postponed the elections until January 1946 in order to give the opposition more time to prepare for it. He also accepted the hardly democratic request of reserving in advance seventy seats in the future assembly for the Vietnamese Nationalist Party and the Vietnamese Revolutionary Alliance, including the reservation of the vice-presidency for Nguyen Hai Than (who was of the Revolutionary Alliance) and three other important ministerial positions for the nationalists. That these non-communist parties backed by the Chinese pushed for this hardly made them any more democratically inclined than their adversaries.[31]

This first flawed experiment in multiparty politics only lasted above the sixteenth parallel until late June 1946. When the Chinese army pulled out, the communists attacked those in the Vietnamese opposition parties (the Vietnamese Nationalist Party, Vietnamese Revolutionary Alliance and Dai Viet) with the police and the army, supported in part by the French army. By September 1946, what was left of the opposition parties fled to southern China, languished in Democratic Republic of Vietnam prison camps, went into hiding, or crossed over to the French. The communist-run security services closed independent opposition newspapers, confiscated their presses, and 'reformed' the remaining Vietnamese non-communist nationalist parties (the Vietnamese Nationalist Party and the Revolutionary Alliance) and integrated them into the Lien Viet as the communist-commanded DRV now moved one step closer to becoming a single-party state. When the national assembly met for the second time on 28 October 1946, of the total number of 444 deputies, only 291 were present (distances were long; war was on in the south). Of this number, the opposition parties counted only thirty-seven delegates. Continued communist-directed operations and violence against their political competitors were such that on 8 November, the day the General Assembly voted for the constitution, only two members of the opposition were present out of the total number of 240 delegates there. Liberal intellectuals and politicians in the DRV parliament accepted this in order to maintain national unity, all the while hoping in secret that Vietnamese communists would respect the constitution guaranteeing parliamentary democracy. They would be disappointed, like their counterparts who had allied with the French colonialists. Indeed, the French leaders may have ridiculed the Democratic Republic of Vietnam's elections in late 1946, but, if they did so, they had conveniently forgotten that in mid-1946 they themselves had named the new leaders of the Cochinchinese 're-public', censored the press, and had been careful to avoid any kind of vote on national unification. Democracy would never come easily to Vietnam, neither under the French, nor their communist adversaries.[32]

Administratively, the DRV government maintained the three regions into which Minh Mang had divided the country in the 1830s. Each region (north, south, and center) was divided into smaller internal zones in early 1948, each of which, in turn, administered its provinces, districts, and villages. The government exercised power through the creation of 'pop-ular committees', then via 'administrative committees', which ultimately became 'administrative and resistance committees' ('*uy ban khang chien hanh chinh*'), with the outbreak of full-scale war. This four-tiered hierar-chy (zones, provinces, districts and villages) constituted the administrative backbone through which the Democratic Republic of Vietnam operated until 1954. The twelve ministries making up the central government trans-mitted instructions downward to their corresponding offices present at each level of the administrative chain (offices for the interior, the economy, justice, education, etc.). Working via this structure, bureaucrats collected taxes, dispensed justice, maintained order, and schooled children. The Viet Minh and Lien Viet also operated parallel offices located within the administrative and resistance committees. State administration and mass mobilization were designed to work in tandem.[33]

While the Viet Minh was the largest political party and nationalist front in late 1945, the communists did not yet rule a single-party state. For one thing, the Indochinese Communist Party was numerically weak, with only 5,000 members in September 1945. Communists maneuvered adroitly in the background, directed the police and the army, and did their best to con-trol the real positions of power in the government and mass organizations. Secondly, in 1945–6, the communists were on the defensive with the arrival of Chinese republican troops and the Vietnamese opposition parties they protected. Fearful of a Chinese-backed coup, the ICP 'dissolved' itself in November 1945 and accepted a coalition government. Of course, the Indo-chinese Communist Party never sacrificed itself and operated secretly; but a party that chooses to dissolve itself, even on paper, is not in a position to be totalitarian.

What worried them most as they scrambled to survive the French onslaught of 1947 and get the Democratic Republic of Vietnam up and running in the countryside was the painful realization of just how dangerously weak the communist hold over the state and the population was at ground level. The ICP's secret parallel administrative hierarchy rarely reached below the provincial level before 1950. Even though mass membership drives increased the number of communists to 500,000 by this date, the overwhelming majority was poorly trained, unreliable, opportunistic, and often illiterate. Indeed, the transformation of the Indochinese Communist Party into the Vietnamese Workers' Party in 1951 was designed in part to give the communist leadership an excuse to purge its bad elements, streamline its size, and improve quality control. Vietnamese communists led by Ho Chi Minh and Truong Chinh were dedicated communists; they dreamed of Lenin's democratic centralism; and they made plans for communizing Vietnam. But communism, like Confucianism before it, did not appear magically everywhere in Vietnam, nor did everyone embrace it. Indeed, the last thing the party wanted to do as it headed for the hills in 1947 was to alienate non-communist social groups whom it direly needed to run ministries, the army, schools, and hospitals. This was even more important as the French and non-communist Vietnamese nationalists started to build alternative Vietnams of an anticommunist kind.

CHAPTER 9

INTERNATIONALIZED
STATES OF WAR

T HE FORMER EMPEROR of Annam knew they would come. They always did. The fact that he had abdicated in 1945, that he had begged de Gaulle not to re-conquer Vietnam by force, and that he remained an advisor to Ho Chi Minh would not stop them. When the French came to court Bao Dai once again, this time to entreat him to be the titular head of state of their future Associated State of Vietnam, Bao Dai understood the Indochina civil servants very well. He knew their mindset and the colonial ideology driving them. Bao Dai even shared with them the same colonial godfathers—Albert Sarraut and Pierre Pasquier. We do not know what the former emperor thought of Nguyen Van Thinh's tragic death in 1946, but we can be sure that whatever Bao Dai's flaws (and they were many), naivety was not among them. The Indochina administrators wanted from him the very things for which Sarraut had fashioned Bao Dai as a child after the First World War—as a colonial weapon to fight anticolonialists, the living symbol of Franco-Vietnamese collaboration, a ruler through whom the French could rally the peasant 'masses', and an administrative instrument through which to rule indirectly. This was not to be the first 'Bao Dai solution'. It was the fourth. But three things distinguished this latest one: the French now agreed to extend the monarchy to all of 'Vietnam', not just central 'Annam'; the Vietnamese head of state would work in tandem with monarchs in Laos and Cambodia; and the French would align all three states with the West in order to use the Cold War to preserve their colonial presence in Indochina.

AN ASSOCIATED STATE OF VIETNAM AS
A WESTERN-BACKED INDOCHINESE PROTECTORATE?[1]

Léon Pignon was the mastermind of colonial monarchy after the Second World War. As early as July 1946, he had castigated French military commanders for joining forces with the Democratic Republic of Vietnam's leaders to run the non-communist nationalists out of Vietnam along with the withdrawing Chinese. Whatever the nationalists' anti-French vitriol in public, the political advisor to the high commissioner said, it was just posturing. The French could and should use the nationalist opposition in order to combat the DRV. With characteristic Machiavellism, Pignon put the strategic goal to his boss in one simple sentence: 'The opposition to the present government of the Democratic Republic of Vietnam must serve the permanent interests of France in this country'. Divide and rule was once again at the core of French colonial policy. To this end, he suggested that his long-time collaborator, Jean Cousseau, travel to Hong Kong to contact Bao Dai. The colonial administrators were certain they could win over the former emperor once again. In January 1947, Thierry d'Argenlieu advised his government to pursue the restoration of the 'traditional monarchical institution'. He immediately dispatched Cousseau and others to contact Bao Dai and initiate informal talks with others.[2]

The outbreak of war between the French and the Democratic Republic of Vietnam and the changing international situation convinced a wide range of non-communist nationalists that they too could play the 'Bao Dai' card against both the French and the DRV. In February 1947, Nguyen Tuong Tam and Nguyen Hai Than created the All-Country National Union Front (Mat Tran Quoc Gia Thong Nhat Toan Quoc) and stepped up their contacts with Bao Dai. They renewed requests for republican Chinese assistance, hoping that the resumption of the long civil war between Chinese communists and nationalists would finally end the united-front strategy that had hurt Vietnamese non-communists so badly since the 1930s. In March, the All-Country National Union Front formally terminated its collaboration with the Democratic Republic of Vietnam and laid out its plans to create a non-communist republic or a constitutional monarchy. The All-Country National Union Front also turned to the new global power emerging from world war—the United States. Nationalists betted that the Americans would help them, as they were helping China's Chiang Kai-shek against the communist party's Mao Zedong, and that they would force the French to decolonize as the Americans had done in the Philippines in July 1946. Ideologically, anticommunism would unify them all. In March 1947, Truman announced his doctrine of containment and began transforming Japan into America's would-be pillar of Asian containment.

We now know the Americans would disappoint, but no one could know this then. A 'third way' thus seemed possible in 1947. Patriots inside Vietnam like Tran Trong Kim and Ngo Dinh Diem travelled back and forth to China to discuss plans with All-Country National Union Front leaders, Bao Dai, and foreign diplomats about what to do next. Vietnamese Catholics also distanced themselves from both the Democratic Republic of Vietnam's communist core and the French colonial hold over the country and joined discussions. Until 1950, the nationalist-minded Bishop Le Huu Tu transformed his diocese in Bui Chu and Phat Diem into an autonomous and armed religious micro-state in the lower Red River delta, complete with its own administration, tax regime, and troops. The idea that Vietnamese Catholics rushed to help the French re-establish colonial rule is wrong. The only religious groups Pignon could turn provisionally against the DRV in early 1947 were in the south, among the Cao Dai and the Hoa Hao, and whom the French immediately recruited into their Cochinchinese state. But Thierry d'Argenlieu was so suspicious of Nguyen Van Xuan's nationalism that he replaced the president of the Cochinchinese republic with the Hoa Hao's seemingly more pliant Le Van Hoach.[3]

Non-communists opposed to the DRV increasingly agreed that they would have to stand together behind Bao Dai and rely on a bloc of like-minded supporters in China and in Vietnam. They turned to the ex-emperor, not just because the French insisted on negotiating with him, but also because they believed that Bao Dai represented their best chance for forcing the French to accept Vietnam's independence and unity and winning American support. In March, the All-Country National Union Front formally pledged its support to Bao Dai. For the time being, the former Nguyen emperor expressed his willingness to step forward for the good of the people, but held his cards close to his chest and left his political options open. He refused to break with the Democratic Republic of Vietnam; talked informally with the French and foreign diplomats; and closely followed international and Indochinese events. Most importantly, he refused to return to his French handlers. He informed them instead that he, like Ho, expected them to honor the accords of 6 March 1946, meaning the independence of Vietnam within the French Union and the creation of a unitary Vietnamese state including Cochinchina. Two competing Bao Dai solutions—not one—thus developed after the Second World War.

In early 1947, the French coalition government in Paris approved financing for the war in Indochina, but announced that it was willing to implement a ceasefire to achieve a negotiated settlement with all of the Vietnamese, including the Democratic Republic of Vietnam. Upon replacing Thierry d'Argenlieu in March, the new socialist high commissioner, Emile Bollaert, dispatched one of the rare liberal-minded Indochina senior government administrators, and head of the Colonial Academy, Paul Mus, to meet with Ho Chi Minh *and* Bao Dai about finding a solution. While both men informed Mus that the French had to recognize Vietnamese independence and unity to move forward, each of these statesmen left the door open to negotiations. What changed over the summer was that anticommunists within the All-Country National Union Front objected to Bollaert and his socialist-led government's willingness to negotiate with the DRV, fearful that such negotiations could see the non-communists taking orders again from Ho Chi Minh in a coalition government as in 1945–6. The colonial-minded Mouvement républicain populaire (MRP, or the Popular Republican Movement), the French army command in Indochina, and the Gaullists regrouping in the Rassemblement du Peuple français (RPF, or the Rally of the French People) agreed. The last thing they wanted to see was Ho return to power peacefully now that they were on the brink of destroying his state for good (Valluy was preparing a large attack over the summer to do precisely that.). The ousting of the French communists from the ruling coalition in Paris in May further convinced the Popular Republican Movement leadership that it could engineer the same thing in Indochina by winning over the anticommunists in the person of Bao Dai. Now in the majority, the MRP firmly backed Bao Dai over Ho Chi Minh, demanding nothing short of the latter's capitulation. Unwilling to break with the Popular Republican Movement over this, in a fateful decision they would repeat in Algeria, the socialists toed the harder line within the coalition government in Paris. Government instructions now ruled out concessions on the questions of Vietnam's independence and unity. Bollaert had initially planned to speak favorably of these matters in a major speech scheduled for 15 August, the very day the British were to accord independence to India and Pakistan. Instead, on 10 September, the high commissioner invited non-communists to negotiate with the French, intentionally excluded the Democratic Republic of Vietnam, but carefully avoided any talk of independence with any Vietnamese.

Although profoundly disappointed by Bollaert's silence on independence, the non-communists had part of what they wanted strategically—the French exclusion of the DRV from negotiations—and that was enough for them to make the next move. A week later, Bao Dai broke formally with the

Democratic Republic of Vietnam in his address to the Vietnamese people
and announced that he was 'ready to enter into contact with [the] French
authorities'. A few weeks later, Valluy launched Opération Léa to capture
the DRV leadership and clear the way for direct negotiations with Bao Dai.
It failed, but the message was clear: the Popular Republican Movement
would not negotiate with the DRV either.[4]

The decision by the 'Third Force' (the term that emerged to describe
these non-communist nationalists coalescing around Bao Dai) to enter
into negotiations with the French in 1947 was a turning point in twentieth-
century Vietnamese political history. It meant that non-communists were
ready to risk continued civil war with the Democratic Republic of Vietnam,
using French military power to do so, instead of remaining within a national
front with the DRV's state and army in order to force the French to decolonize. The communist destruction of the opposition parties in northern
Vietnam in mid-1946 hardly facilitated reconciliation. Indeed, the communists in control of the DRV in 1947 had scored a major military victory over
their Vietnamese rivals in the previous year. Furious with the communist
assault on them that year, Greater Vietnam (Dai Viet) supporters returned
to colonial-controlled Vietnam convinced that the best strategy was to use
the French to get rid of their enemies. As a result, Greater Vietnam members began to join the 'administrative committees' in Hanoi and Hue which
the French had established after ousting the DRV there.[5]

This was, however, a very risky strategy. Unlike the Democratic Republic of Vietnam, the nationalists lining up behind Bao Dai now entered into
negotiations with the French without having an army or a 'resistance' government, neither inside the country nor abroad. The French civil service
directed the administration of the parts of Vietnam controlled by the Expeditionary Corps, mainly in the cities and the surrounding deltas while
the DRV tended to the rest. This 'Third Force' Vietnam would thus be a
graft on to French Cochinchina and the colonial administration committees resuming their work in Annam and Tonkin. Any non-communist national army would be allied with the French. Non-communists like the Dai
Viet were working on the assumption that the communists would lose and
the French would agree to independence. But what would non-communist
nationalists do if the Democratic Republic of Vietnam carried on or the
Popular Republican Movement refused to accord the Vietnamese real independence and power . . . or both? Such an outcome could transform legitimate non-communist nationalists looking for an alternative to communism

and colonialism into colonial puppets. And chronic factionalism among non-communists never helped. Vietnamese communists were many things, but as long as the French refused to negotiate any real independence for Vietnam, they fought on.

When Bao Dai arrived in Ha Long Bay in December 1947 to begin talks with the high commissioner, he discovered to his dismay that the French were just as opposed to the idea of according real independence to him as they had been to Ho. In their formal declaration, Bollaert pronounced the magic word 'independence'; but in a secret protocol initialed by Bao Dai to serve as a basis for negotiations, the French imposed all sorts of legal limitations on it, including the control of any future state's diplomacy, defense, finances, and currency. Bao Dai returned to Hong Kong to discuss the proposals with his allies before resuming talks. Ngo Dinh Diem and others objected to the protocol, demanding that the French respect the March 1946 accords and follow the British lead on India a few months earlier. Constitutional constraints, the French countered, required them to maintain the French Union and thus impose limitations on colonial sovereignty. Diem insisted that an independent, national government had to come first, one which non-communists could then build up nationally and turn against the Democratic Republic of Vietnam, with the French and the West alongside. If the British could accord dominion status to India, Diem insisted, so could the French, despite the clause in the 1946 constitution preventing member states of the French Union from obtaining full sovereignty equal to France. Diem put his case to the French, but the latter were convinced that they could make the Union work and feared that equal independence with the French for the Vietnamese would bring down the entire imperial state they hoped to stitch together via the Union. When Bollaert sent him packing, Diem pulled out of the Third Force Bao Dai solution, convinced that the French were no more serious about recognizing anticommunist nationalists or decolonizing than they had been twenty years earlier. The French creation of special territories for the 'ethnic minorities' under their control in 1948 only reinforced Diem's view (see chapter 14).[6]

Bao Dai carried on, however, convinced he could use his position in exile to continue to work in collaboration with Vietnamese nationalists inside the country to force the French to decolonize and thereby transform the Cochinchinese Republic and the administrative committees for Annam and Tonkin into an independent Vietnam on the Third Force's terms. He left the task of testing whether the French would at least allow for the creation of a unitary Vietnam to Nguyen Van Xuan (a fellow socialist Bollaert had named to head up the Cochinchinese republic). Greater Vietnam personnel went to work in the administrative committees in Annam and Tonkin.

In early 1948, the high commissioner seemed to soften his position, when he accepted the idea of allowing for the creation of a unitary Vietnamese state under Nguyen Van Xuan's leadership. In May, the latter presided over the formation of a Provisional Central Government of Vietnam, combining the Cochinchinese republic with the administrative committees for Tonkin and Annam. In June, Bao Dai and Bollaert met again in Ha Long Bay. After the usual legal word games about the nature of the French Union and national sovereignty, the high commissioner recognized the *de facto* unification of Annam, Tonkin, and Cochinchina, but reiterated the strict limitations on independence needed to preserve the French Union. A few days later, the Popular Republican Movement-led government disappointed nationalists profoundly by declaring that the latest Ha Long Bay accord in no way changed Cochinchina's legal status. The constitution was clear, they said: As it was a colony, only the French National Assembly could approve such a modification. The French thus continued to rule Vietnam at the federal level, and Xuan, like Thinh before him, was starting to look like a colonial puppet. Bao Dai left for France to negotiate directly with the MRP, but he got no further than Ho had at Fontainebleau in 1946. The talks with Bollaert were dead.

Failure, however, was not an option. The refusal of the most important non-communists to collaborate with the French undermined their colonial presence and ability to defeat the Democratic Republic of Vietnam politically (Operation Léa had failed militarily). In October 1948, the French redoubled their efforts to build a state around Bao Dai, when the Popular Republican Movement named Léon Pignon as the new high commissioner. From his office in the Palais Norodom in Saigon, France's most important Indochina administrator since Albert Sarraut was finally in charge. He immediately mobilized his longtime associates in the colonial administration and focused his full attention on solving the Vietnam problem. Like Sarraut, Pignon was also an astute observer of the international scene. He watched carefully as the Berlin Crisis, the communist coup in Prague, and the Marshall Plan brought the superpowers to the brink of war in Europe. The polarization of the post-1945 international system into two blocs was obvious to the high commissioner, as was the growing American commitment to Western Europe, symbolized by the creation of the North Atlantic

Treaty Organization in April 1949. In Asia, Pignon understood that events in China would directly influence the fate of French Indochina. And what he saw in early 1949 did not look good: Mao Zedong was on his way to defeating Chiang Kai-shek and would undoubtedly seal an alliance with the Soviets that would extend the communist bloc to Indochina's northern border. Just as worrisome, decolonization was on the march—Burma, India, and the Philippines were all newly independent. Unimpressed, Pignon watched as the United States, the United Nations, and India pressured the Dutch to let go of Indonesia in 1949.[7]

Against the odds, the high commissioner, his core team, and the government he served remained convinced that the maintenance of French Indochina (and French Africa) was vital to the French national interest and that the Bao Dai solution remained the best way to hold on. Rather than follow the Anglo-American example in India and the Philippines, Pignon pushed a three-pronged strategy designed to placate some of the Third Force's demands but without terminating France's continued colonial presence. First of all, the high commissioner abandoned the pentagonal Indochinese Federation (it had existed *de facto* since late 1945) in favor of creating three separate but associated states of Indochina—Vietnam, Laos, and Cambodia. This meant that the French would accept Cochinchina's unification with Annam and Tonkin, but only on the condition that Bao Dai returned to lead it within the French Union. The French were willing to accord greater independence to all three Indochinese states, provided that each accepted that France would continue to play the role of the 'fourth' member handling relations among them (currency, customs, immigration, etc.) and military affairs. This is what '*quadripartisme*' (a four-party system) meant in the new legal vocabulary introduced by Pignon's team. It was colonial federalism by another name.

Secondly, for the high commissioner, the Associated States of Indochina grand strategy could only work if each state stood behind loyal national monarchs. Like his trusted administrators, Pignon was convinced that the Indochinese peasant majorities remained loyal to their sovereigns and that the best way to attract and rule them against communists and nationalists was through the intermediaries of these monarchs. The young King Sihanouk had already rejoined the French in 1946, while his Laotian mentor, Sisavang Vong, had never left them. To bolster these kings and their legitimacy, Pignon opened negotiations to rally dissenting nationalist groups in each country. This meant winning over the Khmer and Lao nationalist groups whose leaders had taken refuge in Thailand and contested French rule since the Second World War. From 1945 onward, Lao Issara (Free Lao) nationalists had operated a government in exile from Bangkok. The Khmer Issarak (Free Khmer) movement also created a resistance government in 1948. By their very existence (and the quality of their leaders), these governments-in-exile undermined the legitimacy of the Khmer and Lao monarchies allied with the French. Undeterred, Pignon dispatched emissaries to meet rebel leaders and used the French embassy in Bangkok to rally most of the dissident Khmer and Lao freedom leaders to his grand Indochinese strategy of associated states.[8]

But without Bao Dai, there was no royalist solution and time was running short. As the Chinese Red Army marched across the Yangzi River in early 1949, the French government accepted the unification of Cochinchina with Annam and Tonkin. In exchange, Bao Dai had to return to lead the Associated State of Vietnam (ASV) and align himself with kings Sisavang Vong, Sihanouk, and the king-maker himself, Pignon. 'We need a hero, too', the high commissioner sighed to Lucien Bodard one day, 'against Ho Chi Minh, we have to have an anti-Ho Chi Minh'. That Pignon never thought twice about the poverty of what he was saying speaks volumes of the official colonial mind at the time.[9]

The third part of Pignon's strategy focused on the international dimension. Starting in late 1948, the high commissioner began recasting the fight against the Democratic Republic of Vietnam and for the Associated States as an integral part of the West's wider Cold War struggle against the spread of communism. The idea was to win over Atlantic support for the Indochinese states in the fight against communism and to put pressure on Bao Dai to return to run an independent associated state inside Vietnam or risk being left behind. The Americans' strategic desire to contain communism globally at all costs would trump their reluctance to be seen as backing outdated French colonialists. The French repeated to anyone who would listen on the European desk in the US State Department in Washington and to the American Ambassador in Paris that France (Western Europe) and French Indochina (Southeast Asia) were vital to America's global containment strategy. French propaganda changed accordingly. Ho Chi Minh was not a nationalist, but an internationalist communist of the very worst kind—and the French provided all sorts of documents to prove it. The military high command in Indochina chimed in with this, badly in need, as they were, of increased military assistance. The French also targeted the

British, who were dealing with a communist uprising in Malaya in 1948 where the British, too, had refused to relinquish their colonial hold. The French connected the British 'emergency' in Malaya to their war in Indochina, both the result of an alleged Sino-Soviet plot to take over Southeast Asia. The British needed little prodding. Keen on holding on to Malaya and Singapore, they joined the Americans in stepping up their support of the most recent Bao Dai solution as the lesser of two evils. Pignon had a much harder time bringing postcolonial India on board, however. Nehru preferred to steer a neutral course between communists and colonialists and the superpowers standing behind them in Asia.[10]

Pignon's internationalization of the Indochina problem reached its zenith in January 1950, when Mao and Stalin formally recognized the Democratic Republic of Vietnam. Worried that Sino-Soviet support of the DRV could turn the tide against the French militarily, the high commissioner repeated to his government in the clearest possible terms why the French had to internationalize the war now. The French would continue the fight 'to keep Indochina out of the communist grip', but in so doing the 'Anglo-Saxons' had to provide increased military aid, recognize the Associated States of Indochina diplomatically, and accept a continued French colonial presence there. This was, Pignon concluded, 'the price which we can accept for this [our military] commitment'. In reality, his team had already prepared this course of action in collaboration with the Ministry of Foreign Affairs. In February 1950, the British and Americans recognized the Associated States of Indochina, followed by the rest of the Atlantic alliance. The Indians did not, nor did the Indonesians or Burmese. They preferred to remain unaligned.[11]

If one scholar has qualified the Algerian nationalist movement's success in turning the international system against the French as a 'diplomatic revolution', surely Léon Pignon and his Popular Republican Movement backers achieved a successful diplomatic counter-revolution for the colonial side when Bao Dai signed the Elysée accords with President Vincent Auriol on 8 March 1949, creating the less than fully independent Associated State of Vietnam. Similar accords followed for Laos and Cambodia. The seemingly insurmountable constitutional obstacles blocking the unification of Cochinchina with Vietnam disappeared with revealing alacrity. On 22 May the French National Assembly, supported by the hastily convened Cochinchinese Consultative Council, voted in the unification of Cochinchina with the north and the center. French settlers never had a chance. For the first time, they got a taste of what it was like to be on the wrong side of 'colonial democracy'. Within weeks Bao Dai was back in Vietnam, (supported, indeed pressured by the Atlantic alliance), where he formally presided over the creation of the ASV on 2 July 1949. He became head of a single Vietnamese state and allowed his prime minister to run a government that was no longer provisional.[12]

But the French government was still in control. Unlike the Democratic Republic of Vietnam it opposed, or the Republic of Indonesia that obtained its independence that same year from the Dutch, all three associated states remained subject to colonial limitations in the financial, commercial, legal, and military domains. Pignon's three-pronged strategy created what was effectively an internationally backed Indochinese protectorate in the form of three associated monarchs—Bao Dai, Sihanouk, and Sisavang Vong. French colonial federalism remained in effect, as the continued operation of the Indochinese *piastre* by the Bank of Indochina demonstrated. As Bodard put it, '"Quadripartisme" was the extension of [French] Indochina in an indirect form'. From 1948 the communist core of the DRV and the spread of the Cold War across Eurasia allowed the French to exploit American fears of communism in order to prolong their colonial presence in Indochina, whereas the same priorities led Washington to pressure the Dutch increasingly to grant independence to the non-communist-led Indonesian republicans.[13]

This French diplomatic victory in 1949–50 dealt Vietnamese noncommunists a terrible blow. Bao Dai realized it immediately upon his return to Vietnam in April 1949, when the French refused to transfer to him the Palais Norodom in Saigon, the seat of the High Commissioner of Indochina and the center of French colonial power since 1863. Bao Dai knew that Pignon was using the Associated State of Vietnam—like the Cochinchinese republic before it—as a weapon to hold on colonially. He did not take his life in protest as Nguyen Van Thinh had done. Instead the ex-emperor withdrew into his world and holed himself up in Dalat. He resisted the French passively and tried, when he could, to advance the ASV's interests. He placed a palm branch on the monument dedicated to the Vietnamese the French had executed during the battle of Hanoi. He refused all colonial efforts to crown him again. He would rarely dress up in royal garb or tour the countryside to serve as the protectorate's cultural intermediary. His refusal to play his part as head of state drove the Indochina hands up the wall, as his immobility undermined the legitimacy and laid bare the poverty of the French 'Bao Dai solutions' from Sarraut to Pignon, once again. Sitting in Jean Cousseau's Dalat villa, Lucien Bodard later recalled Cousseau's furious words when the latter got off the phone with Bao Dai: '"Tough. So Bao Dai thinks he's so smart. He wants to play what he calls his game. This will perhaps finish badly for us, but it will end even worse for him—don't forget what I said." "He's a lard ass", Cousseau repeatedly told me after having tried to prove unsuccessfully to Bao Dai for hours that the peasants in the delta were awaiting him, that by appearing before them he would become again the Son of Heaven'. But rather than turning the monarchy on the colonizer and the communists by leading a crusade for independence against the French as Norodom Sihanouk and Mohammed V would do in Morocco in 1953, and 1955, respectively. Bao Dai intentionally let it die. In fact, the king of the Nguyen dynasty knew that the French had already killed it. But his French-bred passivity (and possibly French money) ensured that non-communist Vietnamese nationalists could never make the last Nguyen emperor take action against the colonizers, or the communists, much less both. Bao Dai preferred inertia as resistance. It was not enough, though. It prevented him from building up any popular support worthy of notice and ensured that the monarchy would never be revived.[14]

Pignon's Associated States of Indochina were, however, part of larger French efforts to preserve their international standing in the Atlantic alliance. This took on particular importance from 1950 onward when the crisis in Berlin in 1949, followed by the outbreak of the Korean War, sparked Western fears of a communist assault on both sides of Eurasia and accelerated Western efforts to reinforce the defense of Western Europe through the North Atlantic Treaty Organization (NATO) and the creation of a Western European army known as the European Defense Community. French leaders used the Indochina War as a way of demonstrating their commitment to the Atlantic alliance and obtaining American aid to continue prosecuting the war as part of the global effort to contain Eurasian communism. For some scholars, France's blind commitment to the war in Indochina undermined its European ambitions. Others insist that the First Indochina War actually allowed the French to keep themselves at the Great Powers table and promote their ambitions in NATO and European integration and defense. By committing more troops to Indochina in 1951, one of France's strongest defenders of the Atlantic alliance and the maintenance of the French Union, Georges Bidault, pointed out to his colleagues that 'our action in Tonkin preserves us on the Rhine, since it preserves the Atlantic community'.[15]

RECASTING COMMUNIST VIETNAM:
TRANSNATIONAL STATE-MAKING AND MODERN WAR

Vietnamese communists had their own version of the Associated States of Indochina. Mirroring the colonial transformation of the Indochinese Federation into the Associated States of Indochina in 1948–50 was the communist decision to divide the Indochinese Communist Party along national though equally associated lines. In 1949, Vietnamese communists began preparations to create the Vietnamese Workers' Party, formally approved during the second party congress held in 1951. They could have left it and the colonial model of Indochina there and focused on Vietnam. Instead, like their French opponents, they simultaneously approved the establishment of associated states, national fronts, and communist parties for Laos and Cambodia. The fact that there were hardly any non-Viet communists in Laos and Cambodia did not stop them. In 1950, drawing upon Sino-Vietnamese models and experiences, Ho Chi Minh presided over the creation of the Lao and Khmer nationalist fronts—the Pathet Lao (Lao Nation) from the previous Lao Issara (the Free Lao organization) and Khmer Issarak (Independent Khmer, out of the earlier Free Khmer movement). Vietnamese communists then created two respective 'resistance governments' ('*chinh phu khang chien*') to stand next to the Democratic Republic of Vietnam. In order to attract popular support, the Vietnamese turned to disgruntled Laotian royalty in the person of Prince Souphanouvong and to Cambodian Buddhism in the person of a Khmer-Vietnamese monk named Son Ngoc Minh. Both were fluent in Vietnamese. They followed this up with instructions to cadres in western Indochina and among the Vietnamese diaspora in Thailand to create proto-communist parties for Laos and Cambodia, while Vietnamese officers led by Vo Nguyen Giap began building liberation armies. New possibilities and forms of collaboration emerged as Vietnamese communists initiated their own state-building projects. The son of a Vietnamese bureaucrat in Laos, Kaysone Phoumvihane, joined Giap in creating the Pathet Lao army. Thanks to the Vietnamese, he and Souphanouvong would, one day, rule Laos.[16]

What explains communist Vietnam's attraction for the rest of Indochina? On the one hand, it was a matter of national security. The communists needed allies in Laos and Cambodia to help them in the event the French turned their Associated States on DRV Vietnam militarily (with American support). They also needed their own friendly states in Laos and

Cambodia to prevent the West from attacking them diplomatically by accusing DRV troops or cadres in Laos and Cambodia of violating the territorial sovereignty of the states now led by Norodom Sihanouk and Sisavang Vong. The disappearance of French Indochina as a sovereign territorial bloc would now have real legal implications: by creating national borders between Vietnam on the one hand and Laos and Cambodia on the other. This is why the communists needed a policy of association of their own. Despite the fact that Ho Chi Minh's team had changed the party's name from that of the Indochinese Communist Party to the Vietnamese Workers Party, Vietnamese communists still managed to lead revolutionary Indochina through their own (indirect, communist) policy of association.

On the other hand, Vietnamese communists believed in Indochina. They believed in the Comintern-approved model holding them to bring communist modernity, civilization, and socio-political revolution not just to Vietnam, but also to Laos and Cambodia. A devout internationalist, Ho himself had helped create communist parties for Malaya and Thailand two decades earlier (and may well have created the first communist cell in Laos in 1929). The only difference between the French colonialists and the Vietnamese communist internationalists in 1950 was that the latter actually created Lao and Cambodian states where none had existed before. The result was nonetheless the same: two sets of opposing Associated States of Indochina—six in all—came into being during the First Indochina War, one under the French colonialists, the other under the Vietnamese communists ruling through a revolutionary protectorate. Ironically, as Ho Chi Minh and his entourage were hosting Souphanouvong and Son Ngoc Minh in northern Vietnam to celebrate their revolutionary Indochinese ties in 1950, Albert Sarraut explained to their opposites at the Conference of Pau in France why the Indochinese Federation had had to give way to the Associated States of Indochina within a French Union. Sarraut described it as a 'continued creation'. Ho would have agreed. And because men like Truong Chinh, Ho Chi Minh, Léon Pignon, and Jean Cousseau continued to cast their wars and state-making in these Indochinese ways, they guaranteed that war would come to Laos and Cambodia with all of its devastating consequences.[17]

Similar transnational state-making occurred inside DRV Vietnam itself. Mao Zedong and Joseph Stalin's decision to recognize Ho Chi Minh's Vietnam in January 1950 ended the Democratic Republic of Vietnam's international isolation and re-incorporated the Vietnamese communist party into the internationalist fold it had first joined in the early 1930s. Like the French, Vietnamese communists welcomed the internationalization of the conflict. Not only did it provide them with military assistance, but it also provided them with direct access to international communist models for modernization and state-building. While Pignon called on the West to stand united behind the French to keep Vietnam free from communism, Truong Chinh promised the communist bloc that it could count on the Vietnamese to lead the Indochinese revolution and assume the Southeast Asian burden in the global battle against Western capitalism and imperialism. In exchange, he called upon Moscow, Beijing, and their allies to assist the Vietnamese.[18]

Positioned on the Asian front line of the Eurasian communist bloc, the Chinese took the lead. They were determined to ensure their new state's security and expand communism where they could. With Stalin's approval, Mao Zedong supported his longtime communist allies located on China's vulnerable flanks—Ho Chi Minh in Indochina and Kim Il-sung in Korea. A high-ranking Chinese communist emissary, Luo Quibo, travelled to the Democratic Republic of Vietnam in February 1950 to help them make a list of Vietnamese needs. Militarily, the Vietnamese requested modern arms (machine guns, artillery, ammunition) assistance in creating a professional army, and medicines. Politically, they wanted help to build a *bona fide* single-party communist state along the Maoist lines that had just led the Chinese Communist Party to victory. This included the introduction of Sino-Soviet mobilization techniques, land reform, and advice on and models for creating a communist-orientated security service, economy, education system, and culture. A remarkable transnational transformation of Vietnamese statecraft began in the DRV zones in Vietnam in 1950—and this in the middle of a full-blown colonial war which was now turning into one of the hottest conflicts of the Cold War.[19]

Meanwhile, the Americans threw their weight behind the Associated States of Indochina: Laos, Cambodia, and Vietnam. As Luo Guibo was visiting the Democratic Republic of Vietnam, the American State Department dispatched Robert Griffin to tour Indochina at the request of the French government. Accompanying his February visit was the first courtesy call of the Seventh Fleet to Saigon, just as Pignon had requested a few weeks earlier, and which Mao now feared. Griffin met with the high commissioner and the military high command, carefully listing the French economic and military needs for the Associated States of Indochina. On his return to Washington, Griffin urged his government to provide large-scale aid to

Indochina in order to keep it and the rest of Southeast Asia from falling into communist hands. He also warned that if the United States did not aid the French, then they might well cut their losses and pull out of Indo-china completely. Pignon had clearly gotten his message through and was drawing the Americans into protecting the Associated States of Indochina through the French.

Growing anxieties over Korea reinforced the commitment of the main belligerents to support their allies. Within months, as they slid toward war in Korea, the Americans and the Chinese dispatched military advisor groups to Indochina. In September, American General Francis Brink pre-sided over the creation of the Military Assistance Advisory Group (MAAG) in Saigon. Between September 1950 and May 1953, the Americans supplied 286,000 tons of material to French Union forces. In 1952, Washington had assumed around 40 percent of the military financial burden. By 1954, it reached almost 80 percent. It is not so much that the Americans were buy-ing the war from the French, it was rather an indication of the fact that it was becoming their war *too,* and that they were fighting it indirectly through the French-run Associated States of Indochina, the French Expeditionary Corps, and the Indochinese armies the French now agreed to build for Laos, Cambodia, and most importantly, Vietnam itself.

Although the communist bloc could never match the quantity or the modernity of the American military aid to the French, the Chinese commit-ted themselves to helping their allies in Vietnam in order to protect their southern flank, contain American expansionism in the Pacific, and keep a communist-run state alive, as they were doing in Korea. The communist Chinese Advisory Group was created in 1950 and arrived in DRV Viet-nam shortly after the Korean War began. Luo Guibo personally presided over two sub-delegations, the military advisory group led by generals Chen Geng and Wei Guoqing, and the political one he personally directed. The military delegation channeled aid to the Vietnamese army, trained troops and officers in northern DRV Vietnam and southern China, and helped devise battle plans. Between May 1950 and June 1954, the Chinese com-munists provided 21,517 tons of assistance to the DRV Vietnamese. This included machines guns, rifles, ammunition, and artillery. The Chinese aim was not simply to build up the guerilla war, but, as Mao Zedong had in-structed his advisors, to 'organize a professional army'. The Chinese did not create Ho's army, but they wanted to strengthen it in order to oppose the Franco-American threat on their southern flank indirectly.[20]

Meanwhile, the Chinese political delegation helped Vietnamese communists to create a veritable party-state capable of running this new type of war. Chinese advisors introduced comprehensive rectification campaigns. This Maoist brainwashing specialty sought to train communist-minded cadres, a new class of civil servants, to run the party, the state, the army, and mass organizations. 'Reform' and 'instruction' started at the top of the party, thanks to courses organized by the Chinese delegation. Newly formed party schools then trained rectification specialists, who fanned out across the country to inculcate party themes, instructions, and models for mid-level provincial officials and those further down the administrative chain. Together, these 'rectified' and loyal bureaucrats and officers would form the backbone upon which a new party-state would operate vertically, with the army and the security services receiving special attention. In 1952, based on Sino-Soviet communist techniques Luo Guibo's team introduced, Vietnamese communists formally launched the rectification campaigns. As the party began to consolidate its hold over the state, non-communist nationalists unwilling to undergo rectification were sidelined, persecuted, or defected. Ideological loyalty was essential to the functioning of this new single-party state born of war.

To further increase party control and communize society, the Vietnamese accelerated Sino-Soviet inspired 'new hero' worship, patriotic emulation campaigns, and stepped up the cult of personality around Ho Chi Minh. 'New heroes' ('*anh hung moi*') were exemplary men and women whom all Vietnamese were expected to venerate, not only for their patriotic and heroic deeds, but also for their revolutionary virtues and commitment to communism. Since 1948, the party had begun selecting socialist heroes from among the peasants, workers, and soldiers. Locally organized propaganda drives, schools, and the army encouraged all to emulate them. During the first half of the Indochina conflict, the Democratic Republic of Vietnam relied on patriotic emulation campaigns ('*phong trao thi dua ai quoc*') as a way of mobilizing people to support the war against the French by providing labor, rice, and loyalty. Campaigns lasted from a few weeks to several months in length as cadres fanned out into the villages. Relying on local mass organizations, family ties, and propaganda, officials organized local fun and games, urging men and women in one village to try to outdo their counterparts in another for the good of the nation.

In 1952, now engaged in set-piece battles, communists reorganized the emulation campaigns under strict party control, backed up by the army and police and advised by the Chinese, and focused them increasingly on class issues. From this point, patriotic landowners and bourgeois in the Democratic Republic of Vietnam zone, regardless of how much support they might have provided the cause over the years, became ideological impediments to the party's control over the state, territory, people, and its ability to transform them in communist ways. At the summit of the new hero worship and emulation campaigns was the party-sponsored worship of Ho Chi Minh, the perfect embodiment of communism and nationalism. New hero worship, emulation campaigns, and the cult of personality were all tools by which the party sought to increase its control and communize its civil servants and society. Again, this does not mean that all of Vietnam suddenly became or was destined to become 'communist', any more than one can speak of a timeless 'Confucian Vietnam' covering all of the country down to ground level. However, like others centuries before them, Vietnamese communists now willingly looked to China for models to help them in building a new state, in centralizing party control right down to the grassroots, and in establishing ideological homogeneity. And like the Le dynasty's entry into the East Asian Confucian civilization in the fifteenth century, which had distinguished it from its Southeast Asian neighbors, something very similar happened in the mid-twentieth century when Ho Chi Minh's party embraced Maoism and the internationalist communist movement from which it flowed in order to build a new state and army.[21]

This also means that the Chinese (as well as the Americans) were deeply involved in 'nation-building' in Vietnam. Chinese advisors certainly introduced the Sino-Soviet model for communist land reform. It was another instrument by which the party could destroy 'feudal' and other social structures in the countryside in order to replace them with new ones. Maoist land reform further reinforced the party's vertical control over the state and, theoretically, its ability to mobilize peasants. Not only did the party accord the peasants a plot of land in order to generate their support, but it also began recruiting them into the bureaucracy, the army, and the security services. This social revolution in the countryside began in late 1953 as the war against the French reached its denouement and continued until 1956. We will return to this question later.

The Vietnamese used all of these Sino-Soviet techniques to make the transition to modern, conventional war as well. A year before the Chinese advisors arrived in 1950, Vietnamese communists had already begun shifting to the third phase of Maoist military strategy, the 'General Counter

Offensive'. Although the Democratic Republic of Vietnam never abandoned guerrilla operations, these were no longer sufficient. The only way to drive the French out of Indochina and create the conditions for remaking Vietnam was through decisive military force. This meant that the DRV had to field a professional army capable of winning military victory on the battlefield. Thanks to Chinese assistance and instruction, including the outfitting and training of tens of thousands of troops in the safety of Chinese territory, the Democratic Republic of Vietnam was now in a position to push its military revolution forward by building main force regiments and divisions, a much better-trained officer corps, general staff, and by deploying thousands of party-trained political cadres in its ranks. By 1952, Chinese training and military aid had helped the Vietnamese to assemble a regular army consisting of six armed divisions. It operated via expanding and increasingly professionalized intelligence, logistics, supply, and medical services. In mid-1950, and not before, the People's Army of Viet Nam (Quan Doi Nhan Dan Viet Nam), otherwise known as PAVN, was born. Its 'birth' paralleled the emergence of the American-backed one for the Associated State of Vietnam. Both armies now operated on international models coming from opposite sides in the Cold War.

Ho Chi Minh thus presided over a political and a military revolution in a time of war. Between 1950 and 1954, these divisions and the party-state emerging to run them allowed the Democratic Republic of Vietnam to take the fighting to the French across upper Vietnam and into western Indochina during eight set-piece battles. In 1950, Vo Nguyen Giap and his Chinese advisors focused on opening a direct supply route in the border province of Cao Bang in order to create a safe passage to China. Giap threw his best troops against retreating French Union troops, scoring a spectacular victory that cost Léon Pignon his job and made thousands of French Union troops DRV prisoners of war. Emboldened, General Giap turned his attention to the Red River delta and set his sights on Hanoi. The new French high commissioner and commander-in-chief, General Jean de Lattre de Tassigny, welcomed his opponent's willingness to engage in set-piece battle, convinced that superior French air and firepower—now backed up by the Americans—would ensure victory. Giap overreached and paid for it dearly in a bloody defeat during the battle of Vinh Yen in January 1951 and a second one a few months later at Dong Trieu. As the French had themselves learned during the First World War, fervor and attacks made in waves did not guarantee victory in modern war. Wave attacks on the Red

River delta in 1950–51 left tens of thousands of PAVN soldiers maimed and killed, destroyed by the very things the guerilla army had always avoided— artillery, machine guns, and bombers. Thanks to the Americans, the French also dropped napalm for the first time. A People's Army of Vietnam veteran of Vinh Yen later recalled the experience:

> Be on [the] watch for planes. They will drop bombs and machine gun [you]. Cover yourselves, hide yourselves under bamboo. The planes dived. Then hell opened up before my eyes. It was hell in the form of a big clumsy egg, falling from the first plane [. . .] An immense ball of fire, spreading over hundreds of meters, it seemed to me, sowing terror in the ranks of the soldiers. Napalm. Fire that falls from the sky [. . .] My men ran for cover, and I could not stop them. There is no way you can stay put under this rain of fire that spreads out and burns everything in its path. From everywhere the flames leap up. Joining them was the burst of French machine gun fire, mortars and artillery, transforming into a burning tomb what was only ten minutes earlier a small forest [. . .][22]

This phosphorous gel also fell on innocent civilians, including children. As a twelve year-old, Nguyen Cong Hoan, recalled how his best childhood friend, Huu, 'was lying on the ground, burned by napalm. She wasn't dead, but she was dying. We sat around her at night watching her. Her body glowed with phosphorus'.[23]

The Vietnamese and their Chinese advisors abandoned any hope of taking the delta quickly. From late 1951 onward, they shifted their attention to the highlands, where the jungle canopy and long distances would prevent the French from concentrating their firepower on attacking PAVN forces. It was in this context that Giap and his advisors focused on controlling Hoa Binh—a strategic interchange located between the highlands and the plains and between northern and central Vietnam. In November 1951, de Lattre de Tassigny recovered Hoa Binh in order to thwart his enemy's attempts to push through a supply route toward central and southern Vietnam, to infiltrate troops into the delta, and to reassure highland minority groups of French resolve. Giap was determined to take Hoa Binh for all these same reasons and saw an advantage in attacking the French there, given the craggy, mountainous terrain. Attacking at night, hoping to avoid the full brunt of French airpower, in December 1951 Giap threw thousands of men against the French Union forces in a bid to encircle, overwhelm, and destroy the camp. Fighting was intense, with French artillery inflicting heavy losses on the Democratic Republic of Vietnam's troops again. On 22–3 February, as the Vietnamese massed for a final knock-out punch, the French withdrew their troops. It was a victory, but an incomplete one for Giap.

The DRV wanted a decisive win. And so did the French, criticized by their American counterparts for failing to take the battle to the enemy. In late 1952, in a bid to block the Democratic Republic of Vietnam from taking control of northwestern Vietnam and eastern Laos, de Lattre de Tassigny transformed Na San, a small upland village located along the Lao border, into a major entrenched position, which bulldozers cleared of trees while soldiers and thousands of civilian workers marched in to dig trenches, install heavy artillery, and helped to build an airbase to supply the camp from afar. Some 20,000 men turned it into 'a fabulous war industry for the time'. General Giap was confident that he could win, but he miscalculated at Na San. On 30 November, the People's Army of Vietnam commander sent waves of his troops against the camp, but was shocked by the ferocity of the French response. Enemy artillery and air strikes decimated his young PAVN soldiers. No sooner had the battle started than Giap had to call it off. The Vietnamese lacked the artillery needed to knock out such a fortified position. Nor did they have the logistical capacity to transport large quantities of food, arms, and equipment to the front line to sustain such an assault. Giap also realized that his inability to destroy the airstrip meant that the French could continue to supply it. Instead of taking Na San, the Vietnamese ended up going around it. The Vietnamese learned three things from this defeat, however: the need for better logistics, heavy artillery, and the ability to sever the enemy's air supply. Giap would not forget this, as his party began preparations to win at Dien Bien Phu.[24]

TOTAL WAR IN THE GLOBAL SOUTH?

In order to make the transition to modern war and transform the state and society in communist ways, the DRV had to mobilize on an unprecedented social scale and in record time. To do so, the government incorporated mandatory military service in late 1949, declared a state of general mobilization in early 1950, and initiated full-scale land reform to induce its majority peasant population to defeat the French and the feudal, landowning class at the same time. As Truong Chinh spelled it out, 'those who have riches must contribute money, those who have their manpower must contribute their strength, those with talents must donate them [. . .]. This is the time that requires us to apply correctly the method of total people's resistance, total resistance' ('*toan dien*'). 'No one', the secretary general declared, 'can roam the shores of the resistance war'.[25]

In addition, in order to ensure that weapons, ammunition, medicines, and especially food actually reached soldiers on the battlefields, the DRV needed a logistical system. The problem was that the People's Army of Vietnam lacked mechanized transport—no trucks, no planes, no ships. To take the battle to the French, the Democratic Republic of Vietnam thus had to rely disproportionately on human and animal force, drafting hundreds of thousands of civilians as porters, requisitioning tens of thousands of bicycles, rafts, horses, and oxen, all the while pushing peasants to produce more rice to feed the growing army and phalanx of civilian transporters. As a result, the party's decision to fight a modern war and to create a large standing army, but to do so via massive mobilization of people like their Chinese counterparts, made this conflict an ever-more totalizing one in terms of its social reach. The already blurred line between civilians and combatants broke down massively in northern and central Vietnam when the Vietnamese engaged in eight set-piece battles between 1950 and 1954 which relied almost entirely on human (and animal) transport. Not only did the Vietnamese communists maintain the guerilla war as the Algerian and the Indonesian republics' fighters did, but they also doubled it up with a conventional war which carried within it a full-blown social and military revolution.

Starting in early 1950, with military draft and full mobilization laws on the books, the party dispersed its cadres across Democratic Republic of Vietnam territories (backed by the police and the army), to work with district and village authorities to recruit, organize, and mobilize civilian manpower for the war effort. These cadres relied on local mass organizations, kinship ties, personal relations, peasant, youth and women's associations, as well as force, to recruit and requisition labor. Those who balked faced legal prosecution and incarceration. Emulation, rectification, and the 'new heroes' campaigns exhorted local populations to support the army, the state, and the war cause by providing labor. For those who joined the civilian logistical apparatus, efforts were made to take care of their families, replace their labor in the fields, and guarantee financial support to the family in the event of the injury or death of those drafted. Before being mobilized, these civilian laborers received an official military status, that of fighter laborer (*'chien si dan cong'*). These porters received crash courses in patriotism and socialism. Then off they marched under the guidance of the party cadres.

The number of civilians the DRV mobilized into its logistical service is mind-boggling. During the first major battle of the Indochina War which ended in the French retreat from Cao Bang in late 1950, the DRV mobilized 121,700 civilians. In his bid to take the Red River delta from the French at Vinh Yen in early 1951, Vo Nguyen Giap relied on 300,000 porters. The numbers peaked during the Battle of Hoa Binh in late 1951 and early 1952, when there were 333,200 fighter laborers. The burden of this social mobilization occurred in villages running from northwestern Vietnam to areas in the central part of the country. With the shift from the delta to the highlands in late 1951, the Democratic Republic of Vietnam expanded its territorial control over upland rural areas in the northwest, in the highlands in central Vietnam, and into eastern Laos and Cambodia. Mobilization not only brought war to civilians in these ethnically non-Viet territories but, in so doing, it simultaneously introduced the party-state as the People's Army of Vietnam increased its territorial control. In 1954, 200,000 porters followed the PAVN as it engaged French Union and Associated State of Vietnam forces violently in the central highlands. In all, between 1950 and 1954, the DRV mobilized 1,741,381 people as civilian porters, almost all of them peasants.[26]

The PAVN's manpower needs led cadres to recruit more and more women into its logistical ranks. They were made to push rice-laden bikes across rugged territory, carry heavy packs over hundreds of kilometers, and to help rebuild bombed-out roads and bridges. It was grueling work, sometimes lasting several months, six months for the Battle of Dien Bien Phu. And of the 122,000 civilians mobilized for the Battle of Cao Bang in late 1950, the majority were women. This high level of female participation apparently remained the case for the following battles. If true, this would mean that the total number of women civilians involved in military logistics would equal at least half of the total number of all those mobilized (1.7 million), therefore about 850,000 women out of the total Democratic Republic of Vietnam-controlled population of 10 million. While DRV women did not hold combat positions like their Soviet counterparts did during the Second World War, the former often found themselves involved in military operations. Dao Thi Vinh, a female porter who was about twenty-five in 1954, recalled her experience during the Battle of Dien Bien Phu as follows:

> I worked as a porter behind the front lines. I only came to the front lines one time. On the way there, we carried ammunition and on the way back the injured. We had to climb up the slopes of the mountains or passes. Falls were commonplace. To carry a crate of ammunition, it took two volunteers. On the way back, these two could take care of one wounded person. Every two or three kilometers, we stopped and asked the injured person if he wanted to drink or piss. When he wanted water, we had to bring it to his lips. Many soldiers suffered. They moaned out of pain. We didn't know how to take care of them. All we could do was encourage them. Sometimes, they did not survive their wounds and died en route. At night, we marched and during the day we rested. We were careful when we carried the wounded. When we carried supplies and ammunition, we would sometimes sleep while walking, we were so tired.[27]

From 1950 onward, the French too mobilized the Vietnamese population in unprecedented numbers. Upon his arrival in Indochina, General de Lattre de Tassigny pushed Bao Dai to institute the draft in mid-1951 and modernize the Associated State of Vietnam's army with American assistance. Thanks to the obligatory military service, the ASV army numbered 167,000 troops by 1954. To this one must add the 200,000-strong Expeditionary Corps, bringing total French Union forces facing the People's Army of Vietnam in 1954 to 350,000 soldiers. In other words, there were *three* conventional armies now in play—one French, two Vietnamese. All of them were increasingly well armed and competing intensely for Vietnamese recruits and laborers. In all, almost half a million regular troops were in uniform. The two Vietnams each also counted around 300,000 rural militiamen and women in their territories. (DRV militia forces protected their villages from French attacks, but didn't engage with the French army directly.)[28]

From 1950, Franco-Vietnamese forces also recruited Vietnamese labor on a large scale. These civilian porters called '*supplétifs*' ('auxiliaries') accompanied troops into battle zones, often moving with their whole families. In 1954, they numbered in all around 100,000 individuals. As the intensity and cost of the war increased from 1950 onward, the French found themselves looking for other sources of labor. And this led them to begin using prisoners of war ('*Prisonniers internés militaires*') to help them in their fight in what might well have been a violation of the Geneva Convention. While there is no study of this question, the total number of prisoners of war probably numbered in all, between 1950 and 1954, 100,000 men and apparently women too. Like the DRV's logistical fighters, they helped the French repair roads, bridges, and transport supplies and equipment across the rugged terrain which trucks and planes could only access with great difficulty. They also ended up in the line of fire.[29]

ENDING THE WAR?

Dien Bien Phu: Forcing Decolonization in a Set-piece Battle[30]
The Battle of Dien Bien Phu was one of the most important battles of the twentieth century. Between November 1953 and May 1954, the DRV organized and then engaged the Western colonizer in a violent set-piece battle and won. One cannot understand the full significance of this epic clash without situating it in its Franco-Vietnamese, international, and military dimensions. On the French side, Prime Minister René Mayer was a vigorous believer in strengthening France's role in Europe and the Atlantic community. That the Americans were pushing to rearm West Germany in order to better contain the Soviet Union only reinforced the priority of Europe over Asia in French strategic thinking. Financially, France could not afford to continue an ever more costly conventional war in Indochina and still contribute to European defense. So, having invested massively in continuing their Asian empire, the French were now finding themselves in a war against the Democratic Republic of Vietnam backed by the Chinese and the Soviets, when their real priority lay in defense of their homeland half a world away.

An honorable end ('*une sortie honorable*') to the conflict had to be found. In May 1953, René Mayer named General Henri Navarre as commander-in-chief of the armed forces in Indochina. The French government instructed Navarre to create the necessary military conditions on the battlefield so that diplomats could reach a favorable solution at the negotiating table thereafter. Navarre came up with a two-pronged plan. During 1953–4, the army would avoid large-scale battles with the enemy in order to rebuild French Union forces, and then, in 1954–5, deliver a decisive military blow to Giap's army in order to force the adversary to the negotiating table on terms favorable to the French. Second, upon his arrival in Vietnam, Navarre focused his attention less on the northern delta than on areas in central Vietnam controlled by the DRV. One of Navarre's main operations, Operation Atlante, was designed to retake southern central Vietnam from the Democratic Republic of Vietnam and place it under the ASV sovereign control before opening negotiations. At the outset, Navarre had no intention of fighting a major battle in the valley of Dien Bien Phu.

Nor did his adversary, Vo Nguyen Giap. Like the French, the DRV leadership made decisions in 1953 that would affect the direction of the road leading to Dien Bien Phu and the negotiating table in Geneva. In the usual military conundrum, the pause the French gave themselves to rebuild and retrain their forces allowed their opponents to do just the same. In January 1953, the party accelerated preparations to implement land reform and mobilize the logistics needed to win a major battle. Giap's high command decided that not only did the army have to bring in its own artillery and anti-air defense forces to take out an entrenched enemy position in any future battle, but it also had to devise a strategy to disperse the Expeditionary Corps' troops across Indochina so that they would not be able to concentrate forces in the event that the French would try to repeat the strategy they used in the Battle of Na San. Throughout 1953, the DRV reorganized its main artillery regiment, created a new one, and constituted its first anti-air battalion. Most importantly, the Vietnamese and Chinese agreed that the Democratic Republic of Vietnam needed to score a major battle victory in light of the international détente which the death of Joseph Stalin and the armistice in Korea had opened up by mid-1953.

All of this was underway on the Vietnamese side when the French adopted the Navarre Plan in July 1953. By mid-September 1953, the DRV's intelligence services had 'acquired a good understanding of the basic elements of the Navarre Plan'. This allowed the Vietnamese politburo (its supreme policy-making body) to better devise its own strategy. Because Navarre was 'massing his forces to occupy and hold the Tonkin lowlands', the politburo decided, 'we will force him to disperse his forces out to other sectors so that we can annihilate them'. Rather than trying to attack the delta, where the French could easily concentrate their artillery and air power with devastating effect, the politburo decided to disperse the French toward northwestern Vietnam and upper Laos, then toward central and southern Laos, and even as far as northeast Cambodia. In mid-November 1953, the Vietnamese politburo approved its Winter–Spring Plan along these lines.

Thinking that his opponents were bent on taking Laos, Navarre decided to commit troops to Dien Bien Phu (on the main route to Laos) to stop them from moving westward. But Laos was never the DRV's goal. Diversion was, and it worked.[31]

On 20 November, the French began by parachuting six battalions into Dien Bien Phu. Surprised, Giap immediately put two questions to his intelligence people: 'Is the enemy going to withdraw?' and 'How are they deployed?' Navarre's decision to send French Union troops toward southern central Vietnam (in Operation Atlante), Laos, and northwestern Vietnam, and then to take a simultaneous stand at Dien Bien Phu, unexpectedly presented the Vietnamese high command and politburo with exactly the type of battle that they wanted to fight.

Drawing upon the Na San battle experience, General Henri Navarre ordered the creation of an even bigger and more solidly entrenched camp in the valley of Dien Bien Phu. An airstrip would serve as the vital lifeline to supply some 15,000 French Union troops. Many high-ranking French and American military officials and politicians agreed that the camp could hold and break the back of the enemy's main forces ('*casser du Viet*', or 'break the Vietnamese', was the expression). French artillery, air power, and resistance positions, each of which was given a feminine name from A to H (Béatrice, for example), would mow down the attacking enemy soldiers, destroy Giap's core divisions, and thus hand the Vietnamese an even worse defeat than the one they had suffered at Na San. The French stationed twelve battle-hardened battalions to defend the valley in all. Morale ran high. Many were actually worried that the Vietnamese would not attack, mirroring, paradoxically, Vo Nguyen Giap's fear that the French would pull out before he could '*casser du français*' ('break the French').

The answer came on 3 December when Democratic Republic of Vietnam military intelligence informed Giap that Navarre had committed his side to battle. With the international context firmly in mind, the Vietnamese politburo issued orders instructing the army to surround the camp and wipe it out entirely, all the while continuing the other campaigns designed to disperse the French forces as far across Indochina as possible. Massive mobilization began, as hundreds of thousands of peasants started to transport rice, weapons, and artillery to the hills surrounding the camp. Chinese-supplied Soviet trucks hauled in weapons and rice from the Chinese border. The People's Army of Vietnam finally had mechanized logistics, but 250,000 civilian porters still had to carry supplies to the battlefield.

The policy of land reform referred to earlier officially began in earnest in December 1953, in areas in upper-central and northern Vietnam whose laborers supplied Dien Bien Phu. Meanwhile, on 17 December 1953, the politburo approved a resolution about their policy of fighting and negotiation. This effectively meant that losing this battle was not an option. Victory had to be achieved at 'one-hundred-percent' before negotiations to end the war could begin, Ho told Giap. This need for certainty was why the DRV cancelled its initial attack against Dien Bien Phu which had been planned for 25 January 1954.[32]

However, even though Navarre realized in early January that the Vietnamese were successfully bringing artillery into Dien Bien Phu, he refused to cancel Operation Atlante. Moreover, rather than concentrating all his forces there, on 29 January, Navarre launched Operation Atlante against the Democratic Republic of Vietnam in central Vietnam, while Giap concentrated his best divisions on wiping out Dien Bien Phu. At the head of the elite 308th Division was General Vuong Thua Vu, the man who had commanded the Battle of Hanoi. Hubris certainly explains part of the French miscalculation. But preparations, operations, and morale were so advanced by mid-January that it was too late for Navarre to pull out by air or via Laos without repeating the Cao Bang débâcle and handing the adversary a *de facto* victory at a key point in international negotiations. (The Berlin Conference, 25 January–18 February 1954, had brought together the USA, UK, France and the USSR to discuss among other things the need to settle the two 'hot wars' in Asia—those in Korea and Indochina.) On 13 March, the Vietnamese finally let loose their artillery with deadly accuracy. They quickly knocked out a number of unprotected French artillery guns and destroyed the airstrip which severed the camp's lifeline to the outside within days. They also launched their first massive and costly attack on the same day as troops moved under heavy French artillery and machine-gun fire to submerge the advance posts of Béatrice and Gabrielle.

However, in response, the French Union forces dug in—quite literally. Indeed, the battle for Dien Bien Phu strangely resembled the trench warfare of the First World War. Some spoke of Verdun. This is hardly surprising, since each side possessed artillery, which forced men to go underground to hide when they weren't ordered to go over the top and attack. What differentiated the Democratic Republic of Vietnam's use of trenches in 1954 from those at Verdun in 1916 was that the Vietnamese ones were mobile, expanding slowly to surround the enemy camp instead of forming a straight, static line. But like the trench warfare of the First World War, young Vietnamese boys ordered to attack suffered terrible casualties when they ran into intense machine-gun and artillery fire, as did French Union forces counter-attacking. For both sides, torrential rains quickly filled the trenches with mud, water, blood, and disease, as soldiers often had to make their way around rotting corpses. Although American pilots flew supply missions over Dien Bien Phu, Washington refused to try to save the camp by launching what would have been their own, first direct military engagement, Operation Vulture, a major bombing campaign. The White House approved of indirect intervention in the form of advisors, military assistance, intelligence, and covert Central Intelligence Agency (CIA) operations, but not of putting official American troops on the ground or in the air. The French Union soldiers were on their own as the DRV's army launched two more wave attacks, extending their trenches meter by meter, hill by hill, slowly strangling the enemy, until they reached the camp on the valley floor of Dien Bien Phu and it finally fell on 7 May 1954 at 17:00 hours. That same day, negotiations formally began in Geneva to find a political solution to end the war.[33]

Over the next year, negotiations secured the release of tens of thousands of prisoners of war. The French returned 65,000 men and women prisoners to the Vietnamese in late 1954, but internal reports conceded that 9,000 had died in captivity or had been executed. For the 9,000 dead, only 2,080 graves could be identified. The Democratic Republic of Vietnam returned around 20,000 POWs taken between 1945 and 1954, but as many as 20,000 had disappeared in captivity, reported as 'absentees, missing or unreturned'. Thousands died as the DRV marched them for hundreds of kilometers from Cao Bang (in 1950) and Dien Bien Phu (in 1954) to insalubrious and often disease-ridden prisoner-of-war camps with little medical care. Families on both sides pleaded with their governments to find these POWs or their bodies.[34]

Geneva 1954: A Failed Peace[35]

While the Americans resisted, fearful that the communists would win by diplomacy what they could not achieve on the battlefield, the rest of the international community, including the British, were looking to cool down the two hot wars in the international system in Korea and Indochina. The death of Stalin in March 1953 and the end of the shooting in Korea a few months later opened the way for a thaw in what had until now been very bitter East–West relations. The new leadership emerging in Moscow wanted to reduce tensions in both Europe and Asia in order to focus on internal economic matters. Détente would facilitate this process. Their Chinese allies shared this view. The Korean and Indochinese wars had proved a heavy drain on the new Chinese state, as had radical social change and land reform. Zhou Enlai, now the seasoned foreign minister of communist China, announced that a solution to the Indochina conflict could be found based upon the recent Korean model.

Vietnamese communists duly noted Beijing's position, agreeing that the time was right to give peace a chance, all the while strengthening their position on the battlefield. On 26 November 1953, in an interview with the Swedish paper *Expressen* (*The Express*), Ho Chi Minh had indicated his side's willingness to open negotiations to reach an eventual negotiated settlement to the war. The party's official line was now one of simultaneous fighting and negotiating. A month after Ho's interview, Truong Chinh issued a special clarification to cadres across the country explaining that the party's desire to open negotiations with the French was not a ploy. The time had come to negotiate, as part of the Sino-Soviet shift toward international détente (*'hoa hoan quoc te'*).[36]

The Soviets took the lead first. On 28 September 1953, Moscow had sent a note to France, Great Britain, and the United States which proposed to hold an international conference in Geneva to ease international tensions. In Europe, this included the crucial question of Germany. In Asia, the conference would have to discuss the two major wars dividing the two blocs—those in Korea and Indochina. This conference, the Soviets argued, had to include the People's Republic of China, given that it was involved in both Asian wars, directly against the Americans in Korea and indirectly via Beijing's support of the Democratic Republic of Vietnam. On 8 October, Zhou Enlai expressed his support of the Soviet proposal.

Easing tensions over Germany was first on the list of topics when French, British, Soviet, and American foreign ministers convened in Berlin in early 1954. When the Soviet Union failed to get communist China recognized as one of the official powers at the upcoming conference in Geneva, the Americans agreed that the four main powers could invite delegations of their choice, which allowed the Soviets to invite the Chinese to take part in their first major international conference. (The Soviets and British were co-presidents of the Geneva Conference.) Besides the 'four powers plus China', the conference also included the main Indochinese parties concerned: the Associated States of Vietnam, Laos, and Cambodia and the Democratic Republic of Vietnam. Pham Van Dong led the DRV's delegation to Geneva. His government failed in its attempts to get its associated states in Laos and Cambodia (the Pathet Lao and the Khmer Issarak) accepted officially at the negotiating table.

The Sino-American split cast a long shadow over the Geneva Conference (26 April–21 July 1954) from beginning to end. Zhou Enlai wanted an end to the First Indochina War but also to find a solution which would keep the United States from replacing the French on China's southern flank. He had already begun developing a policy of 'peaceful co-existence' toward non-communist countries in Asia in order to neutralize this part of the world against American attempts to bring those states into a collective security alliance to contain and perhaps even 'roll back' communist China. On the American side, Washington threw its weight behind Chiang Kai-shek's Republic of China (now based on the island of Taiwan after its defeat by the Chinese communists), and signed a security treaty with him in 1954. But despite his strong opposition to dealing with the Chinese communists, the Secretary of State, John Foster Dulles, went along with the French desire to try to negotiate an end to the war. Most importantly, the American Secretary of State did not want to endanger French ratification of the European Defense Community by opposing them at the Geneva Conference.

On 8 May 1954, the day after Dien Bien Phu fell, the conference took up the question of Indochina. The French and the Democratic Republic of Vietnam adopted hardline opening positions. The Vietnamese, having timed their military actions perfectly, felt that their historic victory on the battlefield permitted such confidence. The French government led by the Popular Republican Movement's always hawkish Georges Bidault made it clear that the French might have lost a battle, but not necessarily the whole war. Moreover, going into the Geneva Conference, Bidault was deeply involved in holding the French Union together, as Moroccans, Tunisians, and Algerians pressed for independence like the Vietnamese. Committed to the Atlantic alliance, Bidault always connected Indochina to European questions and threatened to rally to the more hardline American position, if need be, to get his way.

With a green light from the Soviets to take the lead on solving this prickly Asian problem, Zhou Enlai immediately went to work behind the scenes to bring the belligerents together to reach an acceptable political solution. He started by getting the French and the DRV delegates to sit down in private on 17 May and discuss the issue of recovering wounded soldiers at Dien Bien Phu. On that same day, Soviet Foreign Minister Viatcheslav Molotov proposed the debut of negotiations on the armistice. In a concession designed to advance negotiations, Zhou Enlai announced on 20 May that the situation in Laos and Cambodia was different from that of Vietnam. In short, the Chinese premier no longer supported the Democratic Republic of Vietnam's right to speak for western Indochina. Not only did this respond to Western demands to reject the 'counter associated states' created by the DRV in 1950, but it was also part of Zhou's plan to neutralize non-communist Asia in relation to the Americans, including Laos and Cambodia, if proved to be necessary. More than anyone else, Zhou Enlai rolled back Vietnamese internationalist claims to western Indochina in order to show his wary Indian, Burmese, and Indonesian counterparts that the communists were no longer serious about exporting communism beyond Vietnam's borders in postcolonial Asia. The Vietnamese agreed and, in so doing, let go of their Indochinese ambitions, at least for the time being.[37]

The second concession was about where to provisionally partition Vietnam. On 10 June, the Democratic Republic of Vietnam delegation informed the French that they would be open to the idea of dividing Vietnam *until* general elections could be held to unify the country. However, negotiations hardly advanced beyond that. There was little agreement as to where, exactly, the line dividing Vietnam should go. And when the conference's discussions on Korea broke down in mid-June, things looked equally bleak for Indochina, where an armistice had not even been reached.

To head off a diplomatic failure, on 16 June 1954 Zhou Enlai informed the British Foreign Secretary, Anthony Eden, that he would be able to get Pham Van Dong to agree to pull DRV troops out of Laos and Cambodia. This coincided with the fall of the French government on 13 June and its replacement by one headed by Pierre Mendès France, who was determined, like Zhou Enlai, to reach a negotiated settlement at all costs. Not only did Mendès France up the ante by announcing that he would personally negotiate at Geneva and resign in one month's time if an agreement were not reached, but he also threatened to institute a national draft and bring in the US in order to put added pressure on his communist counterparts to make a deal. Bluff or not, this seriously alarmed the Chinese, the Soviets, and the DRV. Outstanding issues included determining the line of partition for Vietnam and setting a date for general elections within the country.

As for the Democratic Republic of Vietnam, its leadership was opposed to accepting the seventeenth parallel as the demarcation line, since it would mean surrendering vast territories in central Vietnam the DRV had ruled since 1945. On 23 June 1954, Zhou Enlai informed Mendès France that the questions of elections and partition would have to be negotiated one way or another to reach an agreement. He then left the conference to consult his government, regional neighbors, and the Democratic Republic of Vietnam leadership. In Asia, Zhou Enlai stopped over in New Delhi, where he reassured Nehru of communist China's peaceful intentions, which would be demonstrated in exchange for the implicit neutrality of non-communist Asia. Zhou Enlai informed Nehru that the kingdoms of Laos and Cambodia would be neutral, part of what he and Nehru called 'Southeast Nations of a New Type', that is non-communist and non-aligned postcolonial Asian states. On 29 June 1954, Zhou Enlai signed the 'Five Principles of Peaceful Co-existence' with his Indian and Burmese counterparts.[38]

Zhou then made his way to the southern Chinese city of Liuzhou, where he held a crucial meeting with Ho Chi Minh and Vo Nguyen Giap on the final negotiating strategy to be adopted at Geneva. Between 3 and 5 July 1954, Zhou Enlai argued that direct American intervention was possible, even likely, in the event the Geneva Conference talks failed. Such a scenario, he stressed, would greatly complicate the DRV's war, not to mention China's own security. He explained that neutral countries such as India and Burma were hostile to American intervention in the region, but needed to be reassured that Sino-Vietnamese internationalism remained limited to Vietnam. This meant that the Vietnamese had to let go of their Indochinese ambitions. It was eventually agreed that the sixteenth parallel could serve as the temporary dividing line for Vietnam; a non-communist political solution was to be accepted for Cambodia; and that the Chinese and Vietnamese would negotiate strongly in order to acquire regrouping zones for the Pathet Lao in upper Laos. These areas would be the provisional home to Pathet Lao troops and administrators until elections were held to create a new government for all of Laos. Ho concurred, and both sides agreed to coordinate their policies so as to reach an agreement with Mendès France. Upon his return, Ho argued successfully to his party that these concessions, including the division of Vietnam at the sixteenth parallel, were vital to obtaining an accord and preventing the Americans from intervening directly.[39]

Back in Geneva, Zhou, Eden, Molotov and Mendès France accelerated their efforts to reach an agreement before the Frenchman's deadline arrived. With the clock ticking, the Democratic Republic of Vietnam finally agreed to pull its troops out of Laos and Cambodia and accepted the partition of Vietnam at the seventeenth parallel falling just south of the city of Vinh, a serious further concession of territory. DRV troops and personnel in Cambodia, Laos, and southern Vietnam would be regrouped to northern Vietnam, whereas those of the Associated State of Vietnam and French Union forces would regroup to the south. Son Ngoc Minh's Cambodian forces laid down their arms and were reintegrated into the royalist forces or returned to civilian life. In Laos, regrouping zones were created for the Pathet Lao in the Lao provinces bordering northern Vietnam, Phongsaly and Samneua. The Geneva conference created an International Commission for Supervision and Control for Vietnam, Laos, and Cambodia. Elections were scheduled to be held in mid-1956 in all of Vietnam in order to decide under which Vietnam—the Democratic Republic of Vietnam or the State of Vietnam—the country would be unified. In the early hours of 21 July 1954, the French and the DRV initialed a ceasefire. The first Indochina War had officially come to an end.

Vietnamese communists agreed with the Sino-Soviet decision to shift to détente and open negotiations on Indochina. They also shared the Chinese fear that if an agreement were not reached at Geneva, then it was likely that the Americans would intervene directly. This they did not want. In February 1954, as talks were underway in Berlin, and again on the eve of the opening discussion of Indochina at Geneva, the Vietnamese communists affirmed their commitment to adopting a negotiating strategy to end the war and which would contribute to bringing peace to Asia and the world, in collaboration with the Soviets and Chinese. During the negotiations at Geneva between May and July, the Soviets and Chinese did indeed push the Vietnamese to back off from the international communist model of Indochina and accept the neutrality and reality of royalist governments there. The Chinese put pressure on their counterparts to accept the seventeenth parallel in order to cut the final deal at Geneva. But Vietnamese party documents also show that their politburo had agreed that it could not continue the war. The Battle of Dien Bien Phu was a glorious victory, but the war, especially the shift to conventional warfare and simultaneous social revolution, had exhausted the people and the army.

During the party's sixth plenum held between 15 and 17 July 1954, the Democratic Republic of Vietnam's leaders justified the decision to sign the Geneva accords by shifting from an armed line to one of negotiations. Drawing upon arguments he had developed with Zhou Enlai a week earlier at Liuzhou, Ho explained that the main enemy in Indochina was no longer the French, but the Americans, who were now bent on war at both the global and Indochinese levels. Ho argued that while the victory at Dien Bien Phu demonstrated the increasing strength of the DRV's armed forces, it had also served to draw the attention of the Americans to Vietnam. This had increased Washington's resolve to take a more direct stand against the communists in Indochina and to broker a deal in Geneva in order to prevent the DRV from taking all of Vietnam, either diplomatically or military. Ho insisted that the Democratic Republic of Vietnam had to exploit the contradictions in the international system, especially the reluctance of the British and French to follow the Americans, in order to reach an international agreement that could isolate the USA. If the DRV could achieve unification via elections and negotiations, then all the better. He added that while the Vietnamese had become stronger compared to the French, they did not yet have the decisive (*'khong phai tuyet doi'*) threshold needed to impose a crushing victory in all of Vietnam. Two days later, the communists' general secretary, Truong Chinh, conceded that the DRV's armed forces had become stronger and that increased force had culminated in the Dien Bien Phu victory, but that the change in armed force was not yet a 'fundamental one' (*'nhung chua thay doi ve can ban'*). The armed forces had won a battle, but they were not necessarily in a position to win the war decisively throughout the country. He also pointed out that there was a war faction in French ruling circles, one which was intent on carrying out the war to the end. These leaders were quite ready to use the Geneva Conference as a way of internationalizing the war to isolate the Democratic Republic of Vietnam along Cold War lines. They were also ready to turn to the Americans to help them finish off a war they themselves could not win. This, the general secretary warned, was a reality the leadership simply could not ignore. As Truong Chinh put it, the Americans had already replaced the French as the DRV's 'Enemy no. 1' in the Indochina War. The time, he said, had come to change their strategy from that of an armed line of protracted resistance to one of peaceful negotiations. In short, the Vietnamese had to win by peaceful means that which they could not win on the battlefield in the short term. On 17 July 1954, the Vietnamese politburo officially changed its policy from an armed to a peaceful strategy and agreed to sign the resulting armistice on 21 July.[40]

The Geneva negotiations did not produce a peace accord, but simply an armistice and a declaration, a pledge by those signing it to organize elections to unite Vietnam once and for all, under one sovereign state, the Democratic Republic of Vietnam now based in Hanoi, or as the Associated State of Vietnam operating from Saigon. That in mid-1954 the Americans and the new prime minister of the State of Vietnam, Ngo Dinh Diem, then refused to sign the declaration boded ill for the prospects of peace in Indochina. And the Geneva negotiations provided no concrete ways for requiring either of the two Vietnams or their respective backers to comply with the declaration. The DRV hoped to win by the ballot box in the future what its army had been unable to win on the battlefield, whereas the ASV sought to get rid of the French colonialists in order to build up a viable nationalist alternative to the communists with the backing of the United States. The Geneva negotiations might have achieved a ceasefire, but the declaration it produced could do little to stop the Vietnamese from going to war against each other. Nor could they stop the Americans from transforming their indirect war in Indochina into a direct one.

CHAPTER 10

A TALE OF TWO REPUBLICS

In July 1963, Nguyen Tuong Tam received a summons to report to a nearby military police station to answer questions about his role in a failed coup attempt against the southern republic's president, Ngo Dinh Diem. Tam was one of Vietnam's best-known anticommunist politicians and a cultural giant from the 1930s, better known by his *nom de plume*, Nhat Linh. He had led a cultural revolution based on the liberation of the individual and the renovation of Vietnamese society. In the 1940s, he had helped to revive and lead the Vietnamese Nationalist Party, the VNQDD, which was opposed to both French colonialism and Vietnamese communism. While Tam had briefly worked with Diem to build a non-communist Vietnam during the Indochina conflict, he now despised the man for what he and his family were doing to the country. Instead of unifying non-communists, Diem was attacking anyone who defied him and in so doing, Tam was convinced, ensuring that the cherished republic would fail. Tam was not alone in his hostility to Diem. A Buddhist protest movement against the Ngo family was gathering strength as well.

Nguyen Tuong Tam had no intention of joining Diem's long list of non-communist victims. On the auspicious seventh day of the seventh month of 1963, he sat down with his sons in their home in Saigon to enjoy their customary family chat. It was to be their last one, for their father had mixed a lethal dose of barbiturates into his own drink, a glass of his favorite Johnny Walker scotch whiskey. The champion of individual liberty had decided to take his life to make a political point. In words strangely reminiscent of Nguyen Van Thinh's suicide note of November 1946, Tam wrote a similar message: 'Let history be my judge. I refuse to accept any other judgment. The arrest and detention of nationalist opposition elements is a serious crime, and it will cause the country to be lost into the hands of the communists. I oppose these acts, and sentence myself to death [. . .] as a warning to those who would trample upon freedom of every kind'. Radio services, newspapers, and friends beamed the message far and wide as thousands of people gathered to watch Tam's funeral cortège file by a few days later. Ngo Dinh Diem's security forces carefully monitored the procession as it paused for a prayer service at the Xa Loi Buddhist pagoda before it moved on to Tam's final resting place. (This temple had become the nerve center for Buddhist protests against Ngo rule.) A month later, Ngo Dinh Diem's forces occupied the pagoda in a harsh clampdown on the opposition. As one officer fighting communists in the provinces expressed his anger at the Ngo family to an American friend: 'I'm a Buddhist now.' He was not, but his point was clear, nevertheless.[1]

Things could have been different. Many nationalists who were opposed to Ngo Dinh Diem in 1963 had placed their faith in this man only a few years earlier. Not only had he pushed the French out, but he had also succeeded in getting the Americans to end their support of the French protectorate over the Associated State of Vietnam in favor of a fully decolonized non-communist Vietnam. Many had been happy to see Diem end a century-old French policy of divide and rule in favor of the creation of a modern nation-state, organized top down, capable of taking on Ho Chi Minh's communist state in the north. So what happened? The question divides Vietnamese and non-Vietnamese to this day. But before we try to answer, we need to return to the end of the First Indochina War to understand how the two authoritarian republics, one in the north, the other in the south, had come into being in the shadow of the Cold War.

Resetting Non-Communist Vietnam: The Republic of Ngo Dinh Diem

The Rise of the Ngo and the American Break with France[2]

The American decision to back the French against the Democratic Republic of Vietnam in order to contain global communism had undermined the Associated State of Vietnam's independence bid. When Bao Dai's first prime minister, Nguyen Phan Long, tried to gain American support for a fully decolonized non-communist Vietnam in 1950, it was easy for the French to replace him as the Americans looked the other way. Containing world communism trumped the promotion of decolonization. During a tour of Vietnam in late 1953, Vice-president Richard Nixon cautioned Vietnamese nationalists not to push the French too hard as the showdown at Dien Bien Phu shaped up. And when King Norodom Sihanouk took his independence crusade to the United States that year, John Foster Dulles had infuriated the mercurial monarch by saying that now was not a good time.

There were dissenting American voices, however. One was the Democrat senator from Massachusetts, John F. Kennedy. He personally visited Vietnam in 1951, meeting with a wide range of French and Vietnamese officials. Despite French reassurances that all was fine, Kennedy left with the distinct impression that France was in no rush to relinquish its colonial hold and that by supporting the French instead of the Vietnamese, American policymakers were undermining their own Cold War strategy. Fellow Democratic senator Mike Mansfield also visited Vietnam that year and came away with a similar feeling. From their positions on the Senate Foreign Relations Committee, they called on the White House to put pressure on the French to accord Vietnam complete independence. In July 1953, Kennedy joined Republican senator Barry Goldwater in trying to get the Eisenhower administration to persuade the French to decolonize in exchange for continued US military aid. 'French grants of limited independence to the people of Vietnam', Kennedy pointed out, 'have always been too little and too late'. The Republican majority defeated Kennedy and Goldwater's amendments, fearful that such pressure could lead the French to pull out of the war. Léon Pignon's strategy of containing American pressure to decolonize was working to perfection.[3]

That is, until Ngo Dinh Diem, the man the French had sent packing a few years earlier for demanding dominion status, decided to make the non-communist case directly to the Americans. While Diem had no master plan to present to Washington upon leaving in 1950, he and his brothers wanted to shift US support from the French to non-communist Vietnamese nationalists. Ngo Dinh Thuc, his brother and one of the country's first Vietnamese bishops, put his international Catholic connections at his brother's disposal. This gave Diem the use of several monasteries from which he lobbied both sides of the Atlantic until 1954. In meetings with a wide range of American diplomats, clergy, statesmen, academics, and journalists, Diem began making his case. As McCarthyism shook the American political establishment, he repeated to his listeners that the French failure to decolonize was only helping the communists, while also pointing out that the French colonial powers were playing the Americans for fools.[4]

Despite difficult encounters which repeated the well-known mantra not to push the French on independence right then, Diem slowly built up a network of support extending well beyond that of the Catholics alone. By early 1954, his contacts included some of the most influential Americans of the time—senators Kennedy and Mansfield, statesman Dean Acheson, Supreme Court judge William O. Douglas, renowned intelligence specialist of wartime Eurasia, William Donovan, and the influential cardinal Francis Spellman. Diem also had an active interest in economic development and built up a lasting relationship with specialists in development theory. This networking put him in the right place, as more American officials began to question the strategic wisdom of supporting the French. Mansfield came away from a lunch with Diem in May 1953 'with the feeling that if anyone could hold South Vietnam, it was somebody like Ngo Dinh Diem'.[5]

Inside Vietnam, others in the Diem clan, especially his brother Ngo Dinh Nhu, promoted the nationalist cause among disgruntled Vietnamese politicians, youth groups, Catholics, union leaders, and their workers. A labor activist himself, Nhu was the prime mover in the creation of a new nationalist political party, the Can Lao Nhan Vi Cach Mang, or the Personalist Revolutionary Labor Party, often known as the Personalist Party. Drawing on the ideas of French philosopher Emmanuel Mounier (collectively known as 'Personalism'), and influenced by leftward shifts in French Catholicism in favor of social action and anticolonialism, Nhu imported Personalism to Vietnam. Particularly appealing was Mounier's rejection of liberal capitalism's over-emphasis on individualism at the expense of building up communal ties and shared prosperity. Just as important was Personalism's opposition to communism's abnegation of the human spirit and its embrace of an Orwellian party-state. For the Ngo brothers, communism and capitalism were ideological dead ends when it came to rethinking Vietnam. Personalism provided an appealing middle-of-the-road approach to socio-economic development, was respectful of human beings, and capable of empowering Vietnam's large peasant population, but without unleashing a destructive class war as did the Democratic Republic of Vietnam in the north and Maoism in China. Personalism mixed with a lot of nationalism would put Vietnam on the right postcolonial track and, the Ngos felt, appeal to Catholics and non-Catholics alike.[6]

The Ngo brothers' strategy of positioning themselves and their cause close to the Americans and disaffected Vietnamese paid off when both international and Indochinese situations changed rapidly in 1953–4. Firstly, inside Vietnam, Bao Dai's passivity left many convinced that they had to take the nationalist cause into their own hands or pass for collaborators with the French. Secondly, this frustration manifested itself in an increasingly ardent desire to create real political parties, a national assembly, indeed, a republic, so that nationalists could mobilize party politics and use these institutions of democracy against Bao Dai, his ministers, and their colonial backers. Thirdly, the French government's unilateral decision to devalue the *piastre* in May 1953 in order to boost metropolitan exports outraged all. It was humiliating proof of just how subservient the relationship with France remained; but it also served as a rallying cry for angry national-ists. When the new French government led by Joseph Laniel promised to complete ('*parfaire*') the Associated State of Vietnam's independence, the Ngo brothers were determined to make it happen, even if it meant bringing down the French Union.

However, the rapidly changing international situation in 1953–4 also posed threats, much the same ones that the Democratic Republic of Viet-nam confronted—Stalin's death in March 1953, a rapid Sino-Soviet shift toward peaceful co-existence which culminated in the Korean War's cease-fire, increasing international talk about negotiating the end of the Indochina conflict, and Laniel's declaration to negotiate an 'honorable exit' from In-dochina. The main threat for non-communist nationalists in all this was that as long as the French failed to accord the Associated State of Vietnam full independence, there was nothing to stop the French legally from nego-tiating directly with the communist bloc, including the Democratic Repub-lic of Vietnam, and signing an international agreement over the heads of the ASV's leaders and people.

As international exchanges on ending the Korean and Indochina confla-grations began in September 1953, the Ngo brothers went on the offensive against the French, Bao Dai, and his ministers. In September, relying on his wide range of contacts, Ngo Dinh Nhu presided over something called the 'Congress of National Union and Peace'. This meeting gathered leaders from all of the major socio-religious and political groups who shared a gen-eral disappointment with the present government and its failure to secure complete independence from the French. This meeting intentionally ex-cluded Bao Dai and his cabinet ministers in a move designed to underscore their nationalist illegitimacy, and caught the French off-guard. Once at the congress, delegates vented their frustration with Bao Dai and his associates, while others called on Laniel to negotiate full independence immediately. The message was clear: if Bao Dai would not lead, others would. More than anything else, this congress allowed the Ngo brothers to promote themselves as the architects of an authentic nationalist alternative to failed collaboration. Within a few months, Nhu had created the Personalist Party and used it, and his union contacts, to build up loyal support for his brother as the only untainted Third Force leader who could stand up to the French, unify non-communist nationalists, and convince the Americans to change their policy straight away.

The September congress spurred Bao Dai to action. In October, the head of the Associated State held his own meeting during which he and his allies issued resolutions demanding full independence. The French dragged their feet as always in response, promising to negotiate, but countering that constitutional complexities and internal politics prevented them from moving faster. What the French truly feared was that by according complete independence to the Associated State of Vietnam in 1953-4, they would bring down their entire empire through the domino effect of that action. Indeed, as Diem and Sihanouk were making their cases for independence abroad, the French were engaged in a trans-imperial legal battle against them as well as nationalists in Tunisia, Morocco, Madagascar, and Algeria making similar demands. Even as the French leaders watched Dien Bien Phu fall to the communists, they could not bring themselves to free the ASV from its imperial 'association' for fear of what might happen elsewhere in their Union if they did.

As preparations for the Geneva Conference began in 1954, both Bao Dai and Ngo Dinh Diem left for Europe determined to force the French hand once and for all. This meant convincing American diplomats to change their policy of supporting Paris, or risk losing all of Vietnam to the communist bloc. In early June 1954, as Zhou Enlai did everything he could do to reach a deal with Pierre Mendès France, Bao Dai asked Ngo Dinh Diem to serve as his new prime minister. During the meeting between the two men in Paris, Bao Dai led Diem into a room where a crucifix hung from the wall. Standing before the cross, he told Diem: 'Here's your God. You will swear before Him to maintain the territory that we confide to you. You will defend it against the communists and if necessary against the French'. Diem swore to it. The French, their Vietnamese allies, and the Democratic Republic of Vietnam had every reason to interpret Bao Dai's choice of Ngo Dinh Diem as a hostile action.[7]

More than anything else, Bao Dai's decision was designed to shift American support toward the Vietnamese in order ensure that the ASV survived international negotiations. The Expeditionary Corps had not only lost the battle of Dien Bien Phu in May 1954, but the French command was pulling back its troops. In early July, a communist regiment moving through the southern central highlands annihilated a retreating French airborne group near the town of Pleiku. The Americans realized that there was no guarantee that the French army would stay, and the question of Vietnam's partition or temporary separation was already on the table in Geneva. Moreover, the débâcles of the lost battles at Dien Bien Phu and Pleiku only reinforced a growing stereotype in official American minds which portrayed the French in Indochina in 1954, as it did Europe in 1940, as a second-rate world power. Mendès France only added to the frustration by failing to secure ratification of the treaty that would have created a European army (see chapter 9). To many Americans, the French seemed unreliable in both Europe and Asia.[8]

It was in this complex and rapidly changing context that Dulles, backed by Eisenhower, began resetting American policy on Vietnam in ways already championed by Kennedy and Goldwater. In April 1954, the secretary of state issued instructions stressing the 'extreme importance' of getting the French to sign a treaty according full independence to the Associated State of Vietnam before negotiations on Indochina began. If the French could not do it, then the Americans would have 'to take an active part' in the conflict, but only if they could collaborate with 'an authentic Vietnamese nationalist government'. This was precisely what Diem seemed to offer. And this is why the needs of the Eisenhower administration and those of the Ngo brothers finally converged at Geneva in mid-1954, and not before. As the French signed the ceasefire documents and a declaration to hold elections in two years with their Democratic Republic of Vietnam counterparts, backed by Moscow and Beijing, Prime Minister Diem's government refused to do so, and was fully supported by Washington.[9]

Separation, Peoples, and Choices

Neither the Ngos nor the Americans knew where their new relationship would take them as the ink dried on the ceasefire agreement signed at the Geneva conference. What we do know is that all the parties present in Geneva at the time, including the United States and the Associated State of Vietnam, accepted that the French war for Indochina was over. The three states that had co-existed, intermingled, and competed with each other across all of Vietnam prior to July 1954 now consolidated into two parallel and separate states—the DRV-sovereign 'North Vietnam', and a still less than entirely independent ASV-'South Vietnam'. Although the Geneva agreements never sanctioned the permanent creation of two states—indeed, the declaration called for elections to unify the country into one state—checkpoints appeared along the seventeenth parallel with each side's national flags waving in the wind on either side of what was becoming a *de facto* border.

Before this happened, however, the Geneva agreements required each state's military personnel and administrators to withdraw from their adversary's zone and accorded civilians the right to move freely from one zone to the other until May 1955 (300 days). As a result, from late July 1954 onward, tens of thousands of French Union and Associated State of Vietnam troops, civil servants, and their families began evacuating areas above the seventeenth parallel, while the Democratic Republic of Vietnam relocated around 100,000 military personnel and administrators from lower Vietnam and Cambodia to the north. In all, around 800,000 people departed for the south, while 120,000 DRV personnel moved north. By May 1955, almost a million individuals in all had moved, thanks to French, American, and, a first, communist bloc transport. Never had so many people emigrated so fast at one time in Vietnam's history.[10]

As in Korea, Germany, and China, the impact of partition on the lives of these people was profound. Within days of learning of the results of the Geneva conference's agreements, individuals began making hard decisions. Thousands of makeshift markets popped up across the country as civilians and soldiers, merchants, and peasants, young and old, Viet and non-Viet tried to sell things they could not take with them or buy materials they would need on arrival. Real-estate prices plummeted in the north and skyrocketed in the south as administrators scrambled to find housing and jobs for the hundreds of thousands of arrivals. Landowners in the north sold what land they had and abandoned any hope of recovering that which the war had already taken and the Democratic Republic of Vietnam had redistributed. Most of the 45,000 Chinese and several thousand French residing above the seventeenth parallel relocated to the south, to Asian port cities, to France, or to elsewhere in the empire. Many of the Chinese in Vietnam held Republic of China passports and moved on to Taiwan. Non-Viet soldiers who had fought with the French moved to the south, including 20,000 Nung people. At least 500,000 Catholics left the north and in so doing shifted the center of gravity of Vietnamese Catholicism firmly in the direction of the south. Two hundred thousand Buddhists also went south, including their main leaders.

Heart-wrenching and tearful family conversations, separations, and inner transformations occurred everywhere as people made decisions in circumstances that were almost always beyond their control. Families left loved ones behind, never to see them again. Some were too old to travel, preferring to live out the rest of their lives in their native villages. Others stayed, determined to protect their homes, land, or livestock, gambling that the promised elections in 1956 would return everything to normal. Those moving southward with the Associated State of Vietnam implored relatives in the countryside to leave the Democratic Republic of Vietnam zone before it was too late, while those allied with the DRV pleaded with their kin not to leave now that the colonialists were finally going. A bright future was on the horizon, they said. Such arguments did not always convince those who had already experienced or feared the radical communization the Democratic Republic of Vietnam had implemented since 1950. Thousands of Vietnamese left communist zones, traumatized by violent land reform and the rectification campaigns discussed in the previous chapter. But it could work the other way too. One cocky young anticommunist nationalist on his way out of Hanoi in 1954 was dumbfounded when a beggar boy took his money and thanked him with a word of caution: 'The Viet Minh will come here before long. We poor people will be given property, you dirty rich people will be felled, and you'll beg us for money'.[11]

But things were never so clear-cut in practice. Regardless of class or race, choices were complicated and loyalties blurred. Ever since losing her husband to the famine of 1945 and her only son to suicide, U Mien had worked as a maid for the family of the northern historian Duong Van Mai Elliott. Part of U Mien wanted to stay put in Hanoi out of her pride in the DRV's heroic victory over the French. But another part of her wanted to leave and go south with the only family she knew, the Duongs. In the end, she left. But even within the Duong family, like so many others struck by civil strife, loyalties were divided: 'While we in Hanoi thought our world was crumbling around us', Duong Van Mai Elliot later wrote of her sister, 'Thang and her Viet Minh colleagues exploded in celebration at the news of the victory of Dien Bien Phu'. Thang had dedicated her best years to the Democratic Republic of Vietnam's struggle and couldn't wait to begin a new postwar life building a new Vietnam. Meanwhile, their father, Duong Thieu Chieu, oversaw the withdrawal of the ASV from the north. In April 1955 he left the northern city of Haiphong (on one of the last boats out before the communists were to take over), not knowing what his Vietnam would become. Like his own grandfather, discussed in chapter 3, he had dedicated his life to public service and he had made choices in doing so. Now those choices would take him and his family far from their northern homeland. And then there was Jean Moreau, the son of a pencil-pushing French customs official and a Vietnamese-Italian mother. He grew up speaking Vietnamese, fascinated by the language, culture, and history of the people. In mid-1945, as Vietnamese nationalism surged around him (and almost killed him), he joined the Democratic Republic of Vietnam and worked in military intelligence. French officers who encountered him at the seventeenth parallel could not believe that he could choose the 'other side'. He did and lives there to this day, a Vietnamese citizen.[12]

The United States, Ngo Dinh Diem, and the Making of Another Vietnam[13]

Just as rapid changes in power relations transform the lives of ordinary people in all walks of life, wars and their endings also reshape alliances on high. The Americans, French, and Ngo brothers emerged from Geneva in a very different relationship from the one they had had going in. With Ho Chi Minh's state now set to take over all of 'North Vietnam' from the capital of Hanoi, the Americans were now focused on supporting a fully decolonized, anticommunist, economically vibrant, and heavily armed 'South Vietnam' capable of holding the Indochinese line in the struggle to contain communism. While Eisenhower came remarkably close to going to war over Indochina in 1954, in the end he resisted and turned to building up 'South Vietnam' and spinning a collective security treaty around it, Laos, and Cambodia. No sooner had the president stated his 'domino theory' in April 1954 (that if one country falls to communism in Asia, they all do) than he set Dulles to work creating what became the South East Asia Treaty Organization (SEATO) in September. It was in turn part of a wider web of American treaties, which ran from the Atlantic alliance in the West to bilateral ones in the East with Japan and Taiwan, linked from below by a southern chain going through Iraq, Pakistan, Bangkok, Australia, New Zealand, and the Philippines. The South East Asia Treaty Organization connected up this Eurasian rim of containment for the Eisenhower administration. It also served to block the Chinese from using neutralist-minded, non-communist states like India, Burma, and Indonesia to break this chain. And given that Zhou Enlai sought to neutralize Indochina against the Americans, Washington extended SEATO's protection to the Associated States without formally admitting them to it. Rightly or wrongly, American strategists were convinced that the Sino-Soviet treaty signed by Stalin and Mao in 1950 had not only consolidated communist domination of Eurasia, but that it now would allow Moscow and

Beijing to push into the whole of Southeast Asia via Tonkin as the Japanese had done in 1940. As we saw in chapter 1, the Americans and the Japanese were by no means the first to recognize Vietnam's strategic importance as a gateway to Southeast Asia and the Indian Ocean.[14]

While Ngo Dinh Diem shared American anticommunism, he focused first and foremost on securing a fully decolonized, economically modern, politically centralized, and legitimate nation-state. He and his family were convinced that only they could do this. Given (in their view) that so many nationalists had become compromised since 1947 by gambling on the French or sitting on the fence, they saw themselves as the chosen ones. Their successful actions in 1953-4 seemed only to confirm it. Critics, however, saw a dangerous turn toward authoritarian rule and nepotism, as Diem leaned ever more heavily on his family. But what counted most, the Ngos retorted, was action and results. Time was short. The 'colonialists' and the 'communists' had just bargained away half the country at Geneva. In over his head, Bao Dai kept Diem on as prime minister and gave him precisely what the Ngo family wanted—full powers.

Communists lined up behind Ho Chi Minh remained as convinced as ever that *they* were the rightful masters of all of Vietnam. Neither Bao Dai nor Ngo Dinh Diem had taken up arms against the French. Vietnamese communists easily portrayed the head of state as a puppet, and they rightly pointed out that for all of his tough talk Diem had sat on the fence for years while the Democratic Republic of Vietnam's leaders and people had made huge sacrifices. The Greater Vietnam coalition, the Vietnamese Nationalist Party and Nguyen Tuong Tam had relied on French military power rather than create their own armies to fight both the French colonialists and the Vietnamese communists. Had it not been for French and American military support, Vietnamese communists would be in charge of all of Vietnam. Instead the DRV had fought the American-backed French and Associated State of Vietnam to a draw. In agreement with his allies in Beijing and Moscow, Ho Chi Minh had convinced his party that the Democratic Republic of Vietnam could win via the ballot box and unify what was theirs through political means (in what appeared to be a period of détente in mid-1954). But the communists also knew they had gambled, and perhaps had done so badly, for neither Ngo Dinh Diem nor the Americans had signed any legally binding agreement enforcing them to organize elections in mid-1956. And it remained to be seen if the French would remain as the executor of the agreement, or would they change course along with the Americans?

This is why the Geneva Conference of 1954 may have marked the end of French fighting, but it was potentially only a pause in two separate, though interconnected wars, a Vietnamese and an American one. As long as both Vietnams were content to focus on consolidating their states, one in the north, the other now rebuilding the south, then the ceasefire of 1954 could have held and could have easily produced two separate Vietnamese nation-states today, as in the case of the two Koreas and Chinas. However, if one of the two Vietnams decided that it would renew its claim to sovereignty over or within the other's zone, then the Vietnamese civil war would resume as one continuous conflict, with its origins in the civil violence of 1945–7. The 'French war' might have ended in July 1954, but that did not mean that the one among Vietnamese had.

Similarly, the conference at Geneva can be seen as a pause in the indirect war for Indochina Washington had operated in since 1950. For if the French had manipulated American anticommunism in order to hold on, colonially, in Indochina, the Americans had also used the French army, colonial administration, and their Vietnamese allies to help fight their global anticommunist war along Eurasia's southeastern flank. The Americans had paid for 80 percent of the costs of the First Indochina War by 1954, precisely because it was 'their' war too. Given the high cost of assuring Western European security, not to mention the Marshall Plan, their direct participation in the Korean War, and their maintenance of a global web of military bases, this indirect strategy using the French army and administration in Indochina made good economic sense.

America's global containment operated precisely through such direct and indirect forms of action. The French communists were not the only ones to point out that France 'was exporting soldiers to Indochina in exchange for dollars'. No torch was necessarily passed in late July 1954 from the French to the Americans, no sparks flew from the embers of one empire to light the flames of another. Two empires (three, if we count the Japanese one involved during the Second World War) had already *intertwined* in complex and fascinating ways for decades. Contrary to what is often claimed, the Americans were not newcomers to Asia or Indochina in 1954. Their 'black ships' had 'opened' Japan in the 1850s. They had colonized the Philippines in 1898, at the same time as the French had consolidated their hold over Indochina and the British had taken over Burma. President Franklin Roosevelt had closely followed Japanese colonial expansion down the Chinese coastline from 1937 onward, into Vietnam in 1940–41, and then, from there, deep into Southeast Asia. During the First Indochina War, the Americans operated indirectly through such institutions as the Military Assistance Advisory Group and the creation of French commando operations in the highlands (while the Chinese communists did something remarkably similar in supporting communist Vietnam in order to keep the Americans off their southern flank; see chapter 9). If anything, Washington sought to replace the 'colonialist' French Associated State of Vietnam with a fully decolonized State of Vietnam. And as long as the Americans did not tread on this new Vietnamese nation-state's sovereignty (just as they had previously carefully respected French colonial sovereignty in Indochina) and Vietnamese nationalist leaders did not endanger the US's strategic investment in Vietnam by negotiating with the 'communists', then a new alliance could work in Indochina which would allow the Americans to contain Eurasian communism indirectly and continue to expand the informal empire they had been building across the Pacific Ocean since the nineteenth century. Such a global perspective—taking into account Vietnam's position on Eurasia's eastern façade where so many empires collide—helps to explain why this country remained so important to the Americans right *through* 1954 and arguably to this day. And if one takes the time to consider how China may have viewed the American presence, it's not surprising that Beijing was deeply interested in what happened in Vietnam and Southeast Asia.[15]

But the ASV was not yet fully sovereign. With the Democratic Republic of Vietnam serious about reaching a political solution by 1956, the Ngos understood that they had a two-year breathing space in which to transform the Associated State of Vietnam into an independent nation-state. With the full powers now granted to him by Bao Dai, the prime minister issued decrees which would place the selection of independent-minded regional and provincial authorities in his hands. Village councils lost their centuries-old autonomy to Ngo Dinh Diem's desire to impose top-down rule (though it never worked out so neatly in practice). He also wanted control over the armed forces in order to free it from the French and use it to subdue those Vietnamese opposed to his nation-building. On 11 September 1954, he relieved General Nguyen Van Hinh of his command of the ASV's armed forces. Furious, Hinh immediately began plotting to overthrow his rival, confident that the French would back him. Despite often seething French hostility toward Diem, Nguyen Van Hinh badly overestimated his French partner's ability or desire to help in post-Geneva Vietnam. Hinh also underestimated the Ngo brothers, who were turning younger, frustrated

nationalist officers in the army against him, carefully casting Hinh as a creature of the French. The Ngos required officers and civil servants to join the
Personalist Party and study its ideology. Once again, Bao Dai backed his
prime minister. Hinh lost his army and moved to France.[16]

Despite strong misgivings about Ngo Dinh Diem, the first American
ambassador to the Associated State of Vietnam, General Lawton Collins,
and the last French High Commissioner for Indochina, General Paul Ely,
reached an accord in December 1954, through which the Americans joined
the French in training the Vietnamese army from January 1955 onward,
while the French would start withdrawing their forces from the ASV and
relinquish control of its armed forces by July of that year. In exchange, the
Americans would continue to provide military assistance and training via
the Military Assistance Advisory Group they had created in 1950. While
the overarching goal was to ensure the outfitting and training of a Vietnamese army capable of taking over from the French, the Collins-Ely agreement dovetailed nicely with Diem's determination to push the French out
and take control of the army, with American support. Indeed, this accord
allowed massive amounts of American military aid to flow directly to the
Associated State of Vietnam instead of via the French, effectively ending Pignon's protectorate and America's proxy war enacted through the
French. Emboldened by such direct support, and confident that he could
win more of it, on 28 December 1954 Ngo Dinh Diem requested the French
to withdraw all of their troops from the ASV. In May 1955, as required by
the Geneva conference's agreed date for a ceasefire, the French withdrew
from northern Vietnam (which was now being turned into DRV Vietnam).
In 1956, the Expeditionary Corps left the south, removing one of the most
dangerous threats to Diem's rise to power and ending a century of French
colonial domination.[17]

With Bao Dai's full backing, Ngo Dinh Diem threw himself into creating
a truly independent nation-state in record time. On 20 July 1954, he formally
withdrew the 'Associated State of Vietnam' (ASV) from the French Union,
thereby finally making it the 'State of Vietnam' (SV). He destroyed Indochinese federalism alongside his Lao and Cambodian counterparts when
they all agreed to abolish the Indochinese Office for Currency Affairs (the
Office indochinois des Changes) in December 1954 and with it the colonial
piastre. Each state officially printed its own national money and administered separate customs, immigration, and border patrol offices. *National*
borders now separated Laos, Cambodia, and Vietnam. In February 1955,

the French Ministry of Relations in charge of the Associated States disappeared. Having freed Vietnam from colonial federalism, Diem promulgated strict nationality laws turning 'ethnic minorities' into 'Vietnamese' citizens; required the Chinese (over a half million) to adopt Vietnamese nationality or leave; and denied French nationals most of the legal privileges they had enjoyed since the nineteenth century. Like his communist competitors, he nationalized education, imposed Vietnamese as the national language, and dispatched diplomats across the globe.

However, Ngo Dinh Diem's nationalist partners of 1953–4 did not necessarily embrace the idea of the creation of a centralized nation-state under Ngo rule. This was particularly true in the south of Vietnam, where the DRV's control had always been weakest and the French had long promoted a policy of divide and rule which favored local fiefdoms. Equally important: ethno-cultural diversity had always been greatest in the Mekong delta, where Viet colonialism was not much older than its French successor. In fact, King Sihanouk had lobbied the French intensively to cede Cochinchina to Cambodia in 1949, claiming that most of it—called 'Kampuchea Krom' in Khmer—and its 400,000 ethnic Khmers were historically 'Cambodian'. The French refused to accord the Kampuchean Krom Khmers a separate legal identity, even though they had granted such a status to hundreds of thousands of 'ethnic minority' peoples populating the highlands.

Religious groups also contested Diem's state-building. Economic change and shifting power relations since the 1920s had thoroughly politicized and militarized the Hoa Hao and Cao Dai faiths' supporters. Combined, their leaders commanded over two million followers by 1954 and, thanks to the Japanese and the French, operated their own territories, economies, and militias. Although Diem tried to staff his state with fellow Catholics, even the loyalties of the one and a half million Catholics now in the south were not monolithic. Many of them exceeded Ngo Dinh Diem's own wishes in their desire to avenge their enforced exile from their northern homes in 1954 and to build an uncompromising anticommunist nationalism. Little wonder that so many French, American, and Vietnamese (including the communists) doubted Diem's ability to last.[18]

Ngo Dinh Diem's first taste of the unruliness of the south occurred in early 1955, when he attempted to rein in the 'sects', the pejorative term used to refer collectively and inaccurately to the Binh Xuyen, Hoa Hao, and Cao Dai. Patriotic though their leaders were, they were no more willing to cede their autonomy to Diem's state-building than they had been to that of Ho

Chi Minh a decade earlier. For Ngo Dinh Diem, a professional civil servant by training, this was entirely unacceptable. As he complained to one American confidant: 'I am not content to wait for the chaos around me to turn into order of its own accord. I am going to try to bring order out of chaos myself'. Indeed, one of the things the Ngos admired most in the communists was their ability to do just that—establish order and loyalty and then structure it methodically and forcefully. While powerful Americans including the newly arrived CIA station chief, General Edward Lansdale, certainly sympathized, he and others advised caution, stressing the need for conciliation in dealing with the 'sects'. Meanwhile, the American ambassador sent cable after cable to Washington warning that Diem was not up to the task.[19]

Events came to a head in early 1955, when the French subsidies to the 'sects' dried up and the Ngo brothers moved to take control of them. To do this, they used the army, their contacts, diplomacy, and even American money if it allowed them to re-appropriate loyalties. Those who rallied to the national cause received pretty medals and cushy positions (just as the Democratic Republic of Vietnam and the French had done before them) while the Ngos simultaneously played off one stubborn leader against another. They adroitly exploited the leader of the Cao Dai, General Trinh Minh The's dissatisfaction with the French (he 'defected' from them four times before 1954), to rally his forces to the Ngo national cause. The Ngos cut similar deals with the Hoa Hao and the Catholics.

The Binh Xuyen's Bay Vien, however, refused to relinquish his lucrative business interests. In exchange for he and his followers' defection from the Democratic Republic of Vietnam in 1948, the French had allowed him to carve out a very profitable niche in the Saigon gambling world and in the trafficking of illicit narcotics. By 1954, Bay Vien's riches were enormous and his influence was such that his men had penetrated the upper reaches of the Associated State of Vietnam's police force. Ngo Dinh Diem now called in the army to put a stop to all of this. In late April, fighting broke out in and around Saigon. Despite intense firefights, the Binh Xuyen forces were dispersed within a couple of weeks. Diem closed down Bay Vien's operations and looked on with quiet satisfaction as the Binh Xuyen's legendary Grand Casino burned to the ground. The prime minister then went after the remaining splinter groups. In 1956, his men executed the Hoa Hao's rebel leader, Ba Cut, putting an end to the 'war of the sects'. Civil war in postcolonial Vietnam was more than just a 'communist' versus 'anticommunist' affair.

While France's General Paul Ely called for the prime minister's removal as he watched his southern allies disappear one by one, the high commissioner was no longer in a position to do much without American support. Indeed, high-ranking Americans had come away from the wars against the 'sects' impressed by Ngo Dinh Diem's ability to score victories in such difficult circumstances, convinced that this was the man with whom they could work in building a strong anticommunist state. Dulles now overruled his ambassador in Saigon, instructing diplomats to throw their weight behind Diem. This support was not unconditional and it was often as paternalistic as that of the French had been. Many continued to question Ngo Dinh Diem's capacity to rule. But for American officials keen on containing communism, there was room for optimism. They had few other choices, in any case.

Joint state-building now got underway in full force. American aid helped Diem to train a new generation of technicians, doctors, policemen, and bureaucrats. Young officers traveled to Fort Leavenworth instead of Saint Cyr to study modern military science as American money also poured in for agricultural development and infrastructure projects. By 1956, the Americans provided Ngo Dinh Diem's Vietnam with $270 million annually, placing it among the top recipients of aid per capita in the world. Vietnam, the Eisenhower administration declared, had 'become an example for people everywhere who hate tyranny and love freedom'. *Life* magazine dubbed Diem 'The Tough Miracle Man of Vietnam'. Most importantly, the Americans could continue their containment of communism in Asia with this man, without sending troops and without the French casting a colonial hue over Washington's efforts.[20]

Flushed with victory, the Ngo brothers then moved against the only person who could block them—their former emperor, Bao Dai, who had served as their head of state since 1949. (Although Bao Dai had abdicated as emperor in August 1945, he had remained as head of state of the Associated State of Vietnam, and, since 1955, of the State of Vietnam.) There was something tragic about the Ngo assault on the last emperor of Vietnam. The Ngo family had faithfully served the Nguyen dynasty since the nineteenth century. Diem owed his premiership to the one-time emperor, not to the Americans. And in many ways, Bao Dai had never wanted to lead and the French had already wrecked the monarchy in any case. But his long association with the French and his passivity cast a dangerous shadow of collaboration and weakness over the Vietnam that the Ngos wanted to make. And this is why, over the summer of 1955, the brothers launched a massive propaganda drive to destroy what little remained of the ex-emperor's prestige. They then carefully stage-managed a national referendum so that the 'people' could decide the fate of the erstwhile monarch. In fact, the Ngos decided everything. In a sham vote held on 23 October 1955, marred by arrests and electoral manipulations, Ngo Dinh Diem received 98 percent of the 5.8 million votes cast.[21]

This fraudulent referendum served more than anything else to cover up what was in reality a palace coup and provide Diem with the clean break and 'popular mandate' he wanted to create a new Vietnam divorced from its collaborative past. Three days later, Diem presided over the creation of the Republic of Vietnam under his presidency. He simultaneously declared that there would be no elections to unify 'South Vietnam' and 'North Vietnam'. The Americans backed him on both counts and recognized his government immediately. The French acquiesced, unwilling to reconvene the negotiations at Geneva or to hold the Americans to organizing the elections. Vietnamese communists now had the choice of either accepting that the seventeenth parallel would become a *de jure* border separating two sovereign states or of renewing their fight to create one sovereign Democratic Republic of Vietnam, theirs.

RESETTING COMMUNIST VIETNAM AND THE REPUBLIC OF HO CHI MINH

Extending DRV Sovereignty above the Seventeenth Parallel
In October 1954, Ho's government returned to Hanoi and began administering the previously Franco-ASV territories, towns, and public buildings. At the outset, the People's Army of Vietnam was in charge. It tracked down and crushed armed minority groups that had worked with the French in the highlands. The security services went after real and imagined enemy spies and sleeper cells, worried in particular by those in the Greater Vietnam coalition who had dominated the Associated State of Vietnam bureaucracy. Despite their support of Ho Chi Minh in the early years, Catholics and 'minority peoples' were as suspect as the 'sects' were for Diem in the south. Meanwhile, the People's Army of Vietnam troops received orders to slow down the massive exodus of people to the south via military force if necessary, as its officers carefully extended the Democratic Republic of Vietnam's highly militarized 'resistance administration' into their new

territories in the north. These particular areas (mainly in the river delta valleys and the big cities) were new because they had not formerly been part of the DRV; they had been administered originally by the French, and thereafter by the French in partnership with the Associated State of Vietnam. General Vuong Thua Vu, the man who had led the Battle of Hanoi in late 1946, ruled the capital, until civilian authorities took over about a year later.

Although the Vietnamese Workers Party (VWP) had often been able to recruit communist cadres who had operated covertly in the 'occupied zone' of the Associated State of Vietnam during the conflict itself, after the war the new leadership found it had little choice but to maintain many of the former regime's civil servants as the Democratic Republic of Vietnam opened police stations, schools, tax offices, census bureaus, and hospitals. The government nevertheless carefully collected information on people in the new zone, checked their family backgrounds, listed their occupations, ethnicities, and religions. Officials introduced the DRV's laws, flags, currency, and stamps. Street names in Hanoi changed yet again as old monuments and statues gave way to new ones. Ho Chi Minh's portrait went up on office walls and stamps everywhere (as did Diem's in the south). The Democratic Republic of Vietnam extended its national project through new school manuals, history books, officer- and teacher-training schools, and a host of cultural activities.

From late 1954, the party also went to work communizing all of 'North Vietnam', carefully extending the rectification, emulation, propaganda, and mobilization campaigns to the areas which the French and the ASV had previously administered. Next to Uncle Ho's portrait hung pictures of Marx, Lenin, Stalin, or Mao. Of course, the Democratic Republic of Vietnam never abandoned nationalism and anticolonialism as its official ideologies. But as in the Soviet Union, China, North Korea, and Cuba, the Vietnamese leadership introduced communism as the new state religion and deployed class as the new category for defining social and political identity. Peasants, workers, and those coming from loyal families obtained the best jobs and enjoyed better access to higher education. Since 1950, Vietnamese communists had already imported Marxism-Leninism and a heavy dose of Maoism to structure the party-state in the maquis, indoctrinate a faithful bureaucracy and a fresh military caste, and transform the society and its economy in the communist mold. They now extended this to all of Vietnam above the seventeenth parallel.[22]

Nowhere was this desire to remake Vietnam better seen than in the land reform campaign that lasted from 1953 to 1956. Communist land reform was designed to achieve several essential and interconnected goals: 1) to mobilize the majority peasant population for making war (up until 1954); 2) to increase the party-state's legitimacy and social base; 3) to extend and anchor its bureaucratic control over people and territory; 4) to destroy the heretofore dominant 'feudal' and 'bourgeois' classes and power structures blocking the communist transformation of state, society, and culture; and in doing all this, 5) to prepare the road ahead for eventual full-scale collectivization of agriculture and the concomitant industrialization of the economy along Sino-Soviet lines.

The communists had already started initiating full-blown land reform in the zones it controlled from 1953. Starting in late 1954, cadres dispersed across former Franco-ASV territories to do the same. They had to take control of village society by promoting this top-down social revolution that would allow them to empower the peasants, install a new bureaucratic elite, and take control of the countryside. They carried with them lists of classes to identify and corresponding quotas to fill for land redistribution. The new social categories were: landlords ('*dia chu*'), rich peasants ('*phu nong*'), middle peasants ('*trung nong*'), poor peasants ('*ban nong*'), and agricultural laborers ('*co nong*'). The main idea was to redistribute land and power from the first two categories to the other three. To supervise this socio-economic upending, the Vietnamese Workers Party relied on its cadre-run 'special people's courts', endowed with extraordinary legal powers authorizing arbitrary arrest, capital punishment, the determination of class, the dismissal of local authorities, and the confiscation of individual property and assets. Over the next two years, these mobile courts visited the majority of villages in the new zones. Military cadres identified landholders, brought them before the courts, carefully gathered the villagers around the accused, and encouraged the crowd to denounce their 'cruel' exploiter. These hate-filled 'struggle sessions' often ended in violence. The party leadership authorized this radical transformation of the rural state and society. In late 1952, Ho Chi Minh had travelled to Beijing and Moscow to obtain increased military assistance and to inform Stalin of his determination and his party's plans to embark upon land reform. Upon his return, the land reform campaign began in earnest.[23]

That land reform destroyed the 'feudal' landowning class and redistributed over 2 million acres of land (800,000 hectares) there can be no doubt. But this social revolution also wreaked socio-economic havoc and indescribable psychological pain. The cadres it deployed were often incompetent and brutal. Few knew the villages they visited. Many were excessively zealous and all too eager to please their superiors instead of the poor subjects they had hauled before them. In order to produce enough 'class enemies' in a delta that had never historically produced many feudalists, big landowners or bourgeois merchants to begin with, they began to 'mis-class' middle-class and richer peasants as such (who were often in reality dirt poor), cooking the books as they went, but forgetting that what they were doing had catastrophic consequences. The result was that these powerless people were suddenly stigmatized by the state and ostracized by their former neighbors and friends.

The communists also attacked bourgeois and landowning individuals who had duly paid their taxes, donated land, reduced their rents, supported the war of independence, and sent fathers, sons, and daughters to the front. Nguyen Thi Nam was a case in point. Born into a small business family near Hanoi in 1906, she went into business young in order to make ends meet (her husband had squandered everything they had in the first years of the marriage). Her business savvy was such that she became a highly successful merchant in the emerging steel and cement industries in Haiphong. Before long, the 'Queen of Iron' (as she was known) was investing in land in Thai Nguyen province, where, by the 1940s, she owned the largest plantation there. She took pride in modernizing this plantation with equipment imported from Europe and established the country's first granulated sugar factory. She donated large amounts of money to Ho Chi Minh's government and, during the war against the French, urged her two sons to join the army. They did. A capitalist though she most certainly was, Nguyen Thi Nam's support was such that she was widely referred to as a 'resistance mother' ('*Me khang chien*') in the Democratic Republic of Vietnam.

All of this changed as the Vietnamese communists presided over the Maoist transformation of the Democratic Republic of Vietnam upon Ho Chi Minh's return from Moscow and Beijing in 1952. As Vietnamese communists joined hands with their Chinese advisors to implement land reform, they singled out Nguyen Thi Nam. She was classified as a 'bourgeois trader': she was by then from the wrong class in what was a very virulent class war. This remarkable businesswoman now embodied the enemy class, an obstacle to the party's ability to take the peasantry in hand, remake rural society ideologically and administratively, and prepare for the ultimate collectivization of the countryside. Patriotism was no longer sufficient to save her. In the summer of 1953, the party put Nguyen Thi Nam on trial under a red banner which read: 'Overthrow the despotic landlord Nguyen

Thi Nam, take back the land for the peasants'. To make an example of her, cadres placed Nam before hundreds of poor peasants and led them in hate-filled denunciations of this 'atrocious landlord' and her long list of crimes. Whipped into a frenzy of hate, the crowd jeered at her, spat on her, and slapped her. At some point in July 1953, as land reform officially got under-way, the Vietnamese communists executed her.[24]

Her execution was not the only one. How many occurred? No one knows for sure, but the most reliable estimates put the number of killed between 5,000 and 15,000. Hundreds, possibly thousands, committed suicide, while others fled. Over three years, the Vietnamese Workers Party dispatched tens of thousands of cadres to organize five successive waves of hate and fear that surged through villages, homes, and lives. The commu-nist party encouraged children to spy on their parents, neighbors to de-nounce each other, and required local village officials to follow orders or risk severe sanction. One man has recently recalled how the party marched into his village and turned his world upside down:

> One day while I was out playing, my mother suddenly dragged my younger
> brother and me back to our house and sat us down next to the cooking fire
> [. . .] [S]he said to us, sobbing, 'From now on you need to stay in the house
> and look after your little brother. You cannot go out to play or go to school
> anymore. If you meet your friends you must bow and call them "sir" and
> "madame"'.
>
> When I responded with pouting and sulking, my mother slapped my
> face so hard that I saw stars. After that, she hugged my brother and me and
> cried with all her heart, saying things I did not understand: 'Tan, our fam-
> ily has been assigned a bad class status'. Not until years later did I begin to
> understand the injustice and humiliation my mother had to endure. I also
> began to see that the slap she gave me reflected her resolve to overcome the
> demands of that horrible and pointless period [. . .]
>
> Despite the fact that our family never had enough food, my mother was
> labeled a 'cruel village tyrant'. Moreover, the land reform team forbade us
> from having any relations with our relatives and neighbors in the village.
> That was the most painful and humiliating aspect of the experience for my
> mother. All we had to gnaw on was moldy dried cassava roots. There were
> many meals when we ate only banana root porridge. Every night the sound
> of the village militia marching past the gate of our house put the fear of
> death into my mother.[25]

In November 1956, resistance to land reform was such that the communist party had to send in the People's Army of Vietnam's 325th Division to quell what was a full-blown peasant revolt in Quynh Luu. The situation was so bad that Ho Chi Minh and Vo Nguyen Giap publicly apologized for the errors their party had committed against the people during the last three years. Although Ho took over the leadership of the communist party from Truong Chinh, who was cast as the main author of the disastrous land reform, everyone, including Ho Chi Minh and Vo Nguyen Giap, were to be counted as responsible 'for wanting to apply the coercive Stalinist method of collectivization'. The party promised to right the wrongs, to 're-class' those who had been wrongly categorized, to return land and assets, and dismantle the special courts. But as Ho admitted, the party 'could not bring the dead back to life'. Instead the party organized a massive 'Rectification of Errors Campaign', during which leaders and cadres publicly confessed their sins. This public and highly ritualized act of ideological contrition served to clean the slate, ensure that all had the (new) 'right thinking', and to reassert the legitimacy of communist rule before moving on, again. This *mise-en-scène* fooled none of those who had suffered so much in a revolution in which they had had so little to say. Even those who benefitted from finally obtaining a plot of land would have to give it up in a few short years' time, when the party sought to take it back. As in China and the Soviet Union, what the collectivization of the countryside required trumped any other considerations.[26]

Failed Communist Reformism (1954–9)

The excesses of the land reform program led to unprecedented internal calls for reform. Highest on that list was judicial change. Just as republican voices reacted with shock to the extra-judicial methods used by the French colonial authorities to suppress peasant revolts in 1908 and 1930–31, a number of supporters of the new state of the Democratic Republic of Vietnam couldn't believe that the 'party of the masses' had committed the same sins as the colonizers. Where was the rule of law, many asked? Did the peasants, 80 percent of the population, have any legal rights? If the 1946 constitution had enshrined them, then why had the communists just violated them so blatantly? These were not new questions. Ho himself had personally witnessed the French firing on starving peasants in 1908, the very event that had sent him on the road to republicanism, into the League of Human Rights, and on to revolution. Outraged peasants seeking justice from Vietnamese cadres who had just violated their basic human rights flooded the office of Vietnam's best-known lawyer, the French-trained Nguyen Manh Tuong. People were so outraged that the party responded by allowing newspapers to publish full reports on the land reform abuses which had occurred up to 1957, including information about the use of state-sponsored torture, executions, and the existence of concentration camps. Incensed, the devout party member and well-known journalist of the 1930s, Nguyen Huu Dang, called for the introduction of a legal code, independent of the party-state, that would protect individual rights while still allowing for more effective communization of the countryside. Others petitioned for the reform of the judiciary, the drafting of a new constitution protecting individual liberties, and the awakening of the National Assembly. It had only met once since 1946—in late 1953—in order to approve the land reform unanimously.[27]

This communist reform-minded constitutionalism bumped up against the Vietnamese politburo's simultaneous goal of drafting a new constitution which would codify the DRV's wartime transformation into a communist state and make the necessary preparations for collectivization. The Vietnamese Workers Party's inner core was determined to create a new constitution placing the Democratic Republic of Vietnam officially under the leadership of a 'people's democratic dictatorship'. Unlike the constitution of 1946, which was designed to unite and attract all segments of society, this new constitution would legalize the pre-eminence of the communists' party, put it in charge of a new social alliance between the workers and the peasants, and align the DRV's economy with the international communist model. The 1946 constitution no longer fitted the needs or the reality of this new revolutionary state. As Ho Chi Minh told young children gathered around him in 1959, '[W]hen you grow up, you will have a communist constitution'.[28]

Not everyone inside the Democratic Republic of Vietnam agreed with Ho or wanted a dictatorship of the proletariat. Although the details remain shrouded in mystery, in late 1956, a handful of unidentified deputies (apparently shaken by what had occurred in their constituencies during the land reform campaigns), joined reformist-minded lawyers, jurists, and intellectuals like Tuong and Dang in starting to push for constitutional reform, including the empowerment of the legislative and judiciary branches of the government as set out in the 1946 constitution. In December 1956, when the National Assembly convened for the third time in its existence, members agreed to establish the personnel who would undertake a special commission on constitutional reform, and who would duly submit a new project. The Vietnamese Workers Party's Tran Huy Lieu was in charge, seconded by Ho serving as honorary president. Within weeks, deputies in the National Assembly asserted their theoretical power. In January 1957, the assembly passed three laws: one on the 'inviolability of the home and of correspondence', another ensuring freedom of assembly, and a third on the freedom of religion and the press. Although the 1946 constitution had already guaranteed such rights, the question now was whether would they be enforced, and to what extent. In light of the Vietnamese Workers Party's 'errors', that is its prior violation of its citizens' rights, would the legislature or its judicial branches be able to check the party's power in the post-1954 Democratic Republic of Vietnam? Not one of these three laws was actually promulgated in 1957; but it is clear that intense, behind-the-doors debates had occurred on the nature of the new constitution, the limits of state and party power, and the protection of individual human rights. Like the French before them, the communist leadership feared the implications of allowing a democratically elected national assembly to operate independently. It was the party which ran the state.[29]

Simultaneous and closely related calls for legal reform occurred in the arts. Between 1954 and 1956, a diverse range of artists, writers, poets, playwrights, and intellectuals loyal to the regime increasingly called for greater intellectual and artistic freedoms. This movement started in early 1955, when Tran Dan, a military writer and veteran of Dien Bien Phu, found himself undergoing re-education and rectification when he dared to ask General Nguyen Chi Thanh, head of the PAVN's General Political Directorate, for greater freedom of expression in the stifling Maoist-minded world in which he worked. Tran Dan's case became a rallying cry for intellectuals and artists who published two journals with the express goal of reforming the party's excessive hold over culture and the arts—*Nhan Van* (*Humanism*) and *Giai Pham* (*Fine Arts*). Contributors to these journals came from the army, from among French-trained intellectuals, and included such intellectual heavy weights as the renowned philosopher, Tran Duc Thao. Most were communists, some were not; but they all had supported the regime.[30]

The party's stance oscillated from tolerance and even tacit sympathy for its opponents to open hostility toward them and outright repression. Such indecision was linked as much to the land reform program's errors as to the simultaneous secret speech Nikita Khrushchev had just delivered in early

1956. In it, the head of the Soviet communist party criticized Stalin's crimes against his own people and his cult of personality. Khrushchev also advocated a policy of peaceful co-existence and promoted a wide range of socio-economic *and* legal reforms to regain the support of the 'people', above all the peasants, who had suffered terribly during Stalin's rule. This was one of Khrushchev's big foreign policy changes in 1956 that infuriated Mao and not a few Vietnamese. 'Peaceful co-existence' was the new buzzword for trying to calm down the Cold War and work things out with the capitalists through negotiation. Unsurprisingly, this Soviet-approved 'destalinization' also found supporters in the Democratic Republic of Vietnam as it did across the communist world. The problem was that the VWP's leadership would only go so far. Like their Chinese counterparts, they had only just taken power and were doing all they could to consolidate it (using many of the Stalinist methods Khrushchev now condemned). Ho was not about to abandon his cult of personality when he needed it to win back popular support after the land reform débâcle. The great upheaval was the price to be paid for taking control of the state and society from top to bottom.[31]

Most importantly, the peasants' protest in Quynh Luu in November 1956 coincided with the popular uprising against communist rule in Hungary which started on 23 October. With Ngo Dinh Diem building a southern state and even speaking of a march on the north, the Vietnamese Workers Party welcomed the Soviet invasion of Hungary on 4 November and decided that it could not let its own reformers transform social discontent or even the regime into something no one could predict or control. Though it took them longer than the Soviet's quelling of the popular uprising in Hungary did, by 1959 Ho Chi Minh had stopped legislative attempts to curtail the party's power constitutionally. On 1 January 1960, he promulgated the Democratic Republic of Vienam's new constitution, enshrining the power of the communist party, ensuring its supremacy over that of the National Assembly, and guaranteeing that communism was now the official ideology of the DRV, its economy, and society. And the communist leadership closed the journals *Nhan Van* (*Humanism*) and *Giai Pham* (*Fine Arts*) for good. As in China and the Soviet Union, there had to be ideological homogeneity among cadres, officers, and intellectuals. Toward the end of his life, Tran Duc Thao, one of Vietnam's greatest minds, a man who had collaborated with French philosopher Jean-Paul Sartre earlier in his career, found himself psychologically destroyed by constant party attacks on individual thought.[32]

EXTENDING REPUBLICAN SOVEREIGNTY IN THE SOUTH

Like Ho Chi Minh, Ngo Dinh Diem may have come from a mandarin family, but he was anything but an inward-looking 'Confucian', 'mandarin', or 'traditionalist'. Diem saw himself as a revolutionary. He certainly possessed one of the most modern educations the French could offer, not least of all in administrative practices. He was obsessed with modern sovereignty, nationalism, and state-building. And although the Ngo brothers abhorred the class war the communists had unleashed in the countryside, they agreed that the creation of a new Vietnam did turn on the transformation of rural society, and as Diem had expressed his thinking on rural change in 1949: 'It is also a social revolution for the economic independence of the Vietnamese farmer and laborer. I advocate the most advanced and bold social reforms, while preserving human dignity and respect, in order that all people in the new Viet Nam may earn a living as truly free people'.[33]

In practice, the Ngo brothers had little more respect for the freedom of the people than the communists they so despised. The Ngos were nepotistic, authoritarian and heavy-handed in their rule. If Ho Chi Minh ensured the communist party held a monopoly on power by 1960, Ngo Dinh Diem had already concentrated state power within an authoritarian executive branch of his government. Indeed, the constitution upon which the new republic rested from late 1955 onward was the result of the new National Constitutional Assembly which had been hastily convened under Diem's personal control. This constitution provided extraordinary powers to its government's executive branch by subordinating all legislature to presidential fiat. Everyone knew what article 3 of the constitution meant: 'The activities of the executive and the legislative agencies must be brought into harmony. The president is vested with the leadership of the Nation'. The president enjoyed vast emergency powers. He controlled foreign policy, could declare war, make treaties, commanded the military, and had the power to 'make all military and civil appointments'. The constitution guaranteed the people's freedom of expression, but, as in the north, if any individual was deemed to threaten national security, then he or she forfeited his or her rights. 'Communism' was outlawed, just as 'anticommunism' was in the north. Such labels could and would be used abusively by the state to neutralize all sorts of enemies. Despite paying it lip service, Diem bypassed the National Assembly, preferring to rule by decree, just like Ho Chi Minh had done during the entire Indochina War. The Republic of Vietnam's judiciary was not independent of the state and had few oversight powers, which led to many of the same human rights abuses committed by the communists—arbitrary arrest, censorship, torture, execution, forced labor, and the use of concentration camps. And behind the president stood his family, not any sort of wider political coalition. By smashing, then refusing to open the political doors to religious groups like the Cao Dai and the Hoa Hao, each one as opposed to communism as he was, Diem not only failed to develop a wider, inclusive anticommunism nationalism that could have built up his legitimacy, but he also frustrated such groups and made enemies of them by keeping them out of the political system. The president's mistrust was such that he failed to create anticommunist alliances even with the Vietnamese Nationalist Party and the Greater Vietnam coalition. Diem struggled even to keep on good terms with those followers of his who made up the base of his support—the Catholic refugees.[34]

As in the north, Ngo state-building wreaked the greatest havoc upon the very people it was designed to uplift and save. It was never intended that way, of course. Diem's land reform was top-down, authoritarian, and badly administered. He spoke in the name of the poor masses, but never asked them what they wanted or provided them with the institutional means to make their needs known. If the VWP rammed land reform through its National Assembly in 1953, the Ngos didn't even consult this institution. Diem simply decreed rural revolution. By redistributing land in areas where there had been large landowners, plantations, and abandoned land, he sought to empower the peasantry, expand the Republic of Vietnam's administrative control, promote economic prosperity, and in so doing legitimate his nation-building. Diem could look to successful non-communist models in Japan, Taiwan, and South Korea, where land reform had sparked an increase in agricultural production and created the foundation for export-led growth capable of financing industrialization.

Land reform was an administrative weapon, too. The First Indochina War had convinced the Ngo brothers that the communists had successfully used land reform to extend state control over their people and territory. The Ngos were now confident that they could fight the communists and expand their own socio-political base using the enemy's own methods. The Americans largely agreed and backed them at the outset. In February 1955, the government lowered rent payments (which farmers had to pay landlords) to between 15 percent and 25 percent of the value of the main crops' yield and authorized them to cultivate abandoned land. In 1956, redistribution began in earnest with the expropriation of land from large landowners. Unlike the Red River valley, the Mekong basin was home to many large-landowning families. In fact, around 2,500 landowners possessed around 40 percent of the rice-producing land. In all, two million hectares of tenured land was theoretically available for redistribution.[35]

And yet land reform failed. In all, the government only distributed one-third of tenured land, while almost 50 percent of the RV's land remained concentrated in the hands of 2 percent of the population. Redistribution also occurred unevenly. In many areas, no land ever changed hands. What happened? For one, landowners resisted the government by paying off corrupt officials or threatening to withdraw their political support if Diem did not back down. 'We have been robbed by the Viet Minh over the years', one landowner bemoaned, 'and we resent similar treatment from the national government'. That this individual was the chief of his province revealed another problem—Diem's civil service was not up to such a herculean task. It was badly understaffed, increasingly corrupt, and often administered by people who had no interest in seeing land reform succeed. In all, 400 officials presided over the Republic of Vietnam's attempted land reform, whereas the Democratic Republic of Vietnam had dispatched tens of thousands of cadres (and the Japanese had relied on 400,000 people) to push through rural reform. Diem could have deployed the army to force landowner compliance; but he was loathe to unleash class war and reluctant to risk a coup. In the end, the Ngos backtracked (whereas the communists only feigned doing so via the 'rectification campaign'). In so doing, the Ngos left millions of peasants frustrated, tens of thousands of whom had already enjoyed land reform under the DRV before 1954. These farmers only reluctantly accepted the return of the landlords in late 1954; and would be quite ready to change loyalties if the local power relations were to allow for it.[36]

Land reform failure did not stop Diem in his state-building efforts. In mid-1956, he initiated a massive resettlement program known as 'Planning for Land'. The main goal was to promote state consolidation by moving Vietnamese people into ethnically non-Viet highland zones. Diem wanted to establish the RV's sovereignty in these peripheral yet strategically important areas where the French had separately administered the 'ethnic minorities' until 1954. The central highlands were also areas in which the DRV had extended its own control during the First Indochina War. Just as importantly, Diem also wanted to relieve population pressure in the delta by promoting ethnic Viet migration to the highlands. Immigrants there received plots of land, tools, seeds, and food grants which allowed them to create new settlements in upland areas. By 1959, 125,000 immigrants lived in 84 settlements. In 1962, 230,000 people lived in 173 settlements. The problem was that the resumption of civil war in the south led Diem to go too fast and to use coercion instead of persuasion to move people, build new villages, and construct new roads. Moreover, this policy of internal colonization only exacerbated longstanding tensions between Viet settlers and the still majority non-Viet indigenous peoples in the highlands.[37]

Diem's quest for control over people and their loyalties also led him to decree an 'Anticommunist Denunciation Campaign' in early 1955. The president used this program to root out communist stay-behinds and sleeper cells in the countryside and to re-educate the large number of sympathizers, former bureaucrats, and members of the DRV's nationalist fronts and former administrators during the Indochina War. Republic of Vietnam security personnel and provincial officials received orders to classify the population in terms of family background, political affiliations, attitudes toward communism, the Democratic Republic of Vietnam, and the Republic of Vietnam. For those who posed little threat, the government organized village ceremonies and community self-criticism sessions. Re-education centers dealt with tougher cases. In carefully choreographed rituals, former communist supporters would ask for forgiveness from fellow villagers and local authorities before swearing allegiance to the republican flag and its great leader, Ngo Dinh Diem.

The Ngo brothers then went further. In January 1956, a presidential ordinance authorized the arrest and incarceration of anyone deemed a threat to national security. Concentration camps popped up as the security services and army arrested thousands of suspects, many of them in fact non-communists. Indeed, large numbers of democratic-minded, law-abiding political opponents of the regime found themselves censored or detained. More were rounded up following the promulgation in May 1959 of an even more draconian piece of anticommunist legislation, Law 10/59. It created 'special military tribunals' with the power to arrest, imprison, and execute people for vaguely defined 'revolutionary activities'. Between 1954 and 1960, this anticommunist offensive incarcerated almost 50,000 people. While non-communist journalists, politicians, judges, and artists ended up in jail as well, Ngo Dinh Diem's dragnet did in fact inflict real damage on the communist party's underground organization. The Vietnamese Workers

Party's clandestine membership below the seventeenth parallel fell from 50,000 in 1954 to 15,000 in 1956. By 1959, the party counted only 5,000 remaining members in southern Vietnam. It was in this desperate situation that party cadres began to plead with the leadership in Hanoi to change the VWP's line so that they could pick up arms to defend themselves, even if it meant resuming civil war and risking American intervention.[38]

But it was also in this context that the Ngo family started to go after anyone who defied its power and state-building project, including non-communist nationalists like Nguyen Tuong Tam and politically minded religious movements such as the one coalescing rapidly around the Xa Loi Buddhist pagoda in downtown Saigon. The Ngos also pursued dissidents in their own ranks. Despite their ideological differences, both Ho Chi Minh and Ngo Dinh Diem clearly struggled to impose authoritarian rule and create the legitimacy for these two different Vietnams that had emerged from a century of French colonial rule. Neither brooked any opposition to their right to rule. After all, Diem was not the first to try to crush religious movements and separatism in the south: Ho Chi Minh had first sent Nguyen Binh to try to do this in late 1945. And behind Diem and Ho, of course, stood Minh Mang with his hard-handed efforts to hold Vietnam together in the mid-nineteenth century. This, too, was modern Vietnam.

CHAPTER 11

TOWARD ONE VIETNAM

DESPITE THE MASSIVE levels of propaganda, not everyone in the Democratic Republic of Vietnam believed in the communist party's glorification of war. As in France and Britain after the First World War, the men who had fought were often among the first to speak of the ugly side of war and its terrible toll on soldiers and civilians. As an officer in the People's Army of Vietnam, Phu Thang had witnessed some of the most violent clashes of the Indochina conflagration and the thought of renewed violence depressed him. Influenced by Nikita Khrushchev's moves toward peaceful co-existence in 1956 and inspired by more realistic and critical accounts of massive Soviet suffering during the Second World War, Thang and other veterans dared to express an antiwar message. In his 1963 novel *Breaking the Siege*, Thang's main character, a veteran of the First Indochina War, gives voice to an unmistakably pacifist message: 'Such is the war! It leads to so much suffering among the people [. . .] The war has and will lead to so much more suffering, hardship, disgrace, and hate [. . .] There is nothing praiseworthy about war and a soldier's life is just miserable. If one can gain real fame in combat, then one has to pay a high price for it. One has to stop this bloodshed with its horror early'.[1]

Thang's message was not what the communist leadership wanted to hear from one of its soldiers, not in 1963 as the Vietnamese politburo prepared to go to war against the Republic of Vietnam and, if necessary, the United States. Such a realistic account of war went against the party's heroization of the conflict since the 'glorious victory' at the Battle of Dien Bien Phu. Worse still, this came from a soldier still employed in the armed services. The man in charge of the planning for a new war and the former head of the army's ideological propaganda department during the preceding one, General Nguyen Chi Thanh, went after Phu Thang and others who promoted such a peaceful line. Starting in 1963, veterans who spoke of the 'horrors' of war lost their positions in the army, saw their works banned, and sometimes ended up behind bars. It was a humiliating and often devastating fate for men who had risked their lives for their country; but culture had once again to serve war. From 1963, there could be no peaceful co-existence as in the Soviet Union, not even on the cultural front.

CIVIL WAR RESUMES

Reasserting DRV Sovereignty

Although the absence of elections in 1956 disappointed many in the Vietnamese Workers' Party, the leadership also had its hands full with the land reform fall-out, the administration of new territories, and the modernization of the economy. Moreover, for the time being communist Vietnam's main backers, the Soviet Union and China, continued to caution against war in favor of peaceful co-existence. Nikita Khrushchev discussed this with Dwight D. Eisenhower in two summit meetings in the late 1950s. In April 1955, Zhou Enlai had stolen the show at the Afro-Asian Conference in Bandung by reassuring his listeners that his country had no intention of exporting communism. A year later, a top-ranking Soviet leader explained in Hanoi why in a nuclear world it was important to give peace a chance instead of believing that war with the capitalists could be the only way to communist victory. The Vietnamese side agreed in theory, but Ho Chi Minh warned that because of the presence of the 'American imperialists' in the south, his party could not rule out armed action. Such reservations must have seemed warranted, when, in 1957, Moscow stunned the VWP by proposing the admission of *both* Vietnams to the United Nations.[2]

The Soviet action certainly vindicated those in the party who had doubted the possibility of achieving national unification through peaceful co-existence. One such critic was Le Duan. Born into a modest family in central Vietnam, Le Duan became involved in radical politics as a railway worker in the 1920s. He joined the communists in 1930 and, after serving five years in prison, directed the party in central Vietnam until the French sent him back to Poulo Condor in 1940. He did hard time in the island prison until the Japanese capitulation in August 1945, when, freed, he returned to the mainland and ran the southern party branch. This powerful man remained in the south after 1954 to lead the party's clandestine organization there. He repeatedly informed his party of the desperate situation created by Ngo Dinh Diem's repressive measures and did his best to provide local guidance. In mid-1956, he penned a report on the 'The Path of the Revolution in the South'. In it, he advised imperiled southern cadres against taking up arms right away, explaining that the party had no real administrative structure or armed forces on which to rely. Until it could approve such an important policy change, political struggle had to remain the *mot d'ordre*. However, as the July 1956 deadline for holding elections passed, Duan urged his followers to remain close to the peasant 'masses', ready, as during the August Revolution in 1945, to seize the favorable moment to take power by force.

The problem was that, as it had been in northern Vietnam in 1944–5, the communists in the south were not always in control. More often than not, communist cadres watched from the sidelines as revolts broke out spontaneously in the highlands and in delta provinces like My Tho and Long An. Those who supported such revolts did so in violation of party policy and were more often than not reacting to events rather than directing them. This gave rise to a paradoxical situation: if the party tried to contain the political fall-out of the rural wrath its Maoist-minded cadres had provoked in the north during the land reform program, the refusal of the party to support peasant revolts in the south denied communists their most important social base for conducting their 'people's war'. With their numbers falling fast, southerners begged the leadership to change its policy so that they could deploy some form of armed action to protect themselves and harness the rural discontent surging around them.[3]

This was the message Duan carried with him when he arrived in Hanoi in late 1957. His senior position in the party, long service in the south, and his direct and often combative style made him an excellent advocate of a more aggressive policy. Assisting him in this lobbying effort were many unhappy southerners who had regrouped in the north after 1954 and his former deputy in the south, Le Duc Tho. The latter had joined the politburo and now directed the party's most powerful 'organizational committee' (the one responsible for setting the internal agenda). Le Duan also found important support in the person of Ho Chi Minh, who took him under his wing as the party began discussing seriously what to do about the 'south'.

If Le Duan and Le Duc Tho urged the party to adopt an armed line, everyone was aware of the dangers of such an approach. Indeed, as the politburo debated this question, Vietnamese communists were deeply involved in the resumption of civil war in Laos between their sister-state run by the Pathet Lao, and the Royal Government of Laos (formerly the Associated State of Laos). Fearful of weakening the Indochinese link in their security chain containing Eurasian communism from the south, the Eisenhower administration had opposed the creation of a coalition Lao government in 1957 which would have included the communist Pathet Lao. Instead the Americans joined the Thais in supporting anticommunist Lao leaders who could keep the country within the American orbit. Determined to support their ally, Vietnamese communists had already dispatched hundreds of advisors to Laos to build up the Pathet Lao's army, state, party, and territorial control. By 1960 the civil war in Laos blew into a major Cold War crisis as the Soviets initiated an airlift to their Pathet Lao allies via Hanoi, and the Americans threatened to send troops through Thailand to back their own. Little wonder many in the Vietnamese Workers Party worried that the resumption of war in southern Vietnam could explode into something unpredictable, including direct American military intervention.[4]

But Le Duan also saw a model in Laos. He reassured skeptics that the party could go ahead with a more aggressive policy below the seventeenth parallel by authorizing the incremental, carefully managed, and always-deniable use of a combination of armed and political action—just as the VWP was already doing with the Pathet Lao. Armed action would allow southerners to protect themselves. But a carefully calibrated mix of political and military action would also give them the chance to harness peasant discontent, structure it administratively, protect it militarily, and, through the creation of a broad-based national front, build up an alternative political sovereignty. In late 1957, Le Duan also noted that the election of a coalition government in Laos, which did incorporate the Pathet Lao, could serve as a model for advancing the Vietnamese Workers Party's cause in the south.

By late 1958, the critical situation of the party in the south, internal debate in the north, and Le Duan's lobbying in Hanoi forced the party to choose. This occurred in January 1959 when the party issued its fifteenth plenum. In this historic document, the party leadership reiterated the importance of consolidating the north, but it also confirmed that this revolutionary process could no longer exclude the unification of the two halves of Vietnam under Democratic Republic of Vietnam sovereignty. As a result, the party now authorized increased political action for southern cadres and allowed them to resume armed action on a limited scale to support it. In concrete terms, this meant that the VWP accepted the need to build a new national front, protect it with force, and provide the personnel and weapons to achieve both interconnected goals. This is why, in May 1959, the Vietnamese Workers Party reactivated its work in the south and began extending an increasingly elaborate network of overland paths southward through eastern Laos, the central highlands, and eastern Cambodia, which were collectively known as the Ho Chi Minh Trail. In September, the party created a new advisory group for Laos with the task of helping the Pathet Lao to expand its political and military control down the eastern side of Laos bordering Vietnam—this was vital to the operation of the Ho Chi Minh Trail. Meanwhile, in 1961, vessels began secretly leaving the north for the south to deliver weapons, administrators, and supplies.[5]

Incremental or not, Hanoi had to structure its stepped-up actions in the south. In September 1960, the Vietnamese Workers Party's third national congress elected Le Duan as its new party leader and formally authorized the use of armed force to bring about the liberation of the south. This would mean the overthrow of the Republic of Vietnam, and the creation of a coalition government favorable to reunification with the Democratic Republic of Vietnam. The party would not deploy the People's Army of Viet Nam in the south. Nor would it try to re-establish its pre-1954 DRV civil service there for fear of provoking direct American intervention. The communists in Hanoi would rather expand their political sovereignty and military control indirectly by supporting efforts already underway to form a national front and by providing a southern, armed force to protect it.

The communists moved quickly. In December 1960, the National Liberation Front of South Vietnam, or the NLF, came to life. Over the next year, the VWP transformed it into an operational political entity by recruiting reliable people below the seventeenth parallel and returning thousands of administrators and officers who had relocated to the north after the 1954 ceasefire. By 1964, the total number of returnees amounted to around 40,000 people, including thousands of former DRV civil servants originally from the south. Thanks to these experienced southerners, the National Liberation Front established bases among villages, intensified anti-Diem propaganda, initiated land reform where possible, operated a policing, militia, and taxation system, and began organizing women, children, youth, and peasants into patriotic associations. The appearance of the NLF flag and the circulation of its stamps signified the emergence of an alternative political sovereignty in the south. Nguyen Huu Tho, a well-known anti-colonialist lawyer and a loyal communist, became its chairman. This is how civil war resumed indirectly in the south.[6]

The Vietnamese Workers Party directed this burgeoning state-building project. To do so, in early 1961 the politburo re-activated the office that had been run by Le Duan during the Indochina conflict, now better known by its American acronym, COSVN, the Central Office of South Viet Nam. Le Duan's close confidant from Poulo Condor and a fellow politburo member, Nguyen Van Linh, ran it. The Central Office of South Vietnam also created and directed the 'People's Liberation Armed Force' (or PLAF). Established in February 1961, the PLAF rapidly recruited into its ranks a wide range of disgruntled peasants, youth, religious leaders, and non-Viet peoples, communist or not. Although it focused initially on organizing guerilla units capable of hit-and-run attacks, winning over or assassinating local RV administrators, the PLAF also developed into an increasingly well-armed and trained professional army. Between 1959 and 1961, the People's Liberation Armed Force's troop strength increased from 2,000 to over 10,000. By 1964, it counted over 100,000 people in its ranks, 30,000 of whom were regular troops. Although COSVN carefully monitored the use of force, hoping that Diem's oppressive policies would do the rest, the politburo had to conclude in 1961 that there was 'practically no possibility that the revolution will develop peacefully'. The question now was whether the Americans would intervene directly in order to try and stop the communists from resuming a war to make all of Vietnam theirs.[7]

THE LIMITS OF COLLABORATION

JFK Commits to South Vietnam[8]
The Vietnamese Workers Party in Hanoi had little reason to be optimistic about the election of a Democrat to the White House in November 1960. Upon entering office in January 1961, John F. Kennedy went further than his predecessors in committing to and arming the Republic of Vietnam. Hardly a week after his inauguration, Kennedy adopted the Counter-Insurgency Plan (CIP) to increase the size of the republic's conventional forces and militias. This was part of the president's emerging policy of 'flexible response' which was designed to build up American conventional and special forces capable of fighting any type of war in any type of situation, in particular against communist-backed insurgencies in the non-Western world. Throughout the 1950s, Kennedy had warned Eisenhower of the dangers of supporting European colonialism in a time of rapid decolonization. Now, in 1960, he criticized Eisenhower's support of the French again (this time in Algeria). The US had to take decolonization seriously, he countered, especially in the light of Moscow and Beijing's stepped-up efforts to win over

the support of postcolonial states entering the international system and the United Nations. In January 1961, Nikita Khrushchev declared that the Soviet Union would support movements of national liberation wherever they occurred. And not to be outdone by Moscow, as the Sino-Soviet split widened, Beijing increased its overtures to the Afro-Asian world.[9]

Despite all the talk of peaceful co-existence following the death of Stalin in 1953, the international system remained a highly volatile one. During his first two years in office, Kennedy went to the brink of war with Khrushchev over Berlin and Cuba (and, to a lesser extent, Laos). Although behind-the-scenes cool-headedness and global trade-offs moved Moscow and Washington away from the brink of nuclear Armageddon over Cuba, the Kennedy administration continued to view the communist bloc as the major threat to American global interests and security. Intelligence reports may have shown a more nuanced picture, but Eisenhower's domino theory continued to inform high-level decision-making. The rapidly accelerating split between Moscow and Beijing did little to change this perception. In the wake of the Cuban crisis in October 1962, Mao publicly lambasted Khrushchev for failing to go all the way against the American capitalists, even if it meant using nuclear weapons. (Of course Chinese communists would negotiate themselves if it served their interests, as they did when Beijing helped Moscow broker a solution to the Lao crisis in 1962.) But China's increasing support of Vietnamese communist armed action against the southern republic hardly reassured Kennedy. Moreover, it also obligated the Soviets too to maintain their support of Hanoi for fear of ceding the revolutionary high ground to Mao in the battle over the leadership of the communist bloc.

What concerned Kennedy's administration most in Indochina was the Republic of Vietnam, which the Americans termed South Vietnam. The president accepted the resolution of the Lao crisis at the negotiating table in Geneva at the same time as building up a strong anticommunist state in South Vietnam. Like his predecessors, Kennedy did not want to dispatch American troops, preferring to rely on the republic to serve Washington's containment needs indirectly. Kennedy continued to arm, train, and finance the Army of the Republic of Vietnam (ARVN) through the Military Assistance Advisory Group first established in 1950, and the Counter-Insurgency Plan. In fact, he greatly increased American support. In his first year in office, overall military aid to the republic increased from $50 million annually to $144 million. By 1962, the ARVN fielded a professional army of

220,000 men, while the Soviets and Chinese assisted the DRV in creating a 200,000-strong PAVN. Kennedy multiplied the number of military advisors in Vietnam, allowing them to accompany ARVN troops on combat missions. The 800 advisors in Vietnam in January 1961 more than tripled by the end of the year and stood at 11,000 by late 1962. This rapid military expansion required a new bureaucratic institution to run it as American commitment to Indochina entered its twelfth year. In early 1962, the Military Assistance Command, Vietnam (or MACV) came to life and rapidly replaced the MAAG. To stop the communists from using the complex network of paths they had pushed toward southern Vietnam through eastern Laos, the central highlands and eastern Cambodia (the Ho Chi Minh Trail), Kennedy approved the use of Agent Orange. This chemical defoliant and others facilitated the detection and bombing of enemy supply lines by destroying the jungle canopy. Between 1962 and 1971, the United States sprayed around 80 million liters of herbicides over the jungles of Indochina with devastating ecological and human consequences.[10]

American economic advisors, diplomats, and military officers also brought their models and world views with them, just as both the French and the Chinese had before them. 'You should know one thing at the beginning,' Edward Lansdale prefaced his memoirs, 'I took my American beliefs with me into these Asian struggles, as Tom Paine would have done.' For most American advisors a strong belief in Western-styled modernization was high on this list. Nowhere is this more evident than in the migration from the university to Kennedy's White House of Walt Rostow, a leading advocate of 'modernization theory' and author of *The Stages of Economic Growth: A Non Communist Manifesto*. Modernization theorists believed that societies develop in a series of increasingly complex stages, moving from 'traditional' to increasingly complex states, with the Western industrial democracies being the most advanced. Modernizers in Washington and their acolytes on the ground in Vietnam believed that America could and should help 'traditional' societies evolve through technology transfers, better education, and improved transportation and communications. Drawing upon their own experiences in New Deal America and postwar Japan, American modernizers also firmly believed in the development of democratic political institutions and grassroots civic action as part of this package deal. Only then would Vietnam truly be capable of implementing the complicated demands of industrial development, its division of labor, and free market exchanges, without graft, corruption, and nepotism. Of course, 'modernization theory' was part of a wider containment strategy; but Americans believed in their superior civilizing mission.[11]

Ngo Dinh Diem: A Platoon of de Gaulles . . .

But theory and practice are two very different things and foreign models always run into trouble on the ground. Ho Chi Minh after all had apologized to the Vietnamese people for applying the Maoist model of communist modernization with such disastrous effects. In South Vietnam, American diplomats, military advisors, development officers, and non-governmental organization workers increasingly bemoaned Diem's botched road to modernity, authoritarian ways, and nepotism. Worse, they concurred, his heavy-handed development projects in the countryside and his repression of political opposition alienated the very people needed to fight the communists—the non-communist peasant majority and the members of the urban elite class. Successful land reform programs in Taiwan and Japan had shown the way to economic growth in the countryside. Political pluralization would win over the elite. If the Ngo brothers would just follow the American recipe, all would be fine.[12]

More than in Japan, Taiwan, or even the Republic of (South) Korea, however, time was of the essence in preserving America's fourth ally on the eastern Eurasian rim. In mid-1961, alarmed Americans diplomats reported that the Republic of Vietnam controlled less than half of the country. The Americans pressed Diem hard to implement reforms fast or risk losing everything. Some spoke privately of finding a replacement for the Vietnamese president. But despite the negative reports piling up on his desk, Kennedy decided to give Diem a chance and look the other way when it came to his counterpart's democratic abuses. The Vietnamese president had come through in 1954–7; he could do it again. Moreover, the administration felt confident that its increased military assistance would ensure that indirect containment continued to work.

Many writers opposed to American intervention in Vietnam have not been kind to America's partner in Vietnam. In her Pulitzer prize–winning antiwar book, *Fire in the Lake*, Frances FitzGerald wrote Ngo Dinh Diem off as an American puppet, no more legitimate than the colonial emperor, Bao Dai, had been under the French. She contrasts Diem's reliance on foreigners to Ho Chi Minh's seething indigenous nationalism. Whereas the Americans propped up the besieged Diem regime, Ho's Vietnam fought on alone against all odds, drawing on a timeless Vietnamese culture of resisting foreign invaders. Official Vietnamese communist historians agree entirely, referring then as now to Diem and his regime as an American creation ('*My-Diem*'), entirely illegitimate ('*nguy*'). The problem for the Americans at the time, however, was that Ngo Dinh Diem was not a puppet. This fiercely independent-minded nationalist leader repeatedly rebuffed American advice. He and his brother Ngo Dinh Nhu had their own ideas about nation-building, land reform, and counter-insurgency. And together they often enraged their American backers. As one American diplomat in Saigon in the early 1960s later summed up the difficulties of negotiating with the Ngo family: 'It was like dealing with a whole platoon of de Gaulles'.[13]

Indeed, the Americans never quite grasped the extent to which Diem, like de Gaulle, was obsessed with national sovereignty, protecting it, affirming it, and determined to run the show on his terms, despite the massive assistance he received from Washington. Lest we forget de Gaulle had done everything in his power to bury Vichy France's collaborative past with the Nazis in favor of forging a fiercely independent postwar national identity free of America. Diem wanted to do something similar by erasing his country's collaboration with the French and showing that his country did not take orders from Washington. In order to legitimate his country's claim to the nationalist mantle, Diem was like de Gaulle incredibly sensitive to questions of national sovereignty, both administratively and symbolically, and never hesitated to say so. When the Americans failed to condemn a plot in the Republic of Vietnam's army against the Ngos in 1960, the pro-government, English-language *Times of Vietnam* captured official anger, aptly writing that the 'threat to our independence does not come from our [communist] enemies alone, but also from a number of foreign people who claim to be our friends'.[14]

The Kennedy administration got a taste of Diem's independence when it proposed a 'limited partnership' to the Vietnamese president in late 1961. In exchange for increased military assistance, a possible security treaty, even troops, the Americans requested the right to participate in internal decision-making rather than operating in a purely advisory capacity as they had since 1950. The Americans wanted to use the leverage they felt their assistance entitled them to—in order to push through badly needed political, economic, and military reforms on which effective containment in Vietnam turned—but which Diem kept refusing them. Diem accepted military assistance and sought a security treaty ensuring that the Americans didn't negotiate over his head with the communists, as they were already doing, in his view, in Laos. However, he rejected the introduction of American ground troops and insisted that the American 'limited partnership' was nothing more than another Western attempt to re-establish a protectorate over Vietnam.

Shocked to be treated at the same level as the 'French colonialists', the Americans backed down; but Diem's Gaullism had the Americans livid in the cables they fired back to Washington. How could they save Vietnam if its president would not let them! The two sides now talked past each other more than ever before, each righteously convinced of the validity of its own position. The Americans failed to grasp how their increasingly intrusive efforts to contain communism could translate into a threat to the national sovereignty of their junior partner. The Ngo brothers forgot something just as important: collaboration can provide security, assistance, even revolutionary traction for the smaller partner; but it can also get you into deep trouble, if you or your revolutionary projects jeopardize the larger strategic goals of the stronger power within your alliance. That danger is particularly high in wartime and the more asymmetrical the power relationships are.

Ngo Dinh Diem's Threat to Indirect American Containment

Strategic Hamlets and the Meltdown in US-Vietnamese Relations

Rather than improving relations between Saigon and Washington, the Ngo brothers' embrace of their 'strategic hamlets' program produced the opposite effect. In the face of the National Liberation Front's rapid expansion throughout the countryside in the early 1960s, Diem focused on ways to regain rural support. He reversed his earlier limits on local village elections, increased the effort to root out provincial corruption and graft, and organized the training for a phalanx of younger cadres to run the local administration. These loyal cadres would administer thousands of strategically located villages across the south, which would be regrouped into clusters of larger hamlets, and then connected to each other by roads and waterways. Barbed wire, trenches, cement fortifications, and local militias would protect them. The army and police would be on call to intervene when needed. The 'strategy' would form a (theoretically) impregnable armed, administrative wall protecting against Vietnamese Workers Party/National Liberation Front penetration.

While the Ngo brothers borrowed from French, British, and American experiences in counter-insurgency practices, they were also professionally trained administrators themselves. They knew from the First Indochina War how the communists had gone about building up their revolutionary states village by village. In fact, the communists had administered almost all of the Ngos' (native) central Vietnam during the Indochina War. The brothers were impressed by what they saw in the communist techniques of mass mobilization, rectification, indoctrination, and awed by how their enemies used war to extend political control downward. Like their adversaries, the Ngos wanted to use the current Second Indochina War (or the Vietnam War as it is widely known in the United States) to create a new bureaucratic elite and entrust it with a social revolution capable of winning rural support for their regime. In 1961, they created a mass party, the Republican Youth Movement, which began indoctrinating young people, training them in Personalism, and dispatching them into the countryside to administer the strategic hamlets. Of course, this elite would be firmly anti-communist and often Catholic, but like their communist opponents, they were designed to be carriers of socio-political change and the intermediaries for top-down central control. This new civil service, backed by the military, had the power to overthrow the traditional power structures, stamp out graft and corruption, and promote local elections. Through these cadres, the government and the people would construct a new power structure village by village, rolling back the NLF/VWP as they moved along, creating a new nation.

All of this was in theory, again. In practice, it was catastrophic. Like the Democratic Republic of Vietnam, Diem's Republic of Vietnam adopted highly coercive methods and paid the price in social support and political legitimacy. In order to move fast against its enemies, the government required tens of thousands of peasants to relocate against their will and to provide massive amounts of physical labor clearing land and building roads, bridges, and villages. By September 1962, the Ngo brothers had incorporated over four million people into 3,225 hamlets. By July 1963, some 7,000 hamlets housed over eight and a half million people in a feat of social mobilization matched only by their enemies. While the strategic hamlets certainly caused problems for the communists' Central Office of South Vietnam, the breakneck speed with which the nationalist government had built them outdistanced its capacity to administer them. Over-extended, in practice the army left large portions of the south in enemy hands. As in the north, there were not enough trained civil servants to preside over these massive experiments in social engineering. Many of the 'traditional' bureaucrats the Ngos had sidelined in the past refused to help restore administrative order now. Most peasants did not want to move from their ancestral villages. Who could blame them? And to make matters worse, the Republic of Vietnam's massive labor demands created the very waves of social anger and resistance on which the National Liberation Front's administrative expansion and land reform thrived.[15]

Distraught, Americans watched from the sidelines as Diem seemed to drive the peasantry straight into communist hands. Once again, they bemoaned the president's mad ideas about social revolution, village democracy, nation-building, and Personalism. They also knew that for Ngo Dinh Diem the strategic hamlets project served both to fight the communists and to protect the republic's sovereignty from American efforts to run the show. Washington's frustration also grew as the American-trained and -modernized Army of the Republic of Vietnam seemed incapable or unwilling to take the battle to the insurgents. Advisors were shocked when, in early 1963, 2,000 heavily armed, air-supported, and motorized ARVN troops failed to smash the 300–400 PLAF forces holding the strategic hamlet of Ap Bac in My Tho province. The botched operation sent the American advisor who prepared the battle plan, Colonel John Paul Vann, into a fit of anger symbolic of the wider American frustration with their junior partner: 'It was a miserable damn performance, just like it always is. These people won't listen. They make the same mistake over and over again in the same way'. That was not quite true. The Army of the Republic of Vietnam officers and men could and often did fight bravely and effectively. But growing American frustration with the course of events and with their allies was real.[16]

The Buddhist Crisis and the Overthrow of Ngo Dinh Diem
The tipping point came during the Buddhist crisis which lasted from May to September 1963. While Diem's family was Catholic and the Ngos had tried to use Catholicism and the Catholic refugees to fight the communists and build up their state, the brothers were not bent on creating a 'Catholic republic'. Upon coming to power, the Ngo brothers actively solicited the support of the Buddhists, including the 200,000 mainly anticommunist ones who had migrated from the north after the 1954 ceasefire. Buddhists had served in some of the highest positions in the Republic of Vietnam (as vice-president, foreign minister, and a general, for example). Diem

allowed the General Buddhist Association, created in 1951, to re-establish the Church's monastic headquarters in the republic, and to hold its second national congress in Saigon in 1958. If anything, it was cooperation which characterized the first five years of relations between the Buddhist Church and Diem's government. And Buddhist leaders were not entirely unhappy to see Diem weaken the Buddhist 'sects', the Cao Dai and the Hoa Hao.[17]

What set the Buddhists and Diem on a collision course were a series of errors on the part of the Ngo brothers, unfortunate coincidences, and a nationally assertive Buddhist Church that bumped up against an equally nationalist-minded Catholic one. Since the 1920s, Buddhist leaders, inspired by the predominant place this religion held in neighboring Thailand and Burma, sought to both revive and create a Vietnamese Buddhist nationalism of their own. Reform-minded monks established Buddhist institutions, schools, clerical associations, and youth groups the religion needed to make a comeback and to assert itself at national level. However, by the early 1960s this increasingly politicized and assertive Buddhist Church began to see the Ngos and their reliance on Catholic refugees, institutions, and youth groups less as weapons for fighting communists than as obstacles to realizing this Buddhist nation. Buddhist clergy who had supported Diem for years, like the eminent nationalist and venerable Tri Quang, now began to criticize the president's blatant favoritism toward Catholics. Others saw Archbishop Ngo Dinh Thuc's proselytization in central Vietnam as an offensive against the Buddhist religion. Buddhists interpreted anticommunist laws such as one banning atheism as pro-Catholic (and sometimes it was). While Diem's vague ideology of Personalism had never caused problems before (because no one really understood what it was), Buddhists now fingered its Catholic origins.

With their characteristic arrogance and insensitivity, the Ngo brothers did little to assuage the Buddhists, letting these increasingly hostile perceptions of Catholicism transform into very real socio-political threats. Nor did the Ngos do much to curb their Catholic favoritism. Tensions finally came to a head on 8 May 1963 when a clash between government forces and Buddhist demonstrators calling for religious equality resulted in the death of seven young Buddhists. Angry young monks and lay people took to the streets. Things took a turn for the worse when Diem issued orders banning the flying of religious flags. Always hypersensitive to issues of sovereignty, the president insisted that only the national republican flag could be flown at such events. Despite the fact that Diem had also banned the display of Catholic flags, the Buddhists interpreted this as yet another assault on their faith. Tri Quang and other religious nationalists in Hue and Saigon further mobilized their Church and its followers. Diem's desire to negotiate an end to the standoff got nowhere. In June, an elderly monk, the venerable Quang Duc, volunteered to immolate himself in a sign of protest. The Buddhist leadership agreed and organized media coverage to draw attention to it and the wider cause. On 11 June 1963, Quang Duc serenely sat down in the Buddha position in downtown Saigon. Supporters doused him with petrol and then set him aflame as one of the few photographers on the spot, Malcolm Browne, filmed his immolation for the world to see. More Buddhist demonstrations and immolations followed, leading Diem to crack down in August by seizing pagodas and arresting hundreds, if not thousands, of them.

If the Ngo brothers were convinced that this action was crucial to maintaining order, the Buddhist crisis, coming on the heels of the strategic hamlets' failure, plunged American confidence in the Ngos to its lowest levels as the National Liberation Front continued to expand its hold on the countryside. At the same time, high-level police and army generals informed the Americans that they were no longer supportive of Diem. By alienating large segments of Vietnamese society, they said, the president was ensuring a communist takeover. American diplomats and officers were telling the White House much the same thing. As for Diem, he oscillated between angry defiance and promises of reconciliation with the Americans. But when the Americans learned that some in his entourage were also speaking of opening contacts with the Vietnamese Workers Party in Hanoi in order to reach a settlement among the Vietnamese people, independently of Washington, the Americans concluded that the Ngo family had become a threat to their wider strategic interests. Like Nguyen Van Thinh, the President of the Republic of Cochinchina who had dared to evoke the possibility of speaking directly to Ho Chi Minh in mid-1946, Diem did not fully grasp the extent to which the Americans were as committed as the French had been to using the southern state as a political weapon to preserve their interests. On 2 November 1963, with a green light from Kennedy, Vietnamese military and security officers overthrew Ngo Dinh Diem and his brother, Nhu. Hours before his death at the hands of the coup leaders, holed up in the presidential palace, Diem had pleaded with the American ambassador to understand one thing: 'I am trying to reestablish order'. The Americans no longer believed it. Nor did many Vietnamese.[18]

From Indirect to Direct Interventions

Hanoi Chooses Direct Intervention[19]

Although the politburo welcomed the American-backed overthrow of Diem, the fall of the Ngo brothers did not result in the collapse of the Republic of Vietnam as the Vietnamese Workers' Party leadership had mistakenly expected. And while their NLF/PLAF had further expanded its control over large parts of the countryside, it did not have the necessary might to overthrow the American-backed Army of the Republic of Vietnam on its own. As a result, powerful voices in Hanoi began to push for direct though gradual Democratic Republic of Vietnam military intervention in the south in order to topple the Republic of Vietnam, create a coalition government with the NLF/VWP in it, and unify the whole country under the Democratic Republic of Vietnam before the United States could send in troops. Le Duan, Le Duc Tho, and their allies in the army, especially a general named Nguyen Chi Thanh, led the charge. They advocated carefully calibrated and interconnected conventional and guerilla war.[20]

This military strategy emphasizing conventional war did not command unanimity within the VWP politburo, however. Many—notably General Vo Nguyen Giap—balked. Giap and his allies worried that such an aggressive line risked provoking the Americans directly into joining the war, creating a conflagration that would be infinitely more violent for the Vietnamese army and people than the one they had just fought against the French. This group was not 'pro Soviet' or a bunch of 'doves', but rather believed that the best military strategy *for the time being* was a guerilla, protracted people's war, not a conventional, direct one. Some also worried that such an aggressive line would risk alienating the Soviets whose leaders, even those taking over from Khrushchev in 1964, wanted a negotiated settlement and might not support the communists in Hanoi. Still others wanted to maintain a combined political–military line in the south, while pressing for the reconvening of the Geneva Conference. (The neutralization of Laos which had been accomplished in 1962 seemed to provide reason for hope—a negotiated settlement which allowed the Pathet Lao to take part in a coalition government and avoid a bigger war involving the US had been achieved.) And, lastly, there was an internal debate featuring those who prioritized war against those who were focused on fully communizing the north first.

While the internal archival details on these debates remain unclear, they patently occurred against the backdrop of the widening split between the

Soviets and the Chinese and this affected Hanoi's war strategy. Most importantly, the Chinese increasingly supported the armed line being pushed by Le Duan's entourage. It was an internationalist duty, Mao said, to support the Vietnamese communist revolution and war against the 'American imperialists'. (It was also a way of keeping the Americans off China's vulnerable underbelly.) And of course support for Hanoi's armed struggle allowed the Chinese to advance in their high-stakes contest with the Soviets for the leadership of the communist bloc. Mao now accused the Soviets of 'revisionism', an emotionally charged word in the communist Church, meaning 'apostasy'. The Soviets felt the pressure and increasingly, if reluctantly, leaned toward supporting their fellow communists in Hanoi. Le Duan looked to the Chinese for support, whose military and logistical aid would be essential to an expanded war. He embraced the Chinese side in internal debates, treating those who cautioned against conventional war with the Americans as 'revisionists', again conveying that he meant something very close to treason in the Vietnamese context. Publicly, however, Le Duan, Ho Chi Minh, and others were careful in plotting a neutral course in the Sino-Soviet split, for the DRV needed vital hi-tech weapons which only Moscow could provide.[21]

The advocates of direct though gradual military intervention emerged victorious in early 1964 when the Vietnamese politburo formally approved their ninth plenum. In this historic document, the party concluded that the United States no longer trusted the Republic of Vietnam to do the fighting for possession of Vietnam. The Battle of Ap Bac had shown that. With Diem out of the way and his military successors beholden to the Americans, Washington was now in a position to intervene directly. The VWP had to continue the political struggle and guerilla warfare, the plenum conceded, but the time had come for Hanoi to intervene directly in the south by sending People's Army of Vietnam regular troops. The hope was that together with the National Liberation Front/People's Liberation Armed Force, the communists in Hanoi could bring down the republic in a carefully calibrated way before the Americans intervened. But everyone knew that by dispatching the Democratic Republic of Vietnam army to win the civil war directly, Hanoi might in itself provoke direct American intervention. Debates became so divisive that in March 1964 Ho Chi Minh had to step in to smooth things over, but not before telling the army to prepare for war.[22]

The man in charge was to be General Nguyen Chi Thanh, a jovial yet dedicated communist officer, loved by many, feared by others. Close to Le

Duan and Le Duc Tho, Thanh was a politburo member, head of the army's powerful General Political Directorate during the First Indochina War, and now equal in rank to Vo Nguyen Giap. He had played a key role in creating the People's Army of Vietnam, a professional, politically controlled force, and was convinced that his men could withstand American firepower and win. We met him at the outset of this chapter. He fully supported the politburo's decision to unify the nation under VWP control whatever the cost. The politburo put him in charge of the Central Office of South Vietnam and sent him to the central highlands below the seventeenth parallel to run it. Thanh knew this area like the back of his hand, for he had run clandestine party and military matters there since the 1930s.[23]

Thanh brought with him to the south in 1964 military officers from the First Indochina War. They reorganized the south into military regions (B1, B2, and B3) and extended the pathways of the Ho Chi Minh Trail as far southward as possible in order to arm and feed the PLAF and the rice-consuming PAVN regiments. Thanh, like Le Duan and Le Duc Tho, knew that the Americans knew that their troops and cadres were crossing the seventeenth parallel. The communists denied it publicly, but (internally) they did not care. For them, the seventeenth parallel was not a legally constituted national border and the Americans had sinned first by trying to create a separate, sovereign Vietnam out of the RV. And if the Republic of Vietnam leadership, backed by the Americans, was now determined to cast the war as one sovereign state's violation of another, the Democratic Republic of Vietnam leadership was just as determined to re-establish its pre-1954 administrative presence in the south to reassert its pre-1954 territorial sovereignty. The communists did not see themselves as starting a war; they were determined to finish the one they had been fighting since September 1945. Significantly, the party resumed its direct war where the People's Army of Vietnam had ended it with the French in June 1954, not at Dien Bien Phu, but in the southern highlands, where PAVN regiments had decimated French mobile groups making a run for the shelter of Pleiku. By May 1965, 7,000 PAVN troops under Thanh's command operated in the central highlands overlooking the Mekong delta region. This was no coincidence.

Washington Chooses Direct Intervention[24]

President Lyndon Johnson would have preferred, like his predecessors, to focus on American domestic matters, above all his ideas for the 'Great Society'. He would have preferred to continue the American policy of the last twenty years of fighting communism in Vietnam by proxy. But the military governments replacing Ngo Dinh Diem were unstable and incapable of stopping the insurgency, those in the White House had concluded. The 16,000 military advisors Kennedy left in Vietnam in late 1963 increased to 23,000 in 1964 as Johnson tried to hold the line. The president also rejected the idea of 'neutralizing' South Vietnam (i.e. letting it plot a course independent of the Cold War); it would, in his view, only weaken American containment of China. Like Kennedy in 1963, Johnson had to choose: either the US had to cut its losses and get out or else it had to intervene directly. Most of Kennedy's advisors had stayed on under Johnson and, with very few exceptions, were as hawkish as Le Duan's entourage inside communist Vietnam. Whatever their inner reservations and *post facto* claims, Johnson and his cabinet advisors chose war instead of negotiating or withdrawing from their investment in South Vietnam. And with the French and Diem now gone that could mean only one thing—the end of indirect containment of the communists.[25]

At the same time as the politburo's Nguyen Chi Thanh assumed his command in the highlands, Johnson named General William C. Westmoreland to run the Military Assistance Command, Vietnam, in Saigon. The Americans increased their surveillance of the north by sending vessels into the Gulf of Tonkin and joined their Vietnamese counterparts in organizing covert operations above the seventeenth parallel (commando raids, psychological warfare, sabotage, and communications surveillance). The aggressive course all sides were now adopting made an incident all but inevitable, just as it had in 1946. The first occurred on 2 August 1964, when a DRV ship fired on the intelligence-gathering destroyer *USS Maddox*. Johnson refrained from taking action, but two days later, when reports of a second attack arrived on his desk (although in reality, the second attack had never actually occurred), he ordered retaliatory air raids and brought a historic resolution before Congress asking for authorization to use armed force to protect American forces and stop DRV aggression. On 7 August 1964, the US Congress voted in favor of the resolution almost unanimously. Known as the Gulf of Tonkin resolution, this was the legal document upon which America went to war against the Democratic Republic of Vietnam without declaring it officially. Congress had authorized Johnson to take 'all necessary measures'.

Given that the Republic of Vietnam's leaders allowed the Americans to intervene directly in their territory and also that they were in no position to stop the DRV from going to war against them, they would now have to watch from the sidelines as others started to make decisions for them. This does not mean that republican leaders had surrendered all of their national sovereignty. However, by betting on *direct* American military intervention to win a civil war, the generals in charge of the Republic of Vietnam had repeated the same gamble that their non-communist nationalist predecessors had made in 1947 by joining the French. In both cases, this choice limited their freedom of action. The rare non-communist Vietnamese man to have rejected *both* bargains was the very one the Army of the Republic of Vietnam generals and the Kennedy administration had just overthrown.

Similarly, while the communists did their best to respect the independence of the southern political institutions they had created in the form of the NLF and the PLAF, the leadership of the VWP in Hanoi's decision to fight directly now left little doubt as to who was in charge. The shock was rude for some in the south when non-communists opposed to the generals in Saigon realized that they were not running the NLF. They should have known better from past events of the pre-1954 period. For example, when non-communist southern nationalists challenged the Indochinese Communist Party's self-appointed right to lead the anti-French resistance in a heated meeting in 1949, Le Duc Tho shot back angrily to his astonished listeners that 'anyone who opposed the communists was anti-resistance, a traitor'. To put it another way, if non-communists threatened to pry the National Liberation Front loose from the Vietnamese Workers Party's grip in independent ways, then they would risk the same fate as Ngo Dinh Diem did when he tried to plot a course inimical to Washington's interests. In 1964, both Washington and Hanoi chose war and in so doing expected their respective southern allies to fall into step.[26]

Meanwhile, as American bombs began to fall over North Vietnam, China backed the more aggressive DRV strategy in the south. Mao saw in increased support for the Vietnamese struggle against American 'imperialism' a foreign threat he could use to mobilize internal support for his 'Cultural Revolution'. Moreover, the rapidly deteriorating state of Sino-Soviet relations convinced him that supporting the Vietnamese was an excellent way of pushing back against the Soviets as well as the United States. In October 1964, China successfully tested its first nuclear bomb. Two months later, the leadership in Beijing agreed to send (over a three-year period as it turned out) 300,000 People's Army of China engineering troops to serve in the Democratic Republic of Vietnam's northern provinces building roads,

securing border exchanges via the railways and manning anti-aircraft bat-
teries. This helped free Vietnamese soldiers to fight the war in the south.
With this huge logistical troop presence in the DRV and the acquisition of
the A-bomb, Beijing's message to Washington was crystal-clear: the Chinese would not deploy combat troops in support of the DRV, but any attempt by the US to cross the seventeenth parallel with troops would trigger
direct Chinese intervention just as it had at the thirty-eighth parallel in Korea in 1950.[27]

The Soviets also increased their assistance to the Democratic Republic
of Vietnam in the wake of the Gulf of Tonkin clash, supplying MIG-17s,
surface-to-air missiles (SAMs), radar systems, and real time intelligence
on B-52 bombing routes. Sino-Soviet intervention was indirect but it was
crucial to the DRV's ability to wage war. And by carefully negotiating and
even manipulating Sino-Soviet competition, the leadership in Hanoi successfully obtained the vital military and economic assistance it needed from
the communist bloc to go to war. Just as in 1950, Vietnamese communists
felt that such generous aid was fully justified, given that their armies and
people were bearing the burden of a direct war with the leader of the enemy
capitalist camp, the United States.

Washington found it much more difficult to win over Allied support for
its cause. The spread of decolonization westward from Asia to Africa by
the early 1960s meant that European powers losing their overseas territories were much less supportive of an anticommunist coalition in Southeast
Asia than they had been in the late 1940s. By 1965, meaningful French and
even British participation in the Southeast Asia Treaty Organization was
fast disappearing.[28] Significantly, the countries that most supported the
United States in Vietnam were all in the Asia–Pacific region. To varying
degrees, their governments worried about the threat of communism and,
with recent memories of Japanese expansion through Tonkin still in their
minds, were keen on maintaining the Americans in the region. In 1969, the
Australians had 8,000 combat troops in Vietnam, New Zealand had 552,
the Philippines 2,000, Thailand had 11,568, and South Korea 50,003, while
Taiwan sent counter-insurgency specialists there. Some have written these
countries off as 'mercenaries'. Although Washington exercised real pressure over them and provided all sorts of things to secure their support, each
had its own reasons for joining the US, as did the Cubans, North Koreans,
and East Germans who supported the Democratic Republic of Vietnam.[28]

1965: Direct Parallel Interventions

The Gulf of Tonkin incident allowed President Johnson to initiate the air war in 1964. Some six months later, a second incident, this time in the southern highlands, provided the White House with the pretext it needed to land American ground troops in southern Vietnam. In February 1965, General Nguyen Chi Thanh had authorized People's Liberation Armed Force troops to attack an American helicopter base in Pleiku, killing eight men. In response, Johnson authorized retaliatory airstrikes against military bases in the Democratic Republic of Vietnam, which rapidly expanded into a strategic bombing campaign against northern military and industrial targets known as Operation Rolling Thunder. While the idea was to force the leadership in Hanoi to stop its support of the southern insurgency and negotiate immediately a settlement recognizing the sovereign existence of the Republic of Vietnam, the Americans badly underestimated the DRV's commitment to war and unification on their terms. And the communist leadership made exactly the same mistake about the Americans. On 8 March 1965, 3,500 US marines landed in Danang as American ground forces now entered the war, with their navy and air force providing support. The VWP already had 10,000 PAVN troops on the ground below the seventeenth parallel.

This carefully calculated parallel commitment to direct military intervention inexorably led both Washington and Hanoi to escalate their troop levels rapidly. In July 1965, President Johnson accepted General Westmoreland's request for more men, bringing the total to 125,000. General Thanh did the same. By 1966, the latter commanded 115,000 regular troops, which were evenly divided between the People's Liberation Armed Force and the People's Army of Vietnam. If one adds the guerilla forces, Thanh commanded a total of 225,000 combatants by 1966. In that year, the United States increased its troop level to 350,000, while the Army of the Republic of Vietnam counted 315,000 regular troops and an equal number of auxiliary personnel. The number of United States troops peaked in 1969 at 543,000, meaning that combined American–ARVN troops numbered around a million.[29]

Guerilla and conventional battles combined throughout the Vietnam War, just as they had before 1954. The first direct military encounter between the People's Army of Vietnam and American troops occurred in November 1965 in the Ia Drang valley. This was a conventional, large-unit

confrontation, occurring in the same area where the PAVN had destroyed
the French mobile units in June 1954. Thanh also sent the People's Liberation Armed Force's main forces into battle against the Army of the Republic
of Vietnam, hoping to bring down the republic before the Americans could
arrive in full force. In June 1965, a PLAF regiment attacked an enemy base
in Dong Xoai. ARVN troops responded with a ferocious counter-attack,
as artillery and bombs rained down on their enemy. One PLAF veteran
recalled his superior officer shouting into the field phone as the ground
shook around them: 'My God! It's brutal, brutal'.[30]

A Savage War of Destruction

The determination of the leaders in Washington and Hanoi from 1965 onward to battle each other directly ensured that the war for Vietnam would
become one of the most ferocious conflicts of the twentieth century. The
most industrialized and technologically advanced country in the world
threw everything it had at one of the least developed states on the same
planet, the Democratic Republic of Vietnam, all the while unleashing massive firepower over the very Vietnam it was trying to save, the Republic of
Vietnam. From a string of bases in Thailand, the Philippines, Japan, South
Korea, Guam, and a wall of aircraft carriers perched in the South China
Sea, the Americans bombed relentlessly in order to force the communists
to the negotiating table, destroy the Ho Chi Minh Trail, level the DRV's
small industry and infrastructure to the ground, and support allied ground
forces in the south. Planes sprayed tens of thousands of liters of herbicides
over the jungle canopy in search of the trucks and people who were pushing bikes carrying supplies down the trails. Thousands of hectares of jungle
were 'transformed into the tropical equivalent of a winter forest'. The communists pushed their supply lines and many of their bases (including those
of the Central Office of South Vietnam) into western Indochina. As they
did so, the Americans bombed Laos and Cambodia relentlessly. Indeed, the
bombing of Cambodia began in 1965, not 1969, as is commonly believed.
Laos has the distinction of being the most heavily bombed country in world
history, if calculated in per capita terms (i.e. it is a sparsely populated, small
country). From 50,000 feet above the ground, out of sight, bomb-laden
B-52s dropped mindboggling amounts of explosives. Closer to the ground,
fighter jets (F4s) and low-flying bombers (Skyraiders) attacked targets supported by sophisticated radar and communications systems. Even closer
to the ground, helicopters not only transported troops rapidly from one

remote place to another, as at Ia Drang, but they also became 'gunships' (UH-1 'Hueys') capable of unleashing impressive firepower themselves. In all, over 1.4 million tons of bombs fell over all of Indochina, two times the total dropped during the Second World War. Half of all the bombs fell over the Republic of Vietnam. The rest fell on Laos, the DRV, and Cambodia, in that order. Operation Rolling Thunder bombed the Democratic Republic of Vietnam on an almost daily basis until 1968, destroying bridges, roads, and any remaining industrial installations American intelligence services could locate. The air force executed 25,000 sorties in 1965, 79,000 in 1966, and 108,000 in 1967. What French bombers had dropped during the two-month Battle of Dien Bien Phu was the equivalent of what the Americans dropped in one day. This was hugely asymmetrical warfare.[31]

Despite the important quantities of modern weapons the DRV received from its communist brethren, the communists were never in a position to inflict anything remotely equal to the violence the Americans inflicted on Vietnamese soldiers, civilians, and the environment. While the People's Army of Vietnam and the People's Liberation Armed Force had artillery, carried AK-47s, lugged machine-guns, and later used tanks, they could never drop napalm on American troops or carpet-bomb American cities and industrial complexes with B-52s. Nor did the DRV have sufficient MiGs (Soviet jet fighters), pilots, or surface-to-air missiles capable of stopping American aerial bombing, much less the industries making them. This disproportionate deployment of firepower meant that Vietnamese soldiers and civilians from north to south, including non-Viet peoples, experienced levels of terror and death unknown to the American combat soldiers, let alone the American civilian population. As one senior member of the National Liberation Front of South Vietnam later recalled, the massive American bombing campaign 'translated into an experience of undiluted psychological terror, into which we were plunged, day in, day out, for years on end':

From a kilometer away, the sonic roar of the B-52 explosions tore eardrums, leaving many of the jungle dwellers permanently deaf. From a kilometer, the shock waves knocked their victims senseless. Any hit within a half kilometer would collapse the walls of an un-reinforced bunker, burying alive the people cowering inside. [. . .] Often the warnings would give us time to grab some rice and escape by foot or bike down one of the emergency routes. Hours later we would return to find, as happened on several occasions, that there was nothing left. It was as if an enormous scythe had swept through the jungle, felling the giant teak and go trees like grass in its way, shredding them into billions of scattered splinters. [. . .] The terror was complete. One lost control of bodily functions as the mind screamed incomprehensible orders to get out.[32]

One soldier later recalled that as the ground trembled around him under the weight of B-52 bombs, he could only think of one thing, 'of my mother giving me a checkered scarf the day I first joined the army. It was terrifying'. Young northern soldiers marching south never forgot their first sight of the war-disabled going the other way on stretchers. Each thought about what it portended for the future: 'We used to say to each other, "On arrival in the South, try to keep your faces intact"'. The VWP refused to let many of the maimed and disfigured return home for fear of undermining morale, while desperate parents, wives, and family did everything they could to find out why their loved ones had not returned home. Intense trauma, nonstop worry, and insomnia rode roughshod over all of Vietnam, deep into Laos and Cambodia, and across the highlands. And when such lethal weapons struck their human targets, the result was often complete vaporization, ruling out the chance of bringing home a body for a proper burial. One member of a cultural group in the south recalled how he had lost his close friend to a direct rocket hit: 'Afterward they found a little hair and some scraps of flesh. That was how one of the finest young composers in Vietnam died'. And as in the wake of the Tay Son wars of the late eighteenth century, the spirits of the dead were once again wandering all over Vietnam looking for a place to rest regardless of any political boundaries between north and south.[33]

We know much less about how rural civilians survived this savagery. One year into the bombing campaign, the legendary French veteran of the Second World War and scholar of modern Vietnam, Bernard Fall, was appalled by the brutal effects of the air campaign on civilians. In late 1965, he wrote a damning account of the American assault on Vietnamese civilians, the result of his mind-bending trip with pilots on a bombing mission over the south. When a monsoon ruled out the primary enemy target, the squadron of Skyraiders he accompanied were diverted to a secondary one, a so-called 'communist rest center' where the planes were to dump their ordnance before returning. The rest center was in fact a Vietnamese fishing village on the Ca Mau peninsula. The planes dived and unleashed several thousand tons of napalm and explosives. Peering out of the cockpit, Fall couldn't believe what he saw that day: 'We came down low, flying very fast, and I could see some of the villagers trying to head away from the burning shore in their sampans. The village was burning fiercely. I will never forget the sight of the fishing nets in flames, covered with burning, jellied gasoline'. No one knew how many civilians died that day or were dying in such raids, but Fall was convinced that this 'impersonalized' killing (his term) from the sky was resulting in the deaths of tens of thousands of non-combatants. In all, according to statistics published recently in Hanoi, the war that started in 1965 and ended ten years later took the lives of 3.1 million of the Democratic Republic of Vietnam's PAVN and its National Liberation Front's PLAF people, civilians and military personnel combined. Two hundred thousand ARVN troops perished. While every single life is precious, only 58,000 Americans died in the conflict, that's 1.7 percent of the 3.3 million total number of those who died. At 98.3 percent, death was a profoundly Vietnamese experience.[34]

War militarized both Vietnams. The civil war starting in the south in 1959 had already led the Army of the Republic of Vietnam and the National Liberation Front/People's Liberation Armed Force to arm whole villages against each other and to create local militias and labor teams to fortify hamlets, dig trenches around them, and keep night watch. Snipers, assassins, and soldiers waged a low-level war of attrition that killed tens of thousands of administrators on all sides. Both sides adopted campaigns to rally the enemy soldiers, administrators, and civilians. The communists had long perfected the Maoist proselytizing propaganda campaigns toward the enemy ('*dich van*'), while the republic imported methods used in Malaya and the Philippines to set up the Open Arms ('*Chieu Hoi*') program to achieve the same goal. However, in doing so, each side provoked violent reactions from the other as it tried to stop people from going over to the 'other side'. The same was true of the US-backed Phoenix Program that sought to fight the administrative war in the south between 1965 and 1972 by neutralizing the enemy's civilian administration through persuasion, but also assassination. The Phoenix Program physically eliminated 26,000 people. The VWP/NFL/PLAF sapper, commando, and police teams may well have killed just as many civilian bureaucrats, men and women. Villagers did what they could to stay alive in this ocean of violence and the waves of hate, vengeance, and raw emotions surging all around them. Hundreds of thousands made a dash for the cities. In fact, the percentage of the population living in southern cities had increased from 20 percent in 1960 to 43 percent by 1971, in what Samuel Huntington called 'forced-draft urbanization'. War, not industrialization, explained this modern phenomenon. But not everyone could get out. Those poor souls who hunkered down in their villages, caring for family members or protecting their land, did their best to keep on good terms with both sides in this savage, seemingly never-ending war of sovereignties. As one assassin recalled, 'They were very frightened of us. They didn't dare to say a word'. Who could blame them?[35]

War militarized northern Vietnam too. Sirens, drills, and bomb shelters became familiar sights and sounds. Whereas the bombing sent southern villagers into the cities, American air attacks on urban areas in the north led the government to evacuate much of the civilian population to the countryside. In the northern cities and countryside, the government recruited massive amounts of labor to help repair bombed-out roads, bridges, and dikes. Militia forces re-emerged in northern society, with some two million people participating in them—10 percent of the DRV's total population. The draft increasingly consumed the entire male population aged between eighteen and forty. This was particularly the case as the war of attrition decimated the People's Liberation Armed Force and caused the communists to accelerate the deployment of northern boys to fight in the south (140,000 People's Army of Vietnam troops from above the seventeenth parallel operated in the south in 1968). The draft hit the male peasant population hardest, though. High-ranking administrators and party officials as well as bribe-paying urbanites were always better at finding ways to keep their sons out of combat. Thousands of their children were sent to Moscow or Budapest to study, just like their republican counterparts heading for the US and France.[36]

Women were deeply involved in war, too. Not only did they have to replace their drafted husbands or fathers planting rice, but they also filled many of the local militias and assumed administrative tasks. As during the Indochina conflict, they helped to repair roads and dikes, all the while taking care of children and elders. Unmarried women served in the army as nurses and medics. But many also saw combat. This was particularly the case in the south, where the line between the professional army, the PLAF, and the guerilla fighters was always blurred. It was also in the south where the need for combatants was always highest. Northern women went south too. Many did so by joining the DRV Youth Brigade. They found themselves transporting supplies down the Ho Chi Minh Trail in extraordinarily difficult circumstances. War trauma on the trail was so intense that many women stopped menstruating. Many never married because of the war and later found themselves ostracized for being single. Children too found themselves in the line of fire, especially in the south. Some served as messengers, intelligence agents, and guides—for all sides.[37]

In the north, the totalizing nature of this war not only broke down gender and age barriers, but it also extended state control over society. Communist surveillance in the cities and countryside increased, as the party organized massive mobilization, emulation, and propaganda campaigns. The police were omnipresent. Literature had to serve the war cause. Opposition to the war was crushed. News of massive numbers of battlefield deaths was censored or delayed so as not to sap civilian morale. The Republic of Vietnam never imposed such control over cultural and political expression, allowing for remarkable critiques of the war and government policy which would have been unthinkable in the north (see chapter 12).

The Tet Offensive of 1968: The Limits of Conventional Warfare[38]

If Johnson was dismayed by his failure to force the communists to accept the existence of the Republic of Vietnam, Le Duan was just as frustrated by his inability to topple that state. Neither side, however, was serious about negotiations, despite attempts by just about everybody to bring Hanoi and Washington together. Advocates of war led by Le Duan, Le Duc Tho, and Nguyen Chi Thanh pushed instead for a major offensive that would trigger the general uprising they needed to bring down Nguyen Van Thieu, the president of the enemy Republic, expand the Central Office of South Vietnam's territorial control, and signal to the Americans that they could not win the war militarily and should leave. Such a grandiose offensive would also help turn public opinion against the White House. Le Duan's entourage apparently worried, too, that military officers associated with Vo Nguyen Giap might oppose such a bold strategy in favor of a policy of protracted guerilla warfare. Thus, in order to push through what became the Tet Offensive (a series of conventional military assaults on southern urban centers), Le Duan's allies renewed their 'anti-revisionist' attacks, placing dozens of Giap's allies under house arrest on trumped-up charges of being 'pro-Soviet', indeed 'traitors'.

In December 1967, the Vietnamese politburo approved the final plans for the Tet Offensive. The new commanding officers for this surprise attack were generals Van Tien Dung and Hoang Van Thai (Nguyen Chi Thanh had died of a heart attack that July). The politburo launched its offensive in early 1968 as people celebrated Tet (the new lunar New Year) across the country. Starting in mid-January, 20,000 People's Army of Vietnam troops attacked the American base of Khe Sanh (located just below the seventeenth parallel), in a violent battle designed to drive the Americans out of this strategic area through which supplies flowed to the National Liberation Front. The People's Army of Vietnam finally took the city from the Americans in July 1968, one of the longest and most intense conventional battles since Dien Bien Phu.

But for the Vietnamese Workers Party in Hanoi this offensive on Khe Sanh also sought to pin down the Americans, as the communists unleashed PLAF conventional and commando attacks on cities across the south, including Saigon, Da Nang, and Hue. People's Army of Vietnam soldiers participated mainly in the assault and occupation of Hue. The combined American–Army of the Republic of Vietnam response was rapid as troops participated in street fighting for the first time since the outbreak of the war against the French in 1946–7. The Battle of Hue was particularly violent. Not only did PAVN/PLAF troops go up against American/ARVN ones in the imperial city, but the four week PAVN/PLAF occupation of the imperial city led to the assassination of hundreds of Republic of Vietnam administrators and the massacre of hundreds, perhaps even thousands, of innocent civilians caught in the cross-fire and hate that engulfed the city. The war of sovereignties struck the cities with a vengeance.

In the end, the urbanites did not rise up as Le Duan had predicted and the mainly People's Liberation Armed Force troops were in no position to hold the cities for long against the combined American–Army of the Republic of Vietnam onslaught. Militarily, the various offensives at Tet were massive failures although the People's Army of Vietnam scored a major victory at Khe Sanh. An estimated 40,000 (some PAVN, but mainly PLAF) troops died in the Tet assaults of 1968. The People's Liberation Armed Force never truly recovered from these defeats. And from this point onward, the north had to send its own troops to fight and die in the south. The Vietnamese politburo did, however, score a major public relations victory with 'Tet'. Photographs of American soldiers pinned down in rubble-strewn Hue streets and evening television images of People's Liberation Armed Force commandos penetrating the American embassy in Saigon led many Americans to wonder why victory was not at hand as promised. Journalists became more critical in their reporting, following in Bernard Fall's footsteps. Congressional support declined as the antiwar movement began to gather steam in the US, Western Europe, and Japan. By late 1968, 45 percent of Americans thought intervention was a mistake. Johnson's war had received such bad press that he agreed to halt the bombing and open negotiations with the communists in Hanoi in Paris. The Democratic Republic of Vietnam agreed to talks on 4 April 1968, but not before the American president had made the stunning decision not to run for a second term. A year later, in September 1969, Ho Chi Minh passed away in Hanoi without seeing the Vietnam he had declared independent in 1945 reunited.[39]

THE PARIS ACCORDS AND THE DIFFICULTY OF ENDING WARS[40]

Nixon and the Return to Indirect Containment?

When the Republican Richard Nixon and his national security advisor, Henry Kissinger, arrived in the White House in January 1969, they were confident that they could end this unpopular war, bring American troops home, refocus American foreign policy on more important matters, and do so honorably without losing international credibility. They also recognized that direct intervention had been very expensive. However, Nixon's negotiating position in Paris followed the same objectives as his predecessor—the Democratic Republic of Vietnam had to recognize the Republic of Vietnam's right to exist as an independent sovereign state, end its support of the southern insurgency, and withdraw its troops from republican territory.

The politburo dispatched its special representative, Le Duc Tho, to lead its negotiations in Paris. Tho demanded the withdrawal of US troops from the south, no more bombing, and refused to negotiate with the Nguyen Van Thieu 'regime' now in charge of the republic. To strengthen its negotiating hand, in June 1969 the communist party in Hanoi also created a counter-Republic of Vietnam for the south, the Provisional Revolutionary Government of the Republic of South Vietnam, or the PRG. The politburo had first approved of and handed the creation of this new southern republic to COSVN on 21 January 1968, on the eve of the Tet Offensive (as they had been convinced there would be a successful uprising). The party simultaneously ordered the creation of a second national front, the Alliance of National, Democratic, and Peace Forces. The communists used these two new political entities as well as the already existing NLF to divide their enemies on the diplomatic front and to win over increased southern support for the creation of a coalition government for South Vietnam on their terms. Hanoi would negotiate with Washington while the PRG would serve as the counter-'republican' instrument through which the politburo would position itself to create an alternative to the Republic of Vietnam. As official historians put the double-speak, the party diplomacy 'is one but also two; two but also one'.[41]

In order to achieve what the White House called 'peace with honor', Nixon and Kissinger adopted a four-pronged strategy. Firstly, they saw an opportunity in the violent breakdown of the Sino-Soviet alliance coinciding with their entry into the White House. Things had become so bad between the two Eurasian communist giants by mid-1969 that each had set its nuclear sights on the other. The Soviet-led Warsaw Pact invasion of Czechoslovakia in August 1968 had convinced Mao that the Soviets, not the Americans, had become the number one enemy. In fact, as Mao reined in his Cultural Revolution in early 1969 in order to focus on the Soviet threat, he realized that he needed the Americans to contain his northern neighbor and to help to modernize the badly neglected Chinese economy. Nixon and Kissinger were just as keen on downplaying ideology in favor of *realpolitik*.

The Soviets also wanted détente. High on Moscow's list was ending the costly nuclear arms race in order to focus on improving the domestic economy. Nixon welcomed this idea, too. Starting in late 1969, the White House opened bilateral talks with the Soviets leading to the Strategic Arms Limitation Talks Agreement (SALT I) in May 1972, which was essential to improving relations between Moscow and Washington. This followed after Nixon's trip to Beijing in early 1972, during which he managed to reset Sino-American relations on the road to normalization. In exchange, Nixon asked Mao and Brezhnev to help bring their fellow communists in Hanoi to the negotiating table. Although the Chinese and Soviets continued to support the Democratic Republic of Vietnam, each now cautioned their ally against continuing the war indefinitely.

Secondly, bringing the 'boys home' from Vietnam had been one of Nixon's major campaign pledges. In June 1969, he withdrew the first contingent of American troops. By 1972, only 24,000 American soldiers remained in Vietnam. But in order to compensate for the exiting American troops, Nixon simultaneously implemented a policy of assisting the Republic of Vietnam to train and arm more of its own soldiers. By 1969, thanks to American support, the Army of the Republic of Vietnam had increased its regular divisional army to 400,000 men, while the People's Army of Vietnam forces below the seventeenth parallel exceeded 80,000. Nixon also provided enormous military aid to the ARVN, including new bombers, artillery, ammunition, machine guns, vehicles, and petrol. This is how Nixon sought to 'Vietnamize' the war effort and extricate the United States from its direct involvement in the war.

Thirdly, to push the Democratic Republic of Vietnam further, Nixon and Kissinger expanded the war into western Indochina by making a concerted effort to destroy communist bases in Laos and Cambodia and to sever the Ho Chi Minh Trail. Nixon greatly increased the bombing of Cambodia in 1969, continued the air assault on Laos, and supported US/ARVN incursions into Cambodia and Laos in 1970 and 1971. This policy certainly hurt the DRV's war effort and triggered intense clashes in Laos. B-52 bombing devastated rural Cambodia as the VWP renewed its support of Cambodian communists (which had been on hold since 1954; see chapter 13). And Nixon also made it clear that he would, if necessary, resume bombing the north, the fourth part of his strategy, if the Vietnamese communists did not negotiate in good faith.

Despite the carrots and sticks, negotiations in Paris remained laborious and drawn-out. The Democratic Republic of Vietnam's leaders refused to concede that there could be two Vietnams. Le Duc Tho repeated over and again that the Geneva Conference agreements of 1954 had only provisionally divided Vietnam, and that only the creation of a coalition government, including the PRG, the NLF, and the Republic of Vietnam, could solve the problem. Nixon continued to persistently back only the sovereignty of the Republic of Vietnam led by Nguyen Van Thieu. Hanoi's chief negotiator, Le Duc Tho, however, refused to negotiate with Nguyen Van Thieu or to include him in a coalition government. For the communists, the leaders of the southern republic were illegitimate. And on the question of not joining the coalition, Thieu paradoxically agreed entirely with his communist adversaries. Not only would his participation in a southern coalition undermine the republic's sovereignty, but Thieu was convinced that such a coalition would allow the communists to eventually take control from the inside. Added to this, Thieu, like his predecessors in the run-up to the Geneva Conference, also had to worry about the Americans negotiating a deal behind his back.

However, if Le Duc Tho refused to budge in Paris, it was also because the communists were not in a strong enough position on the ground in the south to negotiate effectively. International opinion may have turned on the Americans, but the Army of the Republic of Vietnam plus the Americans had decimated the communists' People's Liberation Armed Force in the south since 1968 and kept the People's Army of Vietnam on the run. The Open Arms and Phoenix programs had wreaked terrible damage on the administrative front, weakening the Central Office of South Vietnam's ability to control people and territory. Hundreds of thousands of peasants had fled to the cities, while others sought shelter in Army of the Republic of Vietnam-controlled zones. If the communists had controlled over four million people between 1961 and 1969, those numbers dropped to one and a half million by 1969 and then to only 229,000 people by 1971. One communist cadre in the south said that after the Tet Offensive, communists there 'hardly controlled any land at all'; it was a 'nightmare'. Moreover, the Republic of Vietnam's government with Thieu at the helm seemed to be making a comeback with its liberal agrarian policy, 'Land for the Tiller'. The economy had picked up and elections seemed to hold the promise of a brighter future.[42]

Only military force could provide the DRV with the territorial control it needed to negotiate. As a result, before going any further diplomatically in Paris, the politburo launched a massive, conventional-style military attack on the south in early 1972 which was designed to recapture territory, destabilize Thieu's government, and turn American public opinion further against Nixon in the lead-up to the fall elections. With a clear nod to the Soviet Union and thankful for its increased military aid, the Vietnamese politburo asked General Vo Nguyen Giap to lead this offensive. On 30 March, Giap sent twelve heavily armed combat divisions across the seventeenth parallel in what the Americans christened the Easter Offensive. One hundred and twenty thousand communist troops supported by Soviet-supplied tanks and artillery raced southward until the Army of the Republic of Vietnam held them in An Loc, a small town located 140 kilometers north of Saigon. In a very violent battle, the PAVN troops attacked in wave after wave as ARVN artillery fire and American bombers pounded them mercilessly. The battle continued until July, when Giap called off the attack. While the innermost party conflict over strategy remains a mystery, Giap was clearly no more a 'dove' than Le Duan was and it seemed he could abandon guerilla tactics in favor of full-blown conventional war at the cost of tens of thousands of his soldiers' lives.

Furious, Nixon and Kissinger unleashed a massive bombing campaign against Hanoi (Operation Linebacker) and mined Haiphong harbor to stop

Soviet arms shipments coming in by sea. This intensive bombing of Hanoi brought Le Duc Tho back to the negotiating table, but it also provoked international condemnation. Antiwar sentiment exploded on American campuses, while Europeans began to think that the White House had lost its moral compass. Most ominously for Nixon, Congress began to assert its constitutional control over the power of the purse and thus the executive branch's ability to make war.[43]

The End

Although the Easter Offensive had failed to bring down the southern Republic, the communists left 100,000 People's Army of Vietnam troops below the seventeenth parallel whether Washington liked it or not, and in so doing increased its territorial control. These were probably the offensive's real objectives. Having secured their military position in the south, in July 1972 Le Duc Tho dropped the call for Nguyen Van Thieu's removal as leader of the Republic of Vietnam and agreed that he could now join him in an eventual coalition government. Le Duc Tho also played the politburo's political card, the Provisional Revolutionary Government of the Republic of South Vietnam. The politburo had already placed two trusted communists, Huynh Tan Phat and Madame Nguyen Thi Binh, in charge of this counter-republic and its foreign policy. The USSR, China, and other communist states accorded the PRG full diplomatic recognition, as did many non-aligned nations which had refused to support one side or the other in the Cold War since acquiring their independence. Knowing that Nixon desperately wanted to announce a peace agreement before the upcoming presidential elections, Tho demanded that the Provisional Revolutionary Government of the Republic of South Vietnam take part in the creation of a tripartite commission with the Republic of Vietnam and the National Liberation Front to preside over future elections and any accords.[44]

The agreement Kissinger and Le Duc Tho finally hammered out turned on two main conditions: 1) the implementation of a ceasefire and the withdrawal within sixty days of all remaining American troops while Hanoi would return American prisoners of war and 2) the creation of a tripartite commission, the National Council of Reconciliation and Concord, that would consult to resolve the future of the 'south'. It included the Provisional Revolutionary Government of the Republic of South Vietnam, the Republic of Vietnam, and the National Liberation Front. The People's Army of Vietnam troops remained below the seventeenth parallel.

Unsurprisingly, Nguyen Van Thieu opposed the draft agreement submitted to him in October by the Americans. He rejected any deal that left enemy troops in Republic of Vietnam territory and further compromised the republic's sovereignty via the creation of a national council. Having won a landslide presidential victory in early November, Nixon rallied to Thieu's point of view and reneged on the draft agreement. Nixon now insisted that the communists withdraw their troops first before signing the accord. When they refused, Nixon ordered B-52s to rain bombs all over the north in December 1972. In all, the eleven-day Christmas bombing dropped 36,000 tons of explosives over the north, an act that elicited international opprobrium, but failed to reassure Thieu. Nor did it remove People's Army of Vietnam troops from the south or reduce their territorial control. In short, Nixon wanted out, and Thieu could do little to stop the Americans and the Democratic Republic of Vietnam from signing an agreement.

For Thieu, 1973 was starting to look at lot like 1953. There was a major difference, however. Unlike the French, who, after the negotiated end of the First Indochina War in 1954, had made little commitment to supporting the State of Vietnam thereafter, in 1973 Nixon promised continued military assistance to the Republic of Vietnam and pledged to drop bombs once more if the communists violated the agreement and made it very clear that he would not hesitate to do so. The Vietnamese politburo believed him, at least for the time being, as did Nguyen Van Thieu. On 27 January 1973, the US and the DRV signed a ceasefire document identical to the earlier one. The Republic of Vietnam's Nguyen Van Thieu and the Provisional Revolutionary Government of the Republic of South Vietnam's foreign minister, Madame Nguyen Thi Binh, added their signatures.

The agreement lasted only a few months, however. While Army of the Republic of Vietnam and People's Army of Vietnam troops below the seventeenth parallel jockeyed for positions and control of territory, recent scholarship, based on Vietnamese communist documentation, leaves no doubt that the politburo, led by Le Duan and Vo Nguyen Giap, chose to resume war in late March 1973 and made it official, after yet another round of internal debate, in July 1973. Vo Nguyen Giap joined Le Duan to push for a final conventional war to bring down the Republic of Vietnam. Several top-ranking communist leaders in the south had already flaunted the accords, despite the politburo's threat of severe sanctions. But with the party's final decision to go to war, all was forgotten.[45]

The only thing that could now stop the two Vietnams from resuming civil violence was the belief that Nixon would intervene militarily. However, events in Washington rapidly ruled this out. Congress's passing of the War Powers resolution in late 1973 restricted the American president's ability to wage war. Secondly, the Watergate scandal that led to Nixon's resignation in August 1974 suddenly removed him from the picture. Thirdly, in August 1974, Congress slashed military aid to the RV in yet another move to stop an unpopular war and reassert their power as the legislative branch of the American government. Neither the Soviets nor the Chinese communists objected to the Vietnamese communists' plans to take the south by force. And by late 1974, the politburo was convinced that Nixon's replacement, Gerald Ford, would not intervene in their war in Vietnam. This time, they were right. In early 1975, Ford looked on as the Democratic Republic of Vietnam sent another 100,000 People's Army of Vietnam troops pouring across the seventeenth parallel. The Americans began frantically evacuating their personnel. Despite fighting valiantly in some areas and folding lamentably in others, the Republic of Vietnam could not stop the offensive. On 30 April 1975, after brutal battles leading up to Saigon's outskirts, PAVN troops entered and occupied the presidential grounds of the southern capital, ending the most violent Vietnamese civil war in its long, divided history.[46]

CHAPTER 12

CULTURAL CHANGE
IN THE LONG
TWENTIETH CENTURY

I N JANUARY 1968, the famous poet Nha Ca was in Hue to attend her father's funeral when the Tet Offensive struck southern cities. For almost two months, she watched closely as war marched through her hometown. The experience transformed her and her art. She put aside her poetry and, a year later, published *Mourning Headband for Hue*, an emotionally packed account of the suffering the Battle of Hue had inflicted on the city and its people, including the communist massacre of hundreds of civilians. The Democratic Republic of Vietnam condemned her work. The Republic of Vietnam welcomed it. But, like their counterparts in the north, southern authorities soon discovered that controlling culture was no easy matter. In 1971, as the southern republic's war went from bad to worse, Nha Ca began writing the script for the film *Land of Sorrows*, based in part on *Mourning Headband for Hue*. One of modern Vietnam's greatest songwriters, Trinh Cong Son, starred in it. The government banned the film for its pacifism and the communists were no kinder when they took over Saigon in 1975. They sent Nha Ca to a re-education camp and placed a copy of *Mourning Headband* in the Museum of War Crimes.[1]

That almost a half-century of war deeply affected twentieth-century Vietnamese culture, few would disagree. But other forces were at work, too. Nha Ca had after all first distinguished herself by exploring new literary forms in Saigon in the 1950s. In her poetry, novels, and essays, she explored issues such as love, marriage, family, and women's rights. Trinh Cong Son's guitar and songwriting took Vietnamese music in new ways as artistic innovation blossomed. Like Nha Ca's poetry, Son's music often dealt with the role of the individual in society. This was not new. Many artists and intellectuals had been grappling with such questions since the 1930s at least, when a cultural revolution first broke out in Hanoi. What connected these two periods was how the changes generated by colonialism, war, and globalization forced a debate over the freedom of individuals in the making of modern Vietnam. That debate is still going on today.

CULTURAL REVOLUTION IN COLONIAL VIETNAM

Between the Countryside and East Asia

Colonialism has always been a vector of cultural change in Vietnam. Long before the French arrived, a millennium of Chinese rule had deeply influenced Vietnamese civilization. If the Vietnamese rightly celebrate their independence and commemorate the heroes who rose up to oppose foreign invaders, they also know that Chinese imperial rule introduced new forms of dress, art, music, architecture, cuisine, and speech, as well as two character-based writing systems, *Han* ('classical Chinese') and another tailored to spoken Vietnamese called *chu nom*. Similarly, if many Cham, Khmer, and highland peoples celebrate their historic resistance to Vietnamese colonialism, they too know that their colonial encounters created fascinating mixtures of art, language, dress, and technologies. The Viet investiture of the Cham deity Po Nagar near Nha Trang is one famous example among many.[2]

Thanks to the adoption of the character-based writing systems, Vietnamese elite members developed a high level of literacy in areas where the court and its administration operated, as well as in ports, through which texts of all sorts (religious, philosophical, and literary ones) circulated long after the Chinese withdrew. Vietnam's proximity to the Chinese empire guaranteed its higher classes membership in the wider East Asian civilization well into the twentieth century. Inside the country, the Confucian exams and the educational system nourishing them ensured a steady stream of literate elites. In the nineteenth century, around 4,000 men successfully passed the state board examinations. While another 50,000 never actually sat them, their training was nonetheless such that they could read official documents and correspond in classical characters and often in *chu nom*. Several helped channel the rich oral culture in the countryside into a written form, link it to East Asian literary models, and produce unique forms of Vietnamese poetry, folklore, satire, and literature. The Vietnamese national treasure, *The Tale of Kieu*, written by Nguyen Du in 1820, may have owed much to a Chinese literary model, but it tells a Vietnamese story in *chu nom*, one of a woman heroine, Kieu, whose devotion to her family, despite her fall from grace into prostitution, moves Vietnamese readers to this day.[3]

Chinese literature continued to find wide readership in Vietnam. One of the most popular novels in Vietnam was the fourteenth-century Chinese classic, *The Romance of the Three Kingdoms*. While only a minority could actually read it in the original characters, the story, something like the equivalent of the *Tales of Camelot*, percolated into far-flung villages, thanks to gifted storytellers and local mandarins with extraordinary gifts of memory. This in turn fed into a vibrant oral tradition in the countryside that transformed the *Three Kingdoms* into a spoken version of an Asian bestseller. In the twentieth century, *The Tale of Kieu* and *The Romance of the Three Kingdoms* poured off modern printing presses in *quoc ngu* translations, making them among the most widely read stories in Vietnamese literary history. *The Tale of Kieu* has recently been adapted to the big screen, while Chinese adventure stories still appear regularly on Vietnamese television.[4]

Although Vietnam never produced large cities before the mid-twentieth century capable of sustaining commercialized cultural forms such as in Japan and China, court officials, nobles, and kings developed their own musical traditions, such as the *hat tuong or hat boi* (Vietnamese opera) and *ca tru* (chamber music). That is not to say that Vietnamese culture has come exclusively from the court or as a foreign import. The water-puppet culture of the northern countryside has its roots in the tenth-century Red River valley, telling the stories of day-to-day life, and the trials and tribulations of the rural population. By the early nineteenth century, *ca tru* songs were sung in Hanoi teahouses and wine shops and later spread into the countryside. Northern Vietnamese peasants still perform a kind of satirical musical theatre known as *hat cheo*, while an equally popular southern theatrical form, *cai luong*, arrived with ethnic Viet settlers spreading throughout the Mekong delta by the early twentieth century. The people conquered by the Viet—the Cham, Khmer, and highland peoples—possess their own cultural forms, many of which existed long before the Viet moved out of the Red River valley. As we saw in the first chapter, Cham music was a success in the Vietnamese court following their own independence from the Chinese in 939. Several of Vietnam's most stunning architectural sites are to be found in Khmer temples and Cham stupas (holy mounds which are places of worship).

Global Cultural Change in French Vietnam

Although French colonial rule over Vietnam did not last a tenth of that of the Chinese, the French presided over a highly significant period of cultural transformation. They did so by promoting a Romanized written script, introducing a new education system, and stimulating moderate urbanization. They also did so through the introduction of the printing press, print media (newspapers, novels, pamphlets, textbooks), radios, telephones, telegrams, cinema, and new transportation systems. Did this globalization—this accelerated process of integrative, technological change—have to occur via the French colonial connection? No. As many Vietnamese realized at the time, Japan, Turkey, and even the country considered to be their equal, Thailand, had all adopted the changes above to various degrees without becoming formal colonies. The Nguyen royal family or someone else could have presided over such rapid change without the French, relying on foreign models, advisors, investment, finance, and the like.

But the French did colonize Vietnam and in so doing profoundly influenced its culture. Nowhere is this better seen than in the colonial promotion of the Romanized writing system for the Vietnamese national language, *quoc ngu*. Catholic missions had first developed it for spreading the word in the seventeenth century. Colonial authorities mobilized it two centuries later in order to administrate newly conquered Vietnamese territories more efficiently. They terminated the character-based exam system in Cochinchina in the 1860s and in Annam-Tonkin in 1919. What no one could have imagined at the time was the degree to which a new generation of Vietnamese would embrace *quoc ngu*. They saw in it the perfect writing system for capturing the spoken language. It was easier to learn for children and illiterate adults alike. And it was cheaper to print than Chinese characters. Combined, the Romanized language was capable of spreading all sorts of ideas to an unprecedented number of people in record time.

Quoc ngu was such a success that the colonizer's own language, French, never really had a chance, unlike in Algeria and Senegal, where the elites made French theirs. One of France's greatest cultural admirers, the indefatigable Nguyen Van Vinh, grasped this in the early twentieth century, when he quipped that 'the condition of our nation in the future, good or bad, depends on quoc ngu'. The future father of Vietnam, Ho Chi Minh, also understood the power of *quoc ngu* for disseminating new ideas and forms of socio-political organization. Indeed, the growth of all sorts of 'isms' as well as postcolonial state-building depended heavily on the spread of *quoc ngu*, the literacy it generated, and the administrative legibility it allowed. For the first time, the elite and the wider population shared a common written language.[5]

However, the rapid switchover to *quoc ngu* starting at the turn of the twentieth century came at a high price. Unlike the Japanese and Koreans who maintained their character-based writing systems (kanji and hangul), the Vietnamese lost the ability to access directly (i.e., read themselves) their own rich heritage preserved in Han and chu nom, as well as in French. The Romanized system also distanced Vietnamese from the East Asian civilization in which they had moved for centuries. In the early 1900s, the great patriot Phan Boi Chau, might not have spoken Chinese or Japanese, but he could still interact with his East Asian counterparts through a shared ability to read and write classical characters. Few Vietnamese people visiting East Asia today could order from a menu in a Chinese, Korean, or Japanese restaurant without an English translation.[6]

Another factor explaining why the French triggered such important cultural change in Vietnam was the shift from the Sino-Vietnamese educational system to the Franco-Vietnamese one. Worried by the continued pull of East Asia over young minds, from 1905 onward Governor General Paul Beau, followed by Albert Sarraut and others, presided over the creation of a new educational system teaching in *quoc ngu* and, at higher levels, in French, too. By the early 1920s, the Franco-Indigenous educational system had largely replaced the preexisting Confucian one in major urban centers and was moving into rural towns to compete with the remarkably resilient Sino-Vietnamese private schools. In the new system, children of five or six years old could start elementary school, which covered grades one to three, before moving on to primary school (grades four to six) and then into upper primary school (grades seven to ten). Only a small number made it to high school, the lycée, which comprised grades nine to twelve. Colonial authorities opened the French lycées Albert Sarraut in Hanoi and Chasseloup-Laubat in Saigon to qualified Vietnamese, the ticket to advanced studies in France. While the Indochinese University, established in 1906, started off as something of a technical school, by the 1930s it had become much more than that, training the upper and middle-class young in medicine, law, veterinarian science, forestry, and the humanities. Of course when anticolonial trouble arose, as it always did, the French closed classrooms. The Indochinese University shut down after the 1908 revolts; but it reopened and went on to become the Vietnamese National University in 1945 and operates to this day in Hanoi.[7]

Whatever its republican pretensions, French education in colonial Vietnam was not always secular, assimilationist, egalitarian, and much less a nation-building enterprise. Scores of religious schools, Catholic, Protestant, and Buddhist ones, operated quite independently, in contrast to religious school establishments in France. There was no attempt to use education to create a homogeneous Vietnamese identity. By the 1930s, the French had opened classes to train highland bureaucrats and teachers in their own languages or French, but not in Vietnamese. The Ecole Sabatier produced highland nationalists, equipped with their own Romanized languages, who went on to oppose Vietnamese nation-builders. The large Chinese community built their own schools and taught classes in Chinese (and in several dialects).[8]

Moreover, the widespread idea that the Third Republic wanted to turn young Vietnamese schoolchildren into Frenchmen and women is an oversimplification. By the 1930s, Orientalist-minded administrators of the Third Republic sought to use the school to re-root the Vietnamese youth in their patriotic traditions so that they would not become *déracinés* ('uprooted'). Vichy colonial educators followed suit. French schools across Indochina might have taught elite Vietnamese children that their ancestors were the Gauls, but the French were just as content to teach the majority of young Vietnamese in the majority Franco-Vietnamese schools that they were orderly minded Confucians with their roots in the village. And while Vietnamese and French students intermingled and developed friendships in elite lycées, school clubs, and sporting activities, racial lines were real and income disparities overwhelmingly favored the children of the colonizers. Marguerite Duras may have grown up dirt-poor in rural Indochina and transgressed colonial hierarchies in Saigon by dating a rich Vietnamese boy, but her experience was the exception, not the rule.[9]

Nor were Franco-Vietnamese schools democratic in their social reach among the Viet majority. In all, during the interwar period, only 10 percent of the school-aged Vietnamese population actually went to school. Attendance rates were much lower in rural Vietnam, where a lack of financial support forced the poor to make greater sacrifices or forego education for their children altogether, and with it any chance of upward social mobility. The children of the urban Vietnamese bourgeoisie, former mandarins, and new administrators always did better. Better-off and socially well-connected families sent their children to the best schools to take up new positions in the colonial state as lawyers, health officials, nurses, interpreters, telegraph and telephone operators, veterinarians, agricultural specialists, teachers, and journalists. Unsurprisingly, most of modern Vietnam's nationalist elite came from the cities and these better-off classes. Ho Chi Minh and Ngo Dinh Diem were the fortunate sons of mandarins who studied at the National College in Hue, where Paul Beau had first introduced parts of the Franco-Indigenous curriculum.[10]

Despite all these limitations, the colonial educational system still stimulated great change. Although drop-out rates for poorer students were high, the new education system nonetheless spread *quoc ngu* into the countryside and working-class urban neighborhoods, democratizing the written language in ways which the earlier character-based systems had never achieved. General Nguyen Binh had dropped out of school in third grade, but not before learning how to read and write. He had devoured *The Romance of the Three Kingdoms* in his free time as a teenager and went on to wield a pen as effectively as the sword as an adult. Secondly, colonial education fostered the birth of a new urban intelligentsia numbering about 5,000 individuals in the mid-1920s and climbing to 10,000 by the eve of the Second World War. Its members were largely the products of the Franco-Vietnamese schools, at ease in French and *quoc ngu*. They, in turn, could rely on a mainly literate urban population of 550,000 people by 1937 who could buy their newspapers, novels, poems, and paintings. Thirdly, colonial education opened the doors to the other half of the Vietnamese population—women. Vietnamese girls of all ethnicities obtained the right to study, even in the same classrooms with boys, simply unthinkable under the former Sino-Vietnamese system. The daughters of wealthier families always went furthest. Henriette Bui Quang Chieu, the daughter of the Constitutionalist leader, went through this new educational system and on to France to become Vietnam's first woman doctor in 1934. Lastly, through a combination of school teaching, *quoc ngu*, and modern means of communication, more and more Vietnamese discovered for themselves new scientific ideas, technological advances, literary models, poetic forms, and philosophical horizons.[11]

The printing press and newspapers probably did as much as the new education system to clear the way for a cultural *Risorgimento* during the interwar years. The French had first brought printing presses to help run the colonial state in the *quoc ngu* script. Founded in 1865, the government's official bulletin for Cochinchina (the *Gia Dinh Bao*) immediately began circulating decrees, with trusted Vietnamese interpreters and administrative allies at the helm like Truong Vinh Ky and Huynh Tinh Cua. First trained in Catholic missions in Penang, these men also used the government bulletin and the printing press to start publishing on a wide range of sociocultural matters. More presses spread as the colonial state expanded into Annam and Tonkin. Backed by the government, in 1892 François Henri Schneider opened what became the largest private printing and publishing house in Indochina and joined forces with none other than Nguyen Van Vinh to establish a string of newspapers, translations, and diverse publishing projects. Trained as an interpreter and an administrator, Vinh, like so many others, went on to open his own papers like the *Trung Bac Tan Van* (*Northern Central News*) and the *Dong Duong Tap Chi* (*Indochina Review*). While the French helped finance his papers and others in order to detach the Vietnamese from their East Asian cultural orbit and ally them with the French one, Vinh saw in *quoc ngu* print media the chance to unleash a cultural revolution on very Vietnamese terms. Keenly interested in technology, he began pushing ideas first promoted by the leaders of the Tonkin Free School (Dong Kinh Nghia Thuc). Like Phan Chu Trinh, he wanted to do away with Chinese characters, literary allusions, syntax, and what he saw as an embarrassingly outdated Vietnamese tradition and cultural practices. He championed the liberation of the individual from the suffocating hold of Confucianism. He translated scores of articles and books into *quoc ngu*, including the first translations of *The Tale of Kieu* and *The Romance of the Three Kingdoms*, as well as Jonathan Swift's *Gulliver's Travels* and Victor Hugo's *Les Miserables*.[12]

Like the internet today, it is hard to underestimate the importance of the development of modern print media for spreading ideas to larger numbers of people at higher rates of speed. By the mid-1920s, several *quoc ngu* papers had daily print runs of 15,000 copies. The woman's journal, *Phu Nu Tan Van* (*Modern Women's News*), sold 8,500 copies daily between 1929 and 1931. And lest we forget, these papers passed from one reader to another. Actual readerships were always higher than the number of copies sold. Between 1923 and 1944, of the 10,000 published titles on official record, 20 percent dealt with religious topics (prayer books, rituals, bibles), 24 percent were novels and short stories, 19 percent covered traditional literature, folktales, poetry and satire, and 6 percent related to theatre, especially the southern form called *cai luong*. Little wonder that Vietnamese, like the Marxist lexicographer, Dao Duy Anh, no longer had to go abroad to China, Japan, or France to tap into the revolutionary ideas moving across the globe.

Much of it was at his fingertips in *quoc ngu*, French, or in the Chinese papers he could read and buy in Hanoi and Saigon. And like the Vietnamese communist party's security services battling the web today, the French colonial police censored written material heavily, and tightly controlled the licensing of papers and presses, but they could not stop the accelerating globalization of new ideas of which the French themselves were as much a part as their colonies were.[13]

Religious leaders also realized the power of what the French had done by pushing *quoc ngu*, widening education, and introducing the printing press and newspaper. They probably started promoting literacy 'among the masses' a decade before urban-based nationalists launched the Association for the Dissemination of Quoc Ngu (Hoi Truyen Ba Chu Quoc Ngu) in 1938. Unlike the Indian National Congress, however, Vietnamese bourgeois parties like the Constitutionalists never truly grasped the need to use *quoc ngu* print media to reach into the countryside (where 90 percent of the population still lived in 1945). Their newspaper, *La Tribune indochinoise* (*Indochinese Tribune*), never appeared in *quoc ngu*.

Despite attacks from Phan Chu Trinh, Nguyen Van Vinh, and younger cultural militants, Confucianism experienced a revival via the print media. Major cultural figures of the time such as Tran Trong Kim, Pham Quynh, and Phan Khoi, as well as reform-minded mandarins about whom we know less, vigorously debated about Confucianism, its role in Vietnam in the past, how to retailor it to the needs of the country in the rapidly changing present or whether to discard it entirely. Pham Quynh saw in a renovated Confucianism the chance to remake the monarchy up above and hold the family together down below. Through both, he hoped to preserve the country's social fabric in the face of communism, individualism, and rapid Westernization. Always fearful of Vietnamese nationalism, even among their closest collaborators, the French did little to help their bourgeois allies transform Confucianism into a unifying ideology as the President of China, Chiang Kai-shek, was doing with the 'New Life Movement'. In 1934, when Pasquier ended the first Bao Dai solution (see chapters 4 and 5), he also closed Pham Quynh's intellectual journal, *Nam Phong* (*Southern Wind*).

Others, like the inimitable Nguyen Van To or Tran Trong Kim, saw in reformed Confucianism an East Asian humanism capable of reconciling the community and the individual in a new national form. Man was perfectible and Confucianism was not necessarily a conservative ideology, incapable of change. Nguyen Van To may have dressed in Confucian garb and worked at the Ecole française d'Extrême-Orient on ancient history, but he was also deeply involved in his present, organizing *quoc ngu* campaigns in the 1930s, serving as a municipal advisor for Hanoi, and writing prolifically in intellectual journals in the early 1940s. He showed no interest in Vichy's cultural politics during the Second World War and had no faith in the French resurrection of the very monarchy they had killed, repeatedly. He joined Ho Chi Minh's nationalist government in 1945, helped to develop its educational service and literacy campaigns, and served in the first National Assembly. If young Westernized Vietnamese had lampooned his 'traditionalism' in the 1930s, this fiercely anticolonialist Confucian humanist (who was the first to condemn the French use of torture in 1946) commanded only respect from 1945. Sadly, he disappeared during the French attempt to wipe out Ho's government in late 1947.

Despite modest urbanization across the whole of French Vietnam, it was Hanoi and Saigon that were the sites where Westernization, consumerism, and cultural change occurred most intensely. Bicycles and tramways, followed by automobiles and buses, transformed the way people moved about. Rubber-wheeled rickshaws first imported from Japan became a part of everyday urban life for Europeans and Asians alike. Streetlights went up while sewer systems went in. Cafés, theatres, concert halls, botanical gardens, and cinemas appeared, offering films in French, Vietnamese, Chinese, and even English as Hollywood eyed a global market. Charlie Chaplin visited the colony in the 1930s to the thrill of all. European trends in food, drink, and medicines seeped imperceptibly into local practices. The Vietnamese words for butter—'*bo*' and bread—'*banh*' derive from the French words, *beure* and *pain*. The delicious Vietnamese sandwich, *banh mi*, owes much to the French *baguette*. By the 1920s, taking walks, gardening, attending the theatre, and creating clubs seemed only natural for bourgeois Vietnamese and the fashionable youth who could afford it. Even the less fortunate could catch a glimpse of the big screen, though they had to watch from special, partitioned sections, known as *les avancées*.[14]

Vietnamese sartorial tastes Westernized during the colonial period, as wealthy men put on sports coats and buttoned shirts and women slipped into dresses and even wore shorts as sports took off and physical education became mandatory in schools. Tennis and football (soccer) became Vietnamese passions and remain so to this day. Nguyen Cat Tuong (or 'Le Mur') took fashion trends in Europe and combined them with earlier Vietnamese styles of dress like the *ao ngu than* ('five-paneled body gown') to come up with such original creations as the *ao dai*. This 'long dress' falls elegantly over the woman's entire body, descending from a snugly buttoned collar at the top to a more loosely fitted lower robe flowing over the waist, down the legs, and to the ankles. While the *ao dai* first took off in Tonkin, southern women in Saigon were the ones to make it famous and those Vietnamese who were overseas after 1975 ensured that it remained a symbol of national elegance until it made a comeback in post-communist Vietnam. As Le Mur explained his approach: 'In the old days people dressed basically to conceal their bodies, so they always presented a baggy appearance. But now one should dress so the body is present in a natural manner, or sometimes to modify it a bit so it appears more flowing and graceful'.[15]

None of these sartorial trends moved in straight lines, though. Well into the twentieth century, Vietnamese officials and even bourgeois men in 'the more Westernized' Cochinchina could slip into the traditional collar-buttoned tunics and hats when it suited them or the occasion. Nor did trends simply flow 'out' from the metropole to the colonies, but also the other way round, as Vietnamese influences in French fashion, cuisine, and art demonstrate to this day. Asian influences within Vietnam never disappeared. Indian-styled garments continued to find customers in Saigon and Hanoi, among both the Indian community and the Vietnamese. The writer, Vu Trong Phung, loved to sport his Indian-made shirt. The southern Vietnamese often relaxed in Cham or Khmer-inspired *sarongs* at home. While the Vietnamese bourgeoisie may have used Western cutlery as a social signifier when eating à la française, rich and poor alike continued to use chopsticks, eat white rice from a bowl, and enjoy a *pho* soup as they had for centuries. Chinese and Vietnamese cuisine remained as popular as ever and won over many in the French community. Smoking Western-brand cigarettes certainly took off, but many (mainly northern) Vietnamese men still inhale a potent type of nicotine tobacco through bamboo water-pipes, a practice collectively known as *thuoc lao*. My first Vietnamese language instructor brought his water-pipe all the way from Hanoi to Dekalb, Illinois, in the late 1980s. 'I have never missed anyone the way I miss *thuoc lao*' is how one folk song describes its power. My instructor would have agreed entirely. While urban women broke with the practice of chewing betel and areca nuts in favor of cultivating the pearly white teeth they saw in countless advertisements and beauty magazines in the 1920s and 1930s, these nuts still find their place in marriage celebrations, New Year festivities, and as offerings on altars dedicated to deceased family members.[16]

The Cultural Revolution of the 1930s: The Self-reliance Movement[17]

The renowned scholar of Vietnam and China, Alexander Woodside, is right to insist upon the importance for the twentieth-century Vietnamese of finding new ideologies and forms of social organizations which were capable of reconciling the individual with a society that French colonialism and globalizing forces had shaken so deeply. Some sought to find new forms of community along political lines, with modern nationalism never far from their minds. Communism and republicanism attracted others. Religion, millenarianism, and secret societies offered hope for just as many, while charities, sports, and professional associations worked for others. We have touched upon these questions elsewhere in this book. Here we need to add another 'ism', that of individualism, for it was at the heart of the cultural revolution that burst forth in Hanoi in the early 1930s, shifted to Saigon in the 1950s and 1960s, and continues today.

In its simplest form, individualism emphasizes the independence, self-reliance, and liberty of a human being to determine his or her destiny. Freedom of choice and freedom of action serve as guiding principles. Individualism does not necessarily lead to anarchy, but it does require social, religious, and political systems to respect a human being's freedom of choice as long as this person does not harm the liberty of others. Individualism is related to humanism, which stresses the individual worth of human beings as well as their ability to improve themselves and society through rational thought instead of blind trust in religious faith. However, humanism and individualism are not the unique products of the European renaissance. Confucianism in East Asia also stresses the perfectibility of man and does so in secular, rational ways respectful of the individual.[18]

Younger Vietnamese coming of age in the interwar period, however, latched on hardest to Western individualism. Most were largely uninterested in the humanist, reformist-minded take on Confucianism which Nguyen Van To and Tran Trong Kim advocated. By the 1930s, thanks to their mastery of French and *quoc ngu*, young Vietnamese had access to the canon on Western individualism that had spread to East Asia by the early twentieth century. They could read it in French or in *quoc ngu* translations. But there was also a Chinese connection: because many of these Western educated Vietnamese heralded from mandarin families, many could read Chinese characters and would have been able to follow the New Cultural Movement young Chinese had initiated after the First World War. One of the staunchest defenders of human liberty in Vietnam, Phan Khoi, closely

read the works of China's greatest humanist writer and cultural revolutionary, Lu Xun.[19]

Individualism provided young Vietnamese with a new foundation for
creating a culture in which the *tôi* (the 'I', or the 'me') could find his or her
rightful place in the family, society, and world. Confucianism, this generation claimed, had impeded the emergence of individual freedom and in
so doing blocked the modernization of the country and its ability to exist
on an equal footing with the West. Only the Vietnamese youth could lead
this cultural revolution, for their parents, in their view, had failed miserably.
This was certainly the conclusion Lu Xun's generation had reached in the
wake of China's humiliation at the Versailles Peace Conference in 1919. In
his condemnations of Franco-Vietnamese collaboration, Nguyen An Ninh
drew a similar parallel for Vietnamese youth. In 1922, he told young Vietnamese that change could only come about with the liberation of the individual from the suffocating hold of the old order:

> You must struggle against your milieu, against the family that paralyzes your
> efforts, against this vulgar society weighing you down, against the narrow,
> hampering prejudices that stop at every turn your actions, against ignoble,
> humiliating, terribly humiliating and lackluster ideals which lower our race
> with every passing day [. . .] The greatest idealists have always counseled
> those who want to follow them to leave 'the house of their fathers'. And
> we, too, the youth today, must also leave the house of our fathers. We must
> leave our family, free ourselves from this society, separate from our country
> [. . .] That is to say that once we, the Annamese who have been given the
> chance to be conscious of our own worth, the highest possible form of
> worth being that of the individual and the law governing the world, then
> we will return to Annam.[20]

Of course individualism was political. Nguyen An Ninh's efforts to promote individual liberties went hand in hand with national liberation and
landed him in jail on several occasions. The young leader of the Vietnamese Nationalist Party, Nguyen Thai Hoc, shared the republican dream. The
French smashed the VNQDD's uprising in Tonkin in 1930 and executed
Hoc, suppressing a series of peasant revolts concentrated in Annam at the
same time. The severity of this colonial repression was such that it shifted
radical politics to Cochinchina for the rest of the decade. Given the more
liberal press laws in the Cochinchinese colony, Ninh would militate in favor

of political pluralism and workers' rights in the pages of *La Lutte* in Saigon until his final arrest on the eve of the Second World War.

Realizing that politically minded papers in Annam-Tonkin didn't last very long and in the wake of this repression, many young Vietnamese in the north focused their attention on promoting a cultural revolution. Leading the charge was Nguyen Tuong Tam. He joined forces with a core group of like-minded intellectuals, including his brothers, Nguyen Tuong Long (Hoang Dao) and Nguyen Tuong Lan (Thach Lam) and a close friend, Tran Khanh Giu, better known as Khai Hung. Tam adopted an appropriate *nom de plume*, Nhat Linh ('Free Spirit'). The children of former mandarin families, they were all highly educated, perfectly at ease in French and *quoc ngu* (and could read Chinese). Khai Hung had graduated from the Lycée Albert Sarraut, Nhat Linh from the Lycée du Protectorat. The latter initially joined the colonial civil service, but his love of literature and the newspaper world proved too strong. He left for France in the late 1920s, where he pursued his literary interests, discovered the power of humor, and expanded his knowledge of the print media. Famous for its biting satire, defense of individual rights, and state-of-the-art cartoons, the French weekly, *Le canard enchaîné* (*The Chained Duck*), found an enthusiastic admirer in him, his entourage, and a wide variety of Vietnamese readers.

Starting in 1932, this core group established the Literary Self-strengthening Movement. It opened its doors to like-minded intellectuals, artists, writers, poets, and cartoonists. They established two equally notable *quoc ngu* newspapers to administer their assault on Confucian tradition and in defense of the individual—*Phong Hoa* (*Culture*) and *Ngay Nay* (*These Days*). From 1932 to 1940, the editors wrote and commissioned scores of articles on the need to remake Vietnamese culture, overturn Confucianism, promote Westernization in its place, break with antiquated cultural practices, and liberate the individual through poetry, literature, art, film, dress, sports, and the like. Khai Hung put it best when he affirmed that the 'individual is in the process of achieving liberation, of breaking with the oppressive structures that had, by fooling him, led him down the wrong path [. . .] the individual must decide for himself'.[21]

Irreverence flew off the pages of the first issues of *Phong Hoa* and *Ngay Nay* as TLVD's soldiers mobilized. Never had satire and humor been used with such devastating effect. Ly Toet, the woefully outdated Confucian, was an immensely popular figure for caricature, appearing in issue after issue. He served as the visual whipping boy for the group's attack on all that was outmoded. The Tu Luc Van Doan ripped into those whom they judged 'un-modern', wounding egos as they did so and sparking some lively literary debates. As long as satirists steered clear of politics, colonial authorities, and the monarchy, French censors focused their attention elsewhere.[22]

To defeat the Confucian tradition, Vietnamese writers focused their novels on individuals trapped by the oppressive hierarchical 'system'—tyrannical mothers-in-law, arranged marriages, and power-hungry mandarins. Already, by 1925, Hoang Ngoc Phach had latched on to the theme of 'true love' in Vietnam's first modern novel, *To Tam*, in order to bring to life vividly the destructive nature of arranged marriages on individual lives and suggest why cultural change was indispensable to Vietnam's ability to enter the 'modern world'. Phach has his beautiful heroine, To Tam, face the choice of staying with her true love and being happy or bowing to her parents' wishes that she marry another and thereby strengthen the family's future fortunes. But Phach, in a twist, offers To Tam a way out. Rather than accepting her Confucian fate and with it all chance of happiness, she escapes her dilemma through suicide, the ultimate expression of personal liberty. This was not *The Tale of Kieu*.[23]

Other Literary Self-strengthening Movement writers followed suit. In his popular novel, *The Midst of Spring*, Khai Hung used true love to unite his young couple, Loc and Mai, in order to set up the opposition between individual choice and a traditional culture's oppression. Loc's family forbids his marriage to Mai. His love for this woman cannot not be allowed to trump the strategic need to unite him with a provincial mandarin's daughter. Children were to obey their parents; they did not choose freely. Filial piety, or *hieu*, insured order and stability within the family unit. In terms that would have drawn approval from many of 'the older generation' in Europe as well as Asia, Loc's mother told her defiant son: 'You're not satisfied, but I am satisfied. You must know that in marriage, it's essential to look for a house of equal status. Do you intend to force me into a relationship with a bunch of country bumpkins? [. . .] You're a boy without *hieu*, do you hear me!'[24]

Nhat Linh launched a similar offensive in *Breaking the Ties*. Once again, a young, beautiful woman serves as the protagonist to frame the opposition between arranged marriage and the Confucian order on the one hand and free love and individualism on the other. Her name is Loan. She falls deeply in love with one man, but cannot pursue her heart, as her family requires her to marry another, a bad man, and all in the name of *hieu*. Loan accepts her fate, but in so doing descends into a nightmare as her mother-in-law and husband make her life a living hell. Rather than producing order and harmony, Loan's adherence to *hieu* produces the opposite effect. While her husband cheats on her, her mother-in-law covers for him and exploits her at every turn. When Loan finally comes before a jury on murder charges trumped up by her mother-in-law, Nhat Linh can finally step in as the defense lawyer explaining to his readers that this case is part of a bigger problem: 'Vietnamese society today is not the Vietnamese society of the nineteenth century. The Vietnamese family cannot be left intact to be exactly like the Vietnamese families of previous centuries. In all the countries of the Far East—Japan, China, Thailand and especially in China, the original ancestor of Asian civilization, the status of the family is not as it was before'. Nhat Linh sums up his defense of Loan: 'These people who have absorbed the new culture have been imbued with ideas of humanity and individual freedom, so quite naturally, they seek to escape from that system. This desire is very legitimate [. . .]'. The jury declares her not guilty. She, and the generation she represents, could finally walk free.[25]

Poets also broke with Confucian social constraints and Sino-Vietnamese literary forms that had governed poetry in the East Asian civilizational world for centuries. Several (but not all) started to use *tôi*, the 'I' personal pronoun, in order to free up the expression of the individual self from the oppression of family hierarchies and conventional social relations. True love again served as a popular model for setting up the opposition between 'old' and 'new', 'traditional' and 'modern'. Phan Khoi drew the immediate praise of TLVD poets with the publication of his iconoclastic, free verse poem in 1932 called 'Old Love'. In a few beautiful lines, he evokes the chance meeting of the two lovers long after their decision to part ways in order to accept their arranged marriages:

> Twenty-four years later . . .
> A chance encounter far away . . .
> Both heads had turned to silver;
> Had they not known each other well,
> Might they not have passed unknown?
> An old affair was recalled, no more.
> It was just a glance in passing!
>
> . . . There still are corners to the eyes.[26]

Some of the TLVD's best poets, Luu Trong Lu, The Lu, Huy Can, Che Van Lien, Xuan Dieu, Hoai Thanh, and others inside and outside the group joined in the battle against Sino-Vietnamese poetic forms in favor of free verse, Western models, and large doses of individualism. This flowering became widely known as the New Poetry Movement. Xuan Dieu was one of the movement's stars. The son of a schoolteacher, he published over 400 poems and many essays and literary critiques. His artistic originality springs forth from the first lines of his poem, 'Still Too Far Away':

> The other day you stayed too far away from me;
> So I asked you to move over a bit closer.
> You inched over closer, but I demurred.
> To be a good girl you inched still closer.
> As I was boiling over, in haste with a smile
> You scooted closer, soothing, 'Here I am!'
> I brightened up, then scowled at once
> For I thought, you were still too far away.[27]

Xuan Dieu pushed the envelope like few others at the time. In 'Boys' Love', he wrote approvingly of the homoerotic love between the French romantic poets, Rimbaud and Verlaine: 'Drunk with exotic verse and with passion, / Defying worn paths and old ways'. His former classmate from Hanoi, Huy Can, joined him in taking Vietnamese poetry in new ways. Their homosexuality not only raised Confucian eyebrows, but the communists later forced Xuan Dieu to 'correct' his sexuality through intense 'rectification' that almost destroyed him.[28]

The creation of the Academy of Fine Arts in Hanoi in 1925 introduced Western notions of art and their accompanying techniques, including oil painting to Vietnam. Victor Tardieu, the academy's first director, was determined 'to transform the indigenous craftsmen into professional artists'. Vietnamese graduates of the academy such as Nguyen Gia Tri, Bui Xuan Phai, To Ngoc Van, and others, borrowed Western techniques, oil painting in particular, and often imitated French models. But they also adapted them to explore very Vietnamese problems, such as individualism, love, gender differences, nationalism, politics, and the opposition between 'tradition' and 'modernity'. To Ngoc Van contributed regularly to the Literary Self-strengthening Movement's newspapers. Like many poets and writers, several painters trained during the colonial period put their art in the service of national liberation after 1945. Some joined the communists and mobilized their art as part of a wider transformation of state and society. To Ngoc Van led many graduates of the Fine Arts Academy into the resistance. He died of the injuries he sustained during the Battle of Dien Bien Phu and is today considered one of the country's greatest heroes for his sacrifice. However, Bui Xuan Phai's call for artistic freedom in the wake of that historic victory landed him in trouble with the communists who were intent on defining and controlling art. He lost his teaching position in the School of Fine Arts and had to wait until the 1980s to display his work in public again.[29]

Cultural Revolution: Widening and Humanizing Vietnamese Society

As important as the artists of the Literary Self-strengthening Movement were, they cannot serve to sum up all the cultural transformations occurring in Vietnam at this time. Many derided the literary movement for its unbridled romanticism and obsession with Western modernity when pressing social and political issues clamored for attention. What about the downtrodden, the working class, the domestics, the faceless people without whom the modernization of the cities would not have got very far? What about the peasants and agricultural laborers, who, collectively, constituted 90 percent of Vietnam's population? The advent of the leftwing Popular Front government (1936–8) reinforced such social concerns in literary circles, as did loosening constraints on publishing in the north. Vo Nguyen Giap and Truong Chinh took advantage of this to publish their treatise called 'The Peasant Question' in 1938. Southern communists and Trotskyists associated with *La Lutte* published investigations of working-class life. To be fair, the TLVD's leaders had also ventured into politics and begun to move their urban cultural revolution in more social and rural directions. The Literary Self-strengthening Movement's authors were by no means insensitive to the rural life and its problems. They investigated dire peasant poverty, rural indebtedness, and illiteracy.[30]

Some of the best social realism, however, came from remarkable, independent journalists like Nguyen Hong, Nguyen Cong Hoan, and Tam Lang. During the 1930s, Tam Lang moved among the down-and-out of Hanoi. He described in memorable prose the poor, their lives, their hopes, their trials, and, sometimes, their tribulations. He disguised himself as a rickshaw driver for months in order to show to his urban, mainly middle-class readers the destinies of thousands of their compatriots trudging along everyday like animals. 'Society is to blame', Tam Lang concluded his classic piece of reportage, 'I Pulled a Rickshaw': 'Yes, you and me, all of us are equally at fault [. . .]. To lower a powerless person from his status as a human being to that of a horse, to give him two wooden shafts and say "I will sit up here while you pull me" is the same as saying "You are not a human being"'. Tam Lang pointed out that the Human Rights League (Ligue des droits de l'homme) had tried to prevent the use of rickshaws during the Colonial Exhibition in France in 1931. Why could the Vietnamese not do this in their own society, he asked? At the heart of the question was once again the matter of individual rights.[31]

Some of the most sophisticated, penetrating, and original literature came from the burning pen of one eccentric, opium-addicted gadfly named Vu Trong Phung. His articles, investigative reports, and novels covered topics ranging from poverty, prostitution, and disease to sports, fashion, and love. He could move from biting social satire to outrageous humor in the space of a few lines. The originality of his social commentary comes through brilliantly in 'Luc Xi' ('Dispensary'), his newspaper column about venereal disease and prostitution in colonial Hanoi, as it does in his satirical and often side-splitting take on modern bourgeois society in his story *Dumb Luck*. Like Tam Lang, Vu Trong Phung investigated the individual lives of those who had never received any attention. He also knew the poor because he moved among them. He despised armchair social scientists, especially those who intellectualized about these people and their societies without knowing them: 'A rickshaw puller knows all the cruelty of human beings far better than a scholar. A room boy knows more about the debauchery of humanity than a surgeon. A servant understands more clearly the behavior of human beings than a realist writer'. He ends his social-realist reportage on 'household servants', by turning the tables on his bourgeois readers and asking them to 'investigate' themselves. The Vietnamese Communist Party later banned his books, writing him off as a depraved mind. He was probably twentieth-century Vietnam's greatest literary artist and social critic. A brilliant mind, he died in 1939 at the age of twenty-seven.[32]

One of the biggest changes in individual liberties to occur in colonial Vietnam was the expansion of women's rights. While many have insisted that Vietnam differed culturally from China in its empowerment of women down through the centuries, recent research suggests a less optimistic picture. The Le law code did allow couples to separate, but divorce had to be mutually consented to. If the husband disagreed, there was no divorce.

Legally, the husband, followed by the son, remained in control of land and no real estate could change hands without male consent. Inheritance was legally stacked in favor of men. The Gia Long law code of the early nineteenth century reversed many of the advantages women had enjoyed under the earlier one, while the Confucian-based examination system codified inequality by banning women from undertaking the examinations to become civil servants, and thus from entry into positions of power.[33]

The ending of the examination system in Cochinchina in the 1860s and Annam-Tonkin in 1919 and the widening of the colonial education system to include Vietnamese girls stimulated important changes in gender relations and empowered women in notable ways. Following Meiji Japan's example, the reform-minded creators of the Tonkin Free School allowed women to join them. By opening its doors to women, the Franco-Vietnamese schools had the biggest impact of all by increasing their literacy. This was revolutionary, for few Vietnamese women had ever had the chance to master classical characters or participate in the East Asian cultural world, an all-male club. Literacy in *quoc ngu* and, to a lesser degree, in French opened up new realms of knowledge, offered new career tracks, and allowed women to voice and promote their interests in unprecedented ways. Many put pen to paper as journalists, poets, writers, and newspaper editors. Southern journalists led the way in widely read women's dailies like the *Phu Nu Tan Van* (*Women's Modern News*) and the *Phu Nu Thoi Dam* (*Women's Modern Times*). They attacked Confucian constraints on women's rights in the family and wider society. Articles discussed whether widows should be allowed to re-marry, spouses to divorce, and polygamy to continue. Women's associations, charities, and self-help groups multiplied during the interwar period. Groups for girl scouts appeared, joining the associations for boy scouts already in operation. As mandatory physical education spread in schools, young women joined their male counterparts in exercising their bodies. Madame Hoang Xuan Han pioneered the development of women's tennis in Vietnam. Others entered into revolutionary politics and paid dearly for their activities. The French executed the female communist leader Nguyen Thi Minh Khai. One of the best historians of Vietnam today, Professor Hue-Tam Ho Tai, has provided us with a riveting account of the trials and tribulations of revolutionary women in the person of her aunt, Bao Luong.[34]

However, the liberation bourgeois women experienced in urban areas was not necessarily replicated in the countryside, where male mandarins and rich landowners could run roughshod over women's rights. Many abusive mandarins had several wives and subjected them to terrible existences. Rape went largely unpunished. The Literary Self-strengthening Movement's Khai Hung wrote searing critiques of such matters. Colonial law could do little about these abuses of women given that the protectorate status of Annam and Tonkin kept the Gia Long code in operation there until the late 1930s. The termination of the Confucian exam system did little to change village politics and councils, which remained largely in the hands of men under the French.[35]

Gender equality for French settler women was hardly better. A French woman could not run for office in the Cochinchinese Colonial Council. There was never one female French commissioner at any level of the Indochinese bureaucracy during the entire colonial period. The director of the Ecole française d'Extrême-Orient under Vichy, Georges Coedes, used Vichy's anti-Semitic laws to get rid of the only female member of this organization, and a very illustrious one at that, Suzanne Karpelès. And French women, like their colonized sisters, only received the right to vote in France after the Second World War.[36]

CULTURAL REVOLUTION IN POSTCOLONIAL VIETNAMS: WAR, THE STATE AND INDIVIDUAL FREEDOM

Decades of war deeply affected Vietnamese culture and individual liberties. Between 1940, when the Japanese began occupying Tonkin, and 1991, when the Paris peace accords finally ended the conflicts over Indochina, war mobilized, politicized, and militarized Vietnamese culture as a wide range of actors went to battle over the country's soul. The French fought hard to maintain a colonial culture against those who sought to replace it with a nationalist one. The Japanese tried to force their own imperial propaganda upon Indochina during the Second World War, before the Cold War's superpowers, the United States, the Soviet Union, and China next tried to export their own cultural diplomacies in Vietnam. It worked the other way too. Although Ho Chi Minh and Ngo Dinh Diem presided over the nationalization of their respective states within Vietnam, they also tried to adapt foreign ideologies to local needs. Ho's entourage adapted a foreign Sino-Soviet communist ideology to the north while Diem's family tried to tailor French Personalism to the social realities in the south. All of this built on earlier strata of intertwined cultural, religious, and ideological adaptations discussed earlier on in this book, reaching back for centuries in the form of all sorts of 'isms'.[37]

The Poverty of French Colonial Culture

From start to finish, colonial culture was very much an official enterprise, designed to legitimate French conquest and rule to both the vanquished Vietnamese and the French people in France, who cared very little about their empire. This lack of interest at home was such that the French government brought the colonies to the metropolis in a series of colonial exhibitions, culminating in the extraordinary reproduction of the French empire in miniature outside Paris in 1931. Colonial culture also evolved in reaction to external competition for Vietnamese hearts and minds. If Paul Beau established the Indochinese University in Hanoi in 1908, he did so because Vietnamese students were going abroad to study in Tokyo rather than Paris. Other sets of colonizers asserted their influence too. The Japanese, for example, tried to replace the Chinese at the center of a centuries-old East Asian civilization and were often in a more favorable position than the French in their ability to influence Asian opinions. The Japanese defeat of the Russian navy in 1905 only reinforced the sense of their might and thus their potential to influence the Vietnamese, as did their own colonial propaganda machine. In the lead-up to the First World War the Germans also expounded their propaganda throughout Asia (in Chinese and English). And the Americans were in there, too. French security services carefully monitored American Protestant missionaries in Vietnam during the 1920s, while censors tried to limit news of Washington's creation of the Commonwealth of the Philippines in 1935 (as this was the Philippines' first step toward full independence). All of these factors led the French to accelerate their own propaganda efforts. Indeed, the origins of the French *francophonie* project are not to be found only in the decolonization of the 1960s, as is so often claimed, but rather in this earlier inter-imperial cultural competition.[38]

The outbreak of the Second World War in China in 1937 and the Japanese entry into Tonkin in September 1940 brought this competition directly to Indochina on unfavorable terms for the French. The humiliating defeat of the Third Republic in June 1940, followed by France's official collaboration with Hitler and condominium with Germany's Asian ally, Japan, cost the French authorities dearly in the eyes of the Vietnamese. Determined to maintain the fiction of Franco-Vietnamese collaboration, the new Governor General Jean Decoux reactivated the cultural front through the expansion of youth mobilization campaigns, sporting events, and by allying local patriotisms with Vichy's *Révolution nationale*. Even the leader of Vichy France, Marshall Philippe Pétain, found himself dressed in full Vietnamese Confucian garb on the front page of one Vietnamese paper in 1943. Missing from this return to the past, however, was the colonial emperor Bao Dai and the very Vietnamese elites who had transformed culture and with it individual liberty in such profound ways during the interwar period.

Focused on more pressing matters during the Second World War, the Japanese were content to rule Indochina indirectly through the French and accorded the French governor general Jean Decoux a free hand on the cultural front in exchange for his continued political, economic, and administrative collaboration with them. However, this did not stop the Japanese from promoting their own imperial ideology and propaganda within Vietnam through the creation of cultural associations, newspapers, and limited study abroad. While Decoux monopolized the mobilization of urban youth, the Japanese launched their cultural offensive on the religious front in rural areas of Vietnam, mainly among the followers of the Cao Dai and Hoa Hao Buddhist faiths in the south.[39]

The thinness of Vichy's colonial culture was laid bare for all to see on 9 March 1945, when the Japanese finally overthrew the French and with them, their colonial state. Many Vietnamese lost no time developing what had been in the making for decades—a Vietnamese national culture. Thanks to print media, the expansion of *quoc ngu*, and the access to globalizing ideas that had been developing for half a century, thousands of Vietnamese began decolonizing their culture with astonishing alacrity. Newspapers, radios, telegraphs, and photos spread the news of the end of eighty years of French rule. Colonial monuments came tumbling down. Street names changed from French colonial ones to those of Vietnamese national heroes, as composers scrambled to create a national anthem. Nguyen Thai Hoc, the leader of the Vietnamese nationalist party whom the French had guillotined in 1931 for demanding an independent republic, finally received a carefully ritualized resurrection and public homage in June 1945. The photographer Vo An Ninh captured these events on the covers of the *Trung Bac Tan Van* (*Northern Central News*).

Upon taking over a few months later, Ho Chi Minh continued in the same vein, saluting young scouts, solemnly visiting national shrines, and

17. A Cao Dai temple.

18. Saigon Cathedral.

19. The Battle of Dien Bien Phu, 1954.

20. Vietminh medical soldiers at Dien Bien Phu.

21. French troops at Dien Bien Phu, 23 March 1954.

22. Vietnamese child commandos.

23. Independence celebrations in Hanoi, September 1954.

24. Ngo Dinh Diem at a denunciation of communism ceremony, 28 November 1955.

25. A Buddhist monk burns himself to death in protest of government discrimination, Saigon, 11 June 1963.

26. A helicopter picks up a wounded South Vietnamese soldier, Hiep Duc, South Vietnam, November 1965.

27. US marines in the jungle, 4 November 1968.

28. Vietcong soldiers on an abandoned US tank during the Tet Offensive.

29. Captured South Vietnamese soldiers and civilians, Saigon, 30 April 1975.

30. Chinese troops entering Vietnam, 1979.

31. Vietnamese boat people
awaiting rescue in the
South China Sea, May 1984.

32. The Ho Chi Minh Mausoleum, Hanoi.

taking charge of a whole host of cultural associations, presses, newspapers, schools, and radios. He had competition from non-communist nationalists, however, especially when well-known individuals like Nhat Linh and Khai Hung returned to Hanoi determined to promote a nationalist culture as well as an anticommunist one. Since the start of the Pacific War, these men had joined Nguyen Thai Hoc's party, the Vietnamese Nationalist Party, and now opened a new paper in Hanoi, *Viet Nam*. Heated exchanges broke out as Vietnamese nationalists argued over the nature of postcolonial Vietnam. Meanwhile, colonial war spread across the south as Charles de Gaulle's troops began reconquering the Mekong delta in late 1945. From the start, all three sides—communists, nationalists, and colonialists—mobilized, politicized, and militarized culture like never before, via print culture, cinema, and the airwaves.[40]

Cultural Revolution, War and the Democratic Republic of Vietnam (1945-75)

The outbreak of full-scale hostilities in Hanoi in late 1946 between the French and the Vietnamese saw the French embark upon a bloody war of colonial conquest. French artillery and bombers reduced much of the old quarter in Hanoi to rubble, sending the population fleeing into the countryside. Unlike in the nineteenth century, however, foreign correspondents and diplomats monitored this second conquest closely. And despite their efforts to shape public opinion by emphasizing the three pillars of the 'colonial gesture' (the creation of hospitals, schools, and roads), and the 'horrors' committed by the other side, the French press and propaganda services could never stop their critics, not even those coming from inside the colonial office, from challenging the premises of colonial ideology and war. In 1949, the head of the Colonial Academy in Paris, Paul Mus, dropped a bombshell when he published a series of articles condemning the army's use of torture and calling for French negotiations with Ho Chi Minh. He lost his job and ended up in Yale, where he helped get Southeast Asian studies off the ground and influenced the antiwar movement in the United States. One Frances FitzGerald met him there. Her Pulitzer Prize–winning attack on the American war in Vietnam, *Fire in the Lake*, is dedicated to Mus. Emile de Antonio's *In the Year of the Pig*, nominated for an Oscar for 'best documentary feature' in 1969, owes much to Mus, one of the few French intellectuals to have spoken out against the First Indochina War. In this film, one can hear de Antonio's French Orientalist 'expert' defend Ho

Chi Minh passionately, insisting that he was the rightful heir to a timeless Confucian tradition and resistance culture.[41]

Culture remained a battlefield too, because French colonial conquest was never complete during the entire First Indochina War. Ho Chi Minh's Democratic Republic of Vietnam continued to exist as a state, controlling ten million people spread across wide tracts of territory by the end of that war. From its capital in the northern hills to its control over much of central Vietnam, Ho's lieutenants contested every colonial attempt to influence Vietnamese, Asian, and foreign opinion. The government's diplomatic delegations in Bangkok, Rangoon, New Delhi, Prague, and Paris organized interviews with foreign correspondents, countered French propaganda, and promoted their own. The Ministry of Education and Culture, in collaboration with the Vietnamese Workers Party, presided over the continued nationalization of culture in schools, the bureaucracy, the army, the arts, and literature. Hundreds of prewar cultural luminaries joined the 'resistance', including Xuan Dieu, Huy Can, Phan Khoi, and a young singer-songwriter named Pham Duy. They put their individual freedoms on hold for the greater good of achieving Vietnam's national independence. Many found the resistance personally liberating and often exhilarating. It gave their lives new meaning in an extraordinary time of change. They helped organize mass literacy campaigns in the countryside and put their novels, poetry, paintings, and compositions in the service of the war for national liberation.

Ironically, even in war nationalists continued to rely on French Vietnam's print media. Months before full-scale war broke out in December 1946, the Democratic Republic of Vietnam authorities transferred scores of colonial printing presses, typewriters, radios, and paper to the countryside. A phenomenal range of party, government, technical, and educational papers, directives, and messages poured off DRV presses of colonial origin. *Bao Nhan Dan* (*The People's Daily*) had a print run of 20,000 copies; the communists' weekly, *Su That* (*The Truth*), was printed to the tune of 10,000 copies every week. In all, almost nine million books appeared in the Democratic Republic of Vietnam between 1945 and 1954, the majority of which served administrative, educative and military purposes as well as firing a fiercely patriotic resistance culture. The survival of the war state also depended on administrators, educators, and soldiers being able to read and write in the Romanized script. During its first year of operation, free of French interference above the sixteenth parallel, the DRV taught the basics of *quoc ngu* to 2.2 million people. By the end of the war, the government claimed to have taught those fundamentals to all of the ten million people under its control. Hundreds of rudimentary resistance schools (at both primary and secondary levels) operated in the Democratic Republic of Vietnam. During almost a decade of war a new bureaucratic elite emerged from administrative, agricultural, medical, and technical schools (many of them originally having come from a rural and poor milieu) which offered unprecedented social mobility to the rural Vietnamese. They may not have possessed state-of-the-art training in medicine and science, but they were empowered by the DRV and wartime.[42]

The Democratic Republic of Vietnam's communist leadership went further by seeking to introduce a new communist culture to the country. The party's acting General Secretary, Truong Chinh, worked on this during the Second World War, when he penned a series of influential essays outlining the future of communist culture in Vietnam. Based on the Marxist-Leninist creed, Chinh explained, culture would one day have to serve class interests, above all those of the worker and peasant classes. But for the time being, the party focused on creating a large united front via both of its biggest mass organizations, the Viet Minh and the Lien Viet. Heroic, anticolonialist themes dominated in schools, cultural associations, and the army. This changed radically after the Chinese communist victory of October 1949, however. With Sino-Soviet diplomatic recognition in early 1950, Vietnamese communists willingly aligned their country with the communist bloc, much as the Le dynasty had connected Vietnam to the Confucian East Asian world, its culture, canon, and philosophies, in the fifteenth century. To Marx and Lenin, Vietnamese communists now added Mao and Maoism as the newly renamed Vietnamese Workers' Party embarked on transforming culture through ideological rectification sessions, new hero campaigns, and massive amounts of propaganda. To create a new intellectual and bureaucratic class under its firm direction, the party required artists, poets, writers, and teachers to undergo intensive re-education before returning to their teaching positions. Communist propaganda campaigns in Vietnam proposed more and more worker and peasant heroes to emulate, as they did in China, North Korea, Cuba, and the Soviet Union.[43]

No matter how anticolonialist, intellectuals who resisted this ideological homogenization did so at their own risk. Some escaped to the Republic of Vietnam, like the singer and songwriter Pham Duy. Others convinced themselves that things would improve once national liberation was achieved. Many embraced the party's cause and defended its crackdown during the late 1950s on intellectuals who called for the protection of human rights.

This had happened with the *Nhan Van* (*Humanism*) and *Giai Pham* (*Fine Arts*) affair (see chapter 10). Some stood up to the party's assault on individual liberties. The soul of the New Poetry Movement, and an admirer of China's Lu Xun, Phan Khoi, angered the Vietnamese communist leadership by daring to write, in the wake of the disastrous land-reform campaign of 1956, that 'the people have a right to demonstrate'. He died in 1960, shortly before the party was to put him on trial for 'deviationism'.[44]

Not all individual liberties were suspended in the Democratic Republic of Vietnam, however. Women acquired greater rights. In 1945–6, the government legally established the equality of the sexes, including the right to vote for women. In 1950, another law recognized divorce. The 1959 Law on Marriage and the Family further emancipated women by prohibiting forced and premature marriage. Children could choose their partners, not their parents. Laws outlawed violence against women and the exploitation of daughters and daughters-in-law. As they were operating only from remote areas of Vietnam until 1954, DRV gender laws affected areas long left alone by the increased and mainly urban feminism of the interwar period.

But war, not law or ideology, may well have served as the most effective gender equalizer until 1975. Firstly, the mobilization of millions of men for wartime service required more women to assume positions of power in the family, village councils, and the field. Secondly, while the People's Army of Vietnam was all-male, women were massively involved in rural militias, urban commando units, and the human logistics of transportation. They were essential to operating the highly dangerous Ho Chi Minh Trail and did so at a serious cost to themselves. Thirdly, the evacuation of Vietnamese cities in the face of French attack in 1945–7 sent tens of thousands of urban women into the countryside and, with them, all sorts of new ideas about gender and culture. Similar things occurred when American bombs rained down on Hanoi. The feminization of local politics and work during the Vietnam War is particularly noteworthy. In 1962, DRV women only held 0.5 percent of presidencies in the village administrative councils. By 1967, that number had risen to over 15 percent. Between 1965 and 1969, female membership in village people's councils jumped from 19 percent to 44 percent, while the number of women in the labor force reached an astonishing 80 percent or more by the early 1970s. The percentage of women in militias protecting northern villages, and even among the National Liberation Front fighting alongside the all-male People's Army of Vietnam in the south, ran as high as 50 percent.[45]

We know precious little about how gender relations operated with the end of the war and the return of so many men to their villages to find work. It is doubtful women were able to maintain their wartime gains. And male stereotyping of women, communist or not, did not die easily. As the party's Secretary General, Le Duan, disingenuously put it in the early 1970s: 'Women are very good [at] and highly suited to teaching. Good teaching needs good feelings and deep love for children [. . .] there should be many women in this field, because education for children is above all education by emotion'.[46]

Cultural Revolution, War, and the Republic of Vietnam (1945-75)

If Vietnamese communists later regretted their enthusiastic embrace of Maoism and downplayed their dependence on Sino-Soviet support during three decades of war, anticommunist nationalists also found themselves in a similarly uncomfortable position: that of having to rely on the French and the Americans. The situation was complicated from the outset. Unable to defeat Vietnamese communists on their own, non-communist nationalists, including Nhat Linh/Nguyen Tuong Tam, bet that they could play off the French and the Americans against the communists. Instead, the French played them. The result was that the French not only prolonged their colonial rule (with American support), but in so doing they also undermined non-communist attempts to create a separate national culture at the same time. The French thus ensured that Ho Chi Minh's Vietnam remained the unique, viable defender of independence, despite Ho's efforts to communize Vietnamese culture along Sino—Soviet lines.

Unfortunately, we know very little about the cultural changes that occurred within this 'second' Vietnam that emerged on the international scene between 1949 and 1954. One of the most important transformations may well have been the Vietnamization of the education system and the organization of literacy campaigns in the countryside during the battle for the hearts and minds of the people. Understaffed and at war with a competing DRV state, the French supported the spread of *quoc ngu* as the State of Vietnam began taking over their colonial administration and creating a Vietnamese army. Schools operated in remote areas of the country which provided opportunities and upward social mobility as in the Democratic Republic of Vietnam. Dozens of Vietnamese newspapers, presses, and publishing houses reopened in the cities. Novelists, poets, artists, and intellectuals remained active. Although French censors closed papers judged too critical of the war or French colonialism, there was no stopping the nationalization of culture along Vietnamese lines. New histories of Vietnam appeared, written by irreproachable authors like Hoang Xuan Han. Educators may not have achieved political independence, but they forced the French to grant them greater control over the education system and its curriculum.

The French also tried to limit the amount of American cultural influence entering post-1945 Vietnam, especially the flood of Hollywood films, consumer culture, and music, but not always successfully. French reliance on American aid during the second half of the conflict also made it impossible to deny an increasing number of Vietnamese students the right to study abroad in the United States, like the brilliant English-language translator of *The Tale of Kieu*, Huynh Sanh Thong. All of this occurred as the Democratic Republic of Vietnam sent its first students to China and the Soviet Union. Decolonization, the Cold War, and competing state-building realigned modern Vietnam's cultural alliances in new ways.

While the French did their best to hang on culturally in Vietnam after 1954, their withdrawal finally allowed non-communist nationalists to get rid of a century of colonial culture, as the communists had already done in the DRV. Leading the charge was, of course, Ngo Dinh Diem. Working through the ministries of the Interior and Education, Diem promoted an official nationalism based on three 'antis': anticolonialism, antifeudalism, and anticommunism. He lost no time nationalizing colonial museums, research centers, hospitals, schools, universities, presses, and newspapers. Street names changed yet again as a new set of monuments appeared. As in the Democratic Republic of Vietnam, feudalism meant Diem had no love for the monarchy which the French had systematically used for a century. The sham vote Ngo Dinh Diem organized to get rid of Bao Dai in 1955 was designed as much to consolidate his power as it was to bury the monarchy's prestige for good. His disdain for French colonialism and Vietnamese feudalism was exceeded only by his hatred of communism. Indeed, anticommunism became a vital ingredient in the national culture for the fledgling Republic of Vietnam, transmitted by teachers, cadres and textbooks throughout the national education service, the army, and bureaucracy.[47]

This state-sponsored nationalism ran into problems, however. Diem's methods paralleled the harsh methods used by his communist counterparts to forge a new culture. The 'Denounce the Communist' campaign, like communist rectification, sought to inculcate a homogenous anticommunist ideological mindset. Civil-action cadres were dispersed across the country to train teachers, bureaucrats, highlanders, and army officers. Security services organized denunciation campaigns in villages, convinced as the communists and Confucian militants were before them, that they could impose ideology from the top down. Many accepted their fate, but those who resisted did so at great risk. Thousands of southern communists perished at the hands of the Ngo government. But non-communists who resisted would often meet a similar fate.

Indeed, in his nationalist offensive, Ngo Dinh Diem alienated important non-communist groups. Upon coming to power, he attacked the French-backed 'feudal sects', the Hoa Hao and Cao Dai religions. By failing to reincorporate them into the national body, however, Diem missed an opportunity to develop a wider nationalist coalition and cultural identity capable of resisting communist efforts to build up a national front against the fledgling republic. Diem further reduced his base by refusing to work with other anticommunist parties like the Dai Viet and the Vietnamese Nationalist Party, each of which had moved southward after the Geneva armistice. All of these groups and others increasingly contested Diem's nationalist legitimacy and monopoly on national culture. Like the communist crackdown on intellectual freedom in the north, Diem's authoritarianism also impinged on individual liberties and re-ignited a democratically republican-minded resistance in Vietnam (which had its roots in the early twentieth century). Perhaps the parallel of Phan Khoi's unrepentant defiance of the communists in 1960 and Nhat Linh's decision to kill himself in 1963 rather than appear before Ngo Dinh Diem's court captured the disillusion of this generation of intellectuals with postcolonial authoritarianism. The history of individual liberty in Vietnam is a tragic one.

That said, the Republic of Vietnam, at least following Diem's assassination in late 1963, never matched the communist party's ability to control, rectify, and destroy those who defied its leadership in their cultural production and quest for individual liberties. Twenty-seven Vietnamese language papers came off Saigon presses in 1967, most of which were not government-run. This would have been unthinkable under the communist single-party state. Others appeared in French and English. Glossy magazines appeared, filled with gossip and film stars, as well as journals relating the latest political, philosophical, and literary trends in Europe and North America. Trinh Cong Son read Jean-Paul Sartre while in Hanoi Sartre's Vietnamese colleague, the philosopher Tran Duc Thao, suffered rectification that drove him to the brink of madness. Free verse, creative writing, independent social reportage, and individualism were as popular in Saigon in the 1950s as they had been in Hanoi in the 1930s. Nha Ca and Trinh Cong Son's poetry and songs reflected the importance of individualism to the creation of a new society. Nguyen Sa's free-form writing of the 1960s could have appeared in Hanoi in the 1930s: 'Let me speak at once. If not, I will have to go seek myself like a maddened horse galloping down the road at twilight, chasing the sun as it disappears beyond the mountains [...] Let me speak at once'.[48]

War, however, consumed southern Vietnamese culture during the 1960s, as a civil conflict was submerged by massive and intensely violent American intervention. In the north, the Vietnamese Workers Party closely controlled how writers, poets, and artists represented the war in their work. War had to remain sacred. It had to be glorified. It had to be heroic. When Phu Thang, the First Indochina War veteran we met in chapter 9, suggested otherwise in the early 1960s, the party shut him down. In the south, republican authorities certainly censored artists, and, as we saw above, banned the film *Land of Sorrows* for its pacifism. But until the end of what has become known as the Vietnam War, southern artists, poets, and writers could express remarkably candid accounts of the destructive, ugly face of war as it marched through Vietnam, ripping people, societies, and countries apart. Years before the famous Vietnam War veteran Bao Ninh published his international bestselling novel, *The Sorrow of War*, a host of artists in the south had already taken up the theme because, whatever its faults, the southern republic was more open.

These authors found little to glorify in what the war was doing to Vietnam. As the fighting intensified from 1965 onward and bombs rained down over the country, artists wrote with extraordinary power, originality, and lucidity. Singer and songwriter Trinh Cong Son captured a deep desire for peace and a latent fear that all of the Vietnamese were on a road toward self-destruction in his songs. Everyone knew his songs 'Legacy of the Motherland', 'Love Song of a Madman', and 'Lullaby of Cannons for Night'. The poet Tran Da Thu (Nha Ca's husband) found his own way to capture the grotesque nature of war in the opening lines of his poem, 'Some Gifts to Express My Love':

> I give you a roll of barbed wire.
> Some kind of creeping vine of this new age,
> Which has stealthily crept around my soul today.

That is my love, accept it without question.
I give you a truck with plastique.
It explodes in the midst of a crowded street,
Explodes and hurls about chunks of flesh.
That is my life, do you understand it?
[...]
I would like to give you many more things.
But that's enough. I'll just give you a tear-gas grenade,
To force out tears neither happy nor sad,
Like those streaming down my waiting face.[49]

The singer-songwriter Pham Duy, who first became famous in the Democratic Republic of Vietnam for his blood-chilling song which had condemned the French massacre at Gio Linh in 1948, used his powerful songwriting to communicate the fratricidal nature of the Vietnamese civil war. In his 'Tale of Two Soldiers', he sings of two soldiers who 'both loved the fatherland—Vietnam' [. . .] 'From the same village, but divided'. Both were heroes, but both were forced to be fighting machines designed to kill the other. Duy ends his haunting song with them both lying dead on the battlefield, clasping their rifles in their hands. The last line reads: 'There were two soldiers who one rosy dawn killed each other for Vietnam, killed each other for Vietnam'.[50]

CHAPTER 13

THE TRAGEDY AND THE RISE
OF MODERN VIETNAM

Anything seemed possible to the communist leadership in mid-1975. The Vietnam Ho Chi Minh had declared independent and unified in Ba Dinh Square in Hanoi thirty years earlier was finally a reality. The Democratic Republic of Vietnam had prevailed against all odds, first against the French in one of the most violent wars of decolonization of the twentieth century and then against the Americans in arguably the most brutal conflagration of the Cold War. The victors had reason to celebrate when they gathered in downtown Saigon on 15 May as the PAVN marched by. But all did not cheer, for 1975 also marked the end of a bloody thirty-year civil war among the Vietnamese. There were winners and there were losers. And as in post-Civil War America, France, Russia, or China, the divisions did not disappear overnight.

The question now was, having won, what type of Vietnam would Ho Chi Minh's disciples create? How would the leadership heal the wounds of war that had taken the lives of as many as 3.6 million souls since 1945? Would they unite the country immediately or wait for five to ten years before proceeding, as Le Duc Tho had promised? Would Hanoi transform the Republic of Vietnam's market-oriented economy along communist lines or allow two systems to co-exist for a decent interval? Visitors to Vietnam today might marvel at the rapid economic development of this latest 'Asian tiger', but the road leading toward modern Vietnam after 1975 was not a straight line. In fact, for over a decade, it remained a very tragic one.

ONE VIETNAM?

Uniting the South with the North[1]
While the victors in 1975 were understandably determined to unify the country into one nation-state, they had few historical precedents to guide them.

Except for a few weeks in mid-1945, it had been 113 years since a unitary Vietnam running from north to south had existed. A myriad of states, contesting sovereignties, and identities had proliferated. Southern, central, and northern Vietnam had developed in very different ways under the French. Some nationalists, including the communists, had even thought of going pan-Indochinese. The two Vietnams led by Bao Dai and Ho Chi Minh during the Indochina conflict had never controlled all of Vietnam, functioning instead as competing, fragmented war states. The Geneva Conference agreements of 1954 only solidified the existence of two very different postcolonial states, economies, and societies. Nationalists in both areas certainly believed in a unified Vietnamese nation and located each in a faraway heroic past; but in reality such a state had only existed under the Nguyen dynasty during the first half of the nineteenth century. Le Duan's conquest of the south in 1975 and Gia Long's victory over the north in 1802 stand out as the two points in time at which leaders achieved the territorial state we now call 'modern Vietnam'.

Like their Nguyen predecessors, the Vietnamese communists relied on their conquering army to hold this new Vietnam together. In 1975, the People's Army of Vietnam disarmed the enemy, occupied the major cities, roads, and bridges, and administered the south. A military management committee ruled through a hastily convened coalition government known as the 'Republic of South Vietnam'. This was not the 'Republic of Vietnam' the PAVN had just toppled, but rather a manifestation of the Provisional Revolutionary Government of the Republic of South Vietnam created by the Vietnamese Workers' Party in the late 1960s. That said, military authorities maintained many of the lower- and mid-level civil servants of the *ancien régime* until enough communist officials could arrive to take over. And in contrast to earlier periods in Vietnamese history, that did not take long. As former republican personnel quit, were fired, or had to leave in order to undergo re-education, the new authorities introduced thousands of northern cadres to staff upper- and mid-level positions in southern provincial, district, and urban offices. They operated the new police and security services and took over the administration of schools, universities, hospitals, industries, and businesses which they had seized. Secondly, the wartime destruction of the VWP's National Liberation Front in the south only reinforced this 'northernization' of the southern civil service. Thirdly, given the intensity of the long Vietnamese civil war and the communists' distrust of the 'corrupted' and 'debauched' south it had finally conquered, the victors wanted their people in command. They wanted direct rule.[2]

Having demobilized the Republic of Vietnam's army, the new authorities sent tens of thousands of enemy officers to re-education camps, at the same time as confiscating massive amounts of American-supplied war materiel. Over a million-strong by 1975, the People's Army of Vietnam stood unchallenged in postcolonial Indochina and was the fifth largest standing army in the world. It certainly dwarfed its wartime ally, the southern-grown People's Liberation Armed Forces. The war had decimated the latter's ranks, leading Hanoi to increase dramatically the PAVN's presence in the south. In all, between 1965 and 1975, the north had sent 980,000 People's Army of Vietnam troops and personnel to the south. And with the guns now silent, the communists were in no mood to allow this southern army to assert its independence from the very communist party that had created it or risk the chance that it could support a rival southern regional polity. This reality finally dawned on the NLF's non-communist Minister of Justice, Truong Nhu Tang, as he stood proudly next to the PAVN's General Van Tien Dung during the 15 May 1975 victory celebrations in Saigon. These men and their people had suffered together in the jungles and under the bombs. Together they had driven out the Americans and toppled their common Vietnamese enemies. It was supposed to be a day of great joy. For Tang it was, until the People's Army of Vietnam troops had passed by to be followed by People's Liberation Armed Force soldiers now marching under the national flag of the Democratic Republic of Vietnam. When he asked Dung what was going on, meaning why were there not two flags for two different armies, the general curtly replied: 'The army has already been unified'. 'Since when?' Tang shot back. Dung did not answer as he quietly returned his gaze to the parade. The communists had neutralized two armies in the spring of 1975, not one.[3]

They did away with two governments as well, not only the enemy Republic of Vietnam one created by Ngo Dinh Diem, but also the coalition government the communists had themselves created in the form of the Provisional Revolutionary Government of the Republic of South Vietnam. Now the PRG had become one of three main components of the counter-republic in the south along with the National Liberation Front, and the Alliance of National, Democratic, and Peace Forces. As stipulated in the Paris Accords of January 1973 (see chapter 11), this coalition government was supposed to continue to exist as a separate and sovereign state until an agreement could be reached with the DRV to unite the two Vietnams via elections or negotiations into one sovereign, unitary state. Although this republic was a communist creation, many Third Force non-communists like Truong Nhu Tang sincerely believed that they could use this entity to promote a less than wholly communist 'South Vietnam', allied with, but which would be independent of the Democratic Republic of Vietnam's institutional control for at least a decade. Since the founding of the national front in 1960, Vietnamese communists had repeatedly promised this to their partners and assured them that they were in no rush to communize the south.

In many ways, Third Force nationalists like Truong Nhu Tang had made the same dangerous gamble as their non-communist predecessors who had tried to use French military power to thwart the Vietnamese communists during the initial Indochina War. The difference of course was that this second 'Third Force' had wanted to drive out the Americans and their Vietnamese allies by entering into an alliance with the Vietnamese Workers' Party since 1960. But the political risk was the same: would the militarily stronger partner honor its promises to the junior one once the guns fell silent? By joining the communists, Tang and his non-communist allies ran the risk that the politburo in Hanoi in control of the NLF/PRG would one day discard them just as the French had disposed of Nguyen Van Thinh when he had threatened their Cochinchinese republic in 1946 and the Americans had supported the overthrow of Ngo Dinh Diem when he imperiled their hold on the south.

While the politburo never doubted the loyalty of the communists they had put in charge of the Republic of South Vietnam, Nguyen Thi Binh and Huynh Tan Phat, and rewarded them accordingly after 1975, Ho Chi Minh's disciples were not about to let non-communist, democratic-minded southern nationalists turn the coalition government and the 1973 accords on them in order to plot some sort of 'Third Way' out for South Vietnam or to slip political pluralism into the north. There would be no elections, no coalition, and no autonomous 'South Vietnam', inside or outside of the state of the Democratic Republic of Vietnam. For the communists, the 1973 accords were null and void. Power was finally theirs. And those who challenged it, even former allies, would suffer the consequences. This, too, is why the leadership in Hanoi preferred direct control. The communists did not trust their non-communist allies.

The victors also realized that the south was so different from the north economically and ideologically that it was a threat that had to be subdued immediately. Young PAVN soldiers and communist cadres expecting to save their southern brethren from capitalist exploitation and underdevelopment discovered instead an urban population which was not particularly keen on being liberated ideologically. They also encountered a consumerist society in the cities which they had never dreamed possible. In 1981, a very privileged northern party member sent to Saigon to run a medical laboratory described the impact of the south on her mindset in subversive terms: 'It was a dream city for someone coming from the mists of Hanoi, so austere and poor. The contrast was brutal. I saw a plethora of products about which I knew nothing. An electric rice cooker! Who could have imagined an electric rice cooker in Hanoi, under the bombs? We were still in the age of coal and wood. There was such abundance and choice [. . .]'[4]

Meanwhile, as Saigon teenagers shed their bell-bottomed jeans and clipped their long hair to conform to the austere northern 'look', northern cadres and the rank and file in the People's Army of Vietnam in Saigon were trying them on and 'sucking up every loose camera, television, stereo, and motorcycle' they could find. 'They came to purify us', one Saigon citizen remarked with irony, 'but we are corrupting them'. Indeed, the party feared this and struggled to control the psychological fallout from this meeting of two very different Vietnams. And adding to their sense of urgency was the rapid deterioration of relations with Cambodian and Chinese communists which I will discuss below.[5]

By early 1976, the Vietnamese politburo had concluded that if it did not unify and transform the south then, in five to ten years, it might be too late. In April 1976, having disbanded the military management committee which had ruled there, the party organized elections to create a new National Assembly, the first step to creating a new state. Representatives from all over the country then gathered in Hanoi between 24 June and 3 July 1976 to discuss the future nature and workings of such a unitary state. What would be its economic tack, its political constitution, and roadmap for unification? Would the south continue to exist autonomously? In the end, little if any real debate occurred before the party's delegate to the convention announced that the country would now be unified as part of a new state to be known as the Socialist Republic of Vietnam, or SRV.

A number of liberal-minded delegates who had opposed American intervention, Ngo Dinh Diem, and his military successors could not believe their ears. They had expected a debate, discussions, at the least a bit of time. The 'socialization' of the south was supposed to be gradual. That's what the Central Office of South Vietnam leadership had always promised. One of the rare assemblymen to have transitioned from the republic's parliament to the communist one, Nguyen Cong Hoan earnestly told the communist party's representative in the National Assembly that 'most southerners were not used to the idea of socialism' and 'didn't trust it'. But the communist representative, Hoan later recalled, told him that now: 'There's only one road to building the nation, and that's our road'. Even southern attempts to negotiate a new national flag rather than simply adopting the DRV's yellow star on a red banner went nowhere. On 2 July 1976, the Socialist Republic of Vietnam officially came to life. At the end of the year, during their fourth party congress, the communists renamed their party the Vietnamese Communist Party (VCP) and set the entire country on a communist tack under the leadership of a single-party state. For the first time since 1862, one Vietnamese state existed, not a Confucian, Christian, republican, Personalist, or Buddhist-minded one, but a communist dictatorship.[6]

Communist State-making in the South
Official Vietnamese historians in the SRV like to compare their struggle and social revolution in the twentieth century to that of the Tay Son brothers two hundred years earlier. Like the communists, the Tay Son brothers had fought for the poor, driven out foreign invaders, and unified the country against all odds. However, when it comes to state-building, there are equally compelling reasons to compare the communists' methods of the late twentieth century to those used by their neo-Confucian-minded predecessor in the 1820s and 1830s, the Nguyen Emperor Minh Mang. Both groups came to power after some thirty years of civil and interstate wars. Postwar loyalties were divided. Both were determined to create highly centralized, unitary states by tailoring foreign ideologies and techniques to local needs. Both confronted a heterogeneous southern society and economy very different from their northern-centered ones in Hue and Hanoi.

Worried by the fragile nature of their unitary states, the communists and their Confucian predecessor were also remarkably determined to impose unflinching loyalty right down to the lowest levels of state and society. Just as Minh Mang had imposed the dual, interlocking Confucian policies of 'Cultivation' and 'Sino-Vietnamization' to establish loyalty to his court in Hue and homogenize the civil service and his subjects, so too did the communists turn to Sino-Soviet communist techniques such as rectification, emulation campaigns, hero worship, and self-edifying propaganda to take control of the bureaucracy and society from top to bottom, homogenize both ideologically, and subordinate them to the political center, now in Hanoi. Instead of administering a Confucian-based examination system, the Vietnamese Communist Party trained its bureaucrats in Marxist-Leninist thought via carefully controlled coursework given out by a network of academies. Whereas Minh Mang promoted state-sponsored ancestor worship to people at every level of society, often grafting this type of worship on to local cults, and their deities, the communists did much the same thing by establishing an elaborate cult of Ho Chi Minh in an effort to tie people to the party's ideology. Like the Nguyen emperor, the VCP closed competing churches and schools which belonged to the Catholics, the Buddhists, and the religious sects, or placed them under its own careful control. They also required Catholics and Buddhists to place portraits of Ho Chi Minh on their altars. These were not simple decorations.

But such parallels can only go so far before they lose their analytical value. Neither state, even the communist one, was as 'totalitarian' in its social control as so many would like to think. As always, the gulf between theory and practice was real. Moreover, what the communists proposed ideologically in the late twentieth century would have been unimaginable for the Tay Son brothers or even a remarkably modern emperor at the turn of the nineteenth century like Minh Mang. Vietnamese society had also changed dramatically under a century of French colonialism and thirty years of war, while the social revolution the communists proposed in the late twentieth century was radically different from that of the Tay Son brothers in the 1790s. As the constitution of 1980 now proudly announced it, the Socialist Republic of Vietnam was a Marxist-Leninist state led by the dictatorship of the proletariat, the peasants and the workers.[7]

Upon taking the south, Vietnamese communists extended the Sino-Soviet state-building project they had first begun in the north in 1950 to the south. They pushed party cells down to village level, interlocking with and controlling the state in parallel administrative hierarchies. Again, given the destruction southern communist organizations had suffered during the war, northerners tended to dominate the party's civil service. A wide range of VCP-controlled mass associations emerged to organize and mobilize youth groups, peasants, workers, women and children. Tens of thousands of southern young people joined the party's new associations, with the most promising going on to attend the prestigious Nguyen Ai Quoc Academy in Hanoi while others joined provincial chapters of the party. Membership in the Vietnamese Communist Party was the surest way to social ascension in these years, though all sorts of compromises and negotiations occurred in peoples' daily lives.[8]

While Vietnamese communists never tried to murder the 'bad classes' as their Cambodian counterparts were on their genocidal way to doing from 1975 onward, the VCP applied discriminatory social measures in order to take control of the cities, the means of production, and capital resources. In Saigon/Cholon, the party's initial assault on the 'capitalist' and 'comprador' classes translated into an attack on the ethnic Chinese and Vietnamese citizens of Chinese origin living there (who had played a vital role in developing the southern economy since at least the seventeenth century). Of the urban capitalists targeted by the VCP in late 1975, 70 percent were of ethnic Chinese descent. Socialist Republic of Vietnam authorities closed or seized an estimated 50,000 Chinese businesses in the south. Most were medium- and small-sized businesses employing tens of thousands of workers, including many ethnic Viet. Others were among the most important banks and industries in the country. Communist authorities nationalized, for example, the vibrant business empire of Ly Long Than (whose very close ties to Nguyen Van Thieu did not help him avoid this measure). His family had run such important industries as Vienatexco and Vinafilco (textiles), Vicasa steel, and the Nam Do and Trung Nam banks. In all, Chinese in the south lost an estimated two billion dollars in the late 1970s due to the nationalization of their property, businesses, and industries.[9]

While this may have made good ideological sense, putting the party in charge of powerful banks, it also meant that some 650 state-owned enterprises closed, and 130,000 workers (thousands of them highly trained, experienced, and globally connected Chinese and Vietnamese businessmen and women) withdrew, disappeared into re-education camps, or fled the country. In all, 200,000 Chinese (not all of them from the commercial class) fled to southern China, while over 600,000 repatriated to non-communist countries in Asia and elsewhere. Paradoxically, in the very period that communist China's Deng Xiaoping would begin inviting overseas Chinese to invest their capital and know-how into developing the mainland's market economy, Vietnamese communists were driving the Chinese out in order to destroy southern capitalism and the *ancien régime*'s economic hold. The Vietnamese managed this social-racial 'reordering' through changes in law and the use of repression.[10]

However, this assault on the Chinese in Vietnam occurred as diplomatic relations between the communist Chinese and Vietnamese nation-states

melted down. The Chinese communist authorities were furious, for example, when they learned that their counterparts in Vietnam had reversed a
1955 agreement protecting Chinese nationals from having to adopt Vietnamese nationality, which they interpreted as an attack on Chinese national
sovereignty. Vietnamese communists, however, saw citizenship as a powerful instrument for controlling and nationalizing the Chinese under their
control in the north since 1945 and this even larger Chinese population
they had just inherited in the south, whose political loyalty and economic
power posed problems. As diplomatic relations with Beijing worsened, officials (although not necessarily ordinary people) began to see the 'Chinese', including those living in the north, as a potentially dangerous fifth
column. Despite the fact that many Chinese had joined the Vietnamese in
order to fight the French and Americans, Hanoi now required all Chinese
living in the Socialist Republic of Vietnam to become 'Vietnamese nationals' or leave. 'At the end of 1977 the arrests began', recalled Trinh Duc, as
did state-sponsored anti-Chinese discrimination:

> The first sign was when my direct bosses in the Hoa Van [Overseas Chi-
> nese Mobilizing] Committee were ordered to leave the country. (They are
> living in China now). They had been working closely for years with the
> Chinese Communist Party, overseeing the supplies and aid that were com-
> ing from China [for Vietnamese communists]. Then Chinese cadres were
> arrested as 'Chinese spies'. No one had ever heard that charge before. My
> uncle was arrested at that time. He had been working for the revolution
> since before I came to Vietnam, at least forty years [ago]. He had been
> awarded the First Rank Revolution Medal [by the Vietnamese communists
> themselves].[11]

As Asian communists slid toward war once again (the Third Indochina
War), class-based discrimination rapidly morphed into crude, official racism as scores of Cambodian, Chinese, and Vietnamese newspaper editori-
als, posters, cartoons, and a legion of 'white' and 'black' 'truth' books poured
off the state presses, in which each government accused the other of provoking the other into war. An anti-Chinese clause even found its way into
the SRV's 1980 constitution. Like the Khmers Rouges who were concur-
rently transforming the Vietnamese in Cambodia (the pejorative word they
used for them was '*yuon*'), the authorities in Hanoi also began constructing
a historical enemy (which they felt they needed) from the 'Chinese'.

In the countryside, the class assault on 'cruel landowners' was less severe than it had been in the north in the 1950s, because southern landowners had already lost most of their property. Why? Firstly, the communists had begun redistributing land during the First Indochina War and the National Liberation Front had kept it up as part of the war on the Republic of Vietnam. Secondly, the republican government of Nguyen Van Thieu had in fact implemented successful land redistribution in the Land to the Tiller program. Lastly, by 1975, most of the remaining landowners had already left the country or were on their way to re-education camps as the party confiscated their land equipment (and redistributed it). The Buddhist and Catholic churches were arguably the biggest losers when the Socialist Republic of Vietnam nationalized landholdings (Diem had already nationalized vast Cao Dai and Hoa Hao territories). In any case, by 1978 the party agreed that most of the land below the seventeenth parallel had now been redistributed.[12]

The communist state redefined society in other ways than through class. Much like Ngo Dinh Diem's discriminatory policies toward those in the south who had collaborated with the communists before 1954, it was now the SRV's turn to discriminate against those who had collaborated with the now defeated puppet regimes ('*nguy*') which reached back to the 1940s. From 1975 onward (even before that time in NLF/PLAF zones), the Socialist Republic of Vietnam police and security services began establishing lists of suspect people, issuing identity cards, and requiring people to fill out personal biographies ('*ly lich*'). Like their Chinese counterparts, Vietnamese communists used these dossiers to classify and categorize their subjects in terms of their positions in the *ancien régime* and the National Liberation Force /People's Liberation Armed Force. The *ly lich* requirement insisted citizens state their current occupation, family relations, ethnicity, and religious faith. Although people quickly learned how to protect themselves when filling out these forms, the party-state used these categorizing powers to promote 'good' elements and discriminate against 'bad' ones, as they saw them.[13]

Those who came from families loyal to the party or who had sacrificed labor and loved ones to the armed forces during the thirty-year war now found it easier to access jobs in the bureaucracy, the army, and higher education institutions. The party practiced such discrimination also knowing that millions of people expected something in return for the massive sacrifices they had made during the war. Children of parents and grandparents who had 'collaborated' with the French, the Americans, and their

Vietnamese allies found their careers and study abroad opportunities diminished, even if they scored higher on qualifying examinations. The SRV estimated that in 1975, 6.5 million people (of a total southern population of around twenty million) were 'compromised' either directly or by their families' collaboration. Of course class counted too, as the party assigned a privileged place for the workers and the peasants at the top of the social hierarchy which was constitutionally enshrined.[14]

To assist in this transformation of the south, communist authorities took control of schools and universities there. At the top levels, they removed most teachers and professors and replaced them with ideologically reliable and loyal ones. In all, the communists in charge dispatched some two thousand professors to the south. In May 1975, in an extraordinary attempt to destroy the past, communist authorities seized 100,000 books and burned many publicly, whereas in the new textbooks, official historians presented Ho Chi Minh and his victorious Vietnam as the manifestation of a timeless patriotic culture of heroic resistance to foreign aggression against the French, the Americans and, increasingly, the Chinese. The party-state also introduced and propagated Marxism-Leninism throughout southern Vietnam, making it required reading in schools, military academies, and civil service training programs. Each student, Pham Van Dong insisted in 1984, had to come from the right social milieu, 'filled with hatred for capitalism and imperialism and his heart and mind should be bound to socialism and proletarian internationalism'.[15]

With a few, short-lived exceptions, the SRV closed republican newspapers, television stations, and radio shows in order to install communist-run ones. The victors also changed street names yet again, destroyed enemy monuments and symbols, and erected new ones in their places. In September 1977, Ho Chi Minh City officially became the new name for Saigon. Meanwhile, in the north, authorities followed the Soviets' lead by erecting a massive granite mausoleum in which they placed the embalmed body of President Ho Chi Minh. (It had been in storage there since his death in 1969.) They did so against the written wishes of their venerated leader. Tourists can still view the president's body in this sacred state shrine as Vietnamese schoolchildren and citizens file by. This architectural testament to communist power and its pedagogical cult stands in vivid contrast to the modest living quarters of 'Uncle' Ho, preserved just down the road.[16]

Like their French and Vietnamese adversaries, the communists jailed many of their enemies upon taking power. However, Vietnamese communists were not content to simply lock them up; they also wanted to reform them ('*cai tao*'), to purge them of their erroneous thinking, and, theoretically, re-insert them in the new socialist society. In all, more than a million Vietnamese associated with the former southern republic and its antecedents experienced re-education. For the majority of the lower-level bureaucrats and soldiers, this was not much more than an in-house (re)training course. A communist cadre carefully explained to his listeners their errors; provided them with the fundamentals of the new communist society, peppering his lecture with lib-eral citations from the internationalist Marxist canon and Ho Chi Minh. He then repeated the importance of following the correct path before letting ev-eryone go. Such courses could last a few days, a couple of months, even a year or two. However, for higher-ranking cadres in the former government, army, intelligence, and security services, re-education could last much longer and it often occurred in camps. This form of *cai tao* not only entailed countless sessions of brainwashing, rectification, new hero emulation, and propaganda, but it also meant performing forced labor in harsh, disease-ridden parts of the country. Hundreds of Vietnamese still remained in these camps in the late 1980s. An unknown number never returned. Such officially sanctioned retribution did little to heal Vietnam's deep divisions. One of Vietnam's best modern poets, Thanh Tam Tuyen, spent seven years in a communist camp before emigrating to the United States. In his poem 'Resurrection', he de-scribed how 'a shout is a prayer for the waiting centuries, / I want to live like I want to die, / Among the intersecting breaths of a flaming chest'.[17]

While Vietnamese communists avoided the ferocity of their Cambo-dian counterparts, who emptied Phnom Penh of almost all of its inhabi-tants within weeks of taking power in April 1975, the authorities also feared the massive urbanization the war had generated in the south. Forty-three percent of the population lived in urban areas in 1975. Saigon counted four million people in its population in 1975, making it one of the most urbanized places on earth (alongside Phnom Penh!). One million unem-ployed roamed the urban centers of southern Vietnam in 1975. Many were the 'bad elements', who had lost their jobs with the Republic of Vietnam's fall. Added to this number were 300,000 prostitutes and some 800,000 orphans the enemy armies had left behind. Feeding, housing, employing, indeed controlling all of these people posed immediate and daunting chal-lenges for which the new authorities were badly prepared. As a result, the communist regime encouraged millions of wartime refugees to return to their native villages and many did so of their own volition.[18]

But like Ngo Dinh Diem before them, the communists also engineered new economic zones in order to relocate hundreds of thousands of unemployed people and bad elements to the highlands, sometimes forcibly so. The government provided them with a plot of land, seeds, and wished them well. Many left; others, exhausted, returned to the cities. Confronted with chronic demographic pressures in the north, the party-state also sent tens of thousands of northern peasants to these same settlement areas in the south. However, as we know, the highlands were not 'empty' lands just waiting for the Vietnamese to colonize them. Hundreds of thousands of non-Viet people had inhabited these lands for centuries. Now ethnic Viet poured in. In 1977, the new economic zones were home to 120,000 Vietnamese migrants. In 1978, that number rose to almost half a million and by 1985 it reached a million. Some estimates push the total as high as two million by 1988. This internal colonization certainly helped lower the high rates of wartime urbanization from 43 percent in 1975 to 25 percent in 1979, but it also ensured that the indigenous people of the highlands for the first time truly became 'ethnic minorities' in this new Vietnam.[19]

With its second five-year plan (1976–80), the government imposed Stalinist-minded central planning and collectivization on the south. Even though it was distancing itself from just such a policy in the north, the Vietnamese Communist Party applied the model in the south in order to transform the southern capitalist economy into a communist one, neutralize any economic threats, in short, to establish a centrally planned economy and assert control. This is why the confiscation of Chinese capital and centuries-old commercial networks was so important. The state simultaneously organized peasants into cooperatives, terminated private property, trade, and banking, and set prices instead of letting the market do it. Inside the party, ideologues were determined to collectivize and control agriculture so as to create the surplus needed to feed the cities and finance rapid industrialization according to the Stalinist model.[20]

If the leadership in Hanoi asserted its control, it did so at the price of a massive contraction of the economy. By collectivizing agriculture and setting uncompetitive prices, it erased incentives for production in the countryside. Rather than producing more, Vietnamese peasants—like their Chinese and Soviet counterparts before them—simply cultivated enough land upon which to live rather than have to turn over any surplus to the state at fixed prices (i.e. a loss). The fact that individuals no longer possessed their land, equipment, tools, or animals only further discouraged them.

In 1980, farmers cultivated 100,000 hectares of land less than they had in 1978. Food production for 1980 fell short of its target by seven million tons. Gross domestic product only reached 0.4 percent instead of the predicted double-digit estimate. Living standards tanked, famine broke out in several provinces in 1978 and would continue in those and others, including some in the north, well into the 1980s. Tens of thousands of peasants asked to withdraw from the cooperatives. Many resisted collectivization outright.[21]

Vietnam's international isolation hardly helped. Relations with the Khmers Rouges were already going sour by late 1975 and there were tensions with the Chinese, one of communist Vietnam's biggest trading partners and aid donors since 1950. In May 1975, Washington imposed a trade embargo and soon prohibited Americans from even sending humanitarian aid to the country. As Vietnam moved closer to the Soviet Union and the Chinese improved their relations with the Americans, non-communist Asian states, most notably Japan and the Association of South East Asian Nations (ASEAN), distanced themselves from the Socialist Republic of Vietnam. By rebuffing ASEAN's 1973 invitation to join the group as an observer, the Vietnamese communists left the field open to China to improve relations with the rest of Southeast Asia. By 1980, as the two communist states went to war, life for millions in Vietnam became unbearable.[22]

Fleeing Communist Vietnam[23]

Things became so bad that hundreds of thousands of Vietnamese began to risk their lives to get out. Rich and poor, young and old, men and women, peasants and urbanites left the country. Most—but not all—were southerners associated with the *anciens régimes*. In the weeks leading up to the fall of Saigon on 30 April 1975, nearly 150,000 Vietnamese linked to the crumbling Republic of Vietnam evacuated to the US. Around 10,000 who didn't make it out found their way by boat or overland to Hong Kong and mainland Southeast Asian states by late 1975 and later relocated, mainly to the United States. By 1978, in all of Vietnam, hundreds of thousands of ethnic Chinese and Vietnamese of Chinese descent were already on their way out.[24]

The flight from Indochina was a perilous one. For a price, an ever-increasing one, people paid bribes to local police and border patrol agents to let them go, but not before selling their possessions in order to pay the smugglers, even elaborate smuggling syndicates, to get them out. Most went by boat to southern China, Hong Kong, and above all to the shores of the

Southeast Asian states stretching from the Philippines to Singapore by way of Indonesia and Malaysia. In November 1978, the 1,500-ton freighter *Hai Hong* reached its final destination in Malaysia to unload a human cargo of 2,500 Vietnamese 'boat people', as they were now so unfortunately labeled. Tens of thousands more floated across the South China Sea on woefully unsafe vessels. When littoral states began to turn refugees back, often to their deaths, the United Nations High Commissioner for Refugees intervened. Faced with obstacles at every turn, its representatives negotiated the rules, legal categories, and Western support needed to organize the orderly departure of hundreds of thousands of Vietnamese. From 1979, a series of UN-run camps and processing centers appeared in Southeast Asia. In all, the United States, Australia, France, and Canada resettled 623,800 Indochinese refugees between July 1979 and July 1982. In 1980, the Socialist Republic of Vietnam agreed to establish an Orderly Departure Program or ODP with the UNHCR, which was to be based in Bangkok, and to allow those Vietnamese wishing to leave the country for family reunion and other humanitarian reasons to do so. Most went to the United States, the state of California in particular. In all, between 1975 and 1995, when the ODP program ended, 796,310 boat people and 42,918 so-called 'land people' (those who exited via overland routes) had left their native country: in all, 839,228 Vietnamese. This internal hemorrhaging of modern Vietnam was proof that national reconciliation had been a failure. This was true, too, for communist Laos and especially so in Cambodia, where the Khmers Rouges were responsible for the deaths of at least 1.5 million Cambodians by late 1978. In all, 1,436,556 Laotians, Cambodians, Vietnamese, and minority peoples departed communist Indochina. Two hundred thousand Vietnamese individuals are estimated to have died trying.[25]

MISALLIANCES: THE INDOCHINESE MELTDOWN OF EURASIAN COMMUNISM

This human tragedy occurred against the backdrop of yet another, the renewal of war in Indochina. No sooner had the United States withdrawn from Saigon in 1975 than Vietnamese communists found themselves sliding into another conflagration, not with the French 'colonialists' or the American 'imperialists', but with their former communist brethren in Cambodia and China. No one could have imagined in the early 1950s that the communist internationalism binding them all together across Eurasia would disintegrate into yet another bitter conflict over Indochina. And yet it did. So how did this happen? To answer this question, we need to return briefly to the colonial and Cold War periods in order to trace how the breakdown in two communist relationships, one between the Vietnamese and the Cambodians, the other between the Soviets and Chinese, intersected and eventually destroyed the Eurasian communist bloc at its Indochinese fault-line. How this happened is essential to understanding the continued tragedy of modern Vietnam until 1991.

Vietnamese Communists' Nation-building in Laos and Cambodia

In the beginning, the internationalist communist movement led by the Soviet Union supported the creation of the Indochinese Communist Party with the Vietnamese at its helm. The Comintern required local revolutionaries in these countries to turn the colonial state upon the colonizers. Ho Chi Minh fully supported this, and so did his Chinese counterparts whom he knew well. Indeed, Asian communism was a remarkably fraternal, Sino-Vietnamese enterprise during the interwar period. Not only did Chinese and Vietnamese communists create the ICP in Hong Kong in 1930, but they also helped the Comintern establish communist parties for Thailand and Malaya. This transnational collaboration resumed after the Second World War, when Stalin turned over the leadership of the communist movement in Asia to Mao Zedong. The latter sent his army to help Kim Il-sung in Korea and rushed military aid and advisors to Ho in Vietnam. Despite post 1979 claims to the contrary, there is no hard evidence from the time showing that the Sino-Soviet leadership objected in the early 1950s to the Vietnamese-led Indochinese bloc fighting the French 'colonialists' and the American 'imperialists' on the Southeast Asian frontlines of the Cold War.[26]

Vietnamese communists were also fighting in a colonial context and had to adjust their revolutionary plans for Indochina to counter those of the French. This is why, following the French abandonment of the Indochinese Federation in 1948 and recognition of the three Associated States of Indochina a year later, the communists dissolved the Indochinese Communist Party in favor of separate national parties. Instead of creating an Indochinese federation of their own, Vietnamese communists then established sister Laotian and Cambodian parties, states, and armies. In 1950, Ho personally presided over the creation of the Lao and Cambodian 'resistance governments' and national fronts. In 1951, Vietnamese communists helped to form the Khmer People's Revolutionary Party and began work on a Lao one that became official in 1955. Although the Vietnamese let go of the Indochinese Communist Party in favor of the Vietnamese Workers Party the three sister republics remained linked by association of an Indochinese type under indirect Vietnamese control. Like the French and the Americans, Vietnamese communists were also deeply involved in state-making outside their own national borders.

To get their associated states off the ground, Ho's entourage trained, equipped, and dispatched thousands of advisors and bureaucrats to serve in Laos and Cambodia. The VWP created highly secret and all-powerful 'party affairs committees' to build sister parties, nation-states, and people's armies for each country. Run by trusted Vietnamese cadres, the Lao and Cambodian party affairs committees administered tens of thousands of Viet, Lao, Khmer, and ethnic minority civil servants in charge of these parallel state-building projects. The Vietnamese presided over the creation and administration of police services, customs offices, schools, and courts. They installed the Pathet Lao and Khmer Issarak national parties, established 'People's Administrative and Resistance Committees', and sent trustworthy Lao, Khmer, and highland peoples to study in military and party academies in the Democratic Republic of Vietnam. Vietnamese communists divided Laos and Cambodia territorially into administrative and military zones, connecting each by trails and wireless radio to controlling offices across the border in the DRV. Vietnamese advisors also brought Sino-Vietnamese mobilization techniques, such as armed propaganda, rectification campaigns and patriotic emulation to the other communist countries within Indochina, but *not,* to my knowledge, Maoist land reform. 'In short', one Vietnamese advisor involved in these transfers explained, 'armed propaganda is about more than just organizing meetings, gatherings, or putting on theatrical events. Armed propaganda must make propaganda and put in place and direct [party and state] organizations'. This is how the Vietnamese, like the Chinese in northern Vietnam, transferred Sino-Soviet models into western Indochina during wartime—and this enabled them to build war states at the same time.[27]

The Vietnamese recruited allies with whom they could collaborate. In Laos, Ho Chi Minh, Vo Nguyen Giap, and others actively recruited Prince Souphanouvong whose royal blood would attract popular support for the Pathet Lao. They also turned to the son of a Lao mother and an ethnic Viet civil servant in Laos. His name was Kaysone Phoumivihane. In Cambodia, the Vietnamese won over the cooperation of a Buddhist monk named Son Ngoc Minh, who was also the offspring of a Khmer–Vietnamese mixed marriage in the Mekong delta. Bilingual, these individuals could easily read the important Sino-Soviet texts in Vietnamese (and French) translation. Kaysone Poumvihane, Son Ngoc Minh, and countless others saw in collaboration with the Vietnamese and their superior military power the chance to push through their own revolutionary and nationalist projects against their local competitors.

And like the Americans in South Vietnam or the Chinese in the north, thousands of Vietnamese advisors arrived in Laos and Cambodia with modernization theory on their minds. It was of the Marxist-Leninist–Maoist kind but it too stressed the importance of bringing modernity, civilization, and liberation to their less developed neighbors. Vietnamese cadres in Laos taught indigenous peoples the basics of personal hygiene, how to purify water, cook meat, and procure salt. They introduced modern agricultural tools, helped develop local handicraft industries, and showed how to create a revolutionary type of administration. In order to transmit all of this to the 'people', the Vietnamese initiated mass literacy campaigns in Khmer, Lao, and especially highland languages. One French intelligence officer captured it nicely in the early 1950s: 'And the people's revolutionary war has this which is truly paradoxical: it is undertaken by the Vietnamese against the French in the name of the independence of the Cambodian people. The people's revolutionary war is the work of one foreign army fighting against another, the latter contesting the former's right to bring happiness to the country in question'. But there was more to it than just ideology and an imperial sense of *mission civilisatrice*. If the Vietnamese were happy to export communism to Laos and Cambodia, their revolutionary state-building there was also designed to protect the Democratic Republic of Vietnam's vulnerable western flank from French and American attack. This geopolitical reality was, of course, an essential element in Vietnam's actions, as the Americans well understood.[28]

Vietnam's Indochinese Misalliance: The Khmers Rouges and National Sovereignty

The Geneva Conference of 1954 revealed publicly for the first time Vietnamese communist efforts to project two sovereign sister states. The French, backed by the Americans and the British, firmly refused to recognize the reality of these two regimes and, with Soviet and Chinese acquiescence, successfully excluded them from the negotiating table in favor of their own associated states. However, the French and the Americans were not alone in their opposition to the DRV's Indochinese project. In the months leading up to the Geneva Conference, India's Pandit Nehru had repeated to China's chief negotiator, Zhou Enlai, that communist efforts to create revolutionary states under the auspices of the Pathet Lao and Khmer Issarak were hardly neutral acts. If China wanted to improve its diplomatic relations with India and other non-communist states keen on achieving peaceful co-existence in postcolonial Asia (and thereby to allow China to block simultaneous American attempts to contain it via SEATO), then the communist bloc could not support these un-neutral 'resistance governments' in Laos and Cambodia. French Indochina, Nehru lectured Zhou, could no longer serve as a postcolonial model for nation-building of a communist kind. When communist support of these governments immediately became an obstacle to negotiating a ceasefire, Zhou distanced himself from the Democratic Republic of Vietnam's position and finally convinced Ho Chi Minh to abandon his party's attempts—although these had been long supported by the Chinese and the Soviets—to communize the rest of Indochina. A neutral Laos and Cambodia would suffice.[29]

The ceasefire agreements concluded in Geneva in July 1954 had the most damaging effects for Vietnamese–Khmer communist collaboration in Cambodia. Not only did it require Vietnamese communists to withdraw their party, state, and military personnel from southern Vietnam, but it also obligated them to do the same in Cambodia. Son Ngoc Minh and Khmer bureaucrats trained by the Vietnamese relocated to Hanoi. In Laos, however, the ceasefire agreements allowed the Pathet Lao to regroup in the provinces of Samneua and Phongsaly bordering on the Democratic Republic of Vietnam. While the Vietnamese withdrew their army from Laos, they also immediately dispatched hundreds of advisors across the border to help the Pathet Lao to continue building a resistance government, army, and, in 1955, a communist party. The Vietnamese also brought hundreds of Lao students, civil servants, cadres, and officers to study in the DRV. Over the next twenty years, the Vietnamese Workers Party would help the Pathet Lao to create a new bureaucratic elite and military class. Many of those graduates today hold the top positions in the Lao People's Democratic Republic that came to power along with their Vietnamese allies in 1975. This Indochinese nation-building is part of modern Vietnamese—and Laotian and Cambodian—history.[30]

Things turned out very differently in Cambodia. Firstly, by requiring the DRV/VWP to withdraw from all of Cambodia in 1954, the Geneva agreements allowed a different group of Cambodian communists led by a man named Saloth Sar, better known as Pol Pot, to build a separate communist party free of Vietnamese control. Secondly, by shrewdly leaning toward the Democratic Republic of Vietnam during the Vietnam War (for example, by allowing the Ho Chi Minh Trail to run through eastern Cambodia), Cambodia's Norodom Sihanouk effectively ensured that Vietnamese communists would not overthrow him or support his communist opponents, for whom he coined the popular phrase '*les Khmers Rouges*' ('the Red Khmers', i.e., communist Khmers). Thirdly, although Pol Pot and his entourage maintained links with the (militarily stronger) Vietnamese communists, the Cambodians had no intention of letting the Vietnamese recreate their own pre-1954 party-state administration and armed forces within eastern Cambodia. Rather than seeing the Vietnamese communists as allies, as did the Pathet Lao, the Khmers Rouges saw them and their Indochinese state-making as potential threats.

This became clear in 1970, when a military coup ousted Sihanouk from power and combined American and South Vietnamese troops invaded eastern Cambodia in a bid to destroy enemy bases and the Ho Chi Minh Trail's supply lines once and for all. While this certainly complicated the Democratic Republic of Vietnam's war effort, it also aggravated communist relations with the Khmers Rouges by forcing the Vietnamese deeper into Cambodian territory, including the Khmers Rouges zones. Rather than welcoming the new alliance with the DRV and Sihanouk, pushed on them by the Chinese and the Vietnamese, the Khmers Rouges truly feared that the Vietnamese would take over the Cambodian revolution where they had left it in 1954 by resuming their state-building à la laotienne and while having the Cambodian king tour the countryside on their behalf. Although the Democratic Republic of Vietnam never saw itself as bullying or ever entertained the thought of 'colonizing' Cambodia as the Khmers Rouges would later have it, they assumed that Pol Pot's entourage shared their dream of defeating the Americans and creating independent, associated communist regimes in all of Indochina in alliance with the wider communist bloc.

Here the Vietnamese erred massively. What they embraced as a 'policy of association', the Khmers Rouges saw as a new protectorate in the making. As the People's Army of Vietnam penetrated further into Cambodia under enemy bombs and artillery, the Khmers Rouges did their best to assert their national sovereignty not only against Washington and its Cambodians allies, but also against Hanoi and *its* Cambodian allies. The Khmers Rouges insisted that the Democratic Republic of Vietnam adhere strictly to their nationalist laws which governed their territories. The Khmers Rouges issued travel passes, imposed taxes, and tried (with great difficulty) to control PAVN military movements and interactions with local populations. They even asserted their control at the border over supplies coming from China via the Ho Chi Minh Trail. They wanted total sovereignty. That these Cambodian communists owed their territorial control to Vietnamese troops no more distracted them in their efforts to assert national sovereignty than massive American aid to Ngo Dinh Diem allowed Washington to stop Diem from building up south Vietnam on his own terms.[31]

Unsurprisingly, armed incidents occurred on the ground between these purported allies. Moreover, the return of many pre-1954 Vietnamese-trained Cambodians hardly reassured the Khmers Rouges core, fearful of a DRV-sanctioned *coup d'etat*. While it would be wrong to conclude that the two communist parties were already on their way to war, they operated in something very similar to what Edward Miller has described for the American relationship with Ngo Dinh Diem—a 'misalliance'. And at the core of the breakdown of both alliances were the questions of state-building and national sovereignty. Like the Americans before them, the Vietnamese never truly grasped this reality or its implications for them.[32]

If the Pathet Lao leadership relied on Vietnamese military might to come to power in 1975, and dutifully fell into line with the Paris Accords of 1973 and Hanoi's position, the Khmers Rouges were determined to get 'there', to full independence, first or at least alone, whatever the contradictions involved in practice. Unlike the Lao, the Khmers Rouges rejected Le Duc Tho's request that they sign the Paris Accords. Two years later, Pol Pot's party proudly took power in Phnom Penh on 17 April, over a week before Saigon fell to the People's Army of Vietnam. But when the victorious Vietnamese leadership came to congratulate the leaders of Pol Pot's new Democratic Kampuchea in mid-1975, disingenuously speaking of 'Indochinese solidarity' of all things, Cambodian communists interpreted this as yet another Vietnamese attempt to re-establish their domination at the expense of full Cambodian sovereignty. Despite his reassuring smile and words of thanks to the Vietnamese delegations, Pol Pot saw the Vietnamese communists as a threat to his ability to build a communist Cambodia free of the Indochinese model and its architects.

The Meltdown of Eurasian Internationalism
along the Indochinese Faultline

What no one saw coming in the heady days of mid-1975 was how the Sino-Soviet split running along the Eurasian axis of the communist bloc would interact explosively with this Vietnamese–Cambodian misalliance. Like its predecessors, the Third Indochina War cannot be understood without situating it in its global context. Indeed, the chain reaction setting off this Asian conflagration started in Eastern Europe during the 1960s. More than anything else, the Soviet invasion of Czechoslovakia in August 1968 shattered Eurasian communism for good by bringing its two most powerful states to the brink of war. Relations had long been tense between the two, but Moscow's blatant violation of another state's national sovereignty, a communist one at that, convinced Chinese communists that the Soviet Union, not the United States, had become China's principal national security threat. The Soviet declaration a month later on the 'Sovereignty and the International Obligations of Socialist Countries' did nothing to assuage Chinese fears. In fact, the announcement of the 'Brezhnev Doctrine' made them worse. Things got so bad that in March 1969 Chinese and Soviet troops clashed briefly but violently along a shared border crossing in Central Asia. Meanwhile, Mao halted his Cultural Revolution, shifted Chinese foreign policy from proletarian internationalism to realpolitik, and authorized the opening of negotiations with the Americans in an extraordinary volte-face designed to contain the Soviet Union.[33]

This historic shift in Sino-American relations and their reorientation toward Sino-American containment of the Soviets and their allies directly influenced Sino-Vietnamese and Vietnamese–Cambodian relations. The Chinese had first criticized the Vietnamese communists for negotiating with the Americans after the Tet Offensive in early 1968. But shaken by the Soviet invasion of Czechoslovakia a few months later, they then started pushing the Democratic Republic of Vietnam the other way, urging its leaders to talk to the Americans in Paris where secret talks had begun. To be sure, Beijing continued to support Hanoi in its bid to get the Americans to leave; but the Chinese now went ahead with their own simultaneous efforts to improve relations with the DRV's very enemy. Nixon's historic trip to China in early 1972 could not have come at a worse time in Vietnam's war against the Americans and Nixon exploited this leverage for all it was worth. Moscow also urged Hanoi to negotiate so that the Soviets could improve relations with the Americans, but they also provided the modern war material General Vo Nguyen Giap needed to launch the Easter Offensive in April 1972, determined not to let Vietnam lean China's way.

This complex competition among the Chinese, Soviets, and Americans was much more dangerous for the Vietnamese communists than it had ever been before 1969. Unsurprisingly, Chinese leaders proved the hardest to please. In their paranoiac fear of Soviet 'chauvinism', encirclement, and violations of national sovereignty at every turn, they increasingly interpreted any sign—real or imagined—of favoritism on the DRV's part toward Moscow as a national security threat. Meanwhile, the Soviets pushed back against Sino-American attempts to contain them in Eurasia by intensifying their relationship with the Vietnamese communists and consolidating their position in Asia via their naval presence in the eastern port at Vladivostok. In 1971, as Kissinger visited Beijing, the Soviet embassy in Hanoi reported that thanks to Vietnam's strengthening position and victory 'we will possess comparatively more possibilities for establishing our policy in this region. It is not excluded that Indochina may become for us the key to the whole of Southeast Asia. In addition, in that region there is nobody, so far, we could lean on, except the DRV'. It is not certain that the DRV's communist leadership grasped the dangers of what such a Soviet strategic embrace at this volatile conjuncture might entail. This proved to be another error in the Democratic Republic of Vietnam's foreign policy.[34]

But to be fair, it is not sure that anyone at the time grasped three interconnected things when Indochina became communist in 1975: 1) the extent to which the Chinese feared that any move on Hanoi's behalf toward the Soviet Union represented a dire threat to its national security by encirclement; 2) the degree to which the even more paranoid Khmers Rouges leaders, now in control of all of Cambodia, were increasingly convinced that the Vietnamese communists were already a national security threat that had to be opposed at all costs; and 3) how points 1) and 2) could combine dangerously to bring down the entire communist Church.[35]

That is exactly what happened when the Khmers Rouges lit a match at the bottom of this Eurasian communist edifice by attacking southern Vietnam in September 1977. Caught off-guard, Vietnamese communists acted frantically, demanding immediate explanations from their diplomats, intelligence officers, and former advisors as to the causes. Aware of the dangers of letting a hostile Sino-Cambodian alliance turn on him, Le Duan decided to keep the lid on anti-Khmers Rouges propaganda and then travelled to Beijing in October 1977 to plead with his Chinese partners to rein in Pol

Pot's Democratic Kampuchea. But the Chinese maintained their support of the murderous Khmers Rouges, convinced that they needed this country on their side in order to keep the Vietnamese from taking over all of former French Indochina and then handing it to the Soviets. Hanoi, in turn, was now convinced that Beijing was using the Khmers Rouges to encircle the Socialist Republic of Vietnam and reinforced its collaboration with the Lao communists now in power in Vientiane by signing a security treaty at the same time. This only reinforced Beijing's worst fears of a Soviet conspiracy in Indochina. Where brotherly internationalism had once underpinned Eurasian communist collaboration, paranoia, racism, and raw hate now took over as Vietnamese officials expelled the Chinese in their country, the Khmers Rouges ordered the massacre of the Vietnamese in theirs, and the Chinese and Soviet armies faced off across Eurasia, accusing each other of betraying the Marxist-Leninist canon.

Inter-communist war became a real possibility in Indochina sometime in 1977, and with it the equally real possibility that it could set off a wider Eurasian war among communists. Late in that year, Vietnamese communists sent the PAVN deep into Cambodia in a clear warning to Pol Pot to stop the attacks and as a signal to the new leaders taking over in China that Hanoi would overthrow the Khmers Rouges if they persisted in their attacks. It was a question of national security, the Vietnamese insisted. Pol Pot's entourage saw historic Vietnamese imperialism in this and severed relations with his communist neighbor. The Chinese ended their military and economic cooperation with their longtime Vietnamese allies. By early 1978, trust was in terribly short supply in all the communist capitals running from Moscow to Phnom Penh by way of Beijing and Hanoi. If there was ever a time for a communist leader to step forward in the Eurasian communist family and defuse brotherly tensions, this was it.

The Americans were certainly not going to help. Worried by Soviet advances in Africa and central Asia (the Soviet Union was increasing its support of a new regime in Afghanistan and trouble was brewing in Iran), the Carter administration played the 'China card', needing to stay on side with China rather than taking this chance to normalize relations with the DRV, whose leaders now desperately wanted to forget the past as the possibility of another war on a different flank loomed. Isolated, Hanoi signed a mutual defense treaty with Moscow in November 1978 before moving against the Khmers Rouges. But in so doing they confirmed Beijing's fear that all of Indochina would fall to the Soviets. As the Vietnamese prepared to invade

Cambodia and install a new government, Deng Xiaoping decided to play the 'American card' by travelling to Washington in a visit as historic as Nixon's to China in 1972 had been. He carried with him the promise to teach Vietnam a lesson if it invaded Cambodia. The Carter administration gave its blessing, leaning China's way and against Hanoi and Moscow.[36]

On 25 December 1978, the People's Army of Vietnam entered Cambodia and easily overthrew the Khmers Rouges, drove them to the Thai border, and installed a new revolutionary government faithful to Hanoi and Moscow. All of the actors were now on their way to transforming their worst fears—many of them pure fantasies at the start—into deadly and destabilizing realities. While the Socialist Republic of Vietnam did not intervene to save the Cambodian people from genocide, the People's Army of Vietnam did manage to end the Khmers Rouges' destruction of their own people, re-established Vietnam's security in the south, and saw the Vietnamese resume their Indochinese state-building in Cambodia with their Lao model in hand. The Chinese attacked the Vietnamese in the north on 17 February 1979, when five divisions of their army marched across the SRV's border, sending thousands of innocent civilians running for their lives. While satellite imagery provided by the Americans reassured the Chinese that the Soviets would not attack from the north, thereby excluding a two-front Eurasian war, the Chinese Red Army suffered heavy losses in its attempt to teach a lesson to one of the best trained, equipped, and experienced armies in the world. The Chinese army was humiliated.

It was on the diplomatic and economic fronts where Deng Xiaoping dealt the Vietnamese a devastating blow. Despite their unflinching support of the Khmers Rouges, the Chinese successfully isolated the Vietnamese in all of Asia for over a decade, thanks in no small part to their unprecedented collaboration with the United States. Deng Xiaoping, supported by the Americans and the Japanese, also rallied the Association of South East Asian Nations states to his cause and successfully led the charge to keep the Khmers Rouges alive on the Thai-Cambodian border and in the United Nations' General Assembly.[37]

While it may not have been apparent at the time, the Eurasian segment of the Cold War had vanished by 1979—a full decade before the Berlin Wall crumbled in Europe. That it did so in Indochina is no accident, for this is precisely where the Sino-Soviet and Vietnamese-Cambodian fault-lines running through the Eurasian communist bloc intersected. The first fault-lines had appeared in 1969 and 1970, respectively. The result was the first war among communists in world history. Unlike the situation in 1950, the showdown was no longer between the Americans and the Chinese. It was now between the Chinese and Soviets. Nor did it have anything to do with ideology, one of the essential defining components of a 'cold war'. Little wonder the Americans let the South East Asia Treaty Organization quietly die in 1977. For Deng Xiaoping, the Soviet invasion of Afghanistan in 1979, Moscow's support of the Vietnamese in Indochina, and its rapidly increasing naval presence in the South Sea via the deep-water port of Cam Ranh Bay only confirmed his fears of encirclement. The Third Indochina War—viewed as a continuation of the earlier ones reaching back to the start of the Second World War in Asia in 1937—thus confirms the geopolitical importance of Vietnam/Indochina in twentieth-century world history and geopolitics, not just for the Japanese, French, and Americans, but also for the two communist giants who faced off against each other in central Asia— China and the USSR.[38]

The world leader who finally stepped forward to end the Indochina wars and repair relations across the Eurasian bloc was the Soviet statesman, Mikhail Gorbachev. He understood that the only way to set the Soviet Union on the road to domestic prosperity and thus enable him to implement vital reforms internally was to rethink Moscow's foreign policy entirely, from east to west and north to south. Most importantly, he refused to continue bankrolling either an eastern European empire that had little legitimacy or far-flung expeditions in the Afro-Asian world that cost too much and only made it harder for the Soviets to reach a détente with both the Americans *and* the Chinese. The People's Army of Vietnam might have become the fifth largest army in the world (the third if you count all its personnel), but it did so only because Moscow provided it and the Socialist Republic of Vietnam with massive assistance, totaling 3.3 billion in US dollars by 1985—twice the 1978 level. Soviet support of the Vietnamese, their Lao allies, and Vietnamese nation-building in Cambodia was very expensive and only served to alienate Moscow commercially and diplomatically from what was one of the most dynamic regions of the world by the 1980s—non-communist Asia.[39]

Gorbachev thus wanted to normalize relations with Deng Xiaoping's China as much as he did with Ronald Reagan's United States in order to reform his country via the policies of economic restructuring ('*perestroika*'). To this end, he negotiated an end to the Cold War with Reagan and accepted Deng Xiaoping's three main demands for normalizing Sino-Soviet relations—the reduction of Soviet troops on the Sino-Soviet border; the withdrawal of Soviet troops from Afghanistan; and the end of the Soviet-backed Vietnamese occupation of Cambodia. In 1988-9, Sino-Soviet relations improved rapidly as the Soviet army withdrew from Afghanistan and the Vietnamese pulled out of Cambodia. The impact on the Soviets' relationship with Vietnam was immediate as Soviet aid to the SRV fell by 63 percent in 1990. And as communist regimes in Eastern Europe imploded from 1989 onward, taking the Soviet Union with them two years later, the SRV found itself almost totally isolated in the world (and its ties to Cuba, North Korea, Mongolia, and then South Yemen in no way changed this reality). Following the Soviet lead, Hanoi agreed to negotiate a political settlement to end the war in Cambodia and to swallow its pride and improve relations with China. Otherwise, Vietnamese communists had no choice short of isolating themselves from the entire world like North Korea's Kim Il-sung. In October 1991, with the Cold War now terminated in Europe and Asia, all the major players in the Third Indochina War supported a United Nations-backed peace conference in Paris that ended almost fifty years of war. A UN peacekeeping mission brokered and enforced a ceasefire and then presided over elections held in 1993 that created a coalition government of the Royal Cambodian Government. In 1998, Pol Pot died and the Khmers Rouges disbanded. A half-century of war finally ended. But now the Vietnamese had to focus on the well-being of their own people or risk losing it all as the fall of the Berlin Wall in Europe and the pro-democracy demonstrations in Tiananmen Square in Beijing had just demonstrated. The prospects for building communism in Vietnam had never looked bleaker.[40]

THE FAILURE OF COMMUNISM?

A Capitalist Revolution

Communism provided Chinese and Vietnamese leaders with an extraordinary instrument for creating single party-states capable of controlling and mobilizing massive numbers of people and resources for making war. But once the guns finally fell silent, the Vietnamese, like the Chinese, discovered that communism—whether Marxist, Leninist, Stalinist or Maoist in design—offered no miracle for attaining rapid economic, industrial, and technological modernization. 'Waging a war is simple', Pham Van Dong conceded to Western reporters in 1983, 'running a country is difficult'.

Indeed, by 1983, hardcore communists like Pham Van Dong had to admit that their failing socio-economic policies, and not just war and international isolation, were also responsible for their troubles. By that year, hundreds of thousands of Vietnamese were fleeing the country by boat. Hunger, indeed famine in several places, stalked the countryside. Vietnam remained one of the poorest nations on the planet, with a humiliating annual per capita income stuck at below one hundred American dollars. The legitimacy of the party had never been lower at the moment that its international isolation was highest.[41]

Like Deng Xiaoping and Mikhail Gorbachev, Vietnamese communists realized that they had to improve the well-being of their people if they wished to remain in power. Raw peasant hunger had brought the Viet Minh to power in August 1945. The same thing could bring them down fifty years later. It was in this context that Vietnamese communists decided to embark upon a comprehensive reform of their economic policy. Although initial attempts had begun as early as 1979, it was only in 1986 that the Vietnamese Communist Party united behind the veteran communist Nguyen Van Linh to push through a series of reforms known in Vietnamese as *doi moi* ('renovation'). Just like their Sino-Soviet counterparts, the Vietnamese abandoned Stalinist central planning in favor of allowing a market-oriented economy based on supply and demand to operate. This was particularly the case in the agricultural sector, where new laws rolled back collectivization in favor of private initiative, ownership, and market-based incentives. Vietnamese communists may have cursed Deng Xiaoping in public for starting the Third Indochina War, but in private they recognized that his liberal economic policies were a model for reviving agricultural production and holding on to power. The 1986 reforms encouraged the development of the non-state sector too. Entrepreneurship was no longer a dirty word or subject to state-sponsored discrimination. Indeed, while reforming the economy along liberal lines, the politburo rehabilitated many southerners whose experience, contacts, and networks could help turn it around. The discredited Stalinist industrialization model rapidly ceded the way to export-led development using Vietnam's comparative advantage in agriculture and cheap labor.

Over the next decade, the SRV went further in its economic renovation. In 1988, the party approved new laws allowing foreign direct investment and accorded greater decision-making powers to state-owned enterprises while decreasing state subsidies to them. In the countryside, the party presided over the full de-collectivization of agriculture. Peasants recovered their own equipment and land. In 1989, the party stopped fixing agricultural prices altogether, allowing them to fluctuate in response to supply and demand. The government simultaneously devalued its national currency, the *dong*, in order to stimulate exports in particular, all the while tightening fiscal and monetary policy in an effort to control demand, and with it, runaway inflation. The party reformed its communist-minded banking and legal systems, turning them—and the state in charge of them—into something very different. Banks now had to generate capital by increasing savings rates, providing capital investment while at the same time paying competitive interest rates.[42]

Although the implementation of these policies was not without difficulties (especially that of inflation), over the next decade economic development took off in Vietnam. Thanks to market incentives, food production bounced back rapidly, eradicating famine and transforming Vietnam into the third-largest exporter of rice in the world. Between 1990 and 1997, the annual growth rate of the Gross Domestic Product (GDP) averaged around 8 percent as Vietnam clawed its way back from being one of the poorest countries in the world to enter the ranks of the developing nations. Overall economic growth has remained strong over the last fifteen years despite the Asian crash of 1997 and the global crisis of 2008–9. Between 2000 and 2005 the annual growth rate of GDP hovered at around 7 percent before declining to about 5 percent in 2012. Poverty and hunger have declined remarkably in Vietnam—only 11 percent of the population lives below the poverty line, whereas over 50 percent were in that category prior to the reforms which started in 1986.

Export-led development has created a wide variety of jobs in labor-intensive industries such as garment-making, shoe-making, and computer assemblage. Rice, coffee, and tea exports have also grown rapidly, helping to keep the unemployment rate at 4.3 percent in 2012. The agricultural sector's contribution to GDP has declined from 25 percent in 2000 to 22 percent in 2012, whereas industry's share has increased from 36 percent to 41 percent. Tourism and the service industry accounts for the rest. While GDP growth slowed in 2012, the capitalist-minded market reforms begun officially in 1986 have profoundly transformed Vietnamese society and set it on a very different track to the one the founders of the communist party could have ever imagined. The irony of course is that this capitalist-oriented economic model was precisely the one the Republic of Vietnam had trail-blazed first, as in Taiwan and South Korea. Vietnamese communists, like their Chinese counterparts, had effectively abandoned the communist roadmap to modernization in favor of a market-driven one. This was revolutionary.[43]

A Diplomatic Revolution?

The radical transformation of the economy required an equally revolutionary change in diplomacy. Since 1950, Vietnamese communists had aligned themselves with Moscow and Beijing, their two biggest supporters during twenty-five years of war against the French and Americans. By entering the Eurasian communist world, however, Vietnamese communists had effectively severed Vietnam from its closest Southeast Asian connections, with the exception of the party's Indochinese sister-states in Laos and Cambodia. Hanoi had even spurned a 1973 invitation to join the Association of South East Asian Nations as an observer, assuming that it was an Asian cover for the American-run SEATO military alliance. Instead, in 1978, Hanoi had joined the Council for Mutual Economic Assistance (COMECON), the Soviet-led economic organization from which China had already withdrawn. East Germany's Stasi (secret police) played a vital role in turning communist Vietnam into a modern police state under the close watch of Tran Quoc Hoan, Vietnam's legendary security chief. This meant that as of 1979 the communist leadership in Hanoi had, intentionally and unintentionally, reoriented Vietnam's diplomacy from its historic Asian focus to one almost exclusively focused on the eastern European bloc led by the Soviet Union.[44]

Vietnamese communists owe much to Mikael Gorbachev for forcing them to re-orientate their diplomacy from Eastern Europe back to Asia. Most importantly, Gorbachev's decision to improve Sino-Soviet relations required the Vietnamese to mend their own rift with the Chinese. In July 1986, the Soviet leader announced in Vladivostok that his troops would withdraw from Afghanistan and Mongolia. He simultaneously pressed upon the Vietnamese the importance of getting out of Cambodia and normalizing relations 'with the People's Republic of China for the sake of peace in Asia and the world'. The Vietnamese, as we saw above, complied, as Soviet assistance declined sharply and only highlighted their international vulnerability and internal economic crisis. In 1991, the disappearance of the entire European communist bloc, accounting for over 50 percent of the Socialist Republic of Vietnam's foreign trade in 1988, left Vietnamese communists with no choice but to reset their diplomacy entirely.[45]

The Vietnamese had already approved policy changes to this effect, most notably resolution 13 in 1988 on the 'change of the world and our new thinking'. This document officially authorized the party to begin normalizing relations with former enemy states in order to end Vietnam's diplomatic and commercial isolation and support the party's efforts to reform the domestic economy as rapidly as possible. This, too, led to Hanoi's support of the peace conference in Paris that finally ended the Third Indochina War in 1991. It allowed General Vo Nguyen Giap to lead a delegation to Beijing to attend the Asian Games in 1990, during which time he met with Chinese officials to patch up strained Sino-Vietnamese relations. In November 1991, only weeks after the Paris Conference on Cambodia ended successfully, the Chinese and Vietnamese officially normalized their diplomatic relations.[46]

Having cleared this hurdle, the Socialist Republic of Vietnam could then rapidly improve its ties with the rest of Asia and the world. The leadership in Hanoi accepted ASEAN's invitation to join it as an observer and became a full member in 1995. In that same year, Hanoi and Washington also reached an historic agreement establishing diplomatic relations between the two former enemies. Vietnam followed up its opening to the non-communist world by expanding its cooperation with liberal capitalist organizations such as the International Monetary Fund, the World Bank, the Asian Development Bank, and the World Trade Organization, which it joined in 2007. The internationalist communist world in which Ho Chi Minh and his party had circulated for so long was no more.

Non-communist Asia in particular ensured the success of modern Vietnam's renovation at the turn of the twenty-first century. As of 1989, the Soviet Union had accounted for 34 percent of the SRV's exports and 63 percent of its imports. With the disappearance of the communist world by 1991, those same numbers had dropped to 10 percent and 13 percent respectively. Filling the gap were Japan, South Korea, Taiwan, the Association of Southeast Asian Nations, and, increasingly, China, not the French or the Americans. Asian countries provided 82 percent of communist Vietnam's imports in 1992 and absorbed 60 percent of its exports a year later. The advanced economic development and vitality of Asian capitalism and trade in the late twentieth century helped Vietnam modernize in ways colonialism and communism had always blocked.[47]

But, as in China, this internal and external revolution in communist Vietnam raises important questions. For one, the SRV's embrace of capitalist-oriented development means that the communist vision of the world announced by Truong Chinh in 1950, casting Vietnam as the Indochinese frontline communist soldier fighting the capitalist imperialists in Southeast Asia, was a failure. Three-and-a-half decades later the leader of the Vietnamese Communist Party, Truong Chinh (whose name means the 'Long March') made the astonishing statement that the party had to adopt the *doi moi* reforms because the party had erred 'in our desire to achieve transformation at an early date by quickly abolishing non socialist economic components'. This came from the very man who had pushed through radical Maoist reforms in 1950s and had embraced orthodox communism all his life. At the head of the party again, he now embraced capitalist-minded reforms like his counterparts in China. The survival of his Vietnam depended on it.[48]

Secondly, while the communist leadership has celebrated the Socialist Republic of Vietnam's historic entry into the ASEAN and its normalization of relations with the United States in 1995 as diplomatic victories, viewed over a longer span of time the opposite is arguably the case. By joining forces with the Americans and the ASEAN countries, the Vietnamese communist core had in many ways admitted its failure to build a modern Vietnam and to promote an alternative communist-oriented Southeast Asia, as was first pioneered by Ho Chi Minh (himself one of the creators of the Thai and Malayan communist parties back in 1930). If the Vietnamese communists scored an historic victory in 1975 over the Americans and unified the country for the first time in over a century, in 1995 the United States and the ASEAN also won when lifelong communists embraced the global capitalist system against which they had fought for most of their lives. Leaders in Hanoi, Washington, and the Association of South East Asian Nations' capital cities may all share a fear of Chinese expansion into the South China Sea today, but the reason why they can collaborate today is because the SRV abandoned communism during the Third Indochina War and withdrew from Cambodia. And—just as important—the Eurasian communist bloc, of which the Vietnamese communists were once proud and willing members, simply no longer exists.

CHAPTER 14

VIETNAM FROM BEYOND
THE RED RIVER

We must know how to use our military units correctly, so as to send them in
large numbers to open land and create new economic zones. These units must
consist of many soldiers and fighters who are unshakeable and enthusiastic
in their revolutionary spirit and desire to succeed so as to move mountains
and dig rivers that will transform these empty regions and deserts into land
covered with fertile fields supporting a thriving population.[1]
—PRIME MINISTER PHAM VAN DONG, 1977

T HE EMPTY LANDS to which Pham Van Dong referred in this 1977 address were the highlands of modern Vietnam. Rising from the Gulf
of Tonkin in the northeast, this collection of cragged hills and deep valleys stretches westward, looping around the Red River lowlands as it drops
southward down the central coastline before finally vanishing into the Mekong delta. This massif makes up almost half of Vietnam territorially today.
It teems with rivers, forests, animals, and some of Vietnam's most important
natural resources (zinc, ore, bauxite, and silver) and plantation crops (rubber, coffee, and tea). It also offers protection. During the First Indochina
War, the northern highlands were home to the Democratic Republic of
Vietnam and the site of its historic battle victory over the French in 1954. A
few years later, the DRV pushed its supply lines further southward through
the central highlands to feed and arm forces fighting the Americans. Without the highlands, there would have been no victory at Dien Bien Phu and
no operational Ho Chi Minh Trail. Speaking in 1977, as Vietnamese communists prepared to go to war again over Indochina, Pham Van Dong had
good reason to dispatch soldiers into these areas. He erred, however, when
he spoke of the highlands as empty places. They were not and the prime
minister knew it. He had served there during the 1940s.[2]

By now, the astute reader will have noticed that the narrative to this point
has been a very 'lowland' and 'Viet'-centric one. This history of modern

Vietnam began in the Red River delta at the dawn of the first millennium CE to follow a range of lowland Viet kings, settlers, administrators, revolutionaries, missionaries, state-builders, and workers as they made their way south. After the city of Hanoi came that of Hue, followed by Saigon. While the simplicity of the north-to-south take renders it almost irresistible for those trying to order a narrative for Vietnam's unwieldy past, this standard view comes with serious problems. For one, it is a linear, teleological approach, organized around the inexorable expansion of the Viet people from one delta to another. Scholars inside and outside Vietnam refer to it widely as the Nam Tien ('Southward Advance') school of thought. Secondly, this north–south narrative is very ethnocentric. It downplays the importance of the non-Viet peoples who lived in lowland areas of the central coastline and the Mekong delta, most notably the Cham, the Khmer, and the Chinese. It does the same for the highlands, where dozens of non-Viet peoples like the Tai and Jarai constituted the majority populations until the late twentieth century. As we have seen in this book, until recently, there was no one S-like Vietnam running from north to south.[3]

And this brings us back to the tricky question of Vietnamese colonialism. Advocates of the Southern Advance school tend to celebrate ethnic Viet expansion southward as a sign of strength and vitality. Heroism serves as the favorite trope. Like their Euro-American counterparts, Viet settlers were determined, hardy souls, who, through their blood, sweat, and tears, turned all of these blank spaces into productive fields, brought civilization and modernity to its primitive peoples, and ensured that Vietnam would persevere over its rivals. Missing in this frontier myth is any discussion of how the Viet often took these lands from others, how they conquered people by force, or how the Viet colonizers and the non-Viet colonized also interacted in much more complex ways.

Communist historians in Vietnam today still try to avoid this question altogether, knowing that they created a powerful nationalist myth during the Indochina wars by casting the Viet as the heroic colonized people who threw off the yoke of Western imperialism. Like their Chinese counterparts, Vietnamese communists find it terribly hard to admit that they, too, have been colonizers. Each prefers to extend the idea of a unitary Vietnam far back into the past. Many foreign historians supportive of the Democratic Republic of Vietnam's heroic struggle against the French, the Americans, and the Chinese have also conveniently avoided this chapter in modern Vietnam's history.[4]

This will no longer do. Just as no serious student of American history would accept uncritically Frederick Jackson Turner's famous 'frontier thesis' which cast American history as the unique product of the inexorable expansion of settlers westward, so too should we avoid the Southward Advance version organizing the history of modern Vietnam into one single march from southern China to the Gulf of Thailand. Nor should we avoid Vietnam's own colonial history because it places the Viet in the role of conqueror instead of the victim of foreign domination. This also means accepting that the Cham, Khmer, Jarai, Rhadé, Bahnar, Tai, Hmong, and others are central, not marginal, to our story. For centuries, they ruled other Vietnams and resisted the making of a colonial Vietnam. So before ending this book, let us return to the past again. But this time let us reset our narrative and chronology by beginning in areas beyond the Red River delta, in the rich world of the highlands, along the central coast, and in the Mekong delta—before the Viet arrived. And then let us consider how the non-Viet peoples resisted *and* interacted with Viet state-making, including its imperial forms. It is time to let go of Viet exceptionalism and ethnocentrism as much as its French, Chinese, or American variants.[5]

BEFORE THE VIET CAME:
THE COASTAL AND HIGHLAND PEOPLES OF VIETNAM

Where Mainland Southeast Asia and the Indian Ocean Meet[6]

Some ten thousand years ago, two groups of people each with unique linguistic patterns colonized wide swathes of mainland Southeast Asia—the Austronesians and the Austroasiatics. The Austronesians originated from the island of Taiwan between five and seven thousand years ago. While these peoples had brought agricultural techniques with them from southern China, they also developed sophisticated navigational skills and techniques which allowed them to cross the South China Sea and the Indian Ocean from around the third millennium BCE onward. Their movements were such that by the first millennium BCE, many had reached the coasts of Japan, Vietnam, the Philippines, Java, Sumatra, Polynesia, and Hawaii. Others ventured westward into the Indian Ocean. Some got as far as Madagascar off the eastern African coast, making the Austronesians the first people to cross the Indian Ocean, long before the Chinese, Middle Easterners, and Europeans.

Over the centuries, these peoples settled down across large swathes of island and mainland Southeast Asia and contributed to building smaller political units, cultures, and languages. Located at the center of these maritime movements was today's central Vietnam, where Austronesians made landfall sometime before the first millennium CE. Many of them moved into the nearby highlands in search of game, people who eventually became the Jarai, Rhadé, and Raglai. Others, such as the Cham, remained mainly on the coastline, learning to plant rice, fish, and trade. Connections between the high and lowlands continued over time, as did exchanges with the Indian Ocean world. Indeed, it is useful to think of coastal Vietnam as an extension of archipelago Southeast Asia.[7]

To the north, the Austroasiatic family moved overland from today's India to mainland Southeast Asia by way of southern China. This linguistic group emerged in the Neolithic period around 4,000 years ago. The Austroasiatic peoples were agriculturally oriented. They planted rice and taro as they followed fish-laden streams and rivers from one valley to another. Some of the earliest settled agricultural communities emerged around 2000 BCE inside the deltas of the Red, Mekong, and Chao Phyra rivers which drop down from southern China. These peoples may have initially originated in the Mekong River's lower branches around 4,000 years ago. They then followed inland waterways westward and northward into the Chao Phraya (Thailand) and Red River (Vietnam) deltas, foraging, fishing, and planting their way along. The Austroasiatics included the Khmer, Bahnar, Sedang, Hre, and others. Even the future 'Viet' rulers of the Red River delta heralded from this wider world. In fact, linguists place the Viet language in the proto Mon Khmer subcategory of the Austroasiatic linguistic family. Sinization came later with the extension of the Han empire into the Red River area. The arrival of the Austronesians along the coastline tended to keep the Austroasiatics within inland areas. However, the two linguistic families often mixed as Austronesians migrated into upland areas, especially in the central highlands of Vietnam.

This rapid journey into the depths of time allows us to appreciate the extent to which these peoples had spread throughout upland and lowland parts of Vietnam, Thailand, Cambodia, Laos, and southern China and had begun developing their own civilizations and polities. The appearance of a distinctive Austroasiatic style of pottery during the first millennium BCE is a case in point. The production of Dong Son drums is yet another. Although these drums seem to have originated from the Red River valley, attesting to the cultural vitality of this region, they were products of a common cultural core extending into today's Thailand and the southern Chinese massif discussed in chapter 1. Further to the south, the peoples of Austronesian stock presided over the creation of flourishing commercial centers and civilizations anchored along the coast which ran from central Vietnam to the Gulf of Thailand. During the first millennium CE, the spread of the Iron Age and advances in agricultural techniques allowed new coastal polities such as Oc Eo, Funan, and Sa Huynh to emerge. The ability of these coastal polities to tap into Indian Ocean commercial exchanges extending from the Middle East to the Han empire reinforced their state-building, economic development, and cultural expansion. The demand in the Mediterranean, the Middle East, and China for Southeast Asian spices and luxury goods was particularly important. As early as the third century BCE, Chinese annalists wrote of cloves growing in island Southeast Asia, while their Roman counterparts made similar reports some centuries later. Given the vibrancy of the Indian Ocean trade, we should not be surprised that archeologists have unearthed Roman coins in the coastal polity of Oc Eo in today's southern Vietnam.

Thanks to these early maritime connections, local leaders in central and southern Vietnam not only traded with the Eurasian world, but they also adopted foreign religions and writing systems coming from abroad, adapted them to local spiritual, cultural, and political contexts, and, in doing so, often turned them into something unique. Over the centuries, peoples and leaders in Oc Eo, Funan, and Ha Suynh adopted Hinduism, Mahayana, and then Theravada Buddhism. Sanskrit and Indian Brahmanic-based scripts and inscriptions appeared for the first time as local leaders and clergy developed writing systems to express their spoken languages, ideas, and sacred beliefs. Indian concepts of kingship, astronomy, calendric time, music, and philosophy found clients in these early non-Viet civilizations. And this 'Indianization' occurred over centuries, succeeded in some areas, failed in others, but was always tailored to local needs.

This was certainly true of the powerful Khmer leaders who emerged by the end of the first millennium CE. In 802, King Jayavarman II laid the foundations of a mighty Khmer empire based near Tonlé Sap, with the Mekong River feeding it in the rainy season. Thanks to this abundant water supply, Khmer rulers developed an elaborate hydraulic complex in Angkor Wat, capable of irrigating rice plants and thus producing ever-larger amounts of it. This, in turn, supported one of the largest pre-modern urban populations in the world. Khmer rulers also drew their strength from maritime commerce and used combined persuasion and brute force to expand their empire northward into Laos and eastward into the Mekong delta.

Although the Mekong delta, the Vietnamese coastline, and the surrounding highlands were not heavily populated, these were obviously not empty spaces. Nor were they isolated from the wider region and the world. The central Vietnamese coast in particular offered great opportunities to its inhabitants; but it also posed potential threats. After all, if the Han extended their empire into the Red River delta, making it their southernmost province, it was in part because they wanted an opening to the Indian Ocean trade. For one thousand years, the Han empire ruled the Red River valley.

The Linyi and the Cham Coastal States of the Indian Ocean[8]

To the south of China's Jiaozhi province emerged new non-Viet states, each of which benefitted from its maritime connections to India, China, *and* the highlands. Over the course of the first millennium, new polities succeeded those of Funan, Ha Suynh, and Oc Eo. By the fourth and fifth centuries, a new confederation of coastal kingdoms collectively known as Linyi emerged south of the Red River delta. Initially based around Hue, this polity's leaders took full advantage of their maritime position by trading vigorously with the Indian Ocean world. They expanded their trading to include intensive exchanges with their Chinese neighbor, whose growing economic and cultural development offered new opportunities. While Linyi rulers continued to adapt Indian religions and ideas, they also imported Chinese pottery, architectural styles, art, and ideas through China's Jiaozhi province. The line between 'East Asia and China' and 'Southeast Asia and India' was never a sharp one in practice.[9]

Cham polities emerged in the Thu Bon Valley, Nha Trang, and Phan Rang. Like the Austronesians before them, the Cham arrived in Vietnam via the sea, possibly from the Philippines. They traded actively with China, India, and the Middle East. They, too, tailored Hinduism and Buddhism to local needs and used Sanskrit to create a writing system for the Cham language, perhaps the first for Southeast Asia. The Linyi and Cham coastal federations co-existed until around the sixth century, when, for reasons that are not clear, the two states melded into one which was increasingly referred to as Champa. Until the eleventh century, and even later, Champa ruled the coast of central Vietnam, from the southern border of China's

Jiaozhi province to the Khmer empire in the Mekong delta. Again, there was no 'Vietnam' during the first millennium.

Nor was there ever one unified Cham state or empire. 'Champa' was, in reality, an archipelago-like constellation of small, interconnected coastal kingdoms scattered down the central coastline. Over the centuries, these polities divided into five major realms: 1) Indrapura (located in today's provinces of Quang Binh, Quang Tri, and Thua Thien); 2) Amaravati (in Quang Nam, Quang Ngai province and on the Thu Bon River), 3) Vijaya (Binh Dinh and along the Con River; 4) Panduranga (in Ninh Thuan, Binh Thuan, and along the Dinh River); and 5) Kauthara (Phu Yen, Khanh Hoa, and along the Cai River). They were decentralized kingdoms whose populations gravitated around a charismatic monarch in a specific location. Each kingdom possessed its own religious markers and separate commercial and agricultural activities. Borders were fluid and often overlapped; power was diffuse. Champa, like other neighboring polities at the time, was a collection of small territories, 'a patchwork of often overlapping *mandalas*, or "circles of kings"'. Stronger polities could absorb smaller ones, often doing so violently. This federation of small polities had much in common with the coastal states of archipelago Southeast Asia today, such as Majahapit in today's Indonesia, than the imperially structured Chinese state to the north or the more centralized, mainland ones that would later emerge in the Red River (Dai Viet), Chaophraya (Thailand), and Irrawaddy (Burma) deltas. In fact, the Cham dispatched official delegations to Majahapit, married their children into island royal families, and served as the intermediaries for commercial, cultural, and religious transfers across archipelago Southeast Asia. Malay peoples were also present in Cham courts, ports, and armies.[10]

The Cham also interacted with the nearby Austronesian and Austroasiatic peoples living in the highlands—the Rhade, Roglai, Jorai, Bahnar, Hre, and others. The latter provided Cham traders with much-sought-after luxury goods for the Indian Ocean and Chinese markets, such as rhinoceros horns, ivory, cinnamon, and especially aromatic woods. Eaglewood was particularly important. Cham artistic exchanges—sculptures, statues, and steles—spread inward by overland routes and deep into the Indian Ocean islands by sea. At different times, some Cham kings used these connections to extend their political influence far into the massif. *Champassak,* the name of a central Laotian province today, is suggestive of such ties. Some highlanders even became Cham kings. And thanks to their commercial networks, Cham merchants served as the intermediaries for the export of Red River ceramics into Indian Ocean markets.[11]

Cham coastal links eventually brought them into contact with another religion coming from the far western border of the Indian Ocean—Islam. Arab traders had long traded with Southeast Asia in spices and aromatic woods. From the thirteenth and fourteenth centuries onward, these traders and the missionaries traveling with them ('*sufis*') began to spread the Islamic religion rapidly through the coastal polities of island Southeast Asia. Sultanates emerged in such places as Majahapit. Linked commercially, culturally, and matrimonially to archipelago courts, the Cham brought Islam to the Vietnamese coast in the fifteenth century. In so doing, they joined the Khmer and their Austronesian predecessors in transforming areas below the Red River into a fascinating religious mosaic combining Hinduism, Buddhism, Islam, and pre-existing Austronesian animistic beliefs and practices. Meanwhile, in Jiaozhi province, the Chinese introduced characters, Confucianism, Mahayana Buddhism, and new cultural practices.[12]

The Rise and Fall of Po Binasor's Champa[13]

But even the emergence of an independent Dai Viet polity in the eleventh century did not spell the end of the Cham states, the Khmer empire, or the highlands. Nor did it necessarily send the Viet pouring southward to build 'Vietnam' in one fell swoop as the Nam Tien myth claims. Despite the impressive efforts of Dai Viet annalists to locate a shared past in the precolonial period, court politics in the newly born Vietnamese state remained highly unstable, as local leaders competed with each other for power and control of military and economic resources. Moreover, the threat of a Chinese return to the region was always real and the Cham and the Khmer were no regional pushovers. Twentieth-century Cham and Khmer nationalists would like us to believe that they were the pacific victims of Vietnamese colonial aggression; but some centuries earlier their leaders had fought each other and neither had any qualms about attacking the nascent Dai Viet state in the north to expand their own empires. Attracted in large part by Champa's growing trade with Song China (960–1279) discussed in chapter 1, in the late twelfth century the Khmers attacked and occupied Cham territories, setting up their headquarters in the area of Vijaya in Binh Dinh province today. The Cham pushed back and, in 1226, drove out the Khmers, in order to create their own powerbase in Vijaya. The new leaders also took full advantage of the greater Chinese interaction in the Indian Ocean trade to strengthen their own state and finance a large standing army. Following the defeat of the Mongols in China in 1368, the Cham again improved trading and diplomatic relations with China's new leaders, the commercially and expansionist-minded Ming.

It was in this wider context that a remarkably charismatic Cham king named Po Binasor (Che Bong Nga, in Vietnamese) took power and presided over a golden age in Cham history in the late fourteenth century. Not only did Po unite the various Cham polities under his control, but he also sought to regain lands the Cham had ceded or lost to the Dai Viet. In 1371, with a green light from China, Po drove his armies overland into the Red River delta, landed his warships on the coast, and marched his men on the Dai Viet capital of Hanoi. Cham troops looted Hanoi and burnt the enemy's palace to the ground as civilians ran for cover. In 1376, Po Binasor struck again, overpowering the Dai Viet forces and this time even killing the country's king. By the late fourteenth century, the Cham had not only recovered their lands, but they had also pushed their polity into the lower Red River basin and fostered better relations with China in doing so. If the Dai Viet had repelled the Mongol invaders, they nonetheless failed to stop the Cham from sacking their capital, twice.

Although Po Binasor's violent northern advance shook the young Dai Viet state to its core, the Viet held on and clawed their way back. When the Cham monarch went on the warpath again in 1390, Dai Viet forces counter-attacked, killed Po Binasor in battle, and prepared to press further southward. The only forces stopping them were those of the Chinese, whose commercial interests in the Indian Ocean and its trade remained as real as ever. Admiral Zheng He's famous armadas taking him to Africa and to the holy city of Mecca started at this time. In 1406, Ming armies occupied the Red River and transformed it once again into an imperial province, while Zheng He's boats stopped over in Champa. Although the Dai Viet drove the Chinese out once more in 1428 and established the Le dynasty, the country's new leaders, many of them military men coming from areas along the kingdom's southern frontier (the Le, Trinh, and Nguyen), were convinced that the survival of their small state depended on its territorial expansion southward down into the coastal lowlands and the opening of new ground for wet-rice production (and relief from over-population) in the Red River delta. Leaders coming from southern Dai Viet also knew that Vijaya (Qui Nhon today) provided the best opening to the lucrative trade of the Indian Ocean world. No one at the time knew where any of this would go; but it was the start of the Dai Viet colonial project that began with the massive Le attack on Champa in 1471.

The Peoples of the Northern Highlands

While Dai Viet expansion focused mainly on the southern coastal low-lands, war, trade, and migration continued to connect the young Red River state to the surrounding massif in the north and its peoples. Over the cen-turies, new groups of people continued to arrive in the northern highlands from southern China, most notably the peoples of the Tai-Kadai language family. Slash-and-burn agriculture predominated among them, but wet-rice methods were common where valley water was available. Caravan routes crossed the massif, bringing Chinese traders, explorers, missionaries, and eventually imperial armies. Ideas, technologies, and news moved as new opportunities arose for those who would seize them.

Indeed, the Viet were not the only peoples who tried to create their own state when the Tang dynasty collapsed in the tenth century. In the eleventh century, the Tai-speaking Nung people living along both sides of a loosely controlled Sino-Dai Viet frontier found a charismatic leader in the person of Nung Tri Cao. This young man was familiar with Han statecraft, characters, and attracted by the idea of building an independent state. In 1042, he established the Nung kingdom of 'Great Succession' in the areas of today's Cao Bang and Lang Son provinces. Wary of the emergence of a competing kingdom on their northern border, Dai Viet authorities carried him off to Hanoi. Upon his release a few years later, Tri Cao founded the kingdom of the Southern Heavens in 1048 and, when that failed, tried again by forming the kingdom of the Great South in 1052. This time the Chinese imperial army chased him into the Tai area in Yunnan province, where he died. Although Tri Cao's efforts to carve out a new state like that of the Viet on the edges of the Chinese empire ultimately failed, this eleventh-century man demonstrates the extent to which peoples like the Tai and Nung con-tinued to operate in the loosely controlled highlands and had their own state-building projects. And in implementing them, charismatic leaders like Tri Cao obligated Chinese and Vietnamese leaders to intensify their efforts to control, indeed colonize their highland border areas, even joining forces to do so.[14]

More Tai peoples streamed into the Vietnamese highlands in the nine-teenth century as Qing rulers in China struggled to hold their gigantic multiethnic empire together (the Qing were themselves Manchus from the northern steppes bordering today's Russia). Nowhere was this more evident than when Chinese authorities finally smashed the Taiping rebellion that had surged out from its south in the early 1850s and weakened Beijing's control over its part of the highland world rising out of central Indochina. As the Qing armies marched across the southern provinces in the 1860s, their brutal repression sent tens of thousands of mainly Tai and Hmong peoples into the Nguyen kingdom's northern massif. These refugees joined the Nung and other highland groups such as the Khmu, Lolo, Yao, and Man. In all, more than thirty groups lived in Vietnam's northern highlands, operating under their own chiefdoms and confederations and sending tribute at irregular intervals to the Chinese, Vietnamese, and others.

CONFRONTING VIET EMPIRE

As is so often the case in the imperial chapters of world history, the colonized borrow heavily from their former colonizers. The Viet were no exception to this rule. The Ming occupation may have only lasted two short decades (1407–28), but it was a period of intense and rapid military, cultural, and political transfers to the Red River that drew upon a millennium of earlier colonial interactions and structures. The Viet cherished their independence, but they knew their former colonizers intimately and admired them for many things. Little wonder Dai Viet leaders actively sought out Chinese models and technologies: such things could help them prosper and rule. Thanks to the Ming, for example, the Viet obtained some of the most advanced military technology of the time (cannons, gunpowder, and warships). Postcolonial Dai Viet's leaders also embraced the Chinese bureaucratic model for building and expanding a centralized state capable of recruiting, organizing, and deploying manpower and resources. Chinese statecraft served as a powerful weapon for incorporating and administering Dai Viet's own newly conquered territories. By willingly entering a China-centered East Asian civilizational world that placed Confucian-minded states (real or imagined) in a superior cultural position vis-à-vis their 'uncivilized' and 'barbarian' neighbors, Dai Viet leaders now had a powerful ideology to justify a *mission civilisatrice* outside their current borders. And pushing Dai Viet leaders from below were new population pressures, the product of the Red River delta's rapid agricultural expansion.

In 1470–71, the Le dynasty initiated Vietnam's first real war of territorial conquest by launching a massive attack on Vijaya. The Vietnamese mobilized their cannons, navy, and three hundred thousand troops to strike a Cham force of 100,000 men (but who lacked a charismatic leader). Nearby Khmer and Chinese courts stood by idly as the Dai Viet seized Vijaya and turned it into the province of Binh Dinh. The meaning of the province's name was 'pacified'. The Cham polities of Indrapura, Amaravati, and Vijaya were now Dai Viet. While the fall of Vijaya did not trigger the immediate collapse of the other Cham polities located to the south (Panduranga and Kauthara), from the fifteenth century Viet leaders had all sorts of reasons to continue their imperial project southward.[15]

The Cham and the Nguyen Empire-State

However, the Dai Viet state the Le founded in the fifteenth century did not preside over Vietnam's colonial expansion to the Gulf of Thailand. The rebel Nguyen military lords did. The long civil war that broke out between the Trinh and the Nguyen in the early seventeenth century forced the latter further into the south with their leader in the person of General Nguyen Hoang (discussed in our first chapter). Under constant threat of invasion from the Trinh in the north and with little land on which to stand in the southern part of the same state, Hoang and his descendants recognized that their survival depended on taking the rest of the coast from the Cham, promoting Viet settlements in these lands, and taking control of Cham trade with the Indian Ocean and the central highlands. The Nguyen used the Sino-Vietnamese administrative model their forefathers had borrowed from the Chinese. And like them and others, they compromised with it too and devised all sorts of indirect forms of rule to administer far-flung regions and peoples. Pragmatic colonizers are always the most successful.

The Nguyen state was thus born of recurrent civil war, sustained colonial expansion, and military rule. No sooner had the Trinh and Nguyen gone to war in 1627 than the latter struck southward, against the Cham. In 1653, Kauthara fell to the Nguyen, whose territorial domain now extended from the Hai Van pass to the Phan Rang River. Even the last remaining Cham state, Panduranga, found itself under intense pressure as the Nguyen required its leaders to send tribute to Hue as a sign of its vassalage. This also sent a clear message to the Trinh in Hanoi that the Nguyen were heading up a separate state with an imperial project at its state-making core.[16]

As the Nguyen colonial state expanded southward, its leaders focused on the Khmer empire, too. Starting in the late seventeenth century, Hue's leaders adopted an increasingly aggressive line toward the Khmer court (now located in Phnom Penh) and intervened directly in Cambodian court politics. This was designed mostly to promote Nguyen control over the lower Mekong and to prevent another rapidly emerging state to the west (that of the Thai in the Chao Phraya River valley), from moving into the declining Khmer empire at the Nguyens' expense. And as the Thais pushed into Cambodia, the Nguyen rapidly expanded into the Mekong delta and the last remaining Cham state blocking their march to the Gulf of Thailand. This is how modern Vietnam's 'S'-like form emerged. The Nguyen created it through colonial expansion. In fact, by the late seventeenth century, thousands of Viet settlers had already moved into Panduranga and had no intention of leaving.[17]

In 1692, with his back against the wall, Panduranga's King Po Saut decided to attack the Nguyen forces in order to stop the creation of this 'S'-shaped state before it was too late. The Nguyen leader, Nguyen Phuc Chu, welcomed such a move, since it provided him with the pretext he needed to conquer the last Cham state and move his army and more settlers into the Mekong. Confident that the Chinese and Khmers would not intervene, the Nguyen overpowered the Cham, abolished the monarchy, and transformed Panduranga into the province of Thuan Thanh. Convinced of their superiority, the Nguyen required the conquered Cham to adopt Vietnamese customs and dress, speak Vietnamese, and adhere to the Sino-Vietnamese bureaucratic and civilizational models.[18]

Such harsh measures provoked immediate resistance. Viewed from the Cham point of view, Nguyen colonial expansion meant the end of everything that had been theirs for centuries—a unique coastal confederation with close commercial, cultural, and religious ties to island Southeast Asia, a distinct language with its own writing system, very different ways of dress and conceptions of time and space, as well as unique social organizations, land rights, and fiscal administration. Always pragmatic, the Nguyen switched rapidly to indirect rule. They had neither the military forces necessary to ensure such a harsh occupation nor sufficient administrative organizations and civil servants to control these new territories. The new emperor of the Nguyen, Minh Vuong, transformed Thuan Thanh (Champa) into a protectorate and promoted association rather than assimilation as his colonial policy. Instead of putting ethnic Viet administrators in charge of what was still a majority Cham population, he sought out reliable yet loyal indigenous intermediaries. These go-betweens could work with the Nguyen to win over the support of the Cham people, administer them more effectively, and thereby legitimate Viet colonial rule more effectively. The Nguyen found an invaluable ally in the person of Po Saktiraydaputa, a member of the Cham royal family. Po Saktiraydaputa saw in collaboration with the Nguyen the chance to protect his people, preserve Cham ways, and assert his power over rivals. Minh Vuong made him King of Panduranga.

While this last of the Cham kingdoms was not an independent sovereign state, as a Viet protectorate the Cham did recover considerable local powers. In 1712, for example, the Nguyen allowed Cham courts to judge local affairs and set up a court consisting of both Cham and Viet personnel to deal with affairs involving the Viet settlers. The Cham regained the right to speak their language and practice their religions. They also paid lower taxes. Like the Qing rulers who built Tibetan Buddhist temples in Beijing as they pushed China's imperial borders deep into central Asia (Tibet became a protectorate in 1751), Minh Vuong openly associated himself with the Cham king and helped to renovate the sacred Cham temple of Thien Pu in Hue while his Nguyen imperial state expanded deeper into Southeast Asia.[19]

None of this, however, changed the fact that, having taken Panduranga, the Nguyen were strategically placed to expand their colonial control into the Mekong delta, which they progressively did over the next century. By the early nineteenth century, over one hundred thousand Khmers joined another one hundred thousand Cham as subjects of the Nguyen imperial order. Severed from the Angkorian empire now based in Phnom Penh, Cambodians used the term 'Khmer Krom' to refer to themselves, meaning the Khmers living in the 'lower' Mekong River valley. Most were wet-rice growers, cattle farmers, and Theravada Buddhists. Many Cham also fled into Khmer Krom areas, Phnom Penh, and island Southeast Asia. Some joined the Malays and, on one occasion in the seventeenth century, successfully convinced a Cambodian king to convert to Islam.[20]

But changes in the balance of power always change the dynamics of collaborative relationships, as we have repeatedly seen in this book. Nowhere was this more evident here than when the Tay Son rebellion set off another round of Vietnamese civil wars in the late eighteenth century. At the outset, many Cham eagerly joined the Tay Son brothers. In fact, Tay Son (meaning 'Western Mountains') was the village where the revolt started. Significantly, it was located in the central highlands and ethnically mixed. One Nguyen rebel had a Bahnar as his second wife. Some have suggested that the Tay Son brothers were the offspring of mixed marriages. It is quite possible. Upon launching their revolt, the oldest of the three, Nguyen Nhac, proclaimed himself ruler in the ruins of Vijaya and claimed to possess a sacred sword like one of those of the highlanders. In any case, the Tay Son uprising was a product of these longstanding interactions between the Viet and non-Viet peoples and between the lowlands and uplands of Vietnam.[21]

As military operations rolled through the Cham heartlands and then spread to all of Vietnam, the balance of power shifted back and forth over three decades. Cham elites and peasants adjusted their loyalties and alliances accordingly in the hope that such strategies would keep them out of harm's way in the postwar period. Viet belligerents adapted too. Holed up in the south, the new charismatic leader of the Nguyen, Gia Long, carefully stitched together a series of alliances with the Khmer Krom, the local Chinese, various religious groups, and the Cham. In exchange for their collaboration, he promised them all indirect rule, autonomy, and respect for their customs, religions, languages, and local identities. To the Cham, he swore the restoration of the Panduranga monarchy under future protectorate rule. And in 1802, after having victoriously unified all of Vietnam under Nguyen rule, Gia Long made good on his word. He re-established the Panduranga throne and carefully avoided policies that could turn the non-Viet peoples against him. Imperfect as it was, peace largely reigned until the emperor's death in 1820.[22]

Minh Mang and the Rise of Cham Anticolonialism

The same could not be said of his son Minh Mang (1820–41), who intentionally reversed his father's commitment to indirect imperial rule. Much more Confucian-minded than Gia Long, Minh Mang was obsessed with order and determined to deploy the Sino-Vietnamese bureaucratic model to achieve it. This entailed establishing the unflinching loyalty of his subjects, including the hundreds of thousands of non-Viet ones. If that meant assimilating all of his subjects to his Sino-Vietnamese administrative model, political identity, and common culture under his personal control, then so be it. Although one could argue that what Minh Mang was doing was remarkably modern in terms of rationalizing the state, centralizing power, and homogenizing identity, his harsh application of such policies created a sea of resistance and a wall of non-Viet hate.

In 1832, if not earlier, Minh Mang ordered the dismantling of the protectorate over Panduranga, the abolition of the Cham monarchy and its indigenous administration, and their incorporation into the province of Binh
Thuan under a Viet governor named by him. Gone, too, were the Cham
courts and mixed-personnel tribunals. The Vietnamese imperial army arrived to ensure order and enforce new labor, tax, and land laws. As we saw
in chapter 2, the emperor of the Nguyen also applied the same policies to
the Khmer Krom while simultaneously trying to colonize all of Cambodia.
The emperor required the Cham and Cambodians to dress like the Vietnamese, eat like the Vietnamese, and learn Vietnamese. Minh Mang actively
discouraged (and often prohibited) the practice of Islam, Theravada Buddhism, and Hinduism, judged inferior to Sino-Vietnamese civilization and
the Confucian model upon which it turned (in his view).

For the Cham and Cambodians, colonial assimilation not only shattered
their political independence for good, but it also threatened their very existence as separate cultural and religious identities. The Cham have left
records of the hardship they endured under Vietnamese colonial exploitation. As one voice cried out in the 1830s: 'The Cham lords were [forced]
to abandon [the celebration of their] rites for the ancestors. The lords were
made to say that the [Cham] traditions were bad and had to be abandoned
and that the Vietnamese traditions were appropriate and had to be followed'. Desolation was real: 'There is nothing left in front or behind of us.
All the things that we used to produce with hard work [have been taken
away]. Nothing is left for our subsistence.' The Nguyen forcibly recruited
Cham and Khmer labor to build roads, bridges, and canals, just as they did
in Cambodia during the construction of the Vinh Te canal. Colonial *corvée*
was not a French creation. Nor were the French the first to face anticolonial
resistance movements.[23]

It was in these dire circumstances that a Muslim Cham named Katip
Sumat arrived in Pandarunga from Cambodia. He had just returned from
Mecca and was determined to help organize a resistance movement against
the Vietnamese and spread Islam at the same time. To this end, he organized guerilla forces among the Cham and nearby highlanders and declared
jihad ('holy war') on the Nguyen infidels. Furious, Minh Mang rushed in
his troops, armed local Viet settlers, and called upon both to crush the
'rebels' and this foreign faith. Popular support for Katip declined as the
army cracked down violently and several Cham elites realized that this man
might not have had their interests foremost in his mind. Another Muslim

leader, this time a local Cham named Ja Thak, took over and forged alliances with remaining royal family members, a range of highland peoples, and other Viet at odds with Hue (and there were many). But Minh Mang persevered and in early 1835 his army smashed Ja Thak and the rest of the Cham rebels. The result was catastrophic for the Cham, who now became, along with the Khmer Krom, second-class citizens in their own lands. And Thai (not French) intervention in Cambodia at this time may have been the only thing that saved what remained of the Khmer empire from becoming a permanent part of the Vietnamese one.[24]

Highland Vietnam: The Limits of Colonial Assimilation?[25]

While Vietnamese colonial expansion had always focused on the lowlands, the Nguyen were as engaged as their predecessors in Hanoi had been with the surrounding highlands—and vice versa. Although the court found it difficult to recruit people willing to work in the highlands, considered by many Viet to be inhospitable and insalubrious places, the Nguyen regularly sent administrators, merchants, and armies into the highlands to explore and survey the area, and also to repress, and tax non-Viet populations whenever possible. In 1697, for example, the Nguyen created the barbarian tax ('*thue Man*'). Less than a century later, such taxation generated real hardship, enough to stir highland peoples to revolt under the Tay Son.

The Nguyen intensified their relationships with the central and northern highlands when they unified all of the country at the turn of nineteenth century. Often working through Chinese merchants, Nguyen monarchs traded in cinnamon with Jarai headmen. So lucrative was this commerce that Minh Mang made its production a crown monopoly. Also reinforcing Nguyen interest in the highlands was the expansion of the Thais into Lao territories to the west. In the north, as we saw above, the Qing repression of the Taiping and highlander 'rebels' in southern China had sent tens of thousands of Tai and Hmong peoples flowing into northern Vietnam. Joining them were local militias and bandit groups, of which the Black Flags paramilitary forces crossing the Sino-Vietnamese border were important examples (see chapter 2).[26]

Worried by all of this activity in the borderlands, the Nguyen began collecting information on the upland peoples, their languages, customs, and social organization, at the same time as exploring ways of better administering them. In the northern highlands, the Nguyen improved salaries and offered fast-track promotions to Viet administrators who accepted tough posts in these remote parts of the empire. In the north, the Hue court adapted the Chinese '*tusi*' system ('*tho ty*' in Vietnamese) in order to rule rugged Tai areas through local hereditary chiefs. For example, Hue authorized the local strongman, Deo Van Tri, to collect taxes, trade in opium, and administer justice locally on the condition that he ensure security in the northwest, forward tax revenues to the court, and maintain his people under Nguyen sovereignty. With roots in the eleventh century, this classic form of indirect rule allowed loyal hereditary chiefs to rule vast territories alongside ethnic Viet imperial administrators. Even the assimilationist-obsessed Minh Mang had to concede in the 1830s that direct rule was impossible in this part of his empire.[27]

This was also true for the central highlands looking down over Hue, where the Nguyen reinvigorated their tributary relationships as another form of indirect rule. In 1831, Minh Mang applauded the arrival of Jarai emissaries to his court, especially when they solemnly presented him with tribute symbolizing their submission to Nguyen imperial rule. 'Today', Minh Mang gushed on one august occasion in the 1830s, 'enthroned in the royal palace so as to receive tribute from these envoys, I saw with my own eyes that they were properly guarded, and they bowed in the prescribed ceremonial manner'. Nguyen officials sent their emissaries to the Jarai and Rhadé lands to participate in the 'oath ceremony' during which, the Nguyen annals tell us, both sides 'mixed alcohol with clear water, poured it in a vase, and used bamboo tubes to draw it up and drink it'. Performed before hundreds of highland elites, this public ceremony demonstrated lowland Nguyen respect for the highland peoples, while simultaneously confirming Jarai submission to Nguyen imperial sovereignty. The French would re-enact this ceremony for the same reasons. But they did not create it; for they were not the first colonizers in this part of the world.[28]

The highlanders and the Nguyen also built walls to deal with each other, but not just in oppositional terms. In 1819, the Nguyen dynasty erected a 127-kilometer-long wall in Quang Ngai province to protect them from upland attacks coming from the Hre, while the Hre sought to stop Vietnamese from moving into their territories. However, recent research also shows that the Vietnamese and Hre people built this wall together, and that they did so in part to maintain and provide security for inter-zonal trade and diplomatic relations. Such exchanges had been occurring for centuries between the upland and lowland areas. The 'wall' was one site for this. Markets were another. While the balance of power increasingly tilted against the highlanders, the relationships between the two sides were often more complex than we might first imagine.[29]

FROM IMPERIAL TO NATIONAL ORDERS
IN THE HIGHLANDS?

Enter the French Empire

Unsurprisingly, the French faced many of the same problems as their Viet predecessors when it came to incorporating highland territories and peoples into their colonial state, the Indochinese Union. The list is familiar by now: the need to thwart competing powers from moving into the region from the west (the Thais, but also with the British now in the background too), chronic disorder along the Sino-Vietnamese border as the Qing dynasty melted down, an acute lack of knowledge of Indochina's highlands, and a never-ending shortage of civil servants to rule these vast areas.

The crucial difference between the two imperial projects vis-à-vis the highlands is that by toppling the pre-existing Nguyen empire, the French generated an anticolonialist Viet movement opposed to the colonial order the French wanted to build upon it. Viet royalist elites not only fled abroad to Japan, China, and Thailand, but many also headed into the nearby central highlands. This was the case for the Nguyen court scholars turned patriots, Phan Dinh Phung, Ton That Thuyet, and the boy emperor, Ham Nghi, whom they smuggled out of Hue when the French sacked the imperial capital in 1885. In order to contain the emergence of Vietnamese anticolonialism in the highlands, the French immediately adopted policies to turn the non-Viet peoples against their former overlords and to align them with themselves. This meant replacing Viet imperial administrators in the highlands with French commissioners and a new generation of highlander military and administrative elites. It also meant protecting highlander peoples and cultures from ethnic Viet immigration (although that never worked out so nicely in practice). But French imperial strategies also created new highlander identities, territorial spaces, and interethnic oppositions that had never existed before; but which continue to shape modern Vietnam to this day.

The first Frenchmen to administer people in the central highlands were not colonial officials; they were in fact European Catholic missionaries seeking shelter from Minh Mang's persecution. Pushed out of the lowlands, these religious men immediately focused on 'civilizing' and converting the highland peoples to Christianity. As one French priest wrote in 1830s: '[One would have to make men of them first, in order to make Christians of them'. While large-scale conversions of the highlanders came later, these missionaries spread Christianity into the highlands for the first time and in so doing introduced new religious practices, identities, and rituals that mixed with pre-existing beliefs and added to the mosaic discussed above and elsewhere in this book. Missions emerged with their own territorial boundaries, while priests provided another layer of ethnographic knowledge about the non-Viet peoples. The French conquest of Vietnam certainly provided safety for the missionaries and facilitated their work in the highlands. In exchange, military officers and administrators looked to the missionaries to provide them with the information and the help they badly needed to rule in these far-flung areas into which Viet royalists were regrouping and the British, Thais, and Germans were thought to be active.[30]

Colonial rulers were so desperate in the early years for administrative help that they even turned to a fast-talking, megalomaniac adventurer named Marie-Charles David de Mayréna. In 1885, as the anticolonialist Can Vuong or Save the King movement took off, de Mayréna and a handful of priests jointly organized a confederation of non-Viet peoples in the central highlands of Kontum. The problem, however, was a familiar one—ensuring loyalty. In 1888 French officials were aghast when they learned that instead of remaining as one part of the confederation, de Mayréna had decided instead to create his own new, separate 'Kingdom of the Sedang' (its name referred to one of the tribal groups in Kontum). For de Mayréna, his new kingdom was a sovereign, independent state, complete with its own stamps, flag, and customs service. He even declared himself king and made Catholicism his state's official religion. While colonial authorities quickly ended this most embarrassing experiment in indirect rule (clearly, they had been conned), de Mayréna's kingdom, like Nung Tri Cao's before it and others elsewhere, reminded all of the need to take control of the highlands before others did. This fiasco also convinced many French republican officials that they could not trust missionaries. One went so far as to write that the de Mayréna affair showed that French priests wanted to create a 'free state like that of the Jesuits in Paraguay'. Republicans truly feared this, as mad as Mayréna was.[31]

For the time being, the French depended most on their military and its officers to rule as diplomats cobbled together what, by the early 1900s, became known as French Indochina. Like the Nguyen before them, French administrators created military territories in the northern highlands and Laos. They also transferred highland territories (and borders) back and forth between Cochinchina, Annam, Tonkin, Laos, and Cambodia, searching for the best ways to rule over those whom some had started to call the *'moï'* peoples. Of Sino-Vietnamese origin, this term referred to peoples who did not share in the East Asian cultural world discussed above. They were the 'uncivilized', the 'barbarians'. In French hands, however, *moï* became a handy word to refer to the non-Viet central highlanders in Annam in particular, the *montagnards,* later on, for those who dwelled in the entire massif. In 1931, the central highlands covering parts of northern Cochinchina and Annam counted 600,000 *'moïs'.* Further to the north, in the Tonkin highlands, another 700,000 'ethnic minorities' (*'minorités ethniques'*) resided (Tho, Tai, Man, Hmong, Nung, Lolo,and so on). To this tally the French added 312,000 Khmer in the Mekong delta. In all, a population of about 1.7 million non-Viet peoples lived in the highlands of the Annamese Cordillera which ran into the Mekong marshlands.[32]

With the arrival of Paul Doumer and the death of Phan Dinh Phung at the turn of the century, the French focused further on consolidating their control over the highlands. True to style, Doumer created new highland provinces for Pleiku, Darlac, and Haut Donnai. Others soon followed. Impressed by what the Nguyen had created, one subordinate reported that it was important to embrace a 'system of direct rule' for the central highlands: 'I will not hide from you that this seems more practical to manage a people as primitive as the Moï'. By 'direct rule', however, colonial authorities did *not* mean 'assimilation'. Even though Annam was a French protectorate and the French should therefore have been maintaining the pre-existing Nguyen administration and mandarins to rule all of Annam indirectly, including non-Viet areas, this was not desirable in the Annamese highlands because the French did not trust their monarchs or their mandarins there. The French decided instead to withdraw most Viet administrators from the central highlands, and rule themselves through French commissioners, who, in turn, would collaborate with the local headmen like the Jarai leader Khunjanob in Darlac province and Deo Van Tri in the northwestern highlands. Unlike in Laos and Cambodia, where the French relied on ethnic Viet bureaucrats to help them rule, the French largely excluded the Viet from the highland administration.[33]

At the same time, French colonialism triggered changes that ran counter to that very isolationist policy. Firstly, they expanded the number of roads crisscrossing Indochina in unprecedented ways. Secondly, French financial groups, investors, and the Bank of Indochina, keen to open more mines and plantations, promoted the economic development of highland areas after the First World War. Rubber, coffee, and tea could grow well in different parts of the entire Vietnamese massif. Thirdly, thanks to better roads, technology, and modern finance, more settlers and companies moved into the area to stake land claims, establish plantations, and blast open new mines. This, in turn, stimulated an unprecedented demand for labor. And when highland peoples balked at joining this new commercial world, settlers never hesitated to bring in ethnic Viet labor instead or to resort to imposing the *corvée* upon the non-Viet. Viet entrepreneurs also wanted to open up the highlands for similar reasons. Little wonder the patterns of Viet colonialism started to move westward under the French. In 1943, 42,000 ethnic Viet and 5,100 French people resided in the highlands. Although miniscule compared to the larger central highlander population of one million by the Second World War, these Euro-Viet colonialists were the start of an ever-larger influx of workers and settlers. Some Viet plantation owners even had an edge over their French counterparts. But such Franco-Vietnamese intrusions into the highlands often triggered violent resistance from the indigenous populations.[34]

This commercial penetration of the highlands led to another affair that would do much to seal an alliance between colonial officials and highlander elites and stimulate the birth of a separate *moï* identity. The man at the center of this affair was Léopold Sabatier. Between 1913 and 1926, this professionally trained administrator worked tirelessly from his office in Ban Me Thuot, tending to the Rhadé and other highlanders in Dac Lac province. Unlike de Mayréna, Sabatier's loyalty to the French colonial state was unshakeable. Particularly close to Pierre Pasquier (the Commissioner of Annam after the First World War), Sabatier understood the importance of the highlanders in the defense of Indochina and in containing Vietnamese nationalism. (In 1916, another Vietnamese emperor, Duy Tan, had tried to escape the role of puppet monarch which the French had imposed upon him by heading for these same hills.) Pasquier and Sabatier also wanted to protect the 'pristine' highlanders from the Franco-Viet settlers and the commercial economy they represented. Sabatier's originality resided in his efforts to bequeath the highlanders a separate identity, but one which was allied with the French. With Pasquier's backing, he devised and published a romanized Rhadé writing system, presided over the creation of a Rhadé customary law code and justice system, opened Franco-Rhadé schools for thousands of youngsters, recruited men into the French-led colonial army, opened hospitals and introduced modern medicine. He personally participated in the highland oath ceremonies during which he publicly professed his government's unflinching respect for the highlanders in exchange for their recognition of French sovereignty. Similar efforts were made among the highlanders in the north as well as among the Khmer in Cochinchina whose children attended renovated pagoda schools under French, not Vietnamese, control.[35]

But Sabatier's efforts to isolate the highlands landed him in trouble in the 1920s when powerful people with financial interests called for his removal. Most importantly, Sabatier's tenure coincided with the upswing in the world demand for rubber. As prices soared, financial groups pressed the metropolitan and colonial authorities to open up the highlands to further commercial development: rubber trees grew well in the *terres rouges* of the central highlands. French and Viet landowners and settlers joined them in calling for Sabatier to be ousted. Despite Pasquier's efforts to protect his loyal servant, these Franco-Viet groups finally succeeded in dislodging Sabatier from his post in 1926. Once again, the 'colonizers' were not always one monolithic bloc, racially or economically. Here, French and Vietnamese settlers had joined forces.

While Euro-Viet settlers may have mocked Sabatier for defending the highlanders, esteem for him ran high within the colonial administration and army. Indeed, his work with the Rhadé served as the blueprint for subsequent administrators keen to contain Vietnamese nationalists and communists and to protect Indochina from external threats. In 1935, in the wake of massive lowland Viet revolts at Yen Bay and Nghe An a few years earlier (see chapter 5), one French general argued strongly in favor of creating an autonomous *moï* region under the governor general's guidance. Another emphasized the need 'to save this race, to disentangle it from all harmful foreign influences through a direct administration, and to tie these tribes to us [...] These proud peoples with their spirit of independence will provide us with elite troops, [serve] as safety valves in case of internal insurgency, and [act] as powerful combat units in case of external war'. In the late 1930s, Governor General Jules Brévié insisted that the *moï* constituted a unique racial group and as such deserved the creation of separate French territorial administration. In 1939, as the Japanese army moved its troops down the southern China coast, Brévié created the General Inspectorate for the

Moï Region. And while French-controlled Vietnam was under Japanese occupation, Vichy's Governor General Jean Decoux solemnly participated in the oath ceremony and tried to transfer the colonial capital to Dalat. Though never officially considered as such, the highland areas constituted collectively a separate French protectorate, one part in the central highlands of Annam, the other concentrated in northwestern Tonkin. Speaking of the central highlands in 1937, a French administrator insisted that there was more to Indochina than Laos, Cambodia, Tonkin, Annam, and Cochinchina: 'One must, to be entirely accurate, complete this geographical expression [of Indochina] by adding to it a sixth part, that of the *pays moï*'. And as we shall see, from this 'sixth part' a separate highlander identity would emerge.[36]

Maintaining French Control over the Highlands

As attractive as it was for budding highlander nationalists and strongmen, French protectorate rule placed the people of the massifs in a very dangerous position in 1945, when the Japanese overturned the French colonial state before capitulating to the Allies a few months later. Stepping into the vacuum, Vietnamese nationalists seized power. On 2 September 1945, Ho Chi Minh declared the birth of the Democratic Republic of Vietnam. This government immediately decreed laws unifying Tonkin, Annam, and Cochinchina into one sovereign territory and turning the great majority of those born or residing within 'Vietnam's' borders into 'Vietnamese citizens'. This included the two million non-Viet people who were living in the highlands. Ho did not recognize French rule there or any other special colonial arrangements. It was, he insisted, simply 'Vietnamese'.

But the French were not about to relinquish their Indochinese colony or their direct administration of the highlands, not yet. Starting in Saigon in September 1945, they slowly retook their Indochinese colony piece by piece until they had triggered a full-scale war with the DRV in late 1946. The new High Commissioner of Indochina, Georges Thierry d'Argenlieu, immediately renewed efforts to turn the central highlands and peoples against Vietnamese nationalists, relying on a veteran group of Indochinese administrators in order to do so. In May 1946, at the very moment he was piecing together the Provisional Government of the Republic of Cochinchina, Thierry d'Argenlieu also presided over the creation of the Highland Populations of Southern Indochina (Populations montagnardes du Sud-Indochinois). Administered by the French, this autonomous territorial domain consisted of the central highland provinces of Annam. Like his predecessors reaching back to the Nguyen, Thierry d'Argenlieu travelled to Ban Me Thuot to take part in the oath ceremony. Democratic Republic of Vietnam officials protested vigorously, insisting that the highlands were Vietnamese; but to no avail.

Significantly, the French were no more willing to cede the upland regions to the Vietnamese government which they themselves sought to build in the form of the Associated State of Vietnam. Although Léon Pignon, the French high commissioner between 1948 and 1950, had allowed for the unification of this Vietnam, his team intentionally attached the operation of the highlands *to Bao Dai*, convinced that they could control their emperor and, through him, the central massif, as they had done in the past. This is how and why the Crown Domain of the Southern Highlander Country (Domaine de la couronne du pays montagnards du Sud) came to life in 1950. By winning over Bao Dai's collaboration, the French had devised a method to continue to maintain a separate hold over this militarily important part of Indochina. Although the French nominally recognized Vietnamese sovereignty over the highlands, they maintained a 'special status' for the highlands because of 'special French obligations'. In 1950, immaculately dressed in white suits, Léon Pignon *and* Bao Dai stepped before two thousand highland chiefs in Ban Me Thuot to participate in the oath ceremony. But everyone knew that France's longtime Indochina hand, Jean Cousseau, ran the highlands as the 'special delegate', not the Vietnamese monarch. The Crown Domain of the Southern Highlander Country thus serves as a case study in Bao Dai's failure to force the French to decolonize completely, when he could have done so. The Crown Domain was nothing more than a new term for the continuation of the *de facto* French protectorate over the '*sixième pays*' of colonial Indochina.

Until 1954, the French continued to support a separate territorial administration, highlander education, language training, and military service. In so doing, the French brought isolated highlanders together like never before. Hundreds of young men coming from across the central massif met each other in the classrooms of the newly opened Collège Sabatier. Many accepted administrative positions outside their native lands, and in so doing developed long-lasting and often unprecedented relationships extending across the hills. Similar things happened in highlander combat units. Marriage across clan lines increased. French and, increasingly, Rhadé began to serve as a common language. Protestant missionaries, mainly American and

French, started attracting thousands of converts in the highlands. Their schools and missions circulated highlander youth across tribal lines. And from 1950 onward, the French and Americans promoted special agricultural and infrastructure programs for this area.[37]

The French extended these policies to the northern massif. Of particular concern was that the transfer of the Democratic Republic of Vietnam to the northern highlands from late 1946 onward would lead Ho Chi Minh's administrators to turn the large Tai, Hmong, and Nung populations there against the French. And of course the DRV tried. In February 1946, the French moved troops from southern China (where they had fled the Japanese coup in Indochina in March 1945) into the Tai regions of northwestern Vietnam. With the outbreak of full-scale war later that year, French officials renewed their contacts with Tai clans. Foremost among them was Deo Van Tri, whose son Deo Van Long was now in charge. In 1948, in exchange for Tai loyalty and collaboration against the Democratic Republic of Vietnam administratively and militarily, the French granted the northwest autonomous rule in the form of a Tai federation. Led by Deo Van Long, this federation regrouped the strategically important northwestern provinces of Lai Chau, Phong Tho, and Son La together. Here, too, the French promoted the Tai language, education, military training, and created a new generation of ethnic Tai civil servants. As they had done with the central highland domain, the French connected the Tai Federation to the person of Bao Dai, albeit via French officials once more. Many highlander elites, village headmen and colonially trained civil servants and officers embraced the creation of a wider nationalist identity which was separate from the one ethnic Viet leaders sought to impose. And at war over the destiny of Indochina, opposing Vietnamese states, the French, increasingly backed by the Americans, organized and militarized the massif as never before in its long history. Indeed, French and soon American military officers became heavily invested in working with highland peoples, just as did their Vietnamese enemies.[38]

Nationalist Strategies and Highlander Autonomy
War mitigated any hard-handed assimilationist moves on the part of Vietnamese communists, at least during the early years of the Indochina conflict. In order to combat the French and their allies, experts in charge of the Democratic Republic of Vietnam's newly created highlander affairs bureau carefully respected local traditions, languages, and cultures, and promised autonomy. While Ho's specialists might not have had either the

professional training of someone like Léopold Sabatier, nor could they draw upon a pre-existing Vietnamese-run highland civil service, they were hardly neophytes when it came to knowing the massif. Hounded by the French for years, communists had often taken refuge there, like rebel kings before them. Moreover, the communist organization was, to my knowledge, the only modern political party before 1945 to have shown any real interest in highland peoples and actually opened its doors to them (Catholic and Protestant missions were the only exceptions to this). By the Second World War, some of the most important leaders of the communist party were ethnic Tais from the far north—Hoang Van Thu, Hoang Dinh Giong, and Hoang Van Non. Their multilingualism, local contacts, and knowledge of the highlands on both sides of the Sino-Vietnamese border made them priceless intermediaries for building the party. In 1941, for similar reasons, the communists recruited and promoted a Nung to the highest echelons of what became the People's Army of Vietnam. His name was Chu Van Tan. Between 1949 and 1954, Tan ran the administrative zone for all of northern Vietnam, demonstrating how people from a so-called 'ethnic minority' could rise to the very highest levels of the Vietnamese army, state, and party. It is hard to find such a parallel in Bao Dai's Vietnam and in any case the French were opposed to precisely this type of national integration. Few non-Viet elite members served in the Nguyen court under the French. The communists would backtrack in the late twentieth century, when relations with communist China melted down, official racism raised its ugly head once more, and loyalties along the Sino-Vietnamese frontier blurred again. In 1979, the Viet majority of the communist party placed General Chu Van Tan under house arrest, far from his family and friends along the Sino-Vietnamese border. The parallel with Nung Tri Cao must have crossed more than one historically informed mind.

Lastly, Vietnamese communists working outside Indochina before 1941 were well versed in internationalist communist forms of rule toward the 'ethnic minority question'. Lest we forget, the Soviets and Chinese were also the inheritors of pre-existing multi-ethnic empires. During his long stay in Moscow in the 1930s, Ho would have had ample time to study this matter and the federalist ideas communist theorists had devised to rule the USSR. The Indochinese Communist Party sent another ethnic Tai, Hoang Tu Huu, to Moscow to attend the Comintern Congress in 1935. When Ho Chi Minh left Moscow in 1938 to make his way to Vietnam, he travelled overland through the central Asian borderlands of China before making his way into the multiethnic massif that the Yunnan and Guangxi provinces share with Indochina. When he set up the Viet Minh's base in the Pac Bo caves of Cao Bang province, his success depended on non-Viet collaboration, and this would be the case until 1954. Like Pham Van Dong, Ho knew from personal experience that the highlands were not unpopulated regions.[39]

Little wonder flexibility characterized communist work among the highlanders. If local non-Viet elites pledged their loyalty to the Democratic Republic of Vietnam and refrained from aiding the enemy, the communists were content to operate through them to maintain security, obtain food, and recruit laborers and soldiers. Ho and his lieutenants did their best to immerse themselves in local cultures, organized literacy classes, and tried to learn at least some words in local languages. Ho dressed deliberately in local dress, as a sign of communist sensitivity toward borderland peoples. Ho's men entered into contact with non-Viet leaders who had suffered under French rule, carefully exploiting, for example, the Deo family's mistreatment of the Hmong. The DRV avoided imposing onerous taxes, steered clear of cultural assimilation, respected local languages, helped develop French-initiated scripts for them, and, for the time being, delayed land reform and radical social revolution. The communists opened schools for upland children, introduced hygiene and medicines, and trained members of local elites for civil service and military positions, but always treated them as part of the wider 'Vietnamese family', within a process focused on national integration.

The Democratic Republic of Vietnam's shift to conventional warfare from 1950 onward led both the belligerents to rely ever more heavily on Tai, Hmong, and Nung peoples to supply highland battlefields with recruits, porters, intelligence, and food. The political autonomy the people there enjoyed up to this point began to disappear as the communists mobilized for war in the massifs. And the intensification of the war also brought more Americans into the highlands (although American Protestants had been in Vietnam since the 1920s). The Americans pushed the French hard to build up their special forces in the highlands where they jutted into China's underbelly, convinced of the threat of a wider communist thrust into Southeast Asia and now also themselves at war with the Chinese in Korea. As during the Second World War and again during the Vietnam War, the Americans wanted to use the geopolitical area of the massif to gather intelligence, harass the communists, create secure zones for the nationalists, and win over the hearts and minds of the uplands people whose lands ran deep into China. (The CIA also supported Tibetan resistance to the Chinese at this time.) Strapped for funds, the French acquiesced and operated two US-backed special forces teams based in the highlands until 1954, the Commando Forces (Service Action) and the Airborne Mobile Commandos Groups (Groupement de commandos mixtes aéroportés). Deo Van Long joined the latter unit, and in so doing further sealed his Tai Federation's alliance with the French and, indirectly, the Americans.[40]

The Vietnamese and their Chinese advisors went to great lengths to win over Tai support in this strategically vital northwestern part of Vietnam, where the conventional battles of the First Indochina War had culminated at Dien Bien Phu. Moreover, it was the requirements of conventional war that saw the Vietnamese communists incorporate the Tai people into a Vietnamese party-state born of this transition to total war. Dien Bien Phu was first a Tai town before this historic battle between the French and the DRV wiped it from the face of the earth. The upland peoples were anything but marginal to the march of Vietnamese history.[41]

STATES OF WAR: THE MAKINGS AND UN-MAKINGS OF HIGHLAND VIETNAM (1954–75)

Communist Autonomy in North Vietnam?[42]

Following the Geneva Conference agreements, the communist leadership rapidly dismantled what parts of the Tai Federation their armies had not already occupied in the run-up to Dien Bien Phu. The People's Army of Vietnam and security services tracked down 'rebel' leaders who had collaborated with the French, especially those of the Deo family, while many of the most important upland leaders had already evacuated the area along with the French. Deo Van Long was buried in France. Over twenty thousand Nung, Tai, and Hmong emigrated to southern Vietnam. To administer the hundreds of thousands who remained, Vietnamese communists turned to Sino-Soviet federal ideas. In May 1955, for example, Democratic Republic of Vietnam created the 'Tai–Hmong Autonomous Zone'. In 1956, Hanoi expanded this officially into a larger Northern Vietnam Autonomous Zone covering almost all of the northern massif including over one million multi-ethnic people. While autonomous rule respected local languages, administration, religions, and cultures, the communists were in charge through their parallel party administration, Viet and loyal non-Viet cadres, their security services, and, if need be, their army. Like Ngo Dinh Diem in the south, Ho Chi Minh's government also promoted ethnic Viet immigration into the highlands and even implemented land-reform policies which triggered suffering and violent opposition in many areas in the northern highlands. But unlike the situation in the Republic of Vietnam, the communist leadership imposed its rule free of international scrutiny. The Chinese were not going to criticize Hanoi, since Vietnamese communists were often applying their own Maoist methods.

The Geneva ceasefire agreement prevented the DRV from controlling the central highlands, however. In 1954–5, the communists moved several thousand Viet and highlander cadres to the DRV in the north of Vietnam. Things changed when it became clear that there would not be any elections in 1956 (which might have united Vietnam by peaceful means), and civil war broke out once again among the Viet. By 1960, the highlanders in the central massif found themselves in the crossfire as Hanoi infiltrated several thousand cadres back into the central highlands to rebuild bases and a parallel administration below the seventeenth parallel. Communist propaganda focused on Ngo Dinh Diem's assimilation policies in the highlands and promised autonomous rule to those who joined the 'righteous struggle' for national unification. In 1960, the National Liberation Front came to life to serve as the communist party's new Viet Minh and shadow government in the south. The NLF's platform promised political autonomy to the highlander peoples, declaring that 'all nationalities have the right to use and develop their own spoken and written languages and to preserve or change their customs and habits'. Absent, of course, was any mention of Hanoi's land reform and less than autonomous rule in the northern massif. In 1961, the National Liberation Front organized a conference for the highland peoples led by Ibih Aleao, a Rhadé leader and NLF member, which promised autonomy. As they had done during the First Indochina conflict, the communists opened new schools for children, promoted health care and hygiene, and trained highlander bureaucrats and officers, sending many to the north for further training.

The Democratic Republic of Vietnam badly needed these highlanders and the cover of their lands to be able to run people and supplies along the Ho Chi Minh Trail into southern Indochina. Indeed, the central highlands played much the same role as had the northwestern Tai zones during the battles leading up to Dien Bien Phu. To ensure the functioning of this supply line and the highland bases, at which more and more troops were arriving, Hanoi renewed its earlier training of ethnic Viet civil servants in highland languages and customs before assigning them to the areas through which the trail, troops, and supplies flowed, including in eastern Laos and northeast Cambodia. These Viet groups of administrators often spoke flawless Rhadé, Bahnar, Khmu, Lao, and Khmer. They worked alongside highlander elites to penetrate into villages to create safe zones and win over popular support. In 1969, DRV cadres working in the highlands were astonished to find that one of theirs had gone native on them since 1946:

> At first we thought he was ethnic minority. He was thin, and his skin was dark [. . .] He wore his gray hair twisted into a bun like an onion atop his head. His teeth were filed, and he had a large hole pierced through his earlobe. He wore no shirt but only a loincloth; he carried a small bag on his back and a machete in his hand. I was surprised that he spoke fluent Vietnamese; I soon learned that he was originally from Thai Binh and had joined the march to the south in 1946. He had worked as a cadre organizing the masses during the resistance war against France. When peace was restored in 1954, he received orders to stay in the south and continue his activities undercover. After the Saigon administration promulgated the 10/59 decree he was hunted by this administration and so he escaped to the central highlands. He filed his teeth and pierced his ears, so he could look like the ethnic minority people, thereby avoiding enemy suspicion and also facilitating his organizational work.[43]

The fascinating account above also reveals a step beyond the oath ceremony toward a new method for winning hearts and minds on the ground.

Non-Communist Assimilation in the Republic of Vietnam

Ngo Dinh Diem was furious when he learned of the French decision to create the Tai Federation in 1948 and the Crown Domain for the central highlands in 1950. In 1955, first as prime minister and then as president of the Republic of Vietnam, Diem began dismantling the French Crown Domain. He replaced French commissioners with Viet provincial and district leaders who were subordinate to the central government in Saigon. He ran the long-established French colonial administrators out of the country, in particular Jean Cousseau. However, like his French predecessors, Diem solemnly performed the oath ceremony in Ban Me Thuot. But things would be different and difficult for the highlanders under this form of Vietnamese rule. For the first time since Minh Mang in the 1830s, they were now dealing with an ethnic Viet leader determined to assimilate them to a Vietnamese order. Indeed, Diem was convinced of the superiority of the Vietnamese civilizational order, of its advanced modernity, and of his right to place these people under central administrative control. On this note in particular, Diem took republicanism very seriously, discarding federal models in order to hold a multiethnic state together. The Ministry of the Interior took over highland affairs. The central government administered highland education, imposed Vietnamese as the common language, and threw out colonial textbooks in favor of a common Vietnamese curriculum. The Collège Sabatier became the Nguyen Du School. Just as importantly, Diem disbanded the remaining French special forces (which were still in charge of groups of highlanders and thus outside Vietnamese control).[44]

Diem also saw a solution in the central highlands below the seventeenth parallel: to transfer there many of the 800,000 northern refugees who had arrived in the south since 1954. They included Catholics and Buddhists, as well as Nung, Hmong, and Tai soldiers and their families. The idea was to relocate as many of them as possible to the highlands' 'empty spaces'. Diem promoted a land-development program that allotted five hectares to each migrant family, provided them with tools, and gave them some seed. Many families moved there of their own volition. Others had no choice. By July 1959, fifty-seven land-development centers were in operation in the central highlands, as 44,000 new Viet settlers cleared 11,000 hectares of land for rice, coffee, rubber, and cotton production. While many Vietnamese returned to the lowlands, others remained in the highlands, and from this point onward the resumption of a centuries-old practice of Vietnamese colonial expansion was underway again with no French presence to check it. Moreover, American aid allowed the Vietnamese government to create new roads into the highlands, facilitating yet again the arrival of even more ethnic Vietnamese.[45]

Upland peoples did not remain idle, however. As the French withdrew from Vietnam and Diem asserted control, highlander elites began discussing what to do. Leadership mainly came from among those who had studied in colonial schools and Christian missions, circulated as civil servants, teachers, and health workers under the French, or served in the special forces with the French during the First Indochina War. One of the central highlands' best-known Rhadé leaders, Y Thih Eban, studied at the Collège

Sabatier as a teenager. Once he had finished there, he then worked as an accountant in the Darlac provincial health service before serving as a medical assistant in the French army. Opposed to Diem's assimilationist policies, in 1955 he and others joined forces to create the Liberation Front of the Highland Peoples (Front de libération des Montagnards). They submitted a petition to President Diem, calling upon him to honor continued highlander autonomy as set out by the provisions of the Crown Domain, to respect their customs and languages, and to protect their lands. While Diem did try to protect their lands from settlers and corrupt officials, his assimilationist policies and support of increased Viet immigration did not reassure. In 1958, as relations deteriorated further, Y Thih Eban joined Y Bham Enuol and Paul Nur (among others) to create the Bajarka movement (the name was an acronym for the Bahnar, Jarai, Rhadé and Khoho peoples). This movement was broadly based and united in its opposition to centralization along Viet lines. It demanded upland autonomy, an end to Viet immigration, and no more cultural assimilation. Diem responded by increasing police surveillance of the movement's activists, meting out heavy prison sentences to the 'rebels', redoubling his assimilationist policies, and dispatching more ethnic Viet officials to run the central massif. Increasingly, Diem regarded the individuals in the Bajarka movement as rebels, whereas this movement's leaders saw themselves as struggling righteously against a Vietnamese colonial thrust that would end their way of life, like the lowland Cham and Khmers before them.[46]

Tensions boiled over in the early 1960s as civil war intensified and different groups competed for the loyalty of the highlanders. The communists' shadow government, the National Liberation Front, promised autonomy to the highlanders and brought their own members into its administration and armed forces. The Americans were back, too. And the use of special forces was part of John F. Kennedy's war on communist-backed guerilla movements like the NLF. Starting in 1961, the CIA and a range of special forces began working with and recruiting highland peoples to gather intelligence on the National Liberation Front, the Democratic Republic of Vietnam, and the Ho Chi Minh Trail connecting the two through the central highlands. In 1962, the CIA presided over its first highlander schools and, more and more, became involved in local affairs and politics. Fighting the communists necessitated it.

Diem's heavy-handed policies, however, stimulated strong resistance among the Cham and Khmers and undermined American attempts to focus on the communists. Diem closed Khmer religious schools in the delta and prohibited the use of Khmer. In 1960, angry Khmer Krom nationalists created the Liberation Front for Kampuchea Krom (Front de liberation du Kampuchea Krom) first led by Samouk Seng, and then Chau Dara, with the express goal of recovering the territories the Vietnamese had taken from the Khmer empire before the French arrived. Disgruntled Cham found a leader in Colonel Lès Kosem, a Muslim Cham colonel from Cambodia who had presided over the creation of the Liberation front for Champa (Front de libération du Champa). Like the Khmer Krom, he wanted Champa back. Supporting both were high-ranking Cambodian nationalists, including Lon Nol and Norodom Sihanouk, who had deeply resented the French decision in 1949–50 to unite Cochinchina with the rest of Vietnam, instead of returning the lands the Vietnamese imperialists had taken from them. The Cambodians supported Cham and Kampuchea Krom separatists until 1975, hoping to return Cambodia's territorial size to its former glory.[47]

Things came to a head in the turmoil unleashed by Diem's assassination in late 1963 and the simultaneous decisions taken by Hanoi and Washington to go to war. In 1964, the Cham and Khmer Krom, with Phnom Penh leaders maneuvering in the background, saw the chance to advance their independence cause by creating the United Front for the Struggle of Oppressed Races (the Front unifié de lutte des races opprimées, better known as FULRO). This front was designed to combine the liberation aspirations and forces of the Khmer Krom, Cham, and highlanders. The problem was that at the outset the United Front for the Struggle of Oppressed Races's leaders, Lès Kosem and Um Savuth, did not have the official support of the Bajarka movement, whose leaders hesitated between believing post-Diem republican promises of highlander reform and supporting him or pursuing the armed line pushed by the United Front for the Struggle of Oppressed Races. For the latter to work, the Cambodian-based Cham and Khmer Krom badly needed those in the Bajarka movement's support (and that of the one million highlanders of the central highlands they symbolically represented). In the end, the Bajarka movement split when, in mid-1964, Y Bham Enuol joined the United Front for the Struggle of Oppressed Races, bringing with him a few thousand armed supporters, while others tried to work with new reform-minded Viet leaders taking over in Saigon.

Unsurprisingly, FULRO leaders used the highlanders working in the American special forces to make their first attack—not on the Vietnamese communists, but rather on their fellow Viet soldiers. On 20 September

1964, as Lyndon Johnson prepared the Gulf of Tonkin resolution, the United Front for the Struggle of Oppressed Races fighters attacked the Vietnamese soldiers in a US special forces camp in the highlands, killing several, but carefully refraining from harming any Americans. As a member of FULRO's armed forces told the American marine he had temporarily disarmed: 'This is our night! We're going to kill Vietnamese'. The United Front for the Struggle of Oppressed Races fighters raised their flag and called for the independence of the highlands. Outraged, Saigon officials feared this revolt would spread and suspected the Americans might play the same divisive game as the French counter-insurgency specialists had during the First Indochina War. The Americans pushed both sides to back down and to keep their eye on the bigger picture—fighting the communists. Things quieted down for the time being, but the FULRO did not disappear, for there was no ignoring the impact on the highlands and its people of centuries of colonial rule, both in its French and Vietnamese variants.[48]

Until 1975, the Republic of Vietnam leadership oscillated between the carrot (reforms) and the stick (repression). Many highlanders welcomed reformism, but others, including Y Bham Enuol and Lès Kosem, retreated into Cambodia to continue harassing the Vietnamese from there. Well into the 1980s, the United Front for the Struggle of Oppressed Races' hardcore members also rejected communist overtures to negotiate, opposed to all forms of Vietnamese imperialism. Of course, the communists had no intention of letting go of the land the Nguyen had colonized and made part of the present-day Vietnam before the French arrived.[49]

But FULRO's anticolonial guerilla war was but a smaller chapter in the maelstrom the Vietnam War unleashed on the central highlands. For if Johnson chose to start his war in the Gulf of Tonkin in 1964, a year later the armed forces of the DRV struck back in Pleiku, in the central highlands where the PAVN had ended the Indochina War in June of 1954. And if the First Indochina War had wreaked havoc across the northern massif, ending in the obliteration of the Tai town of Dien Bien Phu in 1954, the Second Indochina War would ravage the central highlands in ways no one could have imagined. Of the 80 million liters of herbicides the Americans dropped over Vietnam between 1962 and 1971, much, perhaps more than half of that amount fell over the central highlands through which the Ho Chi Minh Trail ran. From the air, American B-52 bombings devastated the highlands, while Hanoi's Tet Offensive in 1968 ripped through Ban Me Thuot. By 1972, the wars for Indochina which had started in 1945 had displaced a mind-boggling 85 percent of all the central highland villages. In one instance designed to create a free-strike zone, the Americans forcibly relocated 10,000 Jarai people away from their villages. As one officer involved in this later recalled: 'We set the houses on fire before the villagers were taken away to show them we meant business'. Vietnamese communist troops engaged in equally brutal methods with similar results. And when the displaced highlanders and Cham returned to claim their homes when the guns fell silent, they found many ethnic Viet there who refused to leave. Indeed, war and the arrival of American troops, many of them stationed in highland areas, attracted ethnic Viet migrants. (The Americans needed all sorts of Vietnamese entrepreneurs, such as suppliers, restaurant owners, and prostitutes to help them house, feed, and entertain its forces.) The number of Viet living in the highlands increased from around 50,000 in 1954 to 450,000 two decades later. But the non-Vietnamese paid a high price during the Vietnam War. An estimated 200,000 highlanders are thought to have perished during the war. The overwhelming majority of them were civilians. Again, the non-Viet people were not on the margins of modern Vietnamese history, but right in the middle of it. They always had been.[50]

AUTHORITARIANISM, REPUBLICANISM, AND POLITICAL CHANGE

I N 2005, AS an expanding economy pulled Vietnam from the depths of poverty, the communist authorities of the Socialist Republic of Vietnam allowed Hoang Minh Chinh to travel to the United States for medical treatment. Chinh had joined the Indochinese Communist Party in the 1930s and distinguished himself as a commando during the First Indochina War before becoming one of the country's leading experts in Marxist theory. He had worked closely with the leadership in tailoring communism to the Democratic Republic of Vietnam. Chinh had also landed himself in hot water when, in 1963, he had questioned the politburo's ideological dogmatism and decision to go to war. Having studied in Moscow in the late 1950s as de-Stalinization spread across the communist world, he returned home to argue with the leadership that socialism could best be attained through peaceful evolution. But for those in Hanoi who wanted to return to war (and gain Mao's support for it), Hoang Minh Chinh's views made him a 'revisionist'. He was in and out of prison until the 1980s, when a second wave of communist reformism led by the Soviet Union's Mikhail Gorbachev released him from his semi-criminal revisionist status and seemed to vindicate him.

It certainly emboldened him. As Gorbachev allowed home-grown democracies to replace dictatorships of the proletariat in the Soviet Union and Eastern Europe, Chinh urged the Vietnamese communists to do the same. This was the message he carried with him to the United States in 2005. In interviews, speeches, and meetings, he called for the introduction of the rule of law, freedom of speech and religion, liberty of the press, free elections, and multiparty politics. In a comparison designed to remind communist leaders that they were on the wrong side of history, Hoang Minh Chinh praised the nineteenth-century German socialists, who, despite Marx's rebuke of their 'revisionist' moderation, had pushed through a ground-breaking political program at Gotha in 1875 (one of the pillars on which modern social democracy stands). Until his death in 2008, Chinh championed the creation of just such a social democratic state working within the framework of a capitalist economy.[1]

Of course, Vietnamese communists saw things differently. Even though they had authorized a capitalist economy to flourish, Lenin's single-party state still suited them just fine for ruling. Political change has certainly occurred with the introduction of a market economy and with it the opening of the country to the non-communist world, its international organizations, rules, capital flows, and interactions with civil society. However, today's communist leaders have nevertheless carefully defined political change in reformist terms, so as to co-opt those who would do away with the vanguard role of the party. What all this means for the country's political future is anybody's guess. But if the past is any guide to this, the leadership can count on Vietnamese republicans to continue opposing authoritarian rule while Vietnamese citizens will push for more political change in their everyday lives.

MAINTAINING COMMUNIST LEGITIMACY IN A POST-COMMUNIST WORLD

In an economy where the Vietnamese Communist Party pushes capitalism as its policy and has abandoned a centrally planned economy in favor of one allowing private entrepreneurship, its leaders have had to shift their ideological *raison d'être* from defending 'class struggle' and 'proletarian internationalism' to promoting economic prosperity and inclusive nationalism for all social groups. Through school textbooks, official histories, museums, billboards, and the media, the party now highlights its historic role as the defender of national independence against the invading French, Japanese, Americans, and Chinese. School children learn how the party led the August Revolution to victory in 1945, defeated the French colonizers at Dien Bien Phu a decade later, and united the entire country against all odds in 1975. This, in turn, is presented as the latest chapter in an ancient tradition of resistance reaching back two thousand years. The message is clear: the communists are legitimate because, like their ancestors, they are the nation's defenders.

Meanwhile, party chroniclers carefully prune problematic events from the narrative. Close collaboration with Mao's China into the 1960s, for example, fits badly with the country's present problems dealing with their northern neighbor in the South China Sea. Ho Chi Minh may have created the Indochinese Communist Party in 1930, but his role in spreading communism to Thailand, Malaysia, Cambodia, and Laos is not what authorities want to emphasize today in their role as a member of the common market-minded Association of South East Asian Nations. And when a special exhibition on the land-reform campaigns of the 1950s opened in Hanoi in September 2014, authorities closed it within days, as young people gasped at the class violence the party had unleashed against its own people and angry farmers used the occasion to vent their anger about current land disputes.[2]

Party historians have been particularly careful to shield Ho Chi Minh from accusations of any wrongdoing in the carrying out of such grandiose projects designed to remake society in the communist mold. To suggest that the country's president was responsible for assaults on his own people during the land-reform programs weakens the leadership's ability to use its great leader to weave nationalism and communism into a powerful source of legitimation. Indeed, the potential for Ho's life and work to define communist rule in nationalist terms was such that when he died in 1969 his disciples refused to honor the president's request that he be cremated and have his ashes scattered across the country. Instead his followers embalmed him and placed his body on display in a massive mausoleum in downtown Hanoi, where Ho lies to this day. School children, cadets, civil servants, officers, and party cadres all file by at one time or another to pay homage to the father of the nation. Etched into the granite entrance are Ho's famous words: 'Nothing is more precious than freedom and independence'.[3]

This is part of a wider personality cult the party has built around Ho since 1945, in the form of rituals, holidays, museums, iconography, and countless biographies. In 1991, as communism crumbled globally, the leadership extended this to include 'Ho Chi Minh Thought' ('Tu tuong Ho Chi Minh'). Teachers, textbooks, documentaries, stamps and pictures all tell the story of the founding father of the nation. Readers follow Ho as he leaves Saigon on the eve of the First World War in search of ways to free the country from its colonial shackles. After searching far and wide, he discovers the path to independence in the form of Marxism-Leninism. With this light now guiding him, he goes on to create the Indochinese Communist

Party in 1930, the Viet Minh nationalist front in 1941, and leads the country to independence in 1945. Ho's patriotism trumps all in this personification of the nation.[4]

Ho, his life, and his thoughts are still the objects of intense official worship. Civil servants at the Nguyen Ai Quoc Party School study the Ho Chi Minh canon in the form of his *Collected Works*. They learn to imitate his unique leadership 'style', stressing as it does, moral rectitude, incorruptibility, and patriotism. The official slogan is clear enough: 'Study and Follow Ho Chi Minh's Example of Moral Conduct'. Ho Chi Minh Thought asks all to emulate this fatherly, gentle, humanistic, indeed Confucian man in their lives and deeds. And there is an exemplary Ho for everyone—the army, the party, teachers, peasants, workers, the young, and the old. But, as in earlier chapters of Vietnamese history, this political religion seeks above all to establish ideological homogeneity and reinforce party control over the state and society from top to bottom. Whether it does so in practice is questionable. But, as in North Korea's state-sponsored adulation of Kim Il-sung, a communist form of the accusation of *lèse-majesté* awaits those in Vietnam who would challenge the deification of Ho Chi Minh.[5]

Communist rulers have simultaneously prevented living, charismatic competitors from stepping in to claim the nationalist mantle from Ho in a post-communist world. Religious leaders remain subject to close surveillance and official scrutiny. Today, the last thing the authorities want in a rapidly changing society is a religious revival that could resurrect the likes of magical, millenarian leaders like the Hoa Hao's Huynh Phu So in the 1930s, a Buddhist Zen master capable of mobilizing thousands of believers as Thich Nhat Hanh was in the 1960s, or an energized Catholic clergy with Vatican connections. Through a series of officially sanctioned Churches, the party seeks to control its Buddhist, Catholic, Protestant, Hoa Hao, and Cao Dai populations, their clergy, and property. Like their Vietnamese and French predecessors, the communist authorities have not hesitated to arrest religious leaders who fail to follow the rules. Similar controls exist to prevent non-Viet populations from pushing ethno-nationalist and, increasingly, ethno-religious identities which are at odds with the official line emphasizing national harmony of a secular kind. And any Vietnamese equivalent to Czechoslovakia's Václev Havel or Poland's Lech Walesa preaching the end of communist rule will find him or herself subject to arrest. The army, police, and intelligence services remain firmly in the regime's hands. Like the Chinese, the Vietnamese authorities invest heavily in technology which allows them to trawl the web, social media, and emails in search of seditious activities.[6]

Some of the most spectacular challenges to communist legitimacy following the official adoption of the *doi moi* ('renovation') policy in 1986 came from veterans of the Vietnam War. What made their attacks so noteworthy was that they challenged the party's right to define the thirty years' war in patriotic terms at precisely the time when the leadership desperately needed the banner of 'glorious resistance' to divert attention from its failed communist policies. Controlling the meaning of the wars is no minor affair in Vietnam. In a land where upward of three million people may have perished between 1945 and 1975, the party has long done its best to define such massive suffering as a sacred event ('*cuoc khang chien than thanh*') on its terms. The leadership has done this by creating an elaborate system of state rituals and ceremonies to commemorate and render homage to those who have died 'for the fatherland'. Officially run veterans' associations, immaculately groomed cemeteries, solemn memorials and monuments, moving sculptures, and countless documentaries all promote the sacredness of the struggle. Like the British and French leaders who scrambled to define the Great War's bloodletting in heroic terms after the event, Vietnamese authorities have carefully ennobled their past conflicts through all the commemorative tools at their disposal.[7]

The party's monopoly hold over war and remembrance cracked, however, with the economic reforms that began in the 1980s. To some extent, the party had only itself to blame. In order to reinforce its new economic policies, then General Secretary Nguyen Van Linh initially urged intellectuals, civil servants, and journalists to speak their minds, to tell the truth ('*noi that, noi thang*'). The party welcomed, indeed published their constructive criticism of inefficiencies and corruption. What the politburo didn't see coming was how writers would seize upon this invitation to speak openly in order to give their own meaning to the social suffering that thirty years of war had generated.

Nowhere was this more evident than in the title of the bestselling novel published by Bao Ninh in 1991—*The Sorrow of War*. In a few hundred pages, this veteran of the Vietnam War described in detail the terrible toll of the great patriotic war on the Vietnamese people. Where the communists spoke of war as a noble endeavor, Bao Ninh drew on his combat experience to remind readers that the war was, in fact, a very ugly affair. It had maimed and it had killed—combatants and civilians, young and old, Viet and non-

Viet. And there was more, Bao Ninh shows us: the Second Indochina War had spread sorrow so deeply that it still flowed into the present and had even invaded the spiritual world. Appearing throughout Bao Ninh's novel are the souls of hundreds of thousands of Vietnamese fighters who went missing in action. (The novel opens with the protagonist, Kien, searching for them, a figure who clearly represents Bao Ninh himself.) Having lost their bodies, these men and women are unable to receive the proper burial rites required to move their spirits into the next world. Instead, they remain trapped in their 'screaming souls', hurtling in a terrifying no-man's land from one end of the country to the other. Surviving family members know their loved ones are 'there', but they can only see them in dreams: bad ones.[8]

It was a bombshell of a novel, not only for its ability to unveil the deep social suffering the party's official cults, rituals, and official atheism had been unable to heal, but also for its success in redefining the meaning of the war in ways the state could not control. Although Bao Ninh did not intentionally seek to undermine the party's legitimacy with his book (what mattered most to him was unpacking the memories that were driving him mad), he had nevertheless turned the party's war myth on its head when, early on in the story, he had one of his soldiers ask what had been on the author's mind for years: 'So much blood, so many lives were sacrificed for what?' Our Vietnamese veteran had just taken a swipe at what one poet-soldier of the Great War, Britain's Wilfred Owen, had called the 'Old Lie'—'*Dulce et decorum est pro patria mori*'. Bao Ninh was soon under house arrest for suggesting that the party's take on the war was just as deceitful.[9]

Another veteran, Duong Thu Huong, went even further. In the course of equally hard-hitting novels, this fearless writer critiqued not just the brutality and senselessness of the war, but she went on to attack the party's right to rule. She was ruthless in her critique of the violent land-reform programs of the 1950s and the corrupt cadres who had implemented it. In her novels, she made no secret of the fact that she thought the party was out of its league when it came to modernizing the country. In *Zenith*, she even dared to treat Ho Chi Minh as a mere mortal. This was too much for those in power. Hopping mad, Nguyen Van Linh had her thrown out of the party and jailed, but not before publicly insulting her as 'that dissident slut'. After serving time in prison and then living under house arrest, Huong obtained political asylum in France in 2006, from where she calls for the democratization of her country's political system, the introduction of the rule of law, and the protection of individual rights.[10]

BACK TO THE FUTURE? VIETNAMESE REPUBLICANISM
OVER THE LONG TWENTIETH CENTURY

There is nothing new about Duong Thu Huong's embrace of democracy. She is one in a very long line of Vietnamese people opposed to authoritarian regimes. While it is tempting at this point in our journey through modern Vietnam to sum up the political changes that have occurred since 1986, let us step back one last time to remind ourselves that the building tensions between Vietnamese authoritarianism and pluralism today reach back over the long twentieth century. Vietnamese republicanism is not a post-1986 phenomenon. Nor is reformism. It emerged over a century ago, before communism arrived; and therein lies one of the keys to understanding political change in modern Vietnam today and what lies ahead.

As we know, by the early 1900s, a host of republican ideas were entering Vietnam via port cities, through the French colonial state itself, and pouring off printing presses from Hong Kong to Saigon by way of Tokyo. Converts to republicanism were many. Indeed, the pantheon of early converts reads like an early twentieth-century Vietnamese *Who's Who*—Phan Chu Trinh, Phan Boi Chau, Phan Van Truong, Nguyen The Truyen, Huynh Thuc Khang, Nguyen Thai Hoc, Nguyen Tuong Tam, Tran Trong Kim, and perhaps the country's greatest democratic spirit, Nguyen An Ninh. They all embraced the notion of popular sovereignty, rule of law, free elections, and representative government. Even the young emperor Bao Dai had shocked his colonial masters when he proposed the creation of a constitutional monarchy in the early 1930s. After all, no other emperor had ever recognized such a temporal claim on divine right.

Ho Chi Minh was initially a member of this club. While his official biographers prefer to start his story in Paris with his conversion to communism, they conveniently forget that the father of communist Vietnam had first championed the democratic ideas flowing into Vietnam from abroad. He travelled to Europe on the eve of the Great War in the hope of forcing the French to make good on their promise of political change. In France, he joined the League of Human Rights, the Freemasons, and the Socialist Party. In 1919, as the victorious Allies convened at Versailles to determine the fate of the postwar world and, many hoped, its colonial parts, Ho joined fellow republicans in Paris to ask the French to implement reforms respectful of Vietnamese individual rights and provide them with a say in governance. The republican nature of the 'Demands of the Annamese People' in 1919 is unmistakable:

1. General amnesty for political prisoners;
2. Reform of the justice system so as to guarantee equal legal rights between Europeans and Vietnamese, including the complete and definitive eradication of special courts that serve to terrorize and suppress the Vietnamese people;
3. Freedom of the press and freedom of opinion;
4. Freedom of association and freedom for gathering;
5. Freedom to emigrate and travel abroad;
6. Freedom of education and the creation in every province of technical and professional schools;
7. The end of [special] laws;
8. The creation of a permanent delegation within the French parliament that can convey the desiderata of the Vietnamese to the government.[11]

Governor General Albert Sarraut's famous speech in Hanoi in 1919 had held out the hope that the Third Republic would finally reform its authoritarian colonial state in democratic ways. Such hope vanished within a few years, however, as the Vietnamese realized that colonial reformism was designed above all to co-opt and subvert Vietnamese republicanism. Sarraut's liberalization of the press and expansion of voting rights for a select few were real, but such measures also coincided with the creation of the powerful political police, the Sûreté générale. Censorship remained firmly in place. The French licensed printing presses as carefully as the communists monitor the web today. Repression without rule of law remained part and parcel of colonial policy. Governor generals authorized special commissions and courts to try, condemn, incarcerate, and execute 'rebels'. Not even the French leftist coalition that came to power in the 1930s, the Popular Front, could bring itself to create the Indochinese equivalent to the Indian National Congress.

Intensely frustrated, men like Ho Chi Minh converted to Marxism-Leninism. But not all republicans did. Just as many carried on. They used existing institutions to push the limits of colonial reformism and exploit French and international conjunctures to roll back authoritarianism.

Equally important, a proliferation of new associations, clubs, charities, self-help, literacy, and anti-poverty groups recalibrated society and local politics in new ways. Urban planning, taxation, state monopolies, and economic development projects stimulated lively debates and new forms of political culture. The printed word in its *quoc ngu* form moved ideas and connected people together. A new professional class of Vietnamese lawyers emerged to assume a range of briefs (although land disputes probably occupied more of their time than juicy political cases). Intellectuals, writers, journalists, and artists took greater interest in the everyday lives of the urban poor and the majority peasant population. Local municipalities and village councils were often the forums for grassroots change. And during the brief period when the Popular Front was in control in France (1936–8), Nguyen An Ninh rallied a wide array of supporters, including workers, to win political posts in local elections, before the authorities ended this short but important experiment in colonial democracy.[12]

Vietnamese republicanism also had its radical wing. By the late 1920s, a handful of dedicated men and women in the Vietnamese Nationalist Party concluded that only violence could secure an independent and truly democratic state. Colonial reformism was a political dead-end. Days before his execution, Nguyen Thai Hoc, the mastermind of the failed Yen Bay insurrection of 1930, sent a letter to the French National Assembly in Paris in which he explained that the French failure to implement real political reforms in Vietnam had left his party with no choice but to use violence to achieve a 'Vietnamese republic'. Another ranking member told a journalist that what he wanted was what the French had, nothing more, nothing less: 'a democratic government, universal suffrage, freedom of the press, respect of human and citizen rights, and, why not, independence'.[13]

This tension between colonial authoritarianism and Vietnamese republicanism is only half the story, though. Just as important was the clash between Vietnamese republicans and communists over the future of Vietnam. Each side wanted to overturn the colonial state holding them down, but each had a very different ideological road-map for how to get there and what the postcolonial state should look like once they did. Official historians would like us to believe that, in the wake of the Yen Bay fiasco (see chapter 5), the real nationalists in the Vietnamese Nationalist Party and elsewhere became communists. It makes for the seamless story discussed above; but it also forgets that a generation of Vietnamese republicans continued to embrace a representative form of government based on popular sovereignty, universal suffrage, multiparty politics, free elections, and an independent national assembly and judiciary. The communists on the other hand, including Ho Chi Minh, adopted democratic centralism, class struggle, and collectivization via land reform as their road-map. Their postcolonial communist state would draw its legitimacy from the protection of workers and peasants and operate in the form of a dictatorship of the proletariat. In short, from the late 1920s onward (and not from a starting-point in 1986), one group looked to Atlantic republicanism for a model of liberal governance; the other drew upon the Soviet Union's combination of Marxism and Leninism to create a single-party state.[14]

Although the competition between these two types of governance was occurring across much of the globe at the time, it played itself out very differently in the Indochinese context, where an authoritarian colonial state opposed both Vietnamese republicanism and communism. This is why the first debates, indeed, clashes between the two sides occurred in the cell blocks of Poulo Condor (where the French had sent so many of their political prisoners). Similar exchanges surfaced in the press and political campaigns during the brief period of the leftwing government coalition known as the Popular Front. In the end, though, the tensions between the two groups only came into the open in 1945-6 when a fragile coalition government led by Ho Chi Minh struggled to hold itself together in the form of the Democratic Republic of Vietnam. With colonial control absent for the first time in eighty years, and thanks to the Chinese nationalist troops the Allies sent into Vietnam to accept the Japanese surrender in northern Indochina in September 1945, Vietnamese democrats and communists expressed their ideas in a remarkably open press, organized political demonstrations and rallies, and created political parties free of colonial molestation. Some of the liveliest debates in Vietnamese political history occurred during this short period. This was particularly the case in their National Assembly which emerged in March 1946, and whose delegates hammered out the country's first constitution throughout the rest of the year. Although this republican moment was limited to the north (as the French had already attacked in the south), for the first time in the history of modern Vietnam a fragile democratic state was born. Emperor Bao Dai helped on that score, when, in August 1945, he abdicated the throne, thereby ending a millennium of monarchical rule. He intentionally referred to himself thereafter as 'citizen Vinh Thuy'. This was in contrast to Cambodia's King Norodom Sihanouk, who welcomed the French back in order to preserve his rule, save the monarchy, and combat democrats keen on creating a constitutional democracy.[15]

This republican moment in Vietnam did not last for more than a year. With the outbreak of full-scale war in late 1946, the French immediately began rolling back democratic rights as the army restored the colonial regime. A formal 'state of siege' was declared in December 1946 and this authorized the army to take over policing, administrative, and judicial affairs. Censorship returned, as did special commissions and courts to deal with the ever-increasing number of 'rebels' taken prisoner in a war the French refused to declare was going on. To do so would have meant recognizing the existence of a competing state. Tens of thousands of political prisoners thus found themselves in colonial cells or working in military labor camps with few rights.[16]

Meanwhile, the communists had no intention of letting their Vietnamese adversaries use a democratic constitution and a multiparty state to force them to compete in free elections so that they would have to govern like communist parties in republican France and Italy. And to be fair, the Chinese occupying forces and their Vietnamese allies such as Nguyen Hai Than and Vu Hong Khanh were just as willing as the communists to use undemocratic methods to increase their control over the DRV or overthrow it. This is also why, as the Chinese army withdrew in mid-1946, the French colonialists and the Vietnamese communists both moved against their common Vietnamese adversaries before turning on each other. In the north, Vietnamese communists closed down the opposition parties by force or co-optation, took control of all presses and papers, prohibited unauthorized demonstrations, and arrested those who defied them. When the new constitution became law on 8–9 November 1946, only two members of the opposition were present. The French had already done much the same against the Vietnamese nationalists in the south.

The 1946 constitution did, however, enshrine many of the political rights so many Vietnamese had wanted since the turn of the twentieth century—universal suffrage, an independent National Assembly and judiciary, rule of law, freedom of expression, an unfettered press, religious liberty, the right to an education, freedom to travel, private property, and more. It was a milestone in Vietnamese political theory. Moreover, it was an entirely Vietnamese initiative—not a French- or an American-driven one. And it was also a joint Vietnamese effort—not a communist-imposed one. United by their fierce opposition to the return of French colonialism, most republicans who had been dissatisfied with the Chinese-backed parties joined Ho's coalition government in 1945–6, convinced that they would be able to partake in the construction of a multiparty state guaranteed by the 1946 constitution once the guns fell silent and the country was free.[17]

This was not to be. While communists and democrats kept the Democratic Republic of Vietnam alive against all odds, starting in 1950, Mao Zedong's military assistance, political models, and advisors allowed Ho Chi Minh and his followers to transform it into a single-party communist state, regardless of what the 1946 constitution stipulated or non-communists in their ranks said. There was no debate allowed about the (Chinese-modeled) rectification and emulation campaigns which followed. No one voted on the party's confiscation of the state bureaucracy, police, judiciary, and army. The National Assembly met only one time during the entire First Indochina War—in 1953, to approve the land-reform policy the communist core led by Ho Chi Minh had already worked out with their Soviet and, above all, Chinese advisors.

Upon taking over all of northern Vietnam following the Geneva conference in 1954, the communist party continued consolidating its hold over the single-party state it had forged from war. Having taken control of the police and the army, the communists had no real intention of sharing power as they had in 1945–6. Sidelined, republicans could do nothing to stop the promulgation of the new constitution of 1960 that validated the wartime shift in the Democratic Republic of Vietnam away from a parliamentary socialist democracy to a single-party communist state. Based on the Soviet model, the 1960 constitution enshrined 'socialism' as the official ideology (use of the word 'communism' was avoided so as not to play into the hands of the man building an anticommunist state in the south, Ngo Dinh Diem). For the communists today, the 1960 constitution is the founding document for their Vietnam, not the 1946 one. And this is why republicans in Vietnam today push so hard for the restoration of the 1946 constitution, which they consider to be the 'real' one. It would allow them to roll back the communist confiscation of the state during the First Indochina War.[18]

Authoritarianism was not a communist or colonialist monopoly, however. The DRV's competitor, the Associated State of Vietnam led by Bao Dai, failed to create a functioning parliament: in part, because the French refused to let go colonially, but also because of their own ineptitude. Following the French withdrawal, Ngo Dinh Diem took over as the president of the Republic of Vietnam that replaced the State of Vietnam below the seventeenth parallel after the Geneva conference. But he did little better than Ho Chi Minh in respecting individual liberties, the rule of law, representative politics, and the freedom of the press. In what could have easily been mistaken for a communist election, in 1955 Diem received almost one hundred percent of the popular vote, making him president. The president and his family controlled the National Assembly, the judiciary, and ruled by decree. And if Ho's regime went after the 'bourgeois' and the 'landlords' in a class war during the land-reform programs of the 1950s, Diem used special powers and courts to exterminate the 'communists' and forcibly moved hundreds of thousands of peasants into strategic hamlets during the same decade. Diem had no patience with Vietnamese democrats clamoring for rule of law. Scores ended up behind bars or, ironically, crossed over to the other side, convinced, again, that the communists would honor their democratic promises once the war had ended. While recent research suggests that the Republic of Vietnam began evolving in democratic ways after Diem's assassination in 1963, the final communist victory in 1975 denied it the chance to transition from its anticommunist authoritarianism into a functioning parliamentary democracy as in Taiwan and South Korea. That is certainly what those who despise the communists wish to believe today. But it is equally possible that had the state in the south survived, it might have remained an authoritarian one like the military regime in Burma, at least until recently. Counterfactual history moves in many directions, especially for those who use it to fit the needs of the present; but in the end we will never know what could have been.[19]

Republicanism and Communism: A Turning-point?

The Global Wiring of the Vietnamese Public Sphere

What we do know is that the competition between authoritarianism and republicanism is not going away any time soon. By adopting market-oriented policies, the party has set far-reaching change into motion and has made it harder for its own agents to monitor the public sphere, define public opinion, control citizens, and limit their contact with the rest of the world. The party's embrace of capitalism has also limited its own room for manoeuver, by integrating it into a web of institutions ranging from the World Bank and the International Monetary Fund to the Association of Southeast Asian Nations and, in late 2015, the proposed Trans-Pacific Partnership. These institutions impose legally binding rules which the national authorities in them must obey in order to obtain loans, attract investment, and trade. The same goes for the new stock markets in Hanoi and Ho Chi Minh City. They might offer attractive returns to investors and generate much-needed investment capital; but they are also closely tied to world financial markets and are subject to their fluctuations, including downward ones.[20]

The shift to the market economy since 1986 has ushered in an era of economic prosperity that only the south knew for a few years before the war destabilized it in the late 1960s and the communists dismantled it a decade later. The renovation policies have fueled the rise of a middle class that is anxious to buy things—shiny washing machines, big-screen smart televisions, faster cars, bigger houses, and investment property. Families have tightened their belts to place their children in some of the finest private schools in Vietnam and many have shelled out even bigger bucks to send them abroad for study. Thanks to family, governmental, or international support, tens of thousands of Vietnamese are now going abroad to obtain advanced degrees in science, medicine, law, banking, finance, mathematics, engineering, agricultural economics, animal husbandry and the like. At ease with modern economics, law, and governance, these highly educated people are increasingly in charge of modern Vietnam's transformation at many different levels.

Change has not been a solely urban phenomenon, however. If anyone forced the party to backtrack on its grand schemes to collectivize agriculture in the north in the 1960s, and then the south after 1975, it was the peasants resisting in their everyday lives. The renovation policies of the 1980s have reduced rural poverty levels dramatically. Farmers can now produce more to earn more. Rice production took off with the end of the state-planned economy in the 1980s. New technologies, fertilizers, and machinery have been introduced into agriculture, making Vietnam the world's second-largest rice producer today. Household incomes have risen as a result. Farmers have the freedom to diversify their activities into commercial crops such as fruit, vegetables, and coffee. Vietnam is also the second-largest coffee producer in the world after Brazil. Commercial pig farming and fisheries have flourished over the last two decades, as the feed industry expands rapidly to keep up.[21]

Having based its legitimacy on providing economic prosperity based on free-market principles, Vietnamese communists, like their Chinese counterparts, must maintain high levels of growth at all costs. The party's

legitimacy now depends on that, not on the myth of glorious war. The urban middle class, professionals, and farmers all count on sustained growth.
So do the large numbers of young people entering the labor market each
year. In 2015, 50 percent of the country's estimated 94 million people were
aged under twenty-nine. They know little of the war years; their gaze is
turned squarely toward the future. If ever economic problems overwhelm
the ruling communist class, stymying its ability to main expected growth
levels, these groups will use their voices, economically and politically. They
have too much at stake not to do so. Highly trained bankers, investors, lawyers, engineers, scientists, and business elites will have urgent advice for
those in power, in the event that the latter prove unable to keep an increasingly complex economy on track.[22]

This is also why endemic party and state corruption draw such heavy
criticism, not only from diehard republican militants, but also from urban
and rural economic leaders with real economic power and interests to protect. It is hard to predict how the growing working class would react in the
event of an economic downturn, but there is no guarantee that it would
be on the communist side. To date, the party has resisted the unioniza-
tion of labor. The message is, nonetheless, clear: great political risk will
confront those who fail to manage economic development and capitalism
competently.[23]

Globalization, however, is more than the spread of Atlantic capitalism
across the planet. It is also an accelerated process of integrative, technological change. The French presided over an early form of this through the introduction of the printing press, print media (newspapers, novels, pamphlets,
textbooks), radios, telephones, the telegraph, cinema, and new transportation systems. More open to the world than its communist competitor in the
1950s and 1960s, the Republic of Vietnam took it further during its short
lifespan (as discussed in chapter 12). But another technological revolution
starting in the late twentieth century has further accelerated this integrative
process of interconnectedness. It has occurred in Vietnam, as elsewhere,
through the introduction of computers, the internet, email, social media
(Facebook, Twitter, YouTube, and blogs), and mobile phones. As of 2014,
39 percent of the Vietnamese population is online; that is a higher rate
than in Thailand or the Philippines. Twenty-two percent of the population
uses social media, mainly Facebook, with twenty million active accounts.
Of the online adults, a staggering 72 percent use a social network, and 51
percent use the internet on their mobile phones. Thirty-six percent of the

population owns a smartphone. Internet cafés are increasingly a thing of the past, because homes are now wired: indeed, 85 per cent of the online users have internet access at home (though not at comparatively high speeds). Vietnamese start-up companies are now using technology transfers to develop and commercialize their own hi-tech products.[24]

The significance of this global wiring of Vietnam from within and without is obvious. Vietnamese citizens in the cities as well as in the countryside have access to alternative sources of information about their country, the region, and the world. Citizens are also in a situation where they can broadcast their demands and share their view on government policies with friends via email, through social platforms like Facebook, or by circulating online petitions to masses of people with the click of a button. Neighborhood and village communities can connect on very specific local problems, while others can reach out to a larger audience to discuss national matters in real time. In April 2015, for example, tech-savvy Hanoi citizens created a Facebook page that brought hundreds of people into the streets to protest against the local municipality's unilateral decision to start chopping down over 6,000 old trees. The government backed down when petitions flooded in and people took to the streets.[25]

The government has also acquiesced in the emergence of an increasingly vibrant civil society. While the communist party has certainly tried to control associations by placing them within its all-encompassing mass organization, the 'Fatherland Front' (a direct descendant of the communist-controlled Viet Minh), it has allowed hundreds of associations to organize their members around a wide range of different activities: charity, the family, economic development, the environment, ethnic minorities, science and technology, women's issues and professional clubs. Many of these groups operate with considerable independence, while others have negotiated increased room for maneuvering within the state despite their nominal subordination to party control. Informal and community-based networks running online have joined in to express their opinions and give support (often through donations and fund-raising) on a range of socio-economic issues.

Very often, the communist authorities have found it useful to work with these groups to improve their governance and transparency, and thereby increase the state's effectiveness and legitimacy. Local groups have also found it in their interest to work with the government, rather than oppose it, in order to realize their goals. Collaboration on environmental, family,

and women's rights is a case in point. The same is true of international
Non-Governmental Organizations (NGOs). The state may control and
monitor their movements, but it also benefits from collaboration with
NGOs. The number of NGOs operating in Vietnam has increased from
200 in the early 1990s to almost 2,000 today. The party might monopolize
power at the top levels, but its control over society at the lower levels is
hardly totalitarian.[26]

Reform or Revolution?

The problem for the communists today is much like the one facing colonialists during the interwar period: when does state-sponsored reformism
risk turning into outright revolution? It's not that Vietnamese communists
are colonialists. The problem is opposition to political authoritarianism
and economic change. Calls for democratic reform have come in many
forms since the renovation policy of the late 1980s began. In the early years,
the push for political reform came from within the system, first from those
whom the revolution had discarded like Hoang Minh Chinh, then from retired, disillusioned senior leaders who had nothing to lose by speaking out.
Veteran army officers and longstanding party members were also among
the first to criticize the inefficiencies and corruption of the party apparatus.
Most did not seek to overthrow the party through the force of arms. Rather,
they used their prestige and impeccable resistance credentials to urge the
leadership to reform the political system peacefully. Particularly attractive
to them were the multiparty parliamentary systems that had emerged without much bloodshed in Eastern Europe in the 1990s.

General Tran Do was one of the most important members of the communist party to speak out against party corruption and about the need to
introduce a democratic system to check its spread. He had joined the party
in 1940, commanded troops during the historic Battle of Dien Bien Phu,
fought the Americans in the south until 1975, and then became vice-deputy
of the National Assembly. In Do's view, the party had been right to revamp
its economic policy by ending collectivization and central planning. But
he added that equally important political reforms were urgently needed in
light of the demands the people would soon make in this era of prosperity. In letters, articles, petitions, and, by the late 1990s, via the internet, the
general urged the party to lead the democratization of the state by returning to the 1946 republican constitution. This would mean introducing free
elections and legalizing opposition parties. But it would obviously open

up the possibility of ending single-party communist rule. This the leadership refused. In 1999, the politburo expelled Tran Do from the party. There would be no return to the 1946 constitution. The party might have revised its constitution in 1992 to approve its embrace of capitalist economics, but it had not relinquished its monopoly hold on politics (article 4), despite an unprecedented number of voices calling on it to do so. Tran Do was part of this bigger debate.[27]

A growing sense of dissatisfaction has emerged over the last decade as more Vietnamese have become convinced that communist reformism is designed above all to co-opt a century of Vietnamese republicanism. Like Nguyen An Ninh who called Sarraut's reformist bluff in 1925, many Vietnamese today—and not just twenty-somethings as in the 1920s—have begun to adopt a more confrontational approach toward the regime by actually demanding the end of communist rule. Defiance has returned to the Vietnamese political scene and many republican-minded Vietnamese, young and old, seem to be willing to go to jail for their ideas. Whereas Nguyen An Ninh had latched on to *quoc ngu,* print technology, and the newspaper to take his message to the people in the 1920s, democratic activists today have turned to the internet, Facebook, YouTube, mass email, and created web pages and blogs to make their case for revolutionary political and social change in the cities and countryside.

In 2006, a group of Vietnamese democrats using the internet circulated their 'Declaration of Freedom and Democracy' calling on the communist government to accord the people a representative form of government, freedom of the press, freedom of association, freedom of religion, and the protection of individual rights. They went further by calling for regime change. As the declaration put it, the communist regime 'is incapable of being renovated bit by bit or modified" and it should be "completely replaced". One of the 2006 declaration's authors, Do Nam Hai, came from a communist family with an impeccable resistance pedigree, but for him, the party's time was up. It lacked the competence needed to fully modernize the country, and corruption, again, was ruining everything. Hai had studied abroad and admired the ability of South Korea, Taiwan, and ultimately even the Philippines and Indonesia to combine political pluralism with successful market economics. If they could do it, so could Vietnam. Communism, as he wrote in 2004, 'has been, is and will be the problem of all problems, the reason of all reasons for the nation's many painful disasters and shameful laggard status'.[28]

Do Nam Hai also joined other like-minded democrats in 2006 in founding the BLOC 8406 (its number recalls the date of its creation on 8 April
2006) to 'pressure and force' the Vietnamese Communist Party to relinquish its total hold over the political system. BLOC 8406 was an organization which initially consisted of over a hundred people, who ranged from
militant republicans to religious leaders, journalists, doctors, writers, teachers, and others. Its republicans published online and hard-copy journals,
newspapers, and pamphlets of a pro-democracy kind. Although BLOC
8406 didn't last more than a few months before the party sent in the security services to stop its members, they had managed to blur the line between
reform and revolution.

As in earlier periods, lawyers got involved in pushing for individual
rights against authoritarian rule as well. Starting in the late 1990s, Cu Huy
Ha Vu and his wife, Nguyen Thi Duong Ha, dedicated their careers to defending common people from government abuses, malpractice, and corruption. Trained in law at the Sorbonne and the son of a famous communist
cultural icon, Vu relished holding the government accountable to its own
laws. He took the couple's legal offensive to a new level in 2005 when he
sued local authorities in central Vietnam for building a resort complex and
thus violating laws made to protect a heritage site. The couple won the
case. In 2008–10, Vu defended a military officer who had been sentenced to
prison for 'injuring the state'. Vu showed that this honest man had, in fact,
been illegally attacked for revealing high-level corruption in Da Nang. In
2009, Cu Huy Ha Vu took it to a level Nguyen An Ninh could never have
imagined, when he tried to sue Vietnam's prime minister for illegally authorizing Chinese companies to mine bauxite in the highlands. Vu lost when
the powers that be concluded that neither the Hanoi People's Court nor
the country's Supreme Court had the right to judge a prime minister. In the
eyes of many, however, Vu had nonetheless scored a major victory by showing up the party's playing of the system. Determined to stop this gadfly who
openly called for the creation of a republican form of government, the party
had Vu sentenced to a seven-year prison term in 2011. Defiant, Vu went on a
hunger strike in 2013 and in so doing attracted attention inside and outside
Vietnam. In April 2014, the authorities agreed to let Vu and his wife accept
asylum in the United States and quickly scuttled them out of the country.

The bauxite question, however, was much bigger than Vu. The outrage
generated by the party's willingness to allow Chinese companies to strip-
mine a huge portion of the central highlands brought together—on the

ground and online—democracy activists, civil society advocates, scientists and engineers, environmentalists, concerned citizens, dissidents, overseas Vietnamese, and even General Vo Nguyen Giap into a bloc of opposition of historic significance. The genesis of the Bauxite controversy is long and complex. What set off the firestorm, as noted, was the party-state's decision to let Chinese companies extract millions of tons of bauxite from the central highlands. The Chinese were ready to come in with their people to do the job, when a range of concerned scientists and environmentalists within the government joined together to find ways to discuss the issue legally and convince the government to think twice about the potentially disastrous environmental, economic, and political effects of removing the surface of the central highlands to get at this mineral. Leading the incipient coalition were people like Tran Thi Lien, who had been active in running NGOs aimed at helping the environment, women, and the highland areas since the 1990s, and scientists like Nguyen Thanh Son who had been tasked by the government to work on the bauxite project, but who knew from experience that strip-mining was a recipe for disaster. Together they organized workshops and published articles in the press and online which drew attention to the dangers of going in too fast. The former rector of Ho Chi Minh City's Economics University agreed, saying that the 'Central Highlands w[ould] die' because of the government's bauxite project.[29]

When the prime minister appeared to turn a blind eye, a core group of seventeen scientists and researchers, almost all of them tied to the government, submitted an internal petition in November 2008 calling on the leadership to study the question more carefully before proceeding. To strengthen their argument, they also added something new by underscoring the importance of the highlands for Vietnam's 'national security'. Prime Minister Nguyen Tan Dung was determined to go through with the bauxite project. In early 2009, he clamped down on press reports on the matter, reaffirming that the project was good for the country and in line with what the party and the government had already decided. What Dung did not see coming was another general, this time the single most important general in communist Vietnam—Vo Nguyen Giap. He knew the topic and he knew many of the government professionals opposed to it. They had all previously listened to the Soviets when, in the 1980s, the latter had advised them not to destroy the highlands to get at the bauxite (Vietnam may in fact hold some of the largest bauxite deposits in the world). Giap wrote an internal letter to the party reminding his equals of all of this and asking them to stop the project until more studies could be done. He also pointed out that it might not be a good idea to let the Chinese send their own people into the highlands. This letter was leaked within days, and was soon appearing on websites faster than the government could put a firewall around them. A few weeks later another general going rogue left no doubt that the bauxite project was more than just a potential environmental catastrophe. It was a national security issue too. By going ahead with it, the communist party was on the verge of letting the historic enemy, the Chinese, into the country.

Voices from all horizons came together in 2010 in opposition to the project. Overseas Vietnamese, dissidents, BLOC 8406, lawyers, scientists, and NGOs, as well as Catholic priests and Buddhist monks all coalesced in opposition to the bauxite program. This allowed them to turn the nationalist tables on the party by accusing it of caving in to the Chinese at the very time the latter were expanding their territorial claims against Vietnam in the South China Sea. No longer was opposition to the bauxite project limited to government scientists, environmentalists, and famous communist generals. It had now become part of a widening call for freedom of expression and political change couched in anti-Chinese discourse. An online anti-bauxite project petition gathered thousands of signatures from people in all walks of life. Soon usually docile delegates in the National Assembly were debating the issue in heated exchanges not seen since 1946.

With the presence of Chinese companies on site, the bauxite project continues to this day, albeit with the party promising to extract bauxite on Vietnamese terms whilst being respectful of the environment and the highland peoples. Not everyone is convinced, however, and the surge in oppositional politics it generated has not subsided. In 2014, protestors hostile to Chinese actions in the South China Seas descended into the streets across the country, calling on the government to take a harder line against Vietnam's northern neighbor. Despite the party's willingness to arrest those who go too far and to firewall dangerous websites, a disparate coalition of voices has coalesced over the last decade against the government, and what unites them more than anything else is that they are less afraid to adopt more confrontational methods to make their interests heard. For many their interests now include the implementation of a democratic system of government, the only one they feel is capable of reconciling the diverse needs and voices of the Vietnamese people.

Only time will tell what will come of this. In December 2015, prominent Vietnamese republicans—army officers, professors, teachers, communist party members, priests, monks, and others—signed and published an online open letter to the Vietnamese Communist Party on the eve of its congress in January 2016. In a move designed to put the party on the wrong side of Vietnamese nationalism following the bauxite affair, the authors of the petition reminded the party that the leadership had the ultimate duty to protect the country against Chinese expansionism. Secondly, they rejoined Hoang Minh Chinh's critique of the failure of communism to serve as a viable 'ism' in the twenty-first century. As Chinh had argued, the petition's advocates called on the communist leadership to adopt measures to move the country toward a social democracy of a Western European type. The daring required to sign such a provocative document and publish it openly leaves no doubt that Vietnam's republicans are not going to be cowed easily. What remains to be seen is to what extent activists, entrepreneurs, professionals, middle-class urbanites, farmers, and defenders of civil society will remain as a cacophony of disparate voices or whether they will come together to remake Vietnam or to make yet another Vietnam.[30]

NOTES

A NOTE ON TERMS

1. On the question of names, see: 'Naming the Country Viet Nam', in George Dutton, Jayne Werner, and John Whitmore, eds., *Sources of Vietnamese Tradition* (New York: Columbia University Press, 2012), pp. 258–9; 'Naming the Country Dai Nam (1838)', in Dutton et al., *Sources of Vietnamese Tradition*, pp. 259–60; Alexander Woodside, *Vietnam and the Chinese Model: A Comparative Study of Vietnamese and Chinese Government in the First Half of the Nineteenth Century* (Cambridge, MA: Harvard University Press, 1988 [first published in 1971]), pp. 120–21. For an excellent discussion of this matter and more generally of Sino-Vietnamese interactions running to the fifteenth century, see Kathlene Baldanza, *Ming China and Vietnam: Negotiating Borders in Early Modern Asia* (New York: Cambridge University Press, 2016).

INTRODUCTION. THE MANY DIFFERENT VIETNAMS

1. For an overview of this bay, see: Ian Storey and Carlyle Thayer, 'Cam Ranh Bay: Past Imperfect, Future Conditional', *Contemporary Southeast Asia*, vol. 23, no. 3, December 2001. On the 7th Fleet, see Edward Marolda, *Ready Seapower: A History of the U.S. Seventh Fleet* (Washington, DC: Naval History & Heritage Command, Department of the Navy, 2011).

2. I reached the number of forty-three years (for the existence of nineteenth-century Vietnam) by subtracting 1802 (the date at which a unified Vietnam appeared under Gia Long), from 1858, when the French attacked and began colonizing Cochinchina/southern Vietnam. From that total of fifty-six years, I then deducted another thirteen years (the period from 1834 to 1847), which corresponds to the time when Vietnam was part of the larger, Dai Nam imperial states (which also included most of Cambodia and large parts of today's eastern Laos). I did not include in my count the periods of time during which the Democratic Republic of Vietnam led by Ho Chi Minh and the Associated State of Vietnam led by Bao Dai existed. Although both claimed sovereignty over all of Vietnam, neither state ever exercised total territorial control during the entire First Indochina War between 1945 and 1954. The same goes for the post-1954 period. Two Vietnamese states continued to exist. Military force allowed the Democratic Republic of Vietnam to vanquish the Republic of Vietnam in 1975, leading to the official creation of one unitary communist-led nation-state which enjoyed full territorial sovereignty from 1976 onward—the Socialist Republic of Vietnam. This means that an S-like Vietnam existed for forty-three years in the nineteenth century, six months in 1945 and forty years (as of 2016) in the twentieth and twenty-first centuries. The sum of these numbers makes eighty-three years and some months.

3. Until at least the fifteenth century, Viet and non-Viet peoples proliferated along the coast between China and central Vietnam. John Whitmore, 'Ngo (Chinese) Communities and Montane-Littoral Conflict in Dai Viet, ca. 1400–1600', *Asia Major*, 3rd series, vol.

XXVII, part 2 (2014), pp. 53–85; and his 'The Rise of the Coast: Trade, State and Culture in Early Dai Viet', *Journal of Southeast Asian Studies*, vol. 37, no. 1 (2006), pp. 103–22; and Li Tana, 'A View from the Sea: Perspectives on the Northern and Central Vietnamese Coast', in ibid., pp. 83–102.

4. See among others: Jacques Népote, 'Quelle histoire? Pour quels Vietnams?', *Péninsule*, nos. 11/12 (1985/6), http://peninsule.free.fr/articles/peninsule_11_12_article_1 .pdf, accessed 11 January 2016; Liam Kelley, *Beyond the Bronze Pillars: Envoy Poetry and the Sino-Vietnamese Relationship* (Honolulu: University of Hawai'i Press, 2005); Olga Dror, *Cult, Culture, and Authority: Princess Lieu Hanh in Vietnamese History* (Honolulu: University of Hawai'i Press, 2007); Emmanuel Poisson, *Mandarins et subalternes au nord du Viêt Nam, une bureaucratie à l'épreuve* (Paris: Maisonneuve & Larose, 2004); Li Tana, *Nguyen Cochinchina: Southern Vietnam in the Seventeenth and Eighteenth Centuries* (Ithaca: Cornell University Press, Southeast Asia Program Publications, 1998); Keith Taylor, *A History of the Vietnamese* (Cambridge: Cambridge University Press, 2013), pp. 620–26; and Keith Taylor, 'Surface Orientations in Vietnam: Beyond Histories of Nation and Region', *Journal of Asian Studies*, vol. 57 (1998), pp. 949–78.

5. Frances FitzGerald, *Fire in the Lake: The Vietnamese and the Americans in Vietnam* (New York: Little, Brown & Company, 1972).

6. Andrew Delbanco, 'The Civil War Convulsion', *The New York Review of Books* (19 March 2015), at http://www.nybooks.com/articles/archives/2015/mar/19/civil-war -convulsion, accessed 20 April 2015. A highly influential scholar of the Vietnam War, Gabriel Kolko, welcomed the Vietnamese communist victory in his *Anatomy of a War: Vietnam, the United States, and the Modern Historical Experience* (New York: Pantheon Books, 1994 (first published in 1985)), p. xii. In 1999, Robert Templer started to move us beyond the Vietnam War generation's American war-centered take on Vietnam's past. See his *Shadows and Wind: A View of Modern Vietnam* (London: Penguin, 1999).

7. R. B. Wong, 'Redefining the Modern World', at http://afe.easia.columbia.edu/china wh/web/s2/index.html, accessed 3 July 2014 (for the citation); Dror Ze'evi, 'Back to Napoleon? Thoughts on the Beginning of the Modern Era in the Middle East', *Mediterranean Historical Review*, vol. 19, no. 1 (June 2004), pp. 73–94.

8. Pierre Brocheux, *Histoire du Vietnam contemporain: La nation résiliente* (Paris: Editions Fayard, 2011), p. 12; Pierre Brocheux and Daniel Hémery, *Indochina: An Ambiguous Colonization (1858–1954)* (Berkeley: University of California Press, 2010), introduction. See also the roundtable review of this book in the *Journal of Vietnamese Studies*, vol. 4, no. 3 (Fall 2010), pp. 244–58; see Brocheux's epilogue, in *Histoire du Vietnam contemporain*, pp. 251–2; Christopher Goscha, *Vietnam or Indochina? Contesting Concepts of Space in Vietnamese Nationalism* (Copenhagen: NIAS, 1995).

9. For a selection of those who have started rethinking the question of modernity in less Western centric ways, see: John Darwin, *After Tamerlane: The Rise and Fall of Global Empires, 1400–2000* (New York: Bloomsbury Press, 2008), pp. 25–27; Dror Ze'evi, 'Back to Napoleon?', pp. 73–94; R. B. Wong, *China Transformed: Historical Change and the Limits of European Experience* (Ithaca: Cornell University Press, 1997); Kenneth Pomeranz, *The Great Divergence: China, Europe, and the Making of the Modern World Economy* (Princeton: Princeton University Press, 2001); Alexander Woodside, *Lost Modernities: China, Vietnam, Korea and the Hazards of World History* (Cambridge, MA: Harvard University Press, 2006); S. L. Eisenstadt, 'Multiple Modernities', *Daedalus*, 129, 1 (2000), pp. 1–29;

Emmanuel Poisson, 'Les Mandarins sont-ils modernes?', *Revue Histoire*, no. 62 (2014), pp. 22–4. On Voltaire and China, see: Arnold H. Rowbotham, 'Voltaire, Sinophile', *Modern Language Association*, vol. 47, no. 4 (December 1932), pp. 1050–65. For the ways by which Western colonial states pick up on preexisting non-Western ones they take over, see: Christopher Bayly, *Empire and Information: Intelligence Gathering and Social Communication in India, 1780–1870* (Cambridge: Cambridge University Press, 2000); Poisson, *Mandarins et subalterns*; Olivier Tessier, 'Outline of the Process of Red River Hydraulics Development during the Nguyen Dynasty', in Mart Stewart and Peter Coclanis, eds., *Environmental Change and Agricultural Sustainability in the Mekong Delta* (Springer Science, 2011), pp. 45–68; and Jean-Pascal Bassino, 'Indochina', in Joel Mokyr, *The Oxford Encyclopedia of Economic History* (Oxford, Oxford University Press, 2005), online at http://oxfordindex.oup.com/view/10.1093/acref/9780195105070.013.0365, accessed 25 June 2015. For a path-breaking account of Minh Mang's reign, see Choi Byung Wook, *Southern Vietnam under the Reign of Minh Mang (1820–1841): Central Policies and Local Response* (Ithaca: Cornell Southeast Asia Program, 2004). Wynn Wilcox provides a useful critique of the French colonial myth demonizing Minh Mang as a 'cruel tyrant'. Wynn Wilcox, *Allegories of the Vietnamese Past*, Yale Southeast Asia Studies, no. 61 (New Haven: Yale University Press, 2011), pp. 62–83. Contrary to Foucauldian takes on modern discipline and incarceration, Peter Zinoman has shown that in colonial Vietnam the French were quite 'un-modern', content to rely on the pre-existing Vietnamese prison system rather than transform it in panoptic ways. Peter Zinoman, *The Colonial Bastille: A History of Imprisonment in Vietnam, 1862–1940* (Berkeley: University of California Press, 2001).

10. On the need to break with Eurocentric periodizations of modernity and history in general, see: Jack Goody's *The Theft of History* (London: Cambridge University Press, 2012) and Jerry Bentley, 'Cross-cultural Interactions and Periodization in World History', *The American Historical Review*, Vol. 101, No. 3 (June 1996), pp. 749–770.

11. Darwin, *After Tamerlane*; Dominic Lieven, *Empire: The Russian Empire and Its Rivals* (New Haven: Yale University Press, 2002); Jane Burbank, Mark von Hagen, and Anatolyi Remnev, eds., *Russian Empire: Space, People, Power, 1700–1930* (Bloomington: Indiana University Press, 2007); Népôte, 'Quelle histoire?'; Hermann Kulke, 'The Early History and the Imperial Kingdom in Southeast Asian History', in David Marr and A. C. Milner, eds., *Southeast Asia in the 9th to 14th Centuries*, 2nd edn (Singapore: Institute of Southeast Asian Studies, 1990), pp. 1–22; Jane Burbank and Frederick Cooper, *Empires in World History: Power and the Politics of Difference* (Princeton: Princeton University Press, 2010); Gabriel Martinez-Gros, *Brève histoire des empires* (Paris: Seuil, 2014); James Millward, Ruth Dunnell, Mark Elliott, and Philippe Foret, eds. *New Qing Imperial History: The Making of Inner Asian Empire at Qing Chengde* (London: RoutledgeCurzon, 2004); Pierre Boilley and Antoine Marès, 'Empires, Introduction', *Monde(s)*, no. 2 (2012), pp. 7–25; Peter Perdue, *China Marches West: The Qing Conquest of Central Eurasia* (Cambridge, MA: Harvard University Press, 2005); and Millward, *New Qing Imperial History*; and Geoff Wade, 'Ming Chinese Colonial Armies in Southeast Asia', in Karl Hack and Tobias Rettig, eds., *Colonial Armies in Southeast Asia* (London: Routledge, 2006), pp. 73–104.

12. Bernard Fall, *The Two Vietnams* (New York: Frederick A. Praeger, 1963). Ta Chi Dai Truong was the first to take up the question of Vietnam's eighteenth-century civil war being a part of its twentieth-century one. Ta Chi Dai Tuong, *Lich su noi chien Viet Nam tu 1771 den 1802* (Los Angeles: An Tiem, 1991 (first published in 1973)). Wynn Wilcox,

'Allegories of the U.S.-Vietnam War: Nguyen Anh, Nguyen Hue and the "Unification De-bates"', *Crossroads*, vol. 17, no. 1 (2003), pp. 129–60. Upon exiting the Chinese empire in the tenth century, the Vietnamese were hardly a regional superpower. Powerful Tai/Lao, Cham, Khmer and Yunnanese (Nanzhao) states came very close to eliminating the fledgling state in the Red River.

13. See William Cronon et al., *Under an Open Sky: Rethinking America's Western Past* (New York: W. W. Norton, 1992); and Richard White, *The Middle Ground: Indians, Empires, and Republics in the Great Lakes Region, 1650–1815*, 2nd edn (Cambridge: Cambridge University Press, 2011). On Said's discomfort with Frances FitzGerald's *Fire in the Lake*, see: John Carlos Rowe, *The Cultural Politics of the New American Studies*, note 21, online at http://quod.lib.umich.edu/o/ohp/10945585.0001.001/1:4.1/--cultural-politics -of-the-new-american-studies?rgn=div2;view=fulltext, accessed 28 August 2014. Professor Rowe says that Said 'had conceived Orientalism in angry response to the liberal Western scholarship represented by Frances FitzGerald's *Fire in the Lake*. That might be pushing it a bit far, but Edward Said was definitely aware of FitzGerald's heavy reliance on the French Orientalist Paul Mus. See Edward Said, *Culture and Imperialism* (London: Vintage, 1993), p. 252 and p. 423, note 43. For a critique of Orientalism in French Indochina, see: Nola Cooke, 'Colonial Political Myth and the Problem of the Other: French and Vietnamese in the Protectorate of Annam', PhD dissertation (Canberra: Australian National University, 1992).

CHAPTER 1. NORTHERN CONFIGURATIONS

1. Charles Wheeler, 'Buddhism in the Re-ordering of an Early Modern World: Chinese Missions to Cochinchina in the Seventeenth Century', *Journal of Global History*, vol. 2, no. 3 (November 2007), pp. 303–24; Li, *Nguyen Cochinchina*, pp. 108–10; and Liam Kelley, 'Vietnam through the Eyes of a Chinese Abbot: Dashan's Haiwai Jishi (1694–95)', MA dissertation (Honolulu: University of Hawai'i, 1996).

2. Haydon Cherry, 'Digging Up the Past: Prehistory and the Weight of the Present in Vietnam', *Journal of Vietnamese Studies*, vol. 4 (2009), pp. 84–144; and Charles Higham, *The Bronze Age of Southeast Asia* (Cambridge: Cambridge University Press, 1996).

3. On the nature of the early Vietnamese state, see: O. W. Wolters, *History, Culture, and Region in Southeast Asian Perspectives* (Singapore: Institute of Southeast Asian Studies, 1982), pp. 1–33 (the mandala citation is on p. 14); Hermann Kulke, 'The Early History and the Imperial Kingdom in Southeast Asian History', in Marr and Milner, *Southeast Asia in the Ninth to Fourteenth Centuries*, pp. 1–22; Nam C. Kim, 'Lasting Monuments and Durable Institutions: Labor, Urbanism, and Statehood in Northern Vietnam and Beyond', *Journal of Archaeological Research*, vol. 21, no. 3, pp. 217–67; Nam Kim, Lai Van Toi and Trinh Hoang Hiep, 'Co Loa: An Investigation of Vietnam's Ancient Capital', *Antiquity*, no. 84 (2010), pp. 1011–27; and Nam C. Kim, *The Origins of Ancient Vietnam* (New York: Oxford University Press, 2015).

4. On early Chinese imperial expansion, see: Geoff Wade, ed., *Asian Expansions: The Historical Experiences of Polity Expansion in Asia* (London: Routledge, 2015), starting with Wade's insightful introduction, pp. 1–30. For early Eurasian parallels, see: Jane Burbank and Mark von Hagen, eds., *Russian Empire: Space, People, Power, 1700–1930* (Bloomington: Indiana University Press, 2007).

5. See: Peter Bol, 'Geography and Culture: The Middle Period Discourse on the Zhong guo—the Central Country', in Ying-kuei, *Space and Cultural Fields: Spatial Images, Practices and Social Production* (Taibei: Center for Chinese Studies, 2009), pp. 61–106; Kenneth Pomeranz, 'Empire and "Civilising" Missions, Past and Present', *Daedalus* (Spring 2005), pp. 34–45; Keith Taylor, *A History of the Vietnamese* (New York: Cambridge University Press, 2013), pp. 14–29; Philippe Papin, 'Géographie et politique dans le Viêt-Nam ancien', *Bulletin de l'Ecole française d'Extrême-Orient*, vol. 87, no. 2 (2000), pp. 609–28; Philippe Papin, 'Le Pays des Viets du Sud', *L'Histoire*, no. 62 (2014), pp. 7–17; Erica Brindley, 'Representations and Uses of Yue Identity along the Southern Frontier of the Han—200–111 BCE, *Early China*, nos. 33–4 (2010–11), pp. 1–35, and her 'Barbarians or Not? Ethnicity and Changing Conceptions of the Ancient Yue (Viet) Peoples (400–50 BC)', *Asia Major*, vol. 16, no. 1 (2003), pp. 10–15. The names of today's 'Yunnan' and 'Hainan' provinces also reflect this southern orientation in the Middle Kingdom's early imperial gaze. Yunnan means 'South of the Clouds', whereas Hainan means the 'South of the Sea'.

6. I rely heavily in this section on Charles Holcombe, 'Early Imperial China's Deep South: The Viet Regions through Tang Times', *T'ang Studies*, vols. 15–16 (1997–8), pp. 125–56; Papin, 'Géographie et politique dans le Viêt-Nam ancien', pp. 609–28; James Anderson and John Whitmore, eds., *China's Encounters on the South and Southwest* (Leiden: Brill, 2015); Papin, 'Le Pays des Viets du Sud', p. 8; Taylor, *A History of the Vietnamese*, pp. 19–50; Erica Brindley, *Ancient China and the Yue: Perceptions and Identities on the Southern Frontier, c.400 BCE–50 CE* (New York: Cambridge University Press, 2015).

7. The Lac Viet tribe lived in the Red River delta, but they could be found as far north as Hunan and Hebei provinces. Holcombe, 'Early Imperial China's Deep South', pp. 131–2, 145–7.

8. Holcombe, 'Early Imperial China's Deep South', pp. 135–6; Papin, 'Le Pays des Viets du Sud', pp. 612–14; Taylor, *A History of the Vietnamese*, pp. 19–50; Nola Cooke, Li Tana and James Anderson, eds., *The Tongking Gulf Through History* (Philadelphia: University of Pennsylvania Press, 2011), pp. 1–24, 39–52; Papin, 'Géographie et politique dans le Viêt-Nam ancien', pp. 609–28.

9. Li Tana, 'A Geopolitical Overview', in Cook et al., *The Tongking Gulf through History*, pp. 1–24; Bérénice Bellina and Ian Glover, 'The Archaeology of Early Contact with India and the Mediterranean World'; Pierre-Yves Manguin, 'The Archaeology of Early Maritime Polities of Southeast Asia', both in Ian Glover and Peter Bellwood, eds. *Southeast Asia, From Prehistory to History* (London: Routledge, 2004), chapters 4 and 12; O. W. Wolters, 'The Development of Asian Maritime Trade from the Fourth to the Sixth Centuries', in Geoff Wade, ed., *China and Southeast Asia*, vol. 1 (London: Routledge, 2009), pp. 75–104. For the citation, see: Dutton et al., *Sources of Vietnamese Tradition*, pp. 15–16. Lapis lazuli is a deep-blue gemstone that can be ground into a much sought-after pigment.

10. Edward Schafer, *The Vermilion Bird: T'ang Images of the South*, 2nd edn (no place: Floating World Editions, 2008); and for the citation: Xue Zong, 'Customs of the South, 231 AD', in Dutton et al., *Sources of Vietnamese Tradition*, p. 26.

11. Kathlene Baldanza, *Ming China and Vietnam: Negotiating Borders in Early Modern Asia* (New York: Cambridge University Press, 2016); and Kelley, *Beyond the Bronze Pillars*. Nguyen Son made the Long March with Mao Zedong in the 1930s and went on to become a general in the Chinese Red Army before returning to Vietnam in 1945 to become a general during the war against the French.

12. Li Tana, 'Jiaozhi (Giao Chi) in the Han Period Tongking Gulf', and Brigitte Borell, 'Han Period Glass Vessels in the Early Tongking Gulf Region', both in Cooke et al., *The Tongking Gulf Through History*, pp. 39–52 and 53–66.

13. Jürgen Osterhammel and Niels Petersson, *Globalization: A Short History* (Princeton: Princeton University Press, 2003), pp. 31–81; and John D. Phan, 'Re-Imagining "Annam": A New Analysis of Sino-Viet-Muong Linguistic Contact', *Chinese Southern Diaspora Studies*, vol. 4 (2010), pp. 3–24. My thanks to Liam Kelley for drawing out the Norman analogy for me.

14. Woodside, *Lost Modernities*; Benjamin Elman, ed., *Rethinking Confucianism* (Los Angeles: University of California, 2002); Liam Kelley, 'Confucianism in Vietnam: A State of the Field Essay', *Journal of Vietnamese Studies*, vol. 1, nos. 1–2 (2006), pp. 314–70; Kelley, *Beyond the Bronze Pillars*, 1–36. Ralph Smith spoke of 'cycles of Confucianization' in 'The Cycle of Confucianization in Vietnam', in Walter Vella, ed., *Aspects of Vietnamese History* (Honolulu: University of Hawai'i Press, 1973), pp. 1–29.

15. For more on the origins of the Vietnamese language, see: Mark Alves, 'Linguistic Research on the Origins of the Vietnamese Language: An Overview', *Journal of Vietnamese Studies*, vol. 1, nos. 1–2 (2006), pp. 110–11.

16. On linguistic matters, see: Alves, 'Linguistic Research on the Origins of the Vietnamese Language', pp. 104–30 and John Phan, 'Muong Is Not a Subgroup', *Mon-Khmer Studies*, no. 40 (2011), pp. 1–18; and Cuong Tu Nguyen, *Zen in Medieval Vietnam* (Honolulu: University of Hawai'i Press, 1997).

17. On cults and spirits in Vietnam, see Ta Chi Dai Truong, *Than, nguoi va dat Viet* (Westminster, CA: Nha Xuat Ban Van Nghe, 1989); Olga Dror, *Cult, Culture, and Authority, Princess Lieu Hanh in Vietnamese History* (Honolulu: University of Hawai'i Press, 2007), and her translation and discussion of Father Adriano di St Thecla, *A Small Treatise on the Sects among the Chinese and Tonkinese* (Ithaca: Southeast Asia Program Publications, 2002); Alain Forest, Yoshiaki Ishizawa and Leon Vandermeersch, eds., *Cultes populaires et sociétés asiatiques* (Paris: L'Harmattan, 1991); Léopold Cadière, *Croyances et pratiques religieuses des Vietnamiens* (Paris: Publications de l'Ecole française d'Extrême-Orient, 1992); Maurice Durand, 'Recueil des puissances invisibles du pays de Viet de Ly Te Xuyen', *Dan Viet Nam*, no. 3 (1949), pp. 1–44. For Eurasian comparisons, see: Patrick Geary, 'Peasant Religion in Medieval Europe', *Cahiers d'Extrême-Asie*, vol. 12 (2001), pp. 185–209, http://www.persee.fr/web/revues/home/prescript/article/asie_0766-1177_2001_num_12_1_1170, accessed 10 August 2015; Jean-Claude Schmitt, *Le Saint Lévrier, guérisseur d'enfants depuis le XIIIe siècle* (Paris: Flammarion, 1979); and Sanjay Subrahmanyam, 'Connected Histories: Notes towards a Reconfiguration of Early Modern Eurasia', in Victor Lieberman, ed., *Beyond Binary Histories, Re-imagining Eurasia to c. 1830* (Ann Arbor: The University of Michigan Press, 1999), pp. 289–316.

18. Holcombe, 'Early Imperial China's Deep South', pp. 137–41.

19. See Schafer, *The Vermilion Bird*; Holcombe, 'Early Imperial China's Deep South', pp. 135–144; and for the citation: Shen Quanqi, 'Life in the South', in Dutton et al., *Sources of Vietnamese Tradition*, p. 12.

20. Holcombe, 'Early Imperial China's Deep South', pp. 155–6.

21. Ibid., pp. 139–56; Li Tana, *The Tongking Gulf Through History*, pp. 9–10; Li Tana, 'A View from the Sea'; Bin Yang, 'Horses, Silver, and Cowries: Yunnan in Global Perspective', *Journal of World History*, vol. 15, no. 3 (September 2004), pp. 281–322. Perso-Arab trade

with Chinese ports was particularly intense. Claudine Salmon, 'Les Persans à l'extrémité orientale de la route maritime (IIe A.E.–XVIIe siècle),' *Archipel*, vol. 68 (2004), pp. 23–58.

22. I rely heavily on Keith Taylor, 'The "Twelve Lords" in Tenth Century Vietnam', *Journal of Southeast Asian Studies*, vol. 14, no. 1 (March 1983), pp. 46–62.

23. On early statecraft in Southeast Asia and Eurasia, see the essays in Marr and Milner, *Southeast Asia in the 9th to 14th Centuries*; Kenneth Hall and John Whitmore, eds., *Explorations in Early Southeast Asian History: The Origins of Southeast Asian Statecraft* (Ann Arbor: The University of Michigan Press, 1976); Victor Lieberman, *Strange Parallels*, vol. 1: *Integration on the Mainland: Southeast Asia in Global Context, c. 800–1830* (New York: Cambridge University Press, 2003), and his *Beyond Binary Histories*.

24. Liam Kelley, 'The Biography of the Hong Bang Clan as a Medieval Vietnamese Invented Tradition', *Journal of Vietnamese Studies*, vol. 7, no. 2 (2012), pp. 87–130; and more generally Eric Hobsbawm and Terence Ranger, eds., *The Invention of Tradition* (Cambridge: Cambridge University Press, 1983); Patrick Geary, *The Myth of Nations: The Medieval Origins of Europe* (Princeton: Princeton University Press, 2002).

25. Kelley, 'The Biography of the Hong Bang Clan', pp. 87–130; Keith Taylor, 'Authority and Legitimacy in Eleventh Century Vietnam', in Marr and Milner, *Southeast Asia in the 9th to 14th Centuries*, pp. 139–76; John Whitmore, 'Chu Van An and the Rise of "Antiquity" in Fourteenth-Century Dai Viet', *Vietnam Review*, no. 1 (1996), pp. 50–61; and more generally Dror, *Cult, Culture, and Authority*.

26. Taylor, 'Authority'; Dror, *Cult, Culture, and Authority*; and Liam Kelley, 'Constructing Local Narratives: Spirits, Dreams, and Prophecies in the Medieval Red River Delta', in Anderson and Whitmore, *China's Encounters on the South and Southwest*, pp. 78–105; and for the citation, see: Le Te Xuyen, 'The Cult of Phung Hung (1329)', in Dutton et al., *Sources of Vietnamese Tradition*, pp. 37–8.

27. Ly Nhan Tong, 'Poems on a Buddhist Land (*ca.* 1100)', in Dutton et al., *Sources of Vietnamese Tradition*, p. 35 (for the first citation); Le Van Huu, 'Buddhist Cults (1272)', in Dutton et al., *Sources of Vietnamese Tradition*, pp. 46–7 (for the second citation); O. W. Wolters, *Two Essays on Dai-Viet in the Fourteenth Century* (New Haven: Yale University Southeast Asia Studies, 1988); John Whitmore, 'Building a Buddhist Monarchy in Đại Việt: Temples and Texts under Lý Nhân-tông (r. 1072–1127)', in D.C. Lammerts, ed., *Buddhist Dynamics in Premodern and Early Modern Southeast Asia* (Singapore: Institute of Southeast Asian Studies, 2015), pp. 283–306; Nguyen The Anh, 'From Indra to Maitreya: Buddhist Influence in Vietnamese Political Thought', *Journal of Southeast Asian Studies*, vol. 33, no. 2 (June 2002), pp. 225–41; Nguyen The Anh, 'Le Bouddhisme dans la pensée politique du Viêt-Nam traditionnel', *Bulletin de l'Ecole française d'Extrême-Orient*, vol. 89, no. 1 (2002), pp. 127–43. On the Chinese parallel, see Cuong Tu Nguyen, *Zen in Medieval Vietnam*.

28. 'Lady God of the Earth (Late Eleventh Century)', in Dutton et al., *Sources of Vietnamese Tradition*, pp. 47–8.

29. Jacques Gernet, *Le Monde chinois* (Paris: Armand Colin, 1999), pp. 290–306; John Stevenson, John Guy, Louise Cort, eds., *Vietnamese Ceramics: A Separate Tradition* (London: Art Media Resources, 1997); John Guy, 'Vietnamese Ceramics and Cultural Identity, Evidence form the Ly and Tran Dynasties', in Marr and Milner, *Southeast Asia in the 9th to 14th Centuries*, pp. 255–70; Momoki Shiro, 'Dai Viet and the South China Sea Trade from the 10th to the 15th Century', *Crossroads*, vol. 12, no 1 (1998), pp. 1–34; John Whitmore, 'The Rise of the Coast: Trade, State and Culture in Early Dai Viet', *Journal of Southeast*

Asian Studies, vol. 37, no. 1 (February 2006), pp. 103–22. For the immediate postcolonial period, see James Anderson, '"Slipping Through Holes": The Late Tenth- and Early Eleventh-Century Sino-Vietnamese Coastal Frontier as a Subaltern Trade Network', in Cooke et al., *The Tongking Gulf Through History*, pp. 87–100.

30. Le Van Huu, 'Music of Champa (1272)', in Dutton et al., *Sources of Vietnamese Tradition*, pp. 82–3 (for the citation); Shiro, 'Dai Viet and the South China Sea Trade from the 10th to the 15th Century'; Whitmore, 'The Rise of the Coast: Trade, State and Culture in Early Dai Viet'.

31. Shiro, 'Dai Viet and the South China Sea Trade from the 10th to the 15th Century'; Whitmore, 'The Rise of the Coast: Trade, State and Culture in Early Dai Viet'.

32. Jack Weatherford, *Genghis Khan and the Making of the Modern World* (New York: Random House, 2004).

33. Shiro, 'Dai Viet and the South China Sea Trade'; Li Tana, 'A View from the Sea', pp. 83–102; Nola Cooke, 'Nineteenth-Century Vietnamese Confucianization in Historical Perspective: Evidence from the Palace Examinations (1463–1883)', *Journal of Southeast Asian Studies*, vol. 25, no. 2 (September 1994), pp. 270–312; and Shawn McHale, '"Texts and Bodies": Refashioning the Disturbing Past of Tran Vietnam (1225–1400)', *Journal of the Economic and Social History of the Orient*, vol. 42, no. 4 (1999), pp. 494–518.

34. I rely heavily on John Whitmore's research on the role Ming colonization played in the making of a new, postcolonial Vietnam under the Le. Whitmore, 'Literati Culture and Integration in Dai Viet'; his *Vietnamese Adaptations of Chinese Government Structure in the Fifteenth Century*, Yale Southeast Asian Studies (New Haven: Yale University Press, 1970), and his 'The Thirteenth Province: Internal Administration and External Expansion in Fifteenth-Century Dai Viet', in Wade, *Asian Expansions*, pp. 120–43, among others.

35. Geoff Wade and Sun Laichen, eds., *Southeast Asia in the Fifteenth Century: The China Factor* (Singapore: National University of Singapore Press, 2010); Timothy Brook, *The Troubled Empire: China in the Yuan and Ming Dynasties* (Belknap Press, 2013); and Geoff Wade, 'The 'Native Office' System: A Chinese Mechanism for Southern Territorial Expansion over Two Millennia', in Wade, *Asian Expansions*, pp. 69–91.

36. Sun Laichen, 'Military Technology Transfers from Ming China and the Emergence of Northern Mainland Southeast Asia (*c.* 1390–1527)', *Journal of Southeast Asian Studies*, vol. 34 (2003), pp. 495–517; Sun Laichen, 'Saltpetre Trade and Warfare in Early Modern Southeast Asia', in Fujita Kayoko, Momoki Shiro and Anthony Reid, eds., *Offshore Asia* (Singapore: Institute of Southeast Asian Studies, 2013), pp. 130–84; Geoff Wade, 'The Zheng He Voyages: A Reassessment', in Wade, ed., *China and Southeast Asia*, vol. 2 (London: Routledge, 2009), pp. 118–41; Geoff Wade, 'Ming Colonial Armies in Southeast Asia', in ibid., pp. 212–44.

37. Baldanza, *Ming China and Vietnam*, pp. 90–91.

38. Geoff Wade, 'Ming China and Southeast Asia in the 15th Century: A Reappraisal', Working Paper Series no. 28 (Singapore: Asia Research Institute, National University of Singapore, 2004), pp. 1–7; John Whitmore, *Vietnam, Ho Quy Ly and the Ming (1371–1421)* (New Haven: Yale Center for International and Area Studies, 1985).

39. Whitmore, 'The Thirteenth Province', pp. 120–43; Wade, 'Ming China and Southeast Asia in the 15th Century', pp. 1–7; and Woodside, *Lost Modernities*, more generally.

40. Sun Laichen, 'Assessing the Ming Role', in Wade and Sun, *Southeast Asia in the Fifteenth Century*, p. 98; Whitmore, *Vietnam, Ho Quy Ly and the Ming*; and Li Tana, 'The

Ming Factor and the Emergence of the Viet in the 15th Century', in Wade and Sun, *Southeast Asia in the Fifteenth Century*, pp. 83–103.

41. Li, 'The Ming Factor and the Emergence of the Viet in the 15th Century'; and Whitmore, 'Literati Culture and Integration in Dai Viet'.

42. Liam Kelley, 'Vietnam as a "Domain of Manifest Civility" (Van Hien Chi Bang)', *Journal of Southeast Asian Studies*, vol. 34, no. 1 (February 2003), pp. 63–76; Whitmore, 'The Thirteenth Province'; and Kathlene Baldanza, 'De-civilizing Ming China's Southern Border', in Yongtao Du and Jeff Kyong-McClain, eds., *Chinese History in Geographical Perspective* (Lanham: Lexington Books, 2015), pp. 55–69.

43. Le Thanh Tong, 'Edict on Champa (1470)', in Dutton et al., *Sources of Vietnamese Tradition*, p. 142 (for the citation); and Roxanne Brown, *The Ceramics of South-East Asia* (Oxford: Oxford University Press, 1988), pp. 28–9.

44. Li, 'The Ming Factor and the Emergence of the Viet in the 15th Century', pp. 87–90; John Whitmore, 'The Last Great King of Classical Southeast Asia, Che Bong Nga and the Fourteenth Century Chams', in Tran Ky Phuong and Bruce Lockhart, eds., *The Cham of Vietnam: History, Society, and Art* (Singapore: National University of Singapore Press, 2011), pp. 168–203.

45. Alain Forest, *Les Missionnaires français au Tonkin et au Siam, Livres I–III* (Paris: Harmattan, 1998).

46. 'The French', however, did not create the Romanized system alone as is so often assumed. See Roland Jacques, 'Le Portugal et la romanisation de la langue vietnamienne. Faut-il réécrire l'histoire?', *Revue française d'histoire d'outre-mer*, vol. 85, no. 318 (1998), pp. 21–54.

47. See Olga Dror and Keith Taylor, eds., *Views of Seventeenth-Century Vietnam* (Ithaca: Southeast Asia Program Publications, 2006); Forest, *Les Missionnaires français au Tonkin et au Siam, Livre II*, pp. 213–14, and *Les Missionnaires française, livre III*, pp. 289–318; and Jacob Ramsay, *Mandarins and Martyrs: The Church and the Nguyen Dynasty in Early Nineteenth-Century Vietnam* (Stanford: Stanford University Press, 2008), pp. 27–8. Dutton provides higher numbers for Tonkin for an earlier period. George Dutton, *The Tay Son Uprising: Society and Rebellion in Eighteenth-Century Vietnam* (Honolulu: University of Hawai'i Press, 2006), pp. 176–9.

48. See Father Adriano di St Thecla, *A Small Treatise*.

49. George Dutton, *Moses to Lisbon: Philiphê Binh as an Envoy of the Padroado Catholics of Tonkin*, forthcoming.

50. Subrahmanyam, 'Connected Histories'.

51. Father Adriano di St Thecla, *A Small Treatise*; Olga Dror's discussion of this matter on pp. 40–41; and Ueda Shin'ya, 'On the Financial Structure and Personnel Organisation of the Trinh Lords in Seventeenth to Eighteenth-Century North Vietnam', *Journal of Southeast Asian Studies*, vol. 46, no. 2 (June 2015), pp. 246–73.

52. Keith Taylor, 'Nguyen Hoang and Vietnam's Southward Expansion', in Anthony Reid, ed., *Southeast Asia in the Early Modern Era: Trade, Power, and Belief* (Ithaca: Cornell University Press, 1993), p. 64. See also Li, *Nguyen Cochinchina*.

53. 'A comprehensive archaeological map of the world's largest preindustrial settlement complex at Angkor, Cambodia', *Proceedings of the National Academy of Sciences (PNAS)*, vol. 104, no. 36 (September 2007), at www.pnas.org/content/104/36/14277.full, accessed 22 September 2014.

54. Salmon, 'Les Persans à l'extrémité orientale', pp. 23–58.

55. For a fascinating discussion of such things, including Mongol and Arabic perceptions of the region, see Léonard Aurousseau, 'Sur le nom de Cochinchine', *Bulletin de l'Ecole
française d'Extrême-Orient*, vol. 24, no. 1 (1924), pp. 563–79; and Nasir Abdoul-Carime, 'In
memoriam Gabriel Ferrand 1864–1935', *Péninsule*, no. 68 (2014), pp. 213–26.

56. Li Tana, 'The Eighteenth-Century Mekong Delta and Its World of Water Frontier'
in Nhung Tuyet Tran and Anthony Reid, eds., *Viet Nam: Borderless Histories* (Madison:
University of Wisconsin Press, 2006), pp. 147–62; Victor Lieberman, *Strange Parallels*,
vol. 1, and his 'The Southeast Asian Mainland and the World Beyond', in Wade, *Asian
Expansions*, pp. 92–119.

57. Claudine Salmon, 'Réfugiés Ming dans les Mers du sud vus à travers diverses inscriptions (*ca.* 1650–*ca.* 1730)', *Bulletin de l'Ecole française d'Extrême-Orient*, vol. 90, no. 1
(2003), pp. 177–227.

58. Richard White, *The Middle Ground: Indians, Empires, and Republics in the Great
Lakes Region, 1650–1815* (Cambridge: Cambridge University Press, 2010 (first published
in 1991)); Charles Wheeler, 'One Region, Two Histories: Cham Precedents in the History
of the Hoi an Region', in Nhung Tuyet Tran and Reid, eds., *Viet Nam*, p. 183.

59. Nguyen The Anh, 'The Vietnamization of the Cham Deity Po Nagar', in K. W.
Taylor and John K. Whitmore, eds., *Essays into Vietnamese Pasts* (Ithaca: Cornell Southeast Asia Program, 1995), pp. 42–50.

60. Nguyen Hoang 'Deathbed Statement to his Son (1613)', in Dutton et al., *Sources of
Vietnamese Tradition*, p. 155 (for the citation)

61. My discussion of the Tay Son relies heavily on the work of Ta Chi Dai Tuong, *Lich
su noi chien Viet Nam tu 1771 den 1802)* (Los Angeles: An Tiem, 1991 (first published in
1973)); George Dutton, *The Tay Son Uprising*; Li, *Nguyen Cochinchina: Southern Vietnam
in the Seventeenth and Eighteenth Centuries*; and Maurice Durand, *Histoire des Tây Son*
(Paris: Les Indes savantes, 2006).

62. Emmanuel Poisson, 'Ngo The Lan et la crise monétaire au Viet Nam à la fin du
XVIIIe siècle', *Cahiers numismatiques* (2007), pp. 45–59.

63. Keith Taylor, 'Surface Orientations in Vietnam: Beyond Histories of Nation and
Region', *Journal of Asian Studies*, vol. 57, no. 4 (November 1998), p. 965; and Dutton, *The
Tay Son Uprising*, p. 17.

64. Dutton, *The Tay Son Uprising*, p. 3; and Le Quang Dinh, 'Vietnamese Geographical Expansion (1806)' in Dutton et al., *Sources of Vietnamese Tradition*, p. 260 (for the
citation).

65. Nguyen Du, 'A Dirge for All Ten Classes of Beings' (1815?), in Dutton et al., *Sources
of Vietnamese Tradition*, p. 300.

CHAPTER 2. A DIVIDED HOUSE AND A
FRENCH IMPERIAL MERIDIAN LINE?

1. Claudine Salmon and Ta Trong Hiep, 'L'Emissaire vietnamien Cao Ba Quat (1809–
1854) et sa prise de conscience dans les "contrées méridionales"', *Bulletin de l'Ecole
française d'Extrême-Orient*, vol. 81, no. 1 (1994), pp. 125–49; Chen Ching-ho, 'Les "Missions officielles dans les Ha chau" ou "contrées méridionales", de la première période des
Nguyen', *Bulletin de l'Ecole française d'Extrême-Orient*, vol. 81, no. 1 (1994), pp 101–21;

and Liam Kelley, 'Batavia through Vietnamese Eyes', at http://scholarspace.manoa.hawaii
.edu/bitstream/id/11148/license.txt/;jsessionid=4F45DB5950FCD029343C74CDEEE-
ABBFA, accessed 13 August 2015.

2. For two excellent examples of this, see Thien Do, *Vietnamese Supernaturalism:
Views from the Southern Region* (London: RoutledgeCurzon, 2003); Philip Taylor, *Goddess on the Rise: Pilgrimage and Popular Religion in Vietnam* (Honolulu: University of
Hawai'i Press, 2004).

3. Alexander Woodside, *Vietnam and the Chinese Model*, 2nd edn (Cambridge, MA:
Harvard University Press, 1988).

4. On Confucianism and the Nguyen bureaucracy, I rely heavily on Poisson, *Mandarins et subalternes*; his 'L'Infrabureaucratie vietnamienne au Bac Ky (Tonkin) de l'indépendance au protectorat (fin du XIXᵉ-début du XXᵉ siècles)', *Le Mouvement social*, no.
194 (2001), pp. 7–24; Wook, *Southern Vietnam*; Woodside, *Vietnam and the Chinese Model*;
Nola Cooke, 'Nineteenth-Century Vietnamese Confucianism in Historical Perspective:
Evidence from the Palace Examinations (1463–1883)', *Journal of Southeast Asian Studies*,
vol. 25, no. 2 (September 1994), pp. 270–312; and Kelley, 'Confucianism in Vietnam'.

5. Philippe Langlet, *L'Ancienne Historiographie d'Etat au Vietnam* (Paris: Publications de l'Ecole française d'Extrême-Orient, 1990); Nola Cooke, 'The Myth of Restoration:
Dang-Trong Influences in the Spiritual Life of the Early Nguyen Dynasty (1802–1847)', in
Anthony Reid, ed., *The Last Stand of Asian Autonomies* (New York: St Martin's Press,
1997), pp. 269–95; and Nola Cooke, 'Southern Regionalism and the Composition of the
Nguyen Ruler Elite', *Asian Studies Review*, vol. 23, no. 2 (1999), pp. 205–31.

6. Frédéric Mantienne, 'The Transfer of Western Military Technology to Vietnam in
the Late Eighteenth and Early Nineteenth Centuries: The Case of the Nguyen', *Journal
of Southeast Asian Studies*, vol. 34, no. 3 (October 2003), pp. 519–34; Li Tana, 'Ships and
Shipbuilding in the Mekong Delta, *c.* 1750–1840', in Nola Cooke and Li Tana, eds., *Water
Frontier: Commerce and the Chinese in the Lower Mekong Region, 1750–1880* (Singapore:
Rowman and Littlefield, 2004), pp. 119–38.

7. I rely here on Wook, *Southern Vietnam*; Woodside, *Vietnam and the Chinese Model*;
Langlet, *L'Ancienne Historiographie de l'Etat au Vietnam*; Poisson, *Mandarins et subalternes;* Yoshiharu Tsuboï, *L'Empire vietnamien face à la France et à la Chine 1847–1885*
(Paris: L'Harmattan, 1987).

8. Cited in Norman Owen, *The Emergence of Modern Southeast Asia* (Honolulu: University of Hawai'i Press, 2005), p. 115.

9. Lieberman, *Strange Parallels*, vol. 1; and Nguyen The Anh, 'Dans quelle mesure
le XVIIIème siècle a-t-il été une période de crise dans l'histoire de la péninsule indochinoise', in Philippe Papin, ed., *Parcours d'un historien du Viêt Nam: Recueil des articles
écrits par Nguyen The Anh* (Paris: Les Indes savantes, 2008), pp. 159–70.

10. Claudine Salmon and Ta Trong Hiep, 'Li Van Phuc et sa découverte de la cité du
Bengale (1830)', in Frédéric Mantienne and Keith Taylor, eds., *Monde du Viet Nam* (Paris:
Les Indes savantes, 2008), pp. 143–95.

11. Cited in Wook, *Southern Vietnam*, p. 59.

12. Wook, *Southern Vietnam*, chapters 4 and 5; Woodside, *Vietnam and the Chinese
Model*, chapters 1–3; Ramsay, *Mandarins and Martyrs*, chapter 2.

13. Wook, *Southern Vietnam*, chapters 4 and 5; and Ramsay, *Mandarins and Martyrs*,
chapter 2.

14. Woodside, *Vietnam and the Chinese Model*, pp. 234–95; Nguyen The Anh, 'Les Conflits frontaliers entre le Vietnam et le Siam à propos du Laos au XIXe siècle', in *Parcours d'un historien*, pp. 31–43; Nguyen The Anh, 'Siam-Vietnamese Relations in the First Half of the Nineteenth Century as Seen through Vietnamese Official Documents', in *Parcours d'un historien*, pp. 44–57.

15. Woodside, *Vietnam and the Chinese Model*, pp. 234–95; quote cited by David P. Chandler, *A History of Cambodia* (Boulder: Westview Press, 1983), p. 126. See also Li Tana's translation of 'Tran Tay Phong Tho Ky': The Customs of Cambodia', *Chinese Southern Diaspora Studies*, vol. 1 (2007), pp. 148–57.

16. Chandler, *A History of Cambodia*, chapter 7; and David P. Chandler, 'An Anti-Vietnamese Rebellion in Early Nineteenth Century Cambodia: Pre-Colonial Imperialism and a Pre-Nationalist Response', *Journal of Southeast Asian Studies*, vol. 6, no. 1 (March 1975), pp. 16–24.

17. Emmanuel Poisson, 'Les Confins septentrionaux du Viet Nam et leur administration', in Mantienne and Taylor, *Monde du Viet Nam*, pp. 329–39; and especially Nguyen Thi Hai, *Monarchie et pouvoirs locaux au Viêt Nam: Le Cas de la marche frontière de Cao Bang (1820–1925)*, PhD dissertation (Paris: Université Paris Diderot, 2015).

18. Frédéric Mantienne, *Pierre Pigneaux* (Paris: Les Indes savantes, 2012).

19. I rely here on Ramsay, *Mandarins and Martyrs*, pp. 41–91. Langlet, *L'Ancienne Historiographie d'Etat au Vietnam*, pp. 86–9, 131–44; Ta Chi Dai Truong, *Than, Nguoi va Dat Viet* (California: Van Nghe, 1989), pp. 238–9.

20. Ramsay, *Mandarins and Martyrs*, pp. 68–91.

21. Ibid.

22. 'The Society for the Propagation of the Faith,' New Avent, www.newadvent.org/cathen/12461a.htm, accessed 25 September 2014; Nola Cooke, 'Early Nineteenth-Century Vietnamese Catholics and Others in the Pages of the Annales de la Propagation de la foi', *Journal of Southeast Asian Studies*, vol. 35, no. 2 (June 2004), pp. 261–85; and Ramsay, *Mandarins and Martyrs*, chapter 4.

23. Laurent Burel, 'L'Action missionnaire française en Centre et Nord Vietnam (1856–1883)', *Revue française d'histoire d'outre mer*, vol. 82, no. 309 (1995), pp. 489–503.

24. See the contributions by Anthony Reid, Yumio Sakurai, James Kong Chin, Li Tana, Choi Byung Wook, Nola Cooke, Geoff Wade and Carl Trocki, in Cooke and Li, *Water Frontier*; Li, 'Ships and Shipbuilding'; Nguyen The Anh, 'Traditional Vietnam's Incorporation of External Cultural and Technical Contributions: Ambivalence and Ambiguity', in *Parcours d'un historien*, pp. 732–46 (for the citation); Mark McLeod, 'Nguyen Truong To: A Catholic Reformer at Emperor Tu-Duc's Court', *Journal of Southeast Asian Studies*, vol. 25, no. 2 (September 1994), pp. 313–30; Georges Boudarel, 'Un Lettré catholique qui fait problème: Nguyen Truong To', in Alain Forest and Yoshiharu Tsuboi, eds., *Catholicisme et sociétés asiatiques* (Paris/Tokyo: L'Harmattan/Sophia University, 1988), pp. 175–6; and Ta Trong Hiep, 'Le Journal de l'ambassade de Phan Thanh Gian en France (4 juillet 1863–18 avril 1864)', in Claudine Salmon, ed., *Récits de voyage des Asiatiques* (Paris: EFEO, 1996), pp. 335–66.

25. On the destabilizing effects of natural disasters, see Katie Dyt, 'King Tu Duc's "Bad Weather": Nature Disasters in Vietnam, 1847–1883', Conference, Vietnam Update 2011, Australian National University; Nguyen The Anh, 'Quelques aspects économiques et sociaux du problème du riz au Vietnam dans la première moitié du XIXe siècle', and

his 'La Réforme de l'impôt foncier de 1875 au Viet Nam', in *Parcours d'un historien*, pp. 171–83, pp. 202–11, respectively. On rural population growth, see Steve Déry, *La Colonisation agricole du Viet-Nam* (Laval: Presses de l'Université du Québec, 1994), p. 54.

26. Emmanuel Poisson, 'Détruire ou consolider les digues du delta du fleuve Rouge', *Aséanie* (2009), pp. 77–96; Van Nguyen-Marshall, *In Search of Moral Authority: The Discourse on Poverty, Poor Relief, and Charity in French Colonial Vietnam* (Peter Lang Publishing, Inc., 2008), pp. 1–30; Hue-Tam Ho Tai, *Millenarianism and Peasant Politics in Vietnam* (Cambridge, MA: Harvard University Press, 1983); and Ramsay, *Mandarins and Martyrs*.

27. Nguyen-Marshall, *In Search of Moral Authority*, p. 10; Langlet, *L'Ancienne Historiographie de l'Etat au Vietnam*, p. 86; Ramsay, *Mandarins and Martyrs*, p. 117 (for the statistics).

28. For general accounts of the French conquest of Vietnam, see Mark W. McLeod, *The Vietnamese Response to French Intervention, 1862–1874* (New York: Praeger, 1991); Brocheux and Hémery, *Indochina*; and Charles Fourniau, *Vietnam. Domination coloniale et résistance nationale (1858–1914)* (Paris: Les Indes savantes, 2002).

29. Jan de Vries, 'The Industrial Revolution and the Industrious Revolution', *Journal of Economic History*, vol. 54, no. 2 (1994), pp. 249–70; Christopher Bayly, *Imperial Meridian: The British Empire and the World 1780–1830* (New York: Longman, 1989); and John Darwin, *The Empire Project: The Rise and Fall of the British World-System, 1830–1970*, 2nd edn (Cambridge, Cambridge University Press, 2011); David Todd, 'A French Imperial Meridian, 1814–1870', *Past and Present*, no. 210 (February 2011), pp. 155–86; Christopher Bayly, *The Birth of the Modern World 1780–1914: Global Connections and Comparisons* (Oxford: Blackwell, 2004); Kenneth Pomeranz, *The Great Divergence: China, Europe, and the Making of the Modern World Economy* (Princeton: Princeton University Press, 2001). On 'gentlemanly capitalism', see Peter Cain and Anthony Hopkins, *British Imperialism: Innovation and Expansion 1688–1914* (London: Longman, 1993). For a Burmese case study, see Anthony Webster, *Gentlemen Capitalists: British Imperialism in South East Asia 1770–1890)* (London: Tauris Academic Studies, 1998).

30. John Laffey, 'Municipal Imperialism in France: The Lyon Chamber of Commerce, 1900–1914', in *Proceedings of the American Philosophical Society*, vol. 119, no. 1 (February 1975), pp. 8–23 (on 'municipal imperialism'); John Laffey, 'Roots of French Imperialism in the Nineteenth Century: The Case of Lyon', *French Historical Studies*, vol. 6, no. 1 (1969), pp. 78–92; Jean-François Klein, *Un Lyonnais en Extrême-Orient. Ulysse Pila Vice-roi de l'Indo-Chine (1837–1909)* (Lyon: Lugd, 1994); and Hubert Bonin, Catherine Hodeir and Jean-François Klein, eds., *L'Esprit économique impérial? Réseaux et groupes de pressions du patronat colonial en France et dans l'Empire (1830–1962)* (Paris: SFHOM, 2008).

31. See chapter 3 for a discussion of the meaning of 'Cochinchina'.

32. Charles-Robert Ageron, *France coloniale ou parti colonial?* (Paris: Presses Universitaires de France, 1978); Marc Meuleau, *Des pionniers en Extrême-Orient. Histoire de la Banque de l'Indochine (1875–1975)* (Paris: Fayard, 1990).

33. Charles-Robert Ageron, 'L'Exposition coloniale de 1931: Mythe républicain ou mythe impérial', in Pierre Nora, ed., *Les Lieux de mémoire. La République* (Paris: Gallimard, 1997 (first published in 1984)), pp. 493–551, and his 'L'Opinion publique face aux problèmes de l'Union française (étude de sondages)', in *Les Chemins de la décolonisation de l'Empire français, 1936–1956* (Paris: Editions du CNRS, 1986), pp. 33–48; Alice

Conklin, *In the Museum of Man: Race, Anthropology, and Empire in France, 1850–1950* (Ithaca: Cornell University Press, 2013).

34. Pierre Loti in *Le Figaro*, 17 October 1883, published in its original uncensored version in *Gulliver*, no 5 (January, February, March 1991), pp. 211–12. The censored version is also available in this edition. A comparison of the two makes for instructive reading.

35. Cited by Henry McAleavy, *Black Flags in Vietnam: The Story of a Chinese Intervention* (London: George Allen and Unwin, 1968), pp. 213–14.

36. The Japanese began removing Korea from the Chinese orbit at exactly the same time. Like the French, they signed a treaty at Tianjin at almost the same time, forcing the Chinese to recognize that Beijing no longer had exclusive relations with Korea.

37. Despite his critique of Ferry's subjugation of foreign peoples, Georges Clémenceau soon advocated the colonial cause. He even prefaced Auguste Pavie's account of the 'peaceful' conquest of Laos. Agathe Larcher-Goscha, 'On the Trail of an Itinerant Explorer: French Colonial Historiography on Auguste Pavie's Work in Laos', in Christopher Goscha and Soren Ivarsson, eds., *Contesting Visions of the Lao Past* (Copenhagen: NIAS, 2003), pp. 209–38.

38. Thongchai Winichakul, *Siam Mapped: A History of the Geo-Body of a Nation* (Chiang Mai: Silkworm Books, 1994); Patrick Tuck, *The French Wolf and the Siamese Lamb*, 2nd edn (Bangkok: White Lotus, 2009); and Soren Ivarsson, *Creating Laos: The Making of Lao Space between Siam and Indochina, 1860–1945* (Copenhagen: Nordic Institute of Asian Studies, 2008).

CHAPTER 3. ALTERED STATES

1. Mark McLeod, 'Truong Dinh and Vietnamese Anti-Colonialism, 1859–64: A Reappraisal', *Journal of Southeast Asian Studies*, vol. 24, no. 1 (March 1993), pp. 88–105; Mark McLeod, *The Vietnamese Response to French Intervention, 1862–1874* (New York: Praeger, 1991), pp. 66–70; 'Truong Cong Dinh to Phan Thanh Gian', document 6, in Truong Buu Lam, ed., *Patterns of Vietnamese Response to Foreign Intervention, 1858–1900* (New Haven: Yale Southeast Asian Studies, 1967), pp. 23–74.

2. Aurousseau, 'Sur le nom de Cochinchine'.

3. See Peter Zinoman, *The Colonial Bastille: A History of Imprisonment in Vietnam, 1862–1940* (Berkeley: University of California Press, 2001). The Poulo Condor prison closed in 1975 and now serves as a major tourist attraction. In the early eighteenth century, the British East India Company had first operated this island, not the Nguyen. The *Bulletin officiel de la Cochinchine française* appeared for the first time in 1865.

4. Ramsay, *Mandarins and Martyrs*, p. 156; and Fourniau, *Vietnam*, p. 106.

5. Fourniau, *Vietnam*, p. 217. Although he focused on northern Vietnam, Emmanuel Poisson's work on the Nguyen bureaucracy at this conjuncture is required reading: *Mandarins et subalternes*; and his 'L'Infrabureaucratie vietnamienne'.

6. Fourniau, *Vietnam*, p. 108 (for the citation); and Louis Vignon, *Un programme de politique coloniale: Les Questions indigènes* (Paris: Librairie Plon, 1919), pp. 238–9.

7. Fourniau, *Vietnam*, p. 107 for the citation.

8. On his efforts, see document 8, translated and commented by Truong Buu Lam, *Patterns*, pp. 81–6.

9. Poisson, *Mandarins et subalternes*, chapter 5. Quote cited by Milton Osborne, *The*

French Presence in Cochinchina and Cambodia, 1859–1905 (Ithaca: Cornell University Press, 1970), p. 71. See also Vignon, *Un programme de politique coloniale*, pp. 239–40.

10. Fourniau, *Vietnam*, p 573. This mirrored similar take-offs in Chinese immigration to other colonial states in the region, such as British Singapore and Malaya and Dutch Indonesia.

11. Chantal Descours-Gatin, *Quand l'opium finançait la colonisation en Indochine* (Paris: L'Harmattan, 1992), pp. 52–63; Philippe Lefailler, *Monopole et prohibition de l'opium en Indochine. Le pilori des chimères* (Paris: L'Harmattan, 2001); Fourniau, *Vietnam*, pp. 196–7; Gerard Sasges, *Imperial Intoxication: Alcohol, Indochina, and the World (1897–1933)* (Honolulu: University of Hawai'i Press, forthcoming). On the Nguyen reliance on the Chinese Mac family, see chapter 2.

12. Cited by Fourniau, *Vietnam*, p. 103.

13. Fourniau, *Vietnam*, pp. 205, 297; and Ramsay, *Mandarins and Martyrs*, pp. 162–6.

14. Ibid., pp. 193–5; and Osborne, *The French Presence* pp. 84–5. On the alcohol monopoly and its rise, see: Gerard Sasges, 'Scaling the Commanding Heights: The colonial conglomerates and the changing political economy of French Indochina', *Modern Asian Studies*, vol. 49 (2015), pp. 1485–1525.

15. Descours-Gatin, *Quand l'opium*, pp. 97–102; and Fourniau, *Vietnam*, p. 197.

16. Fourniau, *Vietnam*, pp. 217–18.

17. Cited by Osborne, *The French Presence*, p. 38.

18. Cited by Fourniau, *Vietnam*, p. 105; and Osborne, *The French Presence*, pp. 95–6.

19. Cited by Osborne, *The French Presence*, p. 38.

20. Ramsay, *Mandarins and Martyrs*, pp. 163–4; and Osborne, *The French Presence*, chapter 4; Fourniau, *Vietnam*, pp. 104–6.

21. I rely here on Nguyen The Anh, *Monarchie et fait colonial au Viet-Nam (1875–1925): Le Crépuscule d'un ordre traditionnel* (Paris: L'Harmattan, 1992); and Charles Fourniau, *Annam-Tonkin, 1995–1896: Lettrés et paysans vietnamiens face à la conquête coloniale* (Paris: L'Harmattan, 1989).

22. Cited by Fourniau, *Vietnam*, p. 374.

23. In the French empire, the positions of the 'résident supérieur' and that of the 'résident général' were roughly the equivalents of 'commissioners' in the British empire's system. The term 'résident supérieur' replaced that of the 'résident général' at the turn of the twentieth century. This new office and its administrators existed at the regional (Tonkin, Annam, Cochinchina), provincial and district levels. Though an imperfect translation, in this book I make reference to the Commissioner of Annam rather than use the term 'Résident supérieur', and also refer to resident generals rather than 'résidents généraux'.

24. Poisson, *Mandarins et subalternes*, chapter 5 in particular; Pasquier quote cited by Pierre Brocheux and Daniel Hémery, *Indochine, la colonisation ambiguë* (Paris: La Découverte, 2001), p. 93.

25. Jan T. Gross, 'Themes for a Social History of War Experience and Collaboration', in Istvan Deak et al., *The Politics of Retribution in Europe: World War II and Its Aftermath* (Princeton: Princeton University Press, 2000), p. 26; J. Kim Munholland, '"Collaboration Strategy" and the French Pacification of Tonkin, 1885–1897', *The Historical Journal*, vol. 24, no. 3 (September 1981), pp. 629–50; and Michael Kim, 'Regards sur la collaboration coréenne', *Vingtième siècle*, no. 94 (April–June 2007), pp. 35–44.

26. Munholland, "'Collaboration Strategy'", pp. 629–50; Charles Fourniau, *Annam-Tonkin*, chapter 2 in particular; and quote cited by Fourniau, *Annam-Tonkin*, p. 74.

27. Duong Van Mai Elliott, *The Sacred Willow: Four Generations in the Life of a Vietnamese Family* (New York: Oxford University Press, 1999), p. 13 (for the citation). See also: Poisson, *Mandarins et subalternes*, pp. 78–145.

28. Poisson, *Mandarins et subalternes*, pp. 78–9, 88–9, 101, 144–5 (on Hoang Cao Khai); and Fourniau, *Annam Tonkin* pp. 70–71.

29. Brocheux and Hémery, *Indochine*, table 3, p. 98. Indochina also included the small concession of Guangzhouwan (Zhanjiang).

30. On the 'native code', see James Barnhart, 'Violence and the Civilizing Mission: Native Justice in French Colonial Vietnam, 1858–1914', PhD dissertation (Chicago: University of Chicago, 1999); and Emmanuelle Saada, 'Citoyens et sujets de l'empire français: les usages du droit en situation coloniale', *Genèses*, vol. 4, no. 53 (2003/2004), pp. 4–24; Paul Isoart, 'La Création de l'Union indochinoise', *Approches-Asie* (4th trimester, 1992), p. 45. Until 1874, Tu Duc refused to sign any document recognizing the French occupation of western Cochinchina. Until that date, only eastern Cochinchina was a legally recognized colony. The French military administered the western provinces as occupied territories, by force.

31. Hue-Tam Ho Tai, 'The Politics of Compromise: The Constitutionalist Party and the Electoral Reforms of 1922 in French Cochinchina', *Modern Asian Studies*, vol. 18, no. 3 (1984), pp. 374–5; and Osborne, *The French Presence*, table 1, p. 289. Between 1880 and 1904, land alienated from the indigenous population totaled 543,493 hectares.

32. Actually, in the context of the colonial state, Cambodian peasants also carried a heavy fiscal burden and, in so doing, helped finance projects that often included Vietnam.

33. David Marr, *Vietnamese Anticolonialism (1885–1925)* (Berkeley: University of California Press, 1971), pp. 50–52.

34. Cited by Brocheux and Hémery, *Indochine*, p. 57.

35. Cited by Marr, *Anticolonialism*, p. 63.

36. Hoang Cao Khai and Phan Dinh Phung, Document 15, in Truong Buu Lam, *Patterns*, p. 124 (for the citation). See also Marr, *Anticolonialism*, pp. 66–8.

37. See Mark McLeod, 'Nguyen Truong To: A Catholic Reformer at Emperor Tu-Duc's Court', *Journal of Southeast Asian Studies*, vol. 25, no. 2 (September 1994), p. 319, citing Phan Dinh Phung textually to this effect.

CHAPTER 4. RETHINKING VIETNAM

1. Agathe Larcher-Goscha, 'Prince Cuong De and the Franco-Vietnamese Competition for the Heritage of Gia Long', in Gisèle Bousquet and Pierre Brocheux, eds., *Viet Nam Exposé* (Ann Arbor: The University of Michigan Press, 2002), pp. 187–215; and Tran My Van, *A Vietnamese Royal Exile in Japan: Prince Cuong De (1882–1951)* (London: Routledge, 2005).

2. Marr, *Anticolonialism*, p. 107.

3. Both men submitted reforms to the Qing court in 1898. After a '100 days reform', the court reversed course and cracked down on reformers. Liang Qichao and Kang Youwei fled the country for their lives. Lai To Lee, Hock Guan Lee, eds., *Sun Yat-Sen, Nanyang and the 1911 Revolution* (Singapore: ISEAS, 2011); and J. Kim Munholland, 'The French

Connection that Failed: France and Sun Yat-Sen, 1900–1908', *The Journal of Asian Studies*, vol. 32, no. 1 (November 1972), pp. 77–95. Some 15 million Chinese were moving between China and Southeast Asia during the period of Western colonial domination. In the late twentieth century, 80 percent of the global overseas Chinese population resided in Southeast Asia. Pierre Trolliet, *La Diaspora chinoise*, 3rd edn (Paris: PUF, 2000), pp. 16, 43. An overseas Chinese skipper safely transported the future general secretary of the Vietnamese Workers Party, Le Duan, from southern Vietnam to Hanoi shortly after the First Indochina War ended in 1954.

4. Both citations from Marr, *Anticolonialism*, p. 125. For earlier periods, see Li Tana, 'The Imported Book Trade and Confucian Learning in Seventeenth- and Eighteenth-century Vietnam', in Michael Aung-Thwin and Kenneth Hall, eds. *New Perspectives on the History and Historiography of Southeast Asia* (London: Routledge, 2011), pp. 167–82.

5. On Japan's notions of racial and civilizational superiority, see Lionel Babicz, *Le Japon face à la Corée à l'époque de Meiji* (Paris: Maisonneuve & Larose, 2002); and Louise Young, *Japan's Total Empire: Manchuria and the Culture of Wartime Imperialism* (Berkeley: University of California Press, 1998).

6. Cited by Vinh Sinh, introduction, *Overturned Chariot: The Autobiography of Phan-Boi-Chau* (Honolulu: University of Hawai'i Press, 1999), p. 12. See also Hiraishi Masaya, 'Phan Boi Chau in Japan', in Vinh Sinh, ed., *Phan Boi Chau and the Dong-Du Movement* (New Haven: Yale Center for International and Area Studies, 1988), pp. 52–82.

7. Letter to Okuma Shigenobu, cited by Marr, *Anticolonialism*, p. 113. See also Shiraishi Masaya, 'Phan Boi Chau in Japan', pp. 54–6.

8. Vinh Sinh, *Phan Boi Chau and the Dong-Du Movement*, p. 10; Marr, *Anticolonialism*, pp. 104–5, 136, 143–5; Ralph Smith, 'The Development of Opposition to French Rule in Southern Vietnam 1880–1940', *Past & Present*, no. 54 (February 1972), pp. 94–104 (p. 103 for the numbers); Pierre Brocheux, 'Note sur Gilbert Chieu (1867–1919)', *Approches Asie* (4th trimester, 1992), pp. 72–81 (p 77, note 87, for the number of 300 students). Gia Long's primary wife was from the delta and her family tombs were maintained by the Nguyen until 1867. Marr, *Anticolonialism*, p. 102, note 13.

9. Marr, *Anticolonialism*, pp. 114–19.

10. See Vinh Sinh, 'Chinese Characters as the Medium for Transmitting the Vocabulary of Modernization from Japan to Vietnam in the Early Twentieth Century', *Asian Pacific Quarterly* (October 1993), pp. 1–16. Chau's quotes cited by Marr, *Anticolonialism*, p. 129.

11. In 1868, this influential Japanese *philosophe* had created the famous 'public school', *Keio Gijuku*, in Tokyo to promote Western studies. It had become a great success by 1900 and is now one of Japan's most prestigious universities. On Phan Boi Chau and Fukuzawa, see Vinh Sinh, 'Phan Boi Chau and Fukuzawa Yukichi: Perceptions of National Independence', in Vinh Sinh, *Phan Boi Chau and the Dong-Du Movement*, pp. 101–49.

12. Eugene Weber, *Peasants into Frenchmen: The Modernization of Rural France (1870–1914)* (Stanford: Stanford University Press, 1976).

13. Jacques Dalloz, *Francs-Maçons d'Indochine, 1868–1975* (Paris: Editions Maçonniques de France, 2002); Daniel Hémery, 'L'Indochine, les droits humains entre colonisateurs et colonisés, la Ligue des Droits de l'Homme (1898–1954)', *Revue française d'histoire d'Outre-mer*, vol. 88, no. 330–31 (2001), pp. 223–39; J. P. Daughton, *An Empire Divided: Religion, Republicanism, and the Making of French Colonialism, 1880–1914* (New York: Oxford University Press, 2006), pp. 89–93; and Jules Roux, 'Le Triomphe définitif en

Indochine du mode de transcription de la langue annamite à l'aide des caractères romains ou "quôc ngu'", conférence' (Hanoi: Bibliothèque de la 'Revue indigène', 1912). Roux later translated Trinh's *Complete Account of the Peasants' Uprising in the Central Region*, which I have been unable to locate.

14. Phan Boi Chau, *Overturned Chariot*, p. 105.

15. Phan Chu Trinh, 'Lettre de Phan Chu Trinh à Paul Beau', *Bulletin de l'Ecole française d'Extrême-Orient*, nos. 1–2 (1907), pp. 166–75.

16. Cited in Document 10, 'Nguyen Truong To', in Truong Buu Lam, ed., *Patterns of Vietnamese Response to Foreign Intervention, 1858–1900*, monograph series no. 11, Yale Southeast Asia Studies (New Haven: Yale University Press, 1967), pp. 89–103. For more on Nguyen Truong To, see Mark McLeod, 'Nguyen Truong To: A Catholic Reformer at Emperor Tu-Duc's Court', *Journal of Southeast Asian Studies*, vol. 25, no. 2 (September 1994), pp. 313–30. On Chu Nom, see John Phan, 'Rebooting the Vernacular in 17th Century Vietnam,' in *Rethinking East Asian Languages, Vernaculars, and Literacies 1000–1919* (Leiden: Brill, 2014), pp. 96–128, and his 'Chu Nôm and the Taming of the South: A Bilingual Defense for Vernacular Writing in the Chi Nam Ngoc Am Giai Nghia', *The Journal of Vietnamese Studies*, vol. 8, no. 1 (2013), pp. 1–33.

17. Poisson, *Mandarins et subalternes*, pp. 98–9, 135.

18. In fact, Fukuzawa Yukichi's educational policies may well have been the school's driving force: Poisson, *Mandarins et subalternes*, chapter 5. Marr, *Anticolonialism*, p. 164. It was private in the sense that the French did not fund it. It also paralleled pre-existing Chinese and Vietnamese private schools for teaching classical studies. Similar 'free schools' would be created well into the twentieth century. The Constitutionalists began creating just such schools in the 1920s. The colonial authorities restricted them severely from 1924. R. B. Smith, 'Bui Quang Chieu and the Constitutionalist Party in French Co-chinchina, 1917–30', *Modern Asian Studies*, vol. 3, no. 2 (1969), p. 138.

19. Marr, *Anticolonialism*, pp. 166–9.

20. Cited in Ibid., p. 170.

21. A. E. Babut, 'A propos de Phan Chu Trinh', *Nam Phong*, no. 109 (1926), p. 26. On the prison, see Peter Zinoman, *The Colonial Bastille: A History of Imprisonment in Vietnam, 1862–1940* (Berkeley: University of California Press, 2001).

22. Amadine Dabat, 'Ham Nghi artiste: le peintre le sculpteur', at http://aejjrsite .free.fr/goodmorning/gm136/gm136_HamNghiArtistePeintreSculpteur.pdf, accessed 26 January 2016; Lorraine Patterson, *Exiles from Indochina in the Transcolonial World* (Oxford: Oxford University Press, forthcoming), and her 'Prisoners from Indochina in the Nineteenth Century French Colonial World', in Ronit Ricci, ed., *Exile in Colonial Asia: Kings, Convicts, Commemoration* (Honolulu: University of Hawai'i Press, 2016); Hua Dong Sy, *De la Mélanésie au Vietnam: Itinéraire d'un colonisé devenu francophile* (Paris: L'Harmattan, 1993); Danielle Donet-Vincent, 'Les Bagnes des Indochinois en Guyane (1931–1963)', *Outre-mers*, vol. 88, nos. 330–31 (2001), pp. 209–21; Christian Schnaken-bourg, 'Les Déportés indochinois en Guadeloupe sous le Second Empire', *Outre-mers*, vol. 88, nos. 330–31 (2001), pp. 205–8; Pierre Brocheux, 'De l'empereur Duy Tan au prince Vinh San: L'Histoire peut-elle se répeter?', *Approches-Asie*, n.s. (1989–1990), pp. 1–25; Hoang Van Dao, *Viet Nam Quoc Dan Dang: A Contemporary History of a National Struggle: 1927–1954* (Pittsburg: RoseDog Books, 2008), pp. 165–6; Robert Aldrich, 'Imperial

Banishment: French Colonizers and the Exile of Vietnamese Emperors', *French History & Civilization*, vol. 5 (2014), at http://fliphtml5.com/vdxa/dxse, accessed 31 August 2015; and his *Banished Potentates: The Deposition and Exile of Indigenous Monarchs under Colonial Rule, 1815–1945* (forthcoming).

23. Ngo Van, *Au pays de la Cloche Fêlée* (Cahors: L'Insomniaque, 2000), pp. 90–91 (for the citation). For the Atlantic, see Peter Linebaugh and Marcus Rediker, *The Many-Headed Hydra: Sailors, Slaves, Commoners, and the Hidden History of the Revolutionary Atlantic* (Boston, MA: Beacon Press, 2013). Christoph Giebel analyzes the construction of an official historiography about Vietnamese communism through Ton Duc Thang in his *Imagined Ancestries of Vietnamese Communism: Ton Duc Thang and the Politics of History and Memory* (Seattle: University of Washington Press, 2004). Maritime revolutionary connections are completely missing from his study. Indeed, the history of Chinese and Vietnamese maritime labor organization and revolution still await their historians. For an impressive early effort, see Didier de Fautereau, 'Le Nationalisme vietnamien: Contribution des marins vietnamiens au nationalisme vietnamien (période entre deux guerres)', MA dissertation (Paris: Université de Paris, 1975), chapters 1–2.

24. See Mireille Le Van Ho, *Des Vietnamiens dans la grande guerre* (Paris: Vendémiaire, 2014); Tyler Stovall, 'The Color Line behind the Lines: Racial Violence in France during the Great War', *The American Historical Review*, vol. 103, no. 3 (June 1998), pp. 737–69; John Horne, 'Immigrant Workers in France during World War I', *French Historical Studies*, vol. 14, no. 1 (Spring 1985), pp. 57–88; Kim Loan Vu Hill, *Coolies into Rebels* (Paris: Les Indes savantes, 2011); and Li Ma, ed., *Les Travailleurs Chinois en France dans la Première guerre mondiale* (Paris: CNRS Editions, 2012), including Tobias Rettig, 'Prevented or Missed Chinese-Indochinese Encounters during WWI: Spatial Imperial Policing in Metropolitan France', pp. 387–407.

25. CGT is the Confédération générale du Travail.

26. Duong Van Giao, *L'Indochine pendant la guerre de 1914–1918* (Paris: Librairie-Edition, 1925); Mireille Le Van Ho, 'Le Général Pennequin et le projet d'armée jaune (1911–1915)', *Revue française d'histoire d'outre-mer*, vol. 75, no. 279 (2nd trimester 1988), pp. 145–67; and Le Van Ho, *Des Vietnamiens dans la grande guerre*, the most important book published in any language on the Vietnamese in France during the Great War.

27. Agathe Larcher, 'Réalisme et idéalisme en politique coloniale: Albert Sarraut et l'Indochine, 1911–1914', MA dissertation (Paris: Université Paris VII, 1992), pp. 9–30 (citation p. 30). The Section française de l'Internationale ouvrière emerged officially in 1905. Despite his economic critique of colonialism as an extension of capitalism, Jaurès accepted the Republic's empire but insisted that Republicans had to promote a humanist colonial policy with the needs of the colonized in mind. See Jean Jaurès, 'Les Compétitions coloniales', *La Petite République* (17 May 1896), in *Revue Histoire* (2010).

28. Peter Zinoman, 'Colonial Prisons and Anti-Colonial Resistance in French Indochina: The Thai Nguyen Rebellion, 1917', *Modern Asian Studies* 34 (2000), pp. 57–98.

29. Patrice Morlat, *La Répression coloniale au Vietnam, 1908–1940* (Paris: Editions L'Harmattan, 1990); and Larcher, 'Réalisme et idéalisme', p. 131.

30. See Christopher Goscha, '"The Modern Barbarian": Nguyen Van Vinh and the Complexity of Colonial Modernity in Vietnam', *European Journal of East Asian Studies*, vol. 3, no. 1 (2004), pp. 135–69.

31. Agathe Larcher, 'La Voie étroite des réformes coloniales et la "collaboration franco-annamite", 1917–1928', *Revue francaise d'histoire d'outre mer*, vol. 82, no 309 (4th trimester 1995), pp. 387–419.

32. Albert Sarraut, 'Discours prononcé le 17 avril 1919 au Van-Mieu', annex in Larcher, 'Réalisme et idéalisme', p. 1. On the French policy of collaboration, see Larcher, 'La Voie étroite des réformes coloniales', pp. 387–420.

33. See Christopher Goscha, *Going Indochinese* (Honolulu/Copenhagen: University of Hawai'i Press/Nordic Institute of Asian Studies, 2012), p. 23.

34. The western Indochinese bureaucracy was divided into two administrative sub-systems, the first being the 'adminstration française', the Indochinese federal level in which the Vietnamese moved. The second was the protectorate ones under Lao and Khmer royal prerogative, subordinate to French Résident Supérieurs, and staffed by Cambodian *chaifaikhets* and Lao *chaomuongs*. The Indochinese level dealt with such federal matters as customs, immigration, security and the governing administrative matters of Laos and Cambodia in relation to the larger Indochinese system.

35. The French had transported over 5,000 Vietnamese to their New Caledonian colony to work in mines, agriculture and small-scale factories. André Chastain, 'La Main-d'œuvre asiatique en Nouvelle-Calédonie', *La Dépêche coloniale et maritime* (1 October 1929), p. 1.

36. All citations are in Goscha, *Going Indochinese*, chapters 1–2.

37. This is clearly at the heart of Nguyen Van Vinh's political program. Ibid., chapter 2.

38. Christopher Goscha, 'Bao Dai et Sihanouk: La Fabrique indochinoise des rois coloniaux', in François Guillemot and Agathe Larcher-Goscha, eds., *La Colonisation des corps* (Paris: Vendémiaire, 2014), pp. 127–77; 'Phan Chau Trinh, sujet de l'Empire d'Annam adresse cette lettre à l'Empereur régnant de l'Annam', translated from the original in Chinese characters, dated 1922, Marseille, in box 371, Service de Protection du Corps Expéditionnaire (SPCE), Centre des Archives d'Outre-Mer, France; and Pasquier's letter to Sarraut, 9 November 1922, in box 371.

39. Cited by Charles Ageron, *France coloniale ou parti colonial* (Paris: PUF, 1978), pp. 230–31. On Sarraut's anticommunism, see Martin Thomas, 'Albert Sarraut, French Colonial Development, and the Communist Threat, 1919–1930', *The Journal of Modern History*, vol. 77, no. 4 (2005), pp. 917–55. On Euro-American collaboration against Southeast Asian nationalist and communist movements, see Frances Gouda, *American Visions of the Netherlands East Indies/Indonesia* (Amsterdam: Amsterdam University Press, 2002); and Anne Foster, *Projections of Power: The United States and Europe in Colonial Southeast Asia, 1919–1941* (Durham, NC: Duke University Press, 2010).

40. Cited in Goscha, 'Bao Dai et Sihanouk', pp. 137–8.

CHAPTER 5. THE FAILURE OF COLONIAL REPUBLICANISM

1. Based on Agathe Larcher-Goscha, 'Bui Quang Chieu in Calcutta (1928): The Broken Mirror of Vietnamese and Indian Nationalism', *Journal of Vietnamese Studies*, vol. 9, no. 4 (Fall 2014), pp. 67–114.

2. On the Constitutionalists, I have relied on the following: Ralph Smith, 'Bui Quang Chieu and the Constitutionalist Party in French Cochinchina, 1917–30', *Modern Asian Studies*, vol. 3, no. 2 (1969), pp. 131–50; Hue-Tam Ho Tai, 'The Politics of Compromise',

pp. 371–91; Hue-Tam Ho Tai, *Radicalism and the Origins of the Vietnamese Revolution* (Cambridge, MA: Harvard University Press, 1992), pp. 41–3; Megan Cook, *The Constitutionalist Party in Cochinchina: The Years of Decline, 1930–1942* (Melbourne: Centre for Southeast Asian Studies, Monash University, 1977); Milton Osborne, 'The Faithful Few: The Politics of Collaboration in Cochinchina in the 1920s', in Walter Vella, ed., *Aspects of Vietnamese History* (Honolulu: University of Hawai'i Press, 1973), pp. 160–90; Patrice Morlat, *La Répression coloniale au Vietnam, 1908–1940* (Paris: Editions L'Harmattan, 1990), p. 276; Pierre Brocheux, 'Elite, bourgeoisie, ou la difficulté d'être', in Philippe Franchini, ed., *Saigon, 1925–1945* (Paris: Autrement, 1992), pp. 135–61; and especially Philippe Peycam, *The Birth of Vietnamese Political Journalism, Saigon, 1916–1930* (New York: Columbia University Press, 2012).

3. 'L'Echo annamite: The Wish List of the Vietnamese People (1925)', in Truong Buu Lam, *Colonialism Experienced: Vietnamese Writings on Colonialism, 1900–1931* (Ann Arbor: The University of Michigan Press, 2000), pp. 208–27; and Louis Roubaud, *Viet-Nam, la tragédie indo-chinoise* (Paris: Librairie Valois, 1931), p. 262.

4. Huynh Thuc Khang, 'Speech Delivered at the Opening Ceremony of the Third Session of the Chamber of People's Representatives in Annam, 1 October 1928', in Truong Buu Lam, *Colonialism Experienced*, pp. 262–3 (for the citation).

5. Truong Buu Lam, *Colonialism Experienced*, p. 78.

6. On the Constitutionalists and India, see Larcher-Goscha, 'Bui Quang Chieu in Calcutta', pp. 131–50. On the Indian National Congress and the making of the British Empire, see John Darwin, *The Empire Project: The Rise and Fall of the British World-System, 1830–1970* (New York: Cambridge University Press, 2009).

7. On the rise of the youth and its radicalization, I have relied on the following: Hue-Tam Ho Tai, *Radicalism*; David Marr, *Vietnamese Tradition on Trial*, 1920–1945 (Berkeley: University of California Press, 1981); Shawn McHale, *Print and Power: Confucianism, Communism, and Buddhism in the Making of Modern Vietnam* (Honolulu: University of Hawai'i Press, 2004). For the statistics, see Marr, *Vietnamese Tradition*, chapter 1; and McHale, *Print and Power*, chapter 1.

8. Marr, *Vietnamese Tradition*, pp. 30–33. On censorship, see McHale, *Print and Power*, chapter 2. On Ho Chi Minh's use of *quoc ngu* in France, see Sophie Quinn-Judge, *Ho Chi Minh: The Missing Years* (Berkeley: University of California Press, 2002), pp. 39–40.

9. Judith Henchy, 'Performing Modernity in the Writings of Nguyen An Ninh and Phan Van Hum', PhD dissertation (Seattle: University of Washington, 2005); Daniel Hémery, 'Nguyen An Ninh', in Franchini, *Saigon 1925–1945*, pp. 159–88; Hue-Tam Ho Tai, *Radicalism*, chapter 4; and Daniel Hémery, *Révolutionnaires vietnamiens et pouvoir colonial en Indochine: Communistes, trotskystes, nationalistes à Saigon de 1932 à 1937* (Paris: François Maspero, 1975).

10. Nguyen An Ninh, 'The Ideal of the Annamese Youth (1923)', in Dutton et al., *Sources of Vietnamese Tradition*, pp. 382–9 (for the citation).

11. Hue-Tam Ho Tai, *Radicalism*, p. 13; and Nguyen An Ninh, 'France in Indochina (1925)', in Truong Buu Lam, *Colonialism Experienced*, pp. 190–207.

12. Cited by Hue-Tam Ho Tai, *Radicalism*, p. 143.

13. Cognacq quote cited by Hue-Tam Ho Tai in Ibid., pp. 143–144.

14. Agathe Larcher, 'D'un réformisme à l'autre: La Redécouverte de l'identité

culturelle vietnamienne, 1900–1930', Série Etudes et Documents Etudes indochinoises IV (May 1995), pp. 85–96; Herman Lebovics, *True France* (Ithaca: Cornell University Press, 1992).

15. Thanks in no small part to materials that continued to flow into Vietnam via the overseas Chinese community. See chapter 4.

16. On the VNQDD, I have relied on Hy Van Luong, *Revolution in the Village: Tradition and Transformation in North Vietnam, 1925–1988* (Honolulu: University of Hawai'i Press, 1992).

17. Roubaud, *Viet-nam*, p. 120.

18. Ibid., p. 120 (for the citation). See also Paul Monet's *Les Jauniers: Histoire Vraie* (Paris: Gallimard, 1930); Nguyen Thai Hoc, 'Radical Nationalism in Vietnam', in Harry J. Benda, et al., *The World of Southeast Asia: Selected Historical Readings* (New York: Harper & Row, Publishers, 1967), pp. 182–5. Pierre Pasquier argued just the opposite to the Vietnamese on 15 October 1930. See his 'In Defense of the Mission Civilisatrice in Indochina', in Benda, *The World of Southeast Asia*, pp. 137–41.

19. I rely on the following studies for my discussion of Ho Chi Minh: Daniel Hémery, 'Jeunesse d'un colonisé, genèse d'un exil, Ho Chi Minh jusqu'en 1911', *Approches Asie* (4th semester 1992), pp. 114–17, 137; Quinn-Judge, *Ho Chi Minh: The Missing Years*; William Duiker, *Ho Chi Minh: A Life* (New York: Hyperion, 2000); Pierre Brocheux, *Ho Chi Minh: Du révolutionnaire à l'icône* (Paris: Payot, 2003); Daniel Hémery, *Ho Chi Minh: De l'Indochine au Vietnam* (Paris: Gallimard, 1990); and Martin Grossheim, *Ho Chi Minh: Der geheimnisvolle Revolutionär: Leben und Legende* (Munich: Beck, 2011).

20. See Hémery, 'Jeunesse d'un colonisé', p. 151.

21. Pierre Trolliet, *La Diaspora chinoise*, 3rd edn (Paris: PUF, 2000), pp. 11–16; and Fautereau, 'Le Nationalisme vietnamien', chapters 1–2.

22. Quinn-Judge, *Ho Chi Minh*, pp. 15–19. We still know little about how Asians understood and how seriously they actually took Wilson's ideas. For the American side, see Erez Manela, *The Wilsonian Moment: Self-Determination and the International Origins of Anticolonial Nationalism* (New York: Oxford University Press, 2007).

23. This message is at the core of Truong's autobiographical indictment of French colonial policy. Phan Van Truong, *Une histoire de conspirateurs annamites à Paris* (Montreuil: L'Insomniaque, 2003 (first published in 1926–8)). Quote cited by Quinn-Judge, *Ho Chi Minh*, p. 17.

24. Scott McConnell, *Leftward Journey: The Education of Vietnamese Students in France 1919–1939* (New Brunswick: Transaction Publishers, 1989).

25. I rely heavily in this section on Quinn-Judge, *Ho Chi Minh*; and Céline Marangé, *Le Communisme vietnamien 1919–1991: Construction d'un État-nation entre Moscou et Pékin* (Paris: SciencesPo, Les Presses, 2012); and her 'La Politique coloniale du parti communiste français: Le Rôle du Komintern et de Ho Chi Minh, 1920–1926', *Communisme* (2013), pp. 47–76.

26. Christopher Goscha, 'Pour une histoire transnationale du communisme vietnamien', *Communisme* (2013), pp. 19–46.

27. Quinn-Judge, *Ho Chi Minh*, pp. 159–90; and Tobias Rettig, 'Special Issue: Revisiting and Reconstructing the Nghê Tinh Soviets, 1930–2011', *South East Asia Research*, vol. 19, no. 4 (2011), pp. 677–853; Brocheux and Hémery, *Indochine*, pp. 307–9.

28. Christopher Goscha, 'Bao Dai et Sihanouk'.

29. 'Conservative Nationalism in Vietnam', in Benda, *The World of Southeast Asia*, pp. 179–81 (for the citation).

30. Bruce Lockhart, *The End of the Vietnamese Monarchy* (New Haven: Yale Center for International and Area Studies, 1993); Philippe Devillers, *Histoire du Vietnam, de 1940 à 1952* (Paris: Editions du Seuil, 1952), pp. 63–4.

31. Section française de l'Internationale ouvrière, the origin of the French Socialist Party. On Nguyen An Ninh and the Popular Front period in Indochina, see: Judith Henchy, 'Performing Modernity'; Daniel Hémery, *Révolutionnaires vietnamiens*; and his 'A Saigon dans les années trente, un journal militant: "La Lutte" (1933–1937)' *Europe solidaire sans frontières* (2005), at http://www.europe-solidaire.org/spip.php?article2852 accessed on 15 June 2016.

32. Brocheux and Hémery, *Indochina*, p. 334.

33. Charles-Robert Ageron, 'L'Exposition coloniale de 1931: Mythe républicain ou mythe impérial?', in Pierre Nora (ed.), *Les Lieux de mémoire*, vol. 1 (Paris: Gallimard, 1997), pp. 493–515.

CHAPTER 6. COLONIAL SOCIETY AND ECONOMY

1. Simon Creek, *Body Work: Sport, Physical Culture, and the Making of Modern Laos* (Honolulu: University of Hawai'i Press, 2014), pp. 1–3; Agathe Larcher-Goscha, 'Du football au Vietnam (1905–1949): Colonialisme, culture sportive et sociabilités en jeux', *Outre-mers*, vol. 97, no. 363–5 (2009), pp. 61–89; and my reading of the *Annam Nouveau* coverage of this incident.

2. Gerard Sasges, *Imperial Intoxication: Alcohol, Indochina, and the World (1897–1933)* (Honolulu: University of Hawaii Press, forthcoming); Olivier Tessier, 'Outline of the Process of Red River Hydraulics Development during the Nguyen Dynasty', in Mart Stewart and Peter Coclanis, eds., *Environmental Change and Agricultural Sustainability in the Mekong Delta* (New York: Springer Science, 2011), pp. 45–68; and Arthur Dommen, *The Indochinese Experience of the French and the Americans* (Bloomington: Indiana University Press, 2001), p. 27.

3. Paul Mus, *Sociologie d'une guerre* (Paris: Editions du Seuil, 1952), p. 125.

4. Marguerite Duras, *Cahiers de la guerre* (Paris: POL Editeurs, 2006), p. 41; Goscha, *Going Indochinese* (Copenhagen: NIAS/University of Hawaii, 2013), pp. 46–7 (for the citation); Aline Demay, *Tourism and Colonization in Indochina (1898–1939)* (London: Cambridge Scholar Publishing, 2014); and especially Erich DeWald, 'Vietnamese Tourism in Late-Colonial Central Vietnam, 1917–1945', PhD dissertation (London: SOAS, 2012). On colonial Dalat, leisure, and society, see: Eric Jennings, *Imperial Heights: Dalat and the Making and Undoing of French Indochina* (Berkeley: University of California Press, 2011).

5. David Del Testa, 'Imperial Corridor', *Science Technology Society*, vol. 4, no. 2 (September 1999), pp. 319–54; Pierre Brocheux, *Histoire économique du Vietnam de 1860 à nos jours* (Paris: Les Indes savantes, 2009), pp. 63–4; and Brocheux and Hémery, *Indochine*, pp. 127–8; Jean-Pascal Bassino, 'Indochina', p. 2.

6. Brocheux and Hémery, *Indochine*, p. 127; Brocheux, *Histoire économique*, p. 64; and http://transmekong.com/fr_3.5_Messageries_Fluviales. On the Mekong Delta, development and the environment, see David Biggs, *Quagmire: Nation-Building and Nature in the Mekong Delta* (Seattle: University of Washington Press, 2011); and Pierre Brocheux,

The Mekong Delta: Ecology, Economy, and Revolution, 1860–1960 (Madison: Center for Southeast Asian Studies, 2009). On the sea in the making of modern Vietnam, see Charles Wheeler, 'Re-thinking the Sea in Vietnamese History', *Journal of Southeast Asian Studies*, vol. 37, no. 1 (February 2006), pp. 123–53.

7. Brocheux, *Histoire économique*, pp. 64–7.

8. Brocheux and Hémery, *Indochine*, pp. 129–30.

9. Maks Banens, 'Vietnam: A Reconstitution of its 20th Century Population History', *Asian Historical Statistics*, COE Project, Institute of Economic Research (Tokyo: Hitotsubashi University, January 2000), p. 39, appendix 4. See also Bassino, 'Indochina', p. 2.

10. Bassino, 'Indochina', p. 2, 3; and Maks Banens, 'Vietnam: A Reconstitution of its 20th Century Population History', p. 39, appendix 4.

11. Brocheux, *Histoire économique*, pp. 76–7.

12. Ibid., pp. 83–8; Brocheux and Hémery, *Indochine*, pp. 125–6.

13. Tran Tu Binh, *The Red Earth*, Southeast Asia Series no. 66 (Athens: Ohio University, 1985), p. 30 (for the citation). On the rubber economy, see above all Eric Panthou, *Les Plantations Michelin au Viêt-Nam* (Clermont-Ferrand: Editions 'La Galipote', 2013).

14. Brocheux, *Histoire économique*, pp. 82–9; Brocheux and Hémery, *Indochine*, p. 125.

15. Brocheux and Hémery, *Indochine*, pp. 124–5.

16. The first American agent was in fact a Frenchman, Aimée Fonsales, a partner in the trading firm Denis Frères and the local agent for Standard Oil. Other Frenchmen working for Denis Frères operated this US Consular Agency until the first American diplomat arrived in 1907. James Nach, *A History of the U.S. Consulate, Saigon, 1889–1950*, unpublished manuscript kindly provided to the author by Mr. Nach.

17. Tracy C. Barrett, *The Chinese Diaspora in South-East Asia: The Overseas Chinese in Indochina* (New York: I. B. Tauris, 2012), pp. 13–15; Thomas Engelbert, 'Vietnamese-Chinese Relations in Southern Vietnam during the First Indochina Conflict', *Journal of Vietnamese Studies*, vol. 3, no 3 (Fall 2008), pp. 191–230.

18. Frédéric Roustan, 'Français, japonais et société coloniale du Tonkin: L'exemple de représentations coloniales', *French Colonial History*, vol. 6 (2005), pp. 179–204.

19. Nadia Leconte, 'La Migration des Pondichériens et des Karikalais en Indochine ou le combat des Indiens renonçants en Cochinchine pour la reconnaissance de leur statut (1865–1954)', MA dissertation (Rennes: Université de Haute-Bretagne, Rennes 2, 2001); and Jacques Weber, 'Les Pondichériens et les Karikalais en Indochine, 1865 à 1954', http:// cidif.go1.cc/index.php?option=com_content&view=article&id=130:26–261-le-combat -des-renoncants-en-cochinchine-pour-la-reconnaisance-de-leur-statut-de-n-leconte &catid=29:lettre-nd26&Itemid=3, accessed 28 August 2015.

20. For an in-depth study of the 'Indians' in Indochina, see: Natasha Pairaudeau, *Mobile Citizens: French Indians in Indochina, 1858–1954* (Copenhagen: NIAS, 2016), and her 'Vietnamese Engagement with Tamil Migrants in Colonial Cochinchina', *Journal of Vietnamese Studies*, vol. 5, no. 3 (Fall 2010), pp. 1–71.

21. For more on Corsicans, see Pascal Bonacorsi, 'Les Corses en Indochine (XIXème-XXème siècles)', MA dissertation (Paris: Université Paris I Panthéon-Sorbonne, 2013); Jean-Louis Prestini, 'Saigon Cyrnos', in Philippe Franchini, *Saigon, 1925–1945* (Paris: Autrement, 1992), pp. 92–103; Robert Aldrich, 'France's Colonial Island: Corsica and the Empire', at http://www.h-france.net/rude/rudevolumeiii/AldrichVol3.pdf, accessed 20 January 2014.

22. Brocheux and Hémery, *Indochine*, pp. 185–6 for the citation; and Natasha Pairau-deau, 'Vietnamese Engagement', pp. 1–71, second citation at p. 17.

23. Goscha, *Going Indochinese*, p. 68.

24. Vu Trong Phung, *The Industry of Marrying Europeans*, trans. Thuy Tranviet (Ithaca: Southeast Asia Program Publications/Cornell, 2005); and Vu Trong Phung, *Luc Xi*, trans. Shaun Malarney (Honolulu: University of Hawai'i Press, 2011); Malarney's introductory essay to this novel, pp. 1–41; and Isabelle Tracol-Huynh, 'La Prostitution au Tonkin colonial, entre races et genres', *Genre, sexualité & société*, no. 2 (Fall 2009), https://gss.revues.org/1219, accessed 28 August 2015.

25. Kim Lefèvre, *Métisse blanche* (Paris: Editions Bernard Barrault, 1989).Christina Firpo, 'Crises of Whiteness and Empire in Colonial Indochina: The Removal of Abandoned Eurasian Children from the Vietnamese Milieu, 1890–1956', *Journal of Social History*, vol. 43, no. 3 (2010), pp. 587–613. It is no secret that many a soldier or even an administrator just up and left once their time in Indochina had expired.

26. Frederick Cooper and Ann Stoler, eds., *Tensions of Empire: Colonial Cultures in a Bourgeois World* (Berkeley: University of California Press, 1997), pp. 198–237.

27. Duras, *Cahiers*, pp. 41–2 (for the citation).

28. Tsai Maw-Kuey, *Les Chinois au Sud Vietnam* (Paris: Bibliothèque nationale, 1968), p. 54; and Goscha, *Going Indochinese*, chapter 4.

29. On the Minh Huong, see Tsai Maw-Kuey, *Les Chinois au Sud Vietnam* and Elise Virely, 'Métissage "asiatique" au Cambodge et en Cochinchine: Les Métis sino-vietnamiens et sino-cambodgiens, enjeux politiques et identité, 1863–1940', MA dissertation (Lyon: Université de Lyon II, 2005).

30. The author of *Métisse blanche*, Kim Lefevre, owes the first part of her name to her Chinese stepfather. Kim Lefèvre, *Métisse blanche*, pp. 114–15, 174–5. Ho Chi Minh married Tang Tuyen Minh. See his letter to his wife, written in Chinese, in Daniel Hémery, *Ho Chi Minh, de l'Indochine au Vietnam* (Paris: Découvertes Gallimard, 1990), p. 145 and William Duiker, *Ho Chi Minh, A Life* (New York: Hyperion, 2000), pp. 143, 198–9.

31. Jean-Dominique Giacometti, 'Prices and Wages in Vietnam before 1954', Discussion Paper no. D98–14 (Tokyo: Institute of Economic Research, Hitosubahsi University, February 1999), p. 21.

32. See the nuanced study by Solène Granier, *Domestiques indochinois* (Paris: Vendémiaire, 2014) and Le Manh Hung, *The Impact of World War II on the Economy of Vietnam* (Singapore: Eastern University Press, 2004), pp. 77–80.

33. See Nola Cooke, 'Colonial Political Myth and the Problem of the Other: French and Vietnamese in the Protectorate of Annam', PhD dissertation (Canberra: Australian National University, 1992); Christopher Goscha, 'La Fabrique indochinoise des rois coloniaux', in François Guillemot and Larcher-Goscha, eds., *La Colonisation des corps, de l'Indochine au Viet Nam* (Paris: Vendémiaire, 2014), pp. 127–75; and Pascale Bezançon, 'Louis Manipoud, un réformateur colonial méconnu', *Revue française d'Histoire d'Outre-mer*, vol. 82, no. 309 (1995), pp. 455–87.

34. I rely heavily here on Cuong Tu Nguyen, 'Rethinking Vietnamese Buddhist History: Is the Thien Uyen Tap Anh a "Transmission of the Lamp" Text?' in Keith Taylor and John Whitmore, eds., *Essays into Vietnamese Pasts* (Ithaca: Cornell University Press, 1995), pp. 81–115; Shawn McHale, *Print and Power: Confucianism, Communism, and Buddhism in the Making of Modern Vietnam* (Honolulu: University of Hawai'i Press,

2003), pp. 70–151; Charles Wheeler, 'Buddhism in the Re-ordering of an Early Modern World: Chinese Missions to Cochinchina in the Seventeenth Century', *Journal of Global History*, vol. 2, no. 3 (November 2007), pp. 303–24; Li, *Nguyen Cochinchina*, pp. 101–12; Elise Anne de Vido, 'Buddhism for This World: The Buddhist Revival in Vietnam, 1920–1951', in Philip Taylor, ed., *Modernity and Re-Enchantment: Religion in Post-Revolutionary Vietnam* (Singapore: Institute of Southeast Asian Studies, 2007), pp. 256–81; and her 'The Influence of Chinese Master Taixu on Buddhism in Vietnam', *Journal of Global Buddhism*, vol. 10 (2009), pp. 413–58.

35. De Vido, 'The Influence of Chinese Master Taixu on Buddhism in Vietnam', pp. 413–58.

36. De Vido, 'Buddhism for This World', pp. 256–81.

37. Philippe Papin, 'Saving for the Soul: Women, Pious Donations and Village Economy in Early Modern Vietnam', *Journal of Vietnamese Studies*, vol. 10, no. 2 (Spring 2015), pp. 82–102; McHale, *Print and Power*, pp. 179–80; and de Vido, 'Buddhism for This World', pp. 256–81.

38. I rely here on the following: Hue-Tam Ho Tai, *Millenarianism and Peasant Politics in Vietnam* (Cambridge, MA: Harvard University Press, 1983); Jane Werner, *Peasant Politics and Religious Sectarianism: Peasant and Priest in the Cao Dai in Viet Nam* (New Haven: Yale University, Southeast Asia Center, 1981); Jérémy Jammes, *Les Oracles du Cao Dai* (Paris: Les Indes savantes, 2014); Pascal Bourdeaux, 'Approches statistiques de la communauté du bouddhisme Hoa Hao (1939–1954)', in Christopher Goscha et Benoît de Tréglodé, eds., *Naissance d'un Etat parti: le Viet Nam depuis 1945* (Paris: Les Indes savantes, 2004), pp. 277–304; Ralph Smith, 'An Introduction to Caodaism', *Bulletin of the School of Oriental and African Studies*, vol. 33 (1970), pp. 335–49, 574–89; Victor Oliver, *Caodai Spiritism* (Leiden: Brill, 1972); Tran My-Van, 'Beneath the Japanese Umbrella: Vietnam's Hoa Hao during and after the Pacific War', *Crossroads*, vol. 17, no 1 (2003), pp. 60–107.

39. Alexander Woodside, *Community and Revolution in Modern Vietnam* (Boston: Houghton Mifflin, 1976), pp. 120–22; and more generally Nguyen-Marshall, *In Search of Moral Authority*.

40. Frances Hill, 'Millenarian Machines in South Vietnam', *Comparative Studies in Society and History*, vol. 13, no. 3 (July 1971), pp. 325–50; and Hue-Tam Ho Tai, *Millenarianism and Peasant Politics in Vietnam*.

41. Jean Pascal Bassino, 'Indochina', p. 2; and Woodside, *Community and Revolution*, pp. 32–3.

42. I rely here on Daughton, *An Empire Divided*; Owen White and J. P. Daughton, eds., *In God's Empire: French Missionaries and the Modern World* (New York: Oxford University Press, 2012); Charles Keith, *Catholic Vietnam: A Church from Empire to Nation* (Berkeley: University of California Press, 2012); and Charles Keith, 'Catholicisme, bouddhisme et lois laïques au Tonkin (1899–1914)', *Vingtième siècle* (July–September 2005), pp. 113–28.

43. Daughton, *An Empire Divided*, pp. 105–9.

44. Keith, *Catholic Vietnam*, pp. 1–3.

45. Ibid.

46. Charles Keith, 'Annam Uplifted: The First Vietnamese Catholic Bishops and the Birth of a National Church, 1919–1945', *Journal of Vietnamese Studies*, vol. 3, no. 2 (2008), p. 137.

47. Keith, *Catholic Vietnam*, p. 139.

48. Ibid., p. 156.

49. Ibid.; and especially Claire Tran Thi Lien, 'Les Catholiques vietnamiens et la RDVN (1945–1954): Une approche biographique', in Goscha and de Tréglodé, *Naissance d'un Etat Parti*, pp. 253–76, and her 'Les Catholiques vietnamiens, entre la reconquête coloniale et la résistance communiste (1945–1954)', *Approches-Asie*, no. 15 (1997), pp. 169–88.

CHAPTER 7. CONTESTING EMPIRE AND NATION-STATES

1. Christopher Goscha, 'This Is the End? The French Settler Community in Saigon and the Fall of Indochina in 1945', paper delivered at the annual meeting of the French Historical Society, held on 24–6 April 2014.

2. See Akira Iriye, *The Origins of the Second World War in Asia and the Pacific* (Harlow: Longman, 1987), pp. 2–4.

3. Mark Mazower, *Hitler's Empire: How the Nazis Ruled Europe* (London: Penguin, 2008).

4. Robert O. Paxton, *Vichy France, Old Guard and New Order, 1940–1944* (New York: Columbia University Press, 1972).

5. Paul Isoart, ed., *L'Indochine française (1940–1945)* (Paris: PUF, 1982). For a recent in-depth account of the Japanese expansion into Indochine, see: Franck Michelin, 'L'Indochine française et l'expansion vers le sud du Japon à l'orée de la Guerre du Pacifique'. PhD thesis (Paris: Université Paris Sorbonne, 2014).

6. The Go East program was the ancestor of the Viet Nam Phuc Quoc Dong Minh Hoi.

7. On Vichy in Indochina, see Eric Jennings, *Vichy in the Tropics: Pétain's National Revolution in Madagascar, Guadeloupe, and Indochina, 1940–1944* (Stanford: Stanford University Press, 2001); Jacques Cantier and Eric Jennings, eds., *L'Empire sous Vichy* (Paris: Odile Jacob, 2004); Sébastien Verney, *L'Indochine sous Vichy. Entre Révolution nationale, collaboration et identités nationales 1940–1945* (Paris: Riveneuve éditions, 2012); Anne Raffin, *Youth Mobilization in Vichy Indochina and Its Legacies, 1940–1970* (Lanham: Lexington Books, 2005); Chizuru Namba, *Français et Japonais en Indochine (1940–1945)* (Paris: Karthala, 2012); Paul Isoart, 'Aux origines d'une guerre: L'Indochine française (1940–1945)', in Isoart, ed., *L'Indochine française (1940–1945)*, p. 20; and François Guillemot, *Dai Viet indépendence et révolution au Viet-Nam, l'échec de la troisième voie (1938–1955)* (Paris: Les Indes savantes, 2012), pp. 33–168. On fascism and Vietnamese nationalism, see: François Guillemot, 'La tentation «*fasciste*» des luttes anticoloniales Dai Viet', Vingtième Siècle, vol. 4, no. 104 (2009), pp. 45–66.

8. Quote from Jennings, *Vichy in the Tropics*, p. 184. (Interpolations as for the text quoted.) On Vichy politics, see: Philippe Devillers, *L'Asie du Sud-Est*, volume 2 (Paris: Sirey, 1971), p. 794. In 1943, under pressure from the settler community, Decoux transformed the Council into a Mixed Assembly with thirty Indochinese and twenty-five French citizens. *Notabilités indochinoises* at http://indomemoires.hypotheses.org/6926, accessed 26 August 2015.

9. All quotes from Pham Quynh, 'L'Accord politique de Confucius et de Maurras', *La Patrie Annamite* (20 April 1942), pp. 1–4. See also Clive Christie, *Ideology and Revolution in South-East Asia, 1900–1980* (London: Curzon, 2001), pp. 88–9.

10. Norodom Sihanouk, *L'Indochine vue de Pékin* (Paris: Editions du Seuil, 1972), p. 34.

11. Soren Ivarsson, *Creating Laos: The Making of Lao Space between Siam and Indochina, 1860–1945* (Copenhagen: Nordic Institute of Asian Studies, 2008) ; and Thongchai Winichakul, *Siam Mapped: A History of the Geo-Body of a Nation* (Chiang Mai: Silkworm Books, 1994).

12. See excerpts from Jean Deoux's memoirs, 'French Indochina in the Co-Prosperity Sphere', in Harry J. Benda and John A. Larkin, eds., *The World of Southeast Asia, Selected Historical Readings* (New York: Harper & Row, Publishers, 1967), pp. 242–4. On the Tran Trong Kim government, see: Vu Ngu Chieu, 'The Other Side of the 1945 Vietnamese Revolution: The Empire of Viet-Nam (March–August 1945)', *Journal of Asian Studies*, vol. 45 (1986), pp. 293–328.

13. Alec Holcombe, 'Staline et les procès de Moscou vus du Vietnam', *Communisme* (2013), pp. 109–58.

14. In 1934–5, Chinese communists escaped nationalist attacks by fleeing to Yan'an in northern China, where they operated until the end of World War II.

15. David Marr, *Vietnam, 1945* (Berkeley: University of California Press, 1995), p. 174.

16. Ibid.

17. Tung Hiep, 'Pha Tuong Paul Bert', *Trung Bac Chu Nhat* (12 August 1945), p. 1.

18. The seal and sword would return to the French and then to Bao Dai and his family. http://www.vietnamheritage.com.vn/pages/en/1031294845453-Conversation-piece-of -the-Nguyen-Dynasty.html, accessed 26 August 2015. Quote cited by Devillers, *Histoire du Vietnam de 1940 à 1952* (Paris: Editions du Seuil, 1952), p. 138.

19. His Catholic wife, the Empress Nam Phuong, also abdicated and issued a letter the same day, defending her husband's decision and the sacredness of Vietnamese independence. Bernard Fall, *Le Viet Minh* (Paris: Armand Colin, 1960), p. 165.

20. Marr, *Vietnam, 1945*; and Gabriel Kolko, *Un siècle de guerres* (Laval: Presses de l'Université de Laval, 2000), pp. 290–302.

21. This is one of the core arguments of David Marr's book, *Vietnam, 1945*.

22. Martin Thomas, 'Silent Partners: SOE's French Indo-China Section, 1943–1945', *Modern Asian Studies*, vol. 34, no. 4 (October 2000), pp. 943–76.

23. Martin Shipway, *The Road to War: France and Vietnam 1944–1947* (New York: Berghahn Books, 2003); Daniel Hémery, 'Asie du Sud-Est, 1945: Vers un nouvel impérialisme colonial?', in Charles-Robert Ageron and Marc Michel, eds., *L'Ere des décolonisations* (Paris: Karthala, 1995), pp. 65–84; and Stein Tønnesson, *The Vietnamese Revolution of 1945* (London: Sage Publications, 1991).

24. Pierre Brocheux, 'De l'empereur Duy Tan au prince Vinh San: L'Histoire peut-elle se répeter?', *Approches-Asie*, n.s. (1989–90), pp. 1–25.

25. On this process, see Alec Holcombe, 'Socialist Transformation in the Democratic Republic of Vietnam', PhD dissertation (Berkeley: University of California at Berkeley, 2013); Pierre Brocheux, *Ho Chi Minh: du révolutionnaire à l'icône* (Paris: Payot, 2003); and Daniel Hémery, 'Ho Chi Minh: Vie singulière et nationalisation des esprits', in Christopher Goscha and Benoît de Tréglodé, eds., *The Birth of a Party-State: Vietnam since 1945* (Paris: Les Indes savantes, 2004), pp. 135–48.

26. See in particular: Hans van de Ven, Diana Lary and Stephen Mackinnon, *Negotiating China's Destiny in World War II* (Stanford: Stanford University Press, 2014).

27. Initially, given that the Potsdam meeting occurred before the Japanese capitulation, the British and Chinese received authorization to conduct military operations in these two

areas. Upon the Japanese defeat, Harry Truman issued Order no. 1, putting the Chinese and British in charge of accepting the Japanese surrender in their respective operational zones.

28. François Guillemot, *Dai Viet*, pp. 316–21.

29. Peter Dunn, who can hardly be accused of being hostile to the French, demonstrates this in his *The First Vietnam War* (London: C. Hurst & Company, 1985). On de Gaulle and the First Indochina War, see Frédéric Turpin, *De Gaulle, les gaullistes et l'Indochine* (Paris: Les Indes savantes, 2005).

30. See Lin Hua, *Chiang Kai-Shek, De Gaulle contre Hô Chi Minh: Viêt-Nam, 1945–1946* (Paris: L'Harmattan, 1994). Defeated Japanese troops fought on both sides of the colonial/national line. On the one hand, they helped the French reconquer southern Vietnam in late 1945. On the other hand, hundreds crossed over to the DRV and fought against that very colonial reconquest. See Christopher Goscha, 'Alliés tardifs: Le Rôle technico-militaire joué par les déserteurs japonais dans les rangs du Viet Minh (1945–1950)', *Guerres mondiales et conflits contemporains*, nos. 202–3 (April–September 2001), pp. 81–109.

31. Stein Tønnesson, 'La Paix imposée par la Chine: L'Accord franco-vietnamien du 6 mars 1946', *Cahiers de l'Institut d'histoire du temps présent* (1996), pp. 35–56; and Stein Tønnesson, *Vietnam 1946: How the War Began* (Berkeley: University of California Press, 2009), pp. 39–64. The idea that Ho's words show that he harbored early on 'traditional' Vietnamese hostility toward 'historic' Chinese 'imperialism' is inaccurate. Ho made the comment with direct reference to the very difficult negotiations with the French over the annex and its requirement for the French to withdraw their troops within five years. On the 6 March accords, see Shipway, *The Road to War*, pp. 150–75; and Tønnesson, *Vietnam 1946*, pp. 39–64.

32. I rely heavily on Guillemot, *Dai Viet*, chapters 6 and 7.

33. Christopher Goscha, 'Intelligence in a Time of Decolonization', *Intelligence and National Security*, vol. 22, no. 1 (February 2007), pp. 100–138; and Marr, *Vietnam, 1945*, pp. 232–7.

34. Ngo Van Chieu, *Journal d'un combattant Viet-Minh* (Paris: Editions du Seuil, 1955), pp. 84–90; and Nguyen Cong Luan, *Nationalist in the Viet Nam Wars: Memoirs of a Victim Turned Soldier* (Bloomington: Indiana University Press, 2012), p. 66.

35. François Guillemot, 'Autopsy of a Massacre: On a Political Purge in the Early Days of the Indochina War (Nam Bo 1947)', *European Journal of East Asian Studies*, vol. 9, no 2 (2010), pp. 225–65; and Shawn McHale, 'Understanding the Fanatic Mind? The Viet Minh and Race Hatred in the First Indochina War (1945–1954)', *Journal of Vietnamese Studies*, vol. 4, no. 3 (Fall 2009), pp. 98–138.

36. Christopher Goscha, *Vietnam: Un Etat né de la guerre, 1945–1954* (Paris: Armand Colin, 2011), pp. 255–63.

CHAPTER 8. STATES OF WAR

1. Christopher Goscha, 'A Popular Side of the Vietnamese Army: General Nguyen Binh and the War in the South', in Christopher Goscha and Benoit de Tréglodé, eds., *Naissance d'un Etat-Parti* (Paris: Les Indes savantes, 2004), pp. 324–53.

2. I rely here on the following: Devillers, *L'Asie du Sud-Est*, pp. 791–847; his *Vingt ans et plus avec le Viet-Nam, 1945–1969* (Paris: Les Indes savantes, 2010); Jacques Dalloz, *La Guerre d'Indochine, 1945–1954* (Paris: Editions du Seuil, 1987); Shipway, *The Road to*

War; Tønnesson, *Vietnam 1946: How the War Began*; Brocheux and Hémery, *Indochina: An Ambiguous Colonization*.

3. *L'Humanité* (30 August 1944), p. 1, cited by Pierre Daprini, 'From Indochina to North Africa: French Discourses on Decolonisation', in Robert Aldrich and Martyn Lyons, eds., *The Sphinx in the Tuileries and Other Essays in Modern French History* (Sydney: University of Sydney, 1999), p. 223, note 5.

4. A. J. Stockwell, 'Southeast Asia in War and Peace: The End of European Colonial Empires', in Nicholas Tarling, ed., *Cambridge History of Southeast Asia* (Cambridge: Cambridge University Press, 1993), p. 346; Martin Shipway, *Decolonization and Its Impact: A Comparative Approach to the End of the Colonial Empires* (Wiley, 2008); and Martin Thomas, *Fight or Flight: Britain, France, and Their Roads from Empire* (Oxford: Oxford University Press, 2014). Quote from de Gaulle as cited by Jean-Marie Domenach, 'Paul Mus', *Esprit*, no. 10 (October 1969), p. 605.

5. Devillers, *Histoire du Vietnam de 1940 à 1952*, p. 244.

6. Christopher Bayly and Tim Harper, *Forgotten Armies: The Fall of British Asia, 1941–1945* (Cambridge, MA: Harvard University Press, 2005), pp. 419–22; Charles Maurras was a rightwing French nationalist and monarchist who supported Pétain's Vichy France; and Christopher Goscha, *Historical Dictionary of the Indochina War: An International and Interdisciplinary Approach (1945–1954)* (Copenhagen/Honolulu: NIAS/University of Hawai'i Press, 2011), p. 63. In 1942, this man, Camir Biros, published a Fascist-minded article on Vichy's nationalist revolution in *La Gazette de Hue*. On the same page, Pham Quynh published his famous elegy of Maurras and Vietnamese royalist patriotism. See chapter 7.

7. For a glimpse into the mindsets of these administrators, see Pierre Gentil, ed., *Derniers chefs d'un empire* (Paris: Académie des Sciences d'Outre-Mer, 1972), pp. 235–363, especially the text of Albert Torel (pp. 310–15, p. 312 for the citation).

8. Daniel Hémery, 'Asie du Sud-Est, 1945: Vers un nouvel impérialisme colonial?', in Charles-Robert Ageron and Marc Michel, eds., *L'Ere des décolonisations* (Paris: Karthala, 1995), pp. 65–84.

9. Bui Diem, *In the Jaws of History* (with David Chanoff) (Bloomington: Indiana University Press, 1999), p. 44.

10. Dalloz, *Francs-Maçons d'Indochine, 1868–1975*, pp. 94–5.

11. To my knowledge, no scholar has studied the question of Cochinchinese separatism, whether French or Vietnamese. My discussion here relies largely on Devillers' *Histoire du Vietnam de 1940 à 1952*, who had unparalleled access to the historical actors of the time. The francophile Catholic intellectuals Pham Ngoc Thao, Pham Ngoc Thuan, and Thai Van Lung crossed over to the communists on anticolonial grounds. The French tortured Thai Van Lung to death. Goscha, *Historical Dictionary*, pp. 372–4, 443.

12. Reproduced in *Luoc Su Chien Si Quyet Tu: Sai Gon, Cho Lon, Gia Dinh, 1945–1954* (Ho Chi Minh City: Cau Lac Bo Truyen Thong Vu Trang, 1992), p. 149.

13. Readers will recall that the Nguyen refusal to pay taxes to the Trinh in the early seventeenth century set off civil war. On the complex series of events leading to the outbreak of war on 19 December, see Tønnesson, *Vietnam 1946*; Shipway, *The Road to War*; and Turpin, *De Gaulle, les Gaullistes et l'Indochine* (Paris: Les Indes savantes, 2005), p. 310. The new national terms as cited by Philippe Devillers, *Paris, Saigon, Hanoi: Les Archives de la guerre, 1944–1947* (Paris: Gallimard, 1988), p. 334.

14. Devillers, *Paris, Saigon, Hanoi*, pp. 334–5.

15. I borrow here from the title of Alistair Horne's *A Savage War of Peace: Algeria, 1954–1962* (New York: Macmillan, 1977).

16. See Goscha, *Vietnam: Un Etat né de la guerre.*

17. Vo Nguyen Giap, *Muon hieu ro tinh hinh quan su o Tau* (Hanoi: no publisher, 1939); and Truong Chinh, *Khang chien nhat dinh thang loi*, first serialized in the party journal, *Su That*, in 1947. For more on Sino-Vietnamese communist connections, see Greg Lockhart, *Nation in Arms: The Origins of the People's Army of Vietnam* (Sydney: Allen and Unwin, 1989).

18. Goscha, 'A Rougher Side of "Popular" Resistance', in Christopher Goscha and Benoît de Tréglodé, eds., *Naissance d'un État-Parti Le Viêt Nam depuis 1945* (Paris: Les Indes savantes, 2004), pp. 325–53.

19. William Turley, 'Urbanization in War: Hanoi, 1946–1973', *Pacific Affairs*, vol. 48, no. 3 (Autumn 1975), pp. 370–97; and Christopher Goscha, 'Colonial Hanoi and Saigon at War: Social Dynamics of the Viet Minh's "Underground City", 1945–1954', *War in History*, vol. 20, no. 2 (2013), pp. 222–20.

20. Goscha, 'Colonial Hanoi and Saigon at War', p. 246 (for the first citation); and Lucien Bodard, *La Guerre d'Indochine: L'Humiliation* (Paris: Bernard Grasset, 1997), p. 373 (for the second citation).

21. Paul and Marie-Catherine Villatoux. *La République et son armée face au 'péril subversif': Guerre et actions psychologiques (1945–1960)* (Paris: Les Indes savantes, 2005); and Christopher Goscha, 'Vietnam and the World Outside: The Case of Vietnamese Communist Advisors in Laos (1948–1962)', *South East Asian Research*, vol. 12, no. 2 (2004), pp. 141–85.

22. *Annuaire des Etats-Associés, 1953* (Paris: Editions de l'Outre-mer et Havas, 1953), pp. 22, 66, 68. Quote from Nguyen Cong Luan, *Nationalist in the Viet Nam Wars, Memoirs of a Victim Turned Soldier* (Bloomington: Indiana University Press, 2012), p. 86.

23. To listen to the song and follow the words, (as sung by Duy Quang), see http://www.nhaccuatui.com/bai-hat/ba-me-gio-linh-pham-duy-2005-duy-quang.oiKuIKw51s.html accessed on 15 June 2016. No detailed study of torture during the Indochina War exists, but non-communist Vietnamese memoirs provide terrible accounts of French Union violence. See Nguyen Cong Luan, *Nationalist in the Viet Nam Wars*, pp. 1–87 and Duong Van Mai Elliott, *The Sacred Willow* (New York: Oxford University Press, 1999), pp. 148–9 for one example of many. For a Vietnamese account of the My Trach massacre, see: 'Vu Tham Sat Lang My Trach', at http://www2.quangbinh.gov.vn/3cms/?cmd=130&art=1186213703100&cat=1179730730203; and Goscha, *Historical Dictionary*, p. 302.

24. On the population increase of Saigon, see: http://recherche-iedes.univ-paris1.fr/IMG/pdf/200206GubryLeThiHuongPresentationHCMV.pdf, accessed 19 June 2013. For deaths on the Vietnamese side during the Indochina War, see: Ngo Van Chieu, *Journal d'un combattant Viet-Minh*, p. 106; R. J. Rummel provides a very similar number based on an analysis of available Western sources. See http://www.hawaii.edu/powerkills/SOD.CHAP6.HTM, accessed 17 June 2013. For the one million estimate for total Vietnamese deaths during the First Indochina War, see Bernard Fall, 'This Isn't Munich, It's Spain', *Ramparts* (December 1965), p. 23. Given that the DRV administered around ten million people during the conflict, this means it lost 5 percent of its total population. Of the 110,000 French Union deaths, 20,000 French nationals perished, that is 0.05 percent of the total population for 1954 in France (43 million). I am unaware of any Vietnamese attempt to assassinate French officials, sabotage French military installations, bomb or harm

French civilians *in France*, though the DRV did assassinate Vietnamese enemies there. My thanks to Shawn McHale for help on this.

25. Nguyen Cong Luan, *Nationalist in the Viet Nam Wars*, p. 79.

26. Ibid., chapters 6 and 7; Michel Bodin, *Les Africains dans la guerre d'Indochine, 1947–1954* (Paris: L'Harmattan, 2000); and Henri Amoureux, *Croix sur l'Indochine* (Paris: Editions Domat, 1955), p. 33 (for the number of children left behind).

27. I rely here on David Marr, *Vietnam: State, War, and Revolution (1945–46)* (Berkeley: University of California Press, 2013); Bernard Fall, *Le Viet Minh* (Paris: Librairie Armand Colin, 1960); and Goscha, *Vietnam: Un Etat né de la guerre*.

28. 'Oral History Interview of Dinh Xuan Ba, Entrepreneur and Former Assault Youth Member', DVD 03, Hanoi, 5 June 2007 (by Merle Pribbenow).

29. See the ministerial decision of 31 August 1945 in *Viet Nam Dan Quoc Cong Bao* (29 September 1945), p. 13.

30. Politically astute Vietnamese may not have recognized Ho Chi Minh in August–September 1945, but they certainly knew from the Popular Front days that Vo Nguyen Giap, Truong Chinh, Tran Huy Lieu and others running the DRV were ICP members.

31. See Marr, *Vietnam: State, War, and Revolution (1945–46)*, chapter 2.

32. Fall, *Le Viet Minh*, pp. 51–2.

33. Fall, *Le Viet Minh*, pp. 76–79, and Goscha, *Vietnam: Un Etat né de la guerre*, chapter 2.

CHAPTER 9. INTERNATIONALIZED STATES OF WAR

1. I rely on Devillers, *Histoire du Vietnam de 1940 à 1952*; his Book 8, 'Vietnam', in Devillers et al., *L'Asie du Sud-Est*, vol. 2 (Paris: Sirey, 1971), pp. 791–847; his *Vingt ans et plus avec le Viet-Nam, 1945–1969* (Paris: Les Indes savantes, 2010); and Dalloz, *La Guerre d'Indochine, 1945–1954*.

2. Pignon's quote cited in Christopher Goscha, 'Le Premier Echec contre-révolution-naire au Vietnam' (Paris: Mémoire de DEA, Université de Paris VII, 1994), notes 119–20, at p. 38. D'Argenlieu quote cited by Devillers, *Histoire du Vietnam de 1940 à 1952*, p. 367.

3. Claire Tran Thi Lien, 'Les Catholiques vietnamiens pendant la guerre d'indépendance (1945–1954): Entre la reconquête coloniale et la résistance communiste', PhD dissertation (Paris: Institut d'études politiques, 1996); Charles Keith, *Catholic Vietnam: A Church from Empire to Nation* (Berkeley: University of California Press, 2012), pp. 208–41. The French knew, too, that Catholics were often anticolonialists. François Méjan, *Le Vatican contre la France d'outre-mer?* (Paris: Librairie Fischbacher, 1957), pp. 122–30.

4. What the latter couldn't know was that George Bidault's party would maintain that stance all the way to the conference table in Geneva. Jacques Dalloz, 'L'Opposition M.R.P. à la guerre d'Indochine', *Revue d'histoire moderne et contemporaine*, vol. 43, no 1 (January–March 1996), pp. 106–18.

5. On non-communist nationalism and nationalist parties, see François Guillemot, *Dai Viêt, indépendance et révolution au Viêt-Nam: L'Echec de la troisième voie (1938–1955)* (Paris: Les Indes savantes, 2012). On the genesis of the Associated State of Vietnam, see: Marie-Thérèse Blanchet, *La Naissance de l'Etat associé du Viet-Nam* (Paris: Editions M.-Th. Génin, 1954).

6. I have been unable to locate the exact contents of the 'secret protocol'. French

scholar Philippe Devillers states, however, that they limited the Associated State of Vietnam's independence.

7. On Léon Pignon, see Daniel Varga, 'La Politique française en Indochine (1947–50): Histoire d'une décolonisation manquée', PhD dissertation (Aix-en-Provence: Université d'Aix-Marseille I, 2004), and his 'Léon Pignon, l'homme-clé de la solution Bao Dai et de l'implication des États-Unis dans la Guerre d'Indochine', *Outre-mers*, nos. 364–5 (December 2009), pp. 277–313.

8. Christopher Goscha, 'Le Contexte asiatique de la guerre franco-vietnamienne: réseaux, relations et économie (1945–1954)', PhD dissertation (Paris: Ecole Pratique des Hautes Etudes, 2000), section Indochine. On the creation of the Associated State of Laos, see Jean Deuve, *Le Royaume du Laos* (Paris: L'Harmattan, 2003).

9. Lucien Bodard, *La Guerre d'Indochine* (Paris: Bernard Grasset, 1997), p. 131.

10. Varga, 'Léon Pignon, l'homme-clé de la solution Bao Dai', pp. 277–313; Mark Atwood Lawrence, *Assuming the Burden: Europe and the American Commitment to War in Vietnam* (Berkeley: University of California Press, 2005), and his 'Recasting Vietnam: The Bao Dai Solution and the Outbreak of the Cold War in Southeast Asia', in Christopher Goscha and Christian Ostermann, eds., *Connecting Histories: Decolonization and the Cold War in Southeast Asia (1945–1962)* (Stanford: Stanford University Press, 2009), pp. 15–38.

11. Léon Pignon, 'Reconnaissance de Ho Chi Minh par Mao Tse Tung', pp. 10–11, 24 January 1950, no. 16/PS/CAB, signed Léon Pignon, dossier 6, box 11, series XIV, SLOTFOM, Centre des Archives d'Outre-mer, France.

12. Matthew Connelly, *A Diplomatic Revolution: Algeria's Fight for Independence and the Origins of the Post-Cold War Era* (New York: Oxford University Press, 2002).

13. Bodard, *La Guerre d'Indochine*, p. 153.

14. Ellen Hammer, *The Struggle for Indochina* (Stanford: Stanford University Press, 1966), p. 246; Bodard, *La Guerre d'Indochine*, p. 502; Christopher Goscha, 'Colonial Kings and the Decolonization of the French Empire: Bao Dai, Mohammed V, and Norodom Sihanouk', forthcoming; and Bui Diem, *In the Jaws of History* (Bloomington: Indiana University Press, 1999), pp. 67–70.

15. For the international context, see among others: Laurent Césari, *Le Problème diplomatique de l'Indochine, 1945–1957* (Paris: Les Indes savantes, 2013); Pierre Grosser, 'La France et l'Indochine (1953–1956). Une "carte de visite" en "peau de chagrin"', PhD dissertation (Paris: Institut d'études politiques, 2002); Mark Thompson, 'Defending the Rhine in Asia: France's 1951 Reinforcement Debate and French International Ambitions', *French Historical Studies*, vol. 38, no. 3 (August 2015), pp. 473–99 (p. 473 for the citation); Lawrence Kaplan, 'The United States, NATO, and French Indochina', in Lawrence Kaplan and Denise Artaud, *Dien Bien Phu and the Crisis of Franco-American Relations, 1954–1955* (Wilmington: Scholarly Resources, 1990); and Jasmine Aimaq, *For Europe or Empire?*, PhD dissertation (Lund: Lund University, 1994).

16. Goscha, 'Le Contexte asiatique', section Indochine. During his travels through the DRV in the early 1950s, American communist Joseph Starobin confirms the linkage between the French and DRV 'associated states'. Joseph Starobin, *Eyewitness in Indo-China* (New York: Cameron & Kahn, 1954), pp. 50, 61–3.

17. 'L'Union française et les Etats Associés de l'Indochine', speech by Albert Sarraut opening the Conference of Pau, October 1950, p. 20.

18. Tuong Vu, 'From Cheering to Volunteering: Vietnamese Communists and the

Coming of the Cold War, 1940–1951', in Goscha and Ostermann, eds., *Connecting Histories*, pp. 172–206; Goscha, 'Choosing between the Two Vietnams: 1950', in Goscha and Ostermann, eds., *Connecting Histories*, pp. 207–37; Goscha, 'Courting Diplomatic Disaster? The Difficult Integration of Vietnam into the Internationalist Communist Movement (1945–1950)', *Journal of Vietnamese Studies*, vol. 1, nos. 1–2 (Fall 2006), pp. 59–103.

19. For the Chinese side, I rely on Chen Jian, *Mao's China and the Cold War* (Chapell Hill: The University of North Carolina Press, 2001); and Qiang Zhai, *China and the Vietnam Wars, 1950–1975* (Chapel Hill: The University of North Carolina Press, 2000).

20. Goscha, *Vietnam: Un Etat né de la guerre*.

21. Benoît de Tréglodé, *Heroes and Revolution in Vietnam* (Singapore: National University of Singapore Press, 2012); Georges Boudarel, 'L'Idéocratie importée au Vietnam avec le maoïsme', in Daniel Hémery et al., *La Bureaucratie au Vietnam* (Paris: L'Harmattan, 1983), pp. 31–106; and Goscha, *Vietnam: Un Etat né de la guerre,* pp. 434–49.

22. Ngo Van Chieu, *Journal d'un combatant Viet-Minh*, pp. 154–5.

23. Nguyen Cong Hoan, in David Chanoff and Doan Van Toai, *'Vietnam': A Portrait of Its People at War*, 2nd edn (London: Tauris Park Paperbacks, 2009), p. 13.

24. Cited in Goscha, *Historical Dictionary*, p. 304.

25. Cited in Goscha, *Vietnam: Un Etat né de la guerre*, pp. 428–9.

26. Nguyen Ngoc Minh, ed., *Kinh te Viet Nam tu cach mang thang tam den khang chien thang loi (1945–1954)* (Hanoi: Nha Xuat Ban Khoa Hoc, 1966), p. 359, and note 16; Christian Lentz, 'Making the Northwest Vietnamese', *Journal of Vietnamese Studies*, vol. 6, no. 2 (2011), pp. 68–105; his 'Mobilization and State Formation on a Frontier of Vietnam', *Journal of Peasant Studies*, vol. 38, no. 3 (2011), pp. 559–86.

27. Nguyen Ngoc Minh, *Kinh te*, p. 355. Quote from Thanh Huyen Dao, ed., *Dien Bien Phu vu d'en face, paroles de bo doi* (Paris: Nouveau Monde Editions, 2010), p. 37.

28. *Annuaire des Etats-Associés, 1953* (Paris: Editions de l'outre-mer et Havas, 1953), pp. 68–70.

29. Maurice Rives, 'Les Supplétifs indochinois', in Yves Jeanclos, ed., *La France et les soldats d'infortune au XXe siècle* (Paris: Economica, 2003), p. 211–20; Michel Bodin, 'Les Supplétifs du Tonkin, 1946–1954', *Revue historique des Armées*, no. 194 (1994), p. 17; and Ivan Cadeau, *Dien Bien Phu, 13 mars–7 mai 1954* (Paris: Tallandier, 2013).

30. The three classic and unsurpassed studies of the battle of Dien Bien Phu remain to this day: Bernard Fall, *Hell in a Very Small Place* (Cambridge: Da Capo Press, 2002, reprinted); Pierre Rocolle, *Pourquoi Dien Bien Phu?* (Paris: Flammarion, 1968); and Jules Roy, *The Battle of Dien Bien Phu*, 2nd edn (New York: Carroll & Graf Publishers, 2002 (first published in the French in 1963)).

31. Goscha, *Vietnam: Un Etat né de la guerre,* chapter 10 and conclusion.

32. The classic account of Vo Nguyen Giap's decision to cancel the January attack is Georges Boudarel and François Caviglioli, 'Comment Giap a failli perdre la bataille de Dien Bien Phu', *Nouvel Observateur* (8 April 1983), pp. 35–6, 90–92, 97–100. See also Christopher Goscha, 'Building Force: Asian Origins of 20th Century Military Science in Vietnam (1905–1954)', *Journal of Southeast Asian Studies*, vol. 34, no. 3 (2003), pp. 535–60; and Goscha, *Vietnam: Un Etat né de la guerre,* chapters 9, 10 and conclusion.

33. John Prados, *Operation Vulture* (New York: Ibooks, 2002).

34. Goscha, *Historical Dictionary*, pp. 389 and 165.

35. The classic study of the Geneva negotiations on Indochina remains François

Joyaux's *La Chine et le règlement du premier conflit d'Indochine, Genève 1954* (Paris: Publications de la Sorbonne, 1979).

36. Pierre Asselin, 'The Democratic Republic of Vietnam and the 1954 Geneva Conference: A Revisionist Critique', *Cold War History*, vol. 11, no. 2 (2011), pp. 155–95; his 'Choosing Peace: Hanoi and the Geneva Agreement on Vietnam, 1954–55', *Journal of Cold War Studies*, vol. 9, no. 2 (2007), pp. 95–126; Goscha, *Vietnam: Un Etat né de la guerre,* chapters 9, 10, conclusion; Goscha, 'A Total War of Decolonization?', in *War & Society,* vol. 31, no. 2 (August 2012), pp. 136–62; Goscha, 'Cold War and Decolonisation in the Assault on the Vietnamese Body at Dien Bien Phu', *European Journal of East Asian Studies,* vol. 9, no. 2 (2010), pp. 201–23.

37. Christopher Goscha, 'Geneva 1954 and the "De-internationalization" of the Vietnamese Idea of Indochina?', paper delivered during the conference entitled New Evidence on the 1954 Geneva Conference on Indochina, Cold War International History Project 2006, Washington DC, 17–18 February 2006, unpublished paper, pp. 1–47.

38. Ibid.

39. Qiang Zhai, *China and the Vietnam Wars,* pp. 58–60; Chen Jian, *Mao's China and the Cold War,* pp. 142–3.

40. See note 36 for the evidence.

CHAPTER 10. A TALE OF TWO REPUBLICS

1. Neil Jamieson, *Understanding Vietnam* (Berkeley: University of California Press, 1995), pp. 241–446.

2. For this section, I rely heavily on François Guillemot, *Dai Viet, indépendance et révolution au Viet-Nam* (Paris: Les Indes savantes, 2012); Jessica Chapman, *Cauldron of Resistance: Ngo Dinh Diem, the United States, and 1950s Southern Vietnam* (Ithaca: Cornell University Press, 2013); Ellen Hammer, *The Struggle for Indochina* (Stanford: Stanford University Press, 1966); Arthur Dommen, *The Indochinese Experience of the French and the Americans* (Bloomington: Indiana University Press, 2001); and Edward Miller, 'Vision, Power and Agency: The Ascent of Ngo Dinh Diem, 1945–54', *Journal of Southeast Asian Studies,* vol. 35, no. 3 (October 2004), pp. 433–58.

3. Dommen, *The Indochinese Experience,* pp. 282–3. Kennedy quote cited by Dommen, *The Indochinese Experience,* p. 213; and on Kennedy's visit to French Indochina, see especially Fredrik Logevall, *Embers of War* (New York: Random House, 2012), pp. xi–xxii.

4. Miller, 'Vision, Power, Agency', pp. 433–58.

5. Ibid. (citation at page 446).

6. John Hellman, *Emmanuel Mounier and the New Catholic Left* (Toronto: University of Toronto, 1981); and Michel Winock, *Esprit* (Paris: Editions du Seuil, 1996).

7. Bao Dai, *Le Dragon d'Annam* (Paris: Plon, 1980), pp. 328–9 (for the citation). American diplomatic historian Seth Jacobs insists in his book on Ngo Dinh Diem that '[f]rom the beginning, Diem's government was an American creation'. Seth Jacobs, *America's Miracle Man in Vietnam: Ngo Dinh Diem, Religion, Race, and U.S. Intervention in Southeast Asia* (Durham, NC: Duke University Press, 2004). See the round table on this book (p. 26 for the citation) at http://h-diplo.org/roundtables/PDF/AmericasMiracleMan-Roundtable.pdf, accessed 29 August 2015. This is a very American-centered view.

8. Pierre Grosser, 'La France et l'Indochine (1953–1956)', PhD dissertation (Paris:

Institut d'Etudes politiques de Paris, 2002). On French policy toward German rearmament and the European army, see William Hitchcock, *France Restored* (Chapel Hill: University of North Carolina Press, 1998), chapters 5–6.

9. Cited by Philip Catton, *Diem's Final Failure* (Lawrence: University Press of Kansas, 2002), p. 7.

10. John Prados, 'The Numbers Game: How Many Vietnamese Fled South in 1954?', *The VVA Veteran* (January/February 2005), at http://www.vva.org/archive/TheVeteran /2005_01/feature_numbersGame.htm, accessed 16 September 2013.

11. Nguyen Cong Luan, *Nationalist in the Vietnam Wars* (Bloomington: Indiana University Press, 2012), pp. 135–6 (for the citation).

12. Duong Van Mai Elliott, *The Sacred Willow* (New York: Oxford University Press, 1999), pp. 240–42 (for the first citation); and Goscha, *Historical Dictionary*, pp. 297–8 (on Jean Moreau).

13. On the early years of the Republic of Vietnam, I rely on the following: Catton, *Diem's Final Failure*; Edward Miller, *Misalliance: Ngo Dinh Diem, the United States, and the Fate of South Vietnam* (Cambridge, MA: Harvard University Press, 2013); Dommen, *The Indochinese Experience*; Chapman, *Cauldron of Resistance*; and Nu-Anh Tran, 'Contested Identities: Nationalism in the Republic of Vietnam (1954–1963)', PhD dissertation (Berkeley: University of California, 2013).

14. The domino theory holds that if Vietnam falls to communism then the rest of Asia goes as well. It is no accident that Pakistan was a member of both SEATO and the Middle East Treaty Organization created in 1955 (Iran, Iraq, Pakistan, Turkey, and the United Kingdom). Nor is it an accident that India, Burma, and Indonesia were absent from SEATO. Each of these new states had refused Atlantic pressure on them to recognize the Associated State of Vietnam led by Bao Dai or take sides in the Korean War. This also explains why Dulles tended to interpret Indian neutrality as a threat to his web of treaties running along the underside of Eurasia from Baghdad to Manilla.

15. Jean-Jacques Servan-Schreiber, founder of *L'Express* and close to Mendès France, put it this way on 22 July 1953 (citation); Kathryn Statler, *Replacing France: The Origins of American Intervention in Vietnam* (Lexington: University Press of Kentucky, 2009); Fredrik Logevall, *Embers of War*. For a Eurasian perspective instead of an American one, see: Christopher Goscha, 'La Géopolitique vietnamienne vue de l'Eurasie: Quelles leçons de la troisième guerre d'Indochine pour aujourd'hui?', *Hérodote*, no. 157 (2015), pp. 23–38. No one puts their finger on the global, *longue durée* origins of America's informal empire in the Pacific better than William Appleman Williams, *The Tragedy of American Diplomacy* (New York: Norton & Norton, 2009). On early American trading missions visiting the newly created Vietnam born in 1802, see: Robert Hopkins Miller, *The United States and Vietnam, 1787–1941* (Honolulu: University Press of the Pacific, 2005).

16. He was the son of Nguyen Van Tam discussed earlier in this book.

17. Officers now had the task of keeping Algeria French.

18. Phi Van Nguyen, 'Les Résidus de la guerre: La Mobilisation des réfugiés du Nord pour un Vietnam non-communiste, 1954–1965', PhD dissertation (Montreal: Université du Québec à Montréal, 2015); Peter Hansen, 'The Virgin Heads South: Northern Catholic Refugees and their Clergy in South Vietnam, 1954–64', in Thomas Dubois, ed., *Casting Faiths: Imperialism and the Transformation of Religion in East and Southeast Asia* (Basingstoke: Palgrave Macmillan, 2009); his 'Bac Di Cu: Catholic Refugees from the North

of Vietnam, and Their Role in the Southern Republic, 1954–1959', *Journal of Vietnamese Studies*, vol. 4, no. 3 (Fall 2009), pp. 173–211; and Van Nguyen Marshall, 'Tools of Empire?' Vietnamese Catholics in South Vietnam', *Journal of the Canadian Historical Association*, vol. 20, no. 2 (2009), p. 138–59.

19. Catton, *Diem's Final Failure*, p. 32. Lansdale's official job was head of the Saigon Military Mission in Saigon. He worked for the CIA.

20. Cited by Mark Lawrence, *The Vietnam War: A Concise International History* (New York: Oxford University Press, 2010), p. 59.

21. Jessica Chapman, 'Staging Democracy: South Vietnam's 1955 Referendum to Depose Bao Dai', *Diplomatic History*, vol. 30, no. 4 (September 2006), pp. 671–703.

22. On the extension of the DRV's state control to all of northern Vietnam after the Geneva conference, see: Fall, *Le Viet-Minh*, pp. 75–85.

23. See Alex-Thai D. Vo, 'Nguyen Thi Nam and the Land Reform in North Vietnam, 1953', *Journal of Vietnamese Studies*, vol. 10, no. 1 (Winter 2015), pp. 1–62.

24. On the land reform, I rely on a new body of scholarship based on Vietnamese and former East Bloc archives. Olivier Tessier, 'Le "grand bouleversement" (*long troi lo dat*): Regards croisés sur la réforme agraire en République démocratique du Viet Nam', *Bulletin de l'Ecole française d'Extrême-Orient*, nos. 95–96 (2008–2009), pp. 73–134; Alex-Thai D. Vo, 'Nguyen Thi Nam and the Land Reform', *Journal of Vietnamese Studies*, pp. 1–62; Alex Holcombe, 'Socialist Transformation in the Democratic Republic of Vietnam', PhD dissertation (Berkeley: University of California at Berkeley, 2014); Balazs Szalontai, 'Political and Economic Crisis in North Vietnam, 1955–56', *Cold War History*, vol. 5, no. 4 (2006), pp. 325–426.

25. Georges Boudarel, *Cent fleurs écloses dans la nuit du Vietnam* (Paris: Editions Jacques Bertoin, 1991), pp. 202–4; Szalontai, 'Political and Economic Crisis in North Vietnam', p. 401. Quote from Nguyen Trong Tan, 'I Know Mr Cu, Mr Dinh, and Many Other Stories that Land Reform Cadre Boi Has Not Told', *Journal of Vietnamese Studies*, vol. 2, no 2 (Summer 2007), pp. 254–5.

26. Fall, *Le Viet Minh*, pp. 102–3 (for the citation on bringing back the dead); Alec Holcombe, 'The Complete Collection of Party Documents: Listening to the Party's Official Voice', *Journal of Vietnamese Studies*, vol. 3, no. 2 (Summer 2010), pp. 231–8. The party's responsibility is what Lise London said that Ho Chi Minh admitted to her and her husband, both victims of Czech Stalinists, during the Vietnamese president's visit to Prague in November 1957. Lise London, *Le Printemps des camarades* (Paris: Editions du Seuil, 1996), pp. 190–94.

27. Nguyen Manh Tuong, *Un excommunié: Hanoi, 1954–1991* (Paris: Que Me, 1991); and Fall, *Le Viet Minh*, p. 104. For an institutional history of the National Assembly in the 1950s, see Bertrand de Hartingh, *Entre le peuple et la nation: La République démocratique du Viet Nam de 1953 à 1957* (Paris: EFEO, 2003).

28. On Vietnamese constitutionalism, see Mark Sidel, *The Constitution of Vietnam: A Contextual Analysis* (Oxford: Hart Publishing, 2009), chapters 1–3 and Fall, *Le Viet Minh*, pp. 45–61, 75–85, 96–106; and Bernard Fall, 'North Vietnam's Constitution and Government', *Pacific Affairs*, vol. 33, no. 3 (1960), p. 282.

29. Fall, *Le Viet Minh*, pp. 55–8; and Szalontai, 'Political and Economic Crisis', p. 412.

30. See Boudarel, *Cent fleurs*; Peter Zinoman, 'Nhan Van Giai Pham and Vietnamese "Reform Communism" in the 1950s: A Revisionist Interpretation', *Journal of Cold War*

Studies, vol 13, no 1 (Winter 2011), pp. 80–100; Kim N. B. Ninh, *World Transformed: The Politics of Culture in Revolutionary Vietnam, 1945–1965* (Ann Arbor: University of Michigan Press, 2002). Created in 1950, the political directorate served, as in Maoist China, to establish the party's control over the army and the training of political commissars for the army. Nguyen Chi Thanh also served with Vo Nguyen Giap on the party's central military committee, the organ placing the PAVN under party leadership.

31. Conversations with liberal-minded Soviet legal experts in Moscow in mid-1956 emboldened Nguyen Mang Tuong in his calls for legal reform. Nguyen Manh Tuong, *Un Excommunié.*

32. Pushing him were Catholics who had suffered during the land reform of 1953–4, and had fled to the south and now wanted to take back that which they had lost. They often pushed Diem and the Vatican much further than either wanted to go. See Phi Van Nguyen, 'Les Résidus de la guerre'. On Tran Duc Thao, see: Philippe Papin, 'Itinéraire II. Les exils intérieurs', in Jocelyn Benoist and Michel Espagne, eds., *L'Itinéraire de Tran Duc Thao, phénoménologie et transferts culturels* (Paris: Armand Colin, 2013), pp. 62–89.

33. Ngo Dinh Diem, 'Statement of June 16, 1949', in *Major Policy Speeches by President Ngo Dinh Diem* (Saigon: Presidency of the Republic of Viet Nam, Press Office, 1957), p. 3. On Diem, his thinking and background, I rely heavily on Miller, *Misalliance* and Catton, *Diem's Final Failure.*

34. Sidel, *The Constitution of Vietnam*, pp. 15–26. On Diem's internal politics, see: Nu Anh-Tran, *Contested Identities: Nationalism in the Republic of Vietnam (RVN), 1954–1963* (forthcoming); and Phi Van Nguyen, 'Les Résidus de la guerre'.

35. Catton, *Diem's Final Failure*, pp. 52–7; and Miller, *Misalliance*, chapters 4–6.

36. Catton, *Diem's Final Failure*, pp. 55–6; and Miller, *Misalliance*, chapters 2, 4–6; and William Turley, *The Second Indochina War*, 2nd edn (Lanham: Rowman & Littlefield Publishers, 2009), pp. 35–8.

37. Catton, *Diem's Final Failure*, pp. 57–63; and Miller, *Misalliance*, chapters 4–6.

38. Turley, *The Second Indochina War*, pp. 35–8.

CHAPTER 11. TOWARD ONE VIETNAM

1. Cited by Martin Grossheim, 'The Lao Dong Party: Culture and the Campaign against Modern Revisionism: The Democratic Republic of Vietnam before the Second Indochina War', *Journal of Vietnamese Studies*, vol. 9, no. 1 (2013), pp. 80–129, p. 94 (for the citation).

2. William Duiker, *Ho Chi Minh* (New York: Hyperion, 2000), pp. 493–4. On Chinese and Soviet policies, I rely on: Mari Olsen, *Soviet–Vietnam Relations and the Role of China, 1949–1964, Changing Alliances* (London: Routledge, 2006); Ilya V. Gaiduk, *Confronting Vietnam: Soviet Policy towards the Indochina Conflict, 1954–1963* (Stanford: Stanford University Press, 2003); Ilya V. Gaiduk, *The Soviet Union and the Vietnam War* (Chicago: Ivan R. Dee, 1996); Qiang Zhai, *China and the Vietnam Wars, 1950–1975* (Chapel Hill: University of North Carolina Press, 2000); Chen Jian, *Mao's China and the Cold War* (Chapel Hill: The University of North Carolina Press, 2001).

3. Carl Thayer, *War by Other Means: National Liberation and Revolution in Viet-Nam, 1954–60* (Sydney: Allen & Unwin, 1990); David Hunt, *Vietnam's Southern Revolution: From Peasant Insurrection to Total War, 1959–1968* (Amherst: University of Massachu-

setts Press, 2009); and especially David Elliott, *The Vietnamese War: Revolution and Social Change in the Mekong Delta, 1930–1975* (Armonk: M. E. Sharpe, 2007) and Jeffrey Race, *War Comes to Long An* (Berkeley: University of California Press, 1972).

4. The Geneva ceasefire regrouped the Pathet Lao into the two northern Lao provinces bordering the DRV, Phongsaly and Samneua. The Royal Lao Government (RLG) was the former Associated State of Laos. See the contributions in Christopher Goscha and Karine Laplante, eds., *The Failure of Peace, 1954–1962* (Paris: Les Indes savantes, 2010).

5. John Prados, *The Blood Road: The Ho Chi Minh Trail and the Vietnam War* (Wiley, 2000); and Christopher Goscha, 'The Maritime Nature of the Wars for Vietnam: (1945–75): A Geo-Historical Reflection', *War & Society*, vol. 24, no. 2 (November 2005), pp. 53–92.

6. Thayer, *War by Other Means*; Robert Brigham, *Guerrilla Diplomacy: The NLF's Foreign Relations and the Viet Nam War* (Ithaca: Cornell University Press, 1999); William S. Turley, *The Second Indochina War*, 2nd edn (Lantham: Rowman & Littlefield, 2009), p. 65. On PAVN troops numbers, see The Military Institute of Vietnam, *Victory in Vietnam*, translated by Merle L. Pribbenow (Lawrence: University Press of Kansas, 2002), p. 311, endnote 6. In all 50,000 military personnel went south between 1959 and 1964, most of them southerners who had regrouped to the north in 1954–5.

7. The PLAF was an institutional part of the PAVN. Turley, *The Second Indochina War*, pp. 45, 63.

8. See among many others: David Kaiser, *American Tragedy: Kennedy, Johnson, and the Origins of the Vietnam War* (Cambridge, MA: Harvard University Press, 2002); and Fredrik Logevall, *Choosing War: The Lost Chance for Peace and the Escalation of War in Vietnam* (Berkeley: University of California Press, 2001).

9. Lorenz Luthi, *The Sino-Soviet Split* (Princeton: Princeton University Press, 2008), chapter 10.

10. Turley, *The Second Indochina War*, p. 62.

11. Lansdale quote cited in Philip Catton, *Diem's Final Failure* (Lawrence: University Press of Kansas, 2002), p. 20. Walt Rostow, *The Stages of Economic Growth: A Non Communist Manifesto* (Cambridge: Cambridge University Press, 1960). Studies of US modernization theory in the global South are numerous. For a useful historiographical account, see Christopher T. Fisher, 'Nation Building and the Vietnam War: A Historiography', *Pacific Historical Review*, vol. 74 (August 2005), pp. 441–56; and Nick Cullather, 'Development? It's History,' *Diplomatic History* 24 (Fall 2000), pp. 641–53. For a study of the Kennedy era, see Michael E. Latham, *Modernization as Ideology: American Social Science and 'Nation Building' in the Kennedy Era* (Chapel Hill: University of North Carolina Press, 2000). For an excellent discussion of the Republic of Vietnam's attempts at modernization, see: Edward Miller, *Misalliance: Ngo Dinh Diem, the United States, and the Fate of South Vietnam* (Cambridge, MA: Harvard University Press, 2013).

12. For more on the difficulties of putting theory into practice, see Miller, *Misalliance*; and Catton, *Diem's Final Failure*.

13. Frances FitzGerald, *Fire in the Lake: The Vietnamese and the Americans in Vietnam* (Boston: Little, Brown & Company, 1972), especially the first section, 'The Vietnamese', pp. 3–230. The American diplomat quote is cited by Catton, *Diem's Final Failure*, p. 24.

14. On France and collaboration, see Henry Rousso, *The Vichy Syndrome* (Cambridge, MA: Harvard University Press, 1991). The *Times of Vietnam* quote as cited by Catton, *Diem's Final Failure*, p. 79.

15. Race, *War Comes to Long An* on the expansion of the NLF in the south.

16. For more on the strategic hamlets project, see Miller, *Misalliance*; and Catton, *Diem's Final Failure*. Vann's quote as cited in Mark Moyar, *Triumph Forsaken: The Vietnam War, 1954–1965* (Cambridge: Cambridge University Press, 2009), p. 194. See also Neil Sheehan, *A Bright Shining Lie: John Paul Vann and America in Vietnam* (New York: Vintage, 1989).

17. Edward Miller, 'Religious Revival and the Politics of Nation Building: Re-interpreting the 1963 "Buddhist Crisis" in South Vietnam', *Modern Asian Studies* (August 2014), pp. 1–60; Phi Van Nguyen, 'Les Résidus de la guerre'; and Giac Duc, in Chanoff and Toai, *Vietnam*, pp. 39–40.

18. See John Prados, 'Ngo Dinh Diem in the Crosshairs', National Security Archives (2 October 2013), http://nsarchive.wordpress.com/2013/10/02/ngo-dinh-diem-in-the -crosshairs, accessed 21 October 2013. See also his 'Kennedy Considered Supporting Coup in South Vietnam, August 1963', ibid., at http://www2.gwu.edu/~nsarchiv/NSAEBB/ NSAEBB302, accessed 21 October 2013. The coup (though not the assassination) had received a green light from Kennedy.

19. Judy Stowe, 'Révisionnisme au Vietnam', *Communisme*, nos. 65/6 (2001), pp. 233–52; Martin Grossheim, 'Revisionism in the Democratic Republic of Vietnam: New Evidence from the East German Archives', *Cold War History*, vol. 5, no. 4 (2006); Pierre Asselin, *Hanoi's Road to the Vietnam War, 1954–1965* (Berkeley: University of California Press, 2013); Lien-Hang T. Nguyen, *Hanoi's War: An International History of the War for Peace in Vietnam* (Chapel Hill: University of North Carolina Press, 2012); Ang Cheng Guan, *The Vietnam War from the Other Side* (London: Routledge/Curzon, 2002); and Ralph Smith, 'Ho Chi Minh's Last Decade, 1960–69', *Indochina Report*, no. 27 (April June 1991), unpaginated.

20. On the question of conventional vs. guerilla war, see Christopher Goscha, '"A Total War" of Decolonization? Social Mobilization and State-Building in Communist Vietnam (1949–54)', *War & Society*, vol. 31, no. 2 (October 2012), pp. 136–62.

21. Using the Party's recently published documents, Pierre Asselin and Lien-Hang Nguyen have provided us the most up-to-date version of this debate. See: Asselin, *Hanoi's Road to the Vietnam War*; and Nguyen, *Hanoi's War*.

22. Turley, *The Second Indochina War*, p. 83.

23. Nguyen Chi Thanh sent the famous army writer and veteran of Dien Bien Phu, Tran Dan, to re-education camp for daring to call into question the army's war.

24. See among others: Larry Berman, *Lyndon Johnson's War: The Road to Stalemate in Vietnam* (New York: W. W. Norton, 1991); Logevall, *Choosing War*; and Michael Hunt, *Lyndon Johnson's War: America's Cold War Crusade in Vietnam, 1945–1968* (New York: Hill and Wang, 1997).

25. For a detailed, often counterfactual account of Johnson's decision-making, see Logevall, *Choosing War*.

26. On Le Duc Tho's angry reply to non-communist southerners in his entourage in 1949, see: Goscha, *Vietnam: Un Etat né de la guerre,* p. 88.

27. Chen Jian, 'China and the Vietnam Wars', in Peter Lowe, ed., *The Vietnam War* (New York: St Martin's Press, 1998), pp. 170–75; and Qiang Zhai, *China and the Vietnam Wars*, pp. 134–9.

28. Peter Busch argues that British support for Kennedy in Vietnam was intense: *All the Way with JFK?* (Oxford: Oxford University Press, 2003). Malaya became independent in 1957, Singapore in 1965. Turley, *The Second Indochina War*, pp. 98–9. For the mercenary view, see Logevall, *Choosing War* and Robert Blackburn, *Mercenaries and Lyndon Johnson's 'More Flags'* (McFarland & Co., 1994). For a non-mercenary approach, see Richard Ruth, *In Buddha's Company: Thai Soldiers in the Vietnam War* (Honolulu: University of Hawai'i Press, 2010).

29. Turley, *The Second Indochina War*, p. 110.

30. Vu Hung, in Chanoff and Toai, *Vietnam*, p. 160 (for the citation).

31. Fall, 'This Isn't Munich, It's Spain', p. 27. Ibid., p. 24. On the bombing of Cambodia, see: Taylor Owen and Ben Kiernan, 'Bombs over Cambodia', *The Walrus* (October 2006) at http://www.yale.edu/cgp/Walrus_CambodiaBombing_OCT06.pdf, accessed 28 August 2015. For Laos, see Vatthana Pholsena, 'Life under Bombing in Southeastern Laos (1964–1973) through the Accounts of Survivors in Sepon', *European Journal of East Asian Studies*, vol. 9, no. 2 (2010), pp. 267–90; and Turley, *The Second Indochina War*, p. 123. Helping the Americans in the air war were partner countries, such as Australia, New Zealand and the Republic of Vietnam. North Korea flew jets for the DRV.

32. Truong Nhu Tang, with David Chanoff and Doan Van Toai, *A Viet Cong Memoir* (New York: Vintage Books, 1986), pp. 167–8.

33. Citations come from Huong Van Ba, in Chanoff and Toai, *Vietnam*, p. 154; Tran Xuan Niem, in Chanoff and Toai, *Vietnam*, p. 67; Le Thanh, in Chanoff and Toai, *Vietnam*, pp. 63–4; and Xuan Vu, in Chanoff and Toai, *Vietnam*, p. 186.

34. For Hanoi's total death count, see: *Lich su Khang Chien Chong My Cuu Nuoc, 1954–1975, tap VIII Toan Thang* (Hanoi: Nha Xuat Ban Chinh Tri Quoc Gia, 2008), p. 463 (my thanks to Merle Pribbenow for bringing this document to my attention). If one accepts Bernard Fall's estimate that as many as one million people died during the First Indochina War, the total loss of Vietnamese life exceeds four million for the period between 1945 and 1975. Fall, 'This Isn't Munich, It's Spain', p. 23. On Bernard Fall, see: my 'Sorry about that . . . Bernard Fall, the Vietnam War and the Impact of a French Intellectual in the U.S.', in Christopher Goscha and Maurice Vaïsse, eds. *La Guerre du Vietnam et l'Europe (1963–1973)* (Brussels: Bruylant, 2003), pp. 363–82.

35. On the Phoenix Program, see Dale Andradé, *Ashes to Ashes: The Phoenix Program and the Vietnam War* (Lexington: Lexington Books, 1990); Mark Moyar, *Phoenix and the Birds of Prey* (Lincoln: University of Nebraska Press, 1997); and Race, *War Comes to Long An*. On war-driven urbanization, see: Samuel Huntington, 'The Bases of Accommodation', *Foreign Affairs*, vol. 46, no. 4 (July 1968), p. 652; Tam Quach-Langlet, 'Saigon, capitale de la République du Sud Vietnam (1954–1975): Ou une urbanisation sauvage', P. B. Lafont, ed., *Péninsule indochinoise, études urbaines* (Paris: L'Harmattan, 1991), pp. 185–206; and Nguyen Van Thich, in Chanoff and Toai, *Vietnam*, p. 170 (for the citation).

36. Nguyen Tan Thanh, in Chanoff and Toai, *Vietnam*, pp. 44–5.

37. François Guillemot, 'Death and Suffering at First Hand: Youth Shock Brigades during the Vietnam War, 1950–1975', *Journal of Vietnamese Studies*, vol. 4, no. 3 (Fall 2009), pp. 17–63; and François Guillemot, *Des Vietnamiennes dans la guerre civile. L'Autre Moitié de la guerre. 1945–1975* (Paris: Les Indes savantes, 2014).

38. The bibliography on the Tet Offensive is massive. I've relied mainly on the

following: James H. Willbanks, *The Tet Offensive: A Concise History* (New York: Columbia University Press, 2007); Turley, *The Second Indochina War*, pp. 143–4; Merle Pribbenow, 'General Vo Nguyen Giap and the Mysterious Evolution of the Plan for the 1968 Tet Offensive', *Journal of Vietnamese Studies*, vol. 1, no. 2 (Summer 2008), pp. 1–33; Lien-Hang T. Nguyen, 'The War Politburo: North Vietnam's Diplomatic and Political Road to the Tet Offensive', *Journal of Vietnamese Studies*, vol. 1, nos. 1–2 (Fall 2006), pp. 4–58; Sophie Quinn-Judge, 'The Ideological Debate in the DRV and the Significance of the Anti-Party Affair, 1967–1968', *Cold War History*, vol. 5, no. 4 (2005), pp. 479–500; and Lien-Hang T. Nguyen, *Hanoi's War*.

39. This is known as the Khe Sanh riddle: Why did the PAVN commit to Khe Sanh instead of the Tet offensive on southern cities? Did the high command seek to fight a 'Dien Bien Phu' at Khe Sanh or was it just a diversion? Ray Stubbe and John Prados, *Valley of Decision: The Siege of Khe Sanh* (New York: Houghton Mifflin, 1991). On Europe and the Vietnam War, see Goscha and Vaïsse, eds., *La Guerre du Vietnam et l'Europe*.

40. Again, the bibliography on the end of the war is massive. See among others: Larry Berman, *No Peace, No Honor: Nixon, Kissinger and Betrayal in Vietnam* (New York: The Free Press, 2001); Jeffrey Kimball, *Nixon's Vietnam War* (Lawrence: University of Kansas Press, 1998), Ang Cheng Guan, *Ending the Vietnam War* (London: Routledge/Curzon, 2004); Pierre Asselin, *A Bitter Peace: Washington, Hanoi, and the Making of the Paris Agreement* (Chapel Hill: The University of North Carolina Press, 2002); and Lorenz Luthi, 'Beyond Betrayal: Beijing, Moscow, and the Paris Negotiations, 1971–1973', *Journal of Cold War Studies*, vol. 11, no. 1 (Winter 2009), pp. 57–107.

41. See the party documents in *Van Kien Dang, Toan Tap*, vol. 29 (1968) (Hanoi: Nha Xuat Ban Chinh Tri Quoc Gia, 2004), pp. 164–6, 243; Vo Van Sung, *Chien Dich Ho Chi Minh giua long Paris* (Hanoi: Nha Xuat Ban Quan Doi Nhan Dan, 2005), pp. 32–7; and Nguyen Dinh Bin, *Ngoai Giao Viet Nam, 1945–2000* (Hanoi: Nha Xuat Ban Chinh Tri Quoc Gia, 2002), p. 283. On the NLF and the PRG more generally, see Brigham, *Guerrilla Diplomacy*.

42. Xuan Vu, in Chanoff and Toai, *Vietnam*, p. 187. Turley, *The Second Indochina War*, for the numbers, see pp. 177–8; and Charles Stuart Callison, *Land-to-the-Tiller in the Mekong Delta* (Lanham: University Press of America, 1983).

43. See Dale Andradé, *America's Last Vietnam Battle* (Lawrence: University of Press, 2001).

44. The Military Institute of Vietnam, *Victory in Vietnam*, p. 339. On Hanoi's relationship with the PRG and other political entities in the south, see: documents in *Van Kien Dang, Toan Tap*, vol. 30 (1969) (Hanoi: Nha Xuat Ban Chinh Tri Quoc Gia, 2004), pp. 188–90.

45. Asselin, *A Bitter Peace*; Berman, *No Peace, No Honor*; Jeffrey Kimball, 'Decent Interval or Not? The Paris Agreement and the End of the Vietnam War.', *Passport*, vol. 34, no. 3 (December 2003), pp. 26–31; J. Veith, *Black April: The Fall of South Vietnam, 1973–75* (New York: Encounter Books, 2012), pp. 35–52, J. Veith, 'A Short Road to Hell: Thieu, South Vietnam and the Paris Peace Accords', in Nathalie Huynh Chau Nguyen, ed., *New Perceptions of the Vietnam War* (Jefferson: McFarland & Company, 2014), pp. 21–40. Veith cites scores of communist and non-communist Vietnamese documents to make his case.

46. Communist documents do not confirm the widespread myth that the ARVN was a military pushover. See Veith, *Black April*. Lorenz Luthi has nuanced the idea that the

Chinese and Soviets 'sold out' Hanoi in the early 1970s. See: Lüthi, 'Beyond Betrayal', pp. 57–107.

CHAPTER 12. CULTURAL CHANGE IN THE
LONG TWENTIETH CENTURY

1. Olga Dror, *Mourning Headband for Hue: An Account of the Battle for Hue, Vietnam 1968* (Bloomington: Indiana University Press, 2014) and her excellent introductory essay.

2. Nguyen The Anh, 'The Vietnamization of the Cham Deity Po Nagar'.

3. David Marr, *Tradition on Trial (1920–1945)* (Berkeley: University of California Press, 1984), p. 33–4; and Nguyen Du, *The Kim Vân Kieu of Nguyen Du (1765–1820)*, translated by Vladislav Zhukov (Ithaca: Cornell Southeast Asia Program, 2013).

4. For a discussion of the *Romance of the Three Kingdoms* in Vietnam, see Woodside, *Community and Revolution*, pp. 33–4.

5. Neil Jamieson, *Understanding Vietnam* (Berkeley: University of California Press, 1995), p. 67.

6. On the failure of *Nom*, see Marr, *Tradition*, pp. 141–3, 145–8.

7. Marr, *Tradition*, p. 35; and Hue-Tam Ho Tai, *Radicalism*, pp. 33–7, 98.

8. Tracy Barrett, 'A Bulwark Never Failing: The Evolution of Overseas Chinese Education in French Indochina, 1900–1954', in Sherman Cochran and Paul Pickowicz, eds., *China on the Margins* (New York: East Asia Program, Cornell University, 2009), pp. 221–42.

9. Agathe Larcher, 'D'un réformisme à l'autre: La redécouverte de l'identité culturelle vietnamienne, 1900–1930', Série Etudes et Documents Etudes indochinoises IV (May 1995), pp. 85–96.

10. Marr, *Tradition*, p. 35; Hue-Tam Ho Tai, *Radicalism*, pp. 33–7; and Alexander Woodside, 'The Development of Social Organizations in Vietnamese Cities in the Late Colonial Period', *Pacific Affairs*, vol. 44, no. 1 (1971), pp. 39–64.

11. Claire Tran Thi Lien, 'Henriette Bui: The Narrative of Vietnam's First Woman Doctor', in Gisèle Bousquet and Pierre Brocheux, eds., *Vietnam Exposé* (Ann Arbor: The University of Michigan Press, 2002), pp. 278–309.

12. Emmanuelle Affidi, 'Vulgarisation du savoir et colonisation des esprits par la presse et le livre en Indochine française et dans les Indes néerlandaises (1908–1936)', *Moussons*, nos. 13–14 (2009), pp. 95–121, and her 'Créer des passerelles entre les mondes . . . L'œuvre interculturelle de Nguyen Van Vinh (1882–1936)', *Moussons*, no. 21 (2014), pp. 33–55; and Marr, *Tradition*, pp. 31–8.

13. Hue-Tam Ho Tai, *Radicalism*, p. 121; Marr, *Tradition*, p. 176; and Haydon Cherry, 'Traffic in Translations: Dao Duy Anh and the Vocabulary of Vietnamese Marxism', Association for Asian Studies Annual Conference, San Diego, California (21–24 March 2013), copy kindly provided by Dr Cherry.

14. Marguerite Duras, *Cahiers de la guerre* (Paris: POL Editeurs, 2006), p. 92; and Hazel Hahn, 'The Rickshaw Trade in Colonial Vietnam, 1883–1940', *Journal of Vietnamese Studies*, vol. 8, no. 4 (Fall 2013), pp. 47–85.

15. Jamieson, *Understanding Vietnam*, p. 101 (for the citation); Nguyen Van Ky, *La Société vietnamienne face à la modernité* (Paris: L'Harmattan, 1995); and Martina Nguyen,

'The Self-Reliant Literary Group (Tu Luc Van Doan): Colonial Modernism in Vietnam, 1932–1941', PhD dissertation (Berkeley: University of California at Berkeley, 2013).

16. Greg Lockhart, *The Light of the Capital: Three Modern Vietnamese Classics* (Oxford: Oxford University Press, 1996), p. 122; Erica Peters, 'Manger: pratiques vietnamiennes et identités européennes', in François Guillemot and Agathe Larcher-Goscha, *La Colonisation des corps, de l'Indochine au Viet Nam* (Paris: Vendémiaire, 2014), pp. 176–99. The tobacco used is called *Nicotiana rustica*, also known in South America as *mapacho*. Mark McLeod and Nguyen Thi Dieu, *Culture and Customs of Vietnam* (Greenwood, 2001), p. 130 (for the citation); and Nguyen Xuan Hien et al., 'La Chique de bétel au Viet-Nam: Les récentes mutations d'une tradition millénaire', *Péninsule*, no. 58 (2009), pp. 73–125.

17. I rely here on Nguyen Van Ky, *La Société vietnamienne face à la modernité. Le Tonkin de la fin du XIXe siècle à la Seconde Guerre mondiale* (Paris: L'Harmattan, 1995); and Martina Nguyen in her PhD dissertation, 'The Self-Reliant Literary Group'.

18. On non-Western conceptions of the individual, see: Jack Goody, *The Theft of History* (Cambridge: Cambridge University Press, 2012).

19. Lai Nguyen An, ed., *Phan Khoi viet va dich Lo Tan* (Hanoi: Nha Xuat Ban Hoi Nha Van, 2007). My thanks to Peter Zinoman for bringing this publication to my attention.

20. Cited by Daniel Hémery; 'L'Homme, un itinéraire vietnamien. Humanisme et sujet humain au XXe siècle', *Moussons*, nos. 13–14 (2009), pp. 11–12.

21. Ibid., p. 13.

22. Nguyen Van Ky, *La Société vietnamienne*; and George Dutton, 'Ly Toet in the City: Coming to Terms with the Modern in 1930s Vietnam', *Journal of Vietnamese Studies*, vol. 2, no. 1 (February 2007), pp. 80–108.

23. Jamieson, *Understanding Vietnam*, p. 106.

24. Ibid., p. 119 (for the citation).

25. Ibid., pp. 144–5 (for the citations).

26. However, the transition to the use of *tôi* was a slow process and it remained biased towards women. See Ben Tran, 'I Speak in the Third Person: Women and Language in Colonial Vietnam', *Positions: East Asia Cultures Critique*, vol. 21, no. 3 (Summer 2013), pp. 579–605. See also Jamieson, *Understanding Vietnam*, p. 110.

27. Thomas D. Le, 'Vietnamese Poetry' (June 2005), at www.thehuuvandan.org/viet poet.html, accessed 28 August 2015 (for the citation); and Jamieson, *Understanding Vietnam*, p. 171.

28. On Xuan Dieu's life and problems with the communist party during the First Indochina War, see: Lai Nguyen Ai and Alec Holcombe, 'The Heart and Mind of the Poet Xuan Dieu: 1954–1958', *Journal of Vietnamese Studies*, vol. 5, no. 2 (Summer 2010), pp. 1–90.

29. Nora Taylor, *Painters in Hanoi* (Honolulu: University of Hawai'i Press, 2004); and Nadine André-Pallois, *L'Indochine: Un lieu d'échange culturel?* (Paris: Publications de l'Ecole française d'Extrême-Orient, 1998).

30. Martina Nguyen makes this point convincingly in her PhD dissertation, 'The Self-Reliant Literary Group'.

31. For a brilliant social history of the poor of French Saigon, see Haydon Cherry, 'Down and Out in Saigon: The Social History of the Urban Poor and the Making of the Vietnamese Revolution in Late Colonial Saigon, 1918–1954', PhD dissertation (New

Haven: Yale University, 2009), to be published soon; and Lockhart, *Light of the Capital*, p. 113 (for the citation).

32. Lockhart, *Light of the Capital*, pp. 154–6 (for the citation). On Vu Trong Phung, see above all: Peter Zinoman, *Vietnamese Colonial Republican: The Political Vision of Vu Trong Phung* (Berkeley: University of California Press, 2013).

33. Nhung Tuyet Tran, 'Beyond the Myth of Equality: Daughter Inheritance Rights in the Le Code', in Nhung Tuyet Tran and Anthony Reid, eds., *Vietnam Borderless Histories* (Madison: The University of Wisconsin Press, 2006), pp. 121–2; Georges Boudarel, 'L'Evolution du statut de la femme dans la République démocratique du Vietnam', *Revue Tiers Monde*, vol. 11, nos 42–3 (April–September 1976), pp. 493–526; and George Dutton, 'Beyond Myth and Caricature: Situating Women in the History of Early Modern Vietnam', *Journal of Vietnamese Studies*, vol. 8, no. 2 (Spring 2013), pp. 1–36.

34. Hue-Tam Ho Tai, *The Memoirs of Bao Luong* (Berkeley: University of California Press, 2010); and Sophie Quinn-Judge, 'Women in the Early Vietnamese Communist Movement: Sex, Lies, and Liberation', *South East Asia Research*, vol. 9, no. 3 (November 2001), pp. 245–69.

35. Boudarel, 'L'Evolution du statut de la femme', pp. 493–526; Hue-Tam Ho Tai, *Radicalism*, chapter 3; Marr, *Tradition*, chapter 5; and Shawn McHale, 'Printing and Power: Vietnamese Debates over Women's Place in Society, 1918–1934,' in Keith W. Taylor, ed., *Essays into Vietnamese Pasts* (Ithaca: Cornell Southeast Asia Program, 1995), pp. 173–94.

36. Penny Edwards, *Cambodge: The Cultivation of a Nation, 1860–1945* (Honolulu: University of Hawai'i Press, 2007), pp. 227–44.

37. Tony Day and Maya H. T. Liem, eds., *Cultures at War: The Cold War and Cultural Expression in Southeast Asia* (Ithaca: Cornell Southeast Asia Program Publications, 2010); and Tuong Vu and Wasana Wongsurawat, eds., *Dynamics of the Cold War in Asia: Ideology, Identity, and Culture* (Basingstoke: Palgrave Macmillan, 2009).

38. See Christopher Goscha, '"The Modern Barbarian": Nguyen Van Vinh and the Complexity of Colonial Modernity in Vietnam', *European Journal of East Asian Studies*, vol. 3, no. 1 (2004), pp. 135–69.

39. On the cultural politics of Buddhism in Southeast Asia, see: Eugene Ford, *Cold War Monks: An International History of Buddhism, Politics and Regionalism in Thailand and Southeast Asia, 1941–1976* (New Haven: Yale University Press, in press).

40. See Christopher Goscha, 'Wiring Decolonization: Turning Technology against the Colonizer during the Indochina War, 1945–1954', *Comparative Studies in Society and History*, vol. 54, no. 4 (2012), pp. 798–831.

41. *In the Year of the Pig* (1968), directed by Emile de Antonio. On Mus during the Indochina War, see Christopher Goscha, 'So What Did You Learn from War?' Violent Decolonization and Paul Mus's Search for Humanity', *South East Asia Research*, vol. 20, no. 4 (December 2012), pp. 569–93.

42. *Kinh te Viet Nam* (Hanoi: Nha Xuat Ban Khoa Hoc, 1966), pp. 372, 379, 399, 400.

43. See in particular Kim N. B. Ninh, *A World Transformed*.

44. On Pham Duy, see Eric Henry, 'Pham Duy and Modern Vietnamese History' (2005) at http://www.uky.edu/Centers/Asia/SECAAS/Seras/2005/Henry.htm, accessed 28 August 2015; quotes cited by Jamieson, *Understanding Vietnam*, p. 264.

45. William Turley, 'Women in the Communist Revolution in Vietnam', *Asian Survey*, vol. 12, no. 9 (September 1972), pp. 793–805; and François Guillemot, *Des Vietnamiennes*

dans la guerre civile. L'autre moitié de la guerre. 1945–1975 (Paris: Les Indes savantes, 2014).

46. Marr, *Tradition*, p. 251.

47. On cultural change, anticommunism and nationalism in the Republic of Vietnam, I rely heavily on the path-breaking work of Nu-Anh Tran, 'South Vietnamese Identity, American Intervention and the Newspaper *Chinh Luan*, 1965–1969', *Journal of Vietnamese Studies*, vol. 1, no. 1–2 (February/August 2006), pp. 169–209; Nu-Anh Tran, 'Contested Identities: Nationalism in the Republic of Vietnam, 1954–1963', PhD Dissertation (Berkeley: University of California at Berkeley, 2013); Tuan Hoang, 'The Early South Vietnamese Critique of Communism', in Tuong Vu and Wasana Wongsurawat, eds., *Dynamics of the Cold War in Asia: Ideology, Identity, and Culture* (Basingstoke: Palgrave Macmillan, 2009), pp. 17–32; and Phi Van Nguyen, 'Les Résidus de la guerre'.

48. On Tran Duc Thao, see: Philippe Papin, 'Itinéraire II. Les exils intérieurs', pp. 62–89; and Jamieson, *Understanding Vietnam*, p. 249. On Nguyen Sa's poem, Jamieson, *Understanding Vietnam*, p. 253.

49. On Trinh Cong Son, see: John Schafer, 'Death, Buddhism, and Existentialism in the Songs of Trinh Cong Son', *Journal of Vietnamese Studies*, vol. 2, no. 1 (Winter 2007), pp. 144–86. Extracts of the poem come from Jamieson, *Understanding Vietnam*, p. 253.

50. Cited by Jamieson, *Understanding Vietnam*, p. 322.

CHAPTER 13. THE TRAGEDY AND THE RISE OF MODERN VIETNAM

1. I rely here on William J. Duiker, *Vietnam Since the Fall of Saigon*, rev. edn (Athens: Ohio University Center for International Studies, 1985); Nguyen Van Canh (with Earle Cooper), *Vietnam under Communism, 1975–1982* (Stanford: Hoover Institution Press, 1983); Stéphane Dovert and Philippe Lambert, 'La Relation Nord-Sud', in Stéphane Dovert and Benoit de Tréglodé, eds., *Viet Nam contemporain* (Paris: IRASEC/Les Indes savantes, 2009), pp. 90–114.

2. François Guillemot, 'Saigon 1975: La mise au pas', *L'Histoire*, no. 62 (2014), pp. 72–4.

3. Van Tien Dung, *Our Great Spring Victory: An Account of the Liberation of South Vietnam* (New York: Monthly Review Press, 1977), pp. 156, 162, 164; and Truong Nhu Tang, *A Viet Cong Memoir*, pp. 264–5.

4. Quoted in Mai Thu Van, *Vietnam: Un peuple, des voix* (Paris: Pierre Horay, 1982), p. 182.

5. Doan Van Toai, *The Vietnamese Gulag* (New York: Simon & Schuster, 1986), p. 196 (for the citation).

6. Nguyen Cong Hoan, in Chanoff and Toai, *Vietnam*, pp. 190–91 (for the citation).

7. On the gulf between theory and practice, see: Ken MacLean, *The Government of Mistrust: Illegibility and Bureaucratic Power in Socialist Vietnam* (Madison: University of Wisconsin Press, 2013). On peasant resistance to collectivization, see: Benedict Kerkvliet, *The Power of Everyday Politics: How Vietnamese Peasants Transformed National Policy* (Ithaca: Cornell University Press, 2005).

8. On all sorts of compromises in daily life between people and the powers that be, see: Philippe Papin and Laurent Passicousset, *Vivre avec les Vietnamiens* (Paris: L'Archipel, 2010), chapters 1–2 in particular.

9. Vo Nhan Tri, *Vietnam's Economic Policy since 1975* (Singapore: Institute of Southeast

Asian Studies, 1991), p. 69; Dovert and Lambert, 'La Relation Nord-Sud', p. 92; and Ngo Vinh Long, 'The Socialization of South Vietnam', in Odd Arne Westad and Sophie Quinn-Judge, eds., *The Third Indochina War* (London: Routledge, 2006), pp. 127–35.

10. Ngo Vinh Long, 'The Socialization of South Vietnam', p. 135; Dovert and Lambert, 'La Relation Nord-Sud', pp. 92–3; and Alexander Woodside, 'Nationalism and Poverty in the Breakdown of Sino-Vietnamese Relations', *Pacific Affairs*, vol. 52 (1979), pp. 381–409.

11. Trinh Duc, as translated in Chanoff and Toai, *Vietnam*, p. 200.

12. Ngo Vinh Long, 'The Socialization of South Vietnam', p. 135.

13. Ann-Marie Leshkowich, 'Standardized Forms of Vietnamese Selfhood: An Ethnographic Genealogy of Documentation', *American Ethnologist*, vol. 41, no. 1 (2014), pp. 143–62.

14. All citations from Stephen Denney, *Human Rights and Daily Life in Vietnam, Report Prepared for the Lawyers Committee for Human Rights*, 25 March 1990, at http://www.ocf.berkeley.edu/~sdenney/SRV-Discrimination-1990, accessed 28 August 2015; and also see Stephen Denney, *Re-education in Unliberated Vietnam*, at http://www.ocf.berkeley.edu/~sdenney/Vietnam-Reeducation-Camps-1982, accessed 28 August 2015.

15. Denny, *Human Rights and Daily Life in Vietnam*.

16. Philippe Langlet and Quach Thanh Tam, *Introduction à l'histoire contemporaine du Vietnam* (Paris: Les Indes savantes, 2001), pp. 23–28, 45–47; Hue-Tam Ho Tai, 'Monumental Ambiguity: The State Commemoration of Ho Chi Minh', in Keith Taylor and John Whitmore, eds., *Essays into Vietnamese Pasts* (Ithaca: Cornell Southeast Asia Program, 1995), pp. 272–88.

17. United Nations High Commissioner for Refugees (UNHCR), *Flight from Indochina*, chapter 4, p. 82, at http://www.unhcr.org/3ebf9bad0.html, accessed 14 November 2013. On reeducation camps, see among others Minh Tri, *Saigon à l'heure de Hanoï, 1975–1980* (Paris: L'Harmattan, 2000); P. V. Tran, *Prisonnier politique au Viet Nam* (Paris: L'Harmattan, 1990); Nguyen Cong Luan, *Nationalist in the Viet Nam Wars, Memoirs of a Victim Turned Soldier* (Bloomington: Indiana University Press, 2012); and for the poem, Thanh Tam Tuyen, *Resurrection*, translated by Linh Dinh, http://poeticinvention.blogspot.ca/2006/12/poet-and-fiction-writer-thanh-tam.html, accessed 19 January 2014.

18. Ngo Vinh Long, 'The Socialization of South Vietnam', p. 132.

19. Dovert and Lambert, 'La Relation Nord-Sud', p. 92; and Laurent Pandolfi, 'Transition urbaine et formes émergentes de construction de la ville vietnamienne', in Dovert and de Tréglodé, *Viet Nam Contemporain*, p. 359.

20. Dovert and Lambert, 'La Relation Nord-Sud', pp. 95–7 and Langlet and Quach, *Introduction à l'histoire contemporaine du Vietnam*, pp. 43–4.

21. Masahiko Ebashi, 'The Economic Take-off', in James W. Morley and Masashi Nishihara, eds., *Vietnam Joins the World* (Armonk: M. E. Sharpe, 1997), pp. 37–8; Ngo Vinh Long, 'The Socialization of South Vietnam', pp. 142–3; Dovert and Lambert, 'La Relation Nord-Sud', pp. 95–7; Marie Sybille de Vienne, *L'Economie du Viet Nam, 1955–1995, Bilan et prospective* (Paris: CHEAM, 1994). On peasant resistance to collectivization, see Benedict Kerkvliet, *The Power of Everyday Politics*.

22. Ngo Vinh Long, 'The Socialization of South Vietnam', p. 127–32.

23. I rely on the following sources for this section: W. Courtland Robinson, *Terms of Refuge: The Indochinese Exodus and the International Response* (London: Zed Books, 1998); Barry Wain, *The Refused, the Agony of the Indochina Refugees* (New York: Simon &

Schuster, 1981); William Shawcross, *The Quality of Mercy* (New York: Simon & Schuster, 1984); and the UNHCR, *Flight from Indochina*, chapter 4, pp. 80–105, at http://www.unhcr .org/3ebf9bado.html, accessed 14 November 2013.

24. UNHCR, *Flight from Indochina*, p. 81, 82.

25. Ibid., p. 98, figure 4.3.

26. See Christopher Goscha, 'Geneva 1954 and the "De-internationalization" of the Vietnamese Idea of Indochina?', unpublished paper.

27. Christopher Goscha, 'Vietnam and the World Outside: The Case of Vietnamese Communist Advisers in Laos (1948–62)', *South East Asia Research*, vol. 12, no. 2 (July 2004), p. 158.

28. Ibid., p. 141.

29. See Goscha, 'Geneva 1954 and the De-internationalization of the Vietnamese Idea of Indochina', note 1.

30. Significantly, the DRV and French delegates signed the ceasefire documents for Camboda and Laos in the names of the Khmer Issarak and the Royal Government of Cambodia and the Pathet Lao and Royal Government of Laos, respectively. On Laotian cadres sent to Hanoi, see: Vatthana Pholsena, 'Une génération de patriotes: L'Education révolutionnaire du Laos au Nord Vietnam', *Communisme* (2013), pp. 231–58; and also Vatthana Pholsena, 'In the Line of Fire: The Revolution in the Hinterlands of Indo-China (1957–1961)', in Christopher Goscha and Karine Laplante, eds., *The Failure of Peace in Indochina, 1954–1962* (Paris: Les Indes savantes, 2010), pp. 341–59.

31. Karl Jackson, 'The Ideology of Total Revolution', in Karl Jackson, ed., *Cambodia, 1975–1978: Rendezvous with Death* (Princeton: Princeton University Press, 1989), pp. 37–78.

32. I rely heavily on Ben Kiernan, *How Pol Pot Came to Power: Colonialism, Nationalism, and Communism in Cambodia, 1930–1975*, 2nd edn (New Haven: Yale University Press, 2004); Grant Evans and Kelvin Rowley, *Red Brotherhood at War* (London: Verso, 1984), especially chapter 4 on 'perfect sovereignty'; Christopher Goscha, 'Vietnam, the Third Indochina War and the Meltdown of Asian Internationalism', in Westad and Quinn-Judge, eds., *The Third Indochina War*, pp. 152–86; and on the misalliance analogy, Edward Miller, *Misalliance: Ngo Dinh Diem, the United States, and the Fate of South Vietnam* (Cambridge, MA: Harvard University Press, 2013).

33. On the importance of the Soviet invasion of Prague in 1968 for Mao, see Chen Jian, 'China, the Vietnam War, and the Sino-American Rapprochement, 1968–1973', in Westad and Quinn-Judge, *The Third Indochina War*, pp. 32–64. That the Czech 'rebels' wanted to get rid of communism mattered less to the Chinese than the fact that the Soviets had intervened in the internal affairs of another sovereign country. On Sino-Vietnamese and Sino-Soviet rifts over Indochina, I rely heavily on Chen Jian, 'China, the Vietnam War, and the Sino-American Rapprochement, 1968–1973', and his Chen Jian, *Mao's China and the Cold War* (Chapel Hill: The University of North Carolina Press, 2001); Qiang Zhai, *China and the Vietnam Wars, 1950–1975* (Chapel Hill: The University of North Carolina Press, 2000); and Lorenz Lüthi, *The Sino-Soviet Split* (Princeton: Princeton University Press, 2008).

34. Ilya V. Gaiduk, 'The Soviet Union Faces the Vietnam War', in Maurice Vaïsse and Christopher Goscha, *Europe et la guerre du Vietnam 1963–1973* (Paris: Bruylant, 2003), p. 201 (for the citation).

35. The Chinese had no navy worth its name in the 1970s. The Soviets did, in Asia, too.

36. The classic study of the Third Indochina War remains to this day Nayan Chanda, *Brother Enemy: The War After the War* (New York: Harcourt, 1986).

37. Jane Perlez, 'Shadow of Brutal '79 War Darkens Vietnam's View of China Relations', *New York Times* (4 July 2014), at http://www.nytimes.com/2014/07/06/world/asia/06vietnam.html?_r=0, accessed 28 August 2015. For the Chinese side, see: Xiaoming Zhang, *Deng Xiaoping's Long War: The Military Conflict between China and Vietnam, 1979–1991* (Chapel Hill: The University of North Carolina Press, 2015).

38. On the Eurasian nature of this war, see: Goscha, 'La Géo-politique vietnamienne vue de l'Eurasie: Quelles leçons de la Troisième guerre d'Indochine', pp. 23–38.

39. Sophie Quinn-Judge, 'Victory on the Battlefield; Isolation in Asia: Vietnam's Cambodia Decade, 1979–1989', in Westad and Quinn-Judge, *The Third Indochina War,* p. 222.

40. However, Vietnam's ally, Hun Sen, remains in power to this day, at the head of the state the Vietnamese helped him build in post-Khmer Rouge Cambodia.

41. Lee Lescaze, 'Journey into an American Nightmare', *Wall Street Journal* (17 October 1982), p. 28.

42. Masahiko Ebashi, 'The Economic Take-off'.

43. CIA World Factbook, Vietnam, at https://www.cia.gov/library/publications/the-world-factbook/geos/vm.html, accessed 28 August 2015.

44. Martin Grossheim, *Fraternal Support: The East German 'Stasi' and the Democratic Republic of Vietnam during the Vietnam War* (Washington: Cold War International History Project, Working Paper No. 71, September 2014), at https://www.wilsoncenter.org/sites/default/files/CWIHP_Working_Paper_71_East_German_Stasi_Vietnam_War.pdf, accessed 28 August 2015. Nguyen Vu Tung, 'The Paris Agreement and Vietnam–ASEAN Relations in the 1970s', in Westad and Quinn-Judge, *The Third Indochina War*, pp. 103–25.

45. Quinn-Judge, 'Victory on the Battlefield', p. 225; Tatsumi Okabe, 'Coping with China', in Morley and Masashi Nishihara, *Vietnam Joins the World*, p. 140.

46. Quinn-Judge, 'Victory on the Battlefield', pp. 219–20.

47. Morley and Masashi Nishihara, *Vietnam Joins the World*, pp. 45–6.

48. Quinn-Judge, 'Victory on the Battlefield', p. 223.

CHAPTER 14. VIETNAM FROM BEYOND THE RED RIVER

1. Mathieu Guérin, Andrew Hardy, Nguyen Van Chinh and Stan Tan Boon Hwee, eds., *Des montagnards aux minorités ethniques* (Paris/Bangkok: L'Harmattan-Irasec, 2003), p. 110.

2. Administratively and militarily, Interzone V was in charge of almost all of the central highlands, with Pham Van Dong in charge until 1950. Goscha, *Historical Dictionary*, pp. 232–3, 375.

3. Keith Taylor, 'Surface Orientations in Vietnam: Beyond Histories of Nation and Region', *Journal of Asian Studies*, vol. 57 (1998), pp. 949–78.

4. The Third Indochina War only reinforced all of this when Khmer Rouge communists accused their Vietnamese brethren of renewing ancient Vietnamese imperialism.

5. See William Cronon, George Miles and Jay Gitlin, eds., *Under an Open Sky: Rethinking America's Western Past* (New York: W. W. Norton, 1992); Patricia Limerick, *The Legacy of Conquest: The Unbroken Past of the American West* (New York: W. W. Norton,

1987); and Richard White, *The Middle Ground: Indians, Empires, and Republics in the Great Lakes Region, 1650–1815* (New York: Cambridge University Press, 2011 (first published in 1991)). The 'Go South/Nam Tien', heroic version of an expanding Vietnam did not start with the Republic of Vietnam in 1955. A nationalist narrative celebrating Nam Tien took off in the early twentieth century, but existed even before. Nguyen Hoang urged his followers to keep on moving south. See: Hung Giang, 'La Formation du pays d'Annam', *Nam Phong*, no 131 (July 1928), pp. 1–5; Nguyen The Anh, 'Le Nam Tien dans les textes vietnamiens', in *Parcours d'un historien*, pp. 18–22; and Claudine Ang, 'Regionalism in Southern Narratives of Vietnamese History', *Journal of Vietnamese Studies*, vol. 8, no. 3 (Summer 2013), pp. 1–26. A new generation of scholars too numerous to cite exhaustively, but on whose work I rely heavily for this chapter are: Nguyen Van Chinh, Pamela McElwee, Jean Michaud, Andrew Hardy, Philip Taylor, Sarah Turner, Philippe LeFailler, Emmanuel Poisson, Oscar Salemink, Mathieu Guérin, Stan Tan Boon Hwee and so many more. For an overview see: Philip Taylor, 'Minorities at Large: New Approaches to Minority Ethnicity in Vietnam', in Philip Taylor, ed., *Minorities at Large: New Approaches to Minority Ethnicity in Vietnam* (Singapore: Institute of Southeast Asian Studies Center, 2011), pp. 3–43.

6. For this early period, I rely on the work of Peter Bellwood, Ian Glover, James Fox among others. See Ian Glover and Peter Bellwood, eds., *Southeast Asia: From Prehistory to History* (London: Routledge/Curzon, 2004); Peter Bellwood, *First Migrants: Ancient Migration in Global Perspective* (London: John Wiley & Sons, 2013); Peter Bellwood, *Man's Conquest of the Pacific: The Prehistory of Southeast Asia and Oceania* (Oxford: Oxford University Press, 1979). Not all scholars are in agreement over the early settlement of Asia, such as Roger Blench at 'Roger Blench: Papers in Southeast Asian Archaeology' at http:// rogerblench.info, accessed 29 August 2015.

7. Just as we thought of it as an extension of the southern Chinese coast in chapter 1.

8. The scholarship on the Linyi and Champa is massive. Some of the most recent interpretive syntheses—grouping together some of the world's best specialists—and on which I draw extensively are: Andrew Hardy, Mauro Cucarzi and Patrizia Zolese, eds., *Champa and the Archaeology of My Son (Vietnam)* (Singapore/ Honolulu: NUS Press/University of Hawai'i Press, 2009); William Southworth, 'The Archeology of the Indianised States of Champa (Southern Vietnam)', in Glover and Bellwood, *Southeast Asia: From Prehistory to History*, pp. 209–33; Bernard Gay, *Actes du séminaire sur le Campa* (Paris: Travaux du Centre d'Histoire et Civilisations de la Péninsule Indochinoise, 1988); Pierre-Bernard Lafont, ed., *Le Campa, géographie, population, histoire* (Paris: Les Indes savantes, 2007); and Tran Ky Phuong and Bruce Lockhart, eds., *The Cham of Vietnam: History, Society and Art* (Singapore: NUS Press, 2011). For a *longue durée* approach, Jacques Népôte, 'Champa: Propositions pour une histoire de temps long', *Péninsule*, no. 26 and no. 27 (1993), pp. 3–54 and pp. 65–123, respectively. For a bibliography, see http://www.champapura.fr/ mediatheque/bibliographie.html, accessed 29 August 2015.

9. See the texts by Southworth and Vickery in Glover and Bellwood, eds., *Southeast Asia: From Prehistory to History*.

10. O. W. Wolters, *History, Culture, and Region in Southeast Asian Perspectives* (Singapore: Institute of Southeast Asian Studies, 1982), pp. 1–33 (citation on p. 14); Hermann Kulke, 'The Early History and the Imperial Kingdom in Southeast Asian History', in Marr

and Milner, eds., *Southeast Asia in the Ninth to Fourteenth Centuries*, pp. 1–22; Denys Lombard, 'Le Campa vu du Sud', *Bulletin de l'Ecole française d'Extrême-Orient*, vol. 76, no. 1 (1987), pp. 311–17; and Nguyen Quoc Thanh, 'Le Culte de la baleine dans le Centre Vietnam, devenir d'un héritage multiculturel', *Péninsule*, no. 55 (2007), pp. 97–125.

11. Andrew Hardy, 'Eaglewood and the Economic History of Champa and Central Vietnam' and John Guy, 'Artistic Exchange, Regional Dialogue and the Cham Territories', in Andrew Hardy, Mauro Cucarzi, and Patrizia Zolese, eds., *Champa and the Archaeology of My Son (Vietnam)* (Singapore: NUS Press, 2009), pp. 107–26, pp. 127–54 respectively. See the contributions by Michael Vickery, William Southworth, Ian Glover, Nguyen Kim Dung in Glover and Bellwood, eds., *Southeast Asia: From Prehistory to History.*

12. For overviews of the penetration of Islam into Cham lands, see Nasir Abdoul Carime, 'L'Historique de l'islamisation dans le basse vallée du Mékong, note de synthèse et bibliographique', *Péninsule*, vol. 56, no. 1 (2008), pp. 31–50; and Anthony Reid, *Charting the Shape of Early Modern Southeast Asia* (Singapore: Institute of Southeast Asian Studies, 2000), chapter 2.

13. John Whitmore, 'The Last Great King of Classical Southeast Asia: "Che Bong Nga" and Fourteenth-Century Champa', in Tran Ky Phuong and Lockhart, *The Cham of Vietnam*, pp. 168–203.

14. James Anderson, *The Rebel Den of Nung Tri Cao, Loyalty and Identity along the Sino Vietnamese Frontiers* (Seattle: University of Washington Press, 2007).

15. Whitmore, 'The Last Great King of Classical Southeast Asia', pp. 168–203.

16. Danny Wong, 'Vietnam Champa Relations during the Seventeenth and Eighteenth Centuries', in Tran Ky Phuong and Lockhart, *The Cham of Vietnam*, pp. 238–62.

17. Ibid.

18. Nicolas Weber, 'The Destruction and Assimilation of Campa 1832–1835, as seen from Cam Sources', *Journal of Southeast Asian Studies*, vol. 43, no. 1 (February 2012), pp. 158–80.

19. Danny Wong, 'Vietnam Champa Relations'.

20. Carool Kersten, 'Cambodia's Muslim King: Khmer and Dutch Sources on the Conversion of Reameathipadei I, 1642–1658', *Journal of Southeast Asian Studies*, vol. 37, no. 1 (February 2006), pp. 1–22. For Khmer population and relations with the Vietnamese, see Shawn McHale, 'Ethnicity, Violence, and Khmer–Vietnamese Relations: The Significance of the Lower Mekong Delta, 1757–1954', *Journal of Asian Studies*, vol. 72, no. 2 (May 2013), pp. 367–390. Jean-Pascal Bassino puts the number of Cham for 1913 at 20–30,000. See his *Vietnam in Historical Statistics*, p. 31.

21. Li Tana, *Nguyen Cochinchina: Southern Vietnam in the Seventeenth and Eighteenth Centuries* (Ithaca: Southeast Asia Program Publications, Cornell University), pp. 149–50.

22. Li, *Nguyen Cochinchina*, pp. 148–53; Po Dharma, *Le Panduranga (Campa), 1802–1835: Ses rapports avec le Viet Nam* (Paris: Ecole française d'Extrême-Orient, 1987), pp. 84–5; and Weber, 'The Destruction', pp. 158–80.

23. Po Dharma, *Le Panduranga (Campa)*, pp. 93–144 (p. 178 for the citations), 169–70; and David Chandler, 'An Anti-Vietnamese Rebellion in Early 19th Century Cambodia: Precolonial Imperialism and a Pre-nationalist Response', *Journal of Southeast Asian Studies*, vol. 4, no. 1 (March 1975), pp. 16–24.

24. Po Dharma, *Le Panduranga (Campa)*, pp. 127–58.

25. Recent scholarship has greatly advanced our understanding of highland Vietnam. I rely heavily here on the work of Andrew Hardy, *Red Hills: Migrants and the State in the Highlands of Vietnam* (Copenhagen: NIAS, 2005); Gerald Hickey, *Sons of the Mountains: Ethnohistory of the Vietnamese Central Highlands to 1954* (New Haven: Yale University Press, 1982); Gerald Hickey, *Free in the Forest: Ethnohistory of the Vietnamese Central Highlands to 1954–1976* (New Haven: Yale University Press, 1982); Oscar Salemink, *The Ethnography of Vietnam's Central Highlanders: A Historical Contextualization*, 1850–1990 (London: RoutledgeCurzon, 2003); Philippe LeFailler, *La Rivière Noire: L'Intégration d'une marche frontière au Vietnam* (Paris: CNRS Editions, 2014); Stan Tan Boon Hwee, 'Swiddens, Resettlements, Sedentarizations, and Villages: State Formation among the Central Highlanders of Vietnam under the First Republic, 1955– 1961', *Journal of Vietnamese Studies*, vol. 1, no. 2 (February–August 2006), pp. 210–52; Sarah Turner, Christophe Bonnin and Jean Michaud, eds., *Frontier Livelihoods: Hmong in the Sino-Vietnamese Borderlands* (Seattle: University of Washington Press, 2015).

26. Gerald Hickey, *Sons of the Mountains*, pp. 168–78; Guérin, Hardy, Nguyen and Tan, *Des montagnards aux minorités ethniques*, p. 28. On the Hmong, see: Christian Culas, *Le messianisme hmong aux xixe et xxe siècles* (Paris: CNRS-Éditions-Éditions de la Maison des Sciences de l'Homme, 2005) and Mai Na M. Lee, *Dreams of the Hmong Kingdom* (Madison: University of Wisconsin Press, 2015). On the Black Flags, see: Bradley Davis, *Imperial Bandits: Outlaws and Rebels in the China-Vietnam Borderlands* (Seattle: University of Washington Press, 2016).

27. Emmanuel Poisson, 'Unhealthy Air of the Mountains: Kinh and Ethnic Minority Rule on the Sino-Vietnamese Frontier from the Fifteenth to the Twentieth Century', in Martin Gainsborough, ed., *On the Borders of State Power: Frontiers in the Greater Mekong Sub-region* (London: Routledge, 2009), pp. 12–24, and especially Bradley Davis, 'Black Flag Rumors and the Black Flag River Basin', *Journal of Vietnamese Studies*, vol. 6, no. 2 (Summer 2011), pp. 16–41; and his *Imperial Bandits: Outlaws and Rebels in the China-Vietnam Borderlands* (Seattle: University of Washington Press, 2016).

28. Hickey, *Sons of the Mountains*, p. 173, 175 (for the citation). The famous French explorer Auguste Pavie relied on pre-existing Sino-Vietnamese models for ruling distant non-Sinitic and Viet lands, including a Chinese text dating from the thirteenth and fourteenth centuries, signed by the Chinese scholar Ma Duanlin. See Davis, 'Black Flag Rumors', p. 21 and chapter 1 of this book.

29. Andrew Hardy, 'Chams, Khmers, Hrê, la mosaïque ethnique', *L'Histoire*, no. 62 (2014), pp. 18–20; and Andrew Hardy and Nguyen Tien Dong, *Khao co hoc Truong luy: 5 nam nghien cuu* (Hanoi: Nha xuat ban khoa hoc xa hoi, 2011), pp. 17–19.

30. Oscar Salemink, *The Ethnography of Vietnam's Central Highlanders*, chapter 2 (citation on p. 43). For French ethnography, see Jean Michaud, *'Incidental Ethnographers. French Catholic Missions on the Tonkin–Yunnan Frontier, 1880–1930* (Leiden: Brill Academic Publishers, 2007). Global historians who master Chinese, Vietnamese, and a range of other languages, sources, concepts, and theories are making it clear that Western, colonial ethnography is not as new or as modern as we might think. See the work of Bradley Davis, Emmanuel Poisson, Philippe LeFailler and especially that of Geoff Wade, James Anderson, Kathlene Baldanza, John Whitmore and others cited in this chapter and chapters 1 and 2. Salemink, *The Ethnography of Vietnam's Central Highlanders*, chapter 2 (citation on p. 43).

31. Hickey, *Sons of the Mountains*, pp. 230–33; and Salemink, *The Ethnography of Vietnam's Central Highlands*, p. 52.

32. *La Pénétration scolaire dans les minorités ethniques* (Hanoi: Imprimerie d'Extrême-Orient, 1931), p. 5.

33. Salemeink, *The Ethnography of Vietnam's Central Highlanders*, p. 77 (for the citation) and Hickey, *Sons of the Mountains*, p. 311.

34. Hickey, *Sons of the Mountains*, p. 370. See the fascinating study by Olivier Tessier 'Les Faux-semblants de la "révolution du thé" (1920–1945) dans la province de Phú Thọ (Tonkin)', *Annales. Histoire, Sciences Sociales*, vol. 1 (2013), pp. 169–205; and 'Trong mua nay dan Moi o Quang Nam hay ra riet nhieu nguoi Annam', *Trung Bac Tan Van* (29 April 1936), p. 1 (on outbreaks of violence).

35. Oscar Salemink, 'Primitive Partisans: French Strategy and the Construction of a Montagnard Ethnic Identity in Indochina', in Hans Antlov and Stein Tønnesson, eds., *Imperial Policy and South East Asian Nationalism* (Copenhagen: NIAS Press, 1995), pp. 265–6; Guérin, Hardy, Nguyen and Tan, *Des montagnards aux minorités ethiques*, pp. 9–82; Hickey, *Sons of the Mountains*, pp. 297–308; Agathe Larcher-Goscha, 'A rebours de la civilisation: Les transgressions de Léopold Sabatier au Darlac', paper presented at the meeting of the Réseau Asie, Paris, 24 September 2003; Léopold Sabatier, *La Palabre du serment du Darlac* (Paris: Ibis Press, 2012); Pascale Bezançon, 'Louis Manipoud, un réformateur colonial méconnu', *Revue française d'histoire d'outre-mer*, vol. 82, no. 309 (1995), pp. 455–87; and Penny Edwards, *Cambodge, The Cultivation of a Nation, 1860–1945* (Honolulu: University of Hawai'i Press, 2007), pp. 183–209.

36. Salemink, 'Primitive Partisans', p. 267; Eric Jennings, *Imperial Heights: Dalat and the Making and Undoing of French Indochina* (Berkeley: University of California Press, 2011); Hickey, *Sons of the Mountains*, pp. 140–43, 323–43; Salemink, 'Primitive Partisans', pp. 267–74; and on the 'sixth part' of Indochina, M. Guerrini, 'La question moi', dossier Indochine, 1, box 25, Bf, Guernet, Centre des Archives d'Outre-mer.

37. Hickey, *Sons of the Mountains*, pp. 392–7, 406–26; and Salemink, 'Primitive Partisans', pp. 267–82.

38. Mark McLeod, 'Indigenous Peoples and the Vietnamese Revolution, 1930–1975', *Journal of World History*, vol. 10, no. 2 (1999), pp. 353–89.

39. Marr, *Tradition on Trial*, p. 404; Woodside, *Community and Revolution*, p. 219.

40. Goscha, *Vietnam: Un Etat né de la guerre,* chapter 10 and conclusion; Charles Keith, 'Protestantism and the Politics of Religion in French Colonial Vietnam', *French Colonial History*, vol. 13 (2012), pp. 141–74; and Goscha, *Historical Dictionary*, pp. 191–4, especially note 6, p. 192, and pp. 424–5.

41. Christian Lentz provides an excellent account of how the war drove DRV state-making in the Tai highlands of northwestern Vietnam. Christian Lentz, 'Making the Northwest Vietnamese', *Journal of Vietnamese Studies*, vol. 6, no. 2 (2011), pp. 68–105, and his 'Mobilization and State Formation on a Frontier of Vietnam', *Journal of Peasant Studies*, vol. 38, no. 3 (2011), pp. 559–86.

42. I rely heavily here on McLeod, 'Indigeneous Peoples', pp. 353–89.

43. Cited by Vatthana Pholsena, 'Highlanders on the Ho Chi Minh Trail', *Critical Asian Studies*, vol. 40, no. 3 (2008), p. 457.

44. Hickey, *Free in the Forest*, pp. 9–13.

45. Ibid., pp. 18–45.

46. Stan Tan Boon Hwee, 'Swiddens, Resettlements, Sedentarizations, and Villages', pp. 210–52; Hickey, *Free in the Forest*, pp. 47–60; and Po Dharma, *Du FLM au FULRO: une lutte des minorités sud indochinoise, 1955–1975* (Paris: Les Indes savantes, 2006).

47. Shawn McHale, 'Ethnicity, Violence, and Khmer-Vietnamese Relations: The Significance of the Lower Mekong Delta, 1757–1954', *The Journal of Asian Studies*, vol. 72, no. 2 (2013), pp. 367–90; Thomas Engelbert, 'Ideology and Reality: Nationalitätenpolitik in North and South Vietnam of the First Indochina War', in Thomas Engelbert and Andreas Schneider, eds., *Ethnic Minorities and Nationalism in Southeast Asia* (Frankfurt: Peter Lang, 2000), pp. 105–42; Po Dharma, *Du FLM au FULRO*, pp. 34–9; Hickey, *Free in the Forest*, pp. 60–62.

48. Po Dharma, *Du FLM au FULRO*, pp. 41–56; Hickey, *Free in the Forest*, pp. 96–107.

49. Hickey, *Free in the Forest*, p. 116.

50. Ibid., p. 165, 166–7, 253.

CONCLUSION. AUTHORITARIANISM, REPUBLICANISM, AND POLITICAL CHANGE

1. 'Mr. Hoang Minh Chinh speaks at Harvard', *BBC Vietnamese Service* (28 September 2005), at http://www.bbc.com/vietnamese/vietnam/story/2005/09/050930_hoangmchinh speech.shtml, accessed 7 January 2016. On Hoang Minh Chinh, see Sophie Quinn-Judge, 'Hoang Minh Chinh: The Honourable Dissident', *OpenDemocracy* (30 April 2008), at https://www.opendemocracy.net/article/vietnams_1968_dissidents_shadow, accessed 7 January 2016, and her 'Vietnam: The Necessary Voices', *OpenDemocracy* (29 April 2007), at https://www.opendemocracy.net/democracy-protest/vietnam_voices_4576.jsp, accessed 7 January 2016.

2. Martin Rathie has recently revealed that the famous 1966 Vietnamese photo showing Ho Chi Minh and his Lao counterpart, Kaysone Phoumvihane, together in Hanoi actually initially included a third person—the Khmer Rouge's Pol Pot. Andrew Walker, 'Two's Company', *New Mandala* (21 August 2012), at http://asiapacific.anu.edu.au/new mandala/2012/08/21/twos-company, accessed 26 January 2016. On the ASEAN Common Market, see the Asian Development Bank's 'ASEAN Economic Community: 12 Things to Know' http://www.adb.org/features/asean-economic-community-12-things-know, accessed 26 January 2016; 'Special Exhibition: Land Reform, 1946-1957', at http://baotang lichsu.vn/subportal/en/News/Special-exhibition/2014/09/3A9241EC/, accessed 11 January 2016; David Brown, 'Vietnam Quickly Shutters "Land Reform" Exhibit' (13 September 2014), at http://www.asiasentinel.com/politics/vietnam-quickly-shutters-land-reform-exhibit, accessed 11 January 2016; and Alex-Thai D. Vo, 'Nguyen Thi Nam and the Land Reform in North Vietnam, 1953', *Journal of Vietnamese Studies*, vol. 10, no. 1 (2013), pp. 1–62.

3. This recently occurred upon the opening of the 12th party congress. 'Les Délégués au 12e Congrès national du PCV rendent hommage au Président Ho Chi Minh', 20 January 2016', at http://fr.vietnamplus.vn/les-delegues-au-12e-congres-national-du-pcv-rendent-hommage-au-president-ho-chi-minh/71497.vnp, accessed on 21 January 2016.

4. Hue-Tam Ho Tai, 'Monumental Ambiguity: The State Commemoration of Ho Chi Minh', in Keith Taylor and John Whitmore, eds., *Essays into Vietnamese Pasts* (Ithaca: Cornell University Southeast Asia Program, 1995), pp. 272–88. On the political use of

Ho Chi Minh, see the chapters by William Duiker, Daniel Hémery, Benoît de Tréglodé and Sophie Quinn-Judge, in Goscha and de Tréglodé, eds., *The Birth of a Party State*, chapters 6–9. Ho Chi Minh, 'The Path Which Led Me to Leninism' (April 1960), at https ://www.marxists.org/reference/archive/ho-chi-minh/works/1960/04/x01.htm, accessed 14 January 2016. For a glimpse of this world, one need only Google 'tu tuong Ho Chi Minh'.

5. Forgetting to use the capital pronoun, 'He', when referring to 'Him', Ho Chi Minh, in the third person can be a cause for suspicion. It has to be 'N' for '*N*guoi'. Before approving the publication of foreign biographies of Ho Chi Minh, censors require authors to remove all mention of Ho Chi Minh's marriage to a Chinese woman. On North Korea's political cult, see Grace Lee, 'The Political Philosophy of Juche', *Stanford Journal of East Asian Affairs*, vol. 3, no. 1 (2003), at https://web.stanford.edu/group/sjeaa/journal3/korea1 .pdf, accessed 11 January 2016.

6. For an overview, see Claire Tran Thi Lien, 'Communist State and Religious Policy in Vietnam: A Historical Perspective', *Hague Journal on the Rule of Law*, no. 5 (2013), pp. 229–52; Pascal Bourdeaux and Jean Paul Williame, 'Special Issue: Religious Reconfigurations in Vietnam', *Social Compass*, vol. 57, no. 3 (2010), pp. 307–10; Nguyen The Anh, 'Le Sangha bouddhiste et la société vietnamienne d'aujourd'hui', *Institut d'Etudes bouddhiques*, no date, at http://www.bouddhismes.net/node/463, accessed 22 January 2016; Tam T. T. Ngo, 'Protestant Conversion and Social Conflict: The Case of the Hmong in Contemporary Vietnam', *Journal of Southeast Asian Studies*, vol. 46, no. 2 (June 2015), pp. 274–92. On the police and its surveillance of the web, see Carlyle Thayer, 'The Apparatus of Authoritarian Rule in Vietnam', in Jonathan London, ed., *Politics in Contemporary Vietnam: Party, State, and Authority Relations* (Basingstoke: Palgrave Macmillan, 2014), pp. 135–61. On censorship in Vietnam, see Thomas Bass, 'Swamp of Assassins', https://www .indexoncensorship.org/?s=thomas+bass&x=0&y=0, accessed 11 January 2016.

7. Shaun Malarney, 'The Fatherland Remembers Your Sacrifice: Commemorating War Dead in North Vietnam', in Hue-Tam Ho Tai, ed., *The Country of Memory: Remaking the Past in Late Socialist Vietnam* (Berkeley: The University of California Press, 2001), pp. 46–76; Christina Schwenkel, 'Exhibiting War, Reconciling Pasts: Photographic Representation and Transnational Commemoration in Contemporary Vietnam', *Journal of Vietnamese Studies*, vol. 3, no. 1 (2008), pp. 36–77; and de Tréglodé, *Heroes and Revolution in Vietnam*. On the Great War and memory, see Jay Winter, *Sites of Memory, Sites of Mourning: The Great War in European Cultural History* (Cambridge: Cambridge University Press, 1995).

8. Bao Ninh, *The Sorrow of War* (London: Vintage, 1998).

9. Ibid., p. 38 (for the quote). Anthropologists have provided sensitive and often brilliant studies of the impact of war on the spiritual realm of Vietnamese existence. See Shaun Malarney, *Culture, Ritual, and Revolution in Vietnam* (Honolulu: University of Hawai'i Press, 2002); Heonik Kwon, *Ghosts of War in Vietnam* (New York: Cambridge University Press, 2008), and his *After the Massacre: Commemoration and Consolation in Ha My and My Lai* (Berkeley: University of California Press, 2006); and Christina Schwenkel, *The American War in Contemporary Vietnam: Transnational Remembrance and Representation* (Bloomington: Indiana University Press, 2009). '*Dulce et decorum est pro patria mori*' means: 'How sweet and right it is to die for your country' as cited in *Poems of the Great War, 1914–1918* (Harmondsworth: Penguin, 1998), pp. 30–31.

10. See Nina McPherson's entry for Duong Thu Huong on the Viet Nam Litterature

Project website: http://vietnamlit.org/wiki/index.php?title=Duong_Thu_Huong, accessed 11 January 2016. Some of Duong Thu Huong's best-known books abroad are: *Beyond Illusions* (1987), *Paradise of the Blind* (1988), *Novel Without a Name* (1995), *Memories of a Pure Spring* (1996), *No Man's Land* (2002) and her recent venture into the life of Ho Chi Minh, *The Zenith* (2009). For an overview of post-1986 Vietnamese literature, see Cam Thi Poisson, 'La Littérature au Vietnam depuis 1986', in Benoît de Tréglodé and Stéphane Dovert, eds., *Vietnam Contemporain* (Paris: Les Indes savantes/Irasec, 2009).

11. Online at http://indomemoires.hypotheses.org/532, accessed 6 December 2015.

12. Nguyen-Marshall, *In Search of Moral Authority*; Hémery, *Révolutionnaires vietnamiens et pouvoir colonial en Indochine*; Woodside, *Community and Revolution in Modern Vietnam*, and his 'The Development of Social Organizations in Vietnamese Cities in the Late Colonial Period'.

13. Cited by Roubaud, *Viet-Nam*, pp. 119–20 and 147–8.

14. And, lest we forget, millions of religious men and women had—and still do have—their own takes on social organization and politics.

15. Marr, *Vietnam: State, War, and Revolution (1945–1946)*, chapter 2; and Fall, *Le Viet-Minh*, pp. 43–109.

16. 'L'Etat de siège s'étend à tout l'Indochine du Nord', *Le Monde*, no. 624 (24 December 1946), p. 1; and Christopher Goscha, *Historical Dictionary of the Indochina War (1945–1954)* (Honolulu: University of Hawai'i Press, 2011), pp. 165 and 389–90.

17. Marr, *Vietnam: State, War, and Revolution (1945-1946)*, chapter 2; and Fall, *Le Viet Minh*, pp. 43–58. The irony on the French side, of course, is that French Republicans supported the monarchies in Indochina until the very end, including Sihanouk's assault on parliamentary democracy. Many authors like to connect Vietnamese Republicanism at this time to the American model, citing Ho's reliance on the American Declaration of Independence of 1776 to craft his own in 1945. This American-centered view completely overlooks half a century of Vietnamese Republicanism.

18. Sidel, *The Constitution of Vietnam*, chapters 1–3.

19. Bernard Fall, 'Representative Government in the State of Vietnam', *Far Eastern Survey*, vol. 23, no. 8 (August 1954), pp. 122–5. On the Republic of Vietnam, see: the contributions in Keith Taylor, ed., *Voices from the Second Republic of South Vietnam (1967–1975)* (Ithaca: Cornell University Southeast Asia Program, 2015).

20. I rely heavily in this section on the work of many scholars: Benedict Kerkvliet, Carlyle Thayer, Tuong Vu, Ken Maclean, Zachary Abuza, Alexander L. Vuving, Jonathan London, Benoît de Tréglodé, Andrew Wells-Dang, Hy Van Luong, David Marr, Terry Rambo, Michael DiGregario, among others. For some important overviews, see Benedict Kerkvliet, 'Regime Critics: Democratization Advocates in Vietnam, 1999–2014', *Critical Asian Studies*, vol. 47, no. 3 (2015), pp. 359–87; Zachary Abuza, *Renovating Politics in Contemporary Vietnam* (Boulder: Lynne Rienner Publishers, 2001); Anita Chan, Benedict Kerkvliet and Jonathan Unger, eds., *Transforming Asian Socialism: China and Vietnam Compared* (Lanham: Rowman & Littlefield, 1999); Benedict Kerkvliet and David Marr, eds., *Beyond Hanoi: Local Government in Vietnam* (Copenhagen: NIAS Press, 2004).

21. See Benedict Kerkvliet, *The Power of Everyday Politics: How Vietnamese Peasants Transformed National Policy* (Ithaca: Cornell University Press, 2005).

22. CIA Factbook, Vietnam, https://www.cia.gov/library/publications/the-world-factbook/geos/vm.html, accessed 19 January 2016.

23. Benedict Kerkvliet, 'Workers Protests in Contemporary Vietnam', *Journal of Vietnamese Studies*, vol. 5, no. 1 (2010), pp. 162–204. Significantly, one of the stipulations accepted by the government in the Trans-Pacific Partnership of 2015 holds it to legalize collective bargaining rights.

24. Michael Gray, 'Control and Dissent in Vietnam's Online World', *Tia Sang Vietnam Research Report*, February 2015, chart 1, 'Vietnam Internet Use in 2013–2014', p. 2, at http://secdev-foundation.org/wp-content/uploads/2015/02/Vietnam.ControlandDissent .Feb15.pdf, accessed 13 January 2016; 'Vietnam's Internet Connection Speed among Asia-Pacific's Lowest: Report', *Tuoi Tre* (20 January 2015), at http://tuoitrenews.vn/business /25503/vietnams-internet-connection-speed-among-asiapacifics-lowest-report, accessed 22 January 2016; and Shara Tibken, 'Meet the Vietnamese Smartphone Maker Gunning to Be the Next Apple' (31 July 2015), at http://www.cnet.com/news/meet-the-vietnamese -smartphone-maker-gunning-to-be-the-next-apple/, accessed 20 January 2016.

25. Michael Gray, 'Hanoians Use Social Media Tools to Help Save Their Trees', *Flash-Notes*, vol. 3 (20 April 2015), at http://secdev-foundation.org/wp-content/uploads/2015/04 /flashnotes-vietnam-FINAL.pdf, accessed 13 January 2016.

26. Among others: Andrew Wells-Dang, 'The Political Influence of Civil Society in Vietnam', in London, ed., *Politics in Contemporary Vietnam*, pp. 162–83; Mark Sidel, *Law and Society in Vietnam* (Cambridge: Cambridge University Press, 2008), chapter 6; and Christina Schwenkel, 'Reclaiming Rights to the Socialist City: Bureaucratic Artefacts and the Affective Appeal of Petitions', *South East Asia Research* (2015), vol. 23, no. 2, pp. 205–25. On the contrary, see Philippe Papin and Laurent Passicousset, *Vivre avec les Vietnamiens* (Paris: L'Archipel, 2010).

27. Sidel, *The Constitution of Vietnam*, chapter 5; and Bui Hai Thiem, 'Pluralism Unleashed: The Politics of Reforming the Vietnamese Constitution', *Journal of Vietnamese Studies*, vol. 9, no. 4 (2014), pp. 1–32.

28. Both citations in Kerkvliet, 'Regime Critics', pp. 370–71.

29. Jason Morris-Jung, 'The Vietnamese Bauxite Controversy: Towards a More Oppositional Politics', *Journal of Vietnamese Studies*, vol. 10, no. 1 (2015), pp. 63–109; and Jason Morris, *The Vietnamese Bauxite Mining Controversy: The Emergence of a New Oppositional Politics* (Berkeley: University of California Press, 2013), at http://digitalassets.lib .berkeley.edu/etd/ucb/text/Morris_berkeley_0028E_14018.pdf, accessed 26 January 2016.

30. 'Thu gui Bo Chinh tri, Ban Chap hanh Trung uong khoa XI, cac dai bieu du Dai hoi lan thu XII va toan the dang vien Dang Cong san Viet Nam', at http://indomemoires .hypotheses.org/20792, accessed 19 January 2016.

ILLUSTRATIONS

1. A stylized map of Vietnam, from the reign of Minh Mang (Copyright © History/Bridgeman Images)

2. Entrance gate to the Imperial City, Hue, Vietnam (Copyright © MyLoupe/UIG, via Getty Images)

3. Entrance to the tomb of Minh Mang (Copyright © Wenzel-Orf/ullstein bild, via Getty Images)

4. Two captured Black Flag militiamen, 1885 (Copyright © History/Bridgeman Images)

5. Arrival in Saigon of Paul Beau, governor-general of Indochina 1902–7, engraving by Charles Georges Dufresne from *Le Petit Journal*, November 1902 (Copyright © Private Collection Archives Charmet/Bridgeman Images)

6. Man-Tien women at a market, Upper Tonkin, 1902 (Copyright © LL/Roger Viollet/Getty Images)

7. Soldiers and trackers posing with the heads of men accused of poisoning French troops, Tonkin, 1908 (Copyright © Apic/Getty Images)

8. Inauguration on 6 September 1910 of the memorial to French and Annamese soldiers who died during the 1909 campaign (Copyright © Photo12/UIG/Getty Images)

9. Exiting the Colonial Exhibition at Vincennes, 1931: Albert Sarraut (left), Bao Dai (center), and Pierre Pasquier (right) (Copyright © Keystone-France/Gamma-Keystone, via Getty Images)

10. Opening of the Colonial Exhibition, Vincennes, 1931. Bao Dei is seated in center (Copyright © Keystone-France/Gamma-Keystone, via Getty Images)

11. Japanese troops en route to occupy Lang Son, September 1940 (Copyright © The Asahi Shimbun, via Getty Images)

12. Rokuro Suzuki, Japanese Consul (Copyright © Keystone-France/Gamma-Rapho, via Getty Images)

13. A 1944 official French government brochure on Indochina (Copyright © Private Collection Archives Charmet/Bridgeman Images)

14. A Japanese soldier posts the first proclamation issued by the Allied Control Commission, Saigon, 1945 (Copyright © History/Bridgeman Images)

15. Vo Nguyen Giap, Jean Sainteny, and General Philippe Leclerc, Hanoi, 17 June 1946 (Copyright © Keystone-France\Gamma-Rapho, via Getty Images)

16. Vo Nguyen Giap and Ho Chi Minh, Battle of Dien Bien Phu, May 1954 (Copyright © Collection Jean-Claude LABBE/Gamma-Rapho, via Getty Images)

17. A Cao Dai temple (Copyright © AGF/UIG/Bridgeman Images)

18. Saigon Cathedral (Copyright © Carl Mydans/The LIFE Picture Collection/ Getty Images)

19. The Battle of Dien Bien Phu, 1954 (Copyright © Apic/Getty Images)

20. Vietminh medical soldiers at Dien Bien Phu (Copyright © SeM/UIG, via Getty Images)

21. French troops at Dien Bien Phu, 23 March 1954 (Copyright © by RDA/Getty Images)

22. Vietnamese child commandos (Copyright © Howard Sochurek/Time Life Pictures/Getty Images)

23. Independence celebrations in Hanoi, September 1954 (Copyright © Édouard BOUBAT/Gamma-Rapho/Getty Images)

24. Ngo Dinh Diem at a denunciation of communism ceremony, 28 November 1955 (Copyright © PhotoQuest/Getty Images)

25. A Buddhist monk burns himself to death in protest of government discrimination, Saigon, 11 June 1963 (Copyright © Popperfoto/Getty Images)

26. A helicopter picks up a wounded South Vietnamese soldier, Hiep Duc, South Vietnam, November 1965 (Copyright © Rolls Press/Popperfoto/Getty Images)

27. US marines in the jungle, 4 November 1968 (Copyright © Terry Fincher/ Express/Getty Images)

28. Vietcong soldiers on an abandoned US tank during the Tet Offensive (Copyright © AFP/Getty Images)

29. Captured South Vietnamese soldiers and civilians, Saigon, 30 April 1975 (Copyright © AFP/Getty Images)

30. Chinese troops entering Vietnam, 1979 (Copyright © History/Bridgeman Images)

31. Vietnamese boat people awaiting rescue in the South China Sea, May 1984 (Copyright © History/Bridgeman Images)

32. The Ho Chi Minh Mausoleum, Hanoi (Copyright © Dorling Kindersley/ UIG/Bridgeman Images)

INDEX

ABOUT THE AUTHOR

CHRISTOPHER GOSCHA is an associate professor of history at the Université du Québec à Montréal. The author and editor of numerous books on Vietnam, Southeast Asia, and international relations in English and French, he lives in Montreal, Canada.